This book contains a full translation of a major but little-known Soviet work on Soviet national income accounts for a crucial stage in the social and economic transformation of the Soviet economy from 1928 to 1930. These were years of mass collectivisation and the launching of the Soviet industrialisation drive. The USSR was perhaps unique in having a well-developed statistical service able to record the detailed changes in economic relationships that were taking place at this time.

The translation is accompanied by three introductory articles which explain the structure and contents of these materials, what new light these materials throw on the development of the Soviet economy in this period and describe the significance of these materials for the history of Soviet statistics and planning. Amongst other questions this evidence casts some doubt on recent attempts to show that Soviet industrialisation resulted in a change in the net flow of goods between industry and agriculture, in favour of agriculture. It also shows that considerable attempts were made by some influential statisticians and planners in the early 1930s to analyse the relationship between different branches and sectors of the economy. In a foreword Professor Sir Richard Stone places the achievement of the construction of these materials in the history of Western works on national income accounts.

S. G. Wheatcroft is Research Fellow at the Centre for Russian and East European Studies, Birmingham University.

R. W. Davies is Professor of Soviet Economic Studies at the Centre for Russian and East European Studies, Birmingham University.

T0328722

MATERIALS FOR A BALANCE OF THE
SOVIET NATIONAL ECONOMY
1928–1930

SOVIET AND EAST EUROPEAN STUDIES

MATERIALS FOR A BALANCE OF THE SOVIET NATIONAL ECONOMY 1928–1930

edited by

S. G. WHEATCROFT

Research Fellow, Centre for Russian and East European Studies, University of Birmingham

and

R. W. DAVIES

Professor of Soviet Economic Studies, Centre for Russian and East European Studies, University of Birmingham

with a foreword by

RICHARD STONE

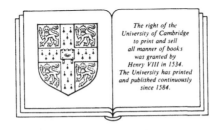

The right of the University of Cambridge to print and sell all manner of books was granted by Henry VIII in 1534. The University has printed and published continuously since 1584.

CAMBRIDGE UNIVERSITY PRESS

CAMBRIDGE

LONDON   NEW YORK   NEW ROCHELLE

MELBOURNE   SYDNEY

CAMBRIDGE UNIVERSITY PRESS
Cambridge, New York, Melbourne, Madrid, Cape Town, Singapore, São Paulo

Cambridge University Press
The Edinburgh Building, Cambridge CB2 2RU, UK

Published in the United States of America by Cambridge University Press, New York

www.cambridge.org
Information on this title: www.cambridge.org/9780521261258

First published 1985
This digitally printed first paperback version 2005

A catalogue record for this publication is available from the British Library

Library of Congress Catalogue Card Number: 85–468

ISBN-13 978-0-521-26125-8 hardback
ISBN-10 0-521-26125-2 hardback

ISBN-13 978-0-521-02016-9 paperback
ISBN-10 0-521-02016-6 paperback

Contents

Foreword

By RICHARD STONE

I. INTRODUCTION

It is a pleasure for me to be writing the preface to this very interesting volume. I learnt of the existence of the original many years ago but being ignorant of Russian could never have got beyond a broad knowledge of its content without an English translation. Now that I have been enabled to read it I find my expectations confirmed: anybody interested in economic history owes a great debt to Professor Davies and Dr Wheatcroft for opening up this hitherto almost unknown page of it.

Official work on economic statistics in early Soviet Russia was considerable. Some information on it and on the personalities involved is given by Naum Jasny in [8, 9], and one of its most remarkable achievements, the 1923–4 input–output table, is reproduced by V. S. Nemchinov in [16]. The present study was originally published in 1932 in 500 copies for official use only. The statistical material it contains relates mainly to 1928, 1929 and 1930 and is of great interest from two points of view. To the student of Russian history it shows the kind of information available as a basis for planning during an important period which saw the unfolding of the first Five-Year Plan, the intensification of the drive towards industrialisation and the introduction of collective farming. And to the student of economic ideas it shows the progress made in Russia during the 1920s towards the construction of national accounts.

The first, specifically Russian aspect is exhaustively dealt with by the editors in the introductory chapters of this book. The second is perhaps best understood if we look at it in the perspective of the development of national accounting from its origins to the present day.

2. THE POLITICAL ARITHMETICIANS

To trace the origins of the concept of national accounting we must go back to seventeenth-century England and to William Petty, one of the most remarkable men of that remarkable age. In 1664, largely with the object of making the tax system more equitable, Petty wrote a tract, entitled *Verbum Sapienti*, in which he gives the first known estimates of what may be called balances of the national economy [19]. Petty equates income to expenditure, which he identifies with 'Expence for Food, Housing, Cloaths,

Table 1 *William Petty's original estimates, 1664 (£ million)*

Income		Expence	
From Land	8	Food, Housing, Cloaths and all other	40
From other Personal Estates	7	necessaries	
From the Labour of the People	25		
Total	40	Total	40

and all other necessaries'. This he estimates at £40 million for the population of England and Wales, which he puts at six million inhabitants. He then estimates the income yielded by land at £8 million and that yielded by 'other Personal Estates' at £7 million. 'Now,' he says, 'if the Annual Proceed of the Stock, or Wealth of the Nation yields but 15 Millions and the Expence be 40, then the Labour of the People must furnish the other 25.' His figures can be set out as an account with four entries, as in table 1.

Table 1 is an example of Petty's 'political arithmetick', which his contemporary Charles Davenant defined as 'the art of reasoning by figures upon things relating to government'. Davenant himself was an enthusiastic practitioner of this art and in his numerous political writings made extensive use of figures to support his arguments. But from our point of view by far the most important of the political arithmeticians was Gregory King.

King was a herald by profession and seems to have worked out his economic estimates for his own curiosity. Had it not been for Davenant, who introduced many of them, with due acknowledgements, in his own books, they would have remained unknown until 1802, when they were rediscovered and published by Chalmers [10].

One of King's most fascinating tables shows the income, expenditure and saving of the population of England, divided into 26 social classes, in the year 1688. A version of it, slightly amended and converted to decimal currency, is set out in table 2. Evidently King's main purpose in working out his balances of income and outlay was to find out the contribution made to 'the wealth of the kingdom' by the various types of 'family', or in modern terms household. To us what is even more interesting is the view it affords of the socio-economic situation of his day.

Another of King's tables which is worth reproducing here is his comparison of England with her two political and commercial rivals, France and Holland, in 1688 and 1695. This is set out with slight amendments in table 3. This table, again, is a mine of information. It contrasts totals with per head figures. It gives a breakdown of consumption. It shows three alternative definitions of income–outlay: as the sum of consumption at market prices plus saving; as the sum of property income plus labour income; and as the sum of consumption at factor cost plus (indirect) taxes plus saving. And by presenting the data within a unified framework it enables many interesting and amusing comparisons to be made both over space and over time. Thus, France, with its relatively large population, has by far the largest income whereas Holland has the smallest; in terms of income per head, however, the position is reversed. The English appear as great consumers of meat and beer, the Dutch seem to prefer poultry and fish to meat and the French definitely prefer wine to beer. In all three countries saving falls in wartime though it remains positive in Holland. Taxes are much higher in Holland than in the other two countries though in all three countries they increase greatly in wartime. King projected his estimates to 1698 and concluded that the war could not be continued beyond that date. He was quite right: the War of the League of Augsburg lasted from 1689 to 1697.

When one reflects that King's estimates were the first of their kind ever to be made one cannot but be amazed at their complexity and sophistication and deplore that they had no sequel. The next step would have been to bring production and foreign trade into the picture, and with the data at his disposal King could indeed have done it: Phyllis Deane has shown in [5, 6] that it is possible to construct a complete set of national accounts using only the estimates made by him or available at the time he was writing. Her totals are brought together in matrix form in table 4.

This table is based on Professor Deane's work but I have stuck my neck out a bit further. She gives five accounts: production, households, government, capital transactions and the rest of the world. I have subdivided government into central and local in order to show the financing and distribution of poor relief, which was one of the responsibilities of local government. King, as we saw in table 2, treats indoor domestic servants as family members and does not impute an income for their services. I have adopted Professor Deane's imputation and shown this as an expenditure of the 'rich'; at the same time I have subtracted an amount equal to servants' income from the expenditure of the 'rich' and added it to the expenditure of the 'poor'. I have also accommodated the £0.2 million of hearth money (a direct tax) by reducing the consumption of the 'rich' by the same amount, thus balancing accounts 1 and 3.

In my table the 'rich' are those who save in table 2 less 215,000 indoor servants; and the 'poor' are those who dissave in table 2 plus the indoor servants. The £2.4 million of saving is the saving of the 'rich' in table 2; and the dissaving of the 'poor' in table 2 is removed by the receipt of £0.6 million of poor relief. Assuming, as I have, that the 'poor' devote all their income to consumption and neither save nor pay taxes, there were in England in 1688 2.461 million 'rich' with an annual income per head of £14, and 3.040 million 'poor' with an annual income per head of £3.7.

Table 4 shows how far King could have got with his political arithmetick. However, he did not pursue the matter, he had no followers, and after his brilliant start all thoughts of balanced accounts seem to have evaporated.

3. FRANÇOIS QUESNAY

The next man we must look to for a quantitative expression of the interdependence of economic flows is François Quesnay, Louis XV's physician. Like many progressive Frenchmen of his day, Quesnay was an advocate of *laisser faire* and tax reforms which he believed would convert French agriculture into a highly capitalised and productive activity such as existed in England. In 1758, at the age of 62, he published his famous *Tableau Économique*, which was illustrated by figures relating to the French economy not

Table 2 A scheme of the income & expence of the several families of England calculated for the year 1688

Ranks, Degrees, Titles and Qualifications	Number of families	Heads per family	Number of persons	Income per family £	Income per head £	Expence per head £	Increase per head £	Total income £'000	Total expence* £'000	Total increase £'000
Temporall Lords	160	40	6400	2800	70	60	10	448	384	64
Spirituall Lords	26	20	520	1300	65	55	10	33.8	28.6	5.2
Baronets	800	16	12800	880	55	51	4	704	652.8	51.2
Knights	600	13	7800	650	50	46	4	390	358.8	31.2
Esquires	3000	10	30000	400	40	37	3	1200	1110	90
Gentlemen	12000	8	96000	240	30	27.5	2.5	2880	2640	240
Persons in greater Offices and Places	5000	8	40000	240	30	27	3	1200	1080	120
Persons in lesser Offices and Places	5000	6	30000	120	20	18	2	600	540	60
Eminent Merchants & Traders by Sea	2000	8	16000	400	50	40	10	800	640	160
Lesser Merchants & Traders by Sea	8000	6	48000	200	33.3	28.3	5	1600	1360	240
Persons in the Law	10000	7	70000	140	20	17	3	1400	1190	210
Eminent Clergy-men	2000	6	12000	60	10	9	1	120	108	12
Lesser Clergy-men	8000	5	40000	45	9	8	1	360	320	40
Freeholders of the better sort	40000	7	280000	84	12	11	1	3360	3080	280
Freeholders of the lesser sort	140000	5	700000	50	10	9.5	.5	7000	6650	350
Farmers	150000	5	750000	44	8.8	8.55	0.25	6600	6412.5	187.5
Persons in Liberal Arts and Sciences	16000	5	80000	60	12	11.5	0.5	960	920	40
Shopkeepers and Tradesmen	40000	4½	180000	45	10	9.5	0.5	1800	1710	90
Artizans and Handicrafts	60000	4	240000	40	10	9.5	0.5	2400	2280	120
Naval Officers	5000	4	20000	80	20	18	2	400	360	40
Military Officers	4000	4	16000	60	15	14	1	240	224	16
	511586	5¼	2675520	67	12.9	12	0.9	34495.8	32048.7	2447.1
Common Seamen	50000	3	150000	21	7	7.5	-0.5	1050	1125	-75
Labouring People & Outservants	364000	3½	1275000	15	4.3	4.4	-0.1	5460	5587	-127
Cottagers & Paupers	400000	3¼	1300000	5	1.5	1.75	-0.25	1950	2275	-325
Common Souldiers	35000	2	70000	14	7	7.5	-0.5	490	525	-35
	849000	3¼	2795000	10.5	3.25	3.45	-0.2	8950	9512	-562
Vagrants	-	-	30000	-	2	4	-2	60	120	-60
	849000	3¼	2825000	10.5	3.19	3.41	-0.22	9010	9632	-622

So the General Account is

Increasing the Wealth of the Kingdom	511586	5¼	2675520	67	12.9	12	0.9	34495.8	32048.7	2447.1
Decreasing the Wealth of the Kingdom	849000	3¼	2825000	10.5	3.19	3.41	−0.22	9010	9632	−622
Neat Totalls [and averages]	1360586	4¹⁄₂₀	5500520	32	7.9	7.55	0.33	43505.8	41680.7	1825.1

Note: This column does not appear in the original.
Source: Gregory King, *Two Tracts*, edited by G. E. Barnett, Johns Hopkins Press, Baltimore, 1936, p. 31 (amended).

Table 3 *The general account of England, France & Holland for the years 1688 & 1695*

	Totals (£ million)						Per head (£'s)					
	1688			1695			1688			1695		
	England	France	Holland	England	France	Holland	England	France	Holland	England	France	Holland
Bread ... & all things made of Meal or Flower				4.3	10.1	1.40				0.79	0.75	0.63
Beef, Mutton, Veal ... Venison, Conies				3.3	5.3	0.80				0.61	0.39	0.36
Butter, Cheese & Milk				2.3	4.0	0.60				0.42	0.30	0.27
Fish, Fowle & Eggs				1.7	3.7	1.10				0.31	0.27	0.49
Fruit, Roots & Garden Stuff				1.2	3.4	0.40				0.22	0.25	0.18
Salt, Oyl, Pickles ... & confectionery Ware				1.1	2.8	0.30				0.20	0.21	0.13
Beer & Ale				5.8	0.1	1.20				1.06	0.01	0.54
Wine, Brandy Spirits ... & made Wines				1.3	8.6	0.40				0.24	0.64	0.18
Dyet [food and drink]	21.3	41.0	6.40	21.0	38.0	6.20	3.87	2.93	2.91	3.85	2.82	2.78
Apparell [clothing]	10.4	18.5	3.00	10.2	16.0	2.80	1.89	1.32	1.36	1.87	1.19	1.25
Incident Charges [expenditure n.e.s.]	10.0	21.0	6.35	14.3	26.0	8.40	1.82	1.50	2.89	2.62	1.93	3.75
Increase [saving]	1.8	3.5	2.00	−3.0	−6.0	0.85	0.33	0.25	0.91	−0.55	−0.44	0.38
General Expence	43.5	84.0	17.75	42.5	74.0	18.25	7.91	6.00	8.07	7.80	5.49	8.15
Rent of Land, Buildings & other Hereditaments	13.0	32.0	4.00									
Produce of Trade, Arts & Labour	30.5	52.0	13.75									
General Income	43.5	84.0	17.75	42.5	74.0	18.25	7.91	6.00	8.07	7.80	5.49	8.15
Consumption besides Taxes	39.7	70.0	11.00	39.0	62.5	10.50	7.22	5.00	5.00	7.16	4.63	4.69
Publick Revenue & Taxes	2.0	10.5	4.75	6.5	17.5	6.90	0.36	0.75	2.16	1.19	1.30	3.08
Increase	1.8	3.5	2.00	−3.0	−6.0	0.85	0.33	0.25	9.01	−0.55	−0.44	0.38
General Expence	43.5	84.0	17.75	42.5	74.0	18.25	7.91	6.00	8.07	7.80	5.49	8.15
Population (millions)	5.5	14.0	2.2	5.45	13.5	2.24						

Source: Gregory King, *Two Tracts*, edited by G. E. Barnett, The Johns Hopkins Press, Baltimore, 1936, p. 55 (amended).

Table 4 *The national accounts of England in 1688 reconstructed from Gregory King's data (£ million)*

	1	2	3	4	5	6	7	8	Totals
1. Agriculture, manufacturing, trade etc.			30.3	11.2	2.3	0.1	1.7	5.1	50.7
2. Indoor domestic service			1.6						1.6
3. Rich	34.5								34.5
4. Poor	9.0	1.6				0.6			11.2
5. Central government	2.1		0.2						2.3
6. Local government	0.7								0.7
7. Capital transactions			2.4						2.4
8. Rest of the world	4.4						0.7		5.1
Totals	50.7	1.6	34.5	11.2	2.3	0.7	2.4	5.1	

as it was but as it might become if his proposals were adopted [20]. Quesnay's writings are not easy to follow and it is helpful if his scheme is set out in the form of an accounting matrix. This was done by Tibor Barna in [1] and his matrix is reproduced here, with slight variations, as table 5.

Table 5 *An imaginary social accounting matrix for France, c.1750 (million livres)*

	1	2	3	4	5	6	7	8	9	Totals
1. Agriculture	525.0	525.0	300.0	525.0	262.5	150.0	75.0	525.0	262.5	3150.0
2. All other activities			300.0	525.0	262.5	150.0	75.0			1312.5
3. Landowners	1050.0									1050.0
4. Farmers	1050.0									1050.0
5. Artisans		525.0								525.0
6. State			300.0							300.0
7. Church			150.0							150.0
8. Capital transactions	525.0									525.0
9. Rest of the world		262.5								262.5
Totals	3150.0	1312.5	1050.0	1050.0	525.0	300.0	150.0	525.0	262.5	

It is clear from the entries in this table that we are dealing with a simplified constructed example and not with empirical data. There are two branches of production, agriculture and manufacturing; three types of household, landowners, farmers and artisans; and two institutions, the state and the church. Finally, there is a capital account for agriculture and an account for foreign trade. There is no saving, and imports balance exports.

From table 5 we can derive a matrix of input-output coefficients and from this we can work out the ratio of the national income (the total of accounts 3, 4 and 5) to agricultural output (the total of account 1) from two equations connecting the national income, agricultural output and manufacturing output (the total of account 2). Thus if we denote the national income by y, agricultural output by x and manufacturing output by z, we can write

$$0.\dot{6}x + 0.4z = y \tag{1}$$

and

$$0.\dot{6}x - 0.6z = 0.5y \tag{2}$$

whence

$$y/x = 1.2 \tag{3}$$

By setting a value on either x or y we could reconstruct table 5. We could also see what would happen to the economy if some of the coefficients were to change.

In addition to describing a static system, Quesnay interested himself in dynamics, particularly in the transition from traditional to modern agriculture. I shall not go into these developments here but an account of them by Barna can be found in [2].

As in the case of Gregory King, Quesnay's innovation made no practical impact on his contemporaries and did not bear fruit until much later.

4. KARL MARX

Marx was aware of the work of the political arithmeticians in so far as it was known in his day and admired it, but his schemes of simple and extended reproduction [15] owe more to Quesnay. In these schemes Marx considers a closed economy in which material production is divided into two branches: industry 1, which produces means of production, and industry 2, which produces consumers' goods. The production of services is not explicitly accounted for, but lies outside the production boundary. The model takes the form of a sequence analysis in which goods are produced in one period and used in the next. Each period possesses at the outset a stock of means of production and a stock of consumers' goods.

Means of production, or 'constant capital', c, consist of intermediate products plus the maintenance of fixed assets used in production. It simplifies matters, but is in no way necessary, if it is assumed that fixed assets have a life of one accounting period, say a year. Labour, or 'variable capital', v, is the only primary input, but in the course of production a 'surplus', s, is generated equal to the excess of sales proceeds over the cost of constant and variable capital. If we are dealing with a socialist economy, the surplus goes not to capitalists in the form of profits, interest and rent, but either to the state to provide for collective consumption or to accumulation to provide for an expansion of production. It is assumed that the workers do not save, but spend the whole of their income on consumption. In terms of cost, the ratio of constant to variable capital is 4:1 in industry 1 and 2:1 in industry 2.

In the simple reproduction scheme the surplus is not large enough to permit of any saving and so no money can be put into accumulation and the economy is stationary. Using Marx's figures, the national accounts and balance sheets will be as in table 6.

Table 6 *The stationary economy (currency units)*

	Opening liabilities	Industry 1	Industry 2	Workers	State	Accumulation	Closing liabilities
Opening assets						8909	
Industry 1		4400	1600				
Industry 2				1900	1009		
Workers		1100	800				
State		500	509				
Accumulation	8909						8909
Closing assets						8909	

At the beginning of the period the economy holds tangible assets worth 8909 units, divided between means of production, 6000 units, and consumers' goods, 2909 units. This opening stock is replaced by industry 1 producing 6000 units and industry 2 producing 2909 units, as shown in the rows for production. The costs and surpluses associated with this production are shown in the corresponding columns. The cost of variable capital, that is wages, in industry 1 is 1100 units, one-quarter of the cost of the constant capital used; and in industry 2 it is 800 units, one-half of the constant capital used. When these expenses have been met, the surpluses in the two industries are 500 and 509 units respectively, and together they are just sufficient to pay for the collective consumption, 1009 units, provided by the state. Although the economy has saved in the past, thus giving rise to the accumulated saving of 8909 units shown in the opening liabilities, it does not save in the present, and so the closing assets and liabilities are the same as the opening ones. It will be noticed that $c_2 = 1600 = v_1 + s_1 = 1100 + 500$, which is the condition that Marx gives for simple reproduction.

If it is possible to save, the economy can grow. Starting from the position shown in table 6, Marx's extended reproduction scheme is illustrated in tables 7 and 8.

Table 7 is similar to table 6 except that the surplus in each industry is now larger. The increases in these surpluses are saved and invested in the industry's own goods, and the closing assets and liabilities exceed the opening ones by the amount of saving. For the second period, therefore, the national accounts will appear in table 8.

In table 8 each industry starts with 10 per cent more constant capital and so has the capacity to produce 10 per cent more output. It can pay out 10 per cent more wages to the workers and 10 per cent more transfers to the state, since the necessary consumers' goods were produced in the preceding period, and it can save 10 per cent more. If the economy continues in this way, all the entries in the national accounts will grow by 10 per cent in each period, and so the scheme provides a simple model of exponential growth.

Looking back on this short survey we see that with the political arithmeticians the idea of national economic balances was first conceived as the equality of income and expenditure and used as a coordinating criterion for understanding the workings of the economy as it was. With Quesnay we have an explicit recognition of the interdependence of economic flows and a rudimentary planning scheme, in which the figures are not

Table 7 *The growing economy: first period (currency units)*

	Opening liabilities	Industry 1	Industry 2	Workers	State	Accumulation	Closing liabilities
Opening assets						8909	
Industry 1		4400	1600			600	
Industry 2				1900	1009	291	
Workers		1100	800				
State		500	509				
Accumulation	8909	600	291				9800
Closing assets						9800	

Table 8 *The growing economy: second period (currency units)*

	Opening liabilities	Industry 1	Industry 2	Workers	State	Accumulation	Closing liabilities
Opening assets						9800	
Industry 1		4840	1760			660	
Industry 2				2090	1100	320	
Workers		1210	880				
State		550	560				
Accumulation	9800	660	320				10780
Closing assets						10780	

observations but targets. With Marx we have a working dynamic model, albeit very simplified, and the figures are merely arithmetical illustrations.

These are the empirical and theoretical strands that converge in the monumental work of the Russian statisticians presented in this book. In their introductory chapters the editors describe its structure and content, its role as a source of information in Soviet economic development, the planning zeal that inspired it and the quicksands of political controversy in which it foundered. Partial sectoral balances continued to be constructed in Russia as aids to planning but the comprehensive vision of Popov and his colleagues was not revived until the late 1950s, as described by Treml and the others in [22]. By then input–output and national accounting had become normal practice all over the world.

5. THE SNA AND THE MPS

Although the notion of organising economic data into an accounting framework had died with Gregory King, sporadic attempts at estimating some of the more important aggregates, especially income, continued to be made throughout the eighteenth century in a number of countries, notably France, England and Russia. In the nineteenth and early twentieth centuries the statistical pace accelerated and the range of data collected broadened considerably. By the time the Russian statisticians embarked on the construction of their balances the statistical material for such an exercise was fairly abundant both in Europe and in America. But nowhere outside Russia was a concerted effort made to bring this material together. Individual researchers went their independent ways, following their own interests. As a result the growing flow of data was insensibly channelled into two separate streams which did not meet until each had swelled into quite a large river. One was the analysis of inter-industry relationships, which might be called the Quesnay stream; the other was the estimation of the components of income and outlay, which might be called the Gregory King stream.

Inter-industry analysis made its first appearance in America in a paper published in 1936 by Wassily Leontief [13]. Leontief had been a student at the university of Leningrad, knew the work of the official statisticians well and in 1925 had written a critique of the 1923–4 balances [12]. He applied his input–output model to US production data for 1919 and 1929 and his first large inter-industry table, with the productive system subdivided into 41 branches and complemented by rather sketchy vectors of final output and value added, appeared in 1941 [14].

On the income and outlay side Simon Kuznets had been making progress in America with income estimation [29] and had published in 1938 a study of commodity outputs and capital formation [11]. And in England Colin Clark, in his *National Income and Outlay* published in 1937, had brought together British data on income, output, consumers' expenditure, government revenue and expenditure, capital formation, saving, foreign trade and the balance of payments, thus covering in some detail both final demand and value added [4]. Although he did not set his figures in an accounting framework it is clear that they came pretty near to consistency.

The time was ripe for the advent of national accounts. In 1941 some highly aggregated balances of the British national income and expenditure, which James Meade and I had worked out while serving in the War Cabinet Offices, were included at the instigation of Keynes in a Budget White Paper [23]. In the same year Ludwig Gruenbaum (Gaathon) brought out his *National Income and Outlay in Palestine, 1936*, which was also cast in an accounting format [7], and Ed van Cleeff in Holland published two papers on a system of national book-keeping [30]. By the end of the war interest had spread. In 1945 I was asked to prepare for the League of Nations a memorandum on the definition and measurement of the national income and related totals, which was published in 1947 [24]. Soon after, the Organisation for European Economic Co-operation set up a National Accounts Research Unit, one of whose tasks was to design a standard system of accounts for use by the member countries [17, 18]. And in 1952 a committee convened by the United Nations formulated the first *System of National Accounts*, which came out the following year and became known as the SNA [25].

At the early stages of national accounting final output and value added were subdivided into their main components but production was treated as a single activity, without any disaggregation into separate branches. However, input–output analysis had also been making considerable advances and the progress continued during the fifties and sixties. In 1951 Leontief published a second, expanded edition of his original input–output tables [14]. Similar tables, more or less detailed, were compiled in many other countries and people began to experiment with the disaggregation of production in the national accounts. The social accounting matrix constructed in 1962 by the Cambridge Growth Project incorporated two industry/commodity submatrices, each containing 31 rows and columns [3]. The integration of input–output into the national accounts finally received its official blessing with the major revision of the SNA published in 1968 [26].

Neither the Soviet Union nor any of the other East European countries had taken part in the formulation of the SNA. Instead, they had developed a system of balances of the national economy, very similar to the balances presented in this book, which was known as the Material Products System, or MPS. The MPS varied from country to country but eventually an agreed formulation was prepared by the Council for Mutual Economic Assistance of the socialist countries and published by the UN in 1971 [27].

The SNA and the MPS both provide an integrated picture of the whole economy. They differ in a number of details, but the most important difference lies in the concept of production, which may be defined in a general way as the bringing into being of goods and services with the ultimate object of satisfying human wants. The question is, where do we draw the production boundary. In the SNA it is drawn widely so as to include all production of goods and services intended for sale (including that part which is not in fact sold but is consumed by the producer) and all non-market production by private non-profit institutions and government departments. What is excluded is the productive activity of household members and amateurs. In the MPS, on the other hand, the production boundary is drawn narrowly so as to include the only material products. The last two words should perhaps be put in inverted commas, since in fact they include the transport of goods but not of people and the services of restaurants but not of hotels; however, their coverage tends to become more inclusive over time. The services excluded from production are relegated to the non-productive sphere and do not appear in the material product balances.

In 1968, on the occasion of the fiftieth anniversary of the Polish Central Statistical Office, I tried to show, with the help of a numerical example based on the revised SNA, that it was possible to form a 'super matrix' from which either system could be derived by an appropriate grouping of the entries [21]. My example was oversimplified and did not deal with all the differences between the two systems; but it went some way towards showing that they represented alternative arrangements of the same basic data.

After the publication of the revised SNA, the Conference of European Statisticians at Geneva started work on links between the SNA and the MPS and eventually a very interesting two-part report was brought out by the UN. The first part, published in 1977, explains in detail how it is possible to pass from one system to the other by adding and subtracting components; the second, published in 1981, contains examples of the national accounting aggregates of SNA countries recast in MPS form and vice versa [28].

And there the matter rests. Progress has been made in formulating and comparing the two systems. It seems clear that they should be considered in terms of their convenience for the purposes for which they are used and not in terms of right and wrong. We may even hope that one day it will be possible to describe the world economy on either basis.

NOTES

[1]   Barna, Tibor. Quesnay's *Tableau* in modern guise. *The Economic Journal*, vol. 85, no. 339, 1975, pp. 485–96.

[2]   Quesnay's model of economic development. *European Economic Review*, vol. 8, no. 4, 1976, pp. 315–38.

[3]   Cambridge, Department of Applied Economics. *A Social Accounting Matrix for 1960*. No. 2 in *A Programme for Growth*. Chapman and Hall, London, 1962.

[4]   Clark, Colin. *National Income and Outlay*. Macmillan, London, 1937.

[5]   Deane, Phyllis. The industrial revolution and economic growth: the evidence of early British national income estimates. *Economic Development and Cultural Change*, vol. 5, 1957, pp. 159–74.

[6]   Deane, Phyllis, and Cole, W. A. *British Economic Growth 1688–1959*. Cambridge University Press, 1962; second edition, 1967.

[7]   Gruenbaum (Gaathon), Ludwig. *National Income and Outlay in Palestine, 1936*. Economic Research Institute of the Jewish Agency for Palestine, Jerusalem, 1941.

[8]   Jasny, N. The Soviet balance of national income and the American input–output analysis. *L'industria*, no. 1, 1962, pp. 51–7.

[9]   *Soviet Economists of the Twenties*. Cambridge University Press, 1972.

[10] King, Gregory. *Natural and Politicall Observations And Conclusions upon the State & Condition of England*. MS copy dated 1696, B.M., Harl. MSS 1898. First printed as an appendix to *An Estimate of the Comparative Strength of Great Britain* by Sir George Chalmers, J. Stockdale, London, 1802; reprinted in *Two Tracts by Gregory King* (ed. G. E. Barnett), Johns Hopkins Press, Baltimore, 1936.

[11] Kuznets, Simon. *Commodity Flow and Capital Formation*. National Bureau of Economic Research, New York, 1938.

[12] Leontief, Wassily W. The balance of the national economy of the USSR (in Russian). *Planovoe Khoziaistvo (The Planned Economy)*, no. 12, 1925. Engl. transl. in *Foundations of Soviet Strategy for Economic Growth* (ed. N. Spulber), Indiana University Press, Bloomington, 1964; reprinted in W. Leontief, *Essays in Economics*, vol. 2, Blackwell, Oxford, 1977.

[13] Quantitative input and output relations in the economic system of the United States. *The Review of Economic Statistics*, vol. XVIII, no. 3, 1936, pp. 105–25.

[14] *The Structure of American Economy*. 1st edn (*1919–1929*), Harvard University Press, 1941; 2nd edn (*1919–1939*), Oxford University Press, New York, 1951.

[15] Marx, Karl. *Das Kapital*. vol. II (ed. F. Engels). Hamburg, 1885.

[16] Nemchinov, V. S. The use of mathematical methods in economics. In *The Use of Mathematics in Economics* (ed. V. S. Nemchinov), Publishing House of Socio-Economic Literature, Moscow, 1959; English transl. (ed. A. Nove), Oliver and Boyd, Edinburgh and London, 1964.

[17] Organisation for European Economic Co-operation. *A Simplified System of National Accounts*. OEEC, Paris, 1950; reprinted, 1951.

[18] *A Standardised System of National Accounts*. OEEC, Paris, 1952; 1958 edn, 1959.

[19] Petty, Sir William. *Verbum Sapienti*. Published with *The Political Anatomy of Ireland*, Browne and Rogers, London, 1691. Reprinted in *The Economic Writings of Sir William Petty* (C. H. Hull ed.), 2 vols., Cambridge University Press, 1899.

[20] Quesnay, François. *Tableau Économique* (ed. and transl. by M. Kuczynski and R. L. Meek). Macmillan, London; Kelley, New York; 1972.

[21] Stone, Richard. A comparison of the SNA and the MPS. In *Mathematical Models of the Economy and Other Essays*. Chapman and Hall, London, 1970.

[22] Treml, Vladimir G., and others. *The Structure of the Soviet Economy*. Praeger, New York, 1972.

[23] UK, Treasury. *An Analysis of the Sources of War Finance and an Estimate of the National Income and Expenditure in 1938 and 1940*. HMSO, London, 1941.

[24] United Nations. *Measurement of National Income and the Construction of Social Accounts*. Studies and Reports on Statistical Methods, no. 7, United Nations, Geneva, 1947.

[25] UN, Statistical Office. *A System of National Accounts for Supporting Tables*. Studies in Methods, series F, no. 2, UN, New York, 1953; rev. 1, 1960; rev. 2, 1964.

[26] *A System of National Accounts*. Studies in Methods, series F, no. 2, rev. 3. UN, New York, 1968.

[27] *Basic Principles of the System of Balances of the National Economy*. Studies in Methods, series F, no. 17. UN, New York, 1971.

[28] *Comparisons of the System of National Accounts and the System of Balances of the National Economy. Part one, Conceptual relationships; Part two, Conversion of aggregates of SNA to MPS and vice versa for selected countries*. Studies in Methods, series F, nos. 20 and 20 (pt II). UN, New York, 1977 and 1981.

[29] US, Senate. *National Income, 1929–32*. Report prepared by Simon Kuznets. US Government Printing Office, Washington, 1934.

[30] Van Cleeff, Ed. Nationale boekhounding: proeve van en jaaroverzicht Nederland 1938, *De Economist*, no. 7/8, 1941, pp. 415–24; Beteekenis en invichtung eener nationale boekhouding, *De Economist*, no. 11, 1941, pp. 608–23.

Preface

The present publication is a translation of *Materialy po balansu narodnogo khozyaistva SSSR za 1928, 1929 i 1933 g.g.*, issued in October 1932 by the Central Administration of National Economic Records of the USSR for official circulation. This important statistical study was made available for general use in several Soviet libraries in the early 1970s; a photocopy may be consulted in the Alexander Baykov Library of the Centre for Russian and East European Studies of the University of Birmingham.

In this edition the translation is preceded by three articles by the British editors. The first article (pp. 3–15) provides a brief guide to the complicated structure of the tables and explanatory notes of the Soviet work; the second (pp. 16–33) discusses the *Materialy* as a source of information on Soviet economic development; the third (pp. 34–48) reviews the place of the *Materialy* in the history of Soviet planning. At the end of the book we have provided a glossary of Russian terms, and of our English-language versions of the difficult Russian.

The initial translation was prepared by Brian Pearce, to whom we are most grateful for his careful work with a difficult text; it was revised by the editors. The translation is complete, except for half a dozen diagrams at the beginning of the book which do not contain new material. Phrases and words added to the text by the British editors are placed in square brackets, as are the numbers and letters of headings which we have changed or added to assist clarity. The tables were prepared from a somewhat blurred copy, and we fear that we may occasionally have misread a figure.

The conclusions of the introductory articles were presented to the Annual Conference of the ESRC Workgroup on Quantitative Methods in Economic History and to the Soviet Industrialisation Project Seminars (SIPS) in Birmingham; we are grateful to Professor C. H. Feinstein, Dr R. M. Harrison and others present at these sessions for their helpful comments. Valuable advice and assistance have also been provided by Professors Holland Hunter and Nobuo Shimotomai, and Dr J. M. Cooper, and by Professor M. Ellman, who first suggested that we should undertake the publication of an English-language edition of *Materialy*. We are particularly grateful to Professor Sir Richard Stone for his interest and encouragement. The heroic labour of preparing the tables was undertaken by Mrs Olga Griffin, and several drafts of the text were painstakingly typed by Mrs Betty Bennett, the Industrialisation Project secretary. The index was prepared by Alison Rowlett.

Preface

This translation was prepared in the course of our project on Soviet industrialisation, which is financed by the British Economic and Social Research Council. Dr Wheatcroft's and Mrs Bennett's salaries, and the cost of the initial translation, were provided by the ESRC; without this support the work would have been impossible. We are also most grateful to the Syndics of Cambridge University Press for taking on the formidable task of publishing this volume, and to Mrs P. Leng for her careful subediting.

S. G. WHEATCROFT

R. W. DAVIES

May 1985
Centre for Russian and East European Studies,
University of Birmingham

ERRATA IN TABLES

p. 136 (3.I. Table 5)   In heading, *for* 'current prices', *read* 'producer's prices'.

p. 169 (3.IIB. Table 2)   Add to footnote [2]:

'All other stock entering the economy before inventorisation has been estimated in inventory prices (less depreciation), and stock entering the economy after inventorisation is estimated at the value of the outlays in the year of entry of the stock. But livestock has been estimated at the average annual prices for each year. Therefore the rate of growth of livestock within each single year in principle corresponds to the rate of growth in fixed prices. But when the live stock at the beginning of 1932 is compared with the stock at the beginning of 1928, the rate of growth reflects the change in prices over these years; as prices for livestock considerably increased in 1928–32, the growth-rate is considerably greater than that in fixed prices.'

p. 426 (App. C. Table 7)   Col. A. Heading I *For* '*Industry* including stock of industry', *read* '*Industry* including stock of housing'.

p. 427 (App. C. Table 7)   In note 1, *for* 'Less' *read* 'All'.

p. 432 (App. C. Table 7a)   In note 1, for 'Excluding' *read* 'All'.

EDITORS' INTRODUCTION

1

The structure and content of the *Materialy*

The ultimate aim of *Materials for a Balance of the Soviet National Economy 1928–1930* was to produce an elaborate *tableau économique* for the whole Soviet economy. The work as completed in 1932 was, as the authors declare in their preface, 'only a first attempt'. The methodology was not fully worked out. Data were often inadequate. The volume was produced in haste. While the authors seek to explain what they are doing quite fully, their explanations are often confused, and they are distributed more or less stochastically between Pervukhin's article and the notes on pp. 256–311, 441–60. The tables themselves are presented in four bundles, reproduced in chapter 3 of *Materialy*: section I (Summary tables), section II (Constituent elements in the balance), section III (Integrated tables in the balance) and the four tabular appendixes of section V. This division has a certain logic, but the logic proves to be complicated and elusive.

We resisted the temptation to rearrange all the tables and the explanatory notes into a systematic order. *Materialy* is an important collection of documents in the history of Soviet planning, and in the circumstances of its time was an outstanding achievement. We have no right to tamper with it; the reader will wish to explore it in its original form.[1] But to spare you from some of the agonies we have suffered in trying to understand the interconnection between the tables and their statistical foundation, we have provided this summary guide to the tables and the explanatory notes.

1.1 GENERAL STRUCTURE OF THE 'MATERIALY'

The process of reproduction in the Soviet economy is examined in a series of linked tables showing the flows of resources between sectors both in money terms (at current prices) and where possible also in real terms (at constant prices). The tables were constructed on the basis of a chess-board division of economic activity, which classified the data in five different ways:

(1) By sector of origin (industry – large-scale and small-scale; building (construction); agriculture; forestry; domestic production; transport; trade).

(2) By product-group (products of building work, or building products; industrial products; agricultural products).[2]

(3) By 'economic end-use'[3] corresponding to the major categories of the Marxist repro-

3

Table 1 *Main stages in preparation of balances in current prices*

Material used for estimation	Main sources of data	Tables in:	Tables appear on pp.	Notes appear on pp.
(1) Balances of products of industry and agriculture in physical and value terms	Industrial and agricultural statistics; family budget surveys	Appendices A and B	314–404	451–60
(2) Production–consumption data for products not available in physical terms	As above	Sections II.C II.D	179–91 192–220	284–309
(3) Trade and transport mark-ups	NKPS and trade data, etc.	Appendices A and B (partial only)	314–404	309–10
(4) Stocks	Various	—	—	285–7, 299–300, 308 (partial)
(5) List of product-groups by type of product-group and economic purpose	—	Appendix D	437–9	101–2
(6) Balance of production and consumption	Compiled from all balances listed above (1)–(5)	III.4 and III.2 (summary)	225–46	448–51
(7) Distribution of annual product	Mainly derived from Table III.4 (item (6) above)	III.3	227–8	450–1
(8) Balances of fixed capital	Industrial census of 1925; various agricultural surveys and censuses; depreciation allowances	II.B Appendix C	167–78 413–22	263–78

(9) Balance of production, consumption and accumulation	Derived from table III.4 (item (6) above) and balances of fixed capital (item (8) above)	III.1	222–4	100–5, 448–50
(10) National income by sector of origin	Derived from table III.4 (item (6) above) and table II.A.4	II.A.1	155	105–10
(11) Production by social sector	Only partially stated	II.A.5–6	160–1	293–8 (Agric.)
(12) National income by social sector	Derived from table II.A.1 (item (10) above) and item (11) above	II.A.2–3	156–8	260–3
(13) Accumulation	From table III.1 (item (9) above)	I.1	127	117–21
(14) 'Real accumulation'	From table III.1 (item (9) above)	I.3 I.4	131–4	121–2
(15) National income by classes and groups of the population	Labour statistics, urban family budgets, rural family budgets, insurance, data, state and local budgets (for social and cultural income in kind)	III.5 II.A.7	247–9 162	110–7, 260–3, 460
(16) Balance of principal indicators of reproduction by social sector	From other balances and national income table	I.2	129–30	122–4

duction schemes (means of production, in turn divided into fixed and circulating means of production; objects of consumption).

(4) By social ownership (the public sector, in turn divided into state and cooperative; and the private sector).

(5) Using this fourfold framework of classification, economic activity in each year was then 'unrolled' into the categories: stocks at beginning of year; production; imports; distribution (consumption) (*a*) in production, (*b*) final consumption by individuals and organisations, (*c*) losses, (*d*) exports; stocks at end of year; production entering into fixed capital.

The exercise of obtaining the data and classifying them in these five ways resulted in a complex series of balances. These are the heart of the *Materialy*, and will be described further below. The balances were used in turn to derive two series of tables showing national income classified by sector of origin and by end-use. The tables showing national income by end-use divided it into consumption (referred to as 'non-productive consumption') and net investment (referred to as 'accumulation'). Accumulation was in turn further divided into net increases in fixed capital ('funds') and in circulating capital ('funds'), each shown separately for the two sectors 'means of production' and 'objects of consumption'. One of the main aims, if not the main aim, of the whole study was to display accumulation and its sources in an economically meaningful way.

Finally, national income was also analysed in terms of the incomes received by different classes and groups of the population, and an attempt was made to tie these estimates in with the estimates of national income by sector of origin and by end-use.

The following account of the way in which these various sets of tables were compiled is summarised in Table 1.

I.2   THE BALANCES

The crucial table in the whole collection is the largest in the volume, table III.4, pp. 229–46, modestly entitled 'The balance of production and consumption'; a summary of this table appears as table III.2. It will be noted that the balance presents in a single table four of the five forms of data classification. The columns of the table unroll the economic activity in each year into stocks, production, consumption, etc. (classification (5) above), dividing each heading by sector of origin (classification (1)). The rows of the table divide economic activities in terms of both product-group (classification (2)) and economic purpose (classification (3)). A categorisation by social ownership (classification (4)) is not presented in this table.

The table in this extended form is presented in the *Materialy* only in current prices; only abbreviated versions of it, and particular sub-sections, are also available in constant prices. Two sets of current prices are used. Production is initially given in producers' prices. Transport and trading costs (as recorded in the transport and trade 'mark-ups' (*nakidki*) on producers' prices) (col. 26), and (where applicable) customs and other duties (col. 27) and excises (col. 28) are then added. Distribution (consumption) is therefore given in consumer prices (producers' prices *plus* cols. 26, 27, 28).

It should be noted that the 'outputs' of transport and trade appear in the table in the form of these mark-ups on production cost, not as a direct measurement of the output of an independent sector.

Table III.4 was itself constructed on the basis of data which appear in *Materialy* in three other sets of tables: (i) the appendix tables grouped in Appendices A and B present balances for particular product groups; (ii) section II.C, Production; and (iii) section II.D, Consumption.

The most reliable core of the data is provided by the product balances in Appendices A and B (pp. 314–405). These show 79 products or product groups in kind as well as in value terms, covering over 50 per cent of total production. The coverage is much fuller for agriculture, where 35 products embrace 80 per cent of all production, than for industry, where 44 products embrace only 30–40 per cent of production (see pp. 101–2; and, for a list of the products, pp. 438–40). In industry the coverage of machinery and other complex producer goods is particularly thin: the only balance in kind for machinery is the tractor balance.

It will be seen from the balances that the data are displayed in a form which corresponds to the headings of the columns in table III.4. Each product balance is located in an appropriate product-group in accordance with classification (2) above, and in an appropriate 'economic purpose' group (classification (3)), both operations being carried out on the basis of the list of products in the classification table of Appendix D (pp. 438–40). In the case of industry the data for the balances came from the current industrial statistics supplied regularly to the statistical agencies of industry and Gosplan by enterprises on an annual standard form (Form B) and on monthly report-cards. These forms and report-cards were also used to provide the data in value terms for the large part of industrial output which was not reported both in kind and in value terms. Special procedures were adopted for the year 1930, for which data in appropriate detail were not available, and for small-scale industry. The data from these sources were checked against other data. The methods used are described in some detail in the notes on pp. 284–92, 304–6 and 308–9.[4]

The procedures for assembling data on agricultural production and consumption were more complicated. Production data often had to be estimated indirectly: grain production was estimated by multiplying estimated productive sown area by estimated yield (see pp. 294–50), livestock production by multiplying number of animals by standard coefficients of production per animal (pp. 295–80). Sown area and number of animals were in turn obtained from the data of sample surveys. Consumption of agricultural production and of industrial consumer goods was evaluated by using the data of family budget surveys. Evaluating production and consumption was more difficult for agriculture than for industry: most industrial production was sold at fixed prices, all agricultural production was either sold at a variety of prices, or not sold at all. In the case of agriculture, the practice followed for estimates in current prices such as those in table III.4 was to use the procurement prices paid by official agencies both for that part of production which was sold to official agencies and for all 'on-farm' production; this included not only production consumed within agriculture but also production consumed by the individual or collective-farm household. Only production actually sold on the market was evaluated at the much higher market prices. For details, see pp. 294–8 (agricultural production), 297–300 (evaluation), 301–7 (consumption), 446–8 (agricultural product balances).

The data on production in industry, construction and agriculture are set out in section II.C (pp. 179–91); the data on the consumption of consumer goods and agricultural products are set out in section II.D (pp. 192–219).

The remaining major items in table III.4 not yet described are the trade and transport mark-ups and the changes in stocks. Trade and transport mark-ups are shown in the product balances for particular products in Appendices A and B, but not in the production tables of section II. Their derivation is described on pp. 309–10. For the economy as a whole the aggregate mark-up was obtained from data on transport incomes, and the trade mark-up by aggregating the trade mark-ups received at various levels of the trading network. Various rather crude devices were used to obtain estimates of the approximate mark-up on a particular product-group. For stocks, the statistical agencies had made increasingly strenuous efforts to record accurate data in the latter half of the 1920s: the procedure and data used in the case of stocks in the trade network are described on pp. 308–9.

We now proceed from table III.4 to the other balances. Table III.3 shows a minor variation on table III.4. It tries to estimate what happens to the annual production of each sector of origin in the course of the year, excluding from the calculations both imports and the stocks at the beginning of the year.

Table III.1, 'Balance of production, consumption and accumulation', is perhaps the most important of the balances. It shows production and consumption by sector of origin (classification (1)) in the rows, and divides economic activity into the three product groups of classification (2) (products of building work, industrial products and agricultural products) in the columns. On the input side, the data on stocks at the beginning of the year, production, imports, trade and transport mark-ups, customs-duties and excises (rows B–G) are taken from table III.4, and on the expenditure side most of the data on 'consumption by the population and institutions', and the data on exports and stocks at the end of the year (rows B, D, E) also come from table III.4. But the table also includes an estimate of the stock of fixed capital at the beginning and end of the year. 'Consumed in production' therefore includes an estimate of the amount of production expended on compensation for depreciation of capital stock during the year, and 'losses' includes an estimate of losses of fixed capital.

The fixed capital tables used for the appropriate rows of table III.1 are set out in Section II.B (pp. 167–78) and Appendix C (pp. 406–37). They are discussed in the notes on pp. 263–78, and the procedures by which they are incorporated in table III.1 are described in Pervukhin's article (pp. 104–5) and in the notes on pp. 449–50. Fixed capital stock in industry as at 1 January 1928, was estimated by applying a standard depreciation allowance (as a percentage) to the estimated value of fixed capital 'at restoration cost' shown in the census of industrial capital of 1 October 1925. Agricultural capital at the same date was estimated on the basis of various sample surveys and censuses described in the text. Similar procedures were used for the other sectors of origin. Then annual data were assembled on capital investment, capital entering into capital stock, and on changes in the amount of incomplete construction in progress at the end of the year. Fairly reliable data were available for industry and transport; in the case of agriculture, particularly in the private sector, various rough guesses had to be made which are described in the notes. A depreciation allowance was then applied to the value of capital stock (in industry this varied between 7.3 and 8.3 per cent). In the case of agriculture, losses of livestock were estimated separately. With these data, the change in capital stock during the year could then be estimated. The procedures are shown in Appendix table C.4 (pp. 414–7) which shows for 1928 (capital stock on 1 January 1928) + (unfinished construction in progress on 1 January 1928) + (capital investment in 1928) − (depreciation and capital worn-out during 1928) − (unfinished construction on 1 January 1929) = (capital stock on 1 January 1929). The estimates for 1929–31 follow the same pattern.

The annual figures for capital stock, with various minor adjustments, are then incorporated in table III.4 to give table III.1.[5] Table III.1 thus in effect includes in the row 'consumed in production' an estimate of the production which was consumed to compensate for the annual depreciation of fixed capital, as well as the production which was consumed in the course of current production.

I.3   NATIONAL INCOME

The table on national income by sector of origin in current prices (table II.A.1) was directly derived from table III.1. Production consumed in production (output, row A) was deducted from production at producers' prices (input, row C) to obtain the net production of each sector (see pp. 222–3). To obtain total national income, transport and trade mark-ups and customs duties were added to the net production of the sectors (in 1928, for example, 51,517.5 − 30,527.9 + 5,181.2 + 271.5 = 26,442.3).

At this stage it may be useful to follow the data through the various tables to demonstrate how a particular set of figures is derived. Let us take census industry in 1928 as an example.

(1)   In table III.4 gross production appears in col. 16, p. 230 (19,245.0). Consumption in production by census industry is in col. 31: 12,981.0 (p. 231), consisting of fixed capital 183.2 (p. 237), circulating capital (11,302.2) (p. 243) and consumer goods 1,495.6 (also p. 243). This reappears in table III.2 (p. 225), where circulating capital is now referred to in col. 4 as 'raw material, materials and fuel'.

(2)   In table II.A.4, p. 159, gross production and productive consumption are set out again in row 2, but with 'unfinished production' shown separately both on the production side and on the consumption side. A depreciation allowance (435.5, col. 6) is also added to productive consumption and deducted from gross production, so as to give net production for the national income series, from which national income used to cover depreciation has already been deducted.

(3)   It is worth noting that the figure for consumption in production which appears in the master table III.1, col. 4 (p. 223) is the same as in table II.A.4, 13,416.5 million rubles in the case of census industry in 1928, as it includes a depreciation allowance in the component product groups (see p. 159, col. 7).

(4)   Net production of census industry in the national income table (table II.A.1, p. 155) is 5,828.5, i.e. gross production of 19,245.0 less consumption in production of 13,416.5,

including unfinished production both in production and in consumption in production, and also including a depreciation allowance in consumption in production.

The next step in preparing the national income tables was to obtain a breakdown of table II.A.1 by social sector. The details of the procedure by which this was done are not described in the text. Agriculture was of course the most important sector of the economy which was predominantly privately owned. The procedure by which net production of agriculture by social sector was estimated is displayed in tables II.A.5 and II.A.6. Consumption in production of materials and fuel, and unfinished production at the end of the year, and a depreciation allowance (see table II.A.6) were deducted from gross production for the three separate sectors 'state farms', 'collective farms', and 'private'. Separate statistical series were used to obtain production in each social sector, as explained in the notes (pp. 293–7), so no special procedure was required to obtain this breakdown. It should be noted that the production of the individual collective-farm household was included not with collective-farm production but in the private sector. Some of the data required for the breakdown of the other sectors of the economy by social sector are scattered about the *Materialy* (e.g. figures for housing-construction in the socialist and private sectors) and the raw data used by the compilers almost invariably collected the data for socialist enterprises and the private sector separately.

All the series were now assembled on the basis of which accumulation (i.e. net investment) could be estimated. The procedures are discussed on pp. 117–21 and the results are shown in table I.1, p. 127. The accumulation fund in each year was obtained simply by deducting consumption net of excises from total national income. The data used for consumption were obtained from the figures for 'consumption by the population and institutions' as given in table III.1, in turn derived from the tables in the Consumption section; but excises were deducted from the totals in rows B 1–4, in order to make them compatible with the national income figure.

The accumulation fund was now adjusted in order to obtain 'real accumulation'. First, losses were deducted: this figure, also obtained from table III.1 (row C) consisted mainly of losses due to premature deaths of animals. The difference was substantial, especially in 1929 and 1930, when accumulation was reduced by over 17 per cent as a result of losses, when measured in current prices. Secondly, the net excess or deficit of imports over exports was also added in. Thus, in table I.1 (p. 127) for 1928, 26,442.3 − 21,305.7 gives accumulation fund of 5,136.6. Now deduct losses (800.9) and add excess of imports over exports (153.6) to obtain real accumulation (4,489.3).

'Real accumulation' was also estimated separately as the sum of the net increase in fixed capital (including the net increase in unfinished construction in progress) and the net increase in stocks. The breakdown of real accumulation into these categories and into social sectors is shown in table I.3 (p. 131) and in more detail in table I.4 (p. 133). The data for this table were all obtained from table III.1 (pp. 222–4), with a slight rearrangement, using other sources to break down the data by social sector.

These various estimates thus provided, in broad categories, a breakdown of national income by end-use as well as by sector of origin. A third and more or less independent set of estimates of national income was made by aggregating the personal income of the various classes and groups of the population, adding in 'income in the socialist sector' not otherwise accounted for. How this was done, and the sources used, are explained in three separate places: pp. 110–7, 260–3 and 460. The basic table is table III.5, 'Balance of distribution and redistribution of the national income, by classes and groups of the population', pp. 247–9; this table is then summarised in table II.A.7 on p. 162. As the definition of national income used throughout is the Marxist definition in terms of material production, incomes have to be handled in two stages. Incomes received by participants in the production process are treated as basic incomes, assumed to be received at the stage of the 'primary distribution' of the national income. These are taken in practice to include all the incomes received in the 'productive' sectors of the economy, including incomes received by non-productive personnel (clerks, accountants, etc.) working in the productive sectors. The total of these basic incomes equals the national income as derived by other methods: thus in table II.A.7 for 1928 the total of col. 1, 26,442.3 equals the total obtained by summing national income by sector of origin in table II.A.1, p. 155, col. 1. To obtain total incomes, 'derivative incomes' received in the non-productive sphere have to be estimated separately (i.e. incomes received in the health, education, defence and administration sectors, etc.): these are summarised in col. 2 of table II.A.7. These two columns are made up of a number of separate items – they include not only wages, but also pensions, the estimated value of education and health services, etc. received without payment, interest on loans, etc. The details are shown in table III.5, cols. 1–17, pp. 247–8. The various forms in which incomes are expended are then also estimated, including purchase of goods, value of education and health services (a self-balancing item), taxes, purchase of loans etc: see table III.5, cols. 20–33. The item 'income of the socialist sector' is not explained: we do not know if it corresponds to the costs of defence and central administration and of persons maintained at the state expense?

In these tables, the income of the agricultural population includes an estimate of the value of farm production consumed by households (at procurement prices). In these tables, unlike the production tables, the income of collective farmers includes both their income as cooperative producers and their income from their household plots, etc., and they are thus comparable with the incomes of individual peasants. In 1930, for example, the incomes of collective farmers were estimated at:

2,656.9	From cooperative production (table III.5(b) p. 253, col. 5)
1,079.9	As independent producer (col. 6)
321.0	As wages in productive sphere (col. 1)
4,057.8	Basic incomes from 'distribution' of national income
10.0	From wages in non-productive sphere (col. 10)
34.0	From insurance (col. 12)
20.0	From pensions etc. (col. 13)
155.4	Estimated value of free social and cultural services (col. 14)
219.4	Derived from 'redistribution' of national income
4,277.2	Total income

I.4   THE BALANCE OF REPRODUCTION AS A WHOLE

We have thus seen that the balance of production, consumption and accumulation (table III.1, derived from table III.4 together with data on capital stock) has been used to derive national income by sector of origin, and hence national income by end-use; and that separate estimates of national income in terms of the incomes of the population have been tied in with these national income estimates. Pervukhin comments with some justice that previous estimates of the national income were made 'in isolation, and not as part of the balance of the national economy', while the present study examined national income as part of the balance of the national economy, and was 'an attempt to study the national income in the process of its movement'.

This attempt was completed only partially in the *Materialy*. The balances and the various approaches to the estimates of national income were tied together in a short table, table I.2, 'Balance of the principal indicators of reproduction by sectors of the national economy' (p. 128). This simply shows two social sectors – socialist and private – and does not attempt to give a breakdown by sector of origin, product-group, etc. Pervukhin claims that this is because the statistical material is inadequate; but more elaborate composite tables could be constructed with the existing data, if a few rough guesses were made for missing items.

The construction of table I.2 is explained on pp. 122–4:

Rows 1 and 2, gross production, consumption in production, are from table II.A.4, p. 159, which as explained above derives the data from tables III.4 and III.2 but breaking them down between the two social sectors

Row 3, derived from rows 1 and 2, is national income as in table I.1, p. 127.

Row 4 shows the transfer of incomes from one sector to another as a result of, for example, workers and collective farmers earning incomes from their independent economies, and in the opposite direction, individual peasants earning wages in the socialist sector. The data are evidently derived from table III.5, pp. 247–9, but with various minor adjustments which are not explained.

Row 5 therefore shows the primary income of each sector.

Row 7 shows transfers from the private sector to the socialist sector in the form of taxes, loans, excises, etc. and from the socialist sector to the private sector in the form of pensions, free social and cultural services, etc. These figures are given only partially in the tables elsewhere in *Materialy*, such as table III.5, and their precise derivation is not explained.

Rows 5 and 8 are obtained by addition or subtraction.

Rows 9–12 allocate magnitudes already available in the other table between the two sectors, culminating in the division of 'real accumulation' between the private and the socialist sector already given elsewhere.

While the balances are incomplete, the various streams of data are coordinated; and the national income estimated in various ways comes to the same total. It should be noted that throughout the whole exercise the objective has been to produce 'balances'; and the various estimates have therefore been adjusted at appropriate points so as to bring them into balance. The different approaches to estimating the balances and the different sources of data do not therefore act as independent checks on one another. But the points at which adjustments have been made are described in Pervukhin's article and

Table 2 *Revaluation into constant prices of 1928*

Price-index	Table	Page	Notes on pp.
Individual product prices	Appendices A and B	314–404	Industry: 290–2
			Agriculture: 299–300
Producers' prices	I.10	146	Consumption: 305–7
			General note: 445–6
Consumer prices	I.10a	147	
Capital investment	I.10b–I.10c	148–9	278–83
National income by sector of origin	I.1–I.1a	127	106–10

in the notes. While the arithmetic has not been provided in the *Materialy*, the adjustments seem usually to have been made in a commonsense and realistic way.

I.5 ESTIMATES IN CONSTANT PRICES

Revaluation of estimates from current prices into constant prices was essential if the *Materialy* were to provide information about the real changes in the economy in 1928–30. This was not only because this was a period of inflation, but also because the inflation affected different aspects of the economy in different degrees. In industry, producers' prices fell slightly in the producer goods' sector, partly because prices were controlled, including the prices of almost all inputs, and partly because until 1930 wages rose less than productivity. Producers' prices of consumer goods rose only by a few per cent. But the consumer prices of industrial consumer goods increased substantially; and average consumer prices of agricultural products rose as much as 90 per cent in the two years 1928–30 owing to the huge increase in prices on the free market.

The revaluation into constant prices of 1928 appears to have been undertaken with care. The main places in *Materialy* where information is given about this revaluation are summarised in table 2.

In the case of both industrial and agricultural production, the index-numbers used for particular products and product-groups were derived where possible from direct information about price-changes. Thus in the case of electric power the average producers' price per 1,000 kWh declined from 103.2 rubles in 1928 to 83.8 rubles in 1930; and the average consumer price declined from 115.8 to 94.6 rubles (see p. 315). These average prices were in turn derived from prices in particular networks. In the case of sugar, the average producers' price fell from 326.6 to 315.8 rubles per tonne, while the average consumers' price rose from 664.7 to 866.3 rubles, but with wide variations for different types of consumer (see pp. 353–4).

Where information was not available about particular products, price indexes were constructed for each product-group. This particularly affected industry, where for many product-groups data were available only in value terms. For some product-groups, the price-index was merely that obtained from data about industrial production in current and in constant 1926/7 prices; for others, where the product-group was manufactured in various branches of industry, weighted price-indexes were constructed depending on the weight of the branch in the product-group concerned (see pp. 291–2). Consumers' prices were obtained from urban and rural family budget studies, which recorded purchases both in kind and in value terms.

In the case of the agricultural population, estimated production and consumption in the case of production consumed within the household were evaluated at official procurement prices in order to obtain the various series in current prices (see pp. 299–300 and pp. 306–7 below). Even in 1928, this meant that on-farm production was given a low value, as official procurement prices were already far below market prices. Consumption of the agricultural population, including the consumption of on-farm production, has therefore been separately revalued at urban prices of 1928, which were over 60 per cent higher than rural prices (see p. 213, cf. p. 215); this enables a more accurate comparison of the real level of urban and rural consumption.

The price-indexes given in tables I.10 and I.10a (pp. 146–7) were derived from the above estimates, not independent of them; they are the final weighted indexes used to revalue production and consumption in current prices into 1928 prices (see p. 110).

Capital investment was the other major item in the tables which was revalued at constant prices. The revaluation was of course in terms of the cost inputs into investment, not of its output. The index of the cost of capital investment was obtained as a weighted index of the cost of 'pure construction' (i.e. building work) and of the cost of capital equipment. Separate indexes were obtained for each major sector of origin. The methods and sources are explained on pp. 278–83; the indexes are given in tables I.10b–I.10e, pp. 148–50. It should be noted that the cost-index for equipment was composed of weighted indexes for imported equipment and equipment produced in the USSR: the cost of imported equipment declined by over 20 per cent between 1927/8 and 1931, while the cost of equipment produced in the USSR declined by only 7 per cent (see p. 149). In the case of agriculture, cost increases in 1931 may be significantly underestimated, as the authors assume that the cost of pure construction did not increase, whereas in sectors for which data are available costs rose by between 12.9 and 20.0 per cent (see p. 148).

National income by sector of origin was revalued into 1928 prices by using the price-indexes for each sector. In the case of both industry and agriculture, the price-index for gross production was used. In the case of transport and trade, the real rate of growth was crudely assumed to be the same as the rate of growth of material production obtained from the tables in the production section of *Materialy*, and the 'price-index' was derived accordingly (see pp. 309–10).

The appropriate price-indexes were also used to revalue production and consumption into 1928 prices in sections II.C and II.D, and the accumulation fund and real accumulation in section I. No attempt was made to revalue into constant prices either national income in terms of the incomes of classes and groups of the population, or the various balances in section III. With the data available, such a revaluation could be made with a reasonable degree of accuracy.

NOTES

Throughout notes, the place of publication of works in Russian is Moscow.

1 We have however changed the confused and inconsistent hierarchy of the tables and sections and added a few new headings. Editorial changes are marked by square brackets [ ].

2 The list of products in Appendix D is divided both by product-group and by economic end-use and the reader will find it necessary to consult this list when working through the tables.

3 Most tables refer to predominant economic end-use, although a few refer to actual economic end-use.

4 For industrial statistics generally, see also E. H. Carr and R. W. Davies, *Foundations of a Planned Economy, 1926–1929*, vol. 1, London, 1969, 934–7.

5 'Unfinished building work in progress' is incorporated in stocks at the beginning and end of the year in table III.1.

2

The *Materialy* as a source of information on Soviet economic development

Materials for a Balance of the Soviet National Economy cover three crucial years of Soviet economic development – 1928, 1929 and 1930 – with some additional information on 1931. By 1928 both industrial and agricultural production already exceeded the pre-war level. In 1928–30 the industrialisation drive was launched; the industrial developments of these years laid the foundations for Soviet victory in the second world war and the emergence of the Soviet Union as a super-power after the war.

The industrialisation drive of 1928–30 was accompanied by dramatic changes in the economic and social structure. On the eve of industrialisation, the Soviet economy was a kind of market economy. All large-scale industry (so-called 'census' industry) was nationalised soon after the Bolshevik revolution of November 1917, and in the simultaneous agrarian revolution the land of private landowners and much of their property were divided up among 20 million individual peasant households. The New Economic Policy (NEP) introduced in 1921 established a market relation between the state sector of the economy and individual peasant agriculture, while retaining and extending important elements of planning in the industrial sector. In 1927 this market relationship broke down, first for grain and then for other agricultural products, and was replaced by the compulsory acquisition of peasant products by the state. During the early 1930s, the socialisation of the economy was completed by the forced collectivisation of agriculture. Millions of peasant householders were joined together into a quarter of a million collective farms, and the state sought to incorporate agriculture into a comprehensive system of central planning. The main stages of collectivisation were completed in 1929–31. *Materialy* thus deal with a period of social as well as economic transformation.

Materialy were a landmark in the development of Soviet statistics, as they were not only more comprehensive than the previous balances, but were also the first balance on an all-USSR scale to cover a series of years rather than a single year. They had a very short public life. The collection was an internal government document 'for official use only', printed in only 500 copies. One or two articles appeared in the press summarising the methodology and results, but it was vigorously condemned almost immediately (see pp. 42–3). Between 1933 and the end of the 1950s it was not mentioned in Soviet publications. When first released for the use of Soviet scholars at the end of the 1950s, *Materialy*, not surprisingly, received a great deal of attention. In 1959, Professor T. V. Ryabushkin explained the methodology of the balance and presented the main data from them in his masterly account of the history of Soviet economic balances.[1] In 1969, Albert Vainshtein used national income data from the *Materialy* as part of his comprehensive study of Russian and Soviet national income.[2] In the same year, A. A. Barsov published his pioneering attempt to analyse transfers between town and country in 1928–32, using *Materialy* as one of his principal sources.[3] Soviet publications have continued to draw on the methodology and the data of the *Materialy*.[4] Its data have also been widely used, either directly or via Barsov, by Western economists in the course of their reconsideration of the nature of the Soviet economic mechanism and its efficiency during this period, especially by Millar, Ellman, Nove and Hunter.[5] We return later to some of the controversial issues considered in these discussions.

Materialy have justifiably been received both in the Soviet Union and in the West with great respect and enthusiasm. If they are to be used fruitfully by scholars, their limitations must be borne in mind. We have shown in the previous chapter (pp. 1–15) that *Materialy* are incomplete in important respects, particularly lacking data presented in constant prices. Much, perhaps most, of the data they contain is also available, albeit in scattered form, in Soviet statistical publications of the early 1930s, which contain, for example, a great deal more information about production, personal incomes and prices, than appears in *Materialy*.

Moreover, the authors of *Materialy* did not undertake any new statistical investigations, but depended on the data available in the files of the central government statistical department TsUNKhU and in the various commissariats. Their estimates for 1929, and particularly for 1930, suffer from the deterioration in the amount and quality of the data available even within the statistical department; the authors of *Materialy* gave frequent examples of this in their notes (see pp. 286–90 below). They tried to fill the gaps by intelligent guesswork. Their guesses were usually conscientious and judicious, but in important instances they did not sufficiently allow for biasses in the underlying data. Thus their material on livestock losses underestimated their extent (we return to this point below, pp. 21–2). And throughout *Materialy* the data for 1929 and 1930 generally suffer from an upward bias because they take no account, or insufficient account, of changes in quality (the underlying prices are usually per unit of physical volume irrespective of quality). In 1929 and 1930 the quality of production in many industries, particularly the consumer goods' industries, deteriorated substantially. A further general deficiency of the data, also a result of the underlying price structure, is that they provide misleading indications of the relationship between the agricultural and industrial sectors. In the series in current prices, the growth of agriculture in 1929 and 1930, and hence the change in its relationship with industry, is exaggerated because agricultural prices increased much more rapidly than industrial prices. The series in constant 1928 prices correct this deficiency. But these series in constant prices possess no absolute validity. In the internal prices of the Russian Empire in 1913, agricultural production was relatively undervalued as compared with world prices, and industrial production relatively over-valued. In 1928 Soviet prices, the 'scissors' between industrial and agricultural prices had opened in favour of industry to a greater extent even than in 1913. The difference of 1913 and 1928 prices from world prices resulted from the relatively high costs and prices of important sub-sectors of industrial production, particularly machine-building. Industry was protected by tariff barriers before the revolution and by foreign trade controls and price controls in the 1920s.

Perhaps the most important structural limitation of the balances presented in *Materialy* is that the data have been grouped into rather crude sectoral divisions. Thus in the tables by sector of origin industry is sub-divided only into 'census' and 'small-scale' industry. Building work – *stroitel' stvo* – also appears as a separate sector, as it is treated as not being part of industry in all Soviet statistics. Agriculture is not sub-divided at all in most of the tables. Products are grouped into only nine (3×3) categories (fixed capital, circulating capital and consumer goods, each in turn divided into 'products of building work', 'industrial products' and 'agricultural products'). It is thus impossible to use the balances to trace interconnections between, say, the metal industries and their industrial or other consumers, or (except in a couple of subsidiary tables) between arable farming and animal husbandry. And in the classification of the data by social group, only 'kulaks' are treated separately from other groups of the peasantry. The production of collective farm households, artisans and others on their personal plots is lumped together in most of the tables with production by individual peasant households in the 'private' sector (though with some difficulty this production can be separated out).

The commentaries by the authors also suffer from a major defect: even in this publication for official use only they had to be very careful not to criticise governmental policy, even by implication: the destruction, for example, of livestock was treated largely in terms of 'wilful slaughtering' for which the peasants and not the government were responsible.

In spite of these limitations, *Materialy* are an outstandingly valuable source of information and provide a very competent analysis of economic processes in this crucial formative stage of the Soviet economic structure. The heroic labours of the authors to integrate scattered and somewhat intractable data have shed a flood of light on obscure places in the economy. Their conclusions, presented in a document intended solely for the eyes of government officials, are very much franker than the published economic literature of that period, which concealed or denied altogether such awkward phenomena as the decline in living standards and the rise in prices.

The central feature of the Soviet economy in these years was of course the unprecedentedly rapid rise in investment. According to *Materialy*, real accumulation in 1931 was 370 per cent of the 1928 level (in constant 1928 prices), and increased from 14.4 per cent of national income in 1928 to 36.0 per cent in 1931. The peak rate of increase was in 1930, when accumulation almost doubled:

Real Accumulation (Previous Year=100)

1929	1930	1931
129.9	192.2	148.1

The pattern of growth of accumulation and its main results are displayed in Tables 3 and 4, which show the increase in capital investment and capital stock during the period covered by *Materialy*.

Table 3 *Gross capital investment in 1928 and 1931 (in million rubles in 1928 prices)*

	1928	1931	1931 (1928 = 100)
All industry (excluding housing)	1560.9	6281.2	402.4
Group 'A' state industry*	995.4	5735.9	576.2
Transport	901.8	2401.6	266.3
Education	117.0	202.9	173.4
Health	89.1	100.7	113.0
Agriculture	2177.7	3287.7	151.0
All housing	1620.6	2156.1	133.0
of which: urban	689.2	1338.1	194.2
rural	931.4	818.0	86.8
Other sectors (residual)	376.6	1235.9	328.2
Total investment	6843.7	15666.1	228.9

*Includes housing, and covers VSNKh and NKSnab industry only.
Source: Appendix D, table 4a, except for Group 'A' industry, which is obtained from table 7a.

Table 4 *Fixed capital stock on 1 January 1928 and 1 January 1932 (in million rubles in 1928 prices)*

	1.1.28	1.1.32	1.1.32 (1.1.28 = 100)
All industry	6481.3	14106.9	217.7
Transport	10520.8	13214.1	125.6
Education	1810.5	2212.9	122.2
Health	939.0	1206.7	128.5
Agriculture	17962.5	19579.2	109.0
All housing	23252.9	25113.6	108.0
of which: urban	12204.6	13484.4	110.5
rural	11048.3	11629.4	105.3
Other sectors (residual)	3360.1	5220.6	155.4
Total capital stock	64327.1	80654.0	125.4

Source: Appendix D, table 4a. As the size of the capital stock in small-scale industry on 1 January 1932, was not available, it was assumed by us to be the same size as on 1 January 1931, and 736.8 million rubles were therefore added both to the figure for 'All industry' and to 'Total capital stock'.

According to the best Western estimates, the vast rate of expansion of investment claimed by *Materialy* is approximately the right order of magnitude in terms of 1928 prices. Moorsteen and Powell estimated that gross investment in fixed capital in 1931 was 247 per cent of the 1928 level (in 1928 prices) and 207 per cent of that level (in 1937 prices).[6] It should be borne in mind that the share of accumulation in national income is much higher in 1928 prices than it would be in world prices, as the inputs into accumulation, which are mainly producer goods, have relatively high prices.

The increase was overwhelmingly concentrated on industry, and particularly on the producer goods' (Group 'A') industries (see table 3). Investment in industry rose from 22.8 per cent of total investment in 1928 to 40.1 per cent in 1931, and amounted to 53.5 per cent of the increase in investment between 1928 and 1931. As a result, industrial capital stock increased at an unprecedented rate. The share of investment allocated to other sectors of the economy, and particularly to education, health, housing and agriculture, greatly declined. Investment in housing in 1930 and 1931 was probably even lower than the level shown in *Materialy*, which more or less arbitrarily assumed that investment in rural building by individual households and non-socialised rural building by collective-farm households in both 1930 and 1931 was sufficient to secure 'simple reproduction' (see pp. 273–7 below). In view of the decline in the supply of building materials to the rural sector (see pp. 30–1) and the great upheavals in the countryside in these years, this seems by no means likely. On the other hand, gross investment in agriculture, at least in 1929 and 1930, is underestimated, owing to the method used to estimate investment in livestock (see pp. 21–2 below).

The expansion of investment, and the shift within the total towards industry, continued trends in Soviet policy already established in the 1920s. In 1928, total investment already exceeded the 1913 level and the proportion of investment allocated to industry was already considerably higher than in 1913, while investment in housing was much lower than in 1913.[7]

A very high proportion of investment in industry was allocated to ambitious large-scale projects, such as the Ural–Kuznetsk iron and steel combine, which took several years to complete. In consequence, a substantial proportion of investment was devoted to projects in progress, and did not result in an immediate increase in fixed capital in operation. This proportion increased throughout 1928–31 (see table 5). In 1931, one-third of the gross investment in census industry was allocated to construction incomplete at the end of the year, and in that year the net increase in fixed capital in census industry, as estimated in *Materialy*, amounted to only 53.5 per cent of gross investment.[8]

The growth in industrial investment was accompanied by major structural changes in the rest of the economy. The share of consumption in national income substantially declined. Early in 1929, the Gosplan journal admitted that the five-year plan would involve 'putting a steel hoop around consumption'.[9] According to the estimate in *Materialy*, the consumption fund in 1931 was only 6.6 per cent higher than in 1928; it had therefore expanded less rapidly than the population; and in 1931 it declined absolutely. These figures certainly do not indicate the full extent of the decline in consumption per head. The family budgets on which they were based are much less complete for 1930 and 1931 than for earlier years (see p. 306 below), and they do not allow for the considerable decline in quality which occurred in 1929–31.

Consumption for the most part consisted of food and food products: these amounted to 70.4 per cent of total personal consumption in 1928 and 68.4 per cent in 1930; including drink and tobacco, these percentages rise to 78.0 per cent in 1928 and 75.7 per cent in

Table 5 *Incomplete construction in 1928–31 (in million rubles in 1928 prices)*

	(1) Stock of incomplete construction on 1 January	(2) Gross investment during year	(3) Increase in stock of incomplete construction during year	(4) Col. (3) as % of col. (2)
All economy				
1928	1380.8	6843.7	657.2	9.6
1929	2038.0	7874.2	959.4	12.2
1930	2997.4	11312.4	1914.6	16.9
1931	4912.0	15666.1	3326.3	21.2
1932	8238.3	–	–	–
Census industry				
1928	880.4	1525.4	354.1	23.3
1929	1234.5	2187.4	488.4	22.3
1930	1722.9	4129.1	1186.7	28.7
1931	2909.6	6281.2	2089.0	33.3
1932	4998.6	–	–	–

Source: Estimated from Appendix C, table 4a.

1930.[10] Petrov stresses in his article that the decline in food consumption in 1930 was entirely a result of the decline in the consumption of livestock products, which declines still further in 1931 (p. 92). This decline was in turn due to the great reduction in the livestock population due to death from disease and lack of fodder, and to premature slaughter, in the course of collectivisation.[11] The decline in livestock did not have its full immediate impact on consumption because premature slaughter temporarily provided more meat, and more leather for the manufacture of footwear. The harmful effects of the livestock crisis on consumption are more or less frankly admitted by Petrov, though he attributes the reduction in stock not to forced collectivisation but to 'wilful slaughtering and squandering by kulak households and, to some extent, under the influence of kulak agitation, by middle peasant households as well'; at one point he also correctly adduces shortage of fodder as a cause of the decline (see p. 77).

The decline in livestock also substantially reduced the net increase in capital stock, and the amount of real capital accumulation. According to *Materialy* the value of livestock fell by 22.7 per cent between 1 January 1929 and 1 January 1932, as measured in 1928 prices (see Appendix C, table 4a). Due to the decline in capital in the form of livestock, in value terms 'real accumulation' was 15.2 per cent less than the accumulation fund (gross accumulation) in 1929 and 9.1 per cent less in 1930 (estimated from data in table I.1a and Appendix C, table 4a). But it should be noted that these tables in *Materialy* do not bring out the full impact of the decline in livestock. This is because 'wilful slaughter' as distinct from 'premature death' is not counted as a 'loss in fixed capital' because it is assumed to be included, together with the normal slaughter of

Table 6 *Livestock investment and capital stock (in million rubles in 1928 prices)*

	1928	1929	1930	1931
1. Capital stock on 1 Jan.	8297.3	8359.4	7648.3	6910.2
2. Capital investment*	868.3	441.3	488.8	494.6
3. Losses**	518.7	880.3	963.1	679.5
4. Estimated depreciation	287.5	272.1	263.8	249.5
5. Net investment (+) or disinvestment (−) (2−(3+4))	+62.1	−711.1	−738.1	−434.4
6. Capital stock on 1 Jan. of following year (1±5)	8359.4	7648.3	6910.1***	6457.8***

Source: Appendix C, table 4a.
Notes: * Value of gross addition to stock less value sent to slaughter for meat.
      ** Premature death; does not include wilful slaughter, which should appear with consumption
         in production.
    *** Original table gives slightly lower amount, as it excludes 11.6 million rubles in 1930 and 9.0
         millions in 1931 transferred to the consumer cooperative organisation Tsentrosoyuz.

livestock, under the heading 'consumption in production' (see p. 449 below). In fact, however, consumption in production would not include the animals eaten by peasants before joining the kolkhozy; this amount simply fails to appear in the balances at all. In table 6, 'capital investment' and 'losses' should therefore both be increased by this unknown but substantial amount of 'wilful slaughter'. This would increase the figures throughout *Materialy* for the accumulation fund, and for capitalist investment in agriculture and in the economy as a whole, probably by some 400 million rubles a year, but would not affect the amount of 'real accumulation' or capital stock.

   The other major development in 1928–30 which receives considerable attention in *Materialy* is the expansion of the socialised sector of the economy at the expense of the private sector; on the Soviet definitions used at that time, the private sector included production by individuals and families. The process of socialisation is displayed in the tables for production, national income, capital stock and elsewhere; tables II.C.2, 2a, 2b, 2c, 2d and 2e show the major changes. In 1928, the private sector was of substantial importance in small-scale industry, building and agriculture. In small-scale industry, production did not expand between 1928 and 1930, and a large number of individual artisans joined handicraft cooperatives. In the building industry, the construction of private housing, especially in the countryside, declined absolutely, while housing construction in the socialist sector, especially in industry increased rapidly. In agriculture, production declined slightly, but in the first collectivisation drive of 1929–30 a substantial proportion of all production was socialised (see table 7). As the production of collective farmers in their private plots is included in the private sector, the extent of collectivisation is minimised. Data for peasant incomes in current prices gave a more precise picture both of the extent to which the traditional individual peasant economy had been invaded by the process of socialisation, and of the extent to which work on the

Table 7 *Private sector as percentage of total production (measured in 1928 prices)*

	1928	1930.
Census industry	1.0	0.2
Small-scale industry	72.0	33.6
All industry	17.6	5.8
Building	40.3	11.4
Agriculture	97.9	78.9
All gross production	52.4	29.5

Source: Table II.C.2d.

Table 8 *Income of agricultural population in 1930*

Type of Income	Total income	Agri-cultural prole-tariat	Collec-tive farmer	Indi-vidual peasant	Kulak
Wages	2684.4	721.3	331.0	1615.1	17.0
Entrepreneurial income	431.4	–	–	–	431.4
From cooperative production	2783.9	–	2656.9	127.0	–
From independent production	11753.2	125.3	1079.9	10548.0	–
Insurance	126.7	7.7	34.0	81.0	4.0
Pensions etc.	68.9	13.0	20.0	35.4	–
Free social services	822.0	47.7	155.4	609.9	9.0
Total	18670.5	915.0	4277.2	13016.4	461.4

Source: Table III.5b Wages obtained by adding cols. 1, 2 and 10; pensions by adding cols. 7 and 13; free services by adding cols. 8 and 14.

personal plot formed a major part of the income of the collective farmer and of the worker on the state farm (the state farm worker is the main category under the heading 'agricultural proletariat'). In 1930, 65.3 per cent of the total income of the agricultural population (11,753.2+431.4=12,184.6 out of 18,670.0 million rubles) was derived from independent production, and the remaining 34.7 per cent from activities in the socialist sector, including 14.4 per cent from wages earned in that sector, and 14.9 per cent from cooperative (collective-farm) production. Of the 12,184.6 million rubles, 1,205.2 million was earned by collective farmers and state farm workers on their personal plots, (see table 8).

Materialy also provide a considerable amount of evidence about the economic mechanism through which the switch of resources to industrial investment was achieved, and the sources from which capital accumulation was obtained.

A series of tables shows that the growth of industrial production and of building work, which provided the physical inputs for the capital investment programme, were the result of increases both in labour productivity and in the number of persons employed (as measured by the total amount of time worked). In census industry, 76 per cent of the increase in output in the three years 1928–30 was attributed to increased labour productivity, 24 per cent to the increase in the labour force. In building work (socialist sector), the percentages were reversed: only 24 per cent was due to productivity, 76 per cent to the increase in the labour force. Moreover, in both industry and building the proportion of the increase due to the expansion of the labour force was substantially higher in 1930 than in 1928, rising to 44 per cent in the case of industry and as much as 83 per cent in the case of building (see tables I.9a and I.9b). Industrialisation during this period thus increasingly relied on extensive rather than intensive growth. The rate of increase in the labour force in these years was very high: according to *Materialy*, the number of workers employed in census industry, building work (all sectors) and state farms increased by 18.7 per cent in 1929 and 35.6 per cent in 1930, from 3.7 to 5.6 million persons (table I.9). The number of building workers in this period more than doubled, from 0.7 to 1.6 millions.[12] The increase in 1931, not given in *Materialy*, was even more rapid: in the three sectors the increase amounted to 44.2 per cent, the number of building workers rising to 2.5 millions.[13] According to *Materialy*, expansion of the non-agricultural population as a whole absorbed 42.5 per cent of the natural increase in the population (3.6 millions) in 1929, and as much as 89.8 per cent of the increase (3.3 millions) in 1930 (estimated from table III.17). These percentages are almost certainly an underestimate, as the official Soviet population figures for these years exaggerated the increase in the population. If we use Lorimer's figures for annual population increase, the increase in the non-agricultural population in these two years was equivalent to 92 per cent of the natural increase in the population and considerably exceeded it in 1930.[14] A large part of the increase in non-agricultural employment was a direct result of the expansion of capital investment in these years: as much as half of the increase in non-agricultural employment was in building work and in the Group 'A' industries.

These shifts in the labour force were accompanied by major changes in the pattern of consumption. As we have seen, in the *Materialy* the total consumption fund increased in 1929, increased slightly in 1930, and declined slightly in 1931; these figures probably conceal a real decline, even leaving aside the deterioration in quality. Simultaneously, the proportion of total consumption acquired by the agricultural population was reduced, while the proportion acquired by the rapidly-expanding non-agricultural population was increased (see table 9). Within the non-agricultural population, consumer goods were concentrated on industrial and other workers. According to *Materialy*, as table 9 shows, consumption of workers per capita continued to rise in absolute terms in 1931 while the consumption of the rest of the population declined. It is probable that the slight decline in per capita consumption for the non-worker population is underestimated, and that the figure for the increase in workers' consumption per capita is exaggerated. It is, however, certain that many industrial workers and their families were partly shielded from the consumption squeeze, as they received higher rations than the mass of urban employees.

While the shift in the labour force, and the accompanying shift in the distribution of consumption between different socio-economic groups, can be traced fairly precisely in *Materialy*, less precise information is provided about the accompanying shift in material

Table 9

	1928	1929	1930	1931
(a) *Consumption by agricultural and non-agricultural population (in million rubles at 1928 urban prices)*				
Total population	33715.8	35333.2	35779.3	(35050.7)
Non-agricultural population:				
All	10959.6	11377.3	12667.3	
Workers	4265.8	4688.9	5763.0	(7486.4)
Others	6973.8	6688.4	6904.6	
Agricultural population:				
All	22756.2	23955.9	23111.8	
Total non-workers	29550.0	30644.3	30016.4	(27564.3)
(b) *Consumption per capita of agricultural and non-agricultural population (in rubles at 1928 urban prices)*				
Total population	222.6	228.1	226.2	(221.8)
Non-agricultural population:				
All	368.2	363.7	369.8	
Workers	361.4	366.9	384.0	(397.4)
Others	(378.1)	(361.5)	(358.0)	
Agricultural population:				
All	187.0	193.8	186.5	
Total non-workers	211.6	215.6	209.6	(197.6)

Source: 1928–30 tables II.D.15 and 15a. Consumption includes public catering, purchase of services, and the value of free social and cultural services. 1931 figures were estimated by the editors using information in Petrov's article (pp. 95–7 below) these data refer to consumption in 1928 prices (less taxes). For workers consumption the 1928–30 rate of growth is identical to that given in Table II.D.15. But for total population the rate of growth is slightly lower. The figure of 35,050.7 is therefore a slight exaggeration.

resources. An interesting set of 'material balances' shows substantial changes in the allocation of building materials. The proportion of roofing iron, cement, brick, window glass and other building materials allocated to industrial construction greatly increased, and the proportion and even the absolute amount allocated to agricultural construction greatly declined. In 1930 industrial construction absorbed almost twice as much of all the listed materials as in 1928 (see Appendix A, table 4). *Materialy* do not provide detailed information about imported and home-produced industrial equipment, the other major input into capital investment. The relevant statistics, showing a large increase in these years, are, however, available in other Soviet sources.[15]

The shifts in resources between different sectors of the economy are set out in tables III.1 and III.4 (for a discussion of the structure of these tables, see pp. 6–9 above). These tables are available only in current prices. It should be borne in mind that agricultural prices rose rapidly in 1928–30 (with consumer prices rising more rapidly than producers' prices), but the prices of industrial manufactured consumer goods rose less rapidly, and industrial producers' prices in the socialist sector actually declined (see tables I.10 and I.10a–e below). With this qualification the changes in relative magnitudes in the course of 1928–30 shown in table III.4 are nevertheless striking. The increase in the

Table 10 *Percentage of production allocated to fixed capital*

	1928	1929	1930
(a) *Products of building work*			
Agriculture	18.4	18.1	18.1
Census industry	17.9	22.4	27.9
Small-scale industry	0.3	0.3	0.3
Transport and communications	9.5	10.1	16.7
Trade	1.1	2.0	3.1
Rural housing	25.3	20.4	10.9
Urban housing	17.7	15.7	14.9
Social (i.e. education, health, etc.)	9.7	10.9	8.2
	100.0	100.0	100.0
(b) *Industrial products*			
Agriculture	34.7	32.3	31.3
Census industry	37.0	38.0	40.5
Small-scale industry	0.6	0.6	0.4
Transport and communications	21.8	22.3	20.5
Trade	1.1	2.2	3.4
Rural housing	–	–	–
Urban housing	–	–	–
Social	4.8	4.7	4.1
Total	100.0	100.0	100.0

Source: Estimated from table III.4.

share of industry in the allocation of products of building work was obtained primarily as a result of the decline in the share of housing. The share of industry in 'industrial products' (which consists almost entirely of machinery and other equipment) increased, and the share of agriculture declined, but the decline of the share of agriculture was not very substantial, because the amount of implements and machinery allocated to agriculture increased substantially in 1928–30.

Table III.4 also shows the changing share of the allocation of industrial and agricultural consumer goods between the agricultural and non-agricultural population (rows B(a) and B(b), cols. 44–7). The share of the non-agricultural population in industrial products rose much more slowly, from 42.0 per cent to 43.0 per cent of the total, than its share in agricultural products, which rose from 37.4 per cent to 48.0 per cent (the latter increase is, however, exaggerated in real terms because urban prices of agricultural products rose more rapidly than rural prices). (See table 10.)

On the basis of *Materialy* and other data, the Soviet economist Barsov has argued that throughout the years 1929–32, with the exception of the single year 1931, the 'balance of payments' between industrial goods supplied to the agricultural sector and agricultural goods supplied to the non-agricultural sector was more favourable to agriculture than in 1928. That part of his estimate which covers the years 1928–30 is reproduced in table 11.

Table 11 *Estimates of exchange between the agricultural and non-agricultural spheres, 1928–30*

	In million rubles at 1928 prices			Index numbers		
	1928	1929	1930	1928	1929	1930
(a) *Barsov*						
Acquired by non-agricultural sphere						
1. Agricultural products less grain and flour returns	3166.5	3467.7	4049.0	100.0	109.5	127.9
Acquired by agricultural sphere						
2. Implements, machinery and equipment ('dead inventory')	600.8	724.2	962.2	100.0	120.5	154.2
3. Non-agricultural consumer goods	3350.6	4100.3	4396.2	100.0	122.4	131.2
4. All acquired by agricultural sphere	3951.4	4824.5	5322.5	100.0	122.2	134.7
(b) *Materialy implicit*						
Acquired by non-agricultural sphere						
1. Agricultural products less grain and flour returns	3397.7	3970.5	3873.6	100.0	116.0	114.0
Acquired by agricultural sphere						
2. Implements, machinery and equipment ('dead inventory')	600.8	724.2	926.2	100.0	120.5	154.2
3. Non-agricultural consumer goods	5781.9	6356.9	6369.7	100.0	109.9	110.2
4. All acquired by agricultural population	6382.7	7081.1	7295.9	100.0	110.9	114.3

Sources: (a) 1. Barsov, *op. cit.* (1969), table opposite p. 112.
    2. Barsov, *op. cit.* (1969), p. 118.
    3. Barsov, *op. cit.* (1969), p. 118.
  (b) 1. calculated from Appendices pp. 314–405.
    2. same as for Barsov above.
    3. see p. 211.

According to Barsov, while the extra-rural marketed production of agriculture increased by 27.9 per cent between 1928 and 1930, the supply of industrial goods to agriculture in the form of machinery and consumer goods increased even more rapidly, by 34.7 per cent. The agricultural population was able to increase its purchases of industrial goods because of the considerable increase in its purchasing power. While both individual peasants aᵗ d ᴋolkhozy were compelled to supply increasing quantities of grain and other agricultural goods to the state at low delivery prices, they sold part of their produce at very high prices in the free market (in 1930 free-market prices were 450 per cent of procurement prices). In his introductory article to *Materialy* Petrov drew attention to the importance of such price differences in the transfer of resources between sectors. While he did not examine the relationship between agriculture and the rest of the economy in this connection, Petrov estimated the transfers between the private and the socialist sector (in 1928 prices), and concluded that in 1930 the transfers from the private to the socialist sector of 2,341.5 million rubles were more than compensated by the 'surplus payment' (primarily to agricultural producers due to high market prices) in the reverse direction of 3,000–3,500 million rubles (see p. 69 below).

It should be noted that these estimates in 1928 prices show relatively high values for industrial as against agricultural products as compared with world prices. Barsov has therefore made alternative calculations in which the absolute amount transferred to the non-agricultural sphere from the agricultural sphere is substantially higher throughout the period than the reverse flow from the agricultural sphere to the non-agricultural sphere. But these alternative calculations use the same underlying data, applying different prices. It is therefore important to check Barsov's estimates in 1928 prices against the data in these prices in the detailed tables of *Materialy*. Our estimates are made within the terms of Barsov's model of the structure of agriculture: non-agriculture economic relations, though his assumptions are controversial and need to be examined on another occasion.

On agricultural products acquired by the non-agricultural population (line 1 in table 9a), *Materialy* provide a great deal of data in the balances of agricultural products, from which an independent estimate can be made. While the data for most products are similar to those given by Barsov, the level of grain transferred from the agricultural sector, even net of the flour and bran returned to agriculture, was higher than in Barsov's data and the rate of growth in 1930 was much lower.

Grain, flour and bran transfers from agriculture to the non-agricultural sectors

	In million tons			In %		
	1928	1929	1930	1928	1929	1930
(a) *Materialy*						
Grain from agriculture	45.1	49.6	52.1	100.0	100.0	115.5
Flour and bran returned to agriculture	38·1	34·1	36·0	100·0	94·5	99·7
Grain from agriculture net of flour and bran returned	9.0	15.5	16.1	100.0	172.2	178.8
(b) *Barsov*						
Extra-rural marketings	15.7	19.5	22.6	100.0	124.2	143.9
Returned rural supply	7.4	9.3	4.8	100.0	125.7	64.9
Extra-rural marketings less rural returns	8.3	10.2	17.9	100.0	122.9	215.7

Sources: (a) Calculated from Appendices A.7 and B.1.
      (b) A. A. Barsov, *ibid.*, p. 103.

The reason for this difference appears to be that Barsov is using an extra-rural procurements classification of agricultural marketings as opposed to the extra-agricultural classification used in *Materialy*. Barsov's data are taken directly from the procurement agencies and exclude non-state grain transfers, whilst the *Materialy* data are based on grain utilisation balances.

The use of these different series of figures for grain makes a major difference to the total value of agricultural produce transferred to the non-agricultural sector, giving an indication of a growth-rate of only 14 per cent in 1928–30 instead of 27.9 per cent (see table below).

Agricultural products acquired by the non-agricultural population exclusive of grain, flour and bran returned to the agricultural sector in million rubles in 1928 prices

	1928	1929	1930	1928	1929	1930
Materialy	3397.7	3970.5	3873.6	100.0	116.9	114.0
Barsov	3166.5	3467.7	4049.0	100.0	109.5	127.9

Sources: *Materialy*, calculated from appendices A.7 and B.1.
Barsov, from Barsov, *ibid.*, pp. 122–3.

As regards the non-agricultural goods acquired by agriculture the *Materialy* data are less complete. Apart from tractors, *Materialy* provide no separate data on agricultural machinery and implements. However, Barsov's data on the supply of agricultural machinery (line 2 of table 9a) are not likely to contain major inaccuracies, and they correspond to the growth rates in the published Soviet statistics on agricultural 'dead inventories'.[16] *Materialy* do, however, provide data on the size and growth of industrial consumer goods acquired by the agricultural population and these data again differ significantly from Barsov's figures. Barsov's data, which indicated an increase of 31.2 per cent in 1928–30, were obtained by applying a price index to official data on rural retail trade in current prices. The data in *Materialy*, in contrast, were obtained from peasant family budgets (see p. 304) and covered all industrial consumer goods including those produced in the countryside and acquired by peasants. With this wider coverage, the increase in industrial goods consumed by the agricultural population, measured in urban prices of 1928, was only 10.2 per cent in 1928–30, as can be seen from the table below:

Industrial consumer goods acquired by the agricultural population in million rubles in 1928 prices

	1928	1929	1930	1928	1929	1930
Materialy	5781.9	6356.9	6369.7	100.0	109.9	110.2
Barsov	3350.6	4100.3	4369.2	100.0	122.4	131.2

Source: *Materialy* p. 211.
Barsov, see above table 11a line 3.

Table 12 *Industrial goods acquired by the agricultural population, 1928–30*

	In million rubles at 1928 prices			As % of total consumption by population and institutions (measured in physical terms)		
(a) *Consumer goods*	1928	1929	1930	1928	1929	1930
Sugar	343.6	294.2	301.2	47.6	46.6	43.5
Tea	67.3	63.0	63.5	58.5	57.4	58.9
Vegetable oil	176.5	180.6	169.7	74.5	72.0	75.1
Salt	54.3	58.4	59.7	86.4	87.2	86.0
Grain spirit	674.2	694.8	751.8	65.3	71.0	66.7
Makhorka	89.2	84.9	77.8	81.5	83.4	78.8
Tobacco and cigarettes	47.7	93.6	113.6	14.6	23.6	24.2
Leather footwear*	739.8	858.0	1020.0	55.4	59.3	60.1
Galoshes	63.5	90.8	79.6	49.0	56.5	51.4
Cotton fabrics	973.5	1078.5	766.7	73.5	73.7	71.7
Woollen fabrics	73.2	62.9	53.0	44.8	45.7	43.2
Household soap	73.6	76.2	59.8	60.2	57.7	54.6
Matches	49.7	56.7	64.4	69.7	68.1	67.4
Total for 13 goods	3426.1	3692.6	3580.8			
1928=100	100.0	107.8	104.5			
Previous year=100	–	107.8	97.0			

	In million metres length			As % of total consumption by population and institutions		
Fabric and clothing in fabric equivalents:						
Cottons	1794.7	1988.4	1514.6	71.3	71.7	68.4
Woollens	42.1	57.1	71.1	43.6	53.6	59.4

	In million rubles at 1928 prices			As % of total consumption (including consumption in production)		
(b) *Producer goods*						
Electric power to agriculture	5.4	6.0	9.3	1.0	0.9	1.5
Coal and coke to agriculture	–	–	–	–	–	–
Kerosene:						
By agriculture	14.8	29.9	60.3	6.2	10.5	16.9
By agricultural population	65.1	61.0	49.7	19.6	15.4	10.0
Total kerosene	79.9	90.9	110.0	25.8	25.9	26.9
Petrol by agriculture	0.5	1.6	25.3	0.3	0.7	7.7

Table 12 (*cont.*)

	In million rubles at 1928 prices			As % of total consumption (including consumption in production)		
Tractors by agriculture (1928 prices per h.p. 180r)	6.8	38.2	96.2	98.9	94.4	92.8
	92.6	136.7	240.8			
Building materials:						
Roofing iron	26.1	24.8	10.0			
Cement	4.3	3.8	3.2			
Bricks	15.6	15.7	11.2			
Glass	21.9	25.8	17.2			
Sawn timber	120.0	110.7	73.8			
Rough timber	294.6	256.6	221.1			
	482.5	437.4	336.5			
Total	4001.2	4266.7	4158.1			

Note: * Includes an estimate for cost of repairs, as price × quantity in table 6 of Appendix A does not equal the total given in value terms. Our figure for 1930 in 1928 prices is approximate, as it includes an estimate for repair.

Sources: (a) Appendix A, table 6.

(b) Appendix A, tables 2 and 3.

The appendix balances in *Materialy*, pp. 314–405, also present data on consumption of specific consumer goods. The data for consumption by the agricultural population of 13 important industrial consumer goods (excluding flour) are given in table 12. For these 13 industrial consumer goods consumption by the agricultural population increased by only 4.5 per cent between 1928 and 1930, as compared with an increase of 10.2 per cent for all industrial consumer goods as given in the table above. The difference is evidently partly due to the substantial increase in the supply of made-up clothing to the countryside. (In these years there was a substantial increase in the factory clothing industry; and a decline in domestic and artisan manufacture. Both urban and rural population received a higher proportion of their clothing in the form of finished clothing made in factories rather than in lengths of textiles.)[17]

These data do not seem compatible with an increase in supplies to the countryside at large as suggested by Barsov. Evidently his data underestimated the importance in 1928 of artisan production not sold through the state retail network, and its decline in 1928–30.[18] His estimate for all industrial goods sold to the agricultural population for personal use in 1928, 3,350.6 million rubles was lower than the figure in *Materialy* for 13 specific goods or groups of goods, 3,426.1 million rubles (see tables 11 and 12).

If we compare the *Materialy* figures for the flow of all agricultural produce to the non-agricultural sector and the flow of all non-agricultural produce to the agricultural sector, then we see a less sharp increase in the flows than indicated by Barsov, and with little overall change in the balance of payments between 1928 and 1930 (see tables 9a and 9b). Unfortunately we have no detailed source of independent data to check the reliability of Barsov's calculations for the years of greater strain in 1931 and 1932.

Materialy are a remarkably competent source of information on a crucially important stage of Soviet economic development. They were produced at a critical period in the re-evaluation of Soviet planning targets and methodology. Because of the intense political sensitivity concerning these matters even these restricted documents failed to state clearly what the economic position was. This was not due to any failure among the statisticians to understand the problem, or due to any shortage of statistical data. It was a consequence of the peculiar political circumstances at the time. *Materialy* provide a sufficient basis upon which an informed and alert reader could calculate the relationships in real terms between the different sectors of the economy and could see that the serious disproportionality of the 1928–30 period was becoming even more serious in 1931. However, contrary to the claims of Barsov and Ellman, it is not possible to conclude that there was any distinct shift in the balance of payments between agriculture and industry in favour of agriculture during 1928–30.

NOTES

1 T. V. Ryabushkin, *Problemy ekonomicheskoi statistiki* (1959), pp. 132–47.
2 A. L. Vainshtein, *Narodnyi dokhod Rossii i SSSR: istoriya, metodologiya ischisleniya, dinamika*, 1969, pp. 95–9; Vainshtein was Kondratiev's principal assistant in the Conjuncture Institute of the People's Commissariat of Finance in the 1920s.
3 A. A. Barsov, *Balans stoimostnykh obmenov mezhdu gorodom i derevnei* (1969); an earlier article by Barsov on the same theme appeared in *Istoriya SSSR*, no. 3, 1969.
4 See for example S. V. Belova, *Fond vozmeshcheniya sredstv truda i dinamiki I podrazdeleniya*, 1977, pp. 28–48.
5 J. R. Millar, 'Soviet Rapid Development and the Agricultural Surplus Hypothesis', *Soviet Studies*, 22 (1970), 'A reply to Alec Nove', *Soviet Studies*, 23 (1971), 'Mass Collectivisation and the Contribution of Soviet Agriculture to the First Five-Year Plan', *Slavic Review*, 23, 1974. A. Nove, 'The Agricultural Surplus Hypothesis; a Comment, *Soviet Studies*, 22 (1971), 'A Reply to a Reply', *Soviet Studies*, 23, 1972, M. Ellman, 'Did the Agricultural Surplus Provide the Resources for the Increase in Investment in the USSR in the First Five-Year Plan?' *Economic Journal*, 85, 1975, and H. Hunter and E. J. Rutan III 'Soviet Investment Choices in the Thirties – Constraints and Costs', paper presented to the Second World Congress for Soviet and East European Studies, Garmisch-Partenkirchen, 1980.
6 Estimated from R. Moorsteen and R. P. Powell, *The Soviet Capital Stock, 1928–1962*, 1966, pp. 358–9.
7 See S. G. Wheatcroft, R. W. Davies and J. M. Cooper, 'Soviet Industrialisation Reconsidered', unpublished paper presented to SSRC Conference on Soviet Economic Development in the 1930s, Centre for Russian and East European Studies, University of Birmingham, 1982, pp. 4–6.
8 The net increase in fixed capital (in census industry in 1928 prices) was estimated at 3,361.5 million rubles (fixed capital entering production, 4,192.2 million rubles, less depreciation, 830.7 millions), while gross investment was 6,282.2 million rubles (see Appendix C, table 4a).

9 *Planovoe khozyaistvo*, no. 3, 1929, p. 283.

10 Estimated from section II.D, table 2, at urban prices; housing and free social services have been excluded from the total.

11 See R. W. Davies, *The Socialist Offensive: the Collectivisation of Soviet Agriculture, 1929–1930*, London and Cambridge, Mass., 1982, pp. 338, 366–8, 420.

12 *Trud v SSSR* (1936), p. 244 (annual average).

13 *Ibid.*, pp. 10–11. These data are not strictly comparable with those in *Materialy*; they include workers in machine-tractor stations, and evidently use a wider definition of census industry than that adopted in *Materialy*. But these differences would have an insignificant effect on the rate of growth.

14 Lorimer estimated that the population increased by only 4.9 millions in 1928–30; other Western estimates for these years coincided with the official Soviet population figures published at the time (see S. G. Wheatcroft, 'The Population Dynamic and Factors Affecting It in the Soviet Union', unpublished *CREES Discussion Papers*, University of Birmingham, SIPS no. 2, 1976, p.61, and accompanying commentary).

15 Moorsteen and Powell estimated that equipment inputs into Soviet investment, measured in 1928 internal prices, increased by 43 per cent in 1929, 87 per cent in 1930, and 35 per cent in 1931, and so amounted to 362 per cent of the 1928 level in 1931 (*ibid.*, pp. 387–9).

16 See *Narodnoe khozyaistvo SSSR* (1932), pp. 142–3. These have been accepted as reasonably accurate by the major Western scholars working in this field (see Moorsteen and Powell, *op. cit.* (1966), pp. 427–42).

17 The supply of clothing to the countryside increased from 104.0 million rubles in 1928–9 to 294.8 millions in 1930, measured in 1926–7 prices. (*Tovarooborot za gody rekonstruktivnogo perioda*, (1932), p. 16; see also the data for cooperative trade in current prices in *ibid.*, pp. 28–9).

18 He estimated sales on the 'unorganised market' at only 360.2 million rubles in 1928, whereas the source he uses gives a figure of 760.4 million rubles (for 1927/8) and states that this covers only 'stationary trade of an intermediary character' (i.e. it excludes sales direct from artisan to peasant, and by private traders without fixed premises). For the figure for 1928, see *Tovarooborot za gody rekonstruktivnogo perioda* (1932), p. 18; we do not have access to the archival sources used by Barsov for private trade in 1929 and 1930.

3

A brief history of the balance of the national economy

In many respects the *Materials for a Balance of the National Economy 1928–1930* represent one of the missing links in the story of the development of Soviet planning. For Soviet economic development to have achieved what it did there had to be a far more serious basis to the planning effort than appears from the available published literature. There was undoubtedly much chaos and unnecessary destruction, especially in agriculture, but nevertheless industry developed on an unparalleled scale; and this growth was based not on market pressure but on a planning process covering an increasingly complex economy.

The planning process was more of a constant administrative process than a genuine attempt to fulfil the targets in specific planning documents, as Professor Zaleski has recently pointed out.[1] But more serious attempts were made to coordinate the separate elements in the plan than appears in most Western accounts of the Soviet planning process of the time.[2]

The present document provides us for the first time with an opportunity to study a major attempt to uncover inter-branch and inter-sector relationships in the economy. It was produced in a limited edition of 500 copies, marked 'For official use only', and circulated among senior planners and officials in the summer of 1932. This was a crucial moment at the end of the first five-year planning period, when the second five-year plan was still under discussion. This was also an extremely complicated political period, when the leadership was gradually coming to accept that it needed to implement more realistic lower planning targets, but when it was still denouncing those who were advocating such a change in policy.

This chapter will attempt to cast more light on the publication (albeit in a restricted circulation) of these materials at this time and will consider both the question of the origins of work on the balances of the national economy in the USSR and their significance for the planning process.

The theoretical origins of the balance of the national economy may be traced to Quesnay's *tableau économique* and Marx's schema of social reproduction.[3] Its practical origins in Russia may be traced to the balances of production and consumption of grain prepared by Shcherbina in the 1880s and Erisman in the 1890s. At the first congress of local government (zemstvo) statisticians, meeting clandestinely in 1894, the eminent statistician A. I. Chuprov drew attention to the lack of statistical work on consumption

34

in both Russia and the West and called for the study of consumption as 'a key factor in production'. In the following years many peasant consumption studies were carried out.[4]

During the First World War, the zemstvo statisticians were for the first time able to undertake statistical work on a national scale. In 1916, led by P. I. Popov (head of the Tula province statistical bureau) and V. G. Groman (Penza), they carried out the first all-Russian agricultural census; and thus, together with the peasant studies already mentioned, provided the basis for food supply plans prepared under Groman's direction in 1916 and 1917. These food production and consumption balances provided a model for the sectoral balances which eventually formed a major part of the balance of the national economy.

After the overthrow of the tsarist regime in the spring of 1917, this work was extended, and a food supply plan was prepared for the whole country, though in conditions of growing food chaos; the leading zemstvo statisticians were promoted to prominent national posts.[5]

Following the Bolshevik revolution, Popov, with support from Lenin, endeavoured to bring together local and central statistical agencies into a single administration. The notion of providing reliable statistics for a coordinated national plan of production and consumption was at the heart of Popov's conception of the role of the new central statistical agency. At a congress of ex-zemstvo statisticians in June 1918 he summarised this approach and made what may be the first recorded use in Soviet Russia of the term 'national economic balance':

It [the central statistical agency] must supply material with which the new state will and must construct a plan of state socialised production and distribution. This plan must be regulated on the basis of a continuous supply to the central statistical agency of data on the changing facts and phenomena in the process of production and redistribution.

Statistical data must provide the basis of a national economic balance. For each given moment it is necessary that society should not only feel the pulsations of its life, but also ... investigate these pulsations, these changes of national economic life.[6]

The idea of the balance therefore preceded the creation of the Central Statistical Administration (TsSU) and was itself an important factor in determining its shape and its work.[7] Six months later, in January 1919, Popov, now head of TsSU, declared that 'we must compile every year a balance of the national economy as a whole and of the separate branches of the economy, based on the work of all the departments of TsSU'.[8]

During the years of civil war, several 'material balances' (balances of production and consumption in physical terms) were prepared in TsSU, but in January 1921, at the end of the war, Popov frankly admitted that the pressure of current work had prevented serious work on an overall national economic balance.[9]

In the meantime, work involving the preparation of sectoral balances had been proceeding in at least two different directions. First, a group of enthusiastic planners attempted to prepare plans or budgets in kind covering the economy as a whole, and were roundly condemned by Lenin for their lack of realism.[10] Secondly, groups of experts led by Krzhizhanovsky, and with the active support of Lenin, prepared in 1920 the famous GOELRO long-term 10–15 year plan for the electrification of Russia. A major feature of the plan was the attempt to programme the production and consumption of major industrial commodities, notably, electric power, on a national and regional basis.

At this time an important difference in approach between Popov's 'balance of the national economy' and the planners' 'material balances' and 'balance method of planning' was already emerging in embryonic form, and acquired much greater importance in subsequent Soviet history. The balance of the national economy as it emerged in the early 1920s was a comprehensive attempt to reveal in value terms the entire process of production and consumption, including fixed capital stock, circulating capital and consumer goods. A *post-factum* accounting balance of the economy was intended to provide the basis or starting point for a national-economic plan in which the economic activity of the different sectors was coordinated or 'balanced'. The uncovering of existing relationships and the provision of a basis for 'balanced' planning: this was the central aim of Popov and his colleagues.[11] In contrast to this approach, the tendency in the State Planning Commission, Gosplan (established in 1921 following the work of the GOELRO commission), and in the industrial commissariat VSNKh, was to rely on plans prepared in each sub-branch of the economy and to coordinate them at the centre.

In an ideal planning system both approaches would be compatible and essential. But in the Soviet Union in the 1920s the process of planning rapidly shifted away from Popov's integrated-balance approach towards the direction followed by Gosplan and GOELRO. Thus the preparation of sectoral plans, and their attempted reconciliation in a national document by Gosplan and the political authorities, became the central feature of Soviet planning even in the mid-1920s. And with the political decision to give overriding priority to industrialisation at the end of the 1920s, 'balance' was for a time altogether thrust aside, and with it the balance of the national economy. But, whether by crude adjustments or by coordinated planning, policy had eventually to adjust to reality; 'balance' imposed itself on the planners. Throughout the period since the end of the 1920s, Soviet planners have hankered to restore the balance of the economy to a central position in planning, as a prerequisite for 'scientific' planning. But the tension between 'plan' and 'balance' has been permanently unresolved, and in the Stalin period was overshadowed and complicated by the extraordinary pace imposed on economic development, and by the hostility of political leaders and administrators to what they saw as the caution, timorousness or sabotage of the advocates of 'balance'.

At first the sharp contrast which eventually emerged between different approaches was not at all obvious. In 1921 after the Civil War a mixed economy was established in which a market relationship between state industry and individual peasant agriculture was the cornerstone. The New Economic Policy (NEP), which lasted until 1928 or 1929, in its early years provided a favourable atmosphere for the development of the balance of the national economy.

The first tentative steps towards the preparation of a national-economic balance were undertaken soon after the beginning of NEP. S. G. Strumilin later claimed that already in 1921, as the responsible senior official in Gosplan, he gave high priority to the preparation of a long-term national-economic balance for the planned utilisation and distribution of labour, and that the first scheme for a *post-factum* balance of the national economy was projected in Gosplan at this time.[12]

In November 1922, Popov presented in TsSU preliminary results of an 'investigation of the national economy as a whole', prepared independently of Gosplan. This concentrated on the peasant market balance. This first practical attempt at compiling the balance of the national economy was already accompanied by a policy clash, the harbinger of greater clashes to come. Gosplan vigorously rejected Popov's proposal to widen the peasant market by increasing grain prices.[13] Almost a year later, Groman, now a senior official in Gosplan, produced a similar market balance for 1922/3, which he rather misleadingly described as a balance of the national economy.[14]

Simultaneously TsSU and Gosplan clashed about the role of the national-economic balance in the planning process. Popov argued that a *post-factum* balance was a prerequisite for coordinated planning, which must be delayed until after a satisfactory balance had been prepared; this could not be done until a series of statistical censuses had been carried out in 1925.[15] Gosplan in contrast proposed to proceed to prepare a coordinated national plan before the balance was available.[16]

Popov's position was temporarily strengthened when A. D. Tsyurupa, a deputy chairman of the Council of People's Commissars, SNK, took on the chairmanship of Gosplan in March 1924. Tsyurupa had considerable personal prestige in the state apparatus and was also greatly respected by the statisticians.[17] Tsyurupa seems to have supported Popov's approach to planning: at the first session of the Gosplan presidium under his leadership he insisted on the need to improve planning methodology and appointed Popov to produce a report on this topic. At this time Popov pressed hard for the authority to carry out the series of censuses which would provide reliable data for a *post-factum* balance of the national economy.[18]

But the ascendancy of the Popovian approach did not last long. At the XIII Party congress in May 1924 Stalin, while insisting on the necessity of reliable statistical records, and praising statisticians in capitalist countries who presented facts correctly irrespective of their political views, condemned Soviet statisticians whose data were unreliable.[19] Shortly afterwards, the Soviet authorities delayed the proposed censuses from 1925 to 1926, but nevertheless accepted a Gosplan proposal that TsSU should compile and complete by 1 October 1924 a balance of the national economy for 1923/4 and a preliminary balance for 1924/5, on a scheme approved by Gosplan.[20]

This decision to push ahead immediately with planning work before new statistical census data would be available clearly indicated a change in priorities. Popov's reaction to this reversal is unknown. He did, however, join the Bolshevik party at about this time and no doubt attempted to argue his case both within and outside the party.

Eventually a report on the summary balance of the national economy for 1923/4 was completed by TsSU at the end of March 1925,[21] six months after the date set by the government. The work in its entirety was only completed and published in the middle of 1926.[22]

This phase in the development of TsSU and the balance of the national economy came to an end in the winter of 1925–6. In the summer of 1925 Gosplan pushed ahead with the preparation of 'control figures' (an annual plan) for the economic year 1925/6 without any firm detailed knowledge of the balance of the national economy and the inter-relationship of the separate sectors and constituents. In November 1925 Tsyurupa was transferred from the chairmanship of Gosplan to another post, and was again replaced by Krzhizhanovsky, the architect of the GOELRO plan.[23] At this time TsSU, weakened by Tsyurupa's departure from Gosplan, also incurred the disfavour of the political authorities because Kamenev, a leader of the 'New Opposition', used TsSU data to claim that there was a dangerous degree of socio-economic differentiation among the peasantry. In January 1926, Popov resigned from the chairmanship of TsSU, which he had occupied since its formation in 1918. The full circumstances of this resignation are not known. For the history of the national economic balance, it is relevant to note that on the day of Popov's resignation Sovnarkom announced a delay in carrying out the censuses which were supposed to be an essential prerequisite of a successful compilation of the balance.[24]

Popov's resignation led to a thorough reform of TsSU, and the loss of much of its pre-revolutionary 'zemstvo' atmosphere. However, there was not a total break with this tradition. Osinskii, the new chairman of TsSU, was an independent-minded person with some pre-revolutionary statistical experience.[25] Osinskii brought Groman into TsSU to head the newly created department 'Statplan', which was to serve as a link between TsSU and Gosplan; Groman simultaneously continued to work in Gosplan.

At the first reported session of the collegium of TsSU under Osinskii's chairmanship in June 1926 he strongly insisted that 'statistics must not be subservient to politics' or 'produced with the aim of supporting preconceived policy conclusions'. He emphasised both that relationships with Gosplan must be improved and that the balances must receive more attention. Work on the balances was 'the synthesis of all statistical activity' and 'must take the same place in the work of TsSU as the control figures occupy in Gosplan'.[26] Groman enthusiastically supported Osinskii's proposed reforms; he declared that 'the control figures of Gosplan are nothing other than a balance of the future national economy'; as a result of the absence of a balance, Gosplan had been 'foredoomed to great inexactitudes'.[27]

Despite these initial statements work on the balance and the proposed series of censuses was gradually reduced. The growing pressures of the accelerated industriali-sation drive and the regime of economy combined against them. During 1926 and 1927 as the party policy moved rapidly in the direction of accepting an acceleration in the pace of industrialisation, Osinskii modified his earlier enthusiasm for the balance of the national economy. His report to a statistical conference in the spring of 1927 indicated a sharp move in TsSU towards a GOELRO–Gosplan goal-oriented view of planning:

The majority of the collegium consider that it is incorrect to hold that all the economic phenomena that surround economic life can be combined into one balance. Rather than seeing all the economic factors like the tributaries of a stream all flowing into one channel, the collegium majority see the relationships of different economic factors more like the solar system, where the central light goes its own way and has planets which move along different orbits, and each of these planets has its own satellites which in turn have their own orbits. And all the system is in a state of inter-related attraction and equilibrium.

He went on to explain that the significance of balances for separate branches, spheres and fields of the economy would increase, and that if the term 'the balance of the national economy' were used to mean 'the inter-related system of different balances for these separate spheres and fields of the economy, then the term could remain'.[28]

This approach was initially shared by many of the enthusiasts for industrialisation in Gosplan such as Strumilin, who argued that the plans for agriculture and other sectors should be fitted into 'engineering projects' setting goals for industry; balances should be a means of not cutting back to bottlenecks but of overcoming them. With this approach, the method of balances ceased to be a means of establishing equilibrium, and itself contributed to the pressure for an increased pace of industrialisation.[29] But others such as Groman, were gradually becoming convinced that the pressure for industrialisation had been allowed to go too far, and they began to defend Popovian balance planning and to insist on the importance of obtaining a *post-factum* balance for the previous year before preparing a balance for a future year.[30]

To the supporters of Strumilin's goal-oriented approach to planning, the censuses which Popov had been struggling to introduce seemed of less importance, and with the increasing predominance of the policies of rapid industrialisation, the censuses were repeatedly postponed,[31] and many senior planning and statistical officials were dismissed. At the end of 1929, in the midst of the drive for the collectivisation of agriculture, TsSU was transformed from a separate government department into the statistical-economic sector (SES) of Gosplan. In the following year, Strumilin himself, who had in turn by this time come to regard the further increases in the plan targets as unrealistic, was to be replaced as head of SES and many of the planners, including Groman, were to be arrested and tried as wreckers.

During the course of these upheavals Stalin, in a speech to a conference of Marxist agrarians in December 1929, made a quite unexpected direct reference to the balance of the national economy:

We also need to raise the question of the popularisation of the marxist theory of reproduction. We need to rework the question of the schema for the construction of the balances of the national economy. What TsSU published in 1926 as a balance of the national economy is not a balance, but merely playing-about with figures. Nor are the tracts of Bazarov and Groman on the problems of the balance of the national economy useful. The schema of the balance of the national economy of the USSR must be worked out by revolutionary marxists if they want to study the question of the economics of the transition period.[32]

Thus Stalin condemned previous work on the balance of the national economy while not dissociating himself from the idea of the balance as such, providing that it was designed by 'revolutionary Marxists'.

In spite of the fierce attacks on the old generation of planners and statisticians, the struggle for reliable statistics and balances continued. Minaev, who replaced Strumilin as head of SES in December 1930, had previously worked on the preparation of a series of balances in the Ukrainian TsSU.[33] He soon emerged as a protagonist of the balance of the national economy and a firm advocate of greater independence for the statistical system.[34]

In November 1930 Gosplan's political leadership was substantially strengthened when Kuibyshev, a full member of the Politburo, was appointed chairman as well as a vice-chairman of SNK.[35] Simultaneously the authority of the People's Commissariat of

Workers' and Peasants' Inspection, NK RKI, was diminished with the departure of Ordzhonikidze for Vesenkha. Minaev, who had called for a central consolidation of planning authority of this kind, was also promoted at this time to be one of Kuibyshev's deputies in Gosplan, replacing Strumilin.[36]

Under Minaev's leadership work was now undertaken on drawing up a new series of balances of the national economy. By the middle of 1931 a preliminary balance of the national economy for 1927/8, 1928/9 and 1929/30 was already being circulated and discussed within Gosplan.[37] Even while some of the planners were being tried as 'bourgeois wreckers'[38] other prominent statisticians continued the attempt to dissociate the balance idea from them.[39]

1931 and 1932 were years of protracted struggle behind the scenes, between more moderate and more extreme economic policies and between different concepts of planning. Much remains unknown about this struggle. During 1932 lower planning targets and better coordinated planning came to prevail. After the official declaration that the first five-year plan had been completed in four years, on 31 December 1932, the annual plan for 1933 marked the victory of more realistic planning. This victory was consolidated a year later with the approval of more modest targets for the 1933–7 second five-year plan at the XVII party congress in January 1934. But this victory in planning policy was accompanied by the further consolidation of the political authority of Stalin and the other leaders who had pressed forward the overambitious targets of 1929–31. Leading planners of the 1920s such as Groman and Bazarov remained in jail or at least out of office. And the move to more realistic planning was also accompanied by a further temporary eclipse of the 'balance of the national economy.'

The present *Materialy* were completed in the midst of this struggle. They were handed to the printer on 27 August 1932, and printed by 17 October.

The immediate background to their preparation was the decision to increase the autonomy and prestige of the central statistical agency. On 17 December 1931, it was renamed the Central Administration of National Economic Records, TsUNKhU, and instead of being administratively a part of Gosplan was merely 'attached' to it. On 11 January 1932, Osinskii was appointed joint deputy chairman of Gosplan and head of TsUNKhU. Minaev remained first deputy chairman of TsUNKhU, and was to some extent strengthened there by the appointment of other supporters of a more moderate approach to the collegium of TsUNKhU: Strumilin was appointed second deputy chairman and Nemchinov, Petrov and Mindlin were appointed members of the collegium. There were several indications at this time of a strong desire amongst some influential groups to return to a more scientific and balanced view of planning. Perhaps the most striking was Osinskii's announcement, within a month of his appointment, that the 1931 grain harvest was lower than had been previously reported.[40]

In June 1932 a clear call for an increase in emphasis on the balance of the national economy and on economic reality came from V. Ignatiev, who wrote in the leading Gosplan journal:

The balance of the national economy was an arena and a weapon of the wreckers and Right opportunists. But now several comrades, completely correctly fighting against the wrecker- and Right-opportunist understanding of the balance, have gone too far in this matter. They have begun to neglect the balance altogether, not noticing that they were throwing out the baby with the bath water. Distrust of the balance must be overcome. It must become one of the most important forms and one of the most important methods of planning the development of the national economy.[41]

The editorial board of the journal, writing later in the year, took a far more conservative line, emphasising that 'we must in the most decisive fashion fight against political speculation from the Right opposition and wreckers on the question of the balance.' 'The proportions in the plan must not be dictated by levelling down to the bottleneck but be dictated by the aims of socialist planning. Certain balancing work must be used in the plan, as in the compilation of separate balances (for grain and fodder, building materials, metals, etc.), as in the sense of the correspondence between such balances as those in physical terms and the financial balance.'[42]

The debate was also visible in an article in the journal of the economics section of the Communist Academy, which strongly emphasised the importance of the balance, insisting that 'in order to correctly build a plan it is necessary to know the real state of affairs, i.e., the concrete reality which it is necessary to change in accordance with the basic tasks of the plan.'[43]

Within TsUNKhU itself Minaev, Petrov and Pervukhin, who were directing the work on the balances, were in a delicate political position. They needed to avoid giving the impression of favouring a reduction of the plan targets. Throughout 1932, Minaev modestly declared that work on the balance and its subsequent publication had only the aims of firstly, to raise for discussion and reworking a series of problems on the theoretical and scientific character of the balance of the national economy, and, secondly, to supply concrete material for the study of the reproduction of the USSR for 1928–30.[44] But only the most naive reader could have failed to realise that the publication of such materials at the time when the Politburo were debating the second five-year plan had political significance.

Petrov, one of the principal compilers of the balance and the head of the TsUNKhU sector on the balance of the national economy, went somewhat further than Minaev. In his introductory section in *Materialy*, Petrov made the normal conventional statements that 'the balance method of economic planning, is a method for synthetically coordinat-ing the plan, with the object of achieving in practice the basic directives of the Party general line.'[45] But at the same time he went on to describe the question of proportiona-lity and dialectical inter-relationships between all the elements of reproduction (both within the socialist sector but also for all the national economy as a whole) as being subordinate but all the same necessary[46] and that the results of the balance, as already calculated, show that the basic questions of the rate and the proportions can be revealed from it.[47]

The figures cited by Petrov clearly drew attention to the disproportion between consumption and accumulation in the economy as a whole, and the lag and partial decline of agriculture as a whole and livestock farming in particular. Petrov attempted to cover himself by stating that this somewhat unhealthy relationship between consump-tion and accumulation could not be considered as being a consequence of high rates of growth of the means of production (accumulation). But he then went on to explain that the lagging behind of the production of articles of consumption was a consequence of the lowering of the output of livestock products, which was itself due to the lowering of the size of herds due to insufficient feed.[48]

Although the balance formally covered only the period 1928–30, several figures, particularly for national income and expenditure, were also given for 1931. Petrov used these figures to demonstrate that the serious disproportionality present in the period 1928–30 was becoming even more serious in 1931, when the position had been reached that all the growth of the national income in 1931 went to accumulation.[49]

A modern Soviet economist, A. Barsov, basing himself on the *Materialy* and on later calculations for 1932, recently drew general conclusions from these data: 'Taking into account all the lowering in the level of agricultural production, it is impossible not to presume that the norm of accumulation in 1931 and 1932 was in all probability extremely high and could hardly correspond to the optimum conditions for resolving the task of the most speedy industrialisation of the country.'[50] In 1932 it was impossible for Soviet economists and statisticians to write with the boldness of Barsov, even in a document prepared for official use and not for publication. But they evidently shared the same impression.

The party leaders apparently made no public comment on *Materialy*, and the balance as such was not directly discussed or commented upon in the press. However, the journal of the economics section of the Communist Academy engineered the publication and criticism of important extracts from *Materialy*. In the issue of their journal for November–December 1932 they published what was said to be an article by one of Petrov's students, Spivak.[51] This was clearly based on *Materialy* and reproduced many of its most important tables. The article was less outspoken than Petrov's article in *Materialy*.[52] Nevertheless in the following issue of the journal (prepared before 1 January 1933, but only published in May of that year) Partigul, in the name of the editorial committee, which included N. Voznesensky, who later became head of Gosplan, vociferously condemned and denounced the work.[53] Moreover, Partigul insisted that the article was sympomatic 'of a series of mistaken positions given in the balance of the national economy for 1928–30'. He particularly condemned their view of agricultural reality, singling out Spivak's statement that there was no expanded production in agriculture and even a small absolute reduction in 1930 in comparison with 1928.[54] The data which showed a decline in agricultural production and means of production needed to be verified, but in any case were averages for the whole of agriculture, and therefore could not show the dynamic of reproduction in the socialist sector. This 'wrecking methodology', based on the zemstvo statisticians and the Right opposition, was 'still deeply rooted in many of our statistical agencies.'[55]

After this article had been written, but before it was published, the Agrarian Institute of the Communist Academy added a further condemnation of Spivak and Petrov in an article devoted to the results of the January 1933 party plenum.[56] In this article Petrov and Spivak were accused of having stated that 'there had so far been no essential movement to liquidate the disproportionality between the development of industry and agriculture in the 1928, 1929 and 1930 period' and that agriculture and small-scale industry were essentially characterised by simple reproduction in contrast to the expanded reproduction of large-scale industry.[57] These alleged statements of Petrov and

Spivak were described as 'antiparty, providing water to the mills of Right opportunists and degenerates' and Petrov and Spivak were likened 'to people who had fully slipped into the position of Right opportunism and degeneration'. It was later added that 'Good-for-nothing theoreticians of the Spivak–Petrov type could not see the qualitative social movements in agriculture for the mist of statistical figures of gross production. They had forgotten their ABC of Leninism, and instead of the dialectical study of social phenomena from all sides, they mechanically placed in the same bracket: the declining kulak sector; the petty commodity sector which is being transformed by collectivisation; and the socialist sector which is developing with expanding reproduction.'[58]

Following these condemnations, little more was heard of the *Materialy* for a considerable time. The more or less realistic data provided in the balance had no doubt played a part in the decision of the Politburo in January 1933 to adopt much more realistic targets for the future annual plan. But these more realistic policies were accompanied by the imposition of tighter political controls over the planning and statistical agencies, to the detriment of the quality of their work. At the beginning of 1933, Minaev and Nemchinov were dismissed from TsUNKhU, and Minaev was replaced by Kraval.[59] Later in the year, the introduction of the 'biological yield', exaggerating the level of grain production, imposed a substantial distortion on the statistics for the agricultural sector which continued until after Stalin's death.

For three years after the dismissal of Minaev and Nemchinov, while a great deal of work was carried out on balances for particular products and sectors, almost no progress was made with the overall balance of the national economy. But in 1936 attitudes changed. The newly established Institute of Economics of the Academy of Sciences set as its prime task the construction of a balance of the national economy.[60] Strumilin and TsUNKhU were criticised for inadequate work on the balance. Strumilin's articles on the balance published in response to this criticism were followed by a heated but inconclusive debate.[61] In November 1936, a special commission was set up in the Academy to work out proposals for expanding work on the balances, headed by Krzhizhanovsky, now a vice-president of the Academy.[62]

The balance of the national economy also came to the fore in the peculiar circumstances surrounding the purges in TsUNKhU in 1937. When 'invited' to make self-criticisms many of TsUNKhU officials drew attention to the lack of work on the balance of the national economy and the failure of TsUNKhU to stand up to departmental pressures.[63] In the atmosphere of 1937 these charges were readily interpreted as conscious wrecking activities of various departmental chiefs, and the statisticians had the dubious pleasure of seeing many of these leaders who had been imposed upon them in order to ensure their conformity with official policy themselves removed and condemned as wreckers.

From this period a more determined effort was made within Gosplan and TsUNKhU to keep a balanced control over the desires of the separate economic agencies and to pay more attention to the balance of the national economy. A series of balances of the national economy for 1935, 1937 and 1938 were produced and issued in mimeographed form in Gosplan from 1937,[64] but little is known about them. The new editorial board of the major Gosplan journal was now insistent in emphasising the significance of coordinating the separate elements in the plan in marked contrast to the attitude of the journal four years earlier.[65]

At the beginning of 1938, N. A. Voznesensky was appointed chairman of Gosplan. Although a scourge of the bourgeois and Right-wing planners as a young party economist in the early 1930s, Voznesensky encouraged the work on the balance of the national economy which had already begun. Voznesensky, more than any other chairman of Gosplan with the possible exception of Tsyurupa, supported a methodology of economic planning based on overall constraints and proportions set by an accounting balance of the national economy and elevated this methodology into official policy. In December 1939, in an article in the party journal *Bolshevik* celebrating Stalin's sixtieth birthday, Voznesensky discussed the task which Stalin had highlighted just ten years earlier, 'the need for the compilation of a balance of the national economy of the USSR'. Voznesensky insisted that one of the tasks of a plan based on a balance of the national economy would be the avoidance of 'departmental-bureaucratic maximalism', and went on to emphasise:

It is impossible to compile a competent plan of the development of the national economy of the USSR if you have not begun with a balance of the national economy. The initial point is to determine the basic economic–political task of the coming period. But once this is determined, it is necessary to begin the compilation of the plan from the balance.[66]

Under Voznesensky there were many signs of renewed work on the balances.[67] The war undoubtedly delayed any such rapid transition, but three years after the end of the war, on 10 August 1948, TsSU was separated from Gosplan and given more independence.[68] In the same period a new scientific–methodological council was formed in TsSU whose members included both P. I. Popov and V. S. Nemchinov,[69] but before much was achieved Voznesensky was arrested and executed in 1949, and work on the balance again went into a decline.

Only after Stalin's death could Nemchinov and many other former TsSU workers, together with other statisticians and economists of the 1920s and 1930s (including Strumilin), lead a movement for the radical improvement of planning methods and statistics.[70] From this time onwards, the balance of the national economy again began to receive much attention.

By the late 1950s Soviet planners were openly explaining to Indian planners the importance of the balance of the national economy for the planning process and its key role in planning methodology:

The economic balance [balance of the national economy] is prepared in the USSR for an aggregate characteristic of the reproduction during the plan or current period. The economic balance characterises the most important economic ratios: [the] ratio between the production of producer goods and that of consumption goods; [the] ratio between different industries (branches of industry) (industry and agriculture and so on); [the] ratio among social sectors in production and consumption of the national product and national income; [the] ratio between consumption and savings; [the] ratio between productive and non-productive spheres, and so on. In Gosplan, the preparation of the plan economic balance is based on the current [*post-factum* accounting] balance which is prepared annually by the Central Statistical Administration of the USSR. The plan economic balance is prepared during all the stages of the preparation of the plan (at the preliminary stage of the preparation of the bench-mark targets and at the final stage of the preparation of the plan-frame).

The formulation of the main indicators of the economic balance is of the highest priority while preparing the plan.[71]

Later in the 1960s G. Sorokin wrote that 'almost all Soviet economists' now accepted this Popov–Voznesensky type of definition of the purpose of the balance:

The problem of the economic balances is one of the most important in the methodology of planning since a general economic balance [balance of the national economy] is needed to plan general proportions...

The balance of the economy should give as complete a survey as possible of the socialist reproduction process. Almost all Soviet economists agree on this definition of the purpose of the economic balance. The balance should help the study of economic proportions and ensure that they are correctly fixed in the economic plan.[72]

However the Soviet economist M. Z. Bor has disputed the emphasis which Sorokin placed on the economic balance method of planning and argued instead for a combination of what he called the 'variant method' (individual branch projects) and the method of the balance of the national economy.[73] And the veteran economist A. D. Kurskii, who had enthused about the central role of the balance of the national economy for planning in his early books written when Voznesensky was in power,[74] totally ignored this balance and concentrated exclusively on separate balances in his later editions of these books on planning.[75]

The practical importance of the balance of the national economy in the planning process continues to be debated, but there can be no doubt of the truth of Naum Jasny's statement that 'the idea of the balance is a great one as such; and that the whole history of Soviet planning is not understandable without it'.[76]

NOTES

1 E. Zaleski, *Stalinist Planning for Economic Growth, 1933–1952*, Chapel Hill, 1980, pp. 484–5.

2 N. Spulber and K. M. Dadkhah, 'The Pioneering Stage in Input–Output Economies: the Soviet National Economic Balances 1923–24, after Fifty Years', *The Review of Economics and Statistics*, February 1975, p. 27 claims that Stalin's speech of 1929 'for decades prevented further work on input–output balances'.

3 On this see P. I. Popov's introduction to the 1923/4 balance, 'Theoretical Foundations of the Balance: Quesnay and Marx', *Trudy TsSU*, xxix (1926), pp. 2–15. One of the Soviet critics of the balance, however, emphasised that its theoretical basis went back not just to Marx but to Gregory King and Adam Smith (S. A. Fal'kner, *Planovoe khozyaistvo*, no. 1, 1928, p. 154).

4 See A. E. Lositskii's informative account in *Trudy TsSU*, xxx, vyp. 2, 1928, pp. 6–12.

5 Lositskii (previously an academic) was appointed head of the statistical department of the newly-created Ministry of Food Supply, and was responsible for preparing this plan. Groman, already in 1916 the representative of the Union of Towns on the governmental Special Council on Food Supply, was placed in charge of the Food Council in March 1917; Popov was appointed head of the statistical department of the Ministry of Agriculture.

6 P. I. Popov, in *Vestnik Statistiki*, no. 1, 1919, p. 32. The new Central Statistical Administration was established shortly after this report, on 25 July 1918.

7 Recent Soviet accounts of the origins of the balance of the national economy have dated the first use of the term to Popov's report of January 1919 and have therefore wrongly concluded that the notion emerged 'during the first months of the organisation of Soviet state statistics', rather than having preceded this organisation (see I. A. Morozova, P. M. Moskvin, M. R. Eidel'man, 'Balans narodnogo khozyaistva SSSR', in *Istoriya Sovetskoi gosudarstvennoi statistiki*, 1969, p. 433, and T. V. Ryabushkin, *Problemy ekonomicheskoi statistiki*, 1959, p. 84.

8 *Byulleten' TsSU*, no. 2, 25 January 1919, cited by I. A. Morozova *et al.*, *loc. cit.*, p. 433.

9 *Ekonomicheskaya zhizn'*, 12 January 1921.

10 See E. H. Carr, *The Bolshevik Revolution, 1917–1922*, vol. 2, Harmondsworth, Middx, 1954, pp. 375–6.

11 Their approach was well summarised by Wassily Leontief, then a young Soviet economist, in *Planovoe khozyaistvo*, no. 12, 1925, p. 254: 'The principal feature of this balance, in comparison with such economic–statistical investigations as the American and English censuses, is the attempt to present in numbers not only the production but also the distribution of the social product, so as to obtain a general picture of the entire process of reproduction in the form of a "tableau économique".' (V. Leontiev, 'Balans narodnogo khozyaistva SSSR', *Planovoe khozyaistvo*, no. 12, 1925, p. 254). Leontief's article has been translated and reprinted in *Foundations of Soviet Strategy for Economic Growth*, ed. N. Spulber, Bloomington, 1964, pp. 88–94.

12 S. G. Strumilin, 'Pervyie opyty perspektivnogo planirovaniya', in S. G. Strumilin, *Izbranniye proizvedeniya*, vol. 2, 1963, p. 180. A note at the head of this article states that it first appeared in *Planovoe khozyaistvo*, no. 12, 1930. However Strumilin's article in that journal entitled 'Pervyie opyty planirovaniya' is much shorter and fails to mention Gosplan's early work on the balance of the national economy. Groman was however mentioned and castigated for his theory of an attenuating curve of growth. The article was written at a time when the senior Gosplan officials associated with planned balances – Bazarov and Groman – were under arrest. It was clearly an attempt to disassociate both Gosplan and himself from Groman.

13 For Popov's analysis and proposals, see *Vestnik statistiki*, nos. 9–12, 1922, pp. 12–13; *Byulleten' Gosplana*, no. 2, 1923, p. 28; *Izvestiya*, 16 February 1923; *Torgovo-promyshlennaya gazeta*, 11 February 1923; for Gosplan objections see *Byulleten' Gosplana*, no. 2 1923, p. 28, nos. 3–6, 1923, pp. 70–2. Whether the 'scissors' crisis of 1923 could have been avoided by increasing grain prices is still a matter of dispute among historians.

14 N. Jasny, 'The Russian Economic "Balance" and Input Output Analysis: A Historical Comment', *Soviet Studies*, 5 July 1962, no. 1, p. 75 claims that 'the idea of a balance of the national economy was fathered in Russia by V. G. Groman', citing this 1923 balance, but ignores Popov's activities concerned with the national-economic balance, which as we have shown can be dated back to July 1918.

15 *Vestnik statistiki*, no. 9–12, 1922, p. 7.

16 *Byulleten' Gosplana*, no. 6–7, 1923, p. 65.

17 He was a former zemstvo statistician, and had worked with Popov in Ufa province statistical office in the late 1890s, where Popov was in exile and was beginning his statistical career (See *Statisticheskoe obozrenie*, no. 5, 1928, p. 5).

18 *Byulleten' Gosplana*, no. 1–2, 1924, p. 74.

19 Stalin, *Sochineniya*, vol. 6, 1952, pp. 214–15.

20 *Stat. Ob.*, no. 2, 1928, p. 109, and *Byulleten' Gosplana*, no. 9–10, 1924, p. 232.

21 *Ekon. zhizn*, 29 March 1925. This was the report that Leontief was later to review.

22 P. I. Popov (ed.), *Balans narodnogo khozyaistva Soiuza SSR 1923/24 goda, Trudy TsSU*, vol. 29, 1926. According to Groman the volume appeared in June 1926 (see *Plan. Khoz.* no. 11, 1926, p. 62). Several of the most important tables appeared somewhat earlier in a special statistical volume produced by TsSU for the International Institute of Statistics in Paris in 1925 (see *Abregé des données statistiques de l'URSS* (Moscow, 1925), pp. 239–42).

23 *Sobranie zakonov*, 1925, part ii, art. 241.

24 *Statisticheskie obozrenie*, no. 2, 1928, p. 109; this was on 5 January 1926. A month earlier, on

1 December 1925, Sovnarkom had agreed to the censuses taking place in 1926; now it resolved to reconsider the matter after a statistical congress in February 1926.

25 Osinskii had belonged to most of the different Opposition groupings at different times and had actually written the platforms for several of them. Before the revolution he worked on a statistical account of Ukrainian grain production as materials for renegotiating a trade agreement with Germany.

26 *Vestnik statistiki*, no. 1, 1927, p. 302.

27 *Ibid.*, p. 312.

28 *Vestnik statistiki*, no. 2, 1927, p. 28.

29 See E. H. Carr and R. W. Davies, *Foundations of a Planned Economy, 1926–1929*, vol. 1, London, 1969, pp. 789–90, 799.

30 *Ekonomicheskaya zhizn'*, 2 April, 1927.

31 See *Statisticheskoe obozrenie*, no. 2, 1928, p. 109.

32 I. Stalin, *Sochineniya*, vol. 12, 1949, pp. 171–2; this was the speech in which Stalin called for the elimination of the kulaks as a class.

33 See T. V. Ryabushkin, *op. cit.* p. 124.

34 See his article in *Statisticheskoe obozrenie*, no. 5, 1930, pp. 7,10.

35 *Sobr. zakonov, 1930*, vol. 2, art. 358.

36 *Sobr. zakonov, 1930*, vol. 2, art. 426.

37 See Minaev in *Plan. khoz.* no. 4, 1931, p. 19 and Ragolskii, in *Plan. khoz.* no. 2–3, 1931, p. 42.

38 Groman and other prominent planners were arrested in September 1930 and put on trial in March 1931. Popov, the author of the earlier 1923/4 balance was not arrested; he had left government service in the late 1920s and worked in the All-Union Agricultural Academy during the 1930s.

39 See Strumilin's article in *Plan. khoz.* December 1930 and an important article by Pervukhin in *Plan. khoz.* no. 5–6, 1931, pp. 227–37.

40 *Izvestiya*, 2 February 1932; he reported a harvest of 78.4 million tons; the plan (which he did not mention) was as high as 98.4 million tons. On 30 October 1931, Molotov had reported that the harvest of 1831 was 'no lower than last year' (*Pravda*, 3 November 1931). In *Sotsialisticheskoe zemledelie*, 5 July 1932, Osinskii reduced his figure further to 70 million tons.

41 V. Ignatiev, *Plan. khoz.*, no. 2, June 1932, p. 136.

42 Editorial in *Plan. khoz.*, no. 6–7, 1932, p. 19. The present-tense warning about Right opposition should be regarded as being quite threatening.

43 G. Kosechenko in *Problemy ekonomiky*, no. 6, 1932, p. 48.

44 See Introduction to *Materialy*, p. 53 below. See also Minaev in *Plan. khoz.*, no. 4, 1931, p. 19, where he expressed a similarly modest and narrow aim.

45 See p. 57 below.

46 *Ibid.*, p. 58 below.

47 *Ibid.*, p. 59 below.

48 *Ibid.*, p. 77 below; he again tried to cover himself by blaming the killing of livestock on to kulaks and their agitation.

49 *Ibid.*, p. 96 below.

50 A. Barsov, *Balans stoimostnykh obmenov mezhdu gorodom i derevnei*, 1969, p. 96.

51 T. Spivak, in *Problemy ekonomiki*, no. 7, 1932, pp. 36–57.

52 For instance Spivak paid far less attention than Petrov to the lack of proportional development in the economy and explained the fall in agricultural production exclusively in terms of class war (compare *ibid.*, p. 42, with Petrov p. 77 below).

53 *Problemy ekonomiki*, no. 8, 1932, p. 201.

54 *Ibid.*, p. 202, citing Spivak, p. 42.

55 *Ibid.*, p. 202.

56 I. Krylov, K. Naumchik, N. Smolin, 'Istoricheskii plenum', *Na Agrarnom Fronte*, no. 1, 1933, pp. 36–7. This article was completed on 15 February 1933 and sent to the printers on 12 March 1933. It would consequently have appeared before Partigul's condemnation.

57 I. Krylov, K. Naumchik, N. Smolin, *ibid.*, p. 36, citing Spivak's article in *Problemy Ekonomiki* but without giving any page reference. In fact these statements do not appear in either Petrov's or Spivak's published work.
58 I. Krylov, K. Naumchik, N. Smolin, *ibid.*, p. 37.
59 *Sobr. zakonov, 1933*, vol. 2, arts. 29, 66. On Kraval', by all accounts a crude administrator, see N. Valentinov, *The NEP and the Party crisis*, Stanford, 1971, pp. 200–1 and E. H. Carr and R. W. Davies, *Foundations of a Planned Economy, 1926–1929*, vol. 1, p. 286.
60 *Problemy ekonomiki*, no. 4, 1936, pp. 145–7. The Institute was formed as a result of the absorption of the Communist Academy by the Academy of Sciences. A. S. Mendel'son was placed in charge of the sector of the balance of the national economy, Strumilin of the industrial sector.
61 *Problemy ekonomiki*, no. 5, 1936, pp. 43–74, *Planovoe khozyaistvo* no. 9–10, 1936, pp. 96–114 and for criticism see *Problemy ekonomiki* no. 6, 1936, pp. 200–2.
62 *Problemy ekonomiki*, no. 6, 1936, p. 201.
63 See *Plan*, no. 7, 1937, pp. 43, 46, 49 and no. 8, 1937, pp. 33–4. It is interesting to note that Popov was reported to have reappeared at these meetings and quite characteristically argued that Gosplan had got its planning methodology wrong (*Plan*, no. 8, 1937, p. 34).
64 A. Vainshtein, *Narodny dokhod Rossii i SSSR* (1969), pp. 79, 80, 161; see also A. Barsov 'NEP i vyravnivanie ekonomicheskikh otnoshenii mezhdu gorodom i derevnei', in *Novaya ekonomicheskaya politika: voprosy teorii i istorii*, ed. M. P. Kim, 1974.
65 *Planovoe khozyaistvo*, no. 5-6, 1937, p. 10.
66 *Bolshevik*, no. 1, 1940, p. 84.
67 See articles on the balance in *Plan. khoz.* nos. 6, 7, 8 and 9, 1940; no. 2, 1941. Voznesensky was elected a candidate member of the Politburo in February 1941 and a full member in February 1947.
68 TsUNKhU had been renamed TsSU somewhat earlier in 1941, see *Istoriya Sovetskoi gosudarstvennoi statistiki*, 1960, p. 12.
69 See P. I. Popov in *Bolshaya Sovetskaya entsiklopaediya*, 2nd edn, vol. 34, col. 163, and V. S. Nemchinov, *Izbranniya proizvedeniya*, vol. 1, p. 10.
70 P. I. Popov did not live to see this happen; he died in 1950 (*BSE*, 2nd edn, vol. 34, col. 163).
71 A. P. Strukov, 'On the Preparation of Balances of the National Economy for Planning in the USSR', in Indian Statistical Institute, *Planning and Statistics in Socialist Countries*, Calcutta, 1963, p. 125.
72 G. Sorokin, *Planning in the USSR*, 1967, pp. 304, 311.
73 M. Z. Bor, *Ocherki po metodologii i metodiki planirovaniya*, 1964, pp. 107–8.
74 A. Kurskii, *Sotsialisticheskoe planirovanie narodnogo khozyaistva SSSR* (1945), pp. 47–8 and A. Kurskii, *Planirovanie narodnogo khozyaistva SSSR* (1947), pp. 92–3.
75 See A. D. Kurskii, *Planirovaniye narodnogo khozyaistva SSSR*, 1955, and A. D. Kurskii, *Nauchniye osnovy Sovetskikh pyatiletok*, 1974.
76 N. Jasny, 'The Russian Economic "Balance" and Input–Output Analysis: a Historical Comment', *Soviet Studies*, 5 1962, no. 1, p. 80.

MATERIALY

Proletarians of all countries unite!
Central Administration for National Economic Records USSR
xxxxxxxxxxxxxxx[*]
xxxxxxxxxxxxxxxxxx

MATERIALS FOR A BALANCE OF THE
SOVIET NATIONAL ECONOMY
1928–1930

Moscow, October 1932

[* The text here has been crossed out, but it would appear to read,
'For official use only'.]

[Soviet publication details]

Delivered for production – 27/VIII [/1932]
Signed for printing – 11/X [/1932]
Printed – 14/X – 32
Number of printer's sheets – 24
Page-format – $\frac{7}{16}$ × $\frac{74}{100}$
Responsible for publication – V. Kvyatkovsky

Glavlit authorisation No. V–31234
Published by the Central Administration of National Economic
Records of the USSR
8th 'Mosoblpoligraf' Press,
46, Friedrich Engels Street
Number of copies printed – 500
Order 2464

1

Introduction

The Central Administration for National Economic Records of the USSR has now completed the very big job of compiling a balance of the USSR national economy for the years 1928–30.

If we leave aside the well-known work by the Central Statistical Administration in 1926, which was unsuccessful, the present work on the balance of the national economy constitutes the first experiment in the practical application of Marxist–Leninist methodology to the study of reproduction as a whole – in the given case, reproduction in the USSR.

We cannot consider the present work as fully finished either methodologically or as a concrete study of reproduction. However, this is only a first attempt, which was made extremely complicated not only by the absence of concrete statistical material but also by the unelaborated state of many theoretical problems of the economy of the transition period. This circumstance is closely connected with the fact that many problems concerning the balance of the national economy still remain insufficiently worked out even now.

For all the reasons mentioned, the present work does not claim to be exhaustive in its elaboration either of concrete economic results or of methodological problems. It is quite obvious that both these economic results and the theoretical premises and practical methods for constructing the balance of the economy must be subjected to detailed discussion. And the more detailed this discussion, the more thorough-going the analysis of the basic methodological propositions on which the present work is based, the sooner will the Central Administration for National Economic Records be able to emerge from the stage of experimentation on to the road of developed and systematic work on the balance of the national economy.

Accordingly, publication of the present work has the aim, first, of bringing forward for discussion and further elaboration a series of problems of the balance of the national economy, both of a general-theoretical and of a more particular character, and, secondly, of providing concrete material for studying reproduction in the USSR in 1928–30 *post-factum*.

It must be mentioned that the statistical materials and calculations published here, which describe synthetically the development of the USSR economy as a whole, are appearing in print in this form for the first time.

To a considerable extent, the separate indexes of reproduction which enter into the system of the balance of the national economy are published here for the first time. Materials which possess independent and serious importance for an analysis of reproduction in the USSR include, for instance, the data on the rate of growth of fixed capital stock of the branches and social sectors of the USSR economy, the data on the distribution of the national income, consumption by classes and groups of the population, accumulation in the USSR, and so on.

Compilation and preparation of the materials of the balance of the national economy has been carried out by all sectors of the Central Administration for National Economic Records under the leadership of the sector concerned with the balance of the national economy, whose task is both the compiling of the balance itself and elaboration of all the basic methodological propositions of the balance. The work was prepared for the press by the sector concerned with the balance of the economy.

The following participated most actively in the compilation of the balance and the preparation of this book: comrades *A. G. Pervukhin* (putting together the balance as a whole; fixed capital stock); *I. A. Morozova* (participated in putting the balance together; consumption; and agriculture); *P. M. Moskvin* (national income). The following prepared particular sections of the balance – comrades *G. A. Al'bitskaya* (stocks; and trade-and-transport mark-up), *V. A. Kvyatkovsky* and *M. A. Tsigel'nitsky* (industrial balances), *G. S. Pollyak* (consumption), *V. P. Nifontov* (livestock), and *I. I. Tutova* (transport).

The work was led by member of the collegium of the Central Administration for National Economic Records of the USSR. *A. I. Petrov.*

Deputy Head of the Central Administration for
National Economic Records of the USSR
S. Minaev

2 Articles

CONTENTS

2

Articles

[1]   GENERAL RESULTS OF THE NATIONAL ECONOMIC BALANCE FOR 1928, 1929
AND 1930

A. Petrov

[A]   Introductory notes[1]

The purpose of the national economic balance of the USSR is to study regularities in the process of reproduction of the economy during the transition period between capitalism and socialism; it examines the actual state of the economy at different stages in the building of socialism.

Economic reproduction during the transition period is planned, and all plans at a national economic level are plans of reproduction. The national economic balance can therefore be used as a synthetic method for studying reproduction both in the past and in economic plans for the future (quarterly, annual, five-year, etc.). The balance method of economic planning is a method for synthetically coordinating the plan, with the object of achieving in practice the basic directives of the Party general line. The synthetically coordinated economic plan will be both a plan and a balance.

At every stage of Soviet economic development reproduction is expanded socialist reproduction and is concerned both with expanded reproduction of the socialist economy in material terms and with expanded reproduction of socialist production relations. Expanded socialist reproduction is a process of struggle against capitalism, restricting, supplanting and eliminating capitalism, and transforming petty commodity economics into socialist economy (the collectivisation of agriculture, the cooperative organisation of small-scale industry). In our investigations it is therefore essential to consider the process of socialist reproduction in the context of the reproduction of the national economy as a whole. Reproduction in the capitalist system is investigated in order to reveal the antagonistic contradictions of the capitalist system. The basic contradiction of capitalism is between the social character of production and the individual character of appropriation. This places the problem of realisation at the centre of the analysis. This problem of the proportionality of reproduction is specific and peculiar to capitalism.

As the Soviet economy is a planned economy, there is no problem of realisation in the

57

form in which it exists for an unorganised economy. This problem is replaced by 'the need for a certain proportionality', achieved through planning. This is not an independent and fundamental law but a subordinate aspect of the general law of the movement towards socialism.

Rates of growth and the sources (factors) of expanded socialist reproduction are the fundamental problems in the theory of the reproduction of the Soviet economy. The problem of proportionality, taking the form of the dialectical interaction between the elements of reproduction within the socialist sector and in the economy as a whole, while necessary, is a subsidiary one.

In short, the balance of the national economy must deal with *the problems of rates of growth, sources and proportions of expanded socialist reproduction*, all of which must be considered in the context of the economy as a whole.

Let us now turn to the design of the balance of the national economy in more specific terms. Is Marx's theory of reproduction relevant in preparing the diagrams and tables of the balance; and are Marx's own reproduction schemas relevant here? The general importance of the Marxist–Leninist theory of reproduction for the problems of the national economic balance is beyond question: initial postulates for the national economic balance are provided by the theory of the Soviet economy, and this theory is itself developed on the basis of the doctrine of Marxism–Leninism. As regards Marx's actual schemas they are not schemas of quantitative relationships which are valid for all time; they are rather illustrations of the contradictory categories of capitalist economy. The schemas as such are not the culmination and end-product of the analysis of reproduction: as Marx and Lenin themselves showed, they are merely material for that analysis. An analysis of Marx's schemas reveals the antagonistic contradictions through which the different elements in capitalist reproduction are interconnected.

The basic principles of the dialectical method of Marxism–Leninism are completely relevant to the study of reproduction in the transitional economy. Many categories of reproduction also retain their importance; however, the relationships between them are different, as they are based on a planned economy, and they also have a different social content. Lenin pointed out, in a well-known passage, that even under a communist economy it is necessary to study the relationship between Departments I and II of social reproduction. [8]

The balance of the national economy is based on the Marxist-Leninist theory of reproduction. It has nothing in common with the rag-bag of rigid formulae used for the notorious equilibrium advocated by the bourgeois wrecker and opportunist 'theoreticians', and purporting to reveal 'the present, the past and the future' automatically. *Do not hunt for a-priori formulae of 'equilibrium', but find out how the dialectical inter-relationship between the elements of reproduction are achieved in practice*: this is the balance method of studying reproduction.

It is obvious that we will not solve the question of how to succeed in synthetically combining all the heterogeneous material, social and economic elements of reproduction by constructing one single schema or table of the balance of the national economy. Although the different aspects of the study of reproduction intersect and are inter-related they cannot be mechanically combined [into a single complex tabular schema]. Nor is this necessary: instead special groups of questions should be considered at the points of inter-section of different aspects of the balance.

The problem of analysing the rates of growth and proportions of expanded socialist reproduction is solved by constructing a balance of production, consumption and accumulation.

The balance of production, consumption and accumulation presents:

(*a*)   a material description of the process of reproduction: the structure of the entire social product in terms of production and consumption; the share of the branches of the economy in total production; the structure of accumulation in physical terms; and the growth of production, consumption and accumulation of material goods in the economy as a whole;

(*b*)   the rates of growth and the share of the social sectors and classes in the production, consumption and accumulation of material goods;

(*c*)   the inter-relationship between branches and sectors of the economy as regards the production and consumption of material goods;

(*d*)   the rates of growth and the shares of the social sectors and branches of the economy in the creation of the national income, i.e., the consumption fund and the accumulation fund for the USSR as a whole.

The basic questions of rates of growth and of proportions can be revealed by a balance of production and consumption based on the elements listed above.

Other problems concerning the sources of expanded socialist reproduction can also be solved by these means. If the balance of production, accumulation and consumption is examined in conjunction with the tables on the distribution of the national income the basic sources of expanded socialist reproduction can be discovered. These services can also be discovered by comparing the data from this balance with materials on the productivity of labour.

The balance also provides a 'by-product' in the form of various price indexes: producer prices and consumer prices, price indexes differentiated according to sector, branch and group of products, etc. These are obtained as a result of using constant prices to revalue production, consumption, etc., in order to obtain the so-called 'physical volume' indicators [indicators in real terms]. The data obtained on 'physical volume' of various items in the balance can also be used in working out the structure and growth of the aggregate of use values.

The following factors are crucial in an investigation of sources of expanded reproduction:

(*a*)   the growth in the productivity of labour in the socialist sector, and

(*b*)   the active policy pursued by the proletarian state in the distribution and redistribution of the national income.

The balance of labour, or, more precisely, the time worked in relation to productivity, can be used to find the first factor. The second factor may be examined by constructing a table showing the balance of the national income, and its distribution and redistribution. This national income table shows:

(*a*)   the primary distribution of the national income between all the participants in production, by social sector of the economy and by class of the population;

(*b*)   the volume and sources of direct redistribution of the national income through various transfers (taxes, services, etc.) between the sphere of production and the non-productive sphere ('the superstructure'), and between the social sectors of the economy. This reveals the volume and sources of the resources allocated to expanded socialist reproduction via the direct redistribution of the national income;

(*c*)   the volume and sources of the relative redistribution of the national income which has been achieved in a given period by means of the price mechanism are calculated by comparing the national income table with data from the balance of production and consumption;

(*d*)   a balance of realisation (supply and demand) can be constructed by means of a comparison with the balance of production and consumption of material goods;

(*e*)   and, finally, the national income tables show the structure and sources of the incomes of classes and groups of the population, the budget of the non-productive sphere, the sources of income of this sphere and their utilisation, and also a number of other indicators which illuminate separate aspects of the process of distribution.

These sets of data allow a full description to be provided of the movement of the elements of reproduction according to social sector: fixed and circulating capital, labour resources and their utilisation, productivity, national income and its elements, the consumption and accumulation funds, redistribution of the national income, and real (final) accumulation.

This brief listing of the aims of the balance of the national economy and the conclusions available from it is far from exhaustive both as regards specific indicators and as regards inter-relationships.

The theory and practice of the balance is obviously closely related to the theory of the Soviet economy and the methodology of planning and record keeping. Comrade Stalin set us the objective of elaborating the problems of the theory of the Soviet economy and of the national economic balance, [9] and this objective still fully retains all its importance; Soviet economists must energetically carry out more work in this direction. As this research is developed, new theoretical objectives will emerge and new methods will be found for their solution.

To a considerable extent, further progress with the balance method depends on reconstructing the whole system of economic records, on providing an adequate amount of reliable and methodologically sound material.

Finally, the introduction of the balances into the practical work of national economic planning is of decisive importance for the further development of the balances. The balances will then become a living reality. Balances regarding the past will become the synthetic description of plan fulfilment, and the national economic plan will itself become a plan-balance. The attention of scientific thought can be concentrated on all the problems of the theory and practice of the national economic balance if they are examined in relation to the current problems of planning.

Since the results of the national economic balance for 1928, 1929 and 1930 have been obtained solely from material already available they cannot claim to be exhaustive.

Several questions on the theory of the Soviet economy are as yet unsolved. But even where the theoretical problems have been cleared up difficulties of a practical nature appear, as a result of the inadequacy of statistical data and their poor quality.

Finally, even when sufficient high-quality primary statistical data are available, problems still arise in the methodology of working up these materials, and particularly in the construction of different synthetic indicators. The methodology for calculating a number of indicators is very weak; these range from comparatively simple indicators like 'output' to considerably more complex ones like 'national income', 'accumulation' and so-called 'physical volume'. Moreover, many of the summary and synthetic indicators cannot be calculated directly, but only indirectly. While the theoretical premises of Marxism–Leninism can be used to provide a sufficiently clear understanding of the nature of every sort of theoretical indicator, the work which has been done on this basis with actual statistical data has been less satisfactory. Past experience of work on synthetic indicators (mainly the Gosplan control figures) was inadequate in both scale and scope. Many methodological questions had to be posed and resolved from scratch. Clearly the results obtained from work on the national economic balance call for extensive and profound discussion of the initial postulates on which the work is based, of the results so far, and of the methods used to work up the statistical data.

The state of statistics and record-keeping has not allowed the full schema of the national economic balance to be applied in its entirety. Thus, it was not possible to provide a break-down into social groups of all items in the balance of production and consumption; a break-down by social groups is given only for the general summary of the balance. Similarly, the state of the material made it impossible to link up the indicators of the balance with the data for specific administrative economic units and for separate branches of the economy. It was found impossible to break down the private enterprise sector into 'capitalist' and 'simple commodity' divisions and to distinguish the class groups in the consumption of the agricultural population. Because of these problems it was impossible to construct a full table of reproduction by sector and so we were limited to the briefer table on 'the balance of the principal indicators of reproduction by sector'.

In the materials and results presented here, the balance of production, consumption and accumulation has been worked out in the greatest detail. The section on the distribution of the national income is presented in somewhat less detail, but it is still sufficiently full to enable general conclusions to be drawn.

Owing to the inadequacy of the statistical materials, the section on the distribution of the national income lacks a division of incomes into money incomes and incomes in kind. Related to this is the total absence of a balance of realisation (supply and demand). A labour balance is also absent; there are no materials at all on this subject for these years. It was possible only to make some general estimates of time worked and labour productivity in census industry, in construction (socialist sector) and in state farms. These gaps must be filled by further work.

As stated above, the general tasks of the national economic balance are to clarify the problem of the rates of growth, sources (factors) and proportions of expanded socialist reproduction. At different stages of socialist construction these questions have been posed and solved in different ways. The period 1928–30 belongs to the reconstruction stage of socialist construction and the stage of the First Five-Year Plan. The basic setting for this entire stage of development was provided by the XV Party Congress, in its Directives for Compilation of the First Five-Year National-Economic Plan. [10].

The general regularities of the Soviet economy were presented in the XV Congress resolution as the main requirements for this stage of our development. 'In compiling the five-year economic plan, as in compiling any kind of economic plan intended to cover a more or less lengthy period of time, it is necessary to try and achieve the most favourable combination of the following elements: expanded consumption by the worker and peasant masses; expanded reproduction (accumulation) in state-owned industry, on the basis of expanded reproduction of the economy generally; a rate of growth of economic development faster than in the capitalist countries; and a systematic and undeviating increase in the relative weight of the socialist economic sector. The latter is a decisive and major element of the whole economic policy of the proletariat.'

The following decisions of the XV Party Congress provided a more specific approach to the period of the First Five-Year Plan: 'It is impossible to maximise both production and consumption at the same time, because this is not feasible. Moreover, one-sided priority should not be given in this period to accumulation ... nor should one-sided priority be given to consumption. It is necessary to achieve an optimum combination of these two factors, bearing in mind both the relative contradiction between them and their mutual impact and interconnection; over a lengthy period these interests coincide.' The Directives then stipulate:

(a) in the sphere of production, while increasing the production of consumer goods, priority must be given to intensifying the production of means of production; and this must be carried out in such a way as to ensure the growth of economic independence of the USSR and to increase its defence capability:

(b) the increase in socialisation of agriculture and small-scale industrial production; the development of state farms:

(c) disproportions are to be overcome by reducing costs in industry, increasing the productivity of labour, and by industrialising agriculture:

(d) the national income is to grow in such a way as to ensure an increased well-being for the working class and the poorest and middle peasants, while at the same time maintaining the maximum possible rate of development for the economy as a whole.

These items must be examined by analysing the national economic balance.

[B]   General description of expanded socialist reproduction

At the most general level, the results of expanded socialist reproduction can be shown by changes in the national income and in its elements – consumption and accumulation.[2]

The percentage shares of consumption and accumulation in the national income (in current prices) have changed in the following way:

	1928	1929	1930
Consumption (by the population and by non-productive institutions)	80.6	80.4	74.3
Accumulation fund	19.4	19.6	25.7

Accumulation takes the form of a growth in physical goods (fixed means of production, raw materials, auxiliary materials, fuel, consumer goods).

A loss of stocks occurred in these years (mainly a decrease in the number of livestock) and this reduced the level of *real* accumulation, i.e. the actual increase in accumulation including changes in stock levels. Allowing for these losses (and for some other insignificant items), real accumulation constituted the following percentages of the national income (in current prices):

1928	1929	1930
17.0	16.1	21.4

National income and accumulation estimates can be checked by an analysis by social sector.

The inter-relationships and connexions between the sectors are disclosed in estimating the following items:

1. the *primary income* of the sector. This is calculated from the distribution of net production;
2. the *total* (*sovokupnyi*) (final) income, received after the redistribution of primary income of the sectors;
3. *non-productive consumption* (individual consumption by the population and consumption by institutions), which shows the fund of accumulation obtained within the sector from the primary income of the sectors;
4. *real accumulation* (in the form of fixed capital, stocks of raw materials, auxiliary materials and fuel). This includes not only the Accumulation Fund formed in each sector, but also the product of the redistribution of the primary income of all the sectors in the current year, and the redistribution of productive forces in the form of fixed capital and stocks created by labour of past years. We use the term 'The balance of the principal indicators of reproduction, by sector' to refer to the method of analysing the reproduction of the sectors by constructing a balance of the sectors according to the elements listed above.

A sector is defined here as the population predominantly engaged in production in the given sector, together with its production-base (enterprises and institutions). This is the only method of deriving the sectors that can provide a description of the reproduction of the sectors and their mutual relationships. This is especially the case since in the private sector the population and the enterprises coincide both juridically and factually.

By primary income we therefore understand income arising in a sector as a result of net production within that sector, plus receipts, in the form of wages, etc., from another sector. Consequently, the primary income of the socialist sector differs from its net production because the earnings which the private agricultural population received from the socialist sector have been deducted from it, while the non-socialist earnings of persons belonging to the socialist sector (mainly collective farmers) have been added.

The primary income of the private sector differs from its net production by the same amount, but the additions and deductions are opposite in sign. Thus, the sum of the primary incomes of all the sectors is equal to the national income for the country as a whole.

The total income (final income) of the socialist sector, in current prices, is formed as a result of the redistribution of primary income through the financial system (transfer payments, taxes, loans, etc.).

It must be borne in mind that what is involved here is a re-distribution from one sector to another of the income of sectors considered as a whole. Transfers from the population within the socialist sector are not considered here, since they involve a redistribution wholly within this sector. A simultaneous analysis of relationships between sectors and intra-sectoral relationships would complicate our understanding of the basic processes governing the relationships between the sectors.

The results of three years of expanded reproduction of socialist production relationships reveal an absolute growth of productive forces in the socialist sector, an ever-increasing share of the socialist sector in primary and final income, and the growth of the accumulated part of the socialist sector.

The percentage shares of the sectors in primary income (in current prices)

	1928	1929	1930
Socialist sector	35.9	46.2	62.1
Private sector	64.1	53.8	37.9

The socialist sector took an even bigger share of final income, since the proletariat gained from the redistribution of the national income through the financial system:

The percentage share of the sectors in final incomes (in current prices)

	1928	1929	1930
Socialist sector	40.8	52.4	68.2
Private sector	59.2	47.6	31.8

Expanded reproduction of the economy in the last two years (1929 and 1930) has been entirely a consequence of reproduction (accumulation) in the socialist sector, which has off-set negative 'reproduction' in the private sector. This fact is vividly reflected in the share of each sector in total accumulation.

The percentage share of the sectors in real accumulation (in current prices)

	1928	1929	1930
Socialist sector	66.6	121.9	145.2
Private sector	33.4	−21.9	−45.2

The expanded reproduction of the socialist sector and its preponderant position in comparison with the private sector are also shown in the changing share of the accumulated and consumed parts of final income. The socialist sector was able to increase the absolute amount of consumption at the same time as increasing the share of final income taken by accumulation (excluding collectivisation) from 27.1 per cent in 1928 to 38.2 per cent in 1930. The private sector, in contrast, was unable to achieve any accumulation at all – there was an actual eating away of capital, and consumption in 1930 exceeded final income by 14.8 per cent.

The percentage share of accumulation in the final income of different sectors (in current prices)

	1928	1929	1930
Socialist sector	27.1	35.3	38.2
Private sector	10.0	−5.2	−14.8

In order to understand these results correctly the following must be taken into account:

In these years agriculture accounted for about four-fifths of the total national income of the private sector. Owing to its low level of economic and technical organisation and production, the petty commodity economy 'is not always able to achieve even simple reproduction' (Stalin, speech to the conference of Marxist agrarians [December 1929]). [11] This last proposition can be confirmed by comparing the net production of agriculture with the level of personal consumption of the agricultural population. This net production (i.e. the net income of the agricultural population, which can be used for both consumption and accumulation) did not even cover consumption:

In million rubles (current prices)

	1928	1929	1930
Consumption by the whole agricultural population	12,440.6	14,298.9	15,820.8
Net production of agriculture	10,409.6	10,694.2	13,630.3
Excess of consumption	2,031.0	3,604.7	2,190.5

The missing part was covered, in the main, by incomes from building work and industry and also from other non-agricultural branches – small-scale industry, and, to some extent, fishing, hunting, etc.

Finally, the 'negative accumulation' of the private sector is explained by the fact that the capitalist sector in town and country, which forms part of this total, was compelled to reduce its production and consume part of its own capital by the policy of restricting it, driving it out and then eliminating it.

The estimates shown above are in current prices. The relationship between consumption and accumulation in the national income was however greatly influenced by the difference in the rates of growth of prices of consumer goods in comparison with the prices of producer goods.

If we take consumption and accumulation in constant prices (1928 prices), we obtain the following (in percentages of the national income):

	1928	1929	1930
Consumption	83.1	79.5	68.5
Accumulation	16.9	20.5	31.5
Real accumulation	14.4	16.9	27.3

The more rapid growth of the accumulated part of the national income as compared with the consumed part (which is itself increasing in absolute terms) is one of the regularities of the reconstruction period and of the socialist economy in general. This is a manifestation of the 'relative contradiction' between production and consumption or, what comes to the same thing, between accumulation and consumption.

The special feature of this contradiction between accumulation and consumption under conditions of planned economy is that, while it is continuously reappearing, at the same time it overcomes and resolves the existing contradiction: a steady growth of consumption can be achieved only if there is a faster growth of accumulation in each period [*sic*].

More important, however, is the fact that neither in the transition period nor in the developed socialist economy does production exist merely for the sake of consumption. Both in the period of the struggle for socialism and in the developed socialist economy there are always broader tasks to be fulfilled than the mere satisfaction of consumption.

'While setting for the Second Five-Year Plan the task of ensuring a considerably more rapid increase in the well-being of the worker and peasant masses, we must, at the same time, reject such arguments as that "socialism means production for consumption."' (Molotov, speech at the sixteenth [*sic* – XVII] Party Conference.) [12]

Estimates of accumulation and consumption by sector (in 1928 prices) show the following:

Real accumulation in the socialist sector (excluding the effect of collectivisation) in percentage of the national income of the sector:

1928	1929	1930
26.5	36.0	41.8

Correspondingly, real accumulation in the private sector constituted the following percentages of the income of that sector:

1928	1929	1930
10.2	−5.1	−12.5

The fundamental question in the study of accumulation is the question of the sources of accumulation (the sources of expanded reproduction).

The following are of decisive importance in this respect:

(a) the growth of labour productivity, which provides an increase in the socialist sector's own resources for accumulation, and

(b) the redistribution of the national income (directly through taxes, etc., and indirectly through the price mechanism), which creates additional resources for accumulation.

Above all, we analysed real accumulation in the economy and in its socialist sector. Real accumulation in the socialist sector comprises: the sector's own investment; utilisation of the income of the private sector; the transfer of property from the private sector to the socialist sector through collectivisation.

The percentage share of the socialist sector's own investment in its real accumulation is as follows (in current prices):

1928	1929	1930
52.7	65.9	67.6

If we exclude the value of collectivised property from the socialist sector's real accumulation, what remains is the amount mobilised for accumulation from the national income. The percentage share contributed by the socialist sector's own investment to its real accumulation [excluding the transfer of collectivised property] will then be (also in current prices):

1928	1929	1930
53.9	69.6	80.4

As for the private sector, we can speak of its 'own' investment only for the year 1928. In that year the final income of the private sector exceeded its consumption by 2,275 million rubles, but in 1929 the excess was a mere 153 million rubles.

In 1930 consumption by the private sector (excluding excises) was not covered by its own final income, despite the increase in prices in the private sector in that year. It is characteristic of the private sector that a rather large share (up to 15 per cent) of its income came from wages and other receipts from the socialist sector (wages earned in industry and building, etc.).

Despite the increase in the absolute amount of the transfers from the private sector, a growing proportion of real accumulation in the socialist sector came from reinvestment within this sector:

Transfers from the private sector in million rubles (in current prices):

1928	1929	1930
1287.3	1878.6	2341.5

The percentage share of these transfers in the final income of the socialist sector declined as follows:

1928	1929	1930
11.9	11.9	8.9

But these transfers steadily increased as a percentage of the primary income of the private sector:

1928	1929	1930
7.6	11.6	16.1

We have taken into account both the redistribution of the national income in favour of the socialist sector and the considerable and growing resources of the socialist sector itself. These took the form of direct redistribution (taxes, etc.) and, partly, of indirect redistribution (excises). This latter form of redistribution does not, however, cover all the redistribution that takes place through prices. The problem of the redistribution of the national income through prices is a very complex one.

Consequently estimates of the relative transfers of national income through prices in a given period are somewhat uncertain. Two methods, using a variety of different materials, have therefore been used in these estimates. The first method compares the shares of the different sectors in the national income as calculated in current and constant prices. The second method utilises data on the price movements of commodities purchased by the urban proletariat in the private sector.

[*First method*] The share of the socialist sector in national income (the final income of the socialist sector, after all adjustments for direct distribution and redistribution) was 52.4 per cent in 1929 and 68.2 per cent in 1930 (in current prices).

These shares show the participation of the socialist sector in the *distribution* of the national income on the basis of existing price relationships.

According to preliminary estimates, the share of the socialist sector's final income in the total national income (in constant 1928 prices) amounted to 55.1 per cent in 1929 and 74.4 per cent in 1930. The amount of the national income transferred from the socialist sector to the private sector in 1929 and 1930 as compared with 1928 is obtained by relating the share of the socialist sector in current and constant prices to the total volume of the national income in constant prices for each of these years.

The amount transferred [above the 1928 level] was 864.2 million rubles in 1929 and 3,014.9 million rubles in 1930 (in current prices).

[*Second method*] Price movements were also analysed, and they indicate a surplus payment to the private sector of 675.0 million rubles in 1929 and 3,523.9 million rubles in 1930.

Since both these estimates indicate a similar amount of transfer by means of the price mechanism they may be accepted as being reliable.

Earlier we showed the scale on which resources were pumped across from the private to the socialist sector through the financial system. These transfers amounted to 2,341.5 million rubles in 1930. When we take into account the surplus payment made by the socialist sector to the private sector through price differences, it emerges that in 1930 the socialist sector's accumulation from the national income took place entirely from its own resources. Part of its own accumulation fund (though only a very small part) had to be surrendered to the private sector.

However, we must keep in mind the assumption upon which the amount of surplus payment to the private sector has been calculated. The assumption is that the 1928 price relationships were 'normal', and that the surplus payments should be estimated in relation to this level.

When we analyse the rates of growth, it is of great importance to determine the relative contribution of different factors to development: 'The productivity of labour is of decisive importance for the victory of the new social order' (Lenin). [13]

Growth of the productivity of labour is a basic factor contributing towards the growth of material production. An increase in the amount of time worked is another factor. Unfortunately it has not proved possible to estimate the growth in labour productivity for the whole socialist sector. We possess data for census industry, building and state farms only.

Census industry (previous year = 100)

	1928	1929	1930
Industrial output per man-hour (constant prices)	121.7	115.0	112.7
Gross industrial output (constant prices)	122.4	124.3	125.8
Man-hours worked (apprentices excluded)	101.0	107.8	111.4

By comparing the rates of growth of time worked and of the physical volume of production, we are able to determine the relative importance of productivity and time worked. The relative importance of these factors are as follows (in percentages):

	1928	1929	1930
Growth through increased productivity of labour	95.5	67.9	55.8
Growth through increase in time worked	4.5	32.1	44.2

For the two years 1929 and 1930, taken together, productivity accounts for 61 per cent of the growth, while the increase in time worked accounts for 39 per cent.

Building (socialist sector) (previous year = 100)

	1929	1930
Gross output per man-day (constant prices)	115.6	108.3
Gross output (constant prices)	145.0	181.0
Man-days worked (including apprentices)	125.3	167.2

The relative importance of labour productivity and the amount of time worked in increasing the volume of building are given in the following table (in percentages):

	1929	1930
Growth through increased productivity of labour	43.8	17.0
Growth through increase in time worked	56.2	83.0

For 1929 and 1930 taken together, increases in productivity accounted for 24.4 per cent of the total growth and increases in the amount of time worked accounted for 75.6 per cent.

State farms (previous year = 100)

	1929	1930	1931
Volume of work per man-day (1928 prices)	128.4	108.7	114.3
Volume of work (1928 prices)	139.3	204.8	227.2
Time worked	108.5	188.4	198.7
Growth in volume of work			
(a) through increased productivity of labour	78.4	15.6	22.4
(b) through increases in time worked	21.6	84.4	77.6

For these three years taken together increases in productivity accounted for [26.5] of the total growth, while the increase in time worked accounted for [73.5] [14].

For the two years [1929 and 1930] if the output of census industry and socialist building are combined (weighted by production in 1928), increases in labour productivity accounted for 50.4 per cent of the total growth. If state farms are also included the proportion falls to 50.3 per cent.

Since industry, building and state farms accounted for 90 per cent of the total output of the socialist sector in 1928 and 80 per cent in 1930, and since there was undoubtedly an increase in labour productivity on collective farms, it follows that productivity increases were the most important factor in increasing the growth of output in the socialist sector.

The growth in labour productivity was quite considerable: over the two years 1929 and 1930 it amounted to 29.6 per cent in industry, to 25.2 per cent in building work, and 39.6 per cent in state farms.

However the amount of time worked played a substantial and increasing role.

This is entirely normal for the transition period. In the conditions of capitalist economy, the utilisation of the most important productive force, man himself, is extremely limited and does not accord with the potential reserves of social labour. The basis of capitalist production is not so much an increase in the army of labour as an intensified exploitation of the wage earners. Capitalist production always retains a high reserve army of labour, either openly or in some concealed form. Only an economy that is building socialism has the possibility and the need to put really into effect 'the right to work'. Therefore a considerable increase takes place in the amount of labour power drawn into production, until the reserves of unemployed labour power are exhausted, and this also facilitates an increase in the rate of growth of production.

It must be remembered, however, that the possibility of increasing production extensively through the additional recruitment of labour power is based, to a considerable degree, on the rates of growth of labour productivity already achieved.

The importance of the higher productivity of labour in the socialist sector is clearly illustrated by the following calculation:

	1928	1929 in %	1930
1. The proportion of net production of census industry, building and state farms in total national income	27.0	33.2	39.4
2. The proportion of workers in these three branches to the total labour force (the active population)	5.0	5.5	7.0

We showed above the distribution of total national income between consumption and accumulation funds. Total consumption consists of two different items: (1) material consumption by the entire productive population (the population engaged in the sphere

of production and circulation, together with their families): (2) consumption by the
non-productive sphere, the 'service' sector.

The latter may be divided, in its turn, into (*a*) administration and defence, and (*b*)
social, cultural and medical services. In a certain sense, expenditure of a social, cultural
and medical character is returned to the productive population in the form of various
services (schools, hospitals, etc.).

Consequently, the population employed in this sphere serves both the productive
population, and also, in a more broad sense, production itself (scientific research work,
etc.). In the capitalist countries this sphere is, in the main, based on private enterprises,
the state is only slightly involved in its organisation, and the share of its services received
by the working population is quite insignificant. To a large extent the working
population of the capitalist countries are obliged to pay for these services out of their
individual incomes. These services include those called by Marx 'imposed services',
those connected with maintaining the apparatus of exploitation.

In the USSR, social, cultural and medical services of the working population are
socialised not only in the sense that they are organised by the proletarian state but also
because these services are provided in addition to incomes distributed to individuals.
The growth of this sphere is associated with the growth of culture in the proletarian state.
Its extension entirely depends on material production, and therefore on the rate of
expanded socialist reproduction.

The percentage share of the national income spent on the non-productive sphere,
compared with the other elements in the national income, is as follows (current prices):

	1929 (% of total)	1930 (% of total)	1930 (1929 = 100)
Administration and defence	5.7	5.4	122.3
Sphere of social, cultural and medical services	8.3	8.3	126.5
Accumulation fund	19.6	25.7	166.8
Consumption of material goods by the population in the productive sphere (including office-workers)	66.4	60.6	116.1
Total	100	100	127.2

The problem of proportions in the economy can be studied on two levels: first from the
price relationships of the mass of products and, secondly, from their relationships in
kind. The complete analysis of the latter is very difficult since the available materials for
the balances in kind are insufficient for a precise study of several aspects of the problems
of proportionality. Summary indicators of proportions in kind can be obtained in
practice (approximately and with certain assumptions) by eliminating price-changes –
in the present case, by making estimates in 1928 prices.

In terms of 'market-price' proportions, only extremely slight changes occurred in the material structure of production. The production of consumer goods (grouped according to their actual utilisation) as a percentage of total production in the economy was as follows (in current prices):

	1928	1929	1930
	41.5	41.2	41.1

But the share of consumer goods in total production measured in constant prices fell by 4.2 per cent in 1930 as compared with 1928. Of similar importance is the fact that the percentage share of agricultural and industrial production in all production used outside its own branch (so-called standard commodity production) when measured in current prices also did not markedly change in these three years:

	1928	1929	1930
Industry	69.8	68.9	68.8
Agriculture	30.2	31.1	31.2

But in constant prices there was a significant reduction in the share of agricultural production, from 30 per cent in 1928 to 25–26 per cent in 1930. This same tendency affecting the relationship between industrial and agricultural production can also be observed when we compare the total production of these branches. While the share of agricultural production in total industrial and agricultural production in current prices merely fell from 43.4 per cent in 1928 to 40.6 per cent, in constant prices it fell to 35.1 per cent.

These differences in estimates made in different prices are wholly due to the role of the private sector in production generally and, in particular, in the production of consumer goods, which was still considerable in those years. The considerable increase in effective demand enabled the private sector to increase its prices while reducing the physical volume of its output. This was especially marked in 1930.

The increase in prices of production of census industry (measured in producers' prices) occurred only for consumer goods; the prices of means of production were reduced. In agriculture prices both of means of production and of consumer goods increased, and the price increase in agriculture was considerably greater than in industry:

Prices (1928 = 100)

	Means of production	Consumer goods
Census industry 1929	98.4	101.5
Census industry 1930	96.0	103.3
Agriculture 1929	103.5	107.0
Agriculture 1930	116.8	144.1

The increase in the prices of agricultural production was principally a consequence of increased prices in the private sector. While the price-index for socialist production amounted to 100.6 in 1929 and to 107.0 in 1930, the index for the private sector amounted to 105.1 and 132.6. A still more considerable disparity appears in the price-index for consumer goods production. In the socialist sector the consumer goods index was 102.0 in 1929 and 105.8 in 1930, while in the private sector the corresponding figures were 107.2 and 150.0.

Changes in the index of consumer goods prices are primarily explained by the increases in producers' prices. The overall price-index for consumption (excluding alcoholic beverages) in 1930 was 124.7 (1928 = 100).

The index for manufactured goods rose by 16.5 per cent, for agricultural products by 164.1 per cent and for industrial food products by 139.3 per cent. Within agriculture the largest increase was for the products of animal husbandry.

The overall price-index (excluding alcoholic beverages) was higher for the non-agricultural population, at 133.8 in 1930, than it was for the agricultural population, at 117.1. The index for manufactured goods was more or less identical: 116.3 for the non-agricultural population and 116.7 for the agricultural. Among the non-agricultural population, the worker households had the lowest indexes (see the tables below [pp. 146–7]).

The indexes quoted are general-trade indexes, that is, they are a weighted index of purchase prices for purchases made in the socialist sector, and from the private trader and middleman, and directly from the producer.

As for the price-index for products produced in the socialist sector, this showed a quite insignificant rise during these years. For instance, the index of prices of consumer goods produced by census industry increased by 3.3 per cent. (This excludes the influence of changes in trade mark-up, which as a whole decreased relative to the other elements.)

The price index for cooperative trade was also more or less stable during this period. Consequently, the above mentioned price increases took place to an overwhelming extent through prices in the private sector, both prices in private trade and prices charged by private producers themselves.

Products from the private sector are received, first, in the form of procurements [by the state] of agricultural produce, and, secondly, through direct purchases by the proletariat of consumer goods from private traders, middlemen and the producers themselves.

When the urban proletariat's consumption is revalued in terms of socialist sector prices a difference emerges amounting to 614.3 million rubles in 1929 and 3,120.1 million rubles in 1930.

Data in kind indicate that the private trader accounted for 17 per cent of the total purchases by the urban proletariat in 1929 and 13.7 per cent in 1930.

The private market price-index (calculated by the sector of trade and supply [of Gosplan]) was 149 for 1929 and 383 in 1930 (1928 = 100).

A comparison of the share of private trade [in total urban proletariat purchases] in 1928 prices and in current prices reveals a surplus payment to the private sector of 675.0 million rubles in 1929 and 3,523.9 million rubles in 1930. Thus, these different sources both present more or less the same picture.

This is the gross amount of the surplus payment. A certain part of it is returned through purchases of goods in the socialist sector: however, these return payments were fairly insignificant since the price-index of the socialist sector had risen only very slightly; commercial trade [of the socialist sector, at higher prices] only began to develop at the end of 1930.

Finally there was also an increase in procurement prices; available data show a gain to the countryside from this increase of 177 million rubles in 1929 and 292 million rubles in 1930.

What part of the surplus-payment made through consumer-goods purchase-prices went directly to the producer, and what part to the professional trader and middleman?

A comparison of the trade mark-up of the private sector with the physical volume of commodity circulation in the private sector indicates an increase in mark-up of 329.5 million rubles in 1929 and 298.1 million rubles in 1930 (these figures refer to professional trade only).

Thus, while in 1929 about a half of the increase in prices was appropriated by private trade, in 1930 the preponderant part of the total gain in prices went directly to the producer, and mainly to the agricultural producer.

The importance of these price changes for the redistribution of the national income has already been mentioned. They enable the private sector to recover part of the transfer payments taken from it in 1929, and to more than recover them in 1930.[3]

The results of these three years have not yet however made a substantial change towards removing the disproportion between the development of industry and that of agriculture. While output of census industry increased by 51.4 per cent over these two years, the output of agriculture actually fell, by 1.5 per cent (in 1928 prices):

| | (Previous year = 100) | | (1928 = 100) |
	1929	1930	1930
Output of census industry	122.6	124.1	151.4
Output of agriculture	100.8	97.9	98.5

This fall in agricultural output was entirely due to the fall in 1930 in the output of animal husbandry. Although arable output in 1929 amounted to 99.9 per cent of the 1928 figure, the 1930 figure increased to 108.8 per cent. The output of animal husbandry, on the other hand, increased to 102.0 per cent [of the 1928 figure] in 1929, but fell by 18 per cent in 1930 (i.e. to 82 per cent of the 1929 figure).

As a result of these changes in the growth of industry and agriculture, the relative share of agriculture fell from 37.4 per cent of all production in 1928 to 29.3 per cent in 1930, while the share of census industry production rose from 37.4 per cent to 45.0 per cent.

During these years the industrial consumption of industrially produced raw and intermediary materials grew by 39 per cent while the consumption of agricultural raw materials increased by a mere 5.3 per cent in 1929 and 9.2 per cent in 1930. This was, of course, a consequence of the inability of agriculture to supply more, rather than of the inability of industry to consume more.

Consequently, the Party pointed to the only correct solution for agriculture. This solution lay in the development of state and collective farming. [15].

Let us now look at the relationship between accumulation and consumption.

The share of consumption in the national income fell from 80.6 per cent in 1928 to 74.3 per cent [in 1930] in current prices. In terms of constant prices the share of consumption fell even further, from 83.1 per cent to 68.5 per cent. Consequently, the share of accumulation increased. In itself this share does not disclose the essence of the accumulation–consumption relation. A fall in the share of consumption might still be accompanied by a considerable increase in the absolute size of consumption. In order to assess the real meaning of these relationships it is necessary to analyse the changes in consumption and in the consumption fund. The background to the fall in the share of consumption in the national income is that consumer goods output increased much more slowly than output as a whole.

The rate of growth of output for the principal economic groups of products (in 1928 prices) over the two years was as follows:

	1930 (1928 = 100)
1. Fixed means of production	154.7
2. Raw materials, auxiliary materials and fuel	129.1
3. Consumer goods	114.1

The grouping of products shown here is given in accordance with their predominant end-use. The rate of growth of the actual consumption fund (in consumer prices) during these years was even lower; in 1930 it was only 7.7 per cent more than in 1928. As the increase in total population in these two years was 4.4 per cent, consumption per head increased by only 3.1 per cent.

The general relationship between consumption and accumulation can be further illustrated by the structure of the increase in the production of material goods in real terms in 1929 and 1930. Thus in 1929 the total increase in the production of material goods amounted to 5,446 million rubles (in 1928 prices). Of this consumer goods accounted for 1,514 million rubles, or 28 per cent. In 1930 out of a total increase of 7,790 million rubles, consumer goods accounted for 1,716 million rubles, or 22 per cent.

The relationships stand out still more sharply when we analyse the material components of accumulation (in 1928 prices).

The shares of the different components of the increase in funds and stocks (real accumulation) were as follows (total increase = 100):

	1928	1929	1930
Increase in means of production	71.2	79.2	82.7
Increase in consumer goods	28.8	20.8	17.3

This disproportion between consumption and accumulation was due entirely to the lag in agricultural output as a whole and in the output of animal husbandry in particular. *If the output of animal husbandry had stayed in 1930 at the average level of the two preceding years, the output of consumer goods would have shown an increase of 20% between 1928 and 1930. And if we exclude the products of animal husbandry from the changes in the population's consumption fund, there would have been an increase of 13.4 per cent (instead of 7.7 per cent). This would have implied a per capita increase of 8.6 per cent (instead of 3.1 per cent).*

Thus the far from favourable ratio between consumption and accumulation are not the result of the high rates of increase in the means of production (accumulation). These high rates do not rule out an increase in consumer goods; on the contrary, in the longer run, they are the only possible basis for an accelerated increase in consumption, and provide the conditions for it. The lag in output of consumer goods was mainly due to the reduced output of products of animal husbandry. This was a consequence of the decrease in the number of livestock, which in turn was a result of the shortage of fodder and especially of wilful slaughter and squandering by kulak households and, to some extent, under the influence of kulak agitation, by middle peasant households as well.

Despite the considerable increase in the output of industrial raw materials, auxiliary materials and fuel, there was a certain lag within this group too. Production of metals and building materials was less than demand.

The shortage of building materials and the shortage and incompleteness of Soviet-made equipment resulted in an increase in building time and an increase in incomplete construction above the desired level. This affected the socialist sector of building to a lesser extent than building as a whole, although here, too, in 1931, there was a slight increase in the share of incomplete work in the total amount of expenditure on building.[4]

Incomplete building as a percentage of expenditure was as follows in current prices:

	1928	1929	1930	1931
Socialist sector	38.4	39.8	39.6	42.1

This process was particularly marked in certain sections of our building work. For example, in the building of dwellings, out of total expenditure (= 100):

	1928	1929	1930	1931
Proportion put into exploitation	75.0	67.0	52.7	43.8
Proportion of unfinished building	25.0	33.0	47.3	56.2
Total	100.0	100.0	100.0	100.0

While the absolute amount of expenditure on the building of dwellings was 114.4 in

1929, 167.0 in 1930, and 138.3 in 1931 (previous year = 100), the amount of finished building put into exploitation lagged: 104.7 in 1929, 135.5 in 1930 and 123.2 in 1931.

The difficulties in building were to a considerable extent caused by the very nature of the expanded reproduction of fixed capital, and are an inevitable accompaniment of our growth. In order to understand these difficulties it is very important to analyse the significance of unfinished construction in the economy.

The amount of unfinished construction measured in current prices, constituted 7.5 per cent of the gross output of census industry (excluding unfinished production) and building in 1928, 12.7 per cent in 1929, 16.2 per cent in 1930, and 20.9 per cent in 1931. Consequently, while in 1928 only 7.5 per cent of current production [was locked up in the construction of means of production], in 1931 this proportion had increased to one-fifth of current output. If we were also to include the consumer goods consumed by workers employed in building, this share would be still larger. These figures indicate both the scope of expanded reproduction of fixed capital and the degree of tension in the supply of means of production and of consumer goods.

The importance of the resources diverted from current production in the form of unfinished building emerges still more sharply if we compare them with the output of Group 'A' of census industry plus building output: they amounted to 19.0 per cent in 1928, 22.2 per cent in 1929, 26.5 per cent in 1930, and 31.7 per cent in 1931.

Thus the amount of unfinished building increased from almost one-fifth of the current output in these branches in 1928 to one-third in 1931: that is, one-third of current output produced no useful effect in the given year. Superficially it seems paradoxical that, in spite of the rapid rate of growth of industrial production, and especially of Group 'A', we nevertheless experienced shortages in both means of production and consumer goods, and even building did not receive all its requirements. It was precisely because we needed to achieve rapid rates of growth of industrial production and, especially, of Group 'A', that we had to rush ahead rapidly with the expanded reproduction of fixed capital. This in its turn provided the only possible basis for high rates of growth of industrial production.

The amount of unfinished building is also important in another respect. Its increase forms part of annual accumulation: it accounted for 20.1 per cent of total accumulation in 1928, 22.0 per cent in 1929, and 23.2 per cent in 1930. *Thus roughly one-fifth of total accumulation in the last two years was only potential accumulation and could not yet serve as a basis for expanded reproduction in the following years.* This is why, despite the enormous growth in capital investment, production is growing more slowly that the rate of growth of capital investment. Factories, plants and production combined provide the basis for the expansion of production only when they are complete. The amount of capital investment, after deducting depreciation and allocations to meet abnormal losses (from, for example, premature slaughter of livestock and natural disasters) consists of the accumulation of both completed fixed capital and unfinished building. The latter accounted for 24.1 per cent of the total in 1928, 38.0 per cent in 1929 and 29.8 per cent in 1930 (in 1928 prices). Thus, of the total amount of capital investment annually allocated to the expanded reproduction of fixed capital, in 1928 more than one-fifth, and in 1930 about one-third was merely potential accumulation.

But even that part of capital investment which was transformed each year into capital stock ready for exploitation did not yet produce its full effect in the first year [of exploitation]. This was due partly to 'infantile disorders' and partly to the fact that the bulk of it usually entered into exploitation only in the middle of the year, and in many cases only at the end of the year.

However, we must keep in mind Comrade Kaganovich's statement:

We are building socialism out of our own proletarian resources [...] We are investing milliards of rubles, and everyone understands that the building of Magnitostroi will take several years, absorbing hundreds of millions of rubles, and that production will begin only after two or three years [...]

There are critics who say: If it is so difficult, wouldn't it be better to take things easier and not to invest milliards of rubles in factories that will only start producing in two or three years time? [...]

That is how petty-bourgeois capitulators and inveterate philistines argue [...]

But these 'sages' are profoundly mistaken. These people cannot see further than their noses. They fail to understand one fundamental thing. They do not realise that we should have lost everything that we had gained in the October Revolution, if we had taken the road that the Right deviators and Trotskyists proposed for us. (Kaganovich, speech to the IX Trade Union Congress [28 April 1932]) [16]

The main features of the process of reproduction in the USSR in 1928–30 are as follows:

(a) the rate of growth of expanded reproduction was rising and was sufficiently high to ensure expanded reproduction of the economy as a whole. It was based on a considerable growth of labour productivity in the socialist sector;

(b) the share of the socialist sector in the production of all groups of material goods increased, particularly in the case of fixed means of production, and to a lesser extent in the case of consumer goods.

The rates of growth of the production of fixed means of production in the socialist sector were the highest; the rate of growth of consumer goods was slightly lower. As a result, the share and also the absolute amount of production in the private sector fell for all groups of products and for all branches of production. Nevertheless, the share of the private sector in the production of consumer goods remained fairly considerable in 1930 (about one-half); the increase in the production of consumer goods in the socialist sector only just exceeded the decrease in the private sector.

Industrialisation also had the effect of changing the proportions of the different groups of products and of the different branches of the economy. Production of fixed means of production considerably outstripped all other groups, and the industrial branches of the economy grew considerably;

(c) there has been tremendous progress in socialist construction, which can be seen in the consolidation of the increased rates of growth of expanded socialist reproduction, in the industrialisation of the country, in the collectivisation of agriculture, in increased labour productivity, in the elimination of unemployment, etc., etc. But there were also some negative aspects affecting consumption and the distribution of the national income. These were mainly due to the complexity of the class struggle against capitalism.

The optimum combination of accumulation and consumption was not fully achieved. This was due not to problems associated with accumulation (its rate of growth and scale) but to specific conditions which affect the production of consumer goods in these years, and particularly the products of animal husbandry. In addition, we were not successful in eliminating the disproportion in relation to agriculture, which lagged behind the other branches of the economy in its rate of growth. This lag was caused by difficulties in the social and technical reconstruction of the petty commodity economy. There was also something of a lag in the production of industrial raw materials and auxiliary materials, which caused a lengthening of construction time, and the 'freezing' of resources.

Another unfavourable outcome of these years was a considerable increase in prices in the private sector, especially in agriculture. This was particularly marked in 1930, and because of this the private sector was able in that year to acquire a considerable share of the national income.

In the following sections a more detailed analysis is provided of various aspects of reproduction (production, capital investment and stock, consumption).

[I] PRODUCTION OF MATERIAL GOODS

In analysing the production of material goods we use estimates of production of the branches producing material goods in real terms, and we assume that they indicate the actual rate of growth and structure of production in the economy.

We have therefore excluded transport, communications and trade from the branches directly producing material goods. Production in real terms has been estimated by revaluing it in terms of 'constant prices' – in the present case, in 1928 prices.

The overall changes in the production of material goods in real terms in 1928, 1929 and 1930[5] were as follows (in 1928 prices):

	1929 (1928 = 100)	1930 (1929 = 100)	1930 (1928 = 100)
Total	110.6	113.7	125.7
Socialist sector	130.7	142.2	185.9
Private sector	92.3	76.9	70.9

The percentage share of the different social sectors in the total production of material goods changed as follows:

	1928	1929	1930
Socialist sector	47.6	56.3	70.5
Private sector	52.4	43.7	29.5

The increase in production of the socialist sector was achieved partly through an expansion of production in existing socialist enterprises, and partly through the socialisation of former private enterprises (collectivisation in agriculture and cooperation in small-scale industry). Of the total increase in production of material goods by the socialist sector in 1929, an expansion of existing enterprises accounted for four-fifths, while socialisation accounted for one-fifth. Most of the total increase came from socialist census industry (57.0 per cent) and from building (15.1 per cent).

In 1930 three-quarters of the increase in production in the socialist sector came from the expansion of existing enterprises and from newly constructed enterprises, while one-quarter was due to socialisation.

The annual rate of growth of production at existing socialist enterprises (indicating expanded socialist reproduction on the 'existing basis') was 23.6 per cent in 1929 and 30.5 per cent in 1930.

These rates of growth exceeded the highest rates of growth of production achieved during the restoration period (27 per cent in 1925/6).

In 1929 there was a 7.7 per cent fall in production in the private sector as compared with 1928 (2,086.2 million rubles in absolute terms). Sixty-two per cent of this decline was due to a fall in production by small-scale industry. The rest was due to a small decline in all other branches. In 1930 production fell in the private sector as compared with 1929 by 5,761.5 million rubles, or 23.1 per cent. Sixty-one per cent of this decrease occurred in agriculture and was due to the transfer of production into the socialist sector as a result of collectivisation.

The following figures show the increase in production for groups of products classified according to end-use (in 1928 prices):

	1929 (1928 = 100)	1930 (1929 = 100)	1930 (1928 = 100)
Fixed means of production	117.4	131.7	154.7
Raw materials, auxiliary materials, fuel	112.7	114.6	129.1
Consumer goods	106.6	107.0	114.1

The percentage of these groups changed as follows:

	1928	1929	1930
Fixed means of production	12.8	13.6	15.8
Raw materials, auxiliary materials, fuel	42.6	43.4	43.8
Consumer goods	44.6	43.0	40.4
Total	100.0	100.0	100.0

The changes in production by social sector for the three groups were as follows (in 1928 prices) (preceding year = 100):

	Socialist sector		Private sector	
	1929	1930	1929	1930
Fixed means of production	148.3	173.6	90.7	72.4
Raw materials, auxiliary materials, fuel	129.5	139.5	93.7	76.0
Consumer goods	126.6	134.2	91.5	78.8

Over the two years 1928–30 production by the socialist sector increased as follows: fixed means of production by 157.5 per cent; raw materials, auxiliary materials and fuel by 80.6 per cent; consumer goods by 69.9 per cent. The private sector declined by 65.6 per cent, 71.2 per cent and 72.1 per cent in these groups in these years.

The decrease in production of means of production by the private sector was considerably exceeded by the growth in production of the socialist sector. For consumer goods, the decrease in private production was also outweighed by an increase in the production of the socialist sector, but to a lesser extent.

Thus the percentage share of fixed means of production in total production increased in the case of the socialist sector and decreased in the case of the private sector:

	Percentage of total production by the socialist sector			Percentage of total production by the private sector		
	1928	1929	1930	1928	1929	1930
Fixed means of production	12.5	14.2	17.3	13.2	12.9	12.1
Raw materials, auxiliary materials, fuel	47.4	46.9	46.0	38.3	38.9	38.5
Consumer goods	40.1	38.9	36.7	48.5	48.2	49.5
Total	100.0	100.0	100.0	100.0	100.0	100.0

As a result of these changes the socialist sector produced the following percentage of total production (in 1928 prices):

	1928	1929	1930
Fixed means of production	46.4	58.6	77.3
Raw materials, auxiliary materials, fuel	52.9	60.8	74.0
Consumer goods	42.8	51.0	63.9
All material goods	47.6	56.3	70.5

The above figures for the production of means of production in the socialist and private sectors adequately show the process of socialist industrialisation. The process can be further illustrated by analysing changes in the structure of the economy by branches. The percentage shares of the different branches in the total production of material goods changed as follows (in 1928 prices):

	1928	1929	1930
Census industry	37.4	41.2	45.0
Small-scale industry	11.4	10.0	9.0
Building	8.2	9.1	11.6
Agriculture	37.4	34.1	29.3
Other branches	5.6	5.6	5.1
Total	100.0	100.0	100.0

The socialist sector mainly consisted of the industrial branches of the economy, but the share of socialist agriculture increased quite significantly:

	Percentage of total production by the socialist sector			Percentage of total production by the private sector		
	1928	1929	1930	1928	1929	1930
Census industry	77.6	72.8	63.7	0.7	0.6	0.3
Small-scale industry	6.7	8.6	8.5	15.7	11.9	10.3
Building work	10.3	11.4	14.5	6.3	6.2	4.5
Agriculture	1.7	2.9	8.8	69.8	74.2	78.2
Other branches	3.7	4.3	7.5	7.5	7.1	6.7
Total	100.0	100.0	100.0	100.0	100.0	100.0

The percentage shares of the sectors in the various branches of the economy are shown in the following table:

	1928	1929	1930
Census industry			
(*a*) socialist sector	99.0	99.4	99.8
(*b*) private sector	1.0	0.6	0.2
Building work			
(*a*) socialist sector	59.7	70.4	88.6
(*b*) private sector	40.3	29.6	11.4
Small-scale industry			
(*a*) socialist sector	28.0	48.5	66.4
(*b*) private sector	72.0	51.5	33.6
Agriculture			
(*a*) socialist sector	2.1	4.8	21.1
(*b*) private sector	97.9	96.2	78.9

Agricultural production

	in current prices, in million rubles			in 1928 prices, in million rubles		
	1928	1929	1930	1928	1929	1930
State farms	242.6	325.8	771.8	243.0	317.8	677.0
(a) arable	206.2	252.1	569.9	206.9	250.8	535.1
(b) animal husbandry	36.4	73.7	201.9	36.1	67.0	141.9
Collective farms	167.9	601.7	3507.6	170.3	604.4	3321.4
(a) arable	152.5	546.4	3100.9	154.3	551.3	3031.6
(b) animal husbandry	15.4	55.3	406.7	16.0	53.1	289.8
Private sector	18830.8	19406.7	19827.8	18828.0	18473.6	14952.9
(a) arable	11002.5	11262.2	9972.6	11000.0	10554.9	8789.6
(b) animal husbandry	7828.3	8144.5	9855.2	7828.0	7918.7	6163.3
Total	19241.3	20334.2	24107.2	19241.3	19395.8	18951.3
(a) arable	11361.2	12060.7	13643.4	11361.2	11357.0	12356.3
(b) animal husbandry	7880.1	8273.5	10463.8	7880.1	8038.8	65950.0
			in % of the preceding year			
State farms	–	134.8	236.9	–	130.8	213.0
(a) arable	–	122.3	226.1	–	121.2	213.3
(b) animal husbandry	–	202.5	273.9	–	185.6	211.8
Collective farms	–	358.4	549.7	–	354.9	549.5
(a) arable	–	358.3	567.5	–	357.3	549.9
(b) animal husbandry	–	359.1	735.4	–	331.9	545.8
Private sector	–	103.1	102.2	–	98.1	80.9
(a) arable	–	102.4	88.5	–	95.6	83.3
(b) animal husbandry	–	104.1	121.0	–	101.2	77.8
Total	–	105.7	118.6	–	100.8	97.7
(a) arable	–	106.2	113.2	–	99.9	108.8
(b) animal husbandry	–	105.0	126.5	–	102.0	82.0

The share of animal husbandry products in the total production of agriculture was 41.0 per cent in 1928 and 41.4 per cent in 1929, and fell to 34.8 per cent in 1930.

The reduction in the production of animal husbandry and in the actual number of livestock was due to the wilful slaughter of livestock which was a consequence of class resistance by the kulaks. The importance of animal husbandry in the economy can be assessed by comparing material production including and excluding production of animal husbandry. Including animal husbandry the growth rate was 10.6 per cent in 1929, 13.7 per cent in 1930, and 25.7 per cent for the two years taken together, while excluding animal husbandry products the growth rate was 12.1 per cent for 1929, 18.9 per cent for 1930 and 33.3 per cent for the two years taken together.

[2]   FIXED CAPITAL STOCK AND CAPITAL INVESTMENT

Expanded reproduction is, above all, expanded reproduction of fixed capital stock (means of labour). Consequently, the construction of fixed capital and its growth are the most important indicators of our progress, of socialist construction and reconstruction.

Summary figures are given below:

Capital stock at beginning of year (preceding year = 100) (in 1928 prices)

	1929	1930	1931
Total stock	103.3	103.6	106.6
Production stock			
(a) Excluding livestock	104.8	107.6	114.3
(b) Including livestock	103.8	103.9	109.4

Thus, contrary to the expectations of those opportunist theoreticians who anticipated a decreasing curve of growth, expanded reproduction of our fixed stock has taken place at an increasing rate. [17] But, apart from the reproduction of stocks for the economy as a whole, we are also interested in the breakdown by social sectors:

Capital stock at beginning of year (preceding year = 100) (in 1928 prices)

	1929	1930	1931
A. *Socialist sector*			
I. *All stocks*			
(a) Excluding livestock	105.2	109.0	118.6
(b) Including livestock	105.3	109.7	120.8
II. *Production stocks*			
(a) Excluding livestock	106.2	111.4	124.9
(b) Including livestock	106.4	112.6	128.4
B. *Private sector*			
III. *All stocks*			
(a) Excluding livestock	101.9	100.6	94.9
(b) Including livestock	101.5	97.6	91.1

The relationship between the socialist sector and the private sector was sharply changed by the different rates of reproduction of fixed capital stock in each sector. There was a rapid growth in the socialist sector in these years, but the private sector did not grow during the first two years of the Five-Year Plan, and in the last of these years [1930] it declined absolutely and additions to stock were not sufficient even for simple reproduction in that year. The percentage share of the different sectors in capital stock was as follows (at the beginning of each year, in 1928 prices):

	1928	1929	1930	1931	1932
Socialist sector					
(a) Excluding livestock	55.2	56.0	58.0	63.3	69.1
(b) Including livestock	48.2	49.1	52.1	59.0	66.8
Private sector					
(a) Excluding livestock	44.8	44.0	42.0	36.7	30.9
(b) Including livestock	51.8	50.9	47.9	41.0	33.2

There was an absolute as well as a relative decline in the fixed stock of the private sector. This absolute decline occurred partly because the private sector consumed its own stock but mainly because it was transferred to the socialist sector, by the process of socialisation.

The increase in the stocks of the socialist sector, however, was mainly due to construction in the socialist sector based on socialist accumulation within the sector, rather than to transfers of stocks from the private sector.

The sources of accumulation were thus both expanded reproduction of the national income within the socialist sector itself and the redistribution of the total national income of the USSR.

While the growth of the capital stock of the socialist sector as a whole took place mainly through new construction within the sector itself, in agriculture the growth of the socialist sector also took place to a considerable extent through the socialisation of the capital stock of the private sector:

Socialisation of agricultural capital stock (in 1928 prices)

	1928	1929	1930	1931
Capital investment in productive capital stock of agriculture in the socialist sector	255.0	637.8	1844.2	2815.7
Socialisation of [agricultural] productive stock	38.7	217.9	914.4	1960.8

As a result of capital construction and socialisation, the relative share of the socialist sector in agriculture changed during these years as follows (in percentages, measured in 1928 prices):

Productive capital stock of agriculture at end of year

	1928	1929	1930	1931
Socialist sector	8.1	12.2	25.3	45.0
Private sector	91.9	87.8	74.7	55.0

The change in the importance of the sectors can be shown still more strikingly by data on the direct construction of new capital stocks, as shown by the changes in capital investment (measured in 1928 prices):

	1928	1929	1930	1931
1. In the economy:				
million rubles	7240.7	8554.5	12507.7	16853.7
Preceding year = 100	–	118.1	146.2	134.7
2. Socialist sector:				
million rubles	4117.4	6041.7	11195.7	15686.9
Preceding year = 100	–	146.7	185.3	140.2
3. Private sector:				
million rubles	3155.7	2610.2	1571.6	1366.4
Preceding year = 100	–	82.7	60.2	86.9

From these figures we see the general pattern of capital investment: increasing rates of growth in the socialist sector, a sharply declining growth in the private sector. This process caused the structure of capital investment by sector to change even more sharply in these years, despite the fact that in 1928 the socialist sector already accounted for more than half of all capital investment.

The share of the sectors in capital investment[6] changed as follows: the share of the socialist sector increased from 54.7 per cent in 1928 to 68.9 per cent in 1929, to 86.6 per cent in 1930 and 91.3 per cent in 1931, and the share of the private sector correspondingly declined from 45.3 per cent in 1928 to only 8.7 per cent in 1931.

Expanded reproduction generally results in expanded reproduction of fixed and circulating capital and of consumer goods. Expanded reproduction (which we will call accumulation for short) in the form of fixed capital is a large proportion of our total accumulation.

The share of accumulation, in the form of fixed capital in the national income, is shown in the following figures (in 1928 prices):

	1928	1929	1930
National income: million rubles	26187.1	29045.1	34637.1
Accumulation in fixed capital stock including incomplete building: million rubles	3042.8	3748.9	7129.6
As % of national income	11.6	12.9	20.6
Increase in fixed capital stock:			
million rubles	2144.2	2369.7	4550.5
As % of national income	8.2	8.2	13.1

The share of accumulation in the form of fixed capital in total real accumulation amounted to 58.0 per cent in 1928, 49.4 per cent in 1929, and 49.2 per cent in 1930. If the amount of unfinished building and the capital investment in unrecorded funds were also included in fixed capital, then the share would be larger and constitute 82.3 per cent in 1928, 78.1 per cent in 1929 and 77.2 per cent in 1930.

Only in our country, where socialism is being constructed, can such a large share of accumulation be found in the form of fixed capital (including unfinished buildings).

Accumulation in fixed capital is one of the basic elements in the construction of the foundations of the socialist economy, which we have now completed. A rapid rate of accumulation in the form of fixed capital took place only in the socialist sector. In 1928 the increase in capital stock in the socialist sector was 1,657.5 million rubles or 77 per cent of the total increase in completed stock (2,144.2 million rubles). In the following year, 1929, the growth in capital stock in the socialist sector was associated with a decline in the stock of the private sector. The former grew by 3,171.6 million rubles while the latter fell by 801.9 million rubles. In 1930 the increase in the socialist sector amounted to 7,466.6 million rubles and the decline in the private sector to 2,926.1 million rubles.

The decline in the private sector reduced the increase of capital stock in the economy as a whole. But it must be noted that part of this decline in the private sector was due to the transfer of capital stock from the private to the socialist sector. This socialisation amounted to 306.5 million rubles in 1929 and 1,354.1 million rubles in 1930.

In order to secure the final victory of socialism, we must also catch up and overtake these (capitalist, A. P.) countries in a technical and an economic respect. Either we do this or they will destroy us. This is necessary not only for the building of socialism, but also in order to uphold the independence of our country in the circumstances of capitalist encirclement. The independence of our country cannot be upheld unless we have an adequate industrial basis for defence. And such an industrial basis cannot be created if our industry is not more highly developed in a technical respect. That is why a fast rate of development of our industry is necessary and imperative. (Stalin, *Problems of Leninism*, p. 434) [18]
A fast rate of development in general, and of the production of the means of production in particular, is the underlying principle and key to . . . the transformation of our entire national economy along the lines of socialist development. (Stalin, *Problems of Leninism*, p. 437) [19]

The implementation of the party line on the industrialisation of the country is illustrated in the material presented below:

If we compare the growth of capital investment in the economy as a whole with the growth of investment in industry, transport and agriculture, we see that the rates of growth of capital investment in industry are higher than the rates for the economy as a whole or for transport or agriculture.

Capital investment (in 1928 prices, preceding year = 100)

	1929	1930	1931
1. Economy as a whole	118.1	146.2	134.7
2. All industry	146.0	185.7	148.8
3. Transport	126.7	143.0	145.6
4. Agriculture	94.8	118.3	128.1

This leads to an increasing share of capital investment going to industry.

If the total capital investment in the economy is taken to be 100, the change in the percentage share of the different branches is as follows:

	1928	1929	1930	1931
1. Industry	22.3	27.8	36.5	40.1
2. Transport	13.1	14.7	14.4	15.3
3. Agriculture	31.8	25.2	22.7	21.0

The sharp fall in the share of agriculture in capital investment was as a result of the contraction of the private sector generally and, in particular, within the private sector, the contraction of investment in livestock.

As a result of the success of our socialist construction and of the industrialisation of the country, the structure of fixed capital has changed. The share of productive capital has increased, the share of the fixed capital of industry, transport and electrification within total productive capital has also increased.

The share of fixed productive capital in total capital stock (beginning of year) amounted to 54.7 per cent in 1928, 55.0 per cent in 1929, 55.2 per cent in 1930, 56.6 per cent in 1931 and 65.5 per cent in 1932.

In the socialist sector the share of fixed productive capital in the total stock of the sector was even greater: it was 57.7 per cent at the beginning of 1928, 58.3 per cent in 1929, 60 per cent in 1930, 63.6 per cent in 1931 and 65.6 per cent in 1932.

Thus the share of productive capital rose from 54.7 per cent at the beginning of 1928 to 58.4 per cent in 1932 for the economy as a whole, while for the socialist sector it increased from 57.7 per cent to 65.6 per cent.

The relative weight of different branches of the economy in fixed productive capital has also changed.

The percentage share of the capital of census industry rose from 15 per cent in 1928 to 25.8 per cent at the beginning of 1932; the share of industry planned by VSNKh (Supreme Council of the National Economy) and by NKSnab (People's Commissariat of Supply) rose from 13.2 per cent to 22.5 per cent, the share of Group 'A' industry rose from 7.2 per cent to 16.5 per cent, and the share of power stations rose from 1.2 per cent to 2.8 per cent.

At the same time the share of agriculture fell somewhat – from 51.0 per cent in 1929 to 41.9 per cent at the beginning of 1932. The share of transport fell to a great extent [*sic*] from 29.9 per cent at the beginning of 1928 to 28.3 per cent at the beginning of 1932. The share of railway transport declined even more substantially from 27.2 per cent at the beginning of 1928 to only 24.4 per cent at the beginning of 1932. The rise in the share of industry and power stations in fixed capital was mainly because their growth rates were higher than those of the other branches.

The active fixed capital at the beginning of the year was as follows (in 1928 prices, previous year = 100):

	1929	1930	1931	1932
1. Census industry	111.6	118.5	130.9	132.5
of which planned by				
VSNKh and NKSnab	113.1	116.9	131.9	129.7
of which in Group 'A'	118.9	125.0	145.7	140.5
2. Power stations (district				
and municipal)	125.1	118.0	135.2	149.3
3. Transport	101.5	103.0	108.1	111.1
of which, railway transport	101.5	102.4	106.1	107.8
4. Agriculture	102.5	99.2	101.2	105.6

The higher growth of fixed capital in industry as compared with other branches of the economy is even more obvious if we compare capital stock on 1 January 1932, with capital stock on 1 January 1928 (1 January 1928 = 100):

1. Census industry	222.8
of which, planned by VSNKh and NKSnab	226.3
of which Group 'A'	304.1
2. Power stations	298.0
3. Transport	125.6
of which, railway transport	118.7
4. Agriculture	108.7

The insignificant increase in fixed capital in agriculture, and its actual reduction in 1930 as compared with 1929, were a consequence of the loss of livestock that took place in those years. Fixed capital in the form of agricultural buildings, agricultural machinery, tractors and implements grew at an increasing annual rate (the stock on 1 January 1928 = 100):

1 January 1929	104.0
1 January 1930	105.8
1 January 1931	109.3
1 January 1932	112.9

It should be pointed out that the low rate of growth of the total fixed capital of agriculture was mainly due to the decrease in capital in the private sector.

This was in turn almost entirely a result of the squandering and 'devouring' of livestock. The transfer of capital from the private to the socialist sector through socialisation or purchase did not influence the changes in agricultural capital in the economy as a whole.

In the socialist sector of agriculture, the growth rates of fixed capital were even higher than in industry. Fixed capital at the beginning of each year increased annually as follows (in 1928 prices, 1 January of previous year = 100):

1929	115.8
1930	148.6
1931	210.2
1932	188.5

This rapid growth in the capital of the socialist sector was due, of course, both to new construction (in the broad sense of the word, that is including the acquisition of new machines, etc.), and to a considerable extent to the expansion of the socialist sector [at the expense of the private sector].

[3] CONSUMPTION OF MATERIAL GOODS

Changes in consumption by the Soviet population in these years were caused first, by changes in the level of production of consumer goods and, secondly, by the distribution of the national income and supplies in accordance with class policy. The average per capita norm of consumption is not a satisfactory indicator of consumption, because it is the result of adding together elements which moved in opposite directions: the incomes and consumption of the working population increased and the incomes and consumption of the capitalist elements in the town and country declined. In an analysis of the incomes and consumption of the working classes, a major feature of the Soviet economy which must be taken into account is the existence of various socio-cultural and medical services which are not paid for by the working people out of their personal incomes. These socio-cultural and similar services (which may be termed 'consumption of non-material goods') cover an important and rapidly increasing share of the total consumption of the working people.

The increase in the total consumption fund of the entire population, 1928 prices (henceforth consumption data are given in 1928 prices throughout) was 7.7 per cent in 1930 in comparison with 1928, and 9.4 per cent if consumption by institutions is included (but excluding services).[7]

Accordingly, the increase in per capita individual consumption was 3.1 per cent in 1930 as compared with 1928, or 5.1 per cent if so-called 'collective consumption' is included (population growth in these two years is taken as 4.4 per cent).

Special features of this period must be borne in mind when we analyse these indicators. Changes took place both in the product-structure of the consumption fund, and in the levels of consumption of different classes and groups of the population. As regards the product structure, there was a decline, in both absolute and relative terms, in the consumption of livestock products. The personal consumption segment of the consumption fund, excluding livestock products, was 11.6 per cent higher in 1930 than in 1928; and consumption including collective consumption but excluding livestock increased by 13.2 per cent. The per capita increase was 6.8 per cent, or 8.2 per cent including collective consumption. (Consumption of alcoholic beverages is excluded: it fell by 3 per cent per capita during these two years.)

The different classes and groups of the population experienced considerably different changes in levels of consumption.

The increase in the consumption fund of the working people of the USSR takes place

both through the increase in the output of consumption goods and through the redistribution of this fund in accordance with a class policy on supplies.

Increase in per capita consumption (including services but excluding alcohol) (in %)

	1929: 1928	1930: 1929	1930: 1928
Workers (manual)	3.4	4.6	8.2
Office workers	2.9	−1.6	1.3
Total urban proletariat	3.5	2.7	6.3
Rural working population	–	–	5.9
All urban and rural working people (bourgeois and kulaks excluded)	–	–	8.2

While the total consumption fund (personal and collective) increased by 9.4 per cent
from 1928 to 1930, the fund for the proletariat and rural working population increased by
14.2 per cent and their per capita consumption by 8.2 per cent.

The total consumption fund of manual workers increased in physical terms by 29.9 per
cent between 1928 and 1930, and, if the value of services is included, by 37.6 per cent
(both these figures exclude the consumption of alcohol). The consumption fund of
manual workers, excluding products of animal husbandry (and excluding alcohol and
services) increased by 43.2 per cent.

The following items of consumption grew considerably: products of arable agriculture
(by 69 per cent), industrial food products (59.4 per cent), clothing and footwear (38 per
cent), household goods and cultural goods (52.1 per cent). But the consumption fund of
livestock products fell by 4.3 per cent during these two years.

The rapid increase in the number of the working population (by 27.2 per cent from
1928 to 1930) reduced the effect of this very considerable increase in their fund of material
consumption with the result that their per capita level of material consumption
(excluding services and alcohol) grew by only 4.1 per cent (by 8.2 per cent if the value of
social-cultural and medical services is included). There was an accelerating increase in
the per capita consumption of manual workers, 3.4 per cent in 1929 and 4.6 per cent in
1930.

Reduced consumption of livestock products lowered the growth of the per capita consumption of manual workers. Their per capita consumption of animal produce fell by
24.8 per cent between 1928 and 1930. If livestock products are excluded, instead of the
8.2 per cent increase in per capita consumption given above, the increase for all the rest
of consumption was 16.1 per cent between 1928 and 1930.

The largest growth in per capita consumption was in arable produce (32.9 per cent),
industrial food products (25.3 per cent), household goods (17.4 per cent) and cultural
goods (19.6 per cent).

Consumption of alcohol per capita fell considerably, by 17.8 per cent in physical terms.

Changes in the composition of the working class also influenced the changes in the per capita consumption of the workers. The number of workers increased by 3.2 millions between 1928 and 1930. Workers fresh from the countryside were a considerable proportion of this figure. For these groups of workers there can be no doubt that their incomes and consumption considerably increased. But at the same time the level of income and consumption of these new and mostly unskilled workers was lower than the average for skilled workers. The lower incomes and consumption of this large number of new workers had the effect of lowering the average level of income and consumption of the working class as a whole. These considerations also apply to some extent to the office workers.

As there are no direct data on the division of fresh labour from the countryside between separate groups of the proletariat, we have made a rough estimate of the increase in per capita consumption for the urban proletariat as a whole. For these purposes the urban proletariat is assumed to be a specific part of the entire working population with a specific and fixed numerical size. For 1928 we have taken a group of the working population which is equivalent in number to the proletariat of 1930 but which is made up of proletarians or of other strata of the working population which subsequently became merged into the urban proletariat.

Taking this specific 1930 urban proletariat, part of which had a lower norm of consumption than the workers in 1928, the increase in per capita consumption of this group was 12.4 per cent (including services). The actual total increase in per capita consumption by the urban proletariat (manual workers, office workers, pensioners, students, etc.) between 1928 and 1930 was only 6.3 per cent (including free services).

The total consumption fund of office workers increased over these two years, in physical terms, by 20.4 per cent (excluding alcohol), or, including free services, by 24.3 per cent. However, as a result of the considerable increase in the size of this group of the proletarian population (22.7 per cent in two years) their average per capita consumption increased by only 1.3 per cent; if consumption of services is excluded, it actually fell by 1.9 per cent between 1928 and 1930.

It must be borne in mind that, throughout these years, per capita consumption (including the consumption of alcohol and services) continued to be higher for office workers than for manual workers – 10.3 per cent higher in 1928, 4.5 per cent higher in 1930.

The low rate of growth of consumption by office workers thus reduced this difference. The class policy applied to the redistribution of the consumption fund ensured that the working class was given priority in the increase of its total and per capita consumption.

There was a marked decline in the per capita consumption by office workers of livestock produce (by 27.1 per cent) and also of clothing and footwear (by 5.6 per cent). When analysing this latter figure one must bear in mind that office workers initially had larger stocks of clothing and footwear than manual workers.

As in the case of manual workers, the fall in the consumption of livestock produce had a marked influence on the growth of the total consumption fund of office workers and on their per capita consumption. The growth of the total consumption fund excluding livestock produce (but including services) enabled an increase in per capita consumption of 9 per cent between 1928 and 1930.

For the urban bourgeoisie there was a marked decrease in both the total amount of consumption and in the per capita norms of consumption. Their total fund fell by almost two thirds; as the numbers of the urban bourgeoisie declined by 50 per cent, their per capita consumption declined by more than 30 per cent.

Owing to the lack of statistical materials, it is not possible to analyse consumption by the different classes of the agricultural population. This must be borne in mind when examining the data on consumption by the agricultural population as a whole. The latter includes different classes and groups which were in different conditions and experienced different tendencies as regards consumption. These classes included both the rural bourgeoisie and the collective farmers, already considerable in numbers in 1930.

The total consumption fund of the agricultural population increased by 5.6 per cent between 1928 and 1930 (excluding alcohol, but including services). With an increase of 1.8 per cent in the numbers of the agricultural population, per capita consumption increased by 3.7 per cent.

The increase in consumption, excluding livestock produce, was 8.4 per cent. Allowing for the decrease in consumption by kulaks, the total consumption fund of the agricultural population increased during these two years by 8.4 per cent and their per capita consumption increased by 5.9 per cent.

As regards different groups of products, between 1928 and 1930 per capita consumption of arable products increased by 9.9 per cent and of industrial goods by 12.3 per cent while per capita consumption of livestock produce decreased by 9.5 per cent between 1928 and 1930. (In 1929 there was an increase of 5.9 per cent in the per capita consumption of livestock produce, as a result of rapacious slaughter of livestock and devouring of stocks.) Per capita consumption of clothing and footwear increased by 16.5 per cent, of household goods by 34.5 per cent and of cultural goods by 20.4 per cent.

It is difficult to compare the physical volume of consumption by the agricultural and non-agricultural populations. The goods consumed varied in quality; and above all the different price levels make it especially difficult to evaluate the products which were consumed by the producers themselves. The position also differed greatly as regards all kinds of services, which were purchased by the urban population in very much larger quantities than by the rural population.

Approximate calculations are given below of the relationship between the agricultural and non-agricultural population in their consumption of material goods.

The total per capita consumption of the agricultural population (excluding services) in physical terms in 1930 amounted to 62 per cent of the per capita consumption of the non-agricultural population.

The following table indicates these relationships for particular groups of products.

Consumption by the agricultural population in relation to the non-agricultural population (non-agricultural population = 100)

(In 1928 prices, with agricultural consumption estimated at urban prices)

	Arable produce	Livestock produce	Cereal products	Industrial goods
1928	161.5	83.7	112.8	29.5
1929	137.3	91.9	123.8	32.6
1930	126.1	100.4	106.9	31.5

The share of the consumption of the agricultural population in the total consumption fund in 1930 was 69.1 per cent. For different products the share was as follows:

arable	82.0%
livestock	78.4%
cereal	79.5%
industrial	53.2%

[C] Some results for 1931

At the moment when this work on the balance of the national economy for 1928–30 was sent to press we did not yet have available all the necessary materials for compiling a balance for 1931. We were only able to make preliminary total estimates of national income, accumulation and consumption.

These results are shown in the following table, in comparison with the corresponding data for the preceding years:

National income and accumulation

	1928	1929	1930	1931	1931 (1928 = 100)
	(in current prices in million rubles)				
National income	26442.3	30135.9	38333.2	47830.8	
Previous year = 100	–	114.0	127.2	124.8	180.9
Accumulation fund	5136.6	5917.1	9870.0	14500.0	
As % of national income	19.4	19.6	25.7	30.3	
Previous year = 100	–	115.2	166.8	146.9	282.3
Consumption fund (net of excises)	21305.7	44218.8	28462.8	33380.8	
As % of national income	80.6	80.4	74.3	69.7	
Previous year = 100	–	113.7	117.5	117.1	156.4
Real accumulation	4489.3	4838.2	8193.4	13100.0	
As % of national income	17.0	16.1	21.4	27.4	
Previous year = 100	–	107.8	169.3	159.8	291.8

Materialy

National income and accumulation(cont.)

	1928	1929	1930	1931	1931 (1928 = 100)
	(in current prices in million rubles)				
1. National income					
1st variant (sum of net production of					
branches in constant prices)	26187.1	29045.1	34637.1	39620.8	
Previous year = 100	–	110.9	119.3	114.4	151.3
2nd variant (sum of consumption and					
accumulation funds in constant prices)	25650.4	28379.2	33811.7	37933.5	
Previous year = 100	–	110.6	119.1	112.2	147.9
2. Accumulation fund	4334.7	5804.0	10634.5	15228.3	
As % of national income					
(2nd variant)	16.9	20.5	31.5	40.1	
Previous year = 100	–	133.6	183.2	143.2	350.5
3. Consumption fund					
(excluding excises)	21305.7	22575.2	23177.2	22705.2	
As % of national income					
(2nd variant)	83.1	79.5	69.5	59.9	
Previous year = 100	–	106.0	102.7	98.0	106.6
4. Real accumulation	3697.4	4801.38	9230.3	13668.6	
As % of national income					
(2nd variant)	14.4	16.9	27.3	36.0	
As % of national income					
(1st variant)	14.1	16.5	26.6	34.5	

As we see, a distinctive feature of the year 1931 is the marked increase of the share of accumulation in the national income, which rose from 27.3 per cent to 36.0 per cent of the total national income. The consumption fund remained at approximately the same level as in the preceding year, 1930.

Thus, the entire increase in the national income in 1931 went into accumulation.

However, despite the lack of growth of the total consumption fund in 1931 (according to these preliminary estimates), the consumption fund and per capita levels of consumption of the workers increased. The total consumption fund of the workers grew by 29.9 per cent in 1931 (in 1928 prices), and the per capita level of consumption (including the socialised wage) grew by 3.5 per cent.

The per capita consumption of workers (including the socialised wage) grew in physical terms by over 12 per cent in comparison with 1928.

The annual growth of the total consumption fund of per capita consumption in 1928–31 is shown in the following table.

The growth of the total consumption fund of workers, 1928–31 (including the socialised wage, in 1928 prices, 1928 = 100)

1928	1929	1930	1931
100.0	109.9	135.1	175.5

The growth in per capita consumption of workers

1928	1929	1930	1931
100.0	101.5	106.2	112.0

When we compare the economic results of our development with the situation in the capitalist countries, the successes of socialist construction are abundantly clear. These successes were achieved because of the advantages of the planned socialist economy, the labour enthusiasm of the broad working masses and the leadership of the Communist Party. In order to compare our results with those in the biggest capitalist countries we can look at the changes in their respective national incomes.

Differences in methods of estimation and of making monetary evaluations in the different countries make it impossible to compare the absolute magnitude of the national incomes; only a comparison of growth rates can be made.

The following table shows changes in the national income (in physical terms) in the USSR, the USA, France and Germany between 1913 and 1931:

	1913	1925	1926	(1913 = 100) 1927	1928	1929	1930	1931
USSR	100.0	103.4	109.9	113.8	123.3	136.2	161.2	182.8
USA	100.0	123.2	129.2	129.2	131.3	137.8	122.9	–
France	100.0	73.1	76.6	83.1	83.7	84.7	80.0	–
Germany	100.0	87.0	90.9	95.8	102.1	103.4	93.8	80.0

While the national income of the USSR increased by 83 per cent between 1913 and 1931, Germany (in 1931) and France (in 1930) had national incomes that were 20 per cent below the pre-war level. Only the USA showed an increase in national income over the pre-war level (by 23 per cent in 1930).

The national incomes of the USA and France undoubtedly suffered further diminution in 1931. This is shown by the decline in the industrial production in real terms in 1931: 16 per cent in USA and 12 per cent in France (this decline continued in 1932 in both cases). The annual changes in the growth of the national income in these years is also significant: the USSR had a steady growth at a rate higher than in the capitalist countries, whereas in the capitalist countries there was a slow growth until 1928–9, and then a decline.

The results of the last few years show particularly clearly the differences between the capitalist and Soviet systems. The general crisis of capitalism has led to a fall in national income, narrowing of reproduction, impoverishment of the mass of the people and a sharpening of contradictions. In the USSR these years were years of new construction, of the implementation of the plan of great works of the First Five-Year Plan; and socialist reproduction expanded at an accelerating rate.

NOTES

The British editors' additional notes are numbered consecutively following the original notes, and are distinguished in the text by the square brackets.

1 It is not possible within the scope of this article to discuss the theoretical problems of the balance of the national economy adequately. The basic premises for constructing the balance are presented here in their most concise form. A critical section of the article has also been omitted; this included an exposure of bourgeois-wrecker and opportunist 'theories' on problems of reproduction in the USSR and in particular on the use of the balance method in constructing the plan and in making specific studies of reproduction.

2 While general estimates of national income have long since been published in various planning and directive documents, and also in economic literature, there have been only a few, very imperfect and conventional calculations of accumulation (one of these calculations was included in the text of the First Five-Year Plan). The basic defect of these estimates is their isolated character, their lack of coordination with all other elements of the national income. In the present work the national income and its constituent parts – consumption and accumulation – are mutually coordinated in the overall balance of production and consumption. By virtue of this, the results obtained differ from previous estimates, both for accumulation and for the national income as a whole. Furthermore, this difference also results from a change in the method of calculation, especially in the estimates in so-called 'constant prices' (here we use 1928 prices). In estimating national income in current prices excises have been excluded. This substantially alters the figure for the national income as compared with the earlier Gosplan estimates. In revaluing the national income in 1928 prices the growth of transport has been taken to have been at the same rate of growth as the branches of material production as a whole.

3 For a number of methodological reasons (see pp. 68–9 above), the estimated amount of redistribution through prices is somewhat problematical.

4 The total amount of expenditure is taken here as expenditure in the given year plus building still incomplete at the beginning of the year.

5 In all these estimates, the balance of production has been calculated by the method of 'gross turnover', i.e., without excluding intra-factory turnover.

6 Capital investment in 1928 prices is taken here as the amount which went into capital stock, whereas the dynamic shown above is for all capital investment (see the tables in Appendix C and in section II, p. 167–78).

7 This figure is at variance with the increase in production of consumer goods shown in the section on production, where the distribution of products is given in accordance with their predominant intended use, and not their actual consumption.

[8] [V. I. Lenin, 'Notes on the book of N. I. Bukharin, "The Economics of the Transition Period", May 1920, reproduced in *Leninskii Sbornik*, Tom XI, 1931, p. 349. In chapter 1 Bukharin had written 'the end of capitalist society will also mark the end of political economy.' In the margin Lenin had written 'Not true. Even under pure Communism will there not be a relationship between Department I (v+m) and Department II (c)? And will there be no accumulation?']

[9] [I. Stalin, *Sochineniya*, vol. 12, 1949, pp. 171–2. Speech on the question of agrarian policy in the USSR to the Conference of Agrarian Marxists, 27 December 1929.]

[10] [See *Pyatnadtsatyii S"ezd VKP(b) Dekabr' 1927g., Stenograficheskii otchet*, II, 1962, pp. 1441–54.]

[11] [Stalin's speech to the Agrarian Marxists was published in I. Stalin, *Sochineniya*, vol. 12, 1949, pp. 141–72 but this particular phrase appears to be missing.]

[12] [*XVII Konferentsiya Vsesoyuznoi Kommunisticheskoi Partii (b), Stenograficheskii otchet*, 1932, p. 148.]

[13] [V. I. Lenin, *Polnoe Sobranie Sochinenii*, (5th edn) vol. 39, p. 21.]

[14] [In original given as 14.2% and 55.8%.]

[15] [Note the first mass collectivisation drive was in the autumn of 1929 and consequently preceded rather than followed these events.]

[16] [L. M. Kaganovich, speech in *Devyatyi vsesoyuznyi s"ezd professional'nykh soyuzov SSSR: stenograficheskii otchet*, 1932, pp. 670–1.]

[17] [The reference here is to the Five-Year Plan prepared under Pyatakov in 1925 and to V. G. Groman and V. A. Bazarov, see I. V. Stalin, *Sochineniya*, vol. 12, 1949, p. 349, and N. Jasny, *Soviet Economists of the Twenties, Names to be remembered*, Cambridge, 1971, pp. 105–16 and 132–4.]

[18] [I. V. Stalin, *Sochineniya*, vol. 12, 1949, p. 145.]

[19] [I. V. Stalin, *Sochineniya*, vol. 11, 1949, p. 248.]

[II]   METHODOLOGICAL QUESTIONS CONCERNING THE BALANCE OF THE
NATIONAL ECONOMY

A. Pervukhin

The statistical groundwork for the balance of the national economy is provided by a series of statistical tables. These include:

(1)   a balance of production, consumption and accumulation;
(2)   a balance of the distribution and redistribution of the national income.

What these balances contain has been explained above.[1] They depict the economy in two of its aspects. The first balance enables us to analyse the physical elements of reproduction. The second covers distribution relationships, and relationships arising from the interaction of the basis and superstructure (redistribution).

In both of these balances the movement of the physical elements of reproduction and of distribution relations is of course shown with a breakdown according to social group. It is also useful to show the indicators from both these tables in an integrated form, with a new breakdown according to reproduction by the different social sectors. For this purpose, a further balance has been constructed from these two balances: the 'Balance of the principal indicators of reproduction by social sector'.

[A]   *The balance of production, consumption and accumulation as a whole*

The construction of a balance of production, consumption and accumulation is a fundamental and most complex task. As our basis for this balance we have taken Marx's reproduction scheme, which we have modified in the following fashion [see table on p. 101 which is a summary of the headings in section 3.III, tables 1–4].

It must be borne in mind that the classification of a product as part of a particular economic group (means of production, consumer good and so on) has been decided in accordance with the predominant way in which it is utilised, since almost all products function in the economy both as means of production and as consumer goods. In practice it is impossible to distribute every product between all the economic groups in which it appears in the economy. In any case, the actual end-use of a product becomes known only after the balance has been constructed.

For this reason, our grouping by predominant end-use does not fully coincide with the actual grouping by end-use.

Nevertheless, it is possible to establish the grouping of products by actual end-use from the balance. But this can be estimated only in consumer prices (see table 6 on page 000, where we have made this estimate). In terms of producers' prices it cannot be calculated because this would require the deduction of the trade and transport mark-up from the consumer price paid by each consumer. Although we know the total amount of this mark-up, we do not know the share of it which falls on each consumer.

The rows in the scheme of the 'Balance of production, consumption and accumulation' were made more specific by presenting within each economic group a breakdown by products; we show individual independent groups and even separate products. Our rows include 135 independent items: of these, 79 are products in kind (balances in

Schema of balance of production, consumption and accumulation

Groups of products	National property at beginning of year				Production in year	Imports	Trade and transport mark-up	Total in consumer prices	Consumed in production		Non-productive consumption		Losses in the economy	Exports	National property at end of year in same categories as at beginning of year	Accumulation (growth in fixed capital and other stocks)
	Fixed Production Funds**	Fixed Consumption Funds*	Stocks of raw materials auxiliary materials, fuel and finished products	Total national property at beginning of year					In production of means of production	In production of consumer goods	Institutions and social organisations	The population				
1	2	3	4	5	6	7	8	9	10	11	12	13	14	15	16	17
A. Means of production																
1. Elements of fixed means of production [fixed capital] (groups of products)																
2. Elements of circulating means of production [working capital] (groups of products)																
B. Consumer goods (groups of products)																
Total																

[* Productive capital stock]
[** Non-productive capital stock]

physical terms) and account for between 56 and 51 per cent of total production [in different years]. A larger proportion has been presented in kind in the case of agricultural products (80 per cent of total agricultural production). Industry is less well covered; production listed in the separate balances in kind was 41.5 per cent of total production in 1928 and 32.9 per cent in 1930.

Even with this breakdown, the classification of the rows suffers from defects. First, in order to distinguish between the individual most important machines and to obtain balances in kind for the principal types of equipment, it would have been necessary to increase still further the number of balances in kind, particularly for products which form elements in fixed capital. Secondly, the failure to obtain a breakdown in kind in the case of a large part of industrial production has resulted in highly aggregated groups of products in value terms, sometimes consisting of 20–30 separate products from the most diverse branches of production. For example, the group 'other building materials' includes a vast range of products (in addition to those separated out in the balances in kind), from sand and gravel to rails and iron structures. Thirdly, it is not always possible to derive a breakdown of production by individual industry from our groupings (for example, the products of the metal industry group etc.).

These defects could be eliminated only by obtaining more detail on more groups of products and by preparing a larger number of balances in physical terms.[2]

The columns of the balance show social sectors, classes and groups of the population; and branches of the economy.

The following points should be noted about particular items in the columns:

1. Capital stock [*osnovnye fondy* – fixed funds] (active) at the beginning and the end of the year, both productive and non-productive capital, is evaluated at cost net of depreciation. It should be noted that in the rows referring to the group 'elements of fixed means of production', products appear as 'active fixed capital stock' only when they have been entered into the column 'fixed capital stock at beginning and end of year': the other items in the columns are stocks, production of stocks, etc.

2. Stocks of products held by producers at the beginning and end of the year are evaluated in producers' transfer prices. Stocks held by producers (and in the channels of distribution) are evaluated at the purchase price paid by each consumer, i.e. at buying price plus delivery costs.

3. Production. Since the balance is built on the basis of balances of separate products, and since one and the same product can appear as a finished product in one enterprise and a semi-fabricated good in another (e.g. yarn is the end product of a spinning mill but only an intermediary product in a weaving mill), we have used the method of gross turnover to calculate agricultural and industrial production. An exception to this rule has been made in industry for those partially completed products which are passed on from one year to another: these are not included in the production of the given year. This exception is due to the fact that in the case of these unfinished products we have not compiled separate balances for each type (for an uncompleted ship for instance).

    Industrial production has been evaluated in transfer prices except in the case of semi-fabricated products that have been produced and wholly consumed within a particular factory, and also in the case of uncompleted products. These have been evaluated at factory cost price. Agricultural production has been evaluated in the prices of actual realisation, except for that part which was consumed on the farm itself, which has been evaluated in procurement prices less transport costs for conveyance from the farm to the reception point.

Building output has been estimated as the sum of expenditure on 'pure construction' [i.e. on building work as such] plus the installation of equipment in a given year, i.e. not by the method of gross turnover but rather by that of gross production. Gross turnover would have included the incomplete construction carried forward from all previous years; and the decision not to use it for the evaluation of building output was due to the fact that the duration of the production process in building is much longer than in all other branches of the economy. The gross turnover of a given year would have included large quantities of incomplete building work from previous years, and this would have hindered an appreciation of the real growth of production. Such calculations were not required by the method used for the calculation of a building output balance. In the building industry both the producer and consumer are known in advance, and we therefore do not need a balance showing buildings of different sizes, or a balance of different types of structures.

The method adopted for estimating building output enables us to show the amount of completed product (ready for use) which enters into the national economy. Only the completed product is recorded in the expenditure part of the balance, unfinished building work in progress being recorded as stocks at the beginning and end of the years.

4. The remaining items in the columns of the input section of the balance, with the exception of imports, show the increase in the prices of products which takes place in the sphere of circulation. Consequently the input section results in the product entering into the economy at consumer prices.

5. From the foregoing it follows that the transfer of a product into the expenditure side of the balance is evaluated in terms of consumer prices. This is true for all types of consumer, whether industry, agriculture, or the different classes and groups of the population.

6. With the exception of the consumption of agricultural products by their actual producers, the term consumption refers purely to the acquisition of products by the consuming population or institutions. Actual consumption by these consumers cannot be evaluated as we have not taken into account their stock levels. In the term 'losses' we have included losses in fixed capital (through fire, premature death of cattle, etc.) and losses from production – losses of agricultural products by the producer during storage, and other items. But we have not included losses suffered in the channels of circulation (shrinkage and spillage) and losses incurred in the course of production. Losses in the course of production were taken into account in estimating the selling price.

In the balances of products included in the category fixed capital, the expenditure section of the balance has a dual character: (1) For those products which are already functioning in the national economy as active fixed capital (entered in the column 'capital stock at the beginning and end of the year') consumption appears in the expenditure section as the amount of depreciation, i.e. consumption here is equivalent to depreciation. (2) For those products which are produced in the given year, it is important to show how the expenditure of these products is distributed between the different branches of the economy, i.e. how they enter into fixed capital. Consequently we have to construct a balance of the production and distribution of these products. So, before constructing the balance of production, consumption and accumulation we have constructed a balance of production and consumption of those particular products which belong, by virtue of their end-use, to the category of fixed capital. In other words, at this stage of the work the balance does not yet include the fixed capital at the beginning and end of the year. Instead of this item, the balance of production and consumption includes the item 'additions to capital stock'. Thus, the balance of production and consumption differs from the balance of production, consumption and accumulation in that it does not show all accumulation but only that part of it which takes the form of increased stocks.

After the balance has been set up in this form, we then construct the balance of production, consumption and accumulation which includes active capital stock at the beginning and end of the year, and its consumption (depreciation). This latter balance covers only the more aggregated groups of products. From the above it will be seen that a further difference between the balance of the production and consumption of the annual product, and the balance of production, consumption and accumulation, is that the former balance shows consumption without deducting depreciation. The latter balance, however, does not show a detailed breakdown of consumption net of depreciation for each separate product.

Data on active capital stock at the beginning and the end of the year were available only for a small number of items. Only three groups are shown: (1) products of building, (2) industrial products, (3) agricultural products. The current state of statistics did not allow a more detailed grouping to be made.

A characteristic feature of our method of research is that we proceed from the construction of a balance for a particular product to the balance of production, consumption and accumulation as a whole.

Our inability to give a detailed breakdown by social group for the production and consumption of *each separate product* (in each separate product balance) is a considerable defect in the present balances of production and consumption, but with the present state of statistics such detail is impossible. We do however have a social breakdown for agricultural production, which is divided into three sectors: state, collective-farm, and individual. For industrial production and building we managed to provide a social breakdown only for the whole branch for the main economic group. In order to achieve this we used the gross production records of industry. Except in the case of agricultural production it was not possible to divide the products consumed in production between the different social sectors, even for these main groups of products, and we had to confine ourselves to setting out the total amount of production. This has nevertheless made it possible for us to give a social breakdown of the national income as a whole.

With the current state of the statistics it has also proved to be impossible to provide a breakdown of personal consumption of the agricultural population by classes and groups.

This is also the reason why trade and transport mark-ups have not been shown separately in the detailed balances, and why the consumption of transport has not been divided between freight and passenger use. These breakdowns have been made only for the total for the branch of the economy, on the basis of various materials from the branch records.

In order to show the inter-connections between production and distribution of the product of a given year we have constructed a balance of distribution of the annual product, on the basis of which a balance of the inter-connections of the different branches has been constructed. This balance of the distribution of the annual product differs from the previous balances in that its input section excludes both imports and stocks at the beginning of the year, and its expenditure section only covers the consumption and distribution of the product produced in the given year. Consequently the expenditure side of the balance – consumption by industry, agriculture, etc. – may add up to less than is shown in the balance of production and consumption. The difference will be stocks consumed and not replaced, plus imports.

[B]   *National income in the balance of production, consumption and accumulation*

To obtain the national income by branches of the economy, or to obtain net production of branches of the economy from the balance of production, consumption and accumulation, it is necessary to deduct the productive consumption of a given branch from the total production for the year of that branch of the economy, evaluated in producers' prices.

For example, in the case of industry in the year 1928, production amounted to 19,245.0 million rubles, but productive consumption was 13,416.5 (see the expenditure section of the balance); consequently net production was $19,245.0 - 13,416.5 = 5,828.5$. In order to obtain the total national income for the given year, it is necessary to aggregate the net production of the different branches of the economy. The trade and transport mark-up will appear as the annual production of transport and trade, for which the net production will have been estimated as described above, by deducting productive consumption in these branches from their total consumption. If we include also customs-duties in the total, we will obtain the national income of the USSR in consumer prices (net of excises).

Excises are included in the input section of the balance only in order to record the size of the product in the input section at actual consumer prices, since the price paid by the consumer for a given product includes excises. But excises are not included in national income, because they represent a *redistribution* of part of the national income which has already been created and accounted for. Excises paid in consumer prices by individuals in the private sector are a form of redistribution of the net production created and accounted for in the private sector. Similarly, excises paid by individuals in the socialist sector (e.g. workers), form part of the net production created in the socialist sector, received initially in the form of wages, and then returned to the state as part of the prices paid for a product by the consumer. Consequently, the excise part of the national income is merely a form of redistribution: it is essentially just a special form of movement of the net production of the socialist sector within the limits of that sector itself. This form of movement of the national income is governed by the specific features of the relations between the socialist and private sectors.

It may be objected that by deducting productive consumption including excises from production (at producers' prices) we under-estimate net production in the branch concerned, because productive consumption is shown in actual consumer prices.

But this objection has no significance. This is because production at producers' prices includes the actual price of the raw materials and auxiliary materials consumed in its creation and consequently also includes the prices of the products subject to excises consumed in this production, if, in general, they enter into productive consumption.

Thus excises have been excluded from the balance when estimating national income. Consequently, in order to calculate the national income directly we have obtained from BNIN the total production of the economy at consumer prices (net of excises) and have deducted from it all productive consumption.

For example, for the year 1928 the national income of 26,442 million rubles was obtained as follows: all production at producers' prices 51,517.5 million rubles, plus trade and transport mark-up 5,181.2 million rubles, plus customs duties 271.5 million rubles, minus consumption in production 30,527.9 million rubles $(51,517.5 + 5,181.2 + 271.5 - 30,527.9 = 26,442)$.

As mentioned above, in the balance of production, consumption and accumulation it proved possible to divide the trade and transport mark-up into separate trade and transport mark-ups only for the total amount. Similarly, we are able to divide up the productive consumption of freight and passenger transport only for the total amount. In the balance, passenger transport has been assigned to the non-productive sphere, so that net production is included in national income only for the transport of goods.

Since we have not included the production of communications [post and telegraphs] in the production of material goods, but have assigned it to the non-productive sphere, we do not include the net production of communications in national income. But this does not mean that our estimate of national income excludes all the net production of communications, because labour expended on those communications related to production is included in the transfer price of the producer.

The net production of public catering is not fully included in the balance.

[C]   *National income in real terms, national income in constant prices*

The value of a social product (a commodity) in capitalist society consists of the following three fundamental parts:
(1)   the embodied value of means of production consumed in production ('C')
(2)   The value of labour power ('V'), and
(3)   surplus value ('M')

The last two elements $(V+M)$ are the value newly created in the given cycle or the given year, and at the level of society as a whole they equal national income. Consequently, if we eliminate the surplus value form [which does not exist in socialist society] national income may be taken to be the sum of labour expended by society in production in the given year.

In establishing the net production of a branch of the economy or the national income of a country, in current prices of the year concerned, we are, essentially, expressing the total labour expended in the given year in monetary terms; this is analogous to a commodity-producing society, which expresses production and national income through money in value terms. Therefore, the actual physical volume of the national income must correspond to the amount of labour expended. But, as we have not yet reached the stage of estimating in direct form in kind either the result of labour or labour itself, we have to estimate labour expenditure indirectly, *expressed as a product of labour*, measured in money terms.

It follows from this that national income in constant prices (the physical volume of the national income [i.e. in real terms]) is *the quantity of use-values (products) that can be ascribed to the labour expended in the given year*. Consequently the task of determining the physical volume of the national income amounts to determining the physical volume of the total output produced in the given year, and estimating what part of this is production (in physical volume terms) which may be ascribed to labour expended in that year.

Recently, the USSR State Planning Commission has estimated the national income in constant prices by assuming that its growth was directly proportional to the growth of gross production in constant prices. This method of estimating assumes that there is a fixed ratio between net production (i.e. production due to newly expended labour) and the product consumed in production. This ignores structural changes due to the increase in productivity of labour. The incorrectness of this method is obvious and requires no detailed criticism.

In the balance of the national economy, net production for each branch and national income as a whole have been estimated in constant prices by applying a *production-price index* to our estimates of net production and national income in current prices. A second national income series in constant prices has been obtained as the sum of consumption and accumulation at constant prices.

National income in the first series is *created* national income [national income by sector of origin]; national income in the second series is national income *realised* in consumption and accumulation [national income by end-use]. The totals differ only when national income is estimated in constant prices. In the national income in prices of the current year there is no difference between what is created and what is realised. This can be demonstrated by the following examples:

Let us call $V + M$ national income (Y).

Let us suppose that in 1928 the scale and value structure of production were as follows (assuming one unit in kind is equivalent to one monetary unit–one ruble):

1st example Department I $60c + 40Y = 100$
            Department II $40c + 80Y = 120$
            Total national income 120

In this example national income equals 120 units, the product of Department II.

Let us now suppose that in 1929 production of Department II is halved, for some reason, and the prices for it are correspondingly doubled. It might seem that the structure would then be as follows:

2nd example Department I $60c + 40Y = 100$ in 1929 and 1928 prices
          Department II $40c + 80Y = 120$ in 1929 prices
                     $40c + 20Y = 60$ in 1928 prices.

But this estimate of the structure of Department II in 1928 prices is erroneous. It has to be remembered that exchange between Department I and Department II takes place in 1929 prices. Since the prices in Department II have doubled the owner of Department

II need only exchange half as many units in kind of his own product in order to receive means of production from Department I.

If we take this circumstance into account, the structure in the second example will actually be as follows:

3rd example Department I $60c + 40 (20) Y = 100 (80)$
              Department II $20 (40)c + 40 (20) Y = 60 (60)$

In Department I the figure 20 in brackets indicates the amount of the product of Department II, expressed in kind (or, what comes to the same thing, in 1928 prices) which has been received in exchange for 40 units in kind (in 1928 prices) of means of production from Department I. Consequently, the $40c$ in brackets in Department II indicates the products of Department I received and consumed in the production of Department II, in exchange for the 20 units supplied in Department I. The figure 80 in brackets in Department I indicates that this category has realised, in productivity and personal consumption, 80 units in 1928 prices, even though 100 units were created. The 20 units in brackets in Department II indicates that in this category 20 units would be left for personal consumption, if 40 units of means of production were paid for with 40 units of its own products, that is, if exchange were carried out at 1928 prices. Thus, while in the product of Department I 40 units remained as the share of net product after the deduction of productive consumption, i.e. as the share of labour expended in the given year, these 40 units were realised in exchange for only 20 units of the product of Department II. Department II, however, consumed in production 40 units of means of production, but in exchange gave only 20 units. As the share of labour expended in the given year, i.e. as its share of net product, it retained 40 units of its own product.

If we add together the total products of Department I and Department II which are left after deducting productive consumption from production (40 from Department I and 40 from Department II), we get 80 units of created national income.

If, however, we add the net production of those two branches actually realised in consumption (20 in Department I and 40 in Department II), we get 60 units of realised national income. This total of realised income is equal to the production of Department II and thus corresponds to simple reproduction.

If net production in current prices is revalued into fixed prices with an index of prices of gross production we obtain national income at fixed prices by sector of origin (the net production created in the given year). In our example, national income is equal to 80 units:

Department I $60c + 40 Y = 100$
Department II $20c + 40 Y = 60$
Total national income 80

In fact, the production price index of Department I equals 100 (see our first and second examples), and net production in 1929, in the prices of that year, equals 40, i.e.:

$$\frac{40}{1} = 40$$

The production price index of Department II is equal to 200. Production in 1929 prices (see our second example) is equal to 120. Consequently, production in 1928 prices is equal to: $120 \div 2 = 60$. Net production (Y) of Department II in 1929 prices is equal to 80 units, and revalued by the index 200 is equal to: $80 \div 2 = 40$.

If, however, we calculate the national income as the sum of consumption and accumulation in constant prices, we get the *realised* national income (see our third example). Personal consumption in 1929, in constant (1928) prices, amounts to 20 units in Department I and 40 units of personal consumption in Department II, i.e. the total sum of consumption is equal to 60 units, and since accumulation, in our example, is equal to zero, the national income is equal to 60 units (60 consumed $+0$ accumulated $= 60\,Y$).

Here, in these examples, realised national income [by end-use] is less than created national income [by sector of origin] by 20 units. But realised national income can also be bigger than created national income. Let us take the same example and suppose that in 1929 (examples 2 and 3), productivity was doubled in Department II, and prices were halved:

Department I $60c + 40\,Y = 100$ in 1929 and 1928 prices

Department II $40c + 80\,Y = 120$ in 1929 prices

$80c + 160\,Y = 240$ in 1928 prices.

Consequently, exchange will take place in the following proportions:

Department I $60c + 40\,(80)\,Y = 100\,(140)$

Department II $80\,(40)c + 160\,Y = 240$

Total created $Y = 200\,(40 + 160)$

Realised national income $= 240\,(160 + 80)$.

Following the conventions of the previous examples, the figures in brackets indicate that in Department I 80 units of articles of consumption were received in exchange for 40 units of means of production, while in Department II 80 units of its own production were exchanged for 40 units of means of production; this is because exchanges took place at current-year prices, and not at base-year (1928) prices.

If we revalue the net production of each branch in accordance with the branch index of production prices, then, in Department I, with the index at 100, we get:

$$\frac{40}{1} = 40\,Y$$

and in Department II, with the index at 0.50, we get:

$$\frac{80}{0.5} = 160,$$

i.e. in all $160 + 40 = 200$ *created* national income.

Here we see that: (1) realised national income is not equal to created national income (in this example the former is bigger than the latter), and (2) realised national income is equal to the production of Department II.

In all these examples, accumulation is equal to zero, but it is not difficult to show that when expanded reproduction takes place, i.e. when accumulation takes place, realised national income will be equal to the sum of consumption and accumulation.

In these examples, when we estimated created national income, net production in current prices was revalued into constant prices by means of a gross-production price index. We should have obtained the same result if we had started not with net production, but with the productive consumption of the branches, and if we had revalued it in terms of the production-price index and had then deducted the resulting sum from production at constant prices to obtain net production.

The net production of trade and goods transport was estimated in 'constant prices' by using the index for the growth of output in physical terms.

The figure of 'net production' of trade and transport in constant prices consequently has no independent significance (it does not measure, for example, the physical volume of the work of transport), and is needed only to complete our estimates of the total volume of the national income as a whole, in constant prices.

Use of this method can be justified on the grounds that trade and transport mark-ups, being the difference between the final price (the consumer price) and the producers' price, do not affect the *physical volume* of production or of the national income. This is quite obvious if revaluation of production, or of national income, is carried out in terms of these constant final prices: the trade and transport mark-ups obviously remain the same share of the total price and, consequently, the rate of growth measured in constant producers' prices coincides with the rate of growth measured in constant final prices.

In order to make a more precise estimate of the trade and transport mark-up in constant prices, it would have been necessary to have established an index of change in the volume of production of each separate product, or group of products, in which each of the separate products would have a different share of the total mark-up. But instead of this, we have made a rough estimate using average indexes for the change in volume of total production.

[D]   The balance of the distribution and redistribution of the national income

The balance of distribution and redistribution of the national income enables us to study the national income in all the phases of its movement. Only on the basis of such a qualitative analysis can a correct quantitative description of the national income be given.

Previous estimates of national income have suffered from the inherent methodological defect of being studied in isolation and not in the context of the balance of the national economy. Consequently the separate elements of the national income have not been linked together. National income has been studied not in its dynamic aspect, but in two distinct isolated phases: the production of the national income, and its distribution. The two methods of estimating national income – the 'real' method [by sector of origin] and the 'personal' method [by end-use] have been treated as alternatives, each considered in isolation, and consequently no coordinated linking of the two has been obtained. The problem was merely seen, quite simply, as obtaining two separate estimates of total national income: total net production of the separate branches of the economy; and total individual incomes. And the problem of the qualitative analysis of national income, with its complex paths of distribution and redistribution, remained unsolved. The absence of such a qualitative analysis also hindered the quantitative study of the national income.

The estimates in the balance of the national economy have been constructed on a different basis. Here an attempt has been made to study the national income in its dynamic aspect, to show the paths followed by the national income in the system of social reproduction.

The process of reproduction is a dialectical unity of the processes of production, distribution, exchange and consumption. In its development, the national income passes through all these stages, each of them being a simple moment in a single process – the reproduction of the economic system. In so far as production and distribution are simply moments of social reproduction, both the 'real' and the 'personal' methods of estimating national income are derived from the same object, which is merely perceived in different phases of its development. There is thus a direct link between them. In previous estimates the methods of estimation are different for each estimate because production and distribution are examined separately; but a more serious fault is that in assuming the process of *distribution* of national income the processes of *redistribution* are not distinguished. In our estimates, however, one of the central problems is the analysis of redistribution.

The main stages in our study of the national income will now be described.

The created national income, perceived as the sum of the net production of the separate branches of the economy, is divided among the basic social classes which participate in social production. These basic social classes are: the proletariat, producers in cooperatives, independent producers, and the bourgeoisie. In this process of primary division of the national income, enterprises of the socialist sector also appear as receivers of income (income of collective farms is given in our estimates together with the incomes of the collective farmers in order to facilitate comparison with the incomes of individual farmers). There is thus a category of income received in the process of distribution – in other words, basic incomes. After the national income has been allocated between the different basic social classes in this process of primary division it then goes through the further stages of redistribution. Part of these incomes is extracted through the financial and budgetary system in order to maintain the non-productive services. We consequently have here processes of redistribution which emerge from the inter-relationship between the basis and the superstructure. Another type of redistribution, which takes place between the participants in social production themselves through the price mechanism, is not distinguished here. The incomes received by the participants in social production are shown in a form which already includes an element of internal redistribution through the price system. Thus, for example, the income from agriculture received by individual farmers appears under the heading of 'income of independent producers', which is primary income received in the stage of distribution of the national income and undoubtedly results as a rule from redistribution as well as distribution. And in principle one should also assign to incomes received through distribution that part of the social product which was actually created in the given sector. But at the present stage it has not been possible to establish this statistically. The problem of redistribution through prices can be solved only by examining it not statistically but dynamically. Incomes of persons engaged in the non-productive sphere, or, performing no social functions at all, appear as incomes received through redistribution.

It should be pointed out that the specific processes of redistribution which are present in our society are governed by the class character of our economy: this applies to both types of redistribution – redistribution due to the existence of a non-productive sphere and redistribution which takes place between the different participating social classes. Under the conditions of developed socialism, redistributive relationships will disappear. The primary distribution of the social product can be counterposed to its redistribution only under the conditions of a class society. In such a society social product from the moment of its production is not social property but the property of particular classes. Production of the national income occurs at the same time as its distribution, with the separate classes each receiving a certain share in the division of the social product. All subsequent transfers of these shares are consequently a redistribution of the national income. In a classless society, however, from the very outset production will belong to society as a whole, and will not constitute the property of separate classes. Persons engaged in the non-productive sphere will participate with equal rights in the division of the social product along with persons directly engaged in production. Hence all shares of the national income received by the separate members of society will be received through distribution.

The division between the productive and non-productive spheres, which leads to the division of incomes into primary and secondary incomes, does not coincide with the division between the spheres in which productive and non-productive labour are applied. There is consequently a further division of income between persons performing productive functions and persons performing non-productive functions or who do not fulfil any social functions (incomes of dependants on society). The category of 'incomes from non-productive functions' is considerably broader than the category 'incomes in the non-productive sphere'. Thus incomes of persons employed in trade (for carrying out the formal functions of circulation) and the credit system, and incomes of statistical, office and minor servicing personnel, in all those branches which form part of the sphere of direct production, are incomes received through distribution, and are at the same time incomes received by persons performing non-productive functions. But obviously all incomes received through redistribution are also incomes received by persons performing non-productive functions. The estimation of these incomes does not therefore require any further work. All that remains is the problem of distinguishing basic incomes in the way we have outlined.

Basic incomes are those incomes received by the separate classes participating in the primary division of the social product and they constitute, in aggregate, the total volume of the national income. But these shares of the national income are not the whole real income of the separate recipients. In order to obtain the amount of real income, we need to trace the subsequent movement of the national income, to trace how the incomes are realised. Here we must introduce two further concepts: (1) incomes realised in the form of accumulation and consumption of material goods and services, and (2) incomes realised in the form of accumulation and consumption of material goods. Incomes realised in the form of accumulation and consumption of material goods and services are obtained as the difference between total basic and derivative incomes and total transfer payments. Incomes realised in the form of accumulation and consumption of material goods are obtained as the difference between (i) incomes realised in the form of accumulation and consumption of material goods and services, and (ii) the value of all the services consumed, both those which have to be paid for and those which are free. The first form of income indicates the level of well-being of particular classes (services increase the well-being of a class), the second form shows the quantitative extent to which particular classes and groups of the population acquire possession of the national income in the form of material consumer goods, after all distributive and redistributive relationships have been taken into account.

Thus analysis of the basic features of the national income may be summarised as requiring: (1) measuring the total volume of the national income and its allocation between branches and sectors of the economy; (2) measuring the volume and structure of the incomes of the classes of society which participate in the primary division of the national income; (3) establishing the distribution of the national income between the productive and non-productive spheres; (4) measuring the total sum of the incomes of the several classes and groups of the population, obtained both from participation in material production and from the performance of functions in the non-productive sphere; (5) measuring the volume and structure of incomes realised in the form of accumulation and consumption of material goods and services; (6) measuring incomes realised in the form of accumulation and consumption of material goods; (7) measuring the incomes of persons performing productive functions and of persons performing non-productive functions; (8) establishing the movement of the national income in relation to productive enterprises in the socialist sector (including accounting relationships between the enterprises themselves, and between the enterprises and the financial and budgetary system); (9) establishing the movement of the national income for non-productive enterprises; and, finally, (10) a general description of the national income, showing the form in which the separate sectors of the economy are inter-connected, that is showing the general conditions of the reproduction of the economic system.

We proceed from these basic features in our construction of the schema for estimating national income. Here we have to bear in mind the following schemas: (1) a schema for estimating national income by the 'real' method [by sector of origin] (see the section 'National income and accumulation'); (2) a schema for calculating national income by the 'personal' method [by end-use] (the distribution and redistribution of the national income); and (3) a synthetic schema in which the movement of the national income shows the connections formed between the separate sectors of the economy during the process of reproduction of the economic system (an example of such a schema is given in the table 'Balance of the basic elements of reproduction of the sectors of the economy').

The second schema – the distribution and redistribution of the national income – is divided into three parts, which are, to some extent, independent of each other: (1) a schema showing the movement of the national income according to classes and groups of the population, (2) a schema showing the movement of the national income for enterprises in the productive sphere, and (3) a schema showing the movement of the national income for non-productive enterprises. Only two parts of these schema have been fully completed – the first and the third. The second part, incomes of enterprises in the productive sphere, is given only as part of the primary division of the national income, together with the incomes of the population; the accounting relationships between the productive sphere and financial and budgetary institutions are not presented in our tables.

We shall now briefly describe the schema, 'Distribution and redistribution of the national income, by classes and groups of the population'. The rows of this schema list the recipients of income. These include classes and groups of the population and enterprises in the productive sphere according to their participation in the primary division of the social product.

The columns are so constructed as to meet all the requirements which we set out above. Thus, on the basis of this schema one can establish the basic and derivative incomes, the incomes realised in the form of accumulation and consumption of material goods and services, and also those incomes realised in the form of accumulation and consumption of material goods alone. From this schema one can also obtain incomes received by persons performing productive functions and incomes received by persons performing non-productive functions.

As can be seen from the schema [see p. 119 below] incomes received through distribution include: (*a*) wages earned in production and in circulation, or, in other words in production as a whole, which includes both branches in the sphere of direct production, and trade and the credit system; (*b*) entrepreneurial incomes, interest and profit; (*c*) incomes of independent producers; (*d*) incomes of cooperative producers; and (*e*) pensions, allowances and the value of social, cultural and medical services received without payment by the entire population except for wage-earners, for whom this item is included in their incomes received through distribution. Payment received from the sale of property is treated as an item outside the balance, since it is not treated here as an element of income. Receipts from the sale of property do not therefore appear either as part of the total incomes or in the residual given in the table. This is based on the premise that receipts from the sale of property cannot be regarded as part of the national income created in the given accounting period. In fact the various social classes and groups of the population, in addition to their basic functions as participants in social production, may also perform functions in the non-productive sphere. Thus the proletariat employed in the productive sphere may be a seller of services. On the other hand, groups of the population employed in the non-productive sphere in their basic function may also be to a certain extent participants in social production. Thus members of the proletariat employed in the non-productive sphere may also have an income from agriculture and from handicraft activities. Part of their incomes will consequently be incomes received through distribution. We consequently see that the division of incomes into basic and derivative incomes does not entirely coincide with the distribution of actual people between the productive and non-productive spheres.

We now analyse the separate items in this schema. The first column: 'wages of persons engaged in production' covers wages of persons fulfilling productive functions. This includes the wages of all workers employed in the branches of the economy which are in the sphere of direct production (i.e. branches in which use-values are created), and also workers employed in goods transport (workers employed in passenger transport, together with those employed in communications, are treated as belonging to the non-productive sphere and receiving incomes through redistribution). This column also includes the wages of engineering and technical personnel. As regards trade, we have made a somewhat arbitrary breakdown of expenses of circulation, including wages, between: (i) expenses connected with the performance of real functions of circulation and (ii) expenses connected with the performance of formal functions. Wages received for the performance of real functions of circulation appear in the first column as wages of persons performing productive functions. Wages received for the performance of formal functions of circulation appear in the second column: 'wages of persons employed in circulation and in servicing production' and are treated as income received by persons performing non-productive functions. The second column also includes the wages of minor staff [MOP] of those branches which belong to the sphere of social circulation, together with the wages of administrative, managerial and record-keeping personnel. The wages of persons employed in the credit system and in the managerial apparatus of branches of the economy also appear in the second column, with the exception of those few workers whose wages appear in the first column. The wages of the workers employed in the economic commissariats, for technical reasons, appear as wages in the non-productive sphere.

The third column shows entrepreneurial income. This includes the incomes of capitalist groups in the sphere of production, including trade. Capitalist incomes from the non-productive sphere, e.g. from letting rooms and apartments, are included with incomes from the sale of services. The next column, 'interest and lottery-loan winners' includes all receipts from the financial system for interest and winnings on loans, current accounts and other similar sources. The recipients of such income may belong to any group of the population. Our estimates cover only the proletariat. Interests and winnings, and entrepreneurial incomes, are all incomes received through distribution and constitute a category of incomes received by persons not performing productive functions.

Pensions and allowances, and the 'value of social, cultural and medical services received without payment' had to be divided between distribution and redistribution. Pensions and allowances [col. 7] and the value of social, cultural and medical services received without payment by wage-earners [col. 8] can be considered as a special form of payment for labour and in relation to these persons can be treated as wages. The total value of these services was divided in proportion to the wages earned by the separate workers employed in the productive and non-productive spheres. That part allocated to income received through distribution is in turn divided into separate sections attributed to persons carrying out productive and persons carrying out non-productive functions. The numerator shows the first group and the denominator the second group.

The category 'incomes of independent producers' [col. 6] covers those incomes which are received from the *function* of being independent producers. Their recipients include both independent producers and other groups of the population, e.g. the proletariat. The category of 'incomes of cooperative producers' covers the incomes received by members of cooperative artels, working in agriculture, industry, transport etc. The whole of the net production of collective farms is treated as part of personal income of the population so that it will be comparable with the incomes of individual peasants. With other groups of the population, only that part of net production which enters into individual use is recorded as personal income and the remaining part of net production is treated as the income of socialised enterprises. 'Incomes of cooperative producers' [col. 5] may also be received by groups of the population who are not members of cartels as their main function: for example, individual farmers who are independent producers as their main function may also be members of cooperative handicrafts organisations and thus receive incomes as cooperative producers. Obviously these should be treated as productive incomes.

'Wages in the non-productive sphere' [col. 10] includes the wages of persons employed in administration and in social and cultural services. 'Incomes from the sale of services' [col. 11] includes incomes in the sphere of non-material production received by special groups of independent producers; this category includes incomes from the free professions and from renting out rooms. The various categories of income received through redistribution were discussed above [pp. 114–16].

On the expenditure side of national income, it should be noted that 'consumption of material goods' [col. 20] covers all forms of individual consumption. For the agricultural population the cost of housing is included under this heading, but the cost of housing used by the non-agricultural population appears as 'rent for accommodation' [col. 21]. 'Consumption of material goods' does not include the value of free social, cultural and medical services, which appears as part of the value of services consumed. This category includes various expenditure items: culture and education, sanitation and hygiene, transport and postal expenses, and the payment of domestic servants. It must be noted however that the material part of these expenses mainly appears under material consumption. Thus material consumption includes the value of material items such as tooth-powder in the case of sanitary-hygienic expenditure, the value of newspapers, books and other products in the case of cultural services. However, in some cases it has been impossible to maintain this principle strictly, and the value of material consumption has in fact been included in the value of so-called 'net services'. Thus, for example, expenditure on passenger transport (the value of transport services) includes the value of material items consumed in the process of creating these services; our estimates treat the whole of passenger transport as 'expenditure on payment for services' [col. 22]. The item 'value of free social, cultural and medical services' [col. 25] is balanced by the corresponding items on the income side.

The remaining forms of expenditure require no specific clarification.

When total expenditure is deducted from total basic and derivative incomes a 'residual' remains [col. 30]. Theoretically, the total sum of all the residuals from all recipients of income (members of the population, productive and non-productive enterprises) indicates the total amount of accumulation in the economy as a whole, i.e. the growth of social wealth in the given production cycle. It will be remembered that the balance of the national income shows personal consumption; consequently the value of the residuals must be equal to accumulation, the difference between national income and consumption.

Among wage earners the residuals are, to an overwhelming extent, monetary in form. But this means that in the economy this sum corresponds to a definite material equivalent. This amount of material goods, belonging economically to various groups of the population, appears in the date on the growth of fixed and circulating capital as an increase in social wealth. Thus, in principle, the schema of distribution also serves the problem of accumulation. (We should note that the residual for the agricultural population is given without deduction of losses; and a considerable part of the residual may be in a monetary form. Consequently these income estimates may differ from the estimates of accumulation in terms of the growth of the fixed and circulating capital of the agricultural population.)

In describing the incomes received in the non-productive sphere we proceeded from the volume and structure of the expenditure side of the balance. Expenditure includes: all material non-productive consumption and capital expenditure in the institutions themselves; all the expenditure connected with servicing the population employed therein (wages, with all additions, with free services, etc.; this also includes expenditures connected with the payment of pensions and allowances to social dependents, pensioners and grant-aided students); expenditure connected with the service of persons maintained by the state (servicemen, the chronically sick, prisoners, etc.). Those expenditures which, although made in the non-productive sphere, are connected with servicing personnel employed in the productive sphere have been excluded from the expenditure of the non-productive sphere. These items include: pensions and allowances, and the value of the free socio-cultural and medical services which are provided to persons employed in the productive sphere. (Strictly speaking, part of the expenditure of the administrative and managerial apparatus should be treated in the same way).[1]

[E] Accumulation

In order to obtain the amount of accumulation, we take the national income, obtained by the methods explained above, and deduct from it the amount consumed by the population and by institutions (having first excluded from consumption the amount of excises charged upon it); this gives the accumulation fund. But the accumulation fund cannot always be fully realised; part of it may be used to cover losses in the economy (e.g. premature deaths of livestock), and these should be deducted from the accumulation fund.

Since accumulation is expressed in the form of products of one sort or another (money is not taken into account from the standpoint of the national economy), a surplus of exports over imports reduces the amount of accumulation remaining in the country in the form of products.

The accumulation fund less losses and less the surplus of exports over imports gives 'real accumulation'. When imports exceed exports, the surplus is added to the accumulation fund.

After these operations we obtain the real accumulation of the country, i.e. accumulation in the form of the increase in fixed capital (both productive and non-productive), the increase in the stocks of products (in the form of raw materials, auxiliary materials, fuel, and finished products), and the increase of incomplete building work in progress.

We can also obtain the same figure for real accumulation by directly estimating from the balance the increase in fixed capital and the increase in stocks. There are some objections to this method of estimating accumulation. First, it is argued that the increase in capital and stocks may not coincide with accumulation because rationalisation may lead to the reduction of stocks and irrational management and delays in circulation may lead to increases in stocks. Secondly, it is argued that if the increase in stocks and capital shows the amount of accumulation in one cycle of production, it cannot show it over several cycles; and in fact several cycles are completed in any one year. Thirdly, it is argued that when we deduct total annual consumption by the population and by institutions from the national income, accumulation will be too low because it excludes the consumption of that section of the workers who enter production as additional workers and whose consumption is provided by the accumulation fund.

All these objections are based on a misunderstanding. First, rationalisation and the resulting reduction of stocks in one part of the economy does not mean that stocks are reduced elsewhere. If stocks with the producer have been reduced, stocks with the consumer will increase; the reduction of stocks throughout the economy means that production and circulation cycles have been reduced and, consequently, the number of cycles in the year has been increased. But if production expands from one cycle to another, even if the production cycles are reduced in length to one day, the increase in production between one cycle and the next will lead to an increase in stocks and the sum of these increases will provide an annual increase in stocks. Therefore the idea that what is true for one production cycle is not true for the sum of the cycles is also unsound. If, for whatever reason, an irrational increase in stocks and delays in circulation take place, this will reduce consumption and therefore increase accumulation. In capitalist society, this will not of course imply any real increase in accumulation. In our economy, a hold-up in stocks in a sector of the economy is conceivable, but it would nevertheless imply an increase in accumulation; whether such accumulation is an effective use of resources is an entirely different question.

The third objection, on the consumption of additional workers, is also unsound, because it ignores the important point that consumption by the workers is reproduced anew in the product that they create. From this it follows that we have a double counting of the created product and that we need to deduct all consumption from the national income in order to get the actual accumulation fund. In order to clarify these matters we show a calculation of accumulation according to Marx's schema over four cycles (see p. 119).

As can be seen from the schema, reproduction begins with stocks amounting to $8,350 = 5,500c + 1,750v + 1,100cfb$ (consumption fund of the bourgeoisie). At the end of the fourth cycle, which corresponds to the completion of production for the year (see col. 4), stocks amount to $11,858 = 7,986c + 2,529v + 1,343cfb$. Thus accumulation in the form of increases in stocks amounts to $11,858 - 8,350 = 3,508$. This is the same as the figure which is obtained by adding together the increases in stocks in each cycle (see col. 5).

Gross production over all four cycles is 41,438, with productive consumption c at 25,360. Deducting productive consumption from gross production, we get a national income of 16,078 ($41,438 - 25,360$). If we deduct from the national income all personal

Schema for the calculation of accumulation over a year consisting of four production cycles

No. of cycles	Stocks at beginning of year or cycle	Production	Stocks at end of year or cycle / Distribution for next cycle	Increase in stocks / Total Constituent elements
1	2	3	4	5
1	I. $5500 = 4000c + 1000v + 500cfb$	$6000 = 4000c + 1000v + 1000m$	$6000 = 4400c + 1100v + 500cfb$	$500 = 400c + 100v$
	II. $2850 = 1500c + 750v + 600cfb$	$3000 = 1500c + 750v + 750m$	$3000 = 1600c + 800v + 600cfb$	$150 = 100c + 50v$
Total	$8350 = 5500c + 1750v + 1100cfb$	$9000 = 5500c + 1750v + 1750m$	$9000 = 6000c + 1900v + 1100cfb$	$650 = 500c + 150v$
2	I. $6000 = 4400c + 1100v + 500cfb$	$6600 = 4400c + 1100v + 1100m$	$6600 = 4840c + 1210v + 550cfb$	$600 = 440c + 110v + 50cfb$
	II. $3000 = 1600c + 800v + 600cfb$	$3200 = 1600c + 800v + 800m$	$3200 = 1760c + 880v + 560cfb$	$200 = 160c + 80v - 40cfb$
Total	$9000 = 6000c + 1900v + 1100cfb$	$9800 = 6000c + 1900v + 1900m$	$9800 = 6600c + 2090v + 1110cfb$	$800 = 600c + 190v + 10cfb$
3	I. $6600 = 4840c + 1210v + 550cfb$	$7260 = 4840c + 1210v + 1210m$	$7260 = 5324c + 1331b + 605cfb$	$660 = 484c + 121v + 55cfb$
	II. $3200 = 1760c + 880v + 560cfb$	$3520 = 1760c + 880v + 880m$	$3520 = 1936c + 968v + 616cfb$	$320 = 176c + 88v + 56cfb$
Total	$9800 = 6600c + 2090v + 1110cfb$	$10780 = 6600c + 2090v + 2090m$	$10780 = 7260c + 2299v + 1221cfb$	$980 = 660c + 209v + 111cfb$
4	I. $7260 = 5324c + 1331v + 550cfb$	$7986 = 5324c + 1331v + 1331m$	$7986 = 5856c + 1464v + 666cfb$	$726 = 532c + 133v + 61cfb$
	II. $3580 = 1936c + 968v + 616cfb$	$3872 = 1936c + 968v + 968m$	$3872 = 2130c + 1065v + 677cfb$	$352 = 194c + 97v + 61cfb$
Total	$10780 = 7260c + 2299v + 1221cfb$	$11858 = 7260c + 2299v + 2299m$	$11858 = 7986c + 2529v + 1343cfb$	$1078 = 726c + 230v + 122cfb$

Total consumption of the bourgeoisie   4531
Total consumption of the workers   8039
Total product over four cycles $41438 = 25360c + 16078Y$ $(8039v + 8039m)$
Total accumulation over cycles $3508 = 2486c + 779v + 243cfb$

Total stocks at end of year   11858
Total stocks at beginning of year   8350
Total increase in stocks   3508

National income   16078
Consumption by the population   12570 $(8039v + 4531$ bourgeoisie)
Total accumulation   3508
of which:
Increase in consumption by bourgeoisie $4771 - 4531 = 243$

cfb = Consumption fund of the bourgeoisie
Y = National income

consumption (all personal consumption 12,570 = workers' consumption 8,039 + consumption of the bourgeoisie 4,531), we get a value of 3,508 as the accumulation fund. This is the same value as was given above for the increase in stocks.

The workers' consumption fund grows by 549 units from 1750 in the first cycle to 2,290 in the fourth cycle. Our opponents consider it incorrect to deduct this increase in consumption fund from the national income, and propose to deduct only the consumption fund of the original workers, i.e. $1,750 \times 4 = 7,000$. We, however, deduct from national income not only these original 7,000, and the increase in consumption of 549, but all actual consumption amounting to 8,039. This is necessary for the following reasons:

(1) The consumption fund of the additional workers employed in the second cycle is 150. This fund is reproduced four times (total 600) and consumed three times (total 450).
(2) The fund of the additional workers employed in the third cycle is 190, and is reproduced three times (total 570), and is consumed twice (total 380).
(3) The fund of the additional workers employed in the fourth cycle, 209, is reproduced twice – once as an accumulation fund and then as the value of labour–power (total 418), and is consumed once (209).

The reproduction fund is consequently equal to 1,588 (600 + 570 + 418) and the consumption fund of the additional workers is 1,039 (450 + 380 + 209). Deducting the latter from the former we get 549 (1,588 − 1,039) as the accumulation (net increase) of the consumption fund. This example shows that our method of calculation does not understate accumulation by excluding consumption of the additional workers (as some of our critics claim).

It must be borne in mind that accumulation obtained by our method, i.e. in the balance, includes the increase in consumption fund in the non-productive sphere. If we were referring to a capitalist society this accumulation would clearly include the increase in consumption fund of the bourgeoisie. (In the example given in the schema above, the increase in consumption by the bourgeoisie would amount to 243 units; see the figures in col. 5.)

In the conditions of our economy, it would be wrong to exclude the total increase in the consumption fund of the non-productive sphere from accumulation, because in our case consumption by the non-productive sphere is to a large extent merely another form of consumption by the workers and by the productive population as a whole. On the one hand, products of material production are consumed in the non-productive sphere; on the other hand, the productive population consumes the services of that sphere in the form of medical and cultural services (hospitals, sanatoria, schools, theatres, etc.).

Consequently, it is a question at most of excluding from accumulation only that part of the non-productive sphere which does not provide medical and cultural services. This includes the administrative apparatus and the army as well as the very small capitalist group. With the exception of the latter group, it would hardly be correct to exclude these groups from accumulation, since the increase, for example, in the buildings and installations of the administrative apparatus is, after all, a real process of accumulation of the material wealth of the country as a result of expanded reproduction. The crucial distinguishing feature of our expanded reproduction in comparison with capitalist reproduction is that it is not the reproduction of capital but the reproduction of use-values.

While our method of calculating accumulation can be used for the economy as a whole, there are difficulties in using this method for calculating accumulation in particular branches of the economy. Here amounts of accumulation obtained by the two methods of estimation – the method of deducting non-productive consumption from the net production of the different branches, and the method of calculating the increase in stocks and fixed capital – do not coincide. This is because redistribution of the national income among branches of the economy may cause the real accumulation of a particular branch to be either smaller or larger than the fund of accumulation. Moreover, at the present stage of our statistics there are other practical problems. The absence of data on consumption for persons employed in specific branches of production makes it impossible to calculate the non-productive consumption of a particular branch. It is also difficult to determine what part of consumption by institutions in the non-productive sphere should be attributed to a particular branch. Consequently, it is extremely difficult to estimate in this way a particular branch's own accumulation fund. Obviously, one could proceed to calculate a given branch's own accumulation fund by calculating the share of net production going in wages to the persons employed in the branch and by calculating the non-productive expenditure of that branch. But then the sum of the branch's own accumulation funds would not coincide with the accumulation fund of the country as a whole. This would be because the estimates of consumption would exclude outlays on non-productive institutions of general state importance. On the other hand, the increase in fixed capital and stocks in a given branch in a number of instances may not coincide with the branch's real accumulation. While the increase in the fixed capital of the branch undoubtedly forms one part of real accumulation, the increase in stocks of raw material, auxiliary materials, fuel and finished products may not coincide with the other part of the real accumulation of the branch. At the moment when the residuals are deduced (i.e. on 1 January), part of them may have only just been transferred to another branch – for example, to the sphere of circulation – in return for money or credit; or, on the other hand, stocks may have only just been received on credit at the moment when residuals are deducted.

We encountered the same type of difficulty when calculating accumulation funds and real accumulation for particular sectors. In this case we managed to overcome the difficulties by estimating the non-productive consumption of the sectors. We assigned the consumption of non-productive institutions to the socialist sector, because the overwhelming majority of them are state, cooperative or social in character. The population and their personal consumption were divided into sectors in accordance with their predominating features. All the primary incomes of the population were also divided into sectors. Thus, the primary income of a sector consists of its net production and the net personal incomes received from or transferred to another sector in the form of wages, etc. For example, the primary income of the socialist sector amounts to its net production, minus the earnings and various other incomes received by the agricultural population of the private sector in the socialist sector (in industry, building, etc.), *plus* incomes of the population in the socialist sector received from the individual part of their economy (this mainly refers to collective farmers).

The primary income of the private sector differs from its net production by the same items, but the sign is reversed. Thus the sum of the primary incomes, like the sum of the net production of the sectors, is equal to the national income.

By deducting the non-productive consumption of a sector from its primary income we obtain its accumulation fund. From this accumulation fund we proceed to calculate the sector's real accumulation in the following way:

(1)   we add or subtract the sum exacted from the national income through the financial system;
(2)   we add or subtract the fixed capital and stocks of products transferred from sector to sector without compensation (e.g. through collectivisation);
(3)   we deduct the losses of the sector (e.g. premature death of livestock);
(4)   we add or subtract the difference between exports and imports (in our calculations these are assumed to be part of the socialist sector).

Consequently, the schema for the calculation of real accumulation of a sector is as follows:

1.   Accumulation fund;
2.   Transfers through the financial system;
3.   Fixed capital and stocks of products transferred without compensation;
4.   Losses of the sector;
5.   Surplus of exports over imports;
6.   Surplus of imports over exports;
7.   Real accumulation.

Real accumulation $(7) = 1 \pm 2 \pm 3 \pm 4 - 5 + 6$
For the socialist sector, the resulting figures show that the formula can be written as follows:

Real accumulation $= 1 + 2 + 3 - 4 - 5 + 6$.

The real accumulation of the sectors, calculated as the increase in fixed capital and in stocks of products, differs from real accumulation, as calculated above, by the amount of net credit. In the published table of basic indicators of reproduction of the sectors we have for technical reasons included net credit when calculating the primary income of the sector, and consequently real accumulation as calculated by both methods is identical. The value of net credit which has been included in the sectors' own accumulation funds in these cases is at most 120–200 million rubles.

[F]   *The balance of principal indicators of reproduction of the sectors*

A 'balance of the principal indicators of reproduction by sectors' (p. 128) can be constructed on the basis of our study of the balance of production, consumption and accumulation and of the balance of distribution and redistribution of the national income. This balance enables us to show the main outlines and the form of inter-relationship between the sectors and to present in summary the crucial results relative to the reproduction of the sectors. Because of defects in the statistical material (referred to above), we have had to limit ourselves to a breakdown into only two sectors: the socialist and the private sectors.

The rows in the balance have five main divisions:

1. The first main division contains the first three rows – gross production of the economy, productive consumption and net production. These show the two basic elements in the production structure of the economy: (i) the part of production consumed in production (forming part of production), and, from the standpoint of value, constituting transferred value, and (ii) net production – production newly created by the labour of the given year, or more correctly, since in terms of production in kind all production was created in the given year, that part of production appertaining to the share of labour expenditure in the given year.

    This production structure is given here primarily in order to show net production, so that it may be possible subsequently to use it to study inter-relationships between the sectors.

2. The second main division contains the fourth and fifth rows. The fourth row indicates what is received and transferred through direct distribution. This shows the way in which the primary income of the sectors is formed, which is itself given as the fifth row (row 3 ± row 4).

    This division thus shows the sectoral inter-relationship in the direct distribution of net production between those participants in production who belong to one sector but participate in the production of another sector. On the one hand, there are members of the agricultural population in the private sector who participate in socialist production and receive from it income in the form of wages. On the other hand, there are collective farmers and some manual and office workers in the socialist sector who carry on an individual economy (mainly agricultural), and consequently participate in the production of the private sector. By measuring this process of direct distribution we are able to obtain the primary income of the sectors. It will be noted that by 'sector' we mean not only the aggregate of enterprises, but also the population which is predominantly employed in the enterprises and institutions of the sector.

3. The third main division contains rows 7 and 8. Row 7 presents the redistribution of primary income through the financial and budgetary system, and row 8 shows the formation of total final income, i.e. the income ultimately received in the sector. We see here the most important aspect of the inter-relationship between the sectors: the extent to which the socialist sector utilises the primary income of the private sector for its reproduction, and hence the extent to which this restricts the reproduction of the private sector.

    Row 8 presents the total (final) income that results from this redistribution and which can be realised by the sector in the form of consumption and accumulation (row 5 ± 7).

4. The fourth main division comprises rows 9, 6 and 5 and provides us with the accumulation funds of the sectors. The accumulation fund of a sector is obtained by deducting the non-productive consumption of the sector from the primary income of the sector. In this division we show the relation between the consumption and accumulation of the sectors from their own primary income and the resources which could be devoted to accumulation in the sector itself if there were no redistribution either of primary income or of the accumulation fund.

5. The final main division contains rows 6, 7, 10, 11, 12 and 13, and gives us the real accumulation of the sectors and its sources. This is equivalent to the following: the

accumulation fund (row 6) plus or minus the balance of redistribution (row 7), plus or minus the property transferred through collectivisation (row 13), minus losses (row 10) plus or minus the difference between exports and imports (row 11).

Thus, in obtaining the reproduction of the sectors as reflected in accumulation, we also uncover the basic features of the inter-relationships between the sectors which precede and accompany real accumulation, i.e. socialist expanded reproduction.

NOTES

1 See pp. 59–60.
2 In our future work proposed for the construction of the balance for 1931 and 1932, we have in mind a more detailed classification of the rows of the balance.
3 Accumulation expressed as total capital investment was included along with consumption in the outlays of the non-productive sphere. As capital construction should be assigned to the productive sphere, that part of capital investment ought to have been excluded. However, given the state of the material this proved impossible.

3. Tables and notes

I GENERAL RESULTS OF THE BALANCE OF THE NATIONAL ECONOMY

CONTENTS

Table 1. National income and accumulation (in million rubles, current prices)

	1928	1929	1930
A	1	2	3
1. National income	26442.3	30135.9	38333.2
2. Non-productive consumption (less excises)	21305.7	24218.8	28462.8
3. Accumulation fund (1-2)	5136.6	5917.1	9870.4
4. Losses	800.9	1035.8	1699.4
5. Surplus of imports over exports (+)	+153.6		+22.4
6. Surplus of exports over imports (-)		-43.1	
7. Real accumulation (growth of fund capital and other stocks) (3-4+5+6)	4489.3	4838.2	8193.4
8. Share of non-productive consumption in national income	80.6	80.4	74.3
9. Share of accumulation fund in national income	19.4	19.6	25.7
10. Share of real accumulation in national income	17.0	16.1	21.4

Table 1a. National income and accumulation (in million rubles, 1928 prices)

	1928	1929	1930
A	1	2	3

1st variant [by sector of origin]

1. National income as sum of net production of branches of national economy in fixed prices	26187.1	29045.1	34637.1

2nd variant [by end use]

1. National income as sum of consumption and accumulation fund in fixed prices	25650.4	28379.2	33811.7
2. Non-productive consumption	21305.7	22575.2	23177.2
3. Accumulation fund (1-2)	4344.7	5804.0	10634.5
4. Losses	800.9	909.1	1154.5
5. Surplus of imports over exports (+)	+153.6		
6. Surplus of exports over imports (-)		-93.6	-249.7
7. Real accumulation (growth of stocks and funds) (3-4+5+6)	3697.4	4801.3	9230.3

In %

1. Accumulation fund as % of national income (2nd variant)	16.9	20.5	31.5
2. Real accumulation as % of national income (2nd variant)	14.4	16.9	27.3
3. Real accumulation as % of national income (1st variant)	14.1	16.5	26.6

Note: National income and consumption - less excises

Table 2. Balance of the principal indicators of reproduction by sectors of the national economy (in million rubles, current prices)

A	1928 Social-ist Sector	1928 Priv-ate Sector	1928 All	1929 Social-ist Sector	1929 Priv-ate Sector	1929 All	1930 Social-ist Sector	1930 Priv-ate Sector	1930 All	In % to previous year 1929 Soc. Sec.	1929 Priv. Sec.	1929 All	1930 Soc. Sec.	1930 Priv. Sec.	1930 All
	1	2	3	4	5	6	7	8	9	10	11	12	13	14	15
1. Gross production of the national economy in consumer prices (less excises)	27458.4	29511.8	56970.2	36080.9	28611.1	64692.0	50872.8	26832.4	77705.2	131.4	96.9	113.6	141.0	93.8	120.1
2. Productive consumption	16436.4	14091.5	30527.9	20567.9	13988.2	34556.1	26947.3	12424.7	39372.0	125.1	99.3	113.2	131.0	88.8	113.9
3. Net production	11022.0	15420.3	26442.3	15513.0	14622.9	30135.9	23925.5	14407.7	38333.2	140.7	94.8	114.0	154.2	98.5	127.2
4. Receipts (+) or payments (-) in the form of direct distribution	-1524.0	+1524.0	-	-1587.5	+1587.5	-	-107.7	+107.7	-	-	-	-	-	-	-
of which: a) wages	-1920.0	+1920.0	-	-2171.0	+2171.3	-	-1868.9	+1868.9	-	113.1	113.1	-	86.1	86.1	-
b) private incomes	+396.0	-396.0	-	+583.5	-583.5	-	+1761.2	-1761.2	-	147.4	147.4	-	301.8	301.8	-
5. Primary income of the sector (3+4)	9498.0	16944.3	26142.3	13925.5	16210.4	30135.9	23817.8	14515.4	38333.2	146.6	95.7	114.0	171.0	89.5	127.2
6. Accumulation fund	1574.1	3562.5	5136.6	3885.3	2031.8	5917.1	8036.3	1834.1	9870.4	246.8	57.0	115.2	206.1	90.3	166.8
7. Receipts (+) or payments (-) by redistribution through the financial budgetary system	+1287.3	-1287.3	-	+1878.6	-1878.6	-	+2341.5	-2341.5	-	145.9	145.9	-	124.6	124.6	-
of which a) taxes, loans etc.	+1107.0	-1107.0	-	+1637.2	-1637.2	-	+1729.2	-1729.2	-	147.9	147.9	-	105.6	105.6	-
b) excises	+812.2	-812.2	-	+1021.0	-1021.0	-	+1377.7	-1377.8	-	125.7	125.7	-	134.9	134.9	-
c) pensions and allowances	-50.5	+50.5	-	-63.8	+63.8	-	-56.5	+56.5	-	126.3	126.3	-	89.6	88.6	-
d) free medical, social and cultural services	-581.4	+581.4	-	-715.8	+715.8	-	-709.0	+709.0	-	123.1	123.1	-	99.1	99.1	-
8. Total income (5+7)	10785.3	15657.0	26442.3	15804.1	14331.8	30135.9	26159.3	12173.9	38333.2	146.5	91.5	114.0	165.5	84.9	127.2
9. Consumption of material wealth by the population and institutions (less excises)	7923.9	13381.8	21305.7	10040.2	14178.6	24218.8	15781.5	12681.3	28462.8	126.7	106.0	113.7	157.2	89.4	117.5
10. Losses	94.2	706.7	800.9	134.5	901.3	1035.8	409.2	1290.2	1699.4	142.8	127.5	129.3	304.2	143.1	164.1
11. Surplus of imports over exports (+)	+153.6	-	+153.6	-43.1	-	-43.1	+22.4	-	+22.4	-	-	-	-	-	-
12. Real accumulation (6+7-10+11+13)	2987.7	1501.6	4489.3	5897.3	-1059.1	4838.2	11893.1	-3699.7	8193.4	127.4	-70.5	107.8	201.7	310.4	169.3
13. Redistributed real accumulation (transfers of fixed capital and other stocks through collectivisation)	+66.9	-66.9	-	+311.0	-311.0	-	+1902.1	-1902.1	-	464.9	464.9	-	611.6	611.6	-

Table 2a. The structure of the balance of the principal indicators in the national economy as a whole and within its sectors
(in percentages)

A	1928			1929			1930		
	Social-ist Sector	Priv-ate Sector	All	Social-ist Sector	Priv-ate Sector	All	Social-ist Sector	Priv-ate Sector	All
	1	2	3	4	5	6	7	8	9
1. Net production in relation to gross production	40.2	52.3	46.4	43.0	51.1	46.6	47.0	53.7	49.3
2. The balance of direct distribution in relation to net production	-13.8	+9.9	-	-10.2	+10.7	-	-0.4	+0.7	-
of which: wages in relation to net production	17.4	12.5	-	14.0	14.8	-	7.8	13.0	-
3. Primary income in relation to net production	86.2	109.9	100.0	85.4	110.9	100.0	99.9	100.8	100.0
4. Accumulation fund in relation to net production	14.3	23.1	19.4	25.1	13.9	19.6	33.6	12.7	25.7
5. Accumulation fund in relation to primary income	16.6	21.0	19.4	27.9	12.5	19.6	32.1	15.4	25.7
6. Balance of redistribution through financial budgetary system in relation to primary income	+17.2	-7.6	-	+13.5	-11.6	-	+9.8	-16.1	-
7. Balance of redistribution through financial budgetary system in relation to accumulation fund	+81.8	36.1	-	+48.4	-92.5	-	-29.1	-127.7	-
8. Aggregate income in relation to primary income	113.6	92.4	100.0	113.5	88.4	100.0	109.8	83.9	100.0
9. Consumption of material goods in relation to primary income	83.4	79.0	80.9	72.1	87.5	80.4	66.3	87.4	74.3
10. Consumption of material goods in relation to aggregate income	73.5	86.0	80.6	63.5	98.9	80.4	60.3	104.2	74.3
11. Real accumulation in relation to net production	27.1	9.7	17.0	38.0	-7.2	16.1	49.7	-25.7	21.4
12. Real accumulation in relation to primary income	31.4	8.9	17.0	42.4	-6.5	16.1	49.9	-25.5	21.4
13. Real accumulation in relation to accumulation fund	189.8	42.2	87.4	151.8	-52.1	81.8	148.0	-201.7	83.0

Table 2b. The relative share of each of the sectors in the balance of the principal indicators (in percentages)

A	1928			1929			1930		
	Social-ist Sector	Priv-ate Sector	All	Social-ist Sector	Priv-ate Sector	All	Social-ist Sector	Priv-ate Sector	All
	1	2	3	4	5	6	7	8	9
1. Gross production of the national economy	48.2	51.8	100.0	55.8	44.2	100.0	65.5	34.5	100.0
2. Net production	41.7	58.3	100.0	51.5	48.5	100.0	62.4	37.6	100.0
3. Primary income of the sectors	35.9	64.1	100.0	46.2	53.8	100.0	62.1	37.9	100.0
4. Accumulation fund	30.6	69.4	100.0	65.7	34.3	100.0	81.4	18.6	100.0
5. Aggregate income	40.8	59.2	100.0	52.4	47.6	100.0	68.2	31.8	100.0
6. Consumption of material goods by the population and by institutions	37.2	62.8	100.0	41.5	58.5	100.0	55.4	44.6	100.0
7. Real accumulation	66.6	33.4	100.0	121.9	-21.9	100.0	145.2	-45.2	100.0

Table 3. National income and real accumulation, by sectors (in million rubles, in current prices)

A	1928			1929			1930		
	Social-ist Sector	Priv-ate Sector	All	Social-ist Sector	Priv-ate Sector	All	Social-ist Sector	Priv-ate Sector	All
	1	2	3	4	5	6	7	8	9
I. National income	11022.0	15420.3	26442.3	15513.0	14622.9	30135.9	23925.5	14407.7	38333.2
II. Real accumulation (increase in fixed capital and other stocks)*	2987.7	1501.6	4489.3	5897.3	-1059.1	4838.2	11893.1	3699.7	8193.4
i) Increase in fixed capital funds, residuals of incomplete building work and investment in unrecorded capital stock	2522.2	520.6	3042.8	4313.0	-819.8	3493.2	9462.0	3411.8	6050.2
of which: a) increase in fixed capital	1657.5	486.7	2144.2	3023.6	-856.6	2167.0	7195.3	-3428.8	3766.5
b) investment in unrecorded capital stock	193.9	-	193.9	322.6	-	322.6	441.6	-	441.6
c) increase in residual of incomplete building work	670.8	33.9	704.7	966.8	36.8	1003.6	1825.1	17.0	1842.1
ii) Increase in stocks	465.5	981.0	1446.5	1584.3	-239.3	1345.0	2432.5	-289.3	2143.2
Real accumulation in %									
a) of the national income of the sector	27.1	9.7	17.0	38.0	-7.2	16.1	49.7	-25.7	21.4
b) of the national income of the USSR	11.3	5.7	17.0	19.6	-3.5	16.1	31.0	-9.6	21.4
*Note: Including transfer through socialisation									
a) of fixed capital	66.9	-66.9	-	311.0	-311.0	-	1502.1	-1502.1	-
b) of stocks	-	-	-	-	-	-	400.0	-400.0	-

Table 3a. National income and real accumulation, by sectors (in million rubles, in 1928 prices)

A	1928 Socialist Sector	1928 Private Sector	1928 All	1929 Socialist Sector	1929 Private Sector	1929 All	1930 Socialist Sector	1930 Private Sector	1930 All
	1	2	3	4	5	6	7	8	9
1. National income (1st variant, i.e. sum of net production of branches in constant prices [by sector of origin])	11069.8	15117.3	26187.1	15910.2	13104.9	29045.1	24396.7	10240.3	34637.1
2. Real accumulation*	3058.3	639.1	3697.4	6152.2	-1350.9	4801.3	12407.1	3177.1	9230.3
of which: a) Growth in fixed capital, residuals of incomplete building work, and investment in unrecorded capital stock	2522.2	520.6	3042.8	4512.9	-764.0	3748.9	10039.1	-2909.8	7129.6
b) Growth in stocks	536.1	118.5	654.6	1639.3	-586.9	1052.4	2368.0	267.3	2100.7
Real accumulation in %									
1. of national income of own sector	26.4	4.4	14.1	38.0	-10.5	16.5	50.5	31.5	26.6
2. of total national income of the USSR	11.7	2.4	14.1	21.2	-4.7	16.5	35.8	-9.2	26.6
*Note: Including transfers through socialisation									
a) of capital	66.9	-66.9	-	306.5	-306.5	-	1354.1	-1354.1	-
b) of stocks	-	-	-	-	-	-	378.1	-378.1	-

Table 4. Material structure of accumulation (in million rubles, in current prices)

A	In million rubles 1928	1929	1930	Structure in % 1928	1929	1930
	1	2	3	4	5	6
A. Increase in means of production	3115.5	3730.6	6957.7	69.4	77.1	84.9
I. Increase in fixed capital, residuals of incomplete building work and investment in unrecorded capital stock	2214.7	2614.5	5357.1	49.3	54.0	65.4
1. Increase in fixed capital and investment in unrecorded capital stock	1510.0	1610.9	3515.0	33.6	33.3	42.9
of which: a) increase in fixed capital*	1348.4	1329.9	3148.8	30.0	27.5	38.4
b) investment in unrecorded capital stock	161.6	281.0	366.2	3.6	5.8	4.5
2. Increase in residuals of incomplete buildings	704.7	1003.6	1842.1	15.7	20.7	22.5
II. Stocks	900.8	1116.1	1600.6	20.1	23.1	19.5
1. Increase in fixed means of production	13.7	18.0	29.8	0.3	0.4	0.4
2. Increase in stocks of raw materials, auxiliary materials and fuel	887.1	1098.1	1570.8	19.8	22.7	19.1
of which: a) agricultural products	899.9	650.1	304.3	20.1	13.4	3.7
b) industrial products	-12.8	448.0	1266.5	-0.3	9.3	15.5
B. Increase in consumer goods	1373.8	1107.6	1235.7	30.6	22.9	15.1
I. Increase in fixed capital and investment in unrecorded capital stock	828.1	878.7	693.1	18.4	18.2	8.5
1. Increase in fixed capital	795.8	837.1	617.7	17.7	17.3	7.6
2. Investment in unrecorded capital stock	32.3	41.6	75.4	0.7	0.9	0.9
II. Stocks - increase in consumer goods	545.7	228.9	542.6	12.2	4.7	6.6
of which: a) agricultural products	228.7	190.9	-78.4	5.1	3.9	-1.0
b) industrial products	317.0	38.0	621.0	7.1	0.8	7.6
Total A + B	4489.3	4838.2	8193.4	100.0	100.0	100.0
of which: a) increase in all fixed capital (including consumption funds)	2144.2	2167.0	3766.5	47.8	44.8	46.0
b) investment in unrecorded capital stock	193.9	322.6	441.6	4.3	6.7	5.4
c) increase in residuals of incomplete building work	704.7	1003.6	1842.1	15.7	20.7	22.5
d) increase in all stocks	1446.5	1345.0	2143.2	32.2	27.8	26.1

*Note: The increase in fixed capital is given for the following branches: census industry and small scale industry, electric power stations, production funds of agriculture, transport, exchange and distribution.

Table 4a. Material structure of accumulation (in million rubles, in 1928 prices)

A	In million rubles			Structure in %		
	1928	1929	1930	1928	1929	1930
	1	2	3	4	5	6
A. Increase in means of production	2633.2	3802.8	7631.0	71.2	79.2	82.7
I. Increase in fixed capital, residuals of incomplete building work and investment in unrecorded capital stock	2214.7	2833.5	6227.0	59.9	59.0	67.5
1. Increase in fixed capital and investment in unrecorded capital stock	1510.0	1791.6	4128.0	40.9	37.3	44.8
of which: a) increase in fixed capital*	1348.4	1497.7	3721.2	36.5	31.2	40.4
b) investment in unrecorded capital stock	161.6	293.9	406.8	4.4	6.1	4.4
2. Increase in residuals of incomplete buildings	704.7	1041.9	2099.0	19.0	21.7	22.7
II. Stocks	418.5	969.3	1404.0	11.3	20.2	15.2
1. Increase in fixed means of production	36.8	12.3	40.8	1.0	0.3	0.4
2. Increase in stocks of raw materials, auxiliary materials and fuel	381.7	957.0	1363.2	10.3	19.9	14.8
of which: a) agricultural products	359.8	423.5	-9.4	9.7	8.8	-0.1
b) industrial products	21.9	533.5	1372.6	0.6	11.1	14.8
B. Increase in consumer goods	1064.2	998.5	1599.3	28.8	20.8	17.3
I. Increase in fixed capital and investment in unrecorded capital stock	828.1	915.4	902.6	22.3	19.1	9.7
1. Increase in fixed capital	795.8	872.0	819.3	21.5	18.2	8.8
2. Investment in unrecorded capital stock	32.3	43.4	83.3	0.8	0.9	0.9
II. Stocks - increase in consumer goods	236.1	83.1	696.7	6.5	1.7	7.6
of which: a) agricultural products	18.1	67.0	207.0	0.5	1.4	2.2
b) industrial products	218.0	16.1	489.7	6.0	0.3	5.4
Total A + B	3697.4	4801.3	9230.3	100.0	100.0	100.0
of which: a) increase in all fixed capital (including consumption funds)	2144.2	2369.7	4540.5	58.0	49.4	49.2
b) investment in unrecorded capital stock	193.9	337.3	490.1	5.2	7.0	5.3
c) increase in residuals of incomplete building work	704.7	1041.9	2099.0	19.0	21.7	22.7
d) increase in all stocks	654.6	1052.4	2100.7	17.8	21.9	22.8

*Note: The increase in fixed capital is given for the following branches: census industry and small scale industry, electric power stations, production funds of agriculture, transport, exchange and distribution.

Table 4b. The material structure of accumulation according to principal groups

A	in 1928 prices in million rubles			structure in %			in current prices in million rubles			structure in %		
	1928	1929	1930	1928	1929	1930	1928	1929	1930	1928	1929	1930
	1	2	3	4	5	6	7	8	9	10	11	12
I. Total increase in fixed capital and other stocks	3697.4	4801.3	9230.3	100.0	100.0	100.0	4489.3	4838.2	8193.4	100.0	100.0	100.0
A. Increase in means of production	2633.2	3802.8	7631.0	71.2	79.2	82.7	3115.5	3730.6	6957.7	69.1	77.1	81.9
B. Increase in consumer goods	1661.2	998.5	1599.3	28.8	20.8	17.3	1373.8	1107.6	1255.7	30.6	22.9	15.1
II. Increase in productive fixed capital and other stocks of raw materials, auxiliary materials and fuel	1891.7	2748.6	5491.2	100.0	100.0	100.0	2397.1	2709.0	5085.8	100.0	100.0	100.0
A. Increase in productive fixed capital funds and investment in unrecorded capital stocks	1510.0	1791.6	4128.0	79.8	65.2	75.2	1510.0	1610.9	3515.0	63.0	59.5	60.1
B. Increase in stocks of raw materials, auxiliary materials and fuel	381.7	957.0	1363.2	20.2	31.8	24.8	887.1	1098.1	1570.8	37.0	40.5	30.9
III. Total increase in fixed capital (including non-productive stock) and residuals of incomplete building work and stocks of fixed means of production	3079.6	3761.2	7170.1	100.0	100.0	100.0	3056.5	3511.2	6080.0	100.0	100.0	100.0
A. Increase in fixed stock (including non-productive stock) and capital investment in unrecorded capital stock	2338.1	2707.0	5030.6	75.9	72.0	70.2	2338.1	2489.6	1208.1	76.5	70.9	69.2
B. Increase in residuals of incomplete building work and stocks of fixed means of production	711.5	1051.2	2139.8	24.1	28.0	29.8	718.4	1021.6	1871.9	23.5	29.1	30.8
IV. Total increase in stocks of raw materials, auxiliary materials, fuel and consumer goods	1445.9	1955.5	2962.5	100.0	100.0	100.0	2260.9	2205.7	2806.5	100.0	100.0	100.0
A. Increase in stocks of raw materials, auxiliary materials and fuel	381.7	957.0	1363.2	26.4	48.9	47.0	887.1	1098.1	1570.8	39.2	49.8	56.0
B. Increase in consumer goods	1064.2	908.5	1599.3	73.6	51.1	51.0	1373.8	1107.6	1255.7	60.8	50.2	41.0

Table 5. Production of material goods, grouped according to sector and [predominant] economic end-use
(in million rubles, in current prices)

Years and groups of products according to [predominant] economic end-use	In current prices			In 1928 prices		
	Socialist Sector	Private Sector	All	Socialist Sector	Private Sector	All
A	1	2	3	4	5	6
1928						
A. Means of production	14672.1	13896.9	28569.0	14689.3	13879.7	28569.0
1. Fixed	3068.7	3541.5	6610.2	3068.7	3541.5	6610.2
2. Raw materials, auxiliary materials and fuel	11603.4	10355.4	21958.8	11620.6	10358.2	21958.8
B. Consumer goods	9821.5	13127.0	22948.5	9853.4	13095.1	22948.4
Total	24493.6	27023.9	51517.5	24542.7	26974.8	51517.5
1929						
A. Means of production	19197.9	13485.2	32683.1	19599.7	12901.6	32501.3
1. Fixed	4444.9	3109.7	7554.6	4551.4	3211.2	7762.6
2. Raw materials, auxiliary materials and fuel	14753.0	10375.5	25128.5	15048.3	9690.4	24738.7
B. Consumer goods	12590.5	13126.6	25717.1	12475.6	11987.0	24462.6
Total	31788.4	26611.8	58400.2	32075.3	24888.6	56963.9
1930						
A. Means of production	27852.4	11545.3	39397.7	28888.8	9685.5	38574.3
1. Fixed	7470.3	3095.1	10565.4	7902.7	2323.5	10226.2
2. Raw materials, auxiliary materials and fuel	20382.1	8450.2	28852.3	20986.1	7362.0	28348.1
B. Consumer goods	16950.7	13478.1	30428.8	16737.8	9441.6	26179.4
Total	44803.1	25023.4	69826.5	45626.6	19127.1	64753.7

Table 5a. Production of material goods, grouped according to sector and [predominant] economic end-use (growth in %)

Years and groups of products according to [predominant] economic end-use	In current prices			In 1928 prices		
	Socialist Sector	Private Sector	All	Socialist Sector	Private Sector	All
A	1	2	3	4	5	6
1929 as % of 1928						
A. Means of production	130.8	97.0	114.4	133.4	93.0	113.8
1. Fixed	145.0	87.8	114.3	148.3	90.7	117.4
2. Raw materials, auxiliary materials and fuel	127.1	100.2	114.4	129.5	93.7	112.7
B. Consumer goods	128.2	100.0	112.1	126.6	91.5	106.6
Total	129.8	98.5	113.4	130.7	92.3	110.6
1930 as % of 1929						
A. Means of production	145.1	85.6	120.5	147.4	75.1	118.7
1. Fixed	168.1	99.5	139.9	173.6	72.4	131.7
2. Raw materials, auxiliary materials and fuel	138.2	81.4	114.7	139.5	76.0	114.6
B. Consumer goods	134.6	102.7	118.3	134.2	78.8	107.0
Total	140.9	94.0	119.6	142.2	76.9	113.7
1930 as % of 1928						
A. Means of production	189.8	83.1	137.9	196.7	69.8	135.0
1. Fixed	243.4	87.4	159.8	257.5	65.6	154.7
2. Raw materials, auxiliary materials and fuel	175.7	81.6	131.3	180.6	71.2	129.1
B. Consumer goods	172.6	102.7	132.6	169.9	72.1	114.1
Total	182.9	92.6	135.5	185.9	70.9	125.7

Table 5b. Production of material goods, grouped according to sector and [predominant] economic end-use
The structure of production according to [predominant] economic end-use, by sectors (in %)

Years and groups of products according to [predominant] economic end-use	In current prices			In 1928 prices		
	Socialist Sector	Private Sector	All	Socialist Sector	Private Sector	All
A	1	2	3	4	5	6
1928						
A. Means of production	59.9	51.5	55.4	59.9	51.5	55.4
1. Fixed	12.5	13.2	12.8	12.5	13.2	12.8
2. Raw materials, auxiliary materials and fuel	47.4	38.3	42.6	47.4	38.3	42.6
B. Consumer goods	40.1	48.5	44.6	40.1	48.5	44.6
Total	100.0	100.0	100.0	100.0	100.0	100.0
1929						
A. Means of production	60.4	50.7	56.0	61.1	51.8	57.0
1. Fixed	14.0	11.7	13.0	14.2	12.9	13.6
2. Raw materials, auxiliary materials and fuel	46.4	39.0	43.0	46.9	38.9	43.4
B. Consumer goods	39.6	49.3	44.0	38.9	48.2	43.0
Total	100.0	100.0	100.0	100.0	100.0	100.0
1930						
A. Means of production	62.2	46.1	56.4	63.3	50.6	59.6
1. Fixed	16.7	12.3	15.1	17.3	12.1	15.8
2. Raw materials, auxiliary materials and fuel	45.5	33.8	41.3	46.0	38.5	43.8
B. Consumer goods	37.8	53.9	43.6	36.7	49.4	40.4
Total	100.0	100.0	100.0	100.0	100.0	100.0

Table 5c. Production of material goods, grouped according to sector and [predominant] economic end-use
Share of sectors in production, in %

Years and groups of products according to [predominant] economic end-use	In current prices			In 1928 prices		
	Socialist Sector	Private Sector	All	Socialist Sector	Private Sector	All
A	1	2	3	4	5	6
1928						
A. Means of production	51.4	48.6	100.0	51.4	48.6	100.0
1. Fixed	46.4	53.6	100.0	46.4	53.6	100.0
2. Raw materials, auxiliary materials and fuel	52.8	47.2	100.0	52.8	47.2	100.0
B. Consumer goods	42.8	57.2	100.0	42.9	57.2	100.0
Total	47.5	52.5	100.0	47.6	52.4	100.0
1929						
A. Means of production	58.7	41.3	100.0	60.3	39.7	100.0
1. Fixed	58.8	41.2	100.0	58.6	41.4	100.0
2. Raw materials, auxiliary materials and fuel	58.7	41.3	100.0	60.8	39.2	100.0
B. Consumer goods	49.0	51.0	100.0	51.0	49.0	100.0
Total	54.4	45.6	100.0	56.3	43.7	100.0
1930						
A. Means of production	70.7	29.3	100.0	74.9	25.1	100.0
1. Fixed	70.7	29.3	100.0	77.3	22.7	100.0
2. Raw materials, auxiliary materials and fuel	70.7	29.3	100.0	74.0	26.0	100.0
B. Consumer goods	55.7	44.3	100.0	63.9	36.1	100.0
Total	64.2	35.8	100.0	70.5	29.5	100.0

Table 6. Production of material goods (grouped according to actual utilisation)
(in million rubles, current prices)

	in million rubles in consumer prices			as a % of preceding year	
	1928	1929	1930	1929	1930
A	1	2	3	4	5
1. Production of means of production	34158.4	39097.4	47550.3	114.5	121.6
2. Production of consumer goods	24274.8	27372.3	33178.4	112.8	121.2
3. Total for national economy	58433.2	66469.7	80728.7	113.8	121.3
As % of the total					
4. Production of means of production	58.5	58.8	58.9	-	-
5. Production of consumer goods	41.5	41.2	41.1	-	-
6. Total	100.0	100.0	100.0	-	-

Table 7. The inter-branch distribution of annual production (in million rubles, current prices)

Branches receiving / Branches producing	Years	Total produced in consumer prices[2] (1)	Retained in own branch (2)	Disposed of outside own branch (in productive sphere) (3)	Including Industry (4)	Agriculture (5)	Building (6)	Transport (7)	Other branches of the economy (8)	Export (9)	Disposed of in non-productive consumption (10)	Including to the agricultural population (11)	to the non-agricultural population, institutions and social organisations (12)
Industry	1928	29869.5	11821.7	4211.2	-	1485.1	1599.6	1119.5	7.0	475.4	13082.7[1]	6758.5	6326.5
	1929	35300.5	14461.8	4925.6	-	1525.4	2004.7	1386.4	9.1	566.8	15211.4[1]	8119.8	6976.4
	1930	43521.9	17364.5	6788.8	-	1977.5	2940.5	1857.8	13.0	561.2	18213.3[1]	9162.0	8904.3
Agriculture	1928	20484.6	8660.5	5027.0	4242.2	-	20.8	86.2	677.8	194.3	6295.6	4000.5	2295.1
	1929	21756.0	7872.9	5606.7	4744.9	-	29.9	81.5	750.4	214.4	7236.4	4474.1	2762.0
	1930	25536.6	8892.9	6579.9	5491.4	-	45.0	152.1	891.4	333.9	9091.1	4908.3	4182.8
Building	1928	4239.1	561.8	1737.3	668.2	677.2	-	391.9	-	-	1940.0[1]	-	-
	1929	5025.3	827.6	2225.7	956.5	758.4	-	510.8	-	-	1972.0[1]	-	-
	1930	6695.1	1560.7	3390.6	1447.2	929.4	-	1014.0	-	-	1743.8[1]	-	-
Other branches of the national economy	1928	3568.5	88.5	1577.1	629.2	71.8	822.3	53.8	-	129.8	1771.1	1048.6	722.5
	1929	4134.3	277.0	1798.0	816.9	68.4	869.2	43.5	-	142.5	1908.1	1027.5	880.6
	1930	4771.4	222.1	2141.1	1060.9	57.2	945.1	77.9	-	141.3	2244.2	967.5	1276.7
Total	1928	58161.7	21132.5	12552.6	5539.6	2234.1	2442.7	1651.4	684.8	799.5	23089.4[1]	11807.6	9254.1
	1929	66216.1	23439.3	14556.0	6518.3	2352.2	2903.8	2022.2	759.5	923.7	26327.9[1]	13621.8	10619.0
	1930	80325.0	28040.2	18900.1	7999.5	2964.1	3930.6	3101.8	904.4	1036.4	31292.4[1]	15037.8	14363.8

Notes: 1. Including, entered into the fixed stock of the non-productive sphere:

products	1928	1929	1930
1. of industry	87.7	115.1	147.0
2. of building	1940.0	1972.0	1743.8
total	2027.7	2087.1	1890.8

2. Column 1 is larger than the sum of columns 2+3+9+10 because some expenditure items have not been included in the table (e.g. losses and increases in stocks in the channels of circulation).

Table 7a. The inter-branch distribution of annual production (in percentages)

Branches producing / Branches receiving	Years	Total	Retained in own branch	Disposed of outside own branch (in productive sphere)	Including					Export	All non-productive consumption	Including	
					Industry	Agriculture	Building	Transport and Trade	Other branches of the economy			Agricultural population	Non-agricultural population, institutions and social organisations
A		1	2	3	4	5	6	7	8	9	10	11	12
Industry	1928	100.0	39.6	14.1	-	5.0	5.4	3.7	0.0	1.6	43.8	22.6	20.9
	1929	100.0	41.0	14.0	-	4.4	5.7	3.9	0.0	1.6	43.1	23.0	19.8
	1930	100.0	40.1	15.7	-	4.6	6.8	4.3	0.0	1.3	42.0	21.1	20.6
Agriculture	1928	100.0	42.3	24.5	20.7	-	0.1	0.4	3.3	0.9	30.7	19.5	11.2
	1929	100.0	36.2	25.7	21.8	-	0.1	0.4	3.4	1.0	33.3	20.6	12.7
	1930	100.0	34.8	25.8	21.5	-	0.2	0.6	3.5	1.3	35.6	19.2	16.4
Building	1928	100.0	13.3	41.0	15.8	16.0	-	9.2	-	-	45.7	-	-
	1929	100.0	16.5	44.3	19.0	15.1	-	10.2	-	-	39.2	-	-
	1930	100.0	23.3	50.6	21.6	13.9	-	15.1	-	-	26.1	-	-
Other branches of national economy	1928	100.0	2.5	44.2	17.6	2.0	23.1	1.5	-	3.6	49.6	29.4	20.2
	1929	100.0	6.7	43.5	19.7	1.7	21.0	1.1	-	3.4	46.2	24.9	21.3
	1930	100.0	4.7	44.8	22.2	1.2	19.8	1.6	-	3.0	47.0	20.3	26.7
Total	1928	100.0	36.3	21.6	9.5	3.9	4.2	2.8	1.2	1.4	39.7	20.3	15.9
	1929	100.0	35.4	22.0	9.8	3.6	4.4	3.1	1.1	1.4	39.8	20.6	16.0
	1930	100.0	34.9	23.5	10.0	3.7	4.8	3.9	1.1	1.3	39.0	18.7	17.9

Note: Column 10 is larger than the sum of columns 11 and 12 because items entered into the fixed funds of the non-productive sphere have not been included in these columns.

Table 8. Actual gross production of the national economy (in current prices)

	In millions of rubles			1929 as percentage of 1928	1930 as percentage of 1929
	1928	1929	1930		
A	1	2	3	4	5
1. Production of the economy (in consumer prices, less excises)	56970.2	64692.0	77705.2	-	-
2. Sent for further processing, from the production of the given year	18677.2	21594.0	25109.6	-	-
3. Actual gross production of the economy (1-2)	38293.0	43098.0	52595.6	112.5	122.0
4. National income	26442.3	30135.9	38333.2	114.0	127.2
5. Actual transferred value of the past year (3-4)	11850.7	12962.1	14262.4	109.4	110.0
6. Share of transferred value in gross production	31.0	30.1	27.1	-	-

Table 9. Role of workers in census industry, building and state farms in the creation of the national income

	1928	1929	1930
A	1	2	3
1. National income (in 1928 prices) in millions of rubles	26187.1	29045.1	34637.1
2. Net production of census industry, building and state farms, in millions of rubles	7058.6	9630.9	13644.0
3. Relative share of these three branches in the total national income of the USSR	27.0%	33.2%	39.3%
4. Number of workers in the USSR, in thousands	75446.0	76800.6	79181.8
5. Number of workers in the three branches, in thousands	3670.0	4105.7	5566.3
6. Relative share of workers in the three branches in the active population as a whole (5:4)	5.0%	5.5%	7.0%

Table 9a. Basic factors in the growth of production - 1. Census industry

	1928	1929	1930
A	1	2	3
1. Rate of growth of output per man-hour in 1926/27 prices	121.7	115.0	112.7
2. Rate of growth of gross production in 1926/27 prices	122.4	124.3	125.8
3. Growth in output:			
(a) through productivity of labour	95.5	67.9	55.8
(b) through time worked	4.5	32.1	44.2
4. Growth in output over the entire period:			
(a) through productivity of labour		for 3 years	76.0
		for 2 years	61.0
(b) through time worked		for 3 years	24.0
		for 2 years	39.0
5. Absolute increase in gross production in 1928 prices:			
1. For the entire period (over 2 years)	-	-	9894.1
(a) through productivity of labour	-	-	6034.3
(b) through time worked	-	-	3859.8
2. By years	-	4243.2	5650.9
(a) through productivity of labour		2881.1	3153.2
(b) through time worked	-	1362.1	2497.7
6. Rate of growth of man-hours worked by all workers, excluding apprentices	101.0	107.8	111.4

Table 9b. Basic factors in the growth of production - 2. Building (socialist sector)

	1929	1930
A	1	2
1. Rate of growth of output of gross production per man-day, in 1928 prices	115.6	108.3
2. Rate of growth of gross production in 1928 prices	145.0	181.0
3. Growth of output		
(a) through productivity of labour	43.8	17.0
(b) through time worked	56.2	83.0
4. Growth of output over the entire period:		
(a) through productivity of labour	-	24.4
(b) through time worked	-	75.6
5. Absolute increase in gross production, in 1928 prices		
1. Over the entire period (2 years)	-	4109.6
(a) through productivity of labour	-	1001.9
(b) through time worked	-	3107.7
2. By years:	1131.7	2977.9
(a) through productivity of labour	495.7	506.2
(b) through time worked	636.0	2471.7
6. Rate of growth of man-days worked by all workers (including apprentices)	125.3	167.2
7. Output of gross production of all building work (of all sectors), in 1928 prices, per man-day	24.2	20.9

Table 9c. Basic factors in growth of production - 3. Agriculture (state farms)

A	1929 1	1930 2
1. Rate of growth of amount of work, per man-day, in percentage of previous year	128.4	108.7
2. Rate of growth of amount of work, in percentages	139.3	204.8
3. Growth in amount of work		
(a) through productivity of labour	78.4	15.6
(b) through time worked	21.6	84.4
4. Rate of growth of time worked	108.5	188.4
5. Rate of growth of gross production, in 1928 prices, per man-day, in percentages	120.7	113.1

Table 10. Indexes of prices of production (producers' prices) (1928 = 100)

Branches of the economy	Years	Socialist sector					Private sector					All sectors				
		A. Means of production			B. Consumer goods	Total production	A. Means of production			B. Consumer goods	Total production	A. Means of production			B. Consumer goods	Total production
		Fixed means of production	Raw material, fuel	All means of production			Fixed means of production	Raw material, fuel	All means of production			Fixed means of production	Raw material, fuel	All means of production		
A	B	1	2	3	4	5	6	7	8	9	10	11	12	13	14	15
For the entire economy	1929	97.7	98.0	97.9	100.9	99.1	96.8	107.1	102.1	109.5	106.9	97.3	101.6	100.6	105.1	102.5
	1930	94.5	97.1	96.4	101.3	98.2	133.2	114.8	119.2	142.8	130.8	103.3	101.7	102.1	116.2	107.8
1. Census industry	1929	102.1	97.8	98.4	101.5	99.5	-	-	-	-	-	102.1	97.8	98.4	101.5	99.5
	1930	98.5	95.5	96.0	103.3	98.4	-	-	-	-	-	98.5	95.5	96.0	103.3	98.4
2. Building	1929	93.4	-	93.4	94.1	93.7	104.3	-	104.3	102.7	103.3	95.4	-	95.4	98.0	96.5
	1930	89.4	-	89.4	85.3	88.2	100.2	-	100.2	100.9	100.7	90.1	-	90.1	88.7	89.7
3. Agriculture	1929	115.5	99.1	100.2	102.0	100.6	94.0	106.5	103.6	107.2	105.1	94.4	106.0	103.5	107.0	104.8
	1930	150.8	104.7	107.4	105.8	107.0	138.1	114.7	120.0	150.0	132.6	139.2	111.7	116.8	144.1	127.2

Table 10a. Indexes of consumer prices paid by the population (1928 = 100)

Groups of products	Total population 1929	1930	A. Non-agricultural population 1929	1930	Manual workers 1929	1930	Office workers 1929	1930	All non-agricultural proletariat 1929	1930	B. Agricultural population 1929	1930
A	1	2	3	4	5	6	7	8	9	10	11	12
All products	108.6	130.4	110.4	135.6	110.1	130.0	110.4	139.1	110.1	134.3	107.4	122.0
of which, industrial goods	107.8	124.7	108.1	121.5	108.0	120.7	106.1	116.5	107.2	119.5	107.6	127.6
All products less alcoholic drink	107.9	124.7	109.7	133.8	109.2	127.4	110.0	138.2	109.5	132.6	106.1	117.1
of which, industrial goods	106.4	116.5	106.5	116.3	106.0	114.4	105.0	113.4	105.7	114.5	105.5	116.7
I. Food products	110.1	137.3	114.4	160.7	113.1	147.6	115.0	171.7	113.7	158.3	107.3	120.5
1. Agricultural products	107.2	150.4	115.4	189.6	112.6	166.3	118.7	210.2	115.2	186.6	102.3	126.1
of which, a) arable	108.7	123.2	107.4	143.6	108.5	133.2	107.3	153.1	108.0	142.4	109.4	110.7
b) livestock	106.8	164.1	118.2	212.3	114.2	183.6	121.9	236.0	117.7	208.6	99.4	133.8
2. Grain products	116.9	110.6	115.5	120.2	115.8	121.7	114.4	117.2	114.9	120.0	117.5	104.7
3. Industrial food products	109.2	139.3	110.9	144.9	111.6	138.2	106.3	140.8	109.1	140.4	107.2	131.6
II. Drink and tobacco	116.1	161.2	114.6	148.2	115.6	149.2	111.6	141.4	114.4	147.1	116.3	172.8
of which, alcoholic drink	119.9	178.5	121.6	165.5	121.4	164.7	123.9	169.9	121.9	165.8	118.8	187.0
III. Clothing and footwear	106.5	111.6	106.8	103.4	104.7	102.2	107.4	101.8	105.7	101.8	106.3	116.5

Table 10b. Building costs indexes ['pure building']

Branches		1925/26	1926/27	1927/28	1928/29	1929/30	1931	Change in index from previous year in % 1929/30	1931
A		1	2	3	4	5	6	7	8
1. Industry (+ housing stock	a)	100.0	95.2	91.1	83.8	77.3	89.2	-7.8	+15.4
of industry)	b)	-	-	100.0	92.0	84.9	97.9	-	-
2. Power station construction	a)	100.0	97.4	91.7	82.6	76.2	87.9	-7.8	+15.4
	b)	-	-	100.0	90.1	83.1	95.9	-	-
3. Railway transport	a)	100.0	96.5	93.8	68.8	92.2	104.1	+3.8	+12.9
	b)	-	-	100.0	94.7	98.3	111.0	-	-
4. Water transport	a)	100.0	94.1	89.4	85.1	85.1	97.4	100.0	+14.5
	b)	-	-	100.0	95.2	95.2	108.9	-	-
5. Other transport	a)	100.0	95.6	93.1	89.6	89.6	101.2	100.0	+12.9
	b)	-	-	100.0	96.2	96.2	108.7	-	-
6. Communications	a)	100.0	96.6	92.8	88.6	81.7	94.3	-7.8	+15.4
	b)	-	-	100.0	95.5	88.0	101.6	-	-
7. Exchange and distribution	a)	100.0	98.0	95.5	90.7	83.6	96.5	-7.8	+15.4
	b)	-	-	100.0	95.0	87.5	101.1	-	-
8. Municipal economy	a)	100.0	98.0	95.5	90.7	83.6	98.9	-7.8	+18.3
	b)	-	-	100.0	95.0	87.5	103.6	-	-
9. Education and administrat-	a)	100.0	98.0	95.5	90.7	83.6	96.5	-7.8	+15.4
ion	b)	-	-	100.0	95.0	87.5	101.0	-	-
10. Public health	a)	100.0	94.3	89.0	84.9	78.8	90.4	-7.8	+15.4
	b)	-	-	100.0	95.4	88.0	101.6	-	-
1. House-building	a)	100.0	93.6	89.0	82.7	73.9	85.3	-10.7	+15.4
(socialist sector)	b)	-	-	100.0	92.9	83.0	95.8	-	-
2. Housing stock of	a)	100.0	94.0	88.3	82.0	73.3	84.6	-10.6	+15.4
industry	b)	-	-	100.0	92.9	83.0	95.8	-	-
3. House building	a)	100.0	100.0	100.0	97.0	103.7	124.4	+3.7	+20.0
(private sector)	b)	-	-	100.0	97.0	103.7	124.4	-	-

Table 10c. Cost indexes for equipment

Equipment, by origin	1925/26	1926/27	1927/28	1928/29	1929/30	1931
A	1	2	3	4	5	6
Imported equipment	100.0	86.6	86.2	85.8	77.2	68.7
Home-produced equipment	100.0	106.8	110.8	108.4	108.4	102.8
Average weighted cost index of equipment	100.0	98.9	99.3	101.1	93.9	88.0

Table 10d. Indexes of capital investment costs

Branches		1925/26	1926/27	1927/28	1928/29	1929/30	1931	Change in index from previous year in %	
								1929/30	1931
A		1	2	3	4	5	6	7	8
1. Industry (+ housing stock of industry)	a)	100.0	-	94.4	90.3	82.7	88.7	-8.4	+7.3
	b)	-	-	100.0	95.7	87.6	94.0	-	-
2. Power station construction	a)	100.0	-	95.1	90.3	82.5	88.0	-8.6	+6.7
	b)	-	-	100.0	95.0	86.8	92.5	-	-
3. Railway transport	a)	100.0	106.6	103.0	103.6	104.4	109.5	+0.8	+4.9
	b)	-	-	100.0	100.6	101.4	106.3	-	-
4. Water transport	a)	100.0	105.3	94.3	89.4	89.4	86.3	100.0	+3.5
	b)	-	-	100.0	94.8	94.8	91.5	-	-
5. Other transport	a)	100.0	95.6	93.1	89.6	89.6	101.2	100.0	+12.9
	b)	-	-	100.0	96.2	96.2	108.7	-	-
6. Communications	a)	100.0	96.6	92.8	88.6	81.7	94.3	-7.8	+15.4
	b)	-	-	100.0	95.5	88.0	101.6	-	-
7. Exchange and distribution	a)	100.0	-	99.3	96.2	90.9	98.7	-3.1	+5.5
	b)	-	-	100.0	96.9	91.5	99.4	-	-
8. Municipal economy	a)	100.0	-	99.5	95.3	90.0	100.0	-5.6	+11.1
	b)	-	-	100.0	95.8	90.5	100.5	-	-
9. Education and administration	a)	100.0	-	96.9	92.2	86.6	97.4	-6.1	+12.5
	b)	-	-	100.0	95.1	89.4	100.5	-	-
10. Public health	a)	100.0	-	90.7	86.8	81.8	91.8	-5.8	+12.2
	b)	-	-	100.0	95.7	90.2	101.2	-	-

Table 10e. Cost indexes of capital investment in agriculture (1925/26 prices = 100)

Types of property	1927/28	1928/29	1929/30	1930/31
A	1	2	3	4
All sectors				
1. Machines and implements	100.0	100.8	98.6	98.2
of which, a) machines and tools	100.0	98.9	98.5	99.5
b) tractors	100.0	100.0	100.0	100.0
c) transport and other agricultural implements	100.0	102.1	98.7	99.4
2. Buildings	94.0	98.4	90.4	88.3
3. Livestock	99.4	90.7	117.6	204.7
4. Land improvement and irrigation	97.2	97.2	94.3	94.8
5. Other measures	96.3	95.2	90.2	89.8
Total	97.4	97.8	100.9	112.0
Including investment in livestock				
Socialist sector	98.3	99.2	102.3	110.9
State sector*	98.0	98.3	102.4	112.5
Collective and cooperative sector*	99.2	100.5	103.9	112.5
Private sector*	97.4	97.5	98.6	114.5
Excluding investment in livestock				
Socialist sector	97.8	96.9	92.4	91.8
State sector*	97.1	94.5	89.0	89.3
Collective and cooperative sector*	98.7	98.5	94.7	93.5
Private sector*	96.3	99.5	96.3	95.8

*Excluding land·improvement and irrigation

3. Tables and notes

II CONSTITUENT ELEMENTS IN THE BALANCE OF THE NATIONAL ECONOMY

CONTENTS

151

Sub-section A: National income

Table 1. National income, by branches of the economy (in current prices)

Branches of the economy	In million rubles			Structure by branches in %			Dynamic as % of previous year		1930 as % of
	1928	1929	1930	1928	1929	1930	1929	1930	1928
A	1	2	3	4	5	6	7	8	9
1. Census industry	5828.5	7831.5	10801.0	22.0	26.0	28.2	134.4	137.9	185.3
2. Small scale industry	1811.9	1848.7	1848.9	6.9	6.1	4.8	102.0	100.0	102.0
3. Building	1869.8	2266.3	3000.1	7.1	7.5	7.8	121.2	132.4	160.5
4. Agriculture	10409.6	10694.2	13630.3	39.4	35.5	35.6	102.7	127.5	131.0
5. Forestry	1404.1	1733.5	1813.2	5.3	5.8	4.7	123.5	104.6	129.1
6. Other branches, fishing, hunting etc.	751.5	747.9	918.4	2.8	2.5	2.4	99.5	122.8	122.2
7. Transport (freight)	1134.9	1488.8	2001.8	4.3	1.9	5.2	131.2	134.5	176.4
8. Trade	2960.5	3271.4	3915.8	11.2	10.9	10.2	110.5	119.7	132.3
9. Customs duties	271.5	253.6	403.7	1.0	0.8	1.1	93.4	159.2	148.7
Total	26442.3	30135.9	38333.2	100.0	100.0	100.0	114.0	127.2	145.0

Sub-section A

Table 1a. National income, by branches of the economy (in 1928 prices)

Branches of the economy	In million rubles			Structure by branches in %			Dynamic as % of previous year		1930 as % of
	1928	1929	1930	1928	1929	1930	1929	1930	1928
A	1	2	3	4	5	6	7	8	9
1. Census industry	5828.5	7835.4	10976.6	22.3	26.9	31.7	134.4	140.1	188.3
2. Small-scale industry	1811.9	1662.0	1620.1	6.9	5.7	4.7	91.7	97.6	89.5
3. Building	1869.8	2346.4	3302.7	7.1	8.1	9.5	125.5	140.8	176.6
4. Agriculture	10154.4	9986.2	10267.2	38.8	34.4	29.6	98.3	102.8	101.1
5. Forestry	1401.1	1695.6	1814.6	5.4	5.7	5.2	120.8	107.0	129.2
6. Other branches (fishing, hunting etc.)	751.5	720.0	884.8	2.9	2.5	2.6	95.8	122.9	117.7
7. Transport (freight)	1131.9	1260.9	1496.7	4.3	4.3	4.3	111.1	118.7	152.3
8. Trade	2960.5	3289.1	3904.2	11.3	11.2	11.3	111.1	118.7	141.5
9. Customs duties	271.5	249.5	370.2	1.0	1.2	1.1	91.9	148.4	136.4
Total	26187.1	29045.1	34637.1	100.0	100.0	100.0	110.9	119.2	132.2

Materialy

Sub-section A

Table 2. National income, by branches and sectors of the economy (in million rubles, in current prices)

Branches of the economy	1928 Socialist sector	Private sector	Total	1929 Socialist sector	Private sector	Total	1930 Socialist sector	Private sector	Total
A	1	2	3	4	5	6	7	8	9
1. Census industry	5764.4	64.1	5828.5	7768.8	62.7	7831.5	10747.0	54.0	10801.0
2. Small-scale industry	307.3	1504.6	1811.9	731.9	1116.8	1818.7	1022.3	826.6	1818.9
3. Building	1088.1	781.7	1869.8	1520.8	745.5	2266.3	2597.7	402.4	3000.1
4. Agriculture	249.7	10159.9	10409.6	566.1	10128.1	10694.2	2498.7	11131.6	13630.3
5. Forestry	592.7	811.4	1404.1	995.2	738.3	1733.5	1262.8	550.4	1813.2
6. Other branches (fishing, hunting etc.)	209.2	512.3	751.1	281.1	466.5	747.9	595.6	322.8	918.4
7. Transport (freight)	893.2	241.7	1134.9	1195.5	293.3	1488.8	1613.5	388.3	2001.8
8. Trade	1645.9	1314.6	2960.5	2199.7	1071.7	3271.4	3184.2	731.6	3915.8
9. Customs duties	271.5	-	271.5	253.6	-	253.6	403.7	-	403.7
Total	11022.0	15420.3	26442.3	15513.0	14622.9	30135.9	23925.5	14407.7	38333.2

Sub-section A

Table 2a. National income, by branches and sectors of the economy (in million rubles, in 1928 prices)

Branches of the economy	1928 Socialist sector	Private sector	Total	1929 Socialist sector	Private sector	Total	1930 Socialist sector	Private sector	Total
A	1	2	3	4	5	6	7	8	9
1. Census industry	5764.4	64.1	5828.5	7788.4	47.0	7835.4	10954.6	22.0	10976.6
2. Small-scale industry	307.3	1504.6	1811.9	667.2	994.8	1662.0	992.5	627.6	1620.1
3. Buildings	1088.1	781.7	1869.8	1623.7	722.7	2316.4	2901.7	401.0	3302.7
4. Agriculture	251.4	9903.0	10154.4	563.5	9422.7	9986.2	2340.1	7927.1	10267.2
5. Forestry	638.8	765.3	1404.1	1014.7	680.9	1695.6	1245.3	529.6	1814.6
6. Other branches (fishing, hunting etc.)	209.2	542.3	751.5	283.6	436.4	720.0	608.2	276.6	884.8
7. Transport (freight)	893.2	241.7	1134.9	1030.2	230.7	1260.9	1285.0	251.4	1496.7
8. Trade	1645.9	1314.6	2960.5	2719.5	569.7	3289.1	3699.2	205.5	3904.2
9. Customs duties	271.5	-	271.5	249.5	-	249.5	370.2	-	370.2
Total	11069.8	15117.3	26187.1	15910.2	13104.9	29015.1	24396.8	10240.3	34637.1

Sub-section A

Table 3. National income, by branches and sectors of the economy (in current prices)

Branches of the economy	Social structures by branches, in %									Branch structure by social sectors, in %						Dynamic, as % of previous year				1930 % of 1928	
	1928			1929			1930			1928		1929		1930		1929		1930			
	Socia-list sector	Pri-vate sector	Total	Socia-list sector	Pri-vate sector	Total	Socia-list sector	Pri-vate sector	Total	Socia-list sector	Pri-vate sector	Socia-list sector	Pri-vate sector	Socia-list sector	Pri-vate sector	Socia-list sector	Pri-vate sector	Socia-list sector	Pri-vate sector	Socia-list sector	Pri-vate sector
A	1	2	3	4	5	6	7	8	9	10	11	12	13	14	15	16	17	18	19	20	21
1. Census industry	98.9	1.1	100.0	99.2	0.8	100.0	99.5	0.5	100.0	52.3	0.4	50.1	0.4	44.9	0.4	134.8	97.8	138.3	86.1	186.4	84.2
2. Small-scale industry	17.0	83.0	100.0	39.6	60.4	100.0	55.3	44.7	100.0	2.8	9.8	4.7	7.7	4.2	5.7	238.2	74.2	140.0	81.2	334.0	54.7
3. Buildings	58.2	41.8	100.0	67.1	32.9	100.0	86.6	13.4	100.0	9.9	5.1	9.8	5.1	10.9	2.8	139.7	95.4	170.9	54.0	238.7	51.5
4. Agriculture	2.4	97.6	100.0	5.3	94.7	100.0	18.3	81.7	100.0	2.3	65.9	3.6	69.3	10.4	77.3	226.7	99.7	441.4	109.9	1000.7	109.6
5. Forestry	42.2	57.8	100.0	57.4	42.6	100.0	69.6	30.4	100.0	5.4	5.3	6.4	5.0	5.3	3.8	167.9	94.0	126.9	74.5	236.9	67.8
6. Other branches (fishing, hunting etc.)	27.8	72.2	100.0	37.6	62.4	100.0	64.9	35.1	100.0	1.9	3.5	1.8	3.2	2.5	2.2	134.5	86.0	211.7	69.2	281.7	59.5
7. Transport (freight)	78.7	21.3	100.0	80.3	19.7	100.0	80.6	19.4	100.0	8.1	1.6	7.7	2.0	6.7	2.7	133.8	121.3	135.0	132.4	180.9	160.7
8. Trade	55.6	44.4	100.0	67.2	32.8	100.0	81.3	18.7	100.0	14.9	8.4	14.2	7.3	13.3	5.1	133.6	81.5	144.8	68.2	193.5	55.6
9. Customs duties	100.0	-	100.0	100.0	-	100.0	100.0	-	100.0	2.4	-	1.7	-	1.8	-	93.4	-	159.2	-	148.7	-
Total	41.7	58.3	100.0	51.5	48.5	100.0	62.4	37.6	100.0	100.0	100.0	100.0	100.0	100.0	100.0	140.7	94.8	154.2	98.5	217.0	98.4

Sub-section A

Table 3a. National income, by branches and sectors of the national economy (in 1928 prices)

Branches of the economy	a) Social structures by branches, in %									b) Branch structure by social sectors, in %						Dynamic, as % of previous year				1930 % of 1928	
	1928			1929			1930			1928		1929		1930		1929		1930			
	Socialist sector	Private sector	Total	Socialist sector	Private sector	Total	Socialist sector	Private sector	Total	Socialist sector	Private sector	Socialist sector	Private sector	Socialist sector	Private sector	Socialist sector	Private sector	Socialist sector	Private sector	Socialist sector	Private sector
A	1	2	3	4	5	6	7	8	9	10	11	12	13	14	15	16	17	18	19	20	21
1. Census industry	98.9	1.1	100.0	99.4	0.6	100.0	99.8	0.2	100.0	52.1	0.4	48.9	0.3	44.9	0.2	135.1	73.3	140.7	46.8	190.0	34.1
2. Small-scale industry	17.0	83.0	100.0	40.1	59.9	100.0	61.3	38.7	100.0	2.8	9.9	4.2	7.6	1.1	6.1	217.1	66.1	149.0	63.1	323.5	41.7
3. Building	58.2	41.8	100.0	69.2	30.8	100.0	87.9	12.1	100.0	9.8	5.2	10.2	5.5	11.9	3.9	149.2	92.5	178.7	55.5	266.7	51.3
4. Agriculture	2.5	97.5	100.0	5.6	94.4	100.0	22.8	77.2	100.0	2.3	65.5	3.5	72.2	9.6	77.4	224.1	95.1	415.3	84.1	930.8	80.0
5. Forestry	45.5	54.5	100.0	59.8	40.2	100.0	70.8	29.2	100.0	5.8	5.1	6.4	5.2	5.3	5.2	158.8	89.0	126.6	77.8	201.2	69.2
6. Other branches (fishing, hunting etc.)	27.8	72.2	100.0	39.4	60.6	100.0	68.7	31.3	100.0	1.9	3.6	1.8	3.3	2.5	2.7	135.6	80.5	214.5	63.4	290.7	51.0
7. Transport (freight)	78.7	21.3	100.0	81.7	18.3	100.0	83.2	16.8	100.0	8.1	1.6	6.5	1.6	5.0	2.5	115.3	95.4	120.9	102.0	139.4	104.0
8. Trade	55.6	44.4	100.0	82.7	17.3	100.0	91.7	8.3	100.0	14.9	8.7	17.0	4.3	15.2	2.0	165.2	43.3	136.0	36.0	224.8	15.6
9. Customs duties	100.0	-	100.0	100.0	-	100.0	100.0	-	100.0	2.3	-	1.5	-	1.5	-	91.9	-	148.4	-	-	-
Total	42.3	57.7	100.0	51.9	48.1	100.0	70.4	29.6	100.0	100.0	100.0	100.0	100.0	100.0	100.0	111.0	86.7	153.1	78.1	220.1	67.7

Sub-section A

Table 4. Structure of production in the branches of the economy (in million rubles, in current prices)

Branches of the economy	Years	Gross production Excluding unfinished production	Unfinished production	Total	Productive consumption Raw material, auxiliary materials, fuel	Unfinished production	Depreciation	Total	Net production
A		1	2	3	4	5	6	7	8
1. Agriculture	1928	18291.0	950.3	19241.3	6789.1	856.2	1186.4	8831.7	10409.6
	1929	19094.4	1239.8	20334.2	7496.3	950.3	1193.4	9640.0	10694.2
	1930	22871.9	1235.3	24107.2	7945.0	1239.8	1292.1	10476.9	31630.3
2. Census industry	1928	18678.9	566.1	19245.0	12523.1	457.9	435.5	13416.5	5828.5
	1929	22673.9	687.9	23361.8	14471.8	686.1	492.4	15530.3	7831.5
	1930	27847.3	838.7	28686.0	16643.4	687.9	553.7	17885.0	10801.0
3. Small-scale industry	1928	5868.7	-	5868.7	4007.3	-	49.5	4056.8	1811.9
	1929	6346.9	-	6346.9	4452.2	-	46.0	4498.2	1848.7
	1930	6592.5	-	6592.5	4695.1	-	48.5	4743.6	1848.9
4. Buildings	1928	4239.1	-	4239.1	2369.3	-	-	2369.3	1869.8
	1929	5025.3	-	5025.3	2759.0	-	-	2759.0	2266.3
	1930	6695.1	-	6695.1	3695.0	-	-	3695.0	3000.1
5. Forestry	1928	1411.3	-	1411.3	2.2	-	5.0	7.2	1404.1
	1929	1741.9	-	1741.9	3.0	-	5.4	8.4	1733.5
	1930	1823.3	-	1823.3	4.1	-	6.0	10.1	1813.2
6. Other branches, (fishing, hunting etc.)	1928	1512.1	-	1512.1	759.4	-	1.2	760.6	751.5
	1929	1590.1	-	1590.1	840.9	-	1.3	842.2	747.9
	1930	1922.4	-	1922.4	1001.5	-	2.5	1004.0	918.4
7. Trade	1928	3198.5	-	3198.5	215.1	-	22.9	238.0	2960.5
	1929	3565.4	-	3565.4	268.0	-	26.0	294.0	3271.4
	1930	4255.3	-	4255.3	307.4	-	32.1	339.5	3915.8
8. Transport (freight)	1928	1982.7	-	1982.7	427.7	-	420.5	847.8	1134.9
	1929	2472.8	-	2472.8	519.8	-	464.2	984.0	1488.8
	1930	3219.7	-	3219.7	741.9	-	476.0	1217.9	2001.8
9. Customs duties	1928	271.5	-	271.5	-	-	-	-	271.5
	1929	253.6	-	253.6	-	-	-	-	253.6
	1930	403.7	-	403.7	-	-	-	-	403.7
Total	1928	55453.8	1516.4	56970.2	27093.2	1314.1	2120.6	30527.9	26442.3
	1929	62761.3	1927.7	64692.0	30811.0	1516.4	2228.7	34556.1	30135.9
	1930	75631.2	2074.0	77705.2	35033.4	1927.7	2410.9	39372.0	38333.2

Sub-section A

Table 5. Gross and net production of agriculture (in current prices)

Social sectors	Years	Gross production in million rubles Excluding unfinished production	Unfinished production	Total	Productive consumption in million rubles Sowing, fodder, etc.	Deprec- iation	Unfinished production	Total	Net production In million rubles	As % of gross production
A		1	2	3	4	5	6	7	8	9
State farms	1928	220.6	22.0	242.6	59.4	22.4	19.0	100.8	141.8	58.5
	1929	267.9	57.9	325.8	93.3	34.3	22.0	149.6	176.2	54.1
	1930	678.7	93.1	771.8	268.0	72.7	57.9	398.6	373.2	48.3
Collective farms	1928	138.8	29.1	167.9	39.4	12.1	8.5	60.0	107.9	64.3
	1929	392.4	209.3	601.7	149.5	33.2	29.1	211.8	389.9	64.8
	1930	3181.7	325.9	3507.6	968.3	167.1	246.7	1382.1	2125.5	60.6
Private sector	1928	17931.6	899.2	18830.8	6690.3	1151.9	828.7	8670.9	10159.9	54.0
	1929	18434.1	972.6	19406.7	7253.5	1125.9	899.2	9278.6	10128.1	52.2
	1930	19011.5	816.3	19827.6	6708.7	1052.3	935.2	8696.2	11131.6	56.1
Total	1928	18291.0	950.3	19241.8	6789.1	1186.4	856.2	8831.7	10409.6	54.2
	1929	19004.4	1239.8	20334.2	7496.3	1193.4	950.3	9640.0	10694.2	52.6
	1930	22871.9	1235.3	24107.2	7915.0	1292.1	1239.8	10476.9	13630.3	56.5

Sub-section A

Table 6. Structure of material outlays in agricultural production (in millions of rubles, in current prices)

Types of material outlay	State farms			Collective farms			Total for socialist sector			Private sector			Total		
	1928	1929	1930	1928	1929	1930	1928	1929	1930	1928	1929	1930	1928	1929	1930
A	1	2	3	4	5	6	7	8	9	10	11	12	13	14	15
A. Auxiliary materials and fuel															
1. Seed	9.7	15.2	39.3	13.0	64.4	261.9	22.7	79.6	301.2	850.8	913.5	733.5	873.5	993.1	1034.7
2. Fodder	36.1	51.9	123.6	14.1	44.7	534.6	50.2	96.6	658.2	3549.3	3675.3	3166.5	3599.5	3771.9	3824.7
3. Mineral fertiliser	2.2	3.0	7.3	0.5	1.9	9.5	2.7	4.9	16.8	8.2	9.9	6.5	10.9	14.8	23.3
4. Fuel for tractors	4.3	10.4	50.7	6.1	19.3	42.4	10.4	29.7	93.1	4.9	3.4	-	15.3	33.1	93.1
5. [Other] Fuel	0.4	0.5	1.1	0.2	0.7	5.2	0.6	1.2	6.3	30.1	30.5	25.5	30.7	31.7	31.8
6. Auxiliary and repair materials	2.4	4.8	15.4	2.3	7.9	41.1	4.7	12.7	56.5	250.6	247.1	230.6	255.3	259.8	287.1
7. Other auxiliary materials	0.0	0.0	0.1	0.2	0.4	2.7	0.2	0.4	2.8	64.3	64.9	67.9	64.5	65.3	70.7
8. Livestock and poultry for slaughter	4.3	7.5	30.5	3.0	10.2	70.9	7.3	17.7	101.4	1932.1	2308.9	2478.2	1939.4	2326.6	2579.6
9. Unfinished production at beginning of year	19.0	22.0	57.9	8.5	29.1	246.7	27.5	51.1	304.6	828.7	899.2	935.2	856.2	950.3	1239.8
Total	78.4	115.3	325.9	47.9	178.6	1215.0	126.3	293.9	1540.9	7519.0	8152.7	7643.9	7645.3	8446.6	9184.8
B. Depreciation of fixed stock	22.4	34.3	72.7	12.1	33.2	167.1	34.5	67.5	239.8	1151.9	1125.9	1052.3	1186.4	1193.4	1292.1
Total	100.8	149.6	398.6	60.0	211.8	1382.1	160.8	361.4	1780.7	8670.9	9278.6	8696.2	8831.7	9640.0	10476.9

Sub-section A

Table 7. Distribution and redistribution of the national income, by classes and groups of the population

A	1928					1929					1930				
	1	2	3	4	5	6	7	8	9	10	11	12	13	14	15
A. Non-agricultural population	8873.7	3916.1	12789.8	11967.0	9602.1	10473.0	4477.2	14950.2	13816.1	11109.8	12980.9	5915.1	18896.0	17617.0	14433.3
I. Proletariat	6217.7	2927.7	9145.4	8911.5	7108.5	7881.7	3439.8	11321.5	10870.6	8652.6	10524.4	4817.0	15341.4	14741.4	12025.8
of which, manual workers	4213.4	379.3	4592.7	4484.3	3661.5	5280.7	401.6	5682.3	5446.5	4430.6	7318.7	552.7	7871.4	7577.8	6212.1
" non-manual workers	1758.3	1859.1	3617.4	3505.4	2721.4	2304.5	2170.4	4474.9	4278.6	3300.5	2960.1	3340.1	6300.2	6010.4	4867.0
" rest of proletarian population	246.0	689.3	935.3	921.8	725.6	296.5	867.8	1164.3	1145.5	921.6	245.6	924.2	1169.8	1153.4	946.7
II. Cooperative producers	512.0	37.5	549.5	505.5	431.4	709.0	48.0	757.0	689.0	595.2	1058.0	70.4	1128.4	992.6	843.3
III. Artisans and craftsmen	1096.3	414.9	1511.2	1398.6	1191.5	1007.5	423.8	1431.3	1271.5	1074.7	830.8	456.5	1287.3	1075.2	901.5
IV. Capitalist groups	1047.7	75.0	1122.7	690.9	417.5	874.8	76.0	950.8	496.5	306.7	567.7	82.2	649.9	320.0	182.7
of which, traders	951.6	-	951.6	-	-	800.0	-	800.0	-	-	511.2	-	511.2	-	-
V. Other population	-	461.0	461.0	460.5	453.2	-	489.6	489.6	488.5	480.5	-	489.0	489.0	487.6	480.0
B. Agricultural population	14560.5	759.6	15320.1	14773.3	14416.3	14988.7	920.7	15909.4	14725.2	13905.1	17576.4	1093.6	18670.0	17246.9	16273.9
of which, proletariat	530.1	60.5	590.6	-	-	668.6	73.7	742.3	734.2	695.3	820.2	94.8	915.0	895.8	842.2
" collective farmers	259.2	8.7	267.9	-	-	728.0	34.0	762.0	730.0	701.5	4057.8	219.4	4277.2	3992.3	3805.8
" individual farmers	12553.4	651.8	13205.2	-	-	12405.0	788.3	13193.3	12273.2	11548.8	12250.0	766.4	13016.4	12080.1	11559.5
" kulaks	1217.8	38.6	1256.4	-	-	1187.1	24.7	1211.8	987.8	959.5	448.4	13.0	461.4	278.7	266.4
Total	23434.2	4675.7	28109.9	26740.3	23718.4	25461.7	5397.9	30859.6	28511.3	25014.9	30557.3	7008.7	37566.0	34863.9	30707.2
C. Income of socialised sector	3008.1	-	-	-	2723.9	4647.2	-	-	-	5121.0	7775.9	-	-	-	7626.0
Total	26442.3	-	-	-	26442.3	30108.9	-	-	-	30135.9	38333.2	-	-	-	38333.2

Column headings (repeating within each year 1928, 1929, 1930):
1, 6, 11 — Incomes received through distribution
2, 7, 12 — Incomes received through redistribution
3, 8, 13 — Total incomes (received) through distribution and redistribution)
4, 9, 14 — Incomes realised as accumulation and consumption of material goods and services
5, 10, 15 — Incomes realised as accumulation and consumption of material goods (without services)

Sub-section A

Table 7a. Structure and rate of growth of incomes of classes and groups of the population and enterprises of the socialist sector

Classes and groups of the population	Share of incomes received through distribution in total volume of national income			Share of incomes realised as accumulation and consumption of material goods in total volume of national income			Rate of growth of total income (received through distribution and redistribution) as % of previous year		1930 as % of 1928
	1928	1929	1930	1928	1929	1930	1929	1930	1928
A	1	2	3	4	5	6	7	8	9
A. Non-agricultural population	33.3	34.8	33.9	36.3	36.9	37.7	116.9	126.4	147.7
I. Proletariat	23.5	26.2	27.4	26.9	28.7	31.4	123.8	135.5	167.8
of which, manual workers	15.9	17.5	19.1	13.9	14.7	16.2	123.7	138.5	171.4
" non-manual workers	6.7	7.7	7.7	10.3	11.0	12.7	123.7	140.8	174.2
" rest of population	0.9	1.0	0.6	2.7	3.0	2.5	124.5	100.5	125.1
II. Cooperative producers	1.9	2.4	2.8	1.6	2.0	2.3	137.8	149.1	205.4
III. Artisans and craftsmen	4.1	3.3	2.2	4.5	3.6	2.3	94.7	89.9	85.2
IV. Capitalist groups	4.0	2.9	1.5	1.6	1.0	0.5	84.7	68.4	57.9
of which, traders	3.6	2.7	1.3	-	-	-	84.1	63.9	53.7
V. Other population	-	-	-	1.7	1.6	1.2	106.2	99.9	106.1
B. Agricultural population	55.1	49.7	45.9	53.4	46.1	42.4	103.8	117.4	121.9
of which, proletariat	2.0	2.2	2.1	-	2.3	2.2	125.7	123.3	154.9
" collective farmers	1.0	2.4	10.6	-	2.3	9.9	284.4	561.3	1596.6
" individual farmers	47.5	41.2	32.0	-	38.3	29.6	99.9	98.7	98.6
" kulaks	4.6	3.9	1.2	-	3.2	0.7	96.6	38.1	36.8
Total	88.6	84.5	79.8	89.7	83.0	80.1	109.8	121.7	133.6
C. Incomes of the socialised sector	11.4	15.5	20.2	10.3	17.0	19.9	-	-	-
Total national income	100.0	100.0	100.0	100.0	100.0	100.0	-	-	-

Sub-section A

Table 8. Distribution and redistribution of material income, by classes and groups of the population (income per head of population)

Column legend (sub-columns repeat in groups of three):
a = Total income received through distribution and redistribution
b = Income realised as accumulation and consumption of material goods and services
c = Income realised as accumulation and consumption of material goods

	In rubles									Dynamic, as % of previous year						1930 as % of 1928		
	1928			1929			1930			1929			1930					
A	1 (a)	2 (b)	3 (c)	4 (a)	5 (b)	6 (c)	7 (a)	8 (b)	9 (c)	10 (a)	11 (b)	12 (c)	13 (a)	14 (b)	15 (c)	16 (a)	17 (b)	18 (c)
A. Non-agricultural population	373.6	349.6	280.5	413.7	382.3	307.4	521.2	486.0	398.1	110.7	109.3	109.6	126.0	127.0	129.5	139.5	139.0	141.9
I. Proletariat	380.5	370.7	295.7	433.9	416.6	331.6	542.6	521.4	425.3	114.0	112.4	112.7	125.1	125.7	128.3	142.6	140.2	143.8
of which, manual workers	390.8	381.6	311.6	446.8	428.2	348.4	517.3	498.0	408.2	114.3	112.2	111.8	115.8	116.3	117.2	132.4	130.5	131.0
" non-manual workers	424.4	411.2	319.3	483.4	462.2	356.5	613.2	585.0	473.7	113.9	112.4	111.7	126.9	126.6	132.9	144.5	142.3	148.4
" rest of proletarian population	248.5	244.9	192.8	282.9	278.4	223.9	420.2	414.3	340.1	113.8	113.7	116.1	148.5	148.8	151.9	169.1	169.2	176.4
II. Cooperative producers	262.9	241.9	206.4	334.2	304.2	262.8	391.7	344.5	312.0	127.8	127.8	127.3	117.2	113.2	118.7	149.0	142.4	151.2
III. Artisans and craftsmen	263.3	243.7	207.6	237.4	210.9	178.2	350.7	292.9	245.6	90.2	86.5	85.8	147.7	138.9	137.8	133.2	120.2	118.3
IV. Capitalist groups	859.0	528.6	319.4	1414.9	738.8	456.4	1662.1	818.4	467.3	164.7	139.8	142.9	117.5	110.8	102.4	193.5	154.8	146.3
of which, traders	790.4	–	–	1353.6	–	–	1612.6	–	–	171.2	–	–	119.1	–	–	204.0	–	–
V. Other population	412.4	411.9	405.4	452.8	451.8	444.5	473.0	471.7	464.3	109.8	109.7	109.6	104.5	104.4	104.5	114.7	114.5	114.5
B. Agricultural population	129.2	124.6	119.0	132.9	123.0	116.2	152.4	140.8	132.9	102.9	98.7	97.6	114.7	114.5	114.4	118.0	113.0	111.7
I. Proletariat	120.6	–	–	165.7	163.9	155.2	191.7	187.6	176.4	137.4	–	–	115.7	114.5	113.7	159.0	–	–
II. Collective farmers	145.5	–	–	182.1	174.4	167.6	183.2	171.0	163.0	125.1	–	–	100.6	98.1	97.2	125.9	–	–
III. Individual farmers	124.1	–	–	124.2	115.5	108.7	142.1	131.9	124.0	100.1	–	–	114.4	114.2	114.1	114.5	–	–
IV. Kulaks	231.8	–	–	251.4	204.9	199.1	166.6	100.7	96.2	108.5	–	–	66.3	49.1	48.3	71.9	–	–
Total	183.9	174.9	155.1	198.0	183.1	160.5	236.7	219.7	193.5	107.7	104.7	103.5	119.5	120.0	120.6	128.7	125.6	124.8

Sub-section A

Table 9. Expenditure of the non-productive sphere (as a whole)

A	1929	1930	Structure in % of total 1929	1930	Dynamic as % of previous year 1930
	1	2	3	4	5
1. Expenditure of non-productive sphere, less accumulation	6027.0	7553.0	100.0	100.0	125.3
of which, received from state and local budgets	3506.0	4698.0	58.2	62.2	134.0
2. Returned as services, in the form of free social, cultural and medical services to the population employed in the productive sphere	1372.1	1811.2	22.8	24.0	132.0
3. Returned as pensions and allowances to the population employed in the productive sphere	446.8	491.6	7.5	6.5	110.0
4. Expenditure of the non-productive sphere 1-(2+3)	4208.1	5250.2	69.7	69.5	124.8
National income in current prices	30135.9	38333.2	-	-	127.2
Share of consumption by the non-productive sphere in total volume of national income	14.0	13.7	-	-	

Sub-section A

Table 9a. Expenditure of the non-productive sphere (administration and defence)

| | 1929 | 1930 | Structure in % of total | | Dynamic as % of previous year |
			1929	1930	1930
A	1	2	3	4	5
1. Total expended in given sphere (less accumulation and capital investment)	1699.3	2078.4	100.0	100.0	122.3
(a) of which, wages	444.1	628.0	26.1	30.2	141.4
(b) of which, material consumption (non-productive), including depreciation	426.6	612.5	25.1	29.5	143.6
2. National income in current prices	30135.6	38333.2	-	-	127.2
Share of expenditure of given sphere in total national income	5.7	5.4	-	-	-

Sub-section A

Table 9b. Expenditure of the non-productive sphere (social cultural services, including central administration of social insurance and trade unions)

| | 1929 | 1930 | Structure in % of total | | Dynamic as % of previous year |
			1929	1930	1930
A	1	2	3	4	5
1. Total expended in given sphere (less accumulation and capital investment)	4327.3	5474.6	100.0	100.0	126.5
(a) of which, returned as free services, in form of social cultural and medical services to the population employed in the productive sphere	1372.1	1811.2	32.4	32.1	132.0
(b) of which, provided as pensions and allowances to workers employed in productive sphere	446.8	491.6	10.6	8.7	110.0
(c) consumed in the given sphere	2508.1	3171.8	57.0	59.2	126.5
2. National income in current prices	30135.6	38333.2	-	-	127.2
Share of consumption by given sphere in total volume of national income	8.3	8.3	-	-	-

Sub-section B: Fixed capital stock

Table 1. Active fixed capital stock by branch of the economy, in value terms, allowing for depreciation (in million rubles, in current prices)

Stock at beginning of year

A	1928			1929			1930			1931			1932		
	Socialist sector	Private sector	Total	Socialist sector	Private sector	Total	Socialist sector	Private sector	Total	Socialist sector	Private sector	Total	Socialist sector	Private sector	Total
	1	2	3	4	5	6	7	8	9	10	11	12	13	14	15
Total in the economy															
a) excluding livestock	30926.7	25103.1	56029.8	32537.1	25574.8	58111.9	35305.7	25778.2	61083.9	41309.7	24441.5	65751.2	49816.4	22703.0	72519.4
b) including livestock[1]	31009.9	33317.2	64327.1	32667.4	33803.9	66471.3	35694.6	33444.5	69139.1	43047.6	32354.3	75401.9	55644.7	30800.0	86444.7
I Productive stock															
a) excluding livestock	16756.1	9093.0	25849.1	17867.1	9268.3	27135.4	19984.7	9285.6	29270.3	24959.3	8360.6	33319.9	–	–	–
b) including livestock[1]	16839.3	17307.1	34146.4	17997.4	17497.4	35494.8	20373.6	16951.9	37325.5	26697.2	16273.4	42970.6	–	–	–
1. In census industry	5712.1	–	5712.1	6436.0	–	6436.0	7547.9	–	7547.9	9568.8	–	9568.8	12713.7	–	12713.7
2. In small-scale industry	130.8	638.4	769.2	168.4	586.7	755.1	267.9	488.9	756.8	552.6	184.2	736.8	n.d.[2]	n.d.[2]	n.d.[2]
3. In agriculture															
a) excluding livestock	1210.6	8454.6	9665.2	1370.1	8681.6	10051.7	1847.7	8796.7	10644.4	3414.7	8176.4	11591.1	6120.8	6907.7	13028.5
b) including livestock[1]	1293.8	16668.7	17962.5	1500.4	16910.7	18411.1	2236.6	16463.0	18699.6	5152.6	16089.2	21241.8	11949.1	15004.1	26953.8
4. In transport	9276.7	–	9276.7	9428.3	–	9428.3	9744.1	–	9744.1	10599.3	–	10599.3	n.d.[2]	n.d.[2]	n.d.[2]
5. In trade	425.9	–	425.9	464.3	–	464.3	577.1	–	577.1	823.9	–	823.9	1299.8	–	1299.8
II Consumption stock	14170.6	16010.1	30180.7	14670.0	16306.5	30976.5	15321.0	16492.6	31813.6	16350.4	16080.9	32431.3	n.d.[2]	n.d.[2]	n.d.[2]
1. Communications stock	229.6	–	229.6	259.7	–	259.7	301.7	–	301.7	370.4	–	370.4	516.5	–	516.5
2. Stock allocated for social purposes	5783.7	–	5783.7	6028.4	–	6028.4	6385.1	–	6385.1	6696.1	–	6696.1	n.d.[2]	–	n.d.[2]
3. Housing stock	8157.3	16010.1	24167.4	8381.9	16306.5	24688.4	8634.1	16492.6	25126.7	9283.9	16080.9	25364.0	n.d.[2]	n.d.[2]	n.d.[2]
a) urban	8077.3	5041.8	13119.1	8279.2	5061.6	13340.8	8497.3	5065.0	13562.3	8894.2	4989.4	13883.6	n.d.[2]	n.d.[2]	n.d.[2]
b) rural	80.0	10968.3	11048.3	102.7	11244.9	11347.6	136.8	11427.6	11564.4	389.7	11091.5	11481.2	718.9	10911.6	11630.5

1. The numerator shows funds at the end of the preceding year, the denominator shows them at the beginning of the year named. This difference between the funds at the beginning and at the end of a year is due to the fact that, in agriculture, livestock were valued according to the average-yearly prices of each year.

[2. n.d. = no data available]

Sub-section B

Table 1a. Active fixed capital stock by branch of the economy, in value terms, allowing for depreciation (in million rubles, in 1928 prices)

Stock at beginning of year

A	1928			1929			1930			1931			1932		
	Socialist sector	Private sector	Total	Socialist sector	Private sector	Total	Socialist sector	Private sector	Total	Socialist sector	Private sector	Total	Socialist sector	Private sector	Total
	1	2	3	4	5	6	7	8	9	10	11	12	13	14	15
Total in the economy															
a) excluding livestock	30926.7	25103.1	56029.8	32537.1	25574.8	58111.9	35470.2	25722.5	61192.7	42081.3	24401.6	66482.9	50789.5	22672.5	73462.0
b) including livestock	31009.9	33317.2	64327.1	32667.4	33803.9	66471.3	35839.0	33002.0	68841.0	43305.6	30075.9	73381.5	53396.2	26521.0	79917.2
I Productive stock															
a) excluding livestock	16756.1	9093.0	25849.1	17867.1	9268.3	27135.4	20084.6	9259.6	29344.2	25464.2	8350.9	33815.1	-	-	-
b) including livestock	16839.3	17307.1	34146.4	17997.4	17497.4	35494.8	20458.4	16539.1	36992.5	26688.5	14025.2	40713.1	-	-	-
1. In census industry	5712.1	-	5712.1	6436.0	-	6436.0	7622.6	-	7622.6	10008.6	-	10008.6	13370.1	-	13370.1
2. In small-scale industry	130.8	638.4	769.2	168.4	586.7	755.1	267.9	488.9	756.8	552.6	184.2	736.8	n.d.	n.d.	n.d.
3. In agriculture															
a) excluding livestock	1210.6	8454.6	9665.2	1370.1	8681.6	10051.7	1862.7	8770.7	10633.4	3455.5	8166.7	11622.2	6207.0	6917.0	13124.0
b) including livestock	1293.8	16668.7	17962.5	1500.4	16910.7	18411.1	2231.5	16050.2	18281.7	4679.8	13841.0	18520.8	8813.7	10765.5	19579.2
4. In transport	9276.7	-	9276.7	9428.3	-	9428.3	9748.8	-	9748.8	10592.7	-	10592.7	n.d.	n.d.	n.d.
5. In trade	425.9	-	425.9	464.3	-	464.3	582.6	-	582.6	854.8	-	854.8	1332.1	-	1332.1
II Consumption stock	14170.6	16010.1	30180.7	14670.0	16306.5	30976.5	15585.6	16462.9	31848.5	16617.1	16050.7	32667.8	n.d.	-	n.d.
1. Communication stock	229.6	-	229.6	259.7	-	259.7	304.4	-	304.4	384.8	-	384.8	527.6	-	527.6
2. Stock allocated for social purposes	5783.7	-	5783.7	6028.4	-	6028.4	6410.2	-	6410.2	6773.6	-	6773.6	n.d.	n.d.	n.d.
3. Housing stock	8157.3	16010.1	24167.4	8381.9	16306.5	24688.4	8671.0	16462.9	25133.9	9458.7	16050.7	25509.4	n.d.	-	n.d.
a) urban	8077.3	5041.8	13119.1	8279.2	5061.6	13340.8	8533.3	5070.8	13604.1	9059.9	4991.2	14051.1	n.d.	n.d.	n.d.
b) rural	80.0	10968.3	11048.3	102.7	11244.9	11347.6	137.7	11392.1	11529.8	398.8	11059.5	11458.3	716.1	10883.3	11629.4

Sub-section B

Table 2. Rate of growth of active fixed capital stock by branch of the economy (in value terms, net of depreciation, in current prices)

Capital stock at start of year, as % of previous year

A	Socialist sector					Private sector					Total				
	1929	1930	1931	1932	1932 in relation to 1928	1929	1930	1931	1932	1932 in relation to 1928	1929	1930	1931	1932	1932 in relation to 1928
	1	2	3	4	5	6	7	8	9	10	11	12	13	14	15
Total in the economy															
a) excluding livestock	105.2	108.5	117.0	122.1	161.1	101.9	100.8	94.8	93.6	90.4	103.7	105.1	107.6	111.5	129.4
b) including livestock	105.3	109.3	120.1	128.2	179.4	101.5	97.5	90.4	85.4	92.4	103.3	103.2	105.3	108.8	134.4
I Productive stock															
a) excluding livestock	106.6	111.9	124.9	-	149.0[1]	109.9	100.2	90.0	-	91.9[1]	105.0	107.9	113.8	-	128.9[1]
b) including livestock	106.9	113.2	130.0	-	158.5[1]	101.1	94.2	84.3	-	94.0[1]	103.9	103.7	107.9	-	125.8[1]
1. In census industry	112.7	117.3	126.8	132.9	222.6	-	-	-	-	-	112.7	117.3	126.8	132.9	222.6
2. In small-scale industry	128.7	159.1	206.3	-	422.1[1]	91.9	83.3	37.7	-	28.9[1]	98.2	100.2	97.4	-	95.8[1]
3. In agriculture															
a) excluding livestock	113.2	134.9	184.8	179.2	505.6	102.7	101.3	92.9	84.5	81.7	104.0	105.9	108.9	112.4	134.8
b) including livestock[2]	116.0	148.7	215.2	197.0	923.6	101.5	94.6	85.6	75.1	90.0	102.5	98.9	100.2	103.5	150.1
5. (sic) In transport	101.6	103.3	108.8	-	114.3[1]	-	-	-	-	-	101.6	103.3	108.8	-	114.3[1]
6. (sic) In trade	109.0	124.3	142.8	157.8	305.2	-	-	-	-	-	109.0	124.3	142.8	157.8	305.2
II Consumption stock	103.5	104.4	106.7	-	115.4[1]	101.9	101.1	97.5	-	100.5[1]	102.6	102.7	101.9	-	107.5[1]
1. Communication stock	113.1	116.2	122.8	139.4	225.0	-	-	-	-	-	113.1	116.2	122.8	139.4	225.0
2. Stock allocated for social purposes	104.2	105.9	104.9	-	115.8[1]	-	-	-	-	-	104.2	105.9	104.9	-	115.8[1]
3. Housing stock	102.8	103.0	107.5	-	113.8[1]	101.9	101.1	97.5	-	100.5[1]	102.2	101.8	101.9	-	105.0[1]
a) urban	102.5	102.6	104.7	-	110.1[1]	100.4	100.1	98.5	-	99.0[1]	101.7	101.7	102.4	-	105.8[1]
b) rural	128.4	133.2	284.9	184.5	898.6	102.5	101.6	97.1	98.4	99.5	102.7	101.9	99.3	101.3	105.3

1. Data at the beginning of 1931 in relation to 1928
2. In agriculture, the calculation of the livestock in current prices differs in method from the calculations of all the other stock

Sub-section B

Table 2a. Rate of growth of active fixed capital stock by branch of the economy (in value terms, allowing for depreciation, in 1928 prices)

Capital stock at start of year, as % of previous year

A	Socialist sector					Private sector					Total				
	1929	1930	1931	1932	1932 in relation to 1928	1929	1930	1931	1932	1932 in relation to 1928	1929	1930	1931	1932	1932 in relation to 1928
	1	2	3	4	5	6	7	8	9	10	11	12	13	14	15
Total in the economy															
a) excluding livestock	105.2	109.0	118.6	120.7	164.2	101.9	100.6	94.9	93.0	90.3	103.7	105.3	108.6	110.5	131.1
b) including livestock	105.3	109.7	120.8	123.3	171.2	101.5	96.7	91.1	88.2	79.6	103.3	103.6	106.6	108.9	124.2
I Productive stock															
a) excluding livestock	106.6	112.4	126.8	-	151.4[1]	101.9	99.9	90.2	-	91.8[1]	105.0	108.1	115.2	-	130.8[1]
b) including livestock	106.9	113.6	130.5	-	158.5[1]	101.1	94.5	84.8	-	86.0[1]	103.9	104.2	110.1	-	119.2[1]
1. In census industry	112.7	118.4	131.3	133.6	234.1	-	-	-	-	-	112.7	118.4	131.3	133.6	234.1
2. In small-scale industry	128.7	159.1	206.3	-	422.5[1]	91.9	83.3	37.7	-	28.9[1]	98.2	100.2	97.3	-	95.8[1]
3. In agriculture															
a) excluding livestock	113.2	136.0	185.5	179.6	512.7	102.7	101.0	93.1	84.7	81.8	104.0	105.8	109.3	112.9	135.8
b) including livestock	116.0	148.7	209.7	188.3	681.2	101.5	94.9	86.2	77.8	64.6	102.5	99.3	101.3	105.7	109.0
4. In transport	101.6	103.4	108.7	-	114.2[1]	-	-	-	-	-	101.6	103.4	108.7	-	114.2[1]
5. In trade	109.0	125.5	146.7	155.8	312.8	-	-	-	-	-	109.0	125.5	146.7	155.8	312.8
II Consumption stock	103.5	104.9	108.0	-	117.3[1]	101.9	101.0	97.5	-	100.3[1]	102.6	102.8	102.6	-	108.2[1]
1. Communications stock	113.1	117.2	126.4	137.1	229.8	-	-	-	-	-	113.1	117.2	126.4	137.1	229.8
2. Stock allocated for social purposes	104.2	107.2	104.9	-	117.1[1]	-	-	-	-	-	104.2	107.2	104.9	-	117.1[1]
3. Housing stock	102.8	103.4	108.9	-	116.0[1]	101.9	101.0	97.5	-	100.3[1]	102.2	101.8	101.5	-	105.6[1]
a) urban	102.5	103.1	106.2	-	112.2[1]	100.4	100.2	98.4	-	99.0[1]	101.7	102.0	103.3	-	107.1[1]
b) rural	128.3	134.1	289.6	187.1	932.6	102.5	101.3	97.1	98.4	99.2	102.7	101.6	99.4	101.5	105.3

1. Data at the beginning of 1931 in relation to 1928.

Sub-section B

Table 3. Share of sectors in fixed capital stock by branch of the economy at beginning of year (in current prices)

A	1928 Socialist sector	Private sector	Total	1929 Socialist sector	Private sector	Total	1930 Socialist sector	Private sector	Total	1931 Socialist sector	Private sector	Total	1932 Socialist sector	Private sector	Total
	1	2	3	4	5	6	7	8	9	10	11	12	13	14	15
Total in the economy															
a) excluding livestock	55.2	44.8	100.0	56.0	44.0	100.0	57.8	42.2	100.0	62.8	37.2	100.0	68.7	31.3	100.0
b) including livestock	48.2	51.8	100.0	48.8	51.2	100.0	50.0	50.0	100.0	54.8	45.2	100.0	64.1	35.6	100.0
I Productive stock															
a) excluding livestock	64.8	35.2	100.0	65.8	34.2	100.0	68.3	31.7	100.0	74.9	25.1	100.0	-	-	-
b) including livestock	49.3	50.7	100.0	50.0	50.0	100.0	51.6	48.4	100.0	57.8	42.2	100.0	-	-	-
1. In census industry	100.0	-	100.0	100.0	-	100.0	100.0	-	100.0	100.0	-	100.0	-	-	-
2. In small-scale industry	17.0	83.0	100.0	22.3	77.7	100.0	35.4	64.6	100.0	75.0	25.0	100.0	100.0	-	100.0
3. In agriculture															
a) excluding livestock	12.5	87.5	100.0	13.6	86.4	100.0	17.4	82.6	100.0	29.5	70.5	100.0	47.0	53.0	100.0
b) including livestock	7.2	92.8	100.0	8.0	92.0	100.0	11.3	88.7	100.0	23.3	76.7	100.0	44.3	55.7	100.0
4. In transport	100.0	-	100.0	100.0	-	100.0	100.0	-	100.0	100.0	-	100.0	-	-	-
5. In trade	100.0	-	100.0	100.0	-	100.0	100.0	-	100.0	100.0	-	100.0	100.0	-	100.0
II Consumption stock	47.0	53.0	100.0	47.4	52.6	100.0	48.2	51.8	100.0	50.4	49.6	100.0	-	-	-
1. Communications stock	100.0	-	100.0	100.0	-	100.0	100.0	-	100.0	100.0	-	100.0	100.0	-	100.0
2. Stock allocated for social purposes	100.0	-	100.0	100.0	-	100.0	100.0	-	100.0	100.0	-	100.0	-	-	-
3. Housing stock	33.8	66.2	100.0	34.0	66.0	100.0	31.4	65.6	100.0	36.6	63.4	100.0	-	-	-
a) urban	61.6	38.4	100.0	62.1	37.9	100.0	62.7	37.3	100.0	64.1	35.9	100.0	-	-	-
b) rural	0.7	99.3	100.0	0.9	99.1	100.0	1.2	98.8	100.0	3.4	96.6	100.0	6.2	93.8	100.0

Sub-section B

Table 3a. Share of sectors in fixed capital stock by branch of the economy at beginning of year (in 1928 prices)

A	1928 Socialist sector	1928 Private sector	1928 Total	1929 Socialist sector	1929 Private sector	1929 Total	1930 Socialist sector	1930 Private sector	1930 Total	1931 Socialist sector	1931 Private sector	1931 Total	1932 Socialist sector	1932 Private sector	1932 Total
	1	2	3	4	5	6	7	8	9	10	11	12	13	14	15
Total in the economy															
a) excluding livestock	55.2	44.8	100.0	56.0	44.0	100.0	58.0	42.0	100.0	63.3	36.7	100.0	69.1	30.9	100.0
b) including livestock	48.2	51.8	100.0	49.1	50.9	100.0	52.1	47.9	100.0	59.0	41.0	100.0	66.8	33.2	100.0
I Productive stock															
a) excluding livestock	64.8	35.2	100.0	65.8	34.2	100.0	68.4	31.6	100.0	75.3	24.7	100.0	-	-	-
b) including livestock	49.3	50.7	100.0	50.7	49.3	100.0	55.3	44.7	100.0	65.6	34.4	100.0	-	-	-
1. In census industry	100.0	-	100.0	100.0	-	100.0	100.0	-	100.0	100.0	-	100.0	100.0	-	100.0
2. In small-scale industry	17.0	83.0	100.0	22.3	77.7	100.0	35.4	64.6	100.0	75.0	25.0	100.0	-	-	-
3. In agriculture															
a) excluding livestock	12.5	87.5	100.0	13.6	86.4	100.0	17.5	82.5	100.0	29.7	70.3	100.0	47.3	52.7	100.0
b) including livestock	7.2	92.8	100.0	8.1	91.9	100.0	12.2	87.2	100.0	25.3	74.7	100.0	45.0	55.0	100.0
4. In transport	100.0	-	100.0	100.0	-	100.0	100.0	-	100.0	100.0	-	100.0	100.0	-	100.0
5. In trade	100.0	-	100.0	100.0	-	100.0	100.0	-	100.0	100.0	-	100.0	100.0	-	100.0
II Consumption stock	47.0	53.0	100.0	47.4	52.6	100.0	48.3	51.7	100.0	50.9	49.1	100.0	-	-	-
1. Communications stock	100.0	-	100.0	100.0	-	100.0	100.0	-	100.0	100.0	-	100.0	100.0	-	100.0
2. Stock allocated for social purposes	100.0	-	100.0	100.0	-	100.0	100.0	-	100.0	100.0	-	100.0	100.0	-	100.0
3. Housing stock	33.8	66.2	100.0	34.0	66.0	100.0	34.5	65.5	100.0	37.1	62.9	100.0	-	-	-
a) urban	61.6	38.4	100.0	62.1	37.9	100.0	62.7	37.3	100.0	64.5	35.5	100.0	-	-	-
b) rural	0.7	99.3	100.0	0.9	99.1	100.0	1.2	98.8	100.0	3.5	96.5	100.0	6.4	93.6	100.0

Sub-section B

Table 4. Investments in fixed capital stock by branch of the economy (in current prices, in millions of rubles)

A	1928 Socialist sector[1]	1928 Private sector	1928 Total	1929 Socialist sector[1]	1929 Private sector	1929 Total	1930 Socialist sector[1]	1930 Private sector	1930 Total	1931 Socialist sector	1931 Private sector	1931 Total
	1	2	3	4	5	6	7	8	9	10	11	12
Total for economy[3]												
a) excluding livestock	3714.9 / 59.1	2260.5	5975.4	5156.0 / 189.1	2137.1	7293.1	8784.0 / 812.9	1176.3	9960.3	13662.0 / 1017.8	1119.6	14781.6
b) including livestock[2]	3763.2 / 66.9	3112.9	6843.7	5305.7 / 311.0	2492.8	7692.6	9367.1 / 1502.1	1577.4	10533.6	14697.8 / 3514.9	1667.9	15823.2
I. Productive stock												
a) excluding livestock	2669.3 / 51.9	1113.1	3782.4	3850.3 / 172.2	1079.5	4929.8	6965.6 / 656.2	600.0	7565.6	-	-	-
b) including livestock[2]	2717.6 / 59.7	1965.5	4650.7	4000.0 / 294.1	1435.2	5329.3	7548.7 / 1345.4	1001.1	8138.9	-	-	-
1. In census industry	1525.5	-	1525.5	2091.2	-	2091.2	3613.0	-	3613.0	5904.3	-	5904.3
2. In small-scale industry	25.0 / 21.0	10.4	35.4	38.4 / 71.4	9.3	47.7	26.1 / 284.9	2.4	28.5	-	-	-
3. In agriculture												
a) excluding livestock	206.7 / 30.9	1102.7	1309.4	486.2 / 100.8	1070.2	1556.4	1442.2 / 371.3	597.6	2039.8	2343.2 / 840.8	386.8	2730.0
b) including livestock[2]	255.0 / 38.7	1955.1	2177.7	635.9 / 222.7	1425.9	1955.9	2025.3 / 1060.5	998.7	2613.1	3379.0 / 3337.9	935.1	3771.6
4. In transport	844.0	-	844.0	1080.3	-	1080.3	1543.7	-	1543.7	n.d.	n.d.	n.d.
5. In trade	68.1	-	68.1	154.2	-	154.2	340.6	-	340.6	595.2	-	595.2
II. Consumption stock	1045.6 / 7.2	1147.4	2193.0	1305.7 / 16.9	1057.6	2363.3	1818.4 / 156.7	576.3	2394.7	-	-	-
1. Communications stock	53.5	-	53.5	70.3	-	70.3	94.4	-	94.4	180.0	-	180.0
2. Stock allocated for social purposes	475.3	-	475.3	643.3	-	643.3	683.4	-	683.4	n.d.	n.d.	n.d.
3. Housing stock	516.8 / 7.2	1147.4	1664.2	592.1 / 16.9	1057.6	1649.7	1040.6 / 156.7	576.3	1616.9	-	-	-
a) urban	496.5	236.3	732.8	568.2	223.3	791.5	932.8	124.5	1057.3	n.d.	n.d.	n.d.
b) rural	20.3 / 7.2	911.1	931.4	23.9 / 16.9	834.3	858.2	107.8 / 156.7	451.8	539.6	176.0 / 177.0	621.0	797.0

1. The denominator of the socialist sector also shows the addition of stock by means of socialisation.

2. The difference between the total and the sum of the separate sectors is due to the fact that, in agriculture, the socialist sector includes purchases of livestock from the private sector, but investment in livestock for the total of the sectors includes only the natural increase of the herd, since the transfer of livestock from sector to sector does not change the total of investment for the economy as a whole. The quantity purchased was, in 1928, 32.4 million rubles; in 1929, 105.9 million rubles; in 1930, 410.9 million rubles; in 1931, 542.5 million rubles.

3. In addition, investment in unrecorded stock, that entered in the balance, was as follows:

	1928	1929	1930
Total	193.9	322.6	441.6
1. In census industry	160.6	260.6	304.4
2. In transport	1.0	29.4	43.1
3. In agriculture	-	-	18.7
4. Stock allocated for social purposes	32.3	41.6	75.4

Sub-section B

Table 4a. Investments in fixed capital stock by branch of the economy (in 1928 prices, in millions of rubles)

A	1928 Socialist sector[1]	Private sector	Total	1929 Socialist sector[1]	Private sector	Total	1930 Socialist sector[1]	Private sector	Total	1931 Socialist sector[1]	Private sector	Total
	1	2	3	4	5	6	7	8	9	10	11	12
Total for economy[3]												
a) excluding livestock	3714.9 / 59.1	2260.5	5975.4	5354.3 / 189.3	2078.6	7432.9	9649.1 / 801.9	1174.5	10823.6	14075.0 / 993.4	1096.5	15171.5
b) including livestock[2]	3763.2 / 66.9	3112.9	6843.7	5491.1 / 306.5	2480.5	7874.2	10018.4 / 1354.1	1553.6	11312.4	14484.4 / 2134.7	1381.3	15666.1
I. Productive stock												
a) excluding livestock	2669.3 / 51.9	1113.1	3782.4	3971.0 / 172.1	1049.3	5020.3	7539.8 / 647.1	603.6	8143.4	-	-	-
b) including livestock[2]	2717.6 / 59.7	1965.5	4650.7	4107.8 / 289.3	1451.2	5461.6	7909.1 / 1199.3	982.7	8632.2	-	-	-
1. In census industry	1525.5	-	1525.5	2187.4	-	2187.4	4129.1	-	4129.1	6281.2	-	6281.2
2. In small-scale industry	25.0 / 21.0	10.4	35.4	38.4 / 71.4	9.3	47.7	26.1 / 284.9	2.4	28.5	-	-	-
3. In agriculture												
a) excluding livestock	206.7 / 30.9	1102.7	1309.4	501.0 / 100.7	1040.0	1541.0	1474.9 / 362.2	601.2	2076.1	2406.3 / 819.5	386.8	2793.1
b) including livestock[2]	255.0 / 38.7	1955.1	2177.7	637.8 / 217.9	1441.9	1982.3	1844.2 / 914.4	980.3	2564.9	2815.7 / 1960.8	671.6	3287.7
4. In transport	844.0	-	844.0	1083.9	-	1083.9	1537.5	-	1537.5	n.d.	n.d.	n.d.
5. In trade	68.1	-	68.1	160.3	-	160.3	372.2	-	372.2	598.8	-	598.8
II. Consumption stock	1045.6 / 7.2	1147.4	2193.0	1383.3 / 17.2	1029.3	2412.6	2109.3 / 154.8	570.9	2680.2	-	-	-
1. Communications stock	53.5	-	53.5	73.6	-	73.6	107.3	-	107.3	177.2	-	177.2
2. Stock allocated for social purposes	475.3	-	475.3	673.7	-	673.7	759.6	-	759.6	n.d.	n.d.	n.d.
3. Housing stock	516.8 / 7.2	1147.4	1664.2	636.0 / 17.2	1029.3	1665.3	1242.4 / 154.8	570.9	1813.3	-	-	-
a) urban	496.5	236.3	732.8	611.6	230.2	841.8	1123.9	120.0	1243.9	n.d.	n.d.	n.d.
b) rural	20.3 / 7.2	911.1	931.4	24.4 / 17.2	799.1	823.5	118.5 / 154.8	450.9	569.4	198.2 / 173.9	619.8	818.0

1. The denominator of the socialist sector also shows the addition of stock by means of socialisation.

2. The difference between the total and the sum of the separate sectors is due to the fact that, in agriculture, the socialist sector includes purchases of livestock from the private sector, but investment in livestock for the total of the sectors includes only the natural increase of the herd, since the transfer of livestock from sector to sector does not change the total of investment for the economy as a whole. The quantity purchased was, in 1928, 32.4 million rubles; in 1929, 97.4 million rubles; in 1930, 259.6 million rubles; in 1931, 199.6 million rubles.

3. In addition, investment in unrecorded stock, that entered in the balance, was as follows:

	1928	1929	1930
Total	193.9	347.3	490.1
1. In census industry	160.6	272.6	347.9
2. In transport	1.0	31.3	47.3
3. In agriculture	-	-	11.6
4. Stock allocated for social purposes	32.3	43.4	83.3

Sub-section B

Table 5. Rate of growth of investment in fixed capital stock by branch of the economy and by sector (in % of previous year, in current prices)

A	Socialist sector[1] 1929	1930	1931	1931 in relation to 1928	Private sector 1929	1930	1931	1931 in relation to 1928	Both sectors 1929	1930	1931	1931 in relation to 1928
	1	2	3	4	5	6	7	8	9	10	11	12
Total for economy												
a) excluding livestock	138.8	170.4	156.0	367.8	94.5	55.0	95.4	49.5	122.1	136.6	148.8	247.4
	141.6	179.5	158.1	389.0								
b) including livestock	141.0	176.5	157.3	390.6	80.1	63.3	105.9	53.6	112.4	136.9	150.6	231.2
	146.6	193.5	172.5	475.5								
I. Productive stock												
a) excluding livestock	144.2	180.9	-	-	97.0	55.6	-	-	130.3	153.5	-	-
	147.8	189.5										
b) including livestock	147.2	188.7	-	-	73.0	69.8	-	-	114.6	152.7	-	-
	154.6	207.1										
1. In census industry	137.1	172.8	163.4	387.0	-	-	-	-	137.1	172.8	163.4	387.0
2. In small-scale industry	153.6	68.0	-	-	89.4	25.8	-	-	134.7	59.7	-	-
	238.7	283.2										
3. In agriculture												
a) excluding livestock	235.2	296.6	162.5	1133.6	97.1	55.8	64.7	35.1	118.9	131.1	133.8	208.5
	247.1	308.9	175.6	1340.1								
b) including livestock	249.4	318.5	166.8	1325.1	72.9	70.0	93.6	47.8	89.8	133.6	144.3	173.2
	292.3	359.4	217.7	2287.0								
4. In transport	128.0	142.9	-	-	-	-	-	-	128.0	142.9	-	-
5. In trade	226.4	220.9	174.8	874.0	-	-	-	-	226.4	220.9	174.8	874.0
II. Consumption stock	124.9	139.3	-	-	92.2	54.5	-	-	107.8	101.3	-	-
	125.6	149.3										
1. Communications stock	131.4	134.3	190.7	336.4	-	-	-	-	131.4	134.3	190.7	336.4
2. Stock allocated for social purposes	135.3	106.2	-	-	-	-	-	-	135.3	106.2	-	-
3. Housing stock	114.6	175.7	-	-	92.2	54.5	-	-	99.1	98.0	-	-
	116.2	196.6										
a) urban	114.4	164.2	-	-	94.5	55.8	-	-	108.0	133.6	-	-
b) rural	117.7	451.0	163.3	867.0	91.6	54.2	137.5	68.2	92.1	65.2	142.4	85.6
	148.4	648.3	133.5	1283.6								

1. In the socialist sector what is shown in the numerator is the growth of capital investment only, but in the denominator what is shown is the growth of capital investment together with receipts through socialisation from the stock of the private sector.

Sub-section B

Table 5a. Rate of growth of investment in fixed capital stock by branch of the economy and by sector (in % of previous year, in 1928 prices)

A	Socialist sector[1]				Private sector				Both sectors			
	1929	1930	1931	1931 in relation to 1928	1929	1930	1931	1931 in relation to 1928	1929	1930	1931	1931 in relation to 1928
	1	2	3	4	5	6	7	8	9	10	11	12
Total for economy												
a) excluding livestock	144.1	180.2	145.9	378.9	92.0	56.5	93.4	48.5	124.4	145.6	140.2	253.9
	146.9	188.5	144.2	399.3								
b) including livestock	145.9	182.4	144.6	384.9	79.7	62.6	88.9	44.4	115.1	143.7	138.5	228.9
	151.4	196.2	146.1	433.9								
I. Productive stock												
a) excluding livestock	148.8	190.0	-	-	94.3	57.5	-	-	132.7	162.2	-	-
	152.3	197.6										
b) including livestock	151.2	192.5	-	-	73.8	67.7	-	-	117.4	158.1	-	-
	158.3	207.1										
1. In census industry	143.4	188.8	152.1	411.7	-	-	-	-	143.4	188.8	152.1	411.7
2. In small-scale industry	153.6	68.0	-	-	89.4	23.8	-	-	134.7	59.7	-	-
	238.7	283.2										
3. In agriculture												
a) excluding livestock	242.4	294.9	163.2	1164.2	94.3	57.8	64.3	35.1	117.7	134.7	134.5	213.3
	253.2	305.3	175.6	1357.7								
b) including livestock	250.1	289.2	152.7	1104.2	73.8	68.0	68.5	34.4	105.0	129.4	128.2	151.0
	291.4	322.4	173.1	1626.3								
4. In transport	128.4	141.8	-	-	-	-	-	-	128.4	141.8	-	-
5. In trade	235.4	232.2	160.9	879.3	-	-	-	-	235.4	232.2	160.9	879.3
II. Consumption stock	132.3	152.5	-	-	89.7	55.5	-	-	110.0	141.1	-	-
	133.0	166.7										
1. Communications stock	137.6	145.8	165.1	331.2	-	-	-	-	137.6	145.8	165.1	331.2
2. Stock allocated for social purposes	141.7	112.8	-	-	-	-	-	-	141.7	112.8	-	-
3. Housing stock	123.1	195.3	-	-	89.7	55.5	--	-	100.1	108.9	-	-
	124.7	213.9										
a) urban	123.2	183.8	-	-	97.4	52.1	-	-	114.9	147.8	-	-
b) rural	120.2	185.7	167.3	976.1	87.7	56.4	137.5	68.0	88.4	69.1	143.7	87.8
	151.3	657.0	136.2	1353.1								

1. In the socialist sector what is shown in the numerator is the rate of growth of capital investment only, but in the denominator what is shown is the growth of capital investment together with receipts through socialisation from the stock of the private sector.

Sub-section B

Table 6. Share of sectors in investments in fixed capital stock by branch of the economy (in current prices)

A	1928			1929			1930			1931		
	Socialist sector	Private sector	Total	Socialist sector	Private sector	Total	Socialist sector	Private sector	Total	Socialist sector	Private sector	Total
	1	2	3	4	5	6	7	8	9	10	11	12
Total for economy												
a) excluding livestock	62.2	37.8	100.0	70.7	29.3	100.0	88.2	11.8	100.0	92.4	7.6	100.0
b) including livestock[1]	54.7	45.3	100.0	68.0	32.0	100.0	85.6	14.4	100.0	89.8	10.2	100.0
I. Productive stock												
a) excluding livestock	70.6	39.4	100.0	78.1	21.9	100.0	92.1	7.9	100.0	-	-	-
b) including livestock[1]	58.0	42.0	100.0	73.6	24.4	100.0	88.3	11.7	100.0	-	-	-
1. In census industry	100.0	-	100.0	100.0	-	100.0	100.0	-	100.0	100.0	-	100.0
2. In small-scale industry	70.6	29.4	100.0	80.5	19.5	100.0	91.6	8.4	100.0	-	-	-
3. In agriculture												
a) excluding livestock	15.8	84.2	100.0	31.2	68.8	100.0	70.7	29.3	100.0	85.6	14.4	100.0
b) including livestock[1]	11.5	88.5	100.0	30.8	69.2	100.0	67.0	33.0	100.0	78.3	21.7	100.0
4. In transport	100.0	-	100.0	100.0	-	100.0	100.0	-	100.0	-	-	-
5. In trade	47.7	52.3	100.0	55.2	44.8	100.0	75.9	24.1	100.0	100.0	-	100.0
II. Consumption stock												
1. Communications stock	100.0	-	100.0	100.0	-	100.0	100.0	-	100.0	100.0	-	100.0
2. Stock allocated to social purposes	100.0	-	100.0	100.0	-	100.0	100.0	-	100.0	-	-	-
3. Housing stock	31.1	68.9	100.0	35.9	64.1	100.0	64.4	35.6	100.0	-	-	-
a) urban	67.8	32.2	100.0	71.8	28.2	100.0	88.2	11.8	100.0	-	-	-
b) rural	2.2	97.8	100.0	2.8	97.2	100.0	19.3	80.7	100.0	22.1	77.9	100.0

1. In calculating the share of the sectors we started from the total obtained by adding the sectors together (see note 2 to Table 4).

Sub-section B

Table 6a. Share of sectors in investments in fixed capital stock by branch of the economy (in 1928 prices)

A	1928 Socialist sector	Private sector	Total	1929 Socialist sector	Private sector	Total	1930 Socialist sector	Private sector	Total	1931 Socialist sector	Private sector	Total
	1	2	3	4	5	6	7	8	9	10	11	12
Total for economy												
a) excluding livestock	62.2	37.8	100.0	72.0	28.0	100.0	89.1	10.9	100.0	92.8	7.2	100.0
b) including livestock[1]	54.7	45.3	100.0	68.9	31.1	100.0	86.6	13.4	100.0	91.3	8.7	100.0
I. Productive stock												
a) excluding livestock	70.6	29.4	100.0	79.1	20.9	100.0	92.6	7.4	100.0	-	-	-
b) including livestock[1]	58.0	42.0	100.0	73.9	26.1	100.0	88.9	11.1	100.0	-	-	-
1. In census industry	100.0	-	100.0	100.0	-	100.0	100.0	-	100.0	100.0	-	100.0
2. In small-scale industry	70.6	29.4	100.0	80.5	19.5	100.0	91.6	8.4	100.0	-	-	-
3. In agriculture												
a) excluding livestock	15.8	84.2	100.0	32.5	67.5	100.0	71.0	29.0	100.0	86.2	13.8	100.0
b) including livestock[1]	11.5	88.5	100.0	30.7	69.3	100.0	65.3	34.7	100.0	80.7	19.3	100.0
4. In transport	100.0	-	100.0	100.0	-	100.0	100.0	-	100.0	-	-	100.0
5. In trade	100.0	-	100.0	100.0	-	100.0	100.0	-	100.0	100.0	-	100.0
II. Consumption stock	47.7	52.3	100.0	57.3	42.7	100.0	78.7	21.3	100.0	-	-	-
1. Communications stock	100.0	-	100.0	100.0	-	100.0	100.0	-	100.0	100.0	-	-
2. Stock allocated to social purposes	100.0	-	100.0	100.0	-	100.0	100.0	-	100.0	-	-	100.0
3. Housing stock	31.1	68.9	100.0	38.2	61.8	100.0	65.5	31.5	100.0	-	-	-
a) urban	67.8	32.2	100.0	72.7	27.3	100.0	90.4	9.6	100.0	-	-	-
b) rural	2.2	97.8	100.0	3.0	97.0	100.0	20.8	79.2	100.0	24.2	75.8	100.0

1. In calculating the share of the sectors we started from the total obtained by adding the sectors together (see note 2 to Table 4a).

Sub-section C: Production

Table 1. Production of material goods (in million rubles, in producer's prices) grouped by branch and by [predominant] economic end-use

A	Years	In current prices					In 1928 prices				
		Means of production			Consumer goods	Total	Means of production			Consumer goods	Total
		Fixed	Raw material, auxiliary material, fuel	Total			Fixed	Raw material, auxiliary material, fuel	Total		
B		1	2	3	4	5	6	7	8	9	10
1. Census industry	1928	1418.2	10793.9	12212.1	7032.9	19245.0	1418.2	10793.9	12212.1	7032.9	19245.0
	1929	2046.4	13029.6	15076.0	8285.8	23361.8	2004.8	13319.6	15324.4	8163.8	23488.2
	1930	2933.7	15572.4	18506.1	10179.9	28686.0	2979.7	16302.5	19282.2	9856.9	29139.1
2. Small-scale industry	1928	229.4	886.1	1115.5	4753.2	5868.7	229.4	886.1	1115.5	4753.2	5868.7
	1929	262.3	927.5	1189.8	5157.1	6346.9	230.4	814.8	1045.2	4660.7	5705.9
	1930	240.6	890.8	1131.4	5461.1	6592.5	206.4	764.8	971.2	4878.1	5849.3
3. Building	1928	2154.9	-	2154.9	2084.2	4239.1	2154.9	-	2154.9	2084.2	4239.1
	1929	2797.3	-	2797.3	2228.0	5025.3	2933.7	-	2933.6	2273.3	5207.0
	1930	4414.9	-	4414.9	2280.2	6695.1	2902.3	-	4902.3	2569.7	7472.0
4. Agriculture	1928	2807.7	9141.7	11949.4	7291.9	19241.3	2807.7	9141.7	11949.4	7291.9	19241.3
	1929	2448.6	9750.6	12199.2	8135.0	20334.2	2593.7	9201.8	11795.5	7600.3	19395.8
	1930	2976.2	10692.2	13668.4	10438.8	24107.2	2137.8	9569.4	11707.2	7244.1	18951.3
5. Forestry	1928	-	703.3	703.3	708.0	1411.3	-	703.3	703.3	708.0	1411.3
	1929	-	946.0	946.0	795.9	1741.9	-	938.3	938.3	765.5	1703.8
	1930	-	1077.1	1077.1	746.2	1823.3	-	1097.1	1097.1	727.6	1824.7
6. Other branches (fishing, hunting, etc.)	1928	-	433.8	433.8	1078.3	1512.1	-	433.8	433.8	1078.3	1512.1
	1929	-	474.8	474.8	1115.3	1590.1	-	464.2	464.2	999.0	1463.2
	1930	-	599.8	599.8	1322.6	1922.4	-	614.3	614.3	903.0	1517.3
Total for economy	1928	6610.2	21958.8	28569.0	22948.5	51517.5	6610.2	21958.8	28569.0	22948.5	51517.5
	1929	7554.6	25128.5	32683.1	25717.1	58400.2	7762.6	24738.7	32501.3	24462.6	56963.9
	1930	10565.4	28832.3	39397.7	30428.8	69826.5	10226.2	28348.1	38574.3	26179.4	64753.7

Sub-section C

Table 1a. Production of material goods (grouped by branch and by [predominant] economic end-use) rate of growth of production in %

		In current prices					In 1928 prices				
		Means of production					Means of production				
	Years	Fixed	Raw material, auxiliary material, fuel	Total	Consumer goods	Total	Fixed	Raw material, auxiliary material, fuel	Total	Consumer goods	Total
A	B	1	2	3	4	5	6	7	8	9	10
1. Census industry											
a) as % of previous year	1929	144.3	120.7	123.5	117.8	121.4	141.4	123.4	125.5	116.1	122.0
	1930	143.4	119.5	122.8	122.9	122.8	148.6	122.4	125.8	120.7	124.1
b) 1930 as % of 1928		206.9	144.3	151.5	144.7	149.1	210.1	151.0	157.9	140.2	151.4
2. Small-scale industry											
a) as % of previous year	1929	114.3	104.7	106.7	108.5	108.1	100.4	92.0	93.7	98.1	97.2
	1930	91.7	96.5	95.1	103.9	103.9	89.6	93.0	92.9	104.7	102.5
b) 1930 as % of 1928		104.9	100.5	101.4	114.9	112.3	90.0	86.3	87.1	102.6	99.7
3. Building											
a) as % of previous year	1929	129.8	–	129.8	106.9	118.5	136.1	–	136.1	109.1	122.8
	1930	157.8	–	157.8	102.3	133.2	167.1	–	167.1	113.0	143.6
b) 1930 as % of 1928		204.9	–	204.9	109.4	157.9	227.5	–	227.5	125.3	176.3
4. Agriculture											
a) as % of previous year	1929	87.2	106.7	102.1	111.6	105.7	92.4	100.7	98.7	104.2	100.8
	1930	121.5	109.7	112.0	128.3	118.6	82.4	104.0	99.3	95.3	97.7
b) 1930 as % of 1928		106.0	117.0	114.4	143.2	125.3	76.1	104.7	98.0	99.3	98.5
5. Forestry											
a) as % of previous year	1929	–	134.5	134.5	112.4	123.4	–	133.4	133.4	108.1	120.7
	1930	–	113.9	113.9	93.8	104.7	–	116.9	116.9	95.0	107.1
b) 1930 as % of 1928		–	153.1	153.1	105.4	129.2	–	156.0	156.0	102.8	129.3
6. Other branches											
a) as % of previous year	1929	–	109.5	109.5	103.4	105.2	–	107.0	107.0	92.6	96.8
	1930	–	126.3	126.3	118.6	120.9	–	132.3	132.3	90.4	103.7
b) 1930 as % of 1928		–	138.3	138.3	122.7	127.1	–	141.6	141.6	83.7	100.3
Total for economy											
a) as % of previous year	1929	114.3	114.4	114.4	112.1	113.4	117.4	112.7	113.8	106.6	110.6
	1930	139.9	114.7	120.5	118.3	119.6	131.7	114.6	118.7	107.0	113.7
b) 1930 as % of 1928		159.8	131.3	137.9	132.6	135.5	154.7	129.1	135.0	114.1	125.7

Sub-section C

Table 1b. Production of material goods (grouped by branch and by [predominant] economic end-use) structure by [predominant] economic end-use, in %

A	B	In current prices Means of production Fixed (1)	Raw material, auxiliary material, fuel (2)	Total (3)	Consumer goods (4)	Total (5)	In 1928 prices Means of production Fixed (6)	Raw material, auxiliary material, fuel (7)	Total (8)	Consumer goods (9)	Total (10)
1. Census industry	1928	7.4	56.1	63.5	36.5	100.0	7.4	56.1	63.5	36.5	100.0
	1929	8.7	55.8	64.5	35.5	100.0	8.5	56.7	65.2	34.8	100.0
	1930	10.2	54.3	64.5	35.5	100.0	10.2	56.0	66.2	33.8	100.0
2. Small-scale industry	1928	3.9	15.1	19.0	81.0	100.0	3.9	15.1	19.0	81.0	100.0
	1929	4.1	14.6	18.7	81.3	100.0	4.0	14.3	18.3	81.7	100.0
	1930	3.7	13.5	17.2	82.8	100.0	3.5	13.1	16.6	83.4	100.0
3. Building	1928	50.8	-	50.8	49.2	100.0	50.8	-	50.8	49.2	100.0
	1929	55.7	-	55.7	44.3	100.0	56.3	-	56.3	43.7	100.0
	1930	65.9	-	65.9	34.1	100.0	65.6	-	65.6	34.4	100.0
4. Agriculture	1928	14.6	47.5	62.1	37.9	100.0	14.6	47.5	62.1	37.9	100.0
	1929	12.0	48.0	60.0	40.0	100.0	13.4	47.4	60.8	39.2	100.0
	1930	12.3	44.4	56.7	43.3	100.0	11.3	50.5	61.8	38.2	100.0
5. Forestry	1928	-	49.8	49.8	50.2	100.0	-	49.8	49.8	50.2	100.0
	1929	-	54.3	54.3	45.7	100.0	-	55.1	55.1	44.9	100.0
	1930	-	59.1	59.1	40.9	100.0	-	60.1	60.1	39.9	100.0
6. Other branches (fishing, hunting etc.)	1928	-	28.7	28.7	71.3	100.0	-	28.7	28.7	71.3	100.0
	1929	-	29.9	29.9	70.1	100.0	-	31.7	31.7	68.3	100.0
	1930	-	31.2	31.2	68.8	100.0	-	40.5	40.5	59.5	100.0
Total for economy	1928	12.8	42.6	55.4	44.6	100.0	12.8	42.6	55.4	44.6	100.0
	1929	13.0	43.0	56.0	44.0	100.0	13.6	43.4	57.0	43.0	100.0
	1930	15.1	41.3	56.4	43.6	100.0	15.8	43.8	59.6	40.4	100.0

Sub-section C

Table 2. Production of material goods (in million rubles, in producer's prices) grouped by branch, sector and [predominant] economic end-use

A	Years	In current prices								
		Socialist sector			Private sector			Total		
		Means of production	Consumer goods	Total	Means of production	Consumer goods	Total	Means of production	Consumer goods	Total
	B	1	2	3	4	5	6	7	8	9
1. Census industry	1928	12085.3	6962.6	19047.9	126.8	70.3	197.1	12212.1	7032.8	19245.0
	1929	14977.3	8239.4	23216.7	98.7	46.4	145.1	15076.0	8285.8	23361.8
	1930	18473.4	10159.5	28632.9	32.7	20.4	53.1	18506.1	10179.9	28686.0
2. Small-scale industry	1928	167.3	1475.9	1643.2	948.2	3277.3	4225.5	1115.3	4753.2	5868.7
	1929	342.7	2513.4	2856.1	847.1	2643.7	3490.8	1189.8	5157.1	6346.9
	1930	627.6	3406.8	4034.4	503.8	2054.3	2558.1	1131.4	5461.1	6592.5
3. Building	1928	1592.9	936.8	2529.7	562.0	1147.4	1709.4	2154.9	2084.2	4239.1
	1929	2261.3	1170.4	3431.7	536.0	1057.6	1593.6	2797.3	2228.0	5025.3
	1930	4130.4	1703.9	5834.3	284.5	576.3	860.8	4414.9	2280.2	6695.1
4. Agriculture	1928	305.0	105.5	410.5	11644.4	7186.4	18830.8	11949.4	7291.9	19241.3
	1929	749.2	178.3	927.5	11450.5	7956.7	19406.7	12199.2	8135.0	20334.2
	1930	3262.9	1016.5	4279.4	10405.5	9422.3	19827.8	13668.4	10458.8	24107.2
5. Forestry	1928	405.7	190.0	595.7	297.6	518.0	815.6	703.3	708.0	1411.3
	1929	711.9	288.1	1000.0	234.1	507.8	741.9	946.0	795.9	1741.9
	1930	962.4	307.4	1269.8	114.7	458.8	553.5	1077.1	746.2	1823.3
6. Other branches (fishing, hunting etc.)	1928	115.9	150.7	266.6	317.9	927.6	1245.5	433.8	1078.3	1512.1
	1929	155.5	200.9	356.4	319.3	914.4	1233.7	474.8	1115.3	1590.1
	1930	395.7	356.6	752.3	204.1	966.0	1170.1	599.8	1322.6	1922.4
Total for economy	1928	14672.1	9821.5	24493.6	13896.9	13127.0	27023.9	28569.0	22948.5	51517.5
	1929	19197.9	12590.5	31788.4	13485.2	13126.6	26611.8	32683.1	25717.1	58400.2
	1930	27852.4	16950.7	44803.1	11545.3	13478.1	25023.4	39397.7	30428.8	69826.5

Sub-section C

Table 2a. Production of material goods (in million rubles, in producer's prices) grouped by branch, sector and [predominant] economic end-use

		In 1928 prices								
		Socialist sector			Private sector			Total		
	Years	Means of production	Consumer goods	Total	Means of production	Consumer goods	Total	Means of production	Consumer goods	Total
A	B	1	2	3	4	5	6	7	8	9
1. Census industry	1928	12085.3	6962.6	19047.9	126.8	70.3	197.5	12212.1	7032.9	19245.0
	1929	15224.2	8118.1	23342.3	100.2	45.7	145.9	15324.4	8163.8	23488.2
	1930	19248.1	9857.1	29085.2	34.1	19.8	53.9	19282.2	9856.9	29139.1
2. Small-scale industry	1928	1167.3	1475.9	1643.2	948.2	3277.3	4225.5	1115.5	4753.3	5868.7
	1929	332.1	2435.4	2767.5	713.1	2225.3	2938.4	1045.2	4660.7	5705.9
	1930	583.7	3297.5	3881.2	387.5	1580.6	1968.1	971.2	4878.1	5849.3
3. Building	1928	1592.9	936.8	2529.7	562.8	1147.4	1709.4	2154.9	2084.2	4239.1
	1929	2420.0	1244.0	3664.0	513.7	1029.3	1543.0	2933.7	2273.3	5207.0
	1930	4618.4	1998.7	6617.1	283.9	571.0	854.9	4902.3	2569.7	7472.0
4. Agriculture	1928	305.7	107.6	413.3	11643.7	7184.3	18828.0	11949.4	7291.9	19241.3
	1929	747.3	174.8	992.2	11048.1	7425.5	18473.6	11795.5	7600.3	19395.8
	1930	3037.2	961.2	3998.4	8670.0	6282.9	14952.9	11707.2	7244.1	18951.3
5. Forestry	1928	422.2	219.8	642.0	281.1	488.2	769.3	703.3	708.0	1411.3
	1929	718.3	301.3	1019.6	220.0	464.2	684.2	938.3	765.5	1703.8
	1930	988.7	303.4	1292.1	108.4	424.2	532.6	1097.1	727.6	1824.7
6. Other branches (fishing, hunting etc.)	1928	115.9	150.7	266.6	317.9	927.6	1245.5	433.8	1078.3	1512.1
	1929	157.7	202.0	359.7	306.5	797.0	1103.5	464.2	999.0	1463.2
	1930	412.7	339.9	752.6	201.6	563.1	764.7	614.3	903.0	1517.3
Total for economy	1928	14689.3	9853.4	24542.7	13879.7	13095.1	26974.8	28569.0	22948.5	51517.5
	1929	19599.7	12475.6	32075.3	12901.6	11987.0	24888.6	32501.3	24462.6	56963.9
	1930	28888.8	16737.8	45626.6	9685.5	9441.6	19127.1	38574.3	26179.4	64753.7

Sub-section C

Table 2b. Production of material goods (grouped by branch, sector and [predominant] economic end-use) rate of growth of production in %

A	In current prices						In 1928 prices					
	Socialist sector			Private sector			Socialist sector			Private sector		
	Means of production	Consumer goods	Total	Means of production	Consumer goods	Total	Means of production	Consumer goods	Total	Means of production	Consumer goods	Total
	1	2	3	4	5	6	7	8	9	10	11	12
1. Census industry												
a) as % of previous year 1929	123.9	118.3	121.9	77.8	66.0	73.6	126.0	116.6	122.5	79.0	65.0	74.0
1930	123.3	123.3	123.3	33.1	44.0	36.6	126.4	121.2	124.6	31.0	43.3	36.9
b) 1930 as % of 1928	152.9	146.0	150.3	25.8	29.0	26.9	159.3	141.3	152.7	26.9	28.2	27.3
2. Small-scale industry												
a) as % of previous year 1929	204.8	170.3	173.8	89.3	80.7	82.6	198.5	165.0	168.4	75.2	67.9	69.5
1930	185.1	135.5	141.3	59.5	77.7	73.3	175.8	135.4	140.2	54.3	71.0	67.0
b) 1930 as % of 1928	375.1	230.8	245.5	53.1	62.7	60.5	348.9	222.0	236.2	40.9	48.2	46.3
3. Building												
a) as % of previous year 1929	142.0	124.9	135.7	95.4	92.	93.2	153.9	132.8	144.8	91.4	89.7	90.3
1930	182.7	145.6	170.0	53.1	54.5	54.0	190.8	160.7	180.6	55.3	55.5	55.4
b) 1930 as % of 1928	259.3	181.9	230.6	50.6	50.2	50.4	289.9	213.4	261.6	50.5	49.8	50.0
4. Agriculture												
a) as % of previous year 1929	245.6	169.0	225.9	98.3	110.7	103.1	244.5	162.5	223.1	94.9	103.4	98.1
1930	435.5	570.1	461.4	90.9	118.4	102.2	406.4	549.9	433.6	78.5	84.6	80.9
b) 1930 as % of 1928	1069.8	963.5	1042.5	89.4	131.1	105.3	993.5	893.3	967.4	74.5	87.5	79.4
5. Forestry												
a) as % of previous year 1929	175.5	151.6	167.3	78.7	98.0	92.0	170.1	137.1	158.8	78.3	95.1	88.9
1930	135.2	106.7	127.0	49.0	86.4	74.6	137.6	100.7	126.7	49.3	91.4	77.8
b) 1930 as % of 1928	237.2	161.8	213.2	38.5	84.7	67.9	234.2	138.0	201.3	38.6	86.9	69.2
6. Other branches												
a) as % of previous year 1929	134.1	133.3	133.4	100.4	98.6	99.1	136.1	134.0	131.9	96.4	85.9	88.6
1930	154.5	177.5	211.1	63.9	105.6	94.8	261.7	168.3	209.2	65.8	70.7	69.3
b) 1930 as % of 1928	341.4	236.6	282.2	64.2	104.1	93.9	356.1	225.5	282.3	63.4	60.7	61.4
Total economy												
a) as % of previous year 1929	130.8	128.2	129.8	97.0	100.0	98.5	133.4	126.6	130.7	93.0	91.5	92.3
1930	145.1	131.6	140.9	85.6	102.7	94.0	147.4	134.2	142.2	75.1	78.8	76.9
b) 1930 as % of 1928	189.8	172.6	182.9	83.1	102.7	92.6	196.7	169.9	185.9	69.8	72.1	70.9

Sub-section C

Table 2c. Production of material goods (grouped by branch, sector and [predominant] economic end-use) in %

		In current prices						In 1928 prices					
		Socialist sector		Private sector		Total		Socialist sector		Private sector		Total	
		Means of produc-tion	Consumer goods	Means of produc-tion	Consumer goods	Means of produc-tion	Consumer goods	Means of produc-tion	Consumer goods	Means of produc-tion	Consumer goods	Means of produc-tion	Consumer goods
A	B	1	2	3	4	5	6	7	8	9	10	11	12
1. Census industry	1928	63.4	36.6	64.3	35.7	63.5	36.5	63.4	36.6	64.3	35.7	63.5	36.5
	1929	64.5	35.5	68.0	32.0	64.5	35.5	65.2	34.8	68.7	31.3	65.2	34.8
	1930	64.5	35.5	61.6	38.4	64.5	35.5	66.2	33.8	63.3	36.7	66.2	33.8
2. Small-scale industry	1928	10.2	89.8	22.4	77.6	19.0	81.0	10.2	89.8	22.4	77.6	19.0	81.0
	1929	12.0	88.0	24.3	75.7	18.7	81.3	12.0	88.0	24.3	75.7	18.3	81.7
	1930	15.6	84.4	19.7	80.3	17.2	82.8	15.0	85.0	19.7	80.3	16.6	83.4
3. Building	1928	63.0	37.0	32.9	67.1	50.8	49.2	63.0	37.0	32.9	67.1	50.8	49.2
	1929	65.9	34.1	33.6	66.4	55.7	44.3	66.0	31.0	33.3	66.7	56.3	43.7
	1930	70.8	29.2	33.1	66.9	65.9	34.1	69.8	30.2	33.2	66.8	65.6	34.4
4. Agriculture	1928	74.3	25.7	61.8	38.2	62.1	37.9	74.0	26.0	61.8	38.2	62.1	37.9
	1929	80.8	19.2	59.0	41.0	60.0	40.0	81.0	19.0	59.8	40.2	60.8	39.2
	1930	76.2	23.8	52.5	47.5	56.7	43.3	76.0	24.0	58.0	42.0	61.8	38.2
5. Forestry	1928	68.1	31.9	36.5	63.5	49.8	50.2	65.8	34.2	36.5	63.5	49.8	50.2
	1929	71.2	28.8	31.6	68.4	54.3	45.7	70.4	29.6	32.2	67.8	55.1	44.9
	1930	75.8	24.2	20.7	79.3	59.1	40.9	76.5	23.5	20.4	79.6	60.1	39.9
6. Other branches (fishing, hunting etc.)	1928	43.5	56.5	25.5	74.5	28.7	71.3	43.5	56.5	25.5	74.5	28.7	71.3
	1929	43.6	56.4	25.9	74.1	29.9	70.1	43.8	56.2	27.8	72.2	31.7	68.3
	1930	52.6	47.4	17.5	82.5	31.2	68.8	54.8	45.2	26.4	73.6	40.5	59.5
Total economy	1928	59.9	40.1	51.4	48.6	55.4	44.6	59.9	40.1	51.4	48.6	55.4	44.6
	1929	60.4	39.6	50.7	49.3	56.0	44.0	61.1	38.9	51.8	48.2	57.0	43.0
	1930	62.2	37.8	46.1	53.9	56.4	43.6	63.3	36.7	50.6	49.4	59.6	40.4

Sub-section C

Table 2d. Production of material goods (grouped by branch, sector and [predominant] end-use) by sector, in %

A	B	In current prices						In 1928 prices					
		Means of production		Consumer goods		Total		Means of production		Consumer goods		Total	
		Socialist sector	Private sector	Socialist sector	Private sector	Socialist sector	Private sector	Socialist sector	Private sector	Socialist sector	Private sector	Socialist sector	Private sector
	Years	1	2	3	4	5	6	7	8	9	10	11	12
1. Census industry	1928	99.0	1.0	99.0	1.0	99.0	1.0	99.0	1.0	99.0	1.0	99.0	1.0
	1929	99.3	0.7	99.4	0.6	99.4	0.6	99.3	0.7	99.4	0.6	99.4	0.6
	1930	99.8	0.2	99.8	0.2	99.8	0.2	99.8	0.2	99.8	0.2	99.8	0.2
2. Small-scale industry	1928	15.0	85.0	31.1	68.9	28.0	72.0	15.0	85.0	31.1	68.9	28.0	72.0
	1929	28.8	71.2	48.7	51.3	45.0	55.0	31.8	68.2	52.3	47.7	48.5	51.5
	1930	55.5	44.5	62.4	37.6	61.2	38.8	60.1	39.9	67.6	32.4	66.4	33.6
3. Building	1928	73.9	26.1	44.9	55.1	59.7	40.3	73.9	26.1	44.9	55.1	59.7	40.3
	1929	80.8	19.2	52.5	47.5	68.3	31.7	82.5	17.5	54.7	45.3	70.4	29.6
	1930	93.6	6.4	74.7	25.3	87.1	12.9	94.2	5.8	77.8	22.2	88.6	11.4
4. Agriculture	1928	2.6	97.4	1.4	98.6	2.1	97.9	2.6	97.4	1.5	98.5	2.1	97.9
	1929	6.1	93.9	2.2	97.8	4.6	95.4	6.3	93.7	2.3	97.7	4.8	95.2
	1930	23.9	76.1	9.7	90.3	17.8	82.2	25.9	74.1	13.3	86.7	21.1	78.9
5. Forestry	1928	57.7	42.3	26.8	73.2	42.2	57.8	60.0	40.0	31.0	69.0	45.5	54.5
	1929	75.3	24.7	36.2	63.8	57.4	42.6	76.6	23.4	39.4	60.6	59.8	40.2
	1930	89.4	10.6	41.2	58.8	69.6	30.4	90.1	9.9	41.7	58.3	70.8	29.2
6. Other branches	1928	26.7	73.3	14.0	86.0	17.6	82.4	26.7	73.3	14.0	86.0	17.6	82.4
	1929	32.8	67.2	18.0	82.0	22.4	77.6	34.0	56.0	20.0	80.0	24.6	75.4
	1930	66.0	34.0	27.0	73.0	39.1	60.9	67.2	32.8	37.6	62.4	49.6	50.4
Total economy	1928	51.4	48.6	42.8	57.2	47.5	52.5	51.4	48.6	42.9	57.1	47.6	52.4
	1929	58.7	41.3	49.0	51.0	54.4	45.6	60.3	39.7	51.0	49.0	56.3	43.7
	1930	70.7	29.3	55.7	44.3	64.2	35.8	74.9	25.1	63.9	36.1	70.5	29.5

Table 2e. Production of material goods (grouped by branch and sector) in %

	In current prices									In 1928 prices								
	Socialist sector			Private sector			Total			Socialist sector			Private sector			Total		
A	1928	1929	1930	1928	1929	1930	1928	1929	1930	1928	1929	1930	1928	1929	1930	1928	1929	1930
	1	2	3	4	5	6	7	8	9	10	11	12	13	14	15	16	17	18
1. Census industry	77.8	73.0	63.9	0.7	0.5	0.3	37.4	40.0	41.1	77.6	72.8	63.7	0.7	0.6	0.3	37.4	41.2	45.0
2. Small-scale industry	6.7	9.0	9.0	15.6	13.1	10.2	11.4	10.9	9.4	6.7	8.6	8.5	15.7	11.9	10.3	11.4	10.0	9.0
3. Building	10.3	10.8	13.0	6.4	6.0	3.4	8.2	8.0	9.6	10.3	11.4	14.5	6.3	6.2	4.5	8.2	9.1	11.0
4. Agriculture	1.7	2.9	9.6	69.7	72.9	79.2	37.4	34.8	34.5	1.7	2.9	8.8	69.8	74.2	78.2	37.4	34.1	29.3
5. Forestry	2.4	3.1	2.8	3.0	2.9	2.2	2.7	3.0	2.6	2.6	3.2	2.8	2.9	2.7	2.8	2.7	3.0	2.8
6. Other branches (fishing, hunting, etc.)	1.1	1.2	1.7	4.6	4.6	4.7	2.9	2.7	2.8	1.1	1.1	1.7	4.6	4.4	3.9	2.9	2.6	2.3
	100.0	100.0	100.0	100.0	100.0	100.0	100.0	100.0	100.0	100.0	100.0	100.0	100.0	100.0	100.0	100.0	100.0	100.0

Sub-section C

Table 3. Gross production of agriculture (in million rubles, in current prices)

A	State farms 1928	State farms 1929	State farms 1930	Collective farms 1928	Collective farms 1929	Collective farms 1930	Total for socialist sector 1928	Total for socialist sector 1929	Total for socialist sector 1930	private sector 1928	private sector 1929	private sector 1930	Total 1928	Total 1929	Total 1930
	1	2	3	4	5	6	7	8	9	10	11	12	13	14	15
I. Arable products	206.2	252.1	569.9	152.5	546.4	3100.9	358.7	798.5	3670.8	11002.5	11262.2	9972.6	11361.2	12060.7	13643.4
A. Means of production (raw material and auxiliary materials).	163.3	205.3	463.8	114.8	474.9	2492.0	278.1	680.2	2955.0	8240.4	8317.7	7069.9	8518.5	8997.9	10025.7
1. grain	72.3	85.0	206.1	57.1	183.5	1337.0	129.4	268.5	1543.9	4320.0	4417.0	3457.1	4449.4	4685.5	5001.0
2. industrial crops	44.3	31.2	73.9	14.3	37.0	372.9	58.6	68.2	446.8	988.0	961.0	968.2	1046.6	1032.2	1415.0
3. fodder crops	24.7	31.2	90.7	14.3	45.1	455.4	39.0	76.3	546.1	2033.2	1964.1	1828.3	2072.2	2040.4	2374.4
4. incomplete production	22.0	57.9	93.1	29.1	209.3	325.9	51.1	267.2	419.0	899.2	972.6	816.3	950.3	1239.8	1235.3
B. Consumer goods (vegetable food products	42.9	46.8	106.1	37.7	71.5	608.9	80.6	118.3	715.0	2762.1	2944.5	2902.7	2842.7	3062.8	3617.7
II. Livestock products	36.4	73.7	201.9	15.4	55.3	406.7	51.8	129.0	608.6	7828.3	8144.5	9855.2	7880.1	8273.5	10463.8
A. Means of production	21.8	45.8	127.8	5.1	23.2	179.3	26.9	69.0	307.1	3404.0	3132.3	3335.6	3430.9	3201.3	3642.7
a) fixed means of production (livestock,poultry and bees in hives)	19.0	41.2	113.9	4.2	20.5	159.7	23.2	61.7	273.6	2784.5	2386.9	2702.6	2807.7	2448.6	2976.2
b) raw material	2.8	4.6	13.9	0.9	2.7	19.6	3.7	7.3	33.5	619.5	745.4	633.0	623.2	752.5	666.5
B. Consumer goods	14.6	27.9	74.1	10.3	32.1	227.4	24.9	60.0	301.5	4424.3	5012.2	6519.6	4449.2	5072.2	6821.1
a) products of slaughter	4.5	7.5	29.8	4.5	11.2	71.7	9.0	18.7	101.5	2033.1	2329.2	2573.1	2042.2	2347.9	2674.6
b) other products	10.1	20.4	44.3	5.8	20.9	155.7	15.9	41.3	200.0	2391.2	2683.0	3946.5	2407.1	2724.3	4146.5
Total	242.6	325.8	771.8	167.9	601.7	3507.6	410.5	927.5	4279.4	18830.8	19406.7	19827.8	19241.3	20334.2	24107.2
of which, A. Means of production	185.1	251.1	591.6	119.9	498.1	2671.3	305.0	749.2	3262.9	11644.4	11450.0	10405.5	11949.4	12199.2	14668.4
a) fixed means of production	19.0	41.2	113.9	4.2	20.5	159.7	23.2	61.7	273.6	2784.5	2386.9	2702.6	2807.7	2448.6	2976.2
b) raw material and auxiliary materials	166.1	209.9	477.5	115.7	477.6	2511.6	281.8	687.5	2989.3	8859.9	9063.1	7702.9	9141.7	9750.6	10692.2
B. Consumer goods	57.5	74.7	180.2	48.0	103.6	836.3	105.5	178.3	1016.5	7186.4	7956.7	9422.3	7291.9	8135.0	10438.8

Sub-section C
Table 4. Rate of growth and structure of production in census industry (in million rubles)

A	Absolute quantities						As % of previous year				Structure in %					
	In current prices			In 1928 prices			In current prices		In 1928 prices		In current prices			In 1928 prices		
	1928	1929	1930	1928	1929	1930	1929	1930	1929	1930	1928	1929	1930	1928	1929	1930
	1	2	3	4	5	6	7	8	9	10	11	12	13	14	15	16
I. Elements of fixed means of production	1418.2	2046.4	2933.7	1418.2	2005.8	2979.7	144.3	143.3	141.3	148.6	7.4	8.7	10.2	7.4	8.5	10.2
1. Machinery and equipment	1303.7	1897.3	2724.2	1303.7	1859.5	2766.2	145.5	143.6	142.6	148.8	6.8	8.1	9.5	6.8	7.9	9.5
including tractors	4.5	17.4	45.2	4.5	13.8	38.6	366.7	259.8	306.7	279.7	0.0	0.1	0.2	0.0	0.1	0.1
" agricultural machinery	157.0	224.1	339.3	157.0	221.4	343.4	142.7	151.4	141.0	155.1	0.8	1.0	1.2	0.8	0.9	1.2
" industrial machinery and equipment	660.9	980.9	1392.4	660.9	962.3	1418.9	148.4	142.0	145.6	147.4	3.4	4.2	4.9	3.4	4.1	4.9
2. Other elements of fixed means of production	114.5	149.1	209.5	114.5	146.3	213.5	129.6	151.3	127.2	156.8	0.6	0.6	0.7	0.6	0.6	0.7
II. Elements of circulating means of production	9900.8	11973.7	13974.1	9900.8	12245.7	14637.6	120.9	116.7	123.7	119.5	51.4	51.3	48.7	51.5	52.1	50.2
1. Raw material, semi-finished goods and auxiliary materials	6823.7	8290.5	9158.7	6823.7	8530.5	9775.9	121.5	110.5	125.0	114.6	35.4	35.5	31.9	35.5	36.3	33.5
a) mineral raw materials	140.0	175.5	207.7	110.0	172.0	210.4	125.4	118.3	122.9	112.3	0.7	0.8	0.7	0.7	0.7	0.7
b) metals and metal articles	1645.0	1923.4	2261.2	1645.0	1971.1	2383.8	116.9	117.6	119.8	120.9	8.5	8.2	7.9	8.6	8.4	8.2
c) products of chemical industry	465.0	538.3	737.0	465.0	544.6	770.0	115.8	136.9	117.1	141.4	2.4	2.3	2.6	2.4	2.3	2.6
d) " of woodworking	309.1	398.9	553.8	309.1	406.4	568.9	129.1	138.8	131.5	140.1	1.6	1.7	1.9	1.6	1.7	1.9
e) " of processing of textile raw material	3156.9	3879.9	3655.9	3156.9	3921.4	3791.3	122.9	94.4	124.2	96.7	16.4	16.6	12.7	16.4	16.7	13.0
f) products of processing of other vegetable raw material	342.0	370.9	456.7	342.0	411.6	462.6	108.5	123.1	120.4	112.4	1.8	1.6	1.6	1.8	1.8	1.6
g) products of processing of animal raw material	639.2	842.6	1087.2	639.2	947.9	1386.2	131.8	129.0	148.3	146.2	3.3	3.6	3.8	3.3	4.0	4.8
h) products of processing of minerals	123.9	159.4	197.1	123.9	153.7	200.6	128.7	123.7	124.1	130.5	0.7	0.7	0.7	0.7	0.7	0.7
i) agricultural products	2.6	1.6	2.1	2.6	1.6	2.1	61.5	131.3	61.5	131.3	0.0	0.0	0.0	0.0	0.0	0.0
2. Building materials	1500.3	1871.4	2592.4	1500.3	1806.1	2480.1	124.7	138.5	120.4	137.3	7.8	8.0	9.1	7.8	7.7	8.5
3. Fuel and electric power	1576.8	1811.8	2223.0	1576.0	1909.1	2381.6	114.9	122.7	121.1	124.7	8.2	7.8	7.7	8.2	8.1	8.2

Sub-section C
Table 4. (cont'd)

A	Absolute quantities						As % of previous year				Structure in %					
	In current prices			In 1928 prices			In current prices		In 1928 prices		In current prices			In 1928 prices		
	1928	1929	1930	1928	1929	1930	1929	1930	1929	1930	1928	1929	1930	1928	1929	1930
	1	2	3	4	5	6	7	8	9	10	11	12	13	14	15	16
III. Consumer goods	7032.9	8285.8	10179.9	7032.9	8163.8	9856.9	117.8	122.9	116.1	120.7	33.5	35.5	35.5	36.5	34.8	33.9
1. Food products	2404.5	2694.0	3348.8	2404.5	2554.4	3031.2	112.0	124.3	106.2	118.7	12.5	11.5	11.7	12.5	10.9	10.4
a) milling and grinding products	953.8	1020.3	1045.6	953.8	897.5	898.1	107.0	102.7	94.1	100.0	4.9	4.4	3.7	4.9	3.8	3.1
b) other industrial products	1438.4	1655.8	2269.7	1438.4	1640.1	2101.9	115.1	137.1	114.0	128.2	7.5	7.1	7.9	7.5	7.0	7.2
c) agricultural products	12.3	17.9	33.6	12.3	16.8	31.2	145.5	187.2	136.6	185.7	0.1	0.0	0.1	0.1	0.1	0.1
2. Beverages and narcotics	569.3	557.6	704.8	569.3	588.1	679.3	97.9	121.4	103.3	115.5	3.0	2.4	2.5	3.0	2.5	2.4
3. Clothing and toiletries	2963.6	3748.2	4458.2	2963.6	3729.9	4432.7	126.5	118.9	125.9	118.8	15.4	16.0	15.5	15.4	15.0	15.2
including fabrics	1841.2	2099.9	1827.9	1841.2	2096.4	1811.7	114.1	87.0	113.9	86.4	9.6	9.0	6.4	9.6	8.9	6.2
" ready made clothes and underwear	431.4	703.1	1205.8	431.4	705.2	1201.0	113.0	171.5	163.5	170.3	2.2	3.0	4.2	2.2	3.0	4.1
4. Articles of household use	260.0	303.1	435.9	260.0	300.0	442.9	116.6	143.8	115.4	147.6	1.3	1.3	1.5	1.3	1.3	1.5
5. Sanitary and hygienic articles	219.0	246.7	242.1	219.5	255.3	252.2	112.4	93.1	116.3	98.8	1.1	1.1	0.8	1.1	1.1	0.9
6. Other consumer goods	616.0	736.2	990.1	616.0	736.1	1018.6	119.5	134.5	119.5	138.4	3.2	3.2	3.5	3.2	3.1	3.5
IV. Unfinished production	566.1	687.9	858.7	566.1	699.6	873.9	121.5	121.9	123.6	124.9	3.0	2.9	2.9	2.9	3.0	3.0
V. Undistributed	327.0	368.0	759.6	327.0	374.3	791.0	112.5	206.4	114.5	211.3	1.7	1.6	2.7	1.7	1.6	2.7
Total	19245.0	23361.8	28686.0	19245.0	23489.2	29139.1	121.4	122.8	122.0	121.1	100.0	100.0	100.0	100.0	100.0	100.0

Sub-section C

Table 5. Gross production of agriculture (in million rubles, in 1928 prices)

A	State farms 1928	1929	1930	Collective farms 1928	1929	1930	Total for socialist sector 1928	1929	1930	Private sector 1928	1929	1930	Total 1928	1929	1930
	1	2	3	4	5	6	7	8	9	10	11	12	13	14	15
I. Arable products	206.9	250.8	535.1	154.3	551.3	3031.6	361.2	802.1	3566.7	11000.0	10554.9	8789.6	11361.2	11357.0	12356.3
A. Means of production (raw material and auxiliary materials)	162.6	205.8	432.1	116.1	481.0	2387.1	278.7	684.8	2819.2	8239.8	7790.3	6146.2	8518.5	8477.1	8965.4
1. grain	71.4	81.7	200.5	56.3	168.8	1321.7	127.7	250.5	1525.2	4321.7	4079.2	3238.6	4449.4	4329.7	4763.8
2. industrial crop	44.6	31.9	57.9	14.5	36.3	338.5	59.1	68.2	396.4	987.5	924.5	754.2	1046.6	992.7	1150.6
3. fodder crops	24.6	31.2	71.8	16.2	52.6	362.6	40.8	83.8	434.4	2031.4	1804.8	1306.7	2072.2	1888.6	1741.1
4. unfinished production	22.0	61.0	101.9	20.1	223.3	361.3	51.1	281.3	463.2	899.2	981.8	846.7	950.3	1266.1	1309.9
B. Consumer goods (vegetable food products)	44.3	45.0	103.0	38.2	70.3	644.5	82.5	115.3	747.5	2760.2	2764.6	2643.4	2842.7	2879.9	3390.9
II. Livestock	36.1	67.0	141.9	16.0	53.1	289.8	52.1	120.1	431.7	7828.0	7918.7	6163.3	7880.1	8038.8	6595.0
A. Means of production	21.8	40.5	88.0	5.2	20.1	130.0	27.0	60.6	218.0	3403.9	3257.8	2523.8	3430.9	3318.4	2741.8
a) fixed means of production (livestock, poultry and bees in hives)	19.0	35.9	72.3	4.2	17.5	109.1	23.2	53.4	181.4	2784.5	2540.3	1956.4	2807.7	2593.7	2137.8
b) raw material	2.8	4.6	15.7	1.0	2.6	20.9	3.8	7.2	36.6	619.4	717.5	567.4	623.2	724.7	604.0
B. Consumer goods	11.3	26.5	53.9	10.8	33.0	159.8	25.1	59.5	213.7	4424.1	4660.9	3639.5	4449.2	4720.4	3853.2
1. products of slaughter	4.3	6.7	26.3	4.8	10.5	55.0	9.1	17.2	81.3	2033.0	2394.5	1742.8	2042.1	2411.7	1824.1
2. other products	10.0	19.8	27.6	6.0	22.5	104.8	16.0	42.3	132.4	2391.1	2266.4	1896.7	2407.1	2308.7	2029.1
Total	243.0	317.8	677.0	170.3	604.4	3321.4	413.3	922.2	3998.4	18828.0	18473.6	14952.9	19241.3	19395.8	18951.3
of which, A. Means of production	184.4	246.3	520.1	121.3	501.1	2517.1	305.7	747.4	3037.2	11643.7	11048.1	8670.0	11949.4	11795.5	11707.2
a) fixed means of production	19.0	35.9	72.3	4.2	17.5	109.1	23.2	53.4	181.4	2784.5	2510.3	1956.4	2807.7	2593.7	2137.8
b) raw material and auxiliary materials	165.4	210.4	447.8	117.1	483.6	2408.0	282.5	691.0	2855.8	8859.2	8507.8	6713.6	9141.7	9201.8	9569.4
B. Consumer goods	58.6	71.5	156.0	49.0	103.3	804.3	107.6	171.8	961.2	7181.3	7425.5	6282.9	7291.9	7600.3	7244.1

Sub-section D: Consumption

Table 1. Consumption fund of material goods

A	In million rubles						As % of previous year				1930 as % of 1928	
	In current prices			In 1928 prices			In current prices		In 1928 prices		In current prices	In 1928 prices
	1928	1929	1930	1928	1929	1930	1929	1930	1929	1930		
	1	2	3	4	5	6	7	8	9	10	11	12
(a) Including consumption of housing measured by annual depreciation												
1. Total consumption fund	22768.7	25996.5	31486.3	22768.7	24030.3	21836.2	111.2	121.1	105.5	103.4	138.3	109.1
including:												
a) non-agricultural population	8925.9	10106.3	13730.2	8925.9	9427.8	9948.1	113.2	135.9	102.3	109.6	153.8	111.5
b) agricultural population	12410.6	14298.9	15820.8	12410.6	13318.2	12966.0	114.9	110.6	107.0	97.1	127.2	104.2
c) institutions	1090.5	1282.4	1548.1	1090.5	1275.8	1550.7	117.6	120.8	117.0	122.0	142.0	142.8
d) passenger transport	341.7	308.9	386.7	341.7	338.5	364.8	99.1	125.2	99.0	118.2	124.1	117.0
(b) Consumption of housing with non-agricultural population measured by quarterly rent payment (net of municipal services)												
1. Total consumption fund	23312.0	26612.4	32164.9	23312.0	21617.1	25611.6	114.2	120.9	105.6	103.6	138.0	109.4
including:												
a) non-agricultural population	9469.2	10722.2	14408.8	9469.2	9714.0	10623.5	113.2	134.4	102.6	109.3	152.2	112.2

Sub-section D

Table 2. Consumption fund of material goods, by groups of products (in million rubles) total population

A	In current prices			In 1928 prices Evaluating fund of agricultural population in rural prices			Evaluating fund of agricultural population in urban prices		
	1928	1929	1930	1928	1929	1930	1928	1929	1930
	1	2	3	4	5	6	7	8	9
I. Food products	12097.4	13773.3	17151.8	12097.4	12515.1	12488.9	21118.0	21760.2	21313.6
1. agricultural products	6787.7	7710.2	10115.1	6787.7	7192.4	6723.0	12726.8	13346.0	12519.8
a)arable products	1774.9	2149.4	2763.6	1774.9	1977.0	2242.9	3886.7	4195.9	4612.8
b)livestock "	5012.8	5560.8	7351.5	5012.8	5215.4	4480.1	8840.1	9150.1	7937.0
2. grain products (flour,groats, baked bread)	3336.3	3825.3	3837.3	3336.3	3273.1	3469.0	6412.4	6359.1	6461.7
3. industrial food products	1973.4	2237.8	3199.4	1973.4	2049.6	2296.9	1978.8	2055.1	2302.1
II. Clothing and footwear	4307.9	5119.8	5467.3	4307.9	4807.9	4898.1	4307.9	4807.9	4898.1
III. Drink and tobacco	1930.2	2211.6	3360.7	1930.2	1913.7	2084.2	2272.2	2238.9	2272.1
IV. Fuel,lighting and water	958.1	1092.0	1196.2	958.1	1028.8	1087.5	1254.1	1329.4	1388.6
V. Household articles	415.2	440.3	563.2	415.2	438.8	565.8	415.2	438.8	565.8
VI. Cultural goods	312.8	360.7	419.6	312.8	360.7	419.6	312.8	360.7	419.6
VII. Other products	315.0	366.0	344.9	315.0	339.5	321.4	315.0	339.5	321.4
Total	20336.6	23363.7	28503.7	20336.6	21404.5	21865.5	29995.2	31275.4	31179.2
VIII. Housing	1573.2	1657.4	1725.9	1573.2	1628.3	1724.6	1573.2	1628.3	1724.6
Total	21909.8	25021.1	30229.6	21909.8	23032.8	23590.1	31568.4	32903.7	32903.8
of which: a) agricultural products	7067.6	8050.8	10368.3	7067.6	7475.9	6927.1	13006.7	13628.5	12753.9
b) industrial goods	9932.7	11487.6	14298.1	9932.7	10656.5	11469.4	10576.1	11287.8	11963.6
Total,less drink	20422.6	23317.6	27532.1	20422.6	21620.3	22078.8	29739.2	31166.0	31204.6
of which: a) agricultural products	7018.1	8010.9	10368.3	7018.1	7439.6	6927.1	12957.2	13593.2	12753.9
b) industrial goods	8495.0	9834.0	11600.6	8495.0	9279.3	9958.1	8796.1	9585.4	10264.4
Numbers of the population (in millions)	151.4	154.9	158.1	-	-	-	-	-	-
Consumption her head (in rubles)	144.7	161.5	191.2	144.7	148.7	149.2	208.5	212.4	208.1

Materialy

Sub-section D

Table 2a. Consumption fund of material goods, by groups of products. Total population. Rate of growth of fund in %

	As % of previous year						1930 as % of 1928		
	In current prices		In 1928 prices					In 1928 prices	
			Evaluating consumption by agricultural population in rural prices		Evaluating consumption by agricultural population in urban prices		In current prices	Evaluating consumption by agricultural population in rural prices	Evaluating consumption by agricultural population in urban prices
	1929	1930	1929	1930	1929	1930			
A	1	2	3	4	5	6	7	8	9
I. Food products	113.8	124.5	103.4	99.8	103.0	97.9	141.8	103.2	100.9
1. Agricultural products	113.6	131.2	106.0	93.5	104.9	94.0	149.0	99.0	98.6
a) arable products	121.2	128.6	111.4	113.5	108.0	109.9	155.7	126.4	118.7
b) livestock products	110.9	132.2	102.0	85.9	103.5	86.7	146.6	89.4	89.8
2. Grain products (flour,groats,baked bread)	114.6	100.3	98.4	106.0	99.2	101.6	115.0	104.0	100.8
3. Industrial food products	113.4	143.0	103.9	112.1	103.9	112.0	162.1	116.4	116.3
II. Clothing and footwear	113.8	106.8	111.6	102.0	111.6	101.9	126.9	113.7	113.7
III. Drink and tobacco	115.1	152.0	99.1	108.9	98.5	101.5	174.1	108.0	100.0
IV. Fuel,lighting,water	114.0	109.5	107.4	105.7	106.0	104.5	124.9	113.5	110.7
V. Household articles	106.0	127.9	105.7	128.9	105.7	128.9	135.6	136.3	136.3
VI. Cultural goods	115.3	116.3	115.3	116.3	115.3	116.3	134.1	134.1	134.1
VII. Other products	116.2	94.2	107.8	95.0	107.8	94.7	109.5	102.0	102.0
Total	114.9	122.0	105.3	102.2	104.3	99.7	140.2	107.5	103.9
VIII. Housing	105.4	104.1	103.5	105.2	103.5	105.9	110.3	109.6	109.6
Total	114.2	120.8	105.1	102.4	104.2	100.0	138.0	107.8	104.2
of which: a) agricultural products	113.9	128.8	105.8	93.0	104.8	93.6	146.7	98.0	98.1
b) industrial goods	115.6	124.5	107.3	107.5	106.5	106.0	143.9	115.5	113.4
Total,less drink	114.2	118.0	105.9	102.1	104.8	100.1	134.8	108.1	104.9
of which: a) agricultural products	114.1	129.4	106.0	93.1	104.9	93.8	147.7	98.7	98.4
b) industrial goods	115.8	118.0	109.2	107.3	109.0	104.1	136.6	117.2	116.7
Numbers of the population	102.3	102.1	-	-	-	-	104.4	-	-
Consumption per head	111.6	118.4	102.8	100.3	101.9	98.0	132.4	103.1	99.8

Note: The dynamic of consumption in constant prices emerges differently as between the two variants because, owing to the different methods of evaluation, there is a marked difference in the share of certain groups of products, and of particular products within a group (see Table 8a.)

Sub-section D

Table 3. Consumption fund of material goods, by groups of products. Manual workers.

A	In millions of rubles						As % of previous year				1930 as % of 1928	
	In current prices			In 1928 prices			In current prices		In 1928 prices		In current prices	In 1928 prices
	1928	1929	1930	1928	1929	1930	1929	1930	1929	1930		
	1	2	3	4	5	6	7	8	9	10	11	12
I. Food products	1828.3	2260.6	3464.2	1828.3	1999.3	2347.7	123.6	153.2	109.4	117.4	189.5	128.4
1. Agricultural products	995.6	1235.7	1862.0	995.6	1097.0	1119.9	124.1	150.7	120.2	102.1	187.0	112.5
including: a) arable products	227.9	329.2	513.0	227.9	303.5	385.1	144.4	155.8	133.2	126.9	225.1	169.0
b) livestock products	767.7	906.5	1349.0	767.7	793.5	734.8	118.1	148.8	103.4	92.6	175.7	95.7
2. Grain products (flour,groats,baked bread)	422.2	499.3	698.2	422.2	431.2	573.5	118.3	140.0	102.1	133.0	165.4	135.8
3. Industrial food products	410.5	525.6	904.0	410.5	471.1	654.3	128.0	172.0	114.8	138.9	220.2	159.4
II. Clothing and footwear	692.7	822.3	976.6	692.7	785.6	956.0	118.7	118.8	113.6	121.7	141.0	138.0
III. Drink and tobacco	447.5	467.3	782.2	447.5	404.4	524.2	104.4	167.4	90.4	129.6	174.8	117.1
IV. Fuel,lighting and water	193.1	232.8	277.9	193.1	216.3	246.1	120.6	119.3	112.0	113.8	143.9	128.0
V. Household articles	103.6	109.5	153.5	103.6	108.9	154.7	105.7	140.2	105.1	142.1	148.2	149.3
VI. Cultural goods	82.4	101.9	125.3	84.2	101.9	125.3	123.7	123.0	123.7	123.0	152.1	152.1
VII. Other products	45.5	57.1	65.9	45.5	57.1	62.2	125.5	115.4	125.5	108.9	144.8	136.7
Total	3393.1	4051.5	5845.6	3393.1	3673.5	4416.2	119.4	144.3	108.3	120.2	172.3	130.1
VIII. Housing	300.2	349.3	391.8	300.2	325.1	381.9	116.4	112.2	108.3	117.5	130.5	127.2
Total	3693.3	4400.8	6237.4	3693.3	3998.6	4798.1	119.2	141.7	108.3	120.0	168.9	129.9
of which: industrial goods	1975.3	2316.5	3285.4	1975.3	2145.3	2722.8	117.3	141.8	108.6	126.9	166.3	137.8
Total,less drink	3370.3	4071.2	5681.4	3370.3	3727.0	4460.6	120.8	139.6	110.6	119.7	168.6	132.4
of which: industrial goods	1652.3	1986.9	2729.4	1652.3	1873.7	2385.3	120.3	137.4	113.4	127.3	165.2	144.4
Numbers (in millions)	11.8	12.8	15.0	-	-	-	108.3	117.4	-	-	127.2	-
Consumption per head (in rubles)	313.0	344.3	415.5	313.0	312.9	319.7	110.0	120.7	100.0	102.2	132.7	102.1

Sub-section D

Table 4. Consumption fund of material goods, by groups of products. Non-manual workers.

A	In millions of rubles						As % of previous year				1930 as % of 1928	
	In current prices			In 1928 prices			In current prices		In 1928 prices		In current prices	In 1928 prices
	1928	1929	1930	1928	1929	1930	1929	1930	1929	1930		
	1	2	3	4	5	6	7	8	9	10	11	12
I. Food products	1460.9	1804.7	2903.3	1460.9	1568.6	1690.7	123.5	160.9	107.4	107.8	198.7	115.7
1. Agricultural products	848.9	1082.3	1864.2	848.9	912.0	887.0	127.5	172.2	107.4	97.3	219.6	104.5
a) arable products	152.5	216.5	404.2	152.5	201.8	264.0	142.0	186.7	132.3	130.8	265.0	173.1
b) livestock products	696.4	865.8	1460.0	696.4	710.2	623.0	124.3	168.6	102.0	87.7	209.6	89.5
2. Grain products (flour,groats,baked bread)	289.9	345.2	458.5	289.9	301.8	391.2	119.1	132.8	104.1	129.6	158.2	134.9
3. Industrial food products	322.1	377.2	580.6	322.1	354.8	412.5	117.1	153.9	110.2	116.3	180.3	128.1
II. Clothing and footwear	477.2	595.0	562.8	477.2	554.1	552.8	124.7	94.8	116.1	99.8	117.9	115.8
III. Drink and tobacco	197.3	220.4	306.2	197.3	197.5	216.6	111.7	138.9	100.1	109.7	155.2	109.8
IV. Fuel,lighting,water	188.3	236.1	279.4	188.3	226.1	259.1	125.4	118.3	120.1	114.6	148.4	137.6
V. Household articles	63.2	70.1	92.7	63.2	69.7	93.4	110.9	132.2	110.3	134.0	146.7	147.8
VI. Cultural goods	115.1	138.3	165.5	115.1	138.3	165.5	120.2	120.0	120.2	120.0	143.8	143.8
VII. Other products	42.7	50.2	57.7	42.7	50.2	55.3	117.6	114.9	107.6	110.2	132.0	129.5
Total	2544.7	3114.8	4367.6	2544.7	2804.5	3033.4	122.4	140.2	110.2	108.2	171.6	119.2
VIII. Housing (quarterly rent payment,less municipal services	340.6	389.3	432.7	340.6	370.4	417.9	114.3	111.1	108.7	112.8	127.0	122.7
Total	2885.3	3504.1	4800.3	2885.3	3174.9	3451.3	121.4	137.0	110.0	108.7	166.4	119.6
of which: industrial goods	1405.9	1687.3	2044.9	1405.9	1590.7	1755.2	120.0	121.2	113.1	110.3	145.5	124.8
Total,less drink	2787.9	3395.4	4638.4	2787.9	3087.2	3356.0	121.8	136.6	107.4	108.7	166.4	120.4
of which: industrial goods	1308.5	1578.6	1883.0	1308.5	1503.0	1659.9	120.7	119.3	114.9	110.4	143.9	126.9
Numbers (in millions)	8.5	9.2	10.4				108.7	112.8			122.7	-
Consumption per head (in rubles)	341.1	380.9	462.5	341.1	345.1	332.5	111.7	121.4	101.2	96.3	135.6	97.5

Sub-section D

Table 5. Consumption fund of material goods. Total non-agricultural proletariat

A	In millions of rubles						As % of previous year				1930 as % of 1928	
	In current prices			In 1928 prices			In current prices		In 1928 prices		In current prices	In 1928 prices
	1928	1929	1930	1928	1929	1930	1929	1930	1929	1930		
	1	2	3	4	5	6	7	8	9	10	11	12
I. Food products	3715.6	4634.8	7119.9	3715.6	4075.4	4497.4	124.7	153.6	109.7	110.3	191.6	121.0
1. Agricultural products	2075.7	2615.6	4154.8	2075.7	2270.6	2226.1	126.0	158.0	109.4	98.0	200.2	107.2
a) arable products	436.7	629.7	1051.6	436.7	583.3	738.3	144.2	167.0	133.6	126.6	240.8	169.1
b) livestock products	1639.0	1985.9	3103.2	1639.0	1687.3	1487.8	121.2	156.3	102.9	83.2	189.3	90.8
2. Grain products (flour,groats,baked bread)	821.1	990.6	1319.9	821.1	862.0	1099.7	120.5	143.3	105.0	127.6	160.7	133.9
3. Industrial food products	818.8	1028.6	1645.2	818.8	942.8	1171.6	125.7	159.9	115.1	124.3	200.9	143.1
II. Clothing and footwear	1302.9	1575.3	1665.3	1302.9	1490.8	1636.4	120.9	105.7	114.4	109.8	127.8	125.6
III. Drink and tobacco	714.1	780.0	1197.0	714.1	681.8	813.7	109.3	153.4	95.5	119.3	167.6	113.9
IV. Fuel, lighting and water	434.5	537.8	623.9	434.5	504.9	562.7	123.8	116.0	116.2	111.4	143.6	129.5
V. Household articles	179.0	192.7	259.7	179.0	191.6	261.7	107.7	134.8	107.0	136.6	150.7	146.2
VI. Cultural goods	211.7	257.0	307.8	211.7	257.0	307.8	121.4	119.8	121.4	119.8	145.4	150.1
VII. Others	99.1	122.4	137.1	99.1	122.4	130.2	123.6	112.0	123.6	106.4	138.3	131.4
Total	6656.9	8100.0	11310.7	6656.9	7323.9	8209.9	121.7	139.6	110.0	112.1	169.9	123.3
VIII. Housing	710.6	819.7	898.4	710.6	778.8	879.0	115.4	109.7	109.6	112.9	126.4	123.7
Total	7367.5	8919.7	12209.1	7367.5	8102.7	9088.9	121.1	136.9	110.0	112.2	165.7	123.4
of which: industrial goods	3760.1	4493.8	5836.0	3760.1	4191.3	4884.1	119.5	129.9	111.5	116.5	155.2	129.9
Total, less drink	6912.2	8428.0	11422.2	6912.2	7699.4	8614.3	121.9	135.5	111.4	111.9	165.2	124.6
of which: industrial goods	3304.8	4002.1	5049.1	3304.8	3788.0	4409.5	121.1	126.2	114.6	116.4	152.8	133.4
Numbers (in millions)	23.9	26.0	29.0	-	-	-	108.7	111.4	-	-	121.0	-
Consumption per head (in rubles)	307.6	342.7	421.1	307.6	311.3	313.5	111.4	122.9	101.2	100.7	136.9	101.9

Sub-section D

Table 6. Consumption fund of material goods, by groups of the population (less drink and livestock products)

| A | In millions of rubles | | | As % of previous year | | 1930 as % |
	1928	1929	1930	1929	1930	of 1928
	1	2	3	4	5	6
A. In current prices						
I. Non-agricultural population	6845.9	7726.1	9748.7	112.9	126.2	142.4
including:						
1) manual workers	2602.6	3164.7	4332.4	122.1	136.9	166.5
2) non-manual workers	2091.5	2529.6	3178.4	120.9	125.6	152.9
3) total proletariat	5273.2	6442.1	8319.0	122.2	129.1	157.8
II. Agricultural population	8450.7	9893.6	10350.9	117.1	104.6	122.5
Total	15296.6	17619.7	20099.6	115.2	114.1	131.4
B. In 1928 prices, with consumption by the agricultural population valued in rural prices						
I. Non-agricultural population	6845.9	7194.4	8296.1	105.1	115.3	121.2
including:						
1) manual workers	2602.6	2933.5	3725.8	112.7	127.0	143.2
2) non-manual workers	2091.5	2377.0	2733.0	113.6	115.0	130.7
3) total proletariat	5273.2	6012.1	7126.5	114.0	118.5	135.1
II. Agricultural population	8450.7	9090.3	9224.1	107.6	101.5	109.2
Total	15296.6	16284.7	17520.2	106.5	107.6	114.5
C. In 1928 prices, with consumption by the agricultural population valued in urban prices						
I. Non-agricultural population	6845.9	7194.4	8296.1	105.1	115.3	121.2
II. Agricultural population	13940.0	14701.3	14893.0	105.5	101.3	106.8
Total	20785.9	21895.7	23189.1	105.3	105.9	111.6

Sub-section D

Table 7. Consumption fund of material goods, by classes and groups of the non-agricultural population

A	Total in millions of rubles						Structure of consumption fund by classes and groups in %				
	In current prices			In 1928 prices			In current prices			In 1928 prices	
	1928	1929	1930	1928	1929	1930	1928	1929	1930	1929	1930
	1	2	3	4	5	6	7	8	9	10	11
I. Proletariat including:	7387.5	8919.7	12209.1	7367.5	8102.8	9089.0	77.8	83.2	84.8	83.4	85.6
1. Manual workers	3693.3	4400.8	6237.4	3693.3	3998.6	4798.1	39.0	41.0	43.3	41.1	45.2
2. Non-manual workers	2885.3	3504.1	4800.3	2885.3	3174.9	3451.3	30.5	32.7	33.3	32.7	32.5
3. Pensioners and grant-aided students	229.5	343.1	528.7	229.5	310.4	376.0	2.4	3.2	3.7	3.2	3.5
4. Other proletarians	559.4	671.7	642.7	559.4	618.9	463.6	5.9	6.3	4.5	6.4	4.4
II. Artisans, craftsmen and small traders	1848.6	1636.0	2016.8	1848.6	1459.0	1408.9	19.5	15.3	13.9	15.0	13.3
III. Capitalist groups	195.7	102.2	102.6	195.7	94.0	67.8	2.1	0.9	0.7	1.0	0.6
IV. Other population	57.4	64.3	80.3	57.4	58.8	57.8	0.6	0.6	0.6	0.6	0.5
	9469.2	10722.2	14408.8	9469.2	9714.6	10623.5	100.0	100.0	100.0	100.0	100.0

Sub-section D

Table 8. Consumption of material goods, per head, as an average for the population as a whole

A	In rubles per head In current prices			In 1928 prices With consumption by agricultural population evaluated in rural prices			With consumption by agricultural population evaluated in urban prices[1]			In 1928 prices, with consumption by agricultural population evaluated in urban prices[1] As % of previous year		1930 as % of 1928
	1928	1929	1930	1928	1929	1930	1928	1929	1930	1929	1930	
	1	2	3	4	5	6	7	8	9	10	11	12
I. Food products	79.9	88.9	108.4	79.9	80.8	79.0	139.5	140.5	134.8	100.7	96.0	96.6
1. Agricultural products	44.9	49.8	64.0	44.9	46.4	42.5	84.1	86.2	79.4	102.5	92.1	94.4
a) arable products	11.7	13.9	17.5	11.7	12.8	14.2	25.7	27.1	29.2	103.4	107.7	113.6
b) livestock products	33.2	35.9	46.5	33.2	33.6	28.3	58.4	59.1	50.2	101.2	84.9	86.0
2. Grain products (flour, groats, baked bread)	22.0	24.7	24.2	22.0	21.2	21.9	42.4	41.0	40.9	96.7	99.8	96.5
3. Industrial food products	13.0	14.4	20.2	13.0	13.2	14.6	13.0	13.3	14.5	102.3	109.0	111.5
II. Clothing and footwear	28.5	33.1	34.5	28.5	31.0	31.0	28.5	31.0	31.0	108.8	100.0	108.8
III. Drink and tobacco	12.7	14.3	21.3	12.7	12.5	13.2	15.0	14.5	14.4	96.7	99.3	96.0
IV. Fuel, lighting and water	6.3	7.0	7.6	6.3	6.6	6.8	8.3	8.6	8.7	103.6	101.2	104.8
V. Household articles	2.7	2.8	3.6	2.7	2.8	3.6	2.6	2.8	3.6	107.7	128.6	138.8
VI. Cultural goods	2.1	2.3	2.7	2.1	2.3	2.7	2.1	2.3	2.7	109.5	117.4	128.6
VII. Other products	2.1	2.4	2.2	2.1	2.2	2.0	2.1	2.2	2.0	104.8	90.9	95.2
Total	134.3	150.8	180.3	134.3	138.2	138.3	198.1	201.9	197.2	101.9	97.7	99.5
VIII. Housing	10.4	10.7	10.9	10.4	10.5	10.9	10.4	10.5	10.9	101.0	103.8	101.8
Total	144.7	161.5	191.2	144.7	148.7	149.2	208.5	212.4	208.1	102.4	98.0	99.8
of which: a) agricultural products	46.7	51.9	65.6	46.7	48.2	43.8	85.8	88.0	80.7	102.6	91.7	94.1
b) industrial products	65.6	74.2	90.5	65.6	68.8	72.6	69.9	72.9	75.6	104.3	103.7	108.2
Total, less drink	134.9	150.6	174.1	134.9	139.6	139.6	196.4	201.2	197.4	102.4	98.1	100.5
of which: a) agricultural products	46.4	51.7	65.6	46.4	48.0	43.8	85.6	87.8	80.7	102.6	91.9	94.3
b) industrial goods	56.1	63.5	73.4	56.1	59.9	63.0	58.0	61.9	64.9	106.7	104.8	111.9

1. In the given variant, consumption by the agricultural population has been re-valued in urban prices for some agricultural products and industrial products of domestic processing.

Sub-section D

Table 8a. Consumption of material goods, total population. Structure of consumption, by groups of products (in %)

A	In current prices			In 1928 prices Evaluating consumption by agricultural population in rural prices			Evaluating consumption by agricultural population in urban prices		
	1928	1929	1930	1928	1929	1930	1928	1929	1930
	1	2	3	4	5	6	7	8	9
I. Food products	55.2	55.0	56.7	55.2	54.4	52.9	66.9	66.2	64.8
1. Agricultural products	31.0	30.8	33.4	31.0	31.2	28.5	40.3	40.6	38.1
a) arable products	8.1	8.6	9.2	8.1	8.6	9.5	12.3	12.8	14.0
b) livestock products	22.9	22.2	24.2	22.9	22.6	19.0	28.0	27.8	24.1
2. Grain products (flour, groats, baked bread)	15.2	15.3	12.7	15.2	14.3	14.7	20.3	19.3	19.7
3. Industrial food products	9.0	8.9	10.6	9.0	8.9	9.7	6.3	6.3	7.0
II. Clothing and footwear	19.7	20.5	18.1	19.7	20.8	20.8	13.7	14.6	14.9
III. Drink and tobacco	8.8	8.9	11.1	8.8	8.4	8.8	7.2	6.9	6.9
IV. Fuel, lighting and water	4.4	4.3	3.9	4.4	4.4	4.6	4.0	4.0	4.2
V. Household articles	1.9	1.8	1.9	1.9	1.9	2.4	1.2	1.3	1.7
VI. Cultural goods	1.4	1.4	1.4	1.4	1.5	1.9	1.0	1.1	1.3
VII. Other products	1.4	1.5	1.2	1.4	1.5	1.3	1.0	1.0	1.0
Total	92.8	93.4	94.3	92.8	92.9	92.7	95.0	95.1	94.8
VIII. Housing	7.2	6.6	5.7	7.2	7.1	7.3	5.0	4.9	5.2
Total	100.0	100.0	100.0	100.0	100.0	100.0	100.0	100.0	100.0
of which: a) agricultural products	32.3	32.1	34.3	32.3	32.4	29.4	41.1	41.4	38.8
b) industrial products	45.3	45.9	47.3	45.3	45.4	48.7	33.6	34.3	36.8
Total, less drink	93.2	93.3	91.1	93.2	93.9	93.6	91.2	94.7	94.9

Sub-section D

Table 9. Consumption of material goods by the non-agricultural population (in rubles per head, in current prices)

A	Manual workers			Non-manual workers			Total proletariat			Total non-agricultural population		
	1928	1929	1930	1928	1929	1930	1928	1929	1930	1928	1929	1930
	1	2	3	4	5	6	7	8	9	10	11	12
I. Food products	154.93	176.88	230.79	172.68	196.16	279.70	155.14	178.06	245.60	158.85	177.69	245.74
1. Agricultural products	84.37	96.69	124.05	100.34	117.64	179.60	86.67	100.48	143.32	85.92	98.97	142.90
including: a) arable products	19.31	25.76	34.18	18.03	23.53	38.94	18.23	24.19	36.27	17.86	23.36	35.79
b) livestock products	65.06	70.93	89.87	82.31	94.11	140.66	68.44	76.29	107.05	68.06	75.61	107.11
2. Grain products (flour, groats, baked bread)	35.77	39.07	46.52	34.27	37.52	44.17	34.28	38.06	45.53	38.39	39.81	46.57
3. Industrial food products	34.79	41.12	60.22	38.07	41.00	55.93	34.19	39.52	56.75	34.54	38.91	56.27
II. Clothing and footwear	58.70	64.33	65.06	56.41	64.67	54.22	54.40	60.52	57.44	57.61	58.80	55.00
III. Drink and tobacco	37.92	36.56	52.11	23.32	23.96	29.51	29.82	29.96	41.29	30.27	30.70	42.29
IV. Fuel, lighting, water	16.35	18.21	18.51	22.26	25.66	26.91	18.14	20.67	21.52	18.50	20.98	21.89
V. Household articles	8.78	8.57	10.23	7.47	7.62	8.93	7.47	7.40	8.96	7.09	6.86	8.28
VI. Cultural goods	6.98	7.97	8.35	13.60	15.03	15.94	8.84	9.87	10.62	8.32	9.17	9.89
VII. Other products	3.86	4.48	4.39	5.05	5.45	5.56	4.14	4.70	4.73	4.71	4.93	4.90
Total	287.52	317.00	389.44	300.79	358.55	420.77	277.95	311.18	390.16	285.35	309.13	387.99
VIII. Housing (quarterly rent-payments, less municipal services)	25.44	27.33	26.10	40.26	42.32	41.69	29.67	31.49	30.99	32.72	33.65	32.72
Total	312.96	344.33	415.54	341.05	380.87	462.46	307.62	342.67	421.15	318.07	342.78	420.71
of which: industrial goods	167.38	181.24	218.87	166.18	183.39	197.00	157.00	172.64	201.31	161.04	170.35	198.52
Total, less drink	285.59	318.54	378.50	329.54	369.05	446.86	288.61	323.28	394.00	298.01	322.60	391.75
of which: industrial goods	140.01	155.45	181.83	154.67	171.57	181.40	137.99	153.75	174.16	110.98	150.17	169.56

Sub-section D

Table 9a. Structure of consumption of material goods by the non-agricultural population (in current prices) as % of total

A	Manual workers			Non-manual workers			Total proletariat			Total non-agricultural population		
	1928	1929	1930	1928	1929	1930	1928	1929	1930	1928	1929	1930
	1	2	3	4	5	6	7	8	9	10	11	12
I. Food products	49.5	51.4	55.5	50.6	51.6	60.5	50.4	52.0	58.3	50.0	51.8	58.4
1. Agricultural products	27.0	28.1	29.9	29.4	30.9	38.8	28.2	29.4	34.0	27.0	28.9	34.0
including: a) arable products	6.2	7.5	8.2	5.3	6.2	8.4	5.9	7.1	8.6	5.6	6.8	8.5
b) livestock products	20.8	20.6	21.7	24.1	24.7	30.4	22.3	22.3	25.4	21.4	22.1	25.5
2. Grain products (flour, groats, baked bread)	11.4	11.4	11.2	10.0	9.9	9.6	11.1	11.1	10.8	12.1	11.5	11.1
3. Industrial food products	11.1	11.9	14.4	11.2	10.8	12.1	11.1	11.5	13.5	10.9	11.4	13.3
II. Clothing and footwear	18.8	18.7	15.6	16.6	17.0	11.8	17.7	17.7	13.6	18.1	17.2	13.0
III. Drink and tobacco	12.2	10.6	12.5	6.8	6.3	6.4	9.7	8.7	9.8	9.5	9.0	10.0
IV. Fuel, lighting, water	5.2	5.3	4.5	6.5	6.7	5.8	5.9	6.0	5.1	5.8	6.1	5.2
V. Household articles	2.8	2.5	2.5	2.2	2.0	1.9	2.4	2.2	2.2	2.2	2.0	2.0
VI. Cultural goods	2.2	2.3	2.0	4.0	3.9	3.4	2.9	2.8	2.5	2.6	2.7	2.4
VII. Other products	1.2	1.3	1.1	1.5	1.4	1.2	1.4	1.4	1.1	1.5	1.4	1.2
Total	91.9	92.1	93.7	88.2	88.9	91.0	90.4	90.8	92.6	89.7	90.2	92.2
VIII. Housing (quarterly rent-payments, less municipal services)	8.1	7.9	6.3	11.8	11.1	9.0	9.6	9.2	7.4	10.3	9.8	7.8
Total	100.0	100.0	100.0	100.0	100.0	100.0	100.0	100.0	100.0	100.0	100.0	100.0
of which: industrial goods	53.5	52.6	52.6	48.8	48.1	42.6	51.1	50.3	47.8	50.6	49.8	47.1

Sub-section D

Table 10. Consumption of material goods by the non-agricultural population, in rubles per head (in 1928 prices)

A	Manual workers			Non-manual workers			Total proletariat			Total non-agricultural population		
	1928	1929	1930	1928	1929	1930	1928	1929	1930	1928	1929	1930
	1	2	3	4	5	6	7	8	9	10	11	12
I. Food products	154.93	156.44	156.41	172.68	170.51	162.88	155.14	156.57	155.14	158.85	155.30	152.96
1. Agricultural products	84.37	85.84	74.61	100.34	99.14	85.45	86.67	87.23	76.79	85.92	85.74	75.37
including: a) arable products	19.31	23.75	25.66	18.03	21.93	25.43	18.23	22.41	25.47	17.86	21.75	24.92
b) livestock products	65.06	62.09	48.95	82.31	77.21	60.02	68.44	64.82	51.32	68.06	63.99	50.45
2. Grain products (flour,groats,baked bread)	35.77	33.74	38.20	34.27	32.80	37.69	34.28	33.12	37.93	38.39	34.48	38.76
3. Industrial food products	34.79	36.86	43.60	38.07	38.57	39.74	34.19	36.22	40.42	34.54	35.08	38.83
II. Clothing and footwear	58.76	61.47	63.69	56.41	60.23	53.26	54.40	57.27	56.45	57.61	55.08	53.20
III. Drink and tobacco	37.92	31.64	34.92	23.32	21.47	20.87	29.82	26.19	28.07	30.27	26.78	28.53
IV. Fuel, lighting, water	16.35	16.92	16.40	22.26	24.58	25.96	18.14	19.40	19.41	18.50	19.75	19.86
V. Household articles	8.78	8.52	10.31	7.47	7.58	9.00	7.47	7.36	9.03	7.09	6.84	8.36
VI. Cultural goods	6.98	7.97	8.35	13.60	15.03	15.94	8.84	9.87	10.62	8.32	9.17	9.89
VII. Other products	3.86	4.47	4.14	5.05	5.47	5.33	4.14	4.70	4.49	4.71	4.93	4.64
Total	287.52	287.43	294.22	300.79	304.87	292.24	277.95	281.36	283.21	285.35	277.85	277.44
VIII. Housing (quarterly rent payments less municipal services)	25.44	25.44	25.44	40.26	40.26	40.26	29.67	29.91	30.32	32.72	32.72	32.72
Total	312.96	312.87	319.66	341.05	345.13	332.50	307.62	311.27	313.53	318.07	310.57	310.16
of which: industrial goods	167.38	167.85	181.41	166.18	172.93	169.10	157.00	161.01	168.49	161.04	157.63	163.31
Total, less drink	285.59	291.62	297.18	329.54	335.60	323.32	288.61	295.79	297.15	298.01	293.99	292.66
of which: industrial goods	140.01	146.60	158.93	154.67	163.40	159.92	137.99	145.52	152.19	140.98	141.05	145.81

Sub-section D

Table 10a. Structure of consumption of material goods by the non-agricultural population (in 1928 prices). As % of total

A	Manual workers			Non-manual workers			Total proletariat			Total non-agricultural population		
	1928	1929	1930	1928	1929	1930	1928	1929	1930	1928	1929	1930
	1	2	3	4	5	6	7	8	9	10	11	12
I. Food products	49.5	50.0	48.2	50.6	49.4	49.0	50.4	50.3	49.5	50.0	50.0	49.3
1. Agricultural products	27.0	27.4	23.3	29.4	28.7	25.7	28.2	28.0	24.5	27.0	27.6	24.3
including: a) arable products	6.2	7.6	8.0	5.3	6.4	7.6	5.9	7.2	8.1	5.6	7.0	8.0
b) livestock products	20.8	19.8	15.3	24.1	22.3	18.1	22.3	20.8	16.4	21.4	20.6	16.3
2. Grain products (flour,groats,baked bread)	11.4	10.8	12.0	10.0	9.5	11.3	11.1	10.7	12.1	12.1	11.1	12.5
3. Industrial food products	11.1	11.8	13.6	11.2	11.2	12.0	11.1	11.6	12.9	10.9	11.3	12.5
II. Clothing and footwear	18.8	19.7	19.9	16.6	17.5	16.0	17.7	18.4	18.0	18.1	17.7	17.2
III. Drink and tobacco	12.2	10.2	10.9	6.8	6.2	6.3	9.7	8.4	8.9	9.5	8.6	9.2
IV. Fuel, lighting and water	5.2	5.4	5.2	6.5	7.0	7.5	5.9	6.2	6.2	5.8	6.4	6.4
V. Household articles	2.8	2.7	3.2	2.2	2.2	2.7	2.4	2.4	2.9	2.2	2.2	2.7
VI. Cultural goods	2.2	2.5	2.6	4.0	4.4	4.8	2.9	3.2	3.4	2.6	3.0	3.2
VII. Other products	1.2	1.4	1.3	1.5	1.6	1.6	1.4	1.5	1.4	1.5	1.6	1.5
Total	91.9	91.9	92.0	88.2	88.3	87.9	90.4	90.4	90.3	89.7	89.5	89.5
VIII. Housing (quarterly rent-payments, less municipal services)	8.1	8.1	8.0	11.8	11.7	12.1	9.6	9.6	9.7	10.3	10.5	10.5
Total	100.0	100.0	100.0	100.0	100.0	100.0	100.0	100.0	100.0	100.0	100.0	100.0
of which: industrial goods	53.5	53.7	56.3	48.8	50.1	50.9	51.1	51.7	53.7	50.6	50.8	52.7

Sub-section D

Table 10b. Rate of growth of consumption of material goods by the non-agricultural population (in 1928 prices) per head

| A | As % of previous year | | | | | | | | 1930 as % of 1928 | | | |
| | Manual workers | | Non-manual workers | | Total proletariat | | Total non-agricultural popln. | | Manual workers | Non-manual workers | Total proletariat | Total non-agricultural population |
	1929	1930	1929	1930	1929	1930	1929	1930				
I. Food products	101.0	100.0	98.7	95.5	100.9	99.1	97.8	98.5	101.0	94.3	100.0	96.3
1. Agricultural products	101.7	86.9	98.8	86.2	100.6	88.0	99.8	87.9	88.4	85.2	88.6	87.7
including: a) arable products	154.1	86.3	121.6	116.0	122.9	113.7	121.8	114.6	132.9	141.0	139.7	189.5
b) livestock products	95.4	78.8	93.8	77.7	94.7	79.2	94.0	78.8	75.2	72.9	75.0	74.1
2. Grain products (flour,groats,baked bread)	94.3	113.2	95.7	114.9	96.6	114.5	89.8	112.4	106.8	110.0	110.6	101.0
3. Industrial food products	105.9	118.3	101.3	103.0	105.9	111.6	101.6	110.7	125.3	104.4	118.2	112.4
II. Clothing and footwear	104.7	103.6	106.8	88.4	105.3	98.6	95.6	96.6	110.4	94.4	103.8	92.8
III. Drink and tobacco	83.4	110.4	92.1	97.2	87.8	107.2	88.5	106.5	92.1	89.5	94.1	94.3
IV. Fuel, lighting and water	103.5	96.9	110.5	101.5	106.9	100.0	106.7	100.6	100.3	112.2	107.0	107.3
V. Household articles	97.0	124.0	101.5	118.7	98.5	122.7	96.5	122.2	117.4	120.5	120.9	117.9
VI. Cultural goods	114.2	104.8	110.4	106.1	111.7	107.6	110.2	107.8	119.6	117.1	120.1	107.8
VII. Other products	115.8	92.6	108.3	97.4	113.5	95.5	104.7	94.1	107.2	105.5	108.4	98.5
Total	99.9	102.4	101.4	95.9	101.2	100.6	97.4	99.8	102.3	97.1	101.9	97.2
VIII. Housing (quarterly rent-payments, less municipal services)	100.0	100.0	100.0	100.0	100.8	101.4	100.0	100.0	100.0	100.0	102.2	100.0
Total	100.3	102.2	101.2	96.3	101.2	100.7	97.6	99.5	102.1	97.5	101.9	97.5
of which: industrial goods	100.3	108.1	104.1	97.8	102.6	104.6	97.9	103.6	108.4	101.8	107.3	101.4
Total, less drink	102.1	101.9	101.8	96.3	102.5	100.4	98.6	99.5	104.1	98.1	102.9	98.2
of which: industrial goods	104.7	108.4	105.6	97.9	105.5	104.5	100.0	103.4	113.5	103.4	110.2	103.4

Sub-section D

Table 11. Consumption of material goods by classes and groups of the non-agricultural population (per head)

A	In rubles						In 1928 prices		1930 as % of 1928
	In current prices			In 1928 prices			As % previous year		
	1928	1929	1930	1928	1929	1930	1929	1930	
	1	2	3	4	5	6	7	8	9
I. Proletariat including:	307.6	342.7	421.2	307.6	311.3	313.5	101.2	100.7	101.9
1. Manual workers	313.0	344.3	415.5	313.0	312.9	319.7	100.0	102.2	102.1
2. Non-manual workers	341.1	380.9	462.5	341.1	345.1	332.5	101.2	96.3	97.5
3. Pensioners and grant-aided students	239.1	288.3	362.1	239.1	260.8	257.5	109.1	98.7	107.7
4. Other proletarians	204.9	234.8	300.3	204.9	216.3	216.6	105.6	100.1	105.7
II. Artisans, craftsmen and small traders	346.2	338.7	415.0	346.2	302.1	289.9	87.3	96.0	83.7
III. Capitalist groups	1171.9	964.1	1236.1	1171.9	886.7	816.8	75.7	92.1	69.7
IV. Other population	181.6	207.4	259.0	181.6	186.1	183.5	102.4	98.6	101.0
Total	318.1	342.8	420.7	318.1	310.6	310.2	97.6	99.9	97.5

Materialy

Sub-section D

Table 12. Consumption of material goods by the agricultural population, in rubles per head

A	In current prices			In 1928 prices					
				Rural			Urban		
	1928	1929	1930	1928	1929	1930	1928	1929	1930
	1	2	3	4	5	6	7	8	9
I. Food products	60.55	66.46	70.50	60.55	61.95	58.52	134.67	136.75	129.74
1. Agricultural products	34.76	37.33	42.14	34.76	36.49	33.44	83.56	86.28	80.45
including: a) arable products	10.21	11.48	12.41	10.21	10.49	11.22	27.57	28.44	30.34
b) livestock products	24.55	25.85	29.97	24.55	26.00	22.22	55.99	57.84	50.11
2. Grain products (flour and groats)	18.02	20.87	18.09	18.02	17.76	17.28	43.30	42.72	41.44
3. Industrial food products	7.77	8.26	10.27	7.77	7.70	7.80	7.81	7.75	7.85
II. Clothing and footwear	21.30	26.54	28.92	21.30	24.96	24.82	21.30	24.96	24.82
III. Drink and tobacco	8.46	10.12	15.44	8.46	8.71	8.93	11.27	11.34	10.45
IV. Fuel, lighting, water	3.34	3.52	3.60	3.34	3.32	3.29	5.78	5.76	5.72
V. Household articles	1.68	1.83	2.26	1.68	1.81	2.26	1.68	1.81	2.26
VI. Cultural goods	0.54	0.60	0.65	0.54	0.60	0.65	0.54	0.60	0.65
VII. Other products	1.43	1.71	1.43	1.43	1.51	1.31	1.43	1.51	1.31
Total	97.30	110.78	122.80	97.30	102.86	99.78	176.67	182.73	174.95
VIII. Housing (depreciation of buildings)	4.92	4.89	4.88	4.92	4.89	4.87	4.92	4.89	4.87
Total	102.22	115.67	127.68	102.22	107.75	104.65	181.59	187.62	179.82
of which: a) agricultural products	37.07	40.08	44.19	37.07	38.78	35.08	85.86	88.57	82.09
b) grain products	18.02	20.87	18.09	18.02	17.76	17.28	43.30	42.72	41.44
c) industrial products	42.21	49.83	60.52	42.21	46.32	47.42	47.51	51.44	51.42
Total, less drink	94.90	107.08	113.91	94.90	100.52	97.29	171.46	177.75	170.94
of which: a) agricultural products	36.66	39.76	44.19	36.66	38.49	35.08	85.45	88.28	82.09
b) industrial goods	35.30	41.56	46.75	35.30	39.38	40.06	37.79	41.86	42.54

Sub-section D

Table 12a. Growth of consumption of material goods by the agricultural population. Structure and rate of growth per head

A	As % of total — In current prices 1928	1929	1930	Rural 1928	1929	1930	Urban 1928	1929	1930	As % of previous year (in 1928 prices) — Rural 1929	1930	Urban 1929	1930	1930 as % of 1928 in 1928 prices — Rural	Urban
	1	2	3	4	5	6	7	8	9	10	11	12	13	14	15
I. Food products	59.2	57.5	56.2	59.2	57.5	55.9	74.2	72.9	72.1	102.3	94.5	101.5	94.9	96.6	96.3
1. Agricultural products	34.0	32.3	33.0	34.0	33.9	31.9	46.0	46.0	44.7	105.0	96.6	103.3	93.2	96.2	96.3
including: a) arable products	10.0	9.9	9.7	10.0	9.7	10.7	15.2	15.2	16.9	102.7	107.0	103.2	106.7	109.9	110.0
b) livestock products	24.0	22.4	23.3	24.0	24.2	21.2	30.8	30.8	27.8	105.9	85.5	103.3	89.6	90.5	89.5
2. Grain products (flour,groats)	17.6	18.0	14.2	17.6	16.5	16.5	23.9	22.8	23.0	98.6	97.3	98.7	97.0	95.9	95.7
3. Industrial food products	7.6	7.2	8.0	7.6	7.1	7.2	4.3	4.1	4.4	99.1	101.3	99.2	101.3	100.4	100.5
II. Clothing and footwear	20.8	22.9	22.7	20.8	23.2	23.7	11.7	13.3	13.8	117.2	99.4	117.2	99.4	116.5	116.5
III. Drink and tobacco	8.3	8.7	12.1	8.3	8.1	8.5	6.2	6.0	5.8	103.0	102.5	100.6	92.2	105.6	92.7
IV. Fuel, lighting	3.3	3.0	2.8	3.3	3.0	3.1	3.2	3.1	3.2	99.4	99.1	99.7	99.3	98.5	98.7
V. Household articles	1.7	1.7	1.8	1.7	1.7	2.2	0.9	1.0	1.3	107.7	124.9	107.7	124.9	134.5	134.5
VI. Cultural goods	0.5	0.5	0.5	0.5	0.6	0.6	0.3	0.3	0.4	111.1	108.3	111.1	108.3	120.4	120.4
VII. Other products	1.4	1.5	1.1	1.4	1.4	1.3	0.8	0.8	0.7	105.6	86.8	105.6	86.8	91.6	91.6
Total	95.2	95.8	96.2	95.2	95.5	95.3	97.3	97.4	97.3	105.7	97.0	103.4	95.7	102.5	99.0
VIII. Housing (depreciation of building)	4.8	4.2	3.8	4.8	4.5	4.7	2.7	2.6	2.7	99.4	99.6	99.4	99.6	99.0	99.0
Total	100.0	100.0	100.0	100.0	100.0	100.0	100.0	100.0	100.0	105.4	97.1	103.3	95.8	102.4	99.1
of which: a) agricultural products	36.2	34.7	34.6	36.2	36.0	33.5	47.8	47.2	45.7	104.6	90.5	103.2	92.7	94.6	95.6
b) grain products	17.6	18.0	14.2	17.6	16.5	16.5	23.8	22.8	23.0	98.6	97.3	98.7	97.0	95.9	95.7
c) industrial goods	41.4	43.1	47.4	41.4	43.0	45.3	26.2	27.4	28.6	109.7	102.4	108.3	100.0	112.3	108.2
Total, less drink	92.8	92.6	89.2	92.8	93.3	93.0	94.4	94.7	95.1	105.9	96.8	103.7	96.2	102.5	99.7
of which: a) agricultural products	-	-	-	-	-	-	-	-	-	105.0	91.1	103.3	93.0	95.7	96.1
b) industrial goods	-	-	-	-	-	-	-	-	-	111.6	101.7	110.8	101.1	113.5	112.6

Materialy

Sub-section D

Table 13. Consumption of material goods per head, by groups of the population (excluding drink and livestock products)

| A | In rubles | | | As % of previous year | | 1930 as % |
	1928	1929	1930	1929	1930	of 1928
	1	2	3	4	5	6
A. In current prices						
I. Non-agricultural population	229.95	246.99	284.64	107.4	115.2	123.8
including:						
1) manual workers	220.53	247.61	288.63	112.3	116.6	130.9
2) non-manual workers	247.23	274.94	306.20	111.2	111.7	123.8
3) total proletariat	220.17	247.49	286.95	112.4	115.9	130.3
II. Agricultural population	69.43	80.05	83.54	115.3	104.4	120.3
Total	101.04	113.75	127.13	112.6	111.8	125.8
B. In 1928 prices with consumption by the agricultural population valued in rural prices						
I. Non-agricultural population	229.95	230.00	242.21	100.0	105.3	105.3
including:						
1) manual workers	220.53	229.53	248.23	104.1	108.1	112.6
2) non-manual workers	247.23	258.39	263.30	104.5	101.9	106.5
3) total proletariat	220.17	230.97	245.83	104.9	106.4	111.7
II. Agricultural population	69.43	73.54	74.45	105.9	101.2	107.2
Total	101.04	105.13	110.82	104.0	105.4	109.7
C. In 1928 prices with consumption by the agricultural population valued in urban prices						
I. Non-agricultural population	229.95	230.00	242.21	100.0	105.3	105.3
II. Agricultural population	114.54	118.94	120.20	103.8	101.1	101.9
Total	137.30	141.35	146.67	102.9	103.8	106.8

Sub-section D

Table 14. Consumption of material goods by the non-agricultural and agricultural population (in 1928 urban prices)

A	Total consumption in millions of rubles			Per head in rubles		
	Non-agric- ultural population	Agricul- tural population	Total	Non-agric- ultural population	Agric- ultural population	Average for total population
	1	2	3	4	5	6
1928						
1. Agricultural products	2557.8	10448.9	13006.7	85.9	85.9	85.9
including: a) arable products	531.7	3521.7	4053.4	17.9	29.0	26.8
b) livestock products	2026.1	6927.2	8953.3	68.0	56.9	59.1
2. Grain products (flour,groats,baked bread)	1143.1	5269.3	6412.4	38.4	43.3	42.3
3. Industrial goods	4794.2	5781.9	10576.1	161.0	47.5	69.8
4. Products of building (depreciation of housing	430.8	599.1	1029.9	14.5	4.9	6.8
Total	8925.9	22099.2	31025.1	299.8	181.6	204.8
1929						
1. Agricultural products	2681.9	10946.6	13628.5	85.7	88.6	87.9
including: a) arable products	680.5	3677.7	4358.2	21.7	29.8	28.1
b) livestock products	2001.4	7268.9	9270.3	64.0	58.8	59.8
2. Grain products (flour,groats,baked bread)	1078.4	5280.7	6359.1	34.5	42.7	41.1
3. Industrial goods	4930.9	6356.9	11287.8	157.6	51.4	72.9
4. Products of building (depreciation of housing	436.6	604.9	1041.5	14.0	4.9	6.7
Total	9127.8	23189.1	32316.9	291.8	187.6	208.7
1930						
1. Agricultural products	2581.4	10172.5	12753.9	75.4	82.1	80.7
including: a) arable products	853.4	3885.0	4738.4	24.9	31.4	30.0
b) livestock products	1728.0	6287.5	8015.5	50.5	50.7	30.7
2. Grain products (flour,groats,baked bread)	1327.5	5134.2	6461.7	38.7	41.4	40.9
3. Industrial goods	5593.9	6369.4	11963.6	163.3	51.4	75.7
4. Products of building (depreciation of housing	445.3	603.9	1049.2	13.0	4.9	6.6
Total	9948.1	22280.3	32228.4	290.4	179.8	203.8

Sub-section D

Table 14a. Consumption of material goods by non-agricultural and agricultural population (in 1928 urban prices) in %

A	Share in total consumption fund in %		Consumption per head by agricultural population as % of consumption by non-agricultural population	Consumption per head as % of previous year			Consumption per head in 1930 as % of 1928		
	Non-agricultural population	Agricultural population		Non-agricultural population	Agricultural population	Total population	Non-agricultural population	Agricultural population	Total population
	1	2	3	4	5	6	7	8	9
1928									
1. Agricultural products	19.7	80.3	99.9	-	-	-	-	-	-
a) arable products	13.1	86.9	161.5	-	-	-	-	-	-
b) livestock products	22.6	77.4	83.7	-	-	-	-	-	-
2. Grain products	17.8	82.2	112.8	-	-	-	-	-	-
3. Industrial goods	45.3	54.7	29.5	-	-	-	-	-	-
4. Products of building	41.8	58.2	34.0	-	-	-	-	-	-
Total	28.8	71.2	60.0	-	-	-	-	-	-
1929									
1. Agricultural products	19.5	80.5	103.3	99.8	103.3	102.6	-	-	-
a) arable products	15.6	84.2	137.3	121.2	103.1	104.9	-	-	-
b) livestock products	21.6	78.4	91.9	94.1	103.3	101.2	-	-	-
2. Grain products	17.0	83.0	123.8	89.9	98.6	97.2	-	-	-
3. Industrial goods	43.7	56.3	32.6	97.8	108.2	104.4	-	-	-
4. Products of building	41.9	58.1	35.0	96.5	100.0	98.5	-	-	-
Total	28.2	71.8	64.0	97.3	103.3	101.9	-	-	-
1930									
1. Agricultural products	20.2	79.8	108.9	88.0	82.7	91.6	87.8	95.7	93.9
a) arable products	18.0	82.0	126.1	114.7	105.4	106.8	139.1	108.7	111.9
b) livestock products	21.6	78.4	100.4	78.9	86.2	84.8	74.3	89.1	85.8
2. Grain products	20.5	79.5	106.9	112.2	97.0	99.5	100.8	95.6	96.7
3. Industrial goods	46.8	53.2	31.5	103.6	100.0	103.8	101.4	108.2	108.5
4. Products of building	42.4	57.6	37.5	92.8	100.0	98.5	89.7	100.0	97.1
Total	30.9	69.1	61.9	99.5	95.8	97.6	96.9	99.0	99.5

Sub-section D

Table 15. Consumption of material goods and services by the population (in millions of rubles, in 1928 urban prices)

A	Recorded in balance	Consumption of material goods Not recorded in balance (value of food prepared in public catering)	Total	Purchase of services	Free social cultural services	Total
	1	2	3	4	5	6
Total population						
1928	31568.4	101.2	31669.6	746.1	1300.1	33715.8
1929	32903.7	133.9	33037.6	841.4	1454.2	35333.2
1930	32903.8	208.5	33112.3	951.4	1715.6	35779.3
A. Non-agricultural population						
1928	9469.2	101.2	9570.4	606.1	783.1	10959.6
1929	9714.6	133.9	9848.5	676.4	852.4	11377.3
1930	10623.5	208.5	10832.0	800.4	1035.1	12667.5
including:						
a) manual workers						
1928	3693.3	33.9	3727.2	152.7	385.9	4265.8
1929	3998.6	52.1	4050.7	198.1	440.1	4688.9
1930	4798.1	93.2	4891.3	249.6	622.1	5763.0
b) non-manual workers						
1928	2885.3	40.4	2925.7	237.9	208.6	3372.2
1929	3174.9	47.0	3221.9	313.3	218.5	3753.7
1930	3451.3	90.7	3542.0	382.5	241.8	4166.3
c) total proletariat						
1928	7367.5	84.7	7452.2	428.8	675.6	8556.6
1929	8102.7	114.2	8216.9	561.7	739.7	9518.3
1930	9088.9	193.9	9282.8	683.3	935.6	10901.7
B. Agricultural population						
1928	22099.2	-	22099.2	140.0	517.0	22756.2
1929	23189.1	-	23189.1	165.0	601.8	23955.9
1930	22280.3	-	22280.3	151.0	680.5	23111.8

Sub-section D

Table 15a. Consumption of material goods and services by the population, per head (in 1928 urban prices)

A	In rubles				As % of previous year				1930 as % of 1928
	Consumption of material goods	Purchase of services	Free social cultural services	Total	Consumption of material goods	Purchase of services	Free social cultural services	Total	
	1	2	3	4	5	6	7	8	9
Total population									
1928	209.1	4.9	8.6	222.6	-	-	-	-	-
1929	213.3	5.4	9.4	228.1	102.0	110.1	109.4	102.5	-
1930	209.4	6.0	10.8	226.2	98.2	110.9	115.5	99.2	101.6
A. Non-agricultural population									
1928	321.5	20.4	26.3	368.2	-	-	-	-	-
1929	314.8	21.6	27.3	363.7	97.9	106.2	103.6	98.8	-
1930	316.2	23.4	30.2	369.8	100.4	108.1	110.9	101.7	100.5
including:									
a) manual workers									
1928	315.8	12.9	32.7	361.4	-	-	-	-	-
1929	317.0	15.5	34.4	366.9	100.4	119.8	105.3	101.5	-
1930	325.9	16.6	41.5	384.0	102.8	107.3	120.4	104.6	106.2
b) non-manual workers									
1928	345.8	28.1	24.7	398.6	-	-	-	-	-
1929	350.2	34.0	23.8	408.0	101.3	121.1	96.3	102.4	-
1930	341.2	36.9	23.3	401.4	97.4	108.2	98.1	98.4	100.7
c) total proletariat									
1928	311.2	17.9	28.2	357.3	-	-	-	-	-
1929	315.7	21.6	28.4	365.7	101.4	120.7	100.7	102.4	-
1930	320.2	23.6	32.3	376.1	101.4	109.3	113.7	102.8	105.3
B. Agricultural population									
1928	181.6	1.1	4.3	187.0	-	-	-	-	-
1929	187.6	1.3	4.9	193.8	103.3	115.7	114.6	103.7	-
1930	179.8	1.2	5.5	186.5	95.8	91.7	112.7	96.2	99.8

Sub-section D

Table 15b. Consumption of material goods and services by the population (in millions of rubles, in 1928 prices, with consumption by the agricultural population valued in rural prices)

A	Consumption of material goods			Purchase of services	Free social cultural services	Total	of which, excluding alcoholic beverages
	Recorded in balance	Not recorded in balance (value of food prepared in public catering	Total				
	1	2	3	4	5	6	7
Total population							
1928	21909.8	101.2	22011.0	746.1	1300.1	24057.2	22570.0
1929	23032.8	133.9	23166.7	841.4	1454.2	25462.3	24049.8
1930	23590.1	208.5	23798.6	951.4	1715.6	26465.6	24954.3
A. Non-agricultural population							
1928	9469.2	101.2	9570.4	606.1	783.1	10959.6	10362.4
1929	9714.6	133.9	9848.5	676.4	852.4	11377.3	10858.5
1930	10623.5	208.5	10832.0	800.4	1035.1	12667.5	12068.1
including:							
a) manual workers							
1928	3693.3	33.9	3727.2	152.7	385.9	4265.8	3942.8
1929	3998.6	52.1	4050.7	198.1	440.1	4688.9	4417.3
1930	4798.1	93.2	4891.3	249.6	622.1	5763.0	5425.5
b) non-manual workers							
1928	2885.3	40.4	2925.7	237.9	208.6	3372.2	3274.8
1929	3174.9	47.0	3221.9	313.3	218.5	3753.7	3666.0
1930	3451.3	90.7	3542.0	382.5	241.8	4165.3	4071.0
c) total proletariat							
1928	7367.5	84.7	7452.2	428.8	675.6	8556.6	8101.3
1929	8102.7	114.2	8216.9	561.7	739.7	9518.3	9115.0
1930	9088.9	193.9	9282.8	683.3	935.6	10901.7	10427.1
B. Agricultural population							
1928	12440.6	-	12440.6	140.0	517.0	13097.6	12207.6
1929	13318.2	-	13318.2	165.0	601.8	14085.0	13191.3
1930	12966.6	-	12966.6	151.0	680.5	13798.1	12886.2

Sub-section D

Table 15c. Consumption of material goods and services by the population, per head (in 1928 prices, with consumption by the agricultural population valued in rural prices)

| | In rubles | | | As % of previous year | | | 1930 as % of 1928 | |
	Total material goods	Total material goods & services	of which, excluding alcoholic beverages	Total material goods	Total material goods & services	of which, excluding alcoholic beverages	Total material goods	of which, excluding alcoholic beverages
A	1	2	3	4	5	6	7	8
Total population								
1928	145.4	158.9	149.1	-	-	-	-	-
1929	149.6	164.4	155.3	102.9	103.5	104.2	-	-
1930	150.5	167.3	157.8	100.6	101.8	101.6	105.3	105.8
A. Non-agricultural population								
1928	321.5	368.2	348.1	-	-	-	-	-
1929	314.8	363.7	347.1	97.9	98.8	99.7	-	-
1930	316.2	369.8	352.4	100.4	101.7	101.5	100.5	101.2
including:								
a) manual workers								
1928	315.8	361.4	334.1	-	-	-	-	-
1929	317.0	366.9	345.6	100.4	101.5	103.4	-	-
1930	325.9	384.0	361.5	102.8	104.7	104.6	106.2	108.2
b) non-manual workers								
1928	345.8	398.6	387.1	-	-	-	-	-
1929	350.2	408.0	398.5	101.3	102.4	102.9	-	-
1930	341.2	401.4	392.2	97.4	98.4	98.4	100.7	101.3
c) total proletariat								
1928	311.2	357.3	338.3	-	-	-	-	-
1929	315.7	365.7	350.2	101.4	102.4	103.5	-	-
1930	320.2	376.1	359.7	101.4	102.8	102.7	105.3	106.3
B. Agricultural population				-	-	-	-	-
1928	102.2	107.6	100.3	-	-	-	-	-
1929	107.8	114.0	106.7	105.5	105.9	106.4	-	-
1930	104.7	111.4	104.0	97.1	97.7	97.5	103.5	103.7

Sub-section D

Table 16. Norms of consumption per head by the population (in kind)

A	Unit of measure-ment (B)	Non-agricultural population Total non-agricultural population			Manual workers			Non-manual workers			Agricultural population		
		1928	1929	1930	1928	1929	1930	1928	1929	1930	1928	1929	1930
		1	2	3	4	5	6	7	8	9	10	11	12
I. Agricultural products													
1. Potatoes	kg	87.63	108.93	146.24	94.12	116.75	141.92	69.31	92.85	134.91	141.04	146.00	147.00
2. Vegetables and melons	"	38.44	54.44	69.11	41.04	56.56	68.66	34.80	56.73	73.52	80.96	85.01	100.77
3. Fruits and berries	"	15.73	15.49	11.30	15.25	16.35	11.98	21.09	17.81	12.59	14.52	14.32	13.19
4. Meat and fat	"	45.25	40.65	27.30	47.93	43.27	29.81	43.78	42.49	27.35	22.80	28.35	23.72
5. Milk and dairy products in milk equivalents	"	173.55	167.53	144.25	152.71	153.83	132.44	237.62	211.54	178.67	176.57	174.89	157.34
6. Eggs	piece	114.9	110.0	76.5	100.2	101.0	69.7	165.1	148.5	104.9	45.03	44.63	32.63
II. Grain products													
1. Rye flour, with baked bread	kg	38.31	42.84	76.55	40.30	44.54	73.90	37.23	42.21	72.45	90.81	86.01	85.58
of which:													
a) in flour	"	14.81	13.27	20.47	17.31	16.39	26.16	10.08	9.62	15.49	90.81	86.01	85.58
b) in baked bread	"	24.00	29.57	56.08	22.99	28.15	47.74	27.15	32.59	57.02	-	-	-
2. Wheat flour, with baked bread	"	101.17	88.91	83.18	113.90	100.05	97.96	82.18	77.37	74.52	89.56	84.48	81.34
of which:													
a) in flour	"	50.29	31.21	22.79	62.89	37.62	28.99	29.93	21.12	20.65	89.56	84.48	81.34
b) in baked bread	"	50.89	57.70	60.39	51.01	62.43	68.97	52.25	56.25	53.87	-	-	-
3. Other flour	"	2.11	2.01	1.65	1.89	2.14	2.03	3.03	2.10	1.69	22.35	29.38	24.61
Total flour	kg	141.59	133.76	161.38	156.09	146.73	173.89	122.44	121.68	148.66	202.72	199.87	191.53
4. Groats of all kinds	"	11.77	13.90	14.61	12.57	15.53	16.18	10.72	12.47	13.81	17.93	17.33	20.51

Sub-section D
Table 16. (cont'd)

A	B	Non-agricultural population									Agricultural population		
		Total non-agricultural population			Manual workers			Non-manual workers					
	Unit of measurement	1928	1929	1930	1928	1929	1930	1928	1929	1930	1928	1929	1930
		1	2	3	4	5	6	7	8	9	10	11	12
III. Industrial goods													
a) food products													
1. Sugar	kg	16.96	14.29	14.86	16.46	15.33	17.55	19.75	14.88	13.90	3.93	3.31	3.38
2. Vegetable oil	"	3.19	3.57	2.53	3.51	4.01	3.15	2.59	3.23	2.00	2.45	2.47	2.31
3. Fresh fish	"	4.15	3.86	4.60	4.13	3.64	4.85	4.70	4.66	4.99	0.63	0.62	0.62
4. Salt fish	"	3.8	6.5	10.1	5.4	7.7	12.4	3.7	5.5	8.3	–	–	–
5. Tea	"	0.33	0.30	0.24	0.32	0.28	0.28	0.38	0.34	0.24	0.13	0.12	0.12
b) Tobacco													
1. Tobacco and cigarettes	piece	1392.0	1434.0	1549.0	1442.0	1466.0	1754.0	1575.0	1599.0	1565.0	60.09	116.06	140.60
2. Makhorka	kg	0.54	0.43	0.49	0.88	0.65	0.78	0.25	0.22	0.21	0.59	0.55	0.50
c) Clothing and toiletries													
1. Cotton fabric including ready made clothing	metres	19.71	19.60	14.06	22.06	21.45	17.87	16.18	19.03	11.38	14.75	16.05	12.23
of which:													
a) fabric	"	16.25	16.36	9.80	18.82	18.10	12.81	12.68	15.78	7.66	13.65	14.79	10.49
b) ready-made clothing in fabric equivalents	"	3.46	3.24	4.26	3.24	3.35	5.06	3.50	3.25	3.72	1.10	1.26	1.74
2. Woollen fabric, including ready made clothing	"	1.50	1.22	0.97	1.52	1.33	1.29	1.34	1.21	0.75	0.35	0.46	0.57
of which:													
a) fabric	"	0.53	0.34	0.17	0.56	0.35	0.22	0.56	0.40	0.15	0.16	0.13	0.11
b) ready made clothing in fabric equivalents	"	0.97	0.88	0.80	0.96	0.98	1.07	0.78	0.81	0.60	0.19	0.33	0.46
3. Leather footwear	pairs	1.25	1.15	1.16	1.11	1.32	1.43	1.21	1.24	1.13	0.41	0.46	0.52
4. Rubber footwear	"	0.56	0.56	0.55	0.62	0.62	0.61	0.54	0.54	0.53	0.13	0.18	0.16
c) household soap	kg	2.67	2.92	2.25	2.88	3.09	2.35	2.51	2.82	2.15	1.07	1.09	0.85

Sub-section D

Table 17. Population data used for estimating consumption (annual average, in thousands)

Classes and groups of the population	1928	1929	1930
A	1	2	3
A. Non-agricultural population	29770	31281	34284
I. Proletariat	23949	26028	28990
including:			
1)manual workers	11802	12781	15006
2)non-manual workers	8461	9203	10376
3)day and casual labourers	1062	1168	1024
4)domestic servants	395	423	430
5)unemployed and transients (living on their own)	1269	1267	696
6)grant-aided students and pensioners (living on their own)	960	1186	1458
II. Artisans, craftsmen and small traders	5338	4831	4860
III. Capitalist groups	167	106	83
IV. Other non-agricultural population	316	316	315
B. Agricultural population	121664	123622	123902
Total	151434	154903	158150
C. Other population (dependent on collective supply)[1]	1022	1093	1182
Total	152456	155996	159332

1. This group of the population includes consumption by [state] institutions [i.e. army and prisoners]

3. Tables and notes

III BASIC INTEGRATED TABLES IN THE BALANCE OF THE NATIONAL ECONOMY

CONTENTS

Table 1. Balance of production, consumption and accumulation, in millions of rubles, in current prices (products grouped by origin)

Item of input	1928 Building products	1928 Industrial products	1928 Agricultural hunting products	1928 Total	1929 Building products	1929 Industrial products	1929 Agricultural hunting products	1929 Total	1930 Building products	1930 Industrial products	1930 Agricultural hunting products	1930 Total
A	1	2	3	4	5	6	7	8	9	10	11	12
INPUT												
A. Fixed capital stock at beginning of year	45853.6	10176.2	8297.3	64327.1	47307.9	10801.6	8862.6	66972.1	49159.8	11938.7	10556.9	71635.4
I. Production	16176.0	9432.1	8297.3	34146.4	17093.2	10039.8	8862.6	35995.6	18130.1	11134.8	10556.9	39821.8
1. In census industry	3238.8	2473.5	-	5712.1	3573.3	2860.3	2.4	6436.0	4092.9	3449.6	5.4	7547.9
2. In small-scale industry	254.9	514.3	-	769.2	250.3	504.8	-	755.1	250.8	506.0	-	756.8
3. In agriculture	6417.3	3247.9	8297.3	17962.5	6650.8	3400.9	8860.2	18911.9	6950.5	3693.9	10551.5	21195.9
4. In transport	6268.6	3008.1	-	9276.7	6349.6	3078.7	-	9428.3	6493.9	3250.2	-	9744.1
5. In trade	237.4	188.5	-	425.9	269.2	195.1	-	464.3	342.0	235.1	-	577.1
II. Consumption	29436.6	744.1	-	30180.7	30214.7	761.8	-	30976.5	31009.7	803.9	-	31813.6
1. Communications stock	111.7	117.9	-	229.6	136.1	123.6	-	259.7	164.0	136.9	-	301.7
2. Stock assigned to social purposes	5157.5	626.2	-	5783.7	5390.2	638.2	-	6028.4	5718.2	667.0	-	6385.2
3. Housing stock	24167.4	-	-	24167.4	24688.4	-	-	24688.4	25126.7	-	-	25126.7
a) urban	13119.1	-	-	13119.1	13340.8	-	-	13340.8	13562.3	-	-	13562.3
b) rural	11048.3	-	-	11048.3	11347.6	-	-	11347.6	11564.4	-	-	11564.4
B. Stocks at beginning of year	1056.7	5882.9	5271.7	12211.3	1618.5	6342.8	6401.2	14562.5	2446.1	7023.5	7241.5	16711.1
1. Means of production	711.3	3545.7	4244.8	8501.8	1128.9	3688.6	5145.6	9963.1	1700.5	4331.3	5795.0	11826.8
2. Consumer goods	345.4	2337.2	1026.9	3709.5	489.6	2654.2	1255.6	4399.4	745.6	2692.2	1446.5	4884.3
C. Production per year (in producer's prices)	4239.1	27162.4	20016.0	51517.5	5025.3	32134.0	21240.9	58400.2	6695.1	37907.9	25223.5	69826.5
1. In agriculture	-	-	19241.3	19241.3	-	-	20334.2	20334.2	-	-	24107.2	24107.2
2. In census industry	-	19231.9	13.1	19245.0	-	23342.8	19.0	23361.8	-	28651.1	34.9	28686.0
3. In small-scale industry	-	5783.4	85.3	5868.7	-	6248.0	98.9	6346.9	-	6517.7	74.8	6592.5
4. In building	4239.1	-	-	4239.1	5025.3	-	-	5025.3	6695.1	-	-	6695.1
5. In forestry	-	1411.3	-	1411.3	-	1741.9	-	1741.9	-	1823.3	-	1823.3
6. In other branches (fishing,hunting, etc.)	-	735.8	778.3	1512.1	-	801.3	788.8	1590.1	-	915.8	1006.6	1922.4
D. Imports	-	750.2	202.9	953.1	-	717.0	163.6	880.6	-	924.9	133.9	1058.8
E. Trade and transport mark-up	-	3761.4	1419.8	5181.2	-	4404.9	1633.3	6038.2	-	5722.6	1752.4	7475.0
a) transport	-	-	-	1982.7	-	-	-	2472.8	-	-	-	3219.7
b) trade	-	-	-	3198.5	-	-	-	3565.4	-	-	-	4255.3
F. Customs duties	-	228.5	43.0	271.5	-	213.9	39.7	253.6	-	364.9	38.8	403.7
G. Excises	-	1463.0	-	1463.0	-	1777.7	-	1777.7	-	3023.5	-	3023.5
Total	51149.4	49424.6	35850.7	135924.7	53951.7	56591.9	38341.3	148684.9	58281.0	66906.0	44947.0	170134.1

Table 1 (cont'd)

Item of output	1928				1929				1930			
	Building products	Industrial products	Agricultural & hunting products	Total	Building products	Industrial products	Agricultural & hunting products	Total	Building products	Industrial products	Agricultural & hunting products	Total
A	1	2	3	4	5	6	7	8	9	10	11	12
OUTPUT												
A. Consumed in production	841.4	17259.6	12426.9	30527.9	885.4	19983.6	13687.1	34556.1	946.1	23029.3	15396.6	39372.0
1. In agriculture	425.9	1272.7	7133.1	8831.7	433.6	1344.1	7862.3	9640.0	448.8	1386.7	8641.4	10476.9
2. In census industry	208.1	11166.2	2042.2	13416.5	235.4	13153.4	2141.5	15530.3	260.6	14964.0	2660.4	17885.0
3. In small-scale industry	16.4	1547.7	2492.7	4056.8	13.0	1642.0	2843.2	4498.2	15.4	1682.6	3045.6	4743.6
4. In building	-	2348.5	20.8	2369.3	-	2729.1	29.9	2759.0	-	3650.0	45.0	3695.0
5. In forestry	-	7.2	-	7.2	-	8.4	-	8.4	-	10.1	-	10.1
6. In trade	10.2	227.8	-	238.0	11.4	282.6	-	294.0	14.8	324.7	-	339.5
7. In transport (freight)	180.8	606.7	60.3	847.8	192.0	732.2	59.8	984.0	206.5	898.6	112.8	1217.9
8. In other branches	-	82.8	677.8	760.6	-	91.8	750.4	842.2	-	112.6	891.4	1004.0
B. Consumption by the population and by institutions	1214.6	14376.5	7177.6	22768.7	1224.9	16588.8	8182.8	25996.5	1244.3	19677.4	10564.4	31486.3
1. Institutions (including communications)	129.2	877.1	84.2	1090.5	133.9	1040.2	108.3	1282.4	142.3	1273.2	133.1	1548.6
2. Passenger transport	55.5	230.4	25.8	311.7	49.5	237.6	21.8	308.9	54.7	292.4	39.6	386.7
3. Agricultural population	599.1	7331.7	4509.8	12440.6	604.9	8738.9	4955.1	14298.9	605.1	9741.5	5474.2	15820.8
4. Non-agricultural population	430.8	5937.3	2557.8	8925.9	436.6	6572.1	3097.6	10106.3	442.2	8370.3	4917.7	13730.2
C. Losses	50.8	74.6	675.5	800.9	61.6	112.6	861.6	1035.8	68.5	175.1	1455.8	1699.4
1. In storage in agriculture	-	-	192.7	192.7	-	-	235.1	235.1	-	-	341.9	341.9
2. In channels of circulation	-	74.6	11.4	86.0	-	107.5	11.7	119.2	-	134.8	170.5	305.3
3. From agricultural stocks: a) livestock	-	-	471.4	471.4	-	-	614.8	614.8	-	-	943.4	943.4
b) others	50.8	-	-	50.8	61.6	5.1	-	66.7	68.5	40.3	-	108.8
D. Exports	-	491.8	307.7	799.5	-	616.0	307.7	923.7	-	652.6	383.8	1036.4
E. Stocks at end of year	1618.5	6342.8	6401.2	14362.5	2446.1	7023.5	7241.5	16711.1	4006.8	9222.4	7467.2	20696.4
1. Means of production	1128.9	3688.6	5145.6	9963.1	1700.5	4331.3	5795.0	11826.8	2724.8	5909.2	6099.1	14733.1
2. Consumer goods	489.6	2654.2	1255.6	4399.4	745.6	2692.2	1446.5	4884.3	1282.0	3313.2	1368.1	5963.3
F. Fixed capital stock at end of year	47307.9	10801.6	8361.8	66471.3	49139.8	11938.7	8060.6	69139.1	51780.2	13961.4	9660.3	75401.9
I. Production	17093.2	10039.8	8361.8	35494.8	18130.1	11134.8	8060.6	37325.5	20209.6	13100.7	9660.3	42970.6
1. In census industry	3513.3	2860.3	2.4	6456.0	4092.9	3449.6	5.4	7547.9	5048.9	4510.3	9.6	9568.8
2. In small scale industry	250.3	504.8	-	755.1	250.8	506.0	-	756.8	250.8	486.0	-	736.8
3. In agriculture	6650.8	3400.9	8359.4	18411.1	6950.5	3693.9	8055.2	18699.6	7400.3	4190.8	9650.7	21241.8
4. In transport	6349.6	3078.7	-	9428.3	6493.9	3250.2	-	9744.1	7023.9	3575.4	-	10599.3
5. In trade	269.2	195.1	-	464.3	342.0	235.1	-	577.1	485.7	338.2	-	823.9

Table 1 (cont'd)

Item of output	1928				1929				1930			
	Building products	Industrial products	Agricultural & hunting products	Total	Building products	Industrial products	Agricultural & hunting products	Total	Building products	Industrial products	Agricultural & hunting products	Total
A	1	2	3	4	5	6	7	8	9	10	11	12
II. Consumption	30214.7	761.8	-	30976.5	31009.7	803.9	-	31813.6	31570.6	860.7	-	32431.3
1. Communications stock	136.1	123.6	-	259.7	164.8	136.9	-	301.7	210.5	159.9	-	370.4
2. Stock assigned to social purposes	5390.2	638.2	-	6028.4	5718.2	667.0	-	6385.9	5995.3	700.8	-	6696.1
3. Housing stock	24688.4	-	-	24688.4	25126.0	-	-	25126.7	25364.8	-	-	25364.8
a) urban	13340.8	-	-	13340.8	13562.3	-	-	13562.3	13883.6	-	-	13883.6
b) rural	11347.6	-	-	11347.6	11564.4	-	-	11564.4	11481.2	-	-	11481.2
G. Investment in unrecorded capital stock	116.2	77.1	-	193.9	193.9	128.7	-	322.6	235.1	187.8	18.7	441.6
1. Census industry	113.8	46.8	-	160.6	188.0	72.6	-	260.6	215.2	89.2	-	304.4
2. Transport	1.0	-	-	1.0	3.5	16.9	-	20.4	8.2	34.9	-	43.1
3. Agriculture	-	-	-	-	-	-	-	-	-	-	18.7	18.7
4. Stock assigned to social purposes	1.4	30.9	-	32.3	2.4	39.2	-	41.6	11.7	63.7	-	75.4
	51149.4	49424.6	85850.7	185924.7	58951.7	56391.9	38841.8	148684.9	58281.0	66906.0	44947.0	170184.0
Increase in fixed capital and other stocks												
I. Increase in fixed capital stocks	1570.5	703.1	64.5	2338.1	2025.8	1265.8	-802.0	2489.6	2875.5	2210.5	-877.9	4208.1
a) production	791.0	654.5	64.5	1510.0	1228.4	1184.5	-802.0	1610.9	2302.9	2090.0	-877.9	3515.0
b) consumption	779.5	48.6	-	828.1	797.4	81.3	-	878.7	572.6	120.5	-	693.1
II. Increase in other stocks	561.8	459.9	1129.5	2151.2	827.6	680.7	840.3	2348.6	1560.7	2198.9	225.7	3985.3
a) means of production	417.6	142.9	900.8	1461.3	571.6	642.7	649.4	1863.7	1024.3	1577.9	304.1	2906.3
b) consumer goods	144.2	317.0	228.7	689.9	256.0	38.0	190.9	484.9	536.4	621.0	-78.4	1079.0
Total increase in fixed capital and other stocks	2132.3	1163.0	1194.0	4489.3	2853.5	1946.5	38.3	4838.2	4436.2	4409.4	-652.2	8193.4
of which: a) means of production	1208.6	797.4	965.3	2971.3	1800.0	1827.2	-152.6	3474.6	3327.2	3667.9	-573.8	6421.3
b) consumer goods	923.7	365.6	228.7	1518.0	1053.4	119.3	190.9	1363.6	1109.0	741.5	-78.4	1772.1

Table 2. Extract from balance of production and consumption, in millions of rubles, in current prices (products grouped by [predominant] economic end-use)

Items of input and output	A. Means of production — a) fixed means of production 1928	1929	1930	b) raw material, auxiliary material and fuel 1928	1929	1930	Total means of production 1928	1929	1930	B. Consumer goods 1928	1929	1930	Total 1928	1929	1930
	1	2	3	4	5	6	7	8	9	10	11	12	13	14	15
INPUT															
A. Stocks at beginning of year	1337.8	1912.0	2677.6	7164.0	8051.1	9149.2	8501.8	9963.1	11826.8	3709.5	4399.4	4884.3	12211.3	14362.5	16711.1
B. Production per year(in producer's prices)	6610.2	7554.6	10565.4	21958.8	25128.5	28832.3	28569.0	32683.1	39397.7	22948.5	25717.5	30428.8	51517.5	58400.2	69826.5
1. In agriculture	2807.7	2448.6	2976.2	9141.7	9750.6	10692.2	11949.4	12199.2	13668.4	7291.9	8135.0	10438.8	19241.3	20334.2	24107.2
2. In census industry	1418.2	2046.4	2933.7	10793.9	13029.6	15572.4	12212.1	15076.0	18506.1	7032.9	8285.8	10179.9	19245.0	23361.8	28686.0
3. In small-scale industry	229.4	262.3	240.6	886.1	927.5	890.8	1115.5	1189.8	1131.4	4753.2	5157.1	5461.1	5868.7	6346.9	6592.5
4. In building	2154.9	2797.3	4414.9	-	-	-	2154.9	2797.3	4414.9	2084.2	2228.0	2280.2	4239.1	5025.3	6695.1
5. In forestry	-	-	-	703.3	946.0	1077.1	703.3	946.0	1077.1	708.0	795.9	746.2	1411.3	1741.9	1823.3
6. In other branches (fishing,hunting,etc.)	-	-	-	433.8	474.8	599.8	433.8	474.8	599.8	1078.3	1115.3	1322.6	1512.1	1590.1	1922.4
C. Imports	235.1	245.2	476.3	593.5	518.5	431.7	828.6	763.7	908.0	124.5	116.9	150.8	953.1	880.6	1058.8
D. Trade and transport mark-up	169.7	228.8	330.1	1611.2	1949.8	2355.8	1780.9	2178.6	2685.9	3400.3	3859.6	4789.1	5181.2	6038.2	7475.0
E. Customs duties	35.9	37.5	121.8	177.8	151.9	190.2	213.7	189.4	312.0	57.8	64.2	91.7	271.5	253.6	403.7
F. Excises	-	-	-	75.0	90.0	136.5	75.0	90.0	136.5	1388.0	1687.7	2887.0	1463.0	1777.7	3023.5
Total entered into producer's prices	8388.7	9978.1	14171.2	31580.8	35889.8	41095.7	39969.0	45867.9	55266.9	31628.6	35844.9	43231.7	71597.6	81712.8	98498.6
OUTPUT															
A. Consumed in production	2159.6	2628.6	3055.9	21963.4	24850.2	28059.7	24123.0	27458.8	31115.6	4419.6	5012.6	6052.6	28542.6	32471.4	37168.2
1. In agriculture	1939.4	2326.7	2579.6	4327.2	4781.7	5283.8	6266.6	7108.4	7863.4	1331.3	1292.8	1267.9	7597.9	8401.2	9131.3
2. In census industry	183.2	244.6	387.7	11302.2	12848.5	14213.3	11485.4	13093.1	14601.0	1495.6	1944.8	2730.3	12981.0	15037.9	17331.3
3. In small-scale industry	12.4	14.0	16.6	3335.1	3712.9	3889.1	3347.5	3726.9	3905.7	659.8	725.3	789.4	4007.3	4452.2	4695.1
4. In building	2.0	3.0	5.0	2352.8	2744.3	3678.6	2354.8	2747.3	3683.6	14.5	11.7	11.4	2369.3	2759.0	3695.0
5. In forestry	-	-	-	2.2	3.0	4.1	2.2	3.0	4.1	-	-	-	2.2	3.0	4.1
6. In trade	-	-	-	166.0	210.5	246.0	166.0	210.5	246.0	49.1	57.5	61.4	215.1	268.0	307.4
7. In transport (freight and passenger)	22.6	40.3	67.0	477.9	529.3	744.8	500.5	569.6	811.8	109.9	139.6	190.7	610.4	709.2	1002.5
8. In other branches	-	-	-	-	-	-	-	-	-	759.4	840.9	1001.5	759.4	840.9	1001.5

Table 2. (cont'd)

Items of input and output	A. Means of production									B. Consumer goods			Total		
	a) fixed means of production			b) raw material, auxiliary material and fuel			Total means of production								
	1928	1929	1930	1928	1929	1930	1928	1929	1930	1928	1929	1930	1928	1929	1930
A	1	2	3	4	5	6	7	8	9	10	11	12	13	14	15
B. Consumed by the population and institutions	12.6	15.7	16.0	865.8	1011.9	1007.8	878.4	1027.6	1023.8	20367.4	23431.1	28829.8	21245.8	24458.7	29853.6
1. Institutions including communications	12.6	15.7	16.0	202.9	232.6	262.7	215.5	248.3	278.7	693.7	846.7	1071.2	909.2	1095.0	1349.9
2. Agricultural population	-	-	-	404.5	461.8	352.7	404.5	461.8	352.7	11437.0	13232.2	14863.0	11841.5	13694.0	15215.7
3. Non-agricultural population	-	-	-	258.4	317.5	392.4	258.4	317.5	392.4	8236.7	9352.2	12895.6	8495.1	9669.7	13288.0
C. Losses	2.6	4.6	-	120.5	157.5	379.1	123.1	162.1	379.1	155.6	192.2	268.1	278.7	354.3	647.2
D. Exports	0.9	2.0	2.1	518.3	655.4	796.6	519.2	657.4	798.7	280.3	266.3	237.7	799.5	923.7	1036.4
E. Stocks at beginning of year	1912.0	2677.6	4013.1	8051.1	9149.2	10720.0	9963.1	11826.8	14733.1	4399.4	4884.3	5963.3	14362.5	16711.1	20696.4
F. Entered into fixed capital stock	4301.0	4649.6	7084.1	61.2	85.6	132.5	4362.2	4735.2	7216.6	2006.3	2058.4	1880.2	6368.5	6793.6	9096.8
I. Production	4224.7	4551.3	6964.5	49.8	68.8	105.1	4274.5	4620.1	7069.6	66.3	86.4	136.4	4340.8	4706.5	7206.0
1. In agriculture	2159.1	1658.6	2406.6	7.3	7.8	11.8	2166.4	1666.4	2418.4	11.2	11.9	18.0	2177.6	1678.3	2436.4
2. In census industry	1272.2	1808.8	2771.5	35.9	45.4	62.7	1308.1	1854.2	2834.2	24.0	30.7	41.9	1332.1	1884.9	2876.1
3. In small-scale industry	21.9	25.6	26.5	1.5	2.1	2.0	23.4	27.7	28.5	-	-	-	23.4	27.7	28.5
4. In transport and communications	712.7	929.8	1503.7	2.6	3.2	5.9	715.3	933.0	1509.6	31.1	43.8	76.5	746.4	976.8	1586.1
5. In trade	58.8	128.5	256.2	2.5	10.3	22.7	61.3	138.8	278.9	-	-	-	61.3	138.8	278.9
II. Consumption	76.3	98.3	119.6	11.4	16.8	27.4	87.7	115.1	147.0	1940.0	1972.0	1743.8	2027.7	2087.1	1890.8
1. Rural housing stock	-	-	-	-	-	-	-	-	-	931.4	858.2	559.6	931.4	858.2	559.6
2. Urban housing stock	-	-	-	-	-	-	-	-	-	652.5	658.1	763.5	652.5	658.1	763.5
3. Stock assigned to social purposes	76.3	98.3	119.6	11.4	16.8	27.4	87.7	115.1	147.0	356.1	455.7	420.7	443.8	570.8	567.7
	8388.7	9978.1	14171.2	31580.8	35889.8	41095.7	39969.0	45867.9	55266.9	31628.6	35844.9	43231.7	71597.6	81712.8	98498.6

Table 3. Distribution of annual production by branch of the economy (in million rubles, in current prices)

A	Year	Production (in producers prices)	Trade and transport mark-up	Excises	Total production (in consumers prices) Total	Consumed in production Total	of which In agriculture	In census industry	In small-scale industry	In building	of which In rural areas	Consumed by the population and institutions Total	of which by the agricultural population
		1	2	3	4	5	6	7	8	9	10	11	12
Total for the economy	1928	51517.5	5181.2	1463.0	58161.7	27648.2	7593.4	12168.6	4007.8	2291.8	867.1	21081.7	11807.6
	1929	58400.2	6038.2	1777.7	66216.1	31787.4	8875.6	14428.2	4452.2	2700.7	865.7	25240.8	13621.8
	1930	69826.5	7475.0	3023.5	80325.0	36487.7	9117.5	16822.1	4695.1	8589.4	816.7	29401.6	15037.8
of which 1. Building	1928	4239.1	-	-	4239.1	-	-	-	-	-	-	-	-
	1929	5025.3	-	-	5025.3	-	-	-	-	-	-	-	-
	1930	6695.1	-	-	6695.1	-	-	-	-	-	-	-	-
2. Industry	1928	25113.7	3292.8	1463.0	29869.5	14251.2	764.5	9910.1	1427.8	1453.2	244.6	12995.0	6758.5
	1929	29708.7	3814.1	1777.7	35300.5	16795.4	793.6	11872.9	1515.9	1801.6	232.2	15096.3	8119.9
	1930	35278.5	5019.9	3023.5	43321.9	19510.4	776.4	13535.8	1543.7	2612.3	174.0	18066.3	9162.0
3. Agriculture	1928	19241.3	1245.3	-	20484.6	11781.7	6757.1	1758.7	2481.1	20.8	20.8	6295.6	4000.5
	1929	20334.2	1421.8	-	21756.0	13108.5	7513.6	1903.4	2829.6	29.9	29.9	7236.4	4474.4
	1930	24107.2	1429.4	-	25536.6	14820.0	8283.9	2417.4	3030.2	45.0	45.0	9091.1	4908.3
4. Forestry	1928	1411.3	351.5	-	1762.8	1092.1	30.7	418.9	81.2	510.6	294.5	588.8	276.7
	1929	1741.9	433.5	-	2175.4	1237.4	31.7	544.3	86.3	522.1	256.5	648.2	285.2
	1930	1823.3	495.7	-	2319.0	1415.2	31.8	655.7	97.0	554.0	219.6	642.1	285.6
5. Fishing & Hunting	1928	323.5	144.0	-	467.5	130.8	-	36.8	17.2	-	-	236.5	135.5
	1929	354.6	201.0	-	555.6	161.6	-	56.7	20.4	-	-	291.1	149.3
	1930	464.3	248.4	-	712.7	237.8	-	112.4	24.2	-	-	366.7	144.7
6. Domestic production	1928	1152.2	143.4	-	1295.0	349.8	41.1	1.5	-	307.2	307.2	945.8	636.4
	1929	1193.1	160.8	-	1353.9	385.1	36.7	1.3	-	347.1	347.1	968.8	593.0
	1930	1372.6	268.7	-	1641.3	405.9	25.4	2.4	-	378.1	378.1	1235.4	537.1
7. Other branches of the economy	1928	36.4	6.2	-	42.6	42.6	-	42.6	-	-	-	-	-
	1929	42.4	7.0	-	49.4	49.4	-	49.4	-	-	-	-	-
	1930	85.5	12.9	-	98.4	98.4	-	98.4	-	-	-	-	-

Table 3. (cont'd)

A	Year	Exports	Imports	Increase in stocks				Entered into fixed capital stock		of which,				Total distributed
				Total	In agriculture	In industry	In building	Total	Into stock of productive branches	Into agricultural stock	Into industrial stock	Into stock of the non-productive sphere	of which, into the rural housing stock	
	B	13	14	15	16	17	18	19	20	21	22	23	24	25
Total for the economy	1928	799.5	287.7	2276.1	1154.4	47.4	712.7	6097.5	4069.8	2146.8	1138.0	2027.7	931.4	58161.7
	1929	928.7	354.8	2449.7	239.7	366.6	1050.7	6510.2	4423.1	1609.8	1733.1	2087.1	858.2	66216.1
	1930	1036.4	647.2	4253.6	424.1	1363.1	1901.9	8498.5	6607.7	2315.4	2483.7	1890.8	559.6	80325.0
of which 1.Building	1928	-	-	561.8	-	-	561.8	3677.3	1737.3	677.2	668.2	1940.0	931.4	4239.1
	1929	-	-	827.6	-	-	827.6	4197.7	2225.7	758.4	956.3	1972.0	858.2	5025.3
	1930	-	-	1560.7	-	-	1560.7	5134.4	3390.6	929.4	1447.2	1743.8	559.6	6695.1
2.Industry	1928	475.4	85.4	509.7	116.0	16.4	146.4	1552.8	1465.1	604.6	467.4	87.7	-	29869.5
	1929	566.8	117.4	531.0	-	298.7	203.1	2190.6	2075.5	731.8	774.5	115.1	-	35300.5
	1930	561.2	142.9	2073.6	210.6	1249.6	328.2	2967.5	2820.5	990.5	1035.4	147.0	-	43321.9
3.Agriculture	1928	194.3	193.3	1152.3	1058.4	-	-	867.4	867.4	865.0	2.4	-	-	20484.6
	1929	214.4	236.9	837.9	239.7	3.5	-	121.9	121.9	119.6	2.3	-	-	21756.0
	1930	333.9	481.7	413.3	213.5	42.7	-	396.6	396.6	395.5	1.1	-	-	25536.6
4.Forestry	1928	33.4	-	48.5	-	29.3	4.5	-	-	-	-	-	-	1762.8
	1929	51.5	-	238.3	-	55.3	-	-	-	-	-	-	-	2175.4
	1930	57.5	-	204.2	-	69.0	13.0	-	-	-	-	-	-	2319.0
5.Fishing & Hunting	1928	96.4	-	3.8	-	1.7	-	-	-	-	-	-	-	467.5
	1929	91.0	-	11.9	-	3.1	-	-	-	-	-	-	-	555.6
	1930	83.8	22.6	1.8	-	1.8	-	-	-	-	-	-	-	712.7
6.Domestic production	1928	-	-	-	-	-	-	-	-	-	-	-	-	1295.6
	1929	-	-	-	-	-	-	-	-	-	-	-	-	1553.9
	1930	-	-	-	-	-	-	-	-	-	-	-	-	1641.3
7.Other branches of the economy	1928	-	-	-	-	-	-	-	-	-	-	-	-	42.6
	1929	-	-	-	-	-	-	-	-	-	-	-	-	49.4
	1930	-	-	-	-	-	-	-	-	-	-	-	-	98.4

Table 4. The balance of production and consumption, in millions of rubles (in current prices)

by origin (A)	Year (B)	In agriculture (1)	In census industry (2)	In small-scale industry (3)	In transport (4)	In forestry (5)	In building — Rural (6)	Industrial (7)	Transport (8)	Trade (9)	Housing (10)	Social purposes (11)	Total in building (12)	In channels of circulation (13)	Total stocks at start of year (14)
Total for the economy	1928	5264.9	3124.8	5.0	315.7	120.4	-	964.2	145.1	42.2	197.8	148.1	1494.9	1885.6	12211.3
	1929	6419.5	3003.4	5.4	334.0	132.1	-	1369.6	302.6	49.0	277.6	212.0	2210.8	2257.8	14362.5
	1930	6603.6	3305.7	6.3	268.4	324.7	9.1	1940.0	478.1	64.4	419.5	326.1	3237.2	2970.2	16711.1
a) Products of building	1928	-	-	-	-	-	-	563.4	105.7	42.2	197.3	148.1	1056.7	-	1056.7
	1929	-	-	-	-	-	-	820.7	259.2	49.0	277.6	212.0	1618.5	-	1618.5
	1930	-	-	-	-	-	9.1	1186.5	440.5	64.4	419.5	326.1	2446.1	-	2446.1
b) Industrial products	1928	491.4	2821.4	5.0	315.7	120.4	-	400.8	37.4	-	-	-	438.2	1690.3	5882.9
	1929	607.4	2721.3	5.4	334.0	132.1	-	548.9	43.4	-	-	-	592.3	1950.3	6342.8
	1930	551.8	3011.0	6.3	263.4	324.7	-	753.5	37.6	-	-	-	791.1	2075.2	7023.5
c) Agricultural products and products of hunting	1928	4773.5	303.4	-	-	-	-	-	-	-	-	-	-	194.8	5271.7
	1929	5812.1	282.1	-	-	-	-	-	-	-	-	-	-	307.0	6401.2
	1930	6051.9	294.7	-	-	-	-	-	-	-	-	-	-	895.0	7241.5
A. Means of production	1928	3786.4	2601.3	5.0	253.6	39.4	-	964.2	145.1	42.2	-	-	1149.5	666.6	8501.8
	1929	4605.6	2495.9	5.4	264.1	52.0	-	1369.6	302.6	49.0	-	-	1721.2	818.9	9963.1
	1930	4686.6	2861.3	6.3	200.2	187.7	9.1	1940.0	478.1	64.4	-	-	2491.6	1393.1	11826.8
a) Products of building	1928	-	-	-	-	-	-	563.4	105.7	42.2	-	-	711.3	-	711.3
	1929	-	-	-	-	-	-	820.7	259.2	49.0	-	-	1128.9	-	1128.9
	1930	-	-	-	-	-	9.1	1186.5	440.5	64.4	-	-	1700.5	-	1700.5
b) Industrial products	1928	23.8	2303.9	5.0	253.6	39.4	-	400.8	37.4	-	-	-	438.2	481.8	3545.7
	1929	35.1	2219.5	5.4	264.1	52.0	-	548.9	43.4	-	-	-	592.3	520.2	3688.0
	1930	16.2	2572.6	6.3	200.2	187.7	-	753.5	37.6	-	-	-	791.1	557.2	4331.3
c) Agricultural products and products of hunting	1928	3762.6	297.4	-	-	-	-	-	-	-	-	-	-	184.8	4244.8
	1929	4570.5	276.4	-	-	-	-	-	-	-	-	-	-	298.7	5145.6
	1930	4670.4	288.7	-	-	-	-	-	-	-	-	-	-	835.9	5795.0

Input of products into the economy — Stocks at beginning of year

Table 4. (cont'd)

Input of products into the economy
Production per year in producer's prices

by [predominant] end-use

by origin	Year	In agri-culture	In census industry	In small-scale industry	In forestry	In hunting	In fishing	In domestic produc-tion	In building	In other branches of the economy	Total produc-tion per year	Imports	Transport and trade mark-up	Customs duties	Excise	Total entered, in consumer's prices
A	B	15	16	17	18	19	20	21	22	23	24	25	26	27	28	29
Total for the economy	1928	19241.3	19245.0	5868.7	1411.3	87.7	235.8	1152.2	4229.1	36.4	51517.5	953.1	5181.2	271.5	1463.0	71597.6
	1929	20334.2	23361.8	6346.9	1741.9	82.3	272.8	1198.1	5025.3	42.4	58400.2	880.6	6058.2	253.6	1777.7	81712.8
	1930	24107.2	28686.0	6592.5	1823.3	129.1	335.2	1372.6	6695.1	85.5	69826.5	1058.8	7475.0	403.7	3023.5	98498.0
a) Products of building	1928	-	-	-	-	-	-	-	4229.1	-	4239.1	-	-	-	-	5295.8
	1929	-	-	-	-	-	-	-	5025.3	-	5025.3	-	-	-	-	6643.8
	1930	-	-	-	-	-	-	-	6695.1	-	6695.1	-	-	-	-	9141.2
b) Industrial products	1928	-	19231.9	5783.4	1411.3	-	235.8	463.6	-	36.4	27162.4	750.2	3761.4	228.5	1463.0	39248.4
	1929	-	23342.8	6248.0	1741.9	-	272.3	486.6	-	42.4	32134.0	717.0	4404.9	213.9	1777.7	45590.3
	1930	-	28651.1	6517.7	1823.3	-	335.2	495.1	-	85.5	37907.9	924.9	5722.6	364.9	3023.5	54967.3
c) Agricultural products and products of hunting	1928	19241.3	13.1	85.3	-	87.7	-	688.6	-	-	20116.0	202.9	1419.8	43.0	-	27053.4
	1929	20334.2	19.0	98.9	-	82.3	-	706.5	-	-	21240.9	163.6	1633.3	39.7	-	29478.7
	1930	24107.2	34.9	74.8	-	129.1	-	877.5	-	-	25223.5	133.9	1752.4	38.8	-	34590.1
A. Means of production	1928	11949.4	12212.1	1115.5	703.3	87.7	-	309.7	2154.9	36.4	28569.0	828.6	1780.9	213.7	75.0	39969.0
	1929	12199.2	15076.0	1189.8	946.0	82.3	-	350.1	2797.3	42.4	32683.1	763.7	2178.6	189.4	90.0	45867.9
	1930	13668.4	18506.1	1131.4	1077.1	129.1	-	385.2	4414.9	85.5	39397.7	908.0	2685.9	312.0	136.5	55266.9
a) Products of building	1928	-	-	-	-	-	-	-	2154.9	-	2154.9	-	-	-	-	2866.2
	1929	-	-	-	-	-	-	-	2797.3	-	2797.3	-	-	-	-	3926.2
	1930	-	-	-	-	-	-	-	4414.9	-	4414.9	-	-	-	-	6115.4
b) Industrial products	1928	-	12211.3	1115.5	703.3	-	-	309.7	-	36.4	14376.2	635.4	1383.0	171.1	75.0	20186.4
	1929	-	15074.9	1189.8	946.0	-	-	350.1	-	42.4	17603.2	607.5	1662.8	150.3	90.0	23802.4
	1930	-	18504.7	1131.4	1077.1	-	-	385.2	-	85.5	21183.9	798.0	2076.7	273.6	136.5	28800.0
c) Agricultural products and products of hunting	1928	11949.4	0.8	-	-	87.7	-	-	-	-	13037.9	193.2	397.9	42.6	-	16916.4
	1929	12199.2	1.1	-	-	82.3	-	-	-	-	12282.6	156.2	515.8	39.1	-	18139.3
	1930	13668.4	1.4	-	-	129.1	-	-	-	-	13798.9	110.0	609.2	38.4	-	20551.5

Table 4 (cont'd)

Distribution of products in the economy
Consumed in production

by [predominant] end-use

by origin (A)	Year (B)	In agriculture (30)	In census industry (31)	In small-scale industry (32)	In transport (33)	In forestry (34)	In fishing (35)	In domestic production (36)	In trade enterprises (37)	In building				Total building (42)	Total consumed in production (43)
										Industrial (38)	Rural (39)	Transport (40)	Housing, social purposes and trade (41)		
Total for the economy	1928	7597.9	12981.0	4007.8	610.4	2.2	81.6	677.8	215.1	537.2	867.1	280.4	684.6	2309.3	28542.6
	1929	8401.2	15037.9	4452.2	709.2	3.0	90.5	750.4	268.0	746.6	865.7	338.4	808.8	2759.0	32471.4
	1930	9181.8	17331.8	4695.1	1002.5	4.1	110.1	891.4	307.4	1310.7	816.7	523.0	1044.6	3695.0	37168.2
a) Products of building	1928	–	–	–	–	–	–	–	–	–	–	–	–	–	–
	1929	–	–	–	–	–	–	–	–	–	–	–	–	–	–
	1930	–	–	–	–	–	–	–	–	–	–	–	–	–	–
b) Industrial products	1928	799.7	10938.8	1514.6	524.2	2.2	81.6	–	215.1	537.2	846.3	280.4	684.6	2348.5	16424.7
	1929	850.9	12896.4	1609.0	627.7	3.0	90.5	–	268.0	746.6	835.8	338.4	808.3	2729.1	19074.6
	1930	822.0	14670.9	1649.5	850.4	4.1	110.1	–	307.4	1310.7	771.7	523.0	1044.6	3650.0	22064.4
c) Agricultural products and products of hunting	1928	6798.2	2042.2	2492.7	86.2	–	–	677.8	–	–	20.8	–	–	20.8	12117.9
	1929	7550.3	2141.5	2843.2	81.5	–	–	750.4	–	–	29.9	–	–	29.9	13396.8
	1930	8309.3	2660.4	3045.6	152.1	–	–	891.4	–	–	45.0	–	–	45.0	15103.8
A. Means of production	1928	6266.6	11485.4	3347.5	500.5	2.2	–	–	166.0	532.8	867.1	280.4	674.5	2354.8	24123.0
	1929	7108.4	13093.1	3726.9	569.6	3.0	–	–	210.5	743.1	865.7	333.4	800.1	2747.3	27458.8
	1930	7863.4	14601.0	3905.7	811.8	4.1	–	–	246.0	1307.3	816.7	523.0	1036.6	3683.6	31115.6
a) Products of building	1928	–	–	–	–	–	–	–	–	–	–	–	–	–	–
	1929	–	–	–	–	–	–	–	–	–	–	–	–	–	–
	1930	–	–	–	–	–	–	–	–	–	–	–	–	–	–
b) Industrial products	1928	341.5	9562.8	977.7	414.3	2.2	–	–	166.0	532.8	846.3	280.4	674.5	2334.0	13798.5
	1929	377.7	11107.6	1020.4	488.1	3.0	–	–	210.5	743.1	835.8	338.4	800.1	2717.4	15924.7
	1930	443.9	12163.2	1025.1	659.7	4.1	–	–	246.0	1307.3	771.7	523.0	1036.6	3638.6	18180.6
c) Agricultural products and products of hunting	1928	5925.1	1922.6	2369.8	86.2	–	–	–	–	–	20.8	–	–	20.8	10324.5
	1929	6730.7	1985.5	2706.5	81.5	–	–	–	–	–	29.9	–	–	29.9	11534.1
	1930	7419.5	2437.8	2880.6	152.1	–	–	–	–	–	45.0	–	–	45.0	12935.0

Table 4. (cont'd)

Distribution of products in the economy
Consumed by institutions and by
the population

by [predominant] end-use by origin	Year	Institutions and social organis- ations	Population Agricul- tural	Non- agricul- tural	Total consumed by institutions and pop- ulation	Losses In stor- age in agricul- ture	In channels of circ- ulation	Total	Exports	Stocks at end of year In agric- ulture	In census industry	In small scale industry	In trans- port	In forestry
A	B	44	45	46	47	48	49	50	51	52	53	54	55	56
Total for the economy	1928	909.2	11841.5	8495.1	21245.8	192.7	86.0	278.7	799.5	6419.5	3003.4	5.4	334.0	132.1
	1929	1095.0	13691.0	9669.7	24458.7	235.1	119.2	354.4	923.7	6603.6	3303.7	6.8	263.4	324.7
	1930	1349.9	15215.7	13288.0	29853.6	341.9	305.3	647.2	1036.4	6910.2	4659.5	7.6	190.3	445.6
a) Products of building	1928	-	-	-	-	-	-	-	-	-	-	-	-	-
	1929	-	-	-	-	-	-	-	-	-	-	-	-	-
	1930	-	-	-	-	-	-	-	-	-	-	-	-	-
b) Industrial products	1928	825.0	7331.7	5937.3	14094.0	-	74.6	74.6	491.8	607.4	2721.3	5.4	334.0	132.1
	1929	986.7	8738.9	6572.1	16297.7	-	107.5	107.5	616.0	551.8	3011.0	6.3	263.4	324.7
	1930	1216.8	9741.5	8370.3	19328.6	-	134.8	134.8	652.6	755.7	4319.4	7.6	190.3	445.6
c) Agricultural products and products of hunting	1928	84.2	4509.8	2557.8	7151.8	192.7	11.4	204.1	307.7	5812.1	282.1	-	-	-
	1929	108.3	4955.1	3097.6	8161.0	235.1	11.7	246.8	307.7	6051.8	294.7	-	-	-
	1930	133.1	5474.2	4917.7	10525.0	341.9	170.5	512.4	383.8	6154.5	340.1	-	-	-
A. Means of production	1928	215.5	404.5	258.4	878.4	52.2	70.9	123.1	519.2	4605.6	2495.9	5.4	264.1	52.0
	1929	218.3	461.8	317.5	1027.6	63.6	98.5	162.1	657.4	4686.6	2861.3	6.3	200.2	187.7
	1930	278.7	352.7	392.4	1023.8	91.3	287.8	379.1	798.7	4893.4	4040.2	7.6	146.3	274.4
a) Products of building	1928	-	-	-	-	-	-	-	-	-	-	-	-	-
	1929	-	-	-	-	-	-	-	-	-	-	-	-	-
	1930	-	-	-	-	-	-	-	-	-	-	-	-	-
b) Industrial products	1928	190.2	103.5	254.0	547.7	-	70.8	70.8	326.6	35.1	2219.5	5.4	264.1	52.0
	1929	214.2	101.8	308.2	624.2	-	98.3	98.3	439.3	16.2	2572.6	6.3	200.2	187.7
	1930	240.7	94.3	368.8	703.8	-	128.4	128.4	449.3	9.5	3707.0	7.6	146.3	274.4
c) Agricultural products and products of hunting	1928	25.3	301.0	4.4	330.7	52.2	0.1	52.3	192.6	4570.5	276.4	-	-	-
	1929	34.1	360.0	9.3	403.4	63.6	0.2	63.8	218.1	4670.4	288.7	-	-	-
	1930	38.0	258.4	23.6	320.0	91.3	159.4	250.7	348.8	4883.9	333.2	-	-	-

Table 4. (cont'd)

Distribution of products in the economy
Stocks at end of year

by [predominant] end-use

by origin	Year	In building						Total in building	In channels of circulation	Total stocks at end of year
		Rural	Industrial	Transport	Trade	Housing	Social purposes			
A	B	57	58	59	60	61	62	63	64	65
Total for the economy	1928	-	1369.6	302.6	49.0	277.6	212.0	2210.8	2257.5	14362.5
	1929	9.1	1940.0	478.1	64.4	419.5	326.1	3237.2	2970.2	16711.1
	1930	6.0	3174.1	550.9	126.1	764.8	517.2	5139.1	3344.1	20696.4
a) Products of building	1928	-	820.7	259.2	49.0	277.6	212.0	1618.5	-	1618.5
	1929	9.1	1186.5	440.5	64.4	419.5	326.1	2446.1	-	2446.1
	1930	6.0	2076.8	515.9	126.1	764.8	517.2	4006.8	-	4006.8
b) Industrial products	1928	-	548.9	43.4	-	-	-	592.3	1950.3	6342.8
	1929	-	753.5	37.6	-	-	-	791.1	2075.2	7023.5
	1930	-	1097.3	35.0	-	-	-	1132.3	2371.5	9222.4
c) Agricultural products and products of hunting	1928	-	-	-	-	-	-	-	307.0	6401.2
	1929	-	-	-	-	-	-	-	895.0	7241.5
	1930	-	-	-	-	-	-	-	972.6	7467.2
A. Means of production	1928	-	1369.6	302.6	49.0	-	-	1721.2	818.9	9963.1
	1929	9.1	1940.0	478.1	64.4	-	-	2491.6	1393.1	11826.8
	1930	6.0	3174.1	550.9	126.1	-	-	3857.1	1514.1	14733.1
a) Products of building	1928	-	820.7	259.2	49.0	-	-	1128.9	-	1128.9
	1929	9.1	1186.5	440.5	64.4	-	-	1700.5	-	1700.5
	1930	6.0	2076.8	515.9	126.1	-	-	2724.8	-	2724.8
b) Industrial products	1928	-	548.9	43.4	-	-	-	592.3	520.2	3688.6
	1929	-	753.5	37.6	-	-	-	791.1	557.2	4331.3
	1930	-	1097.3	35.0	-	-	-	1132.3	632.1	5909.2
c) Agricultural products and products of hunting	1928	-	-	-	-	-	-	-	298.7	5145.6
	1929	-	-	-	-	-	-	-	835.9	5795.0
	1930	-	-	-	-	-	-	-	882.0	6099.1

Table 4. (cont'd)

Distribution of products in the economy
Entered into fixed capital stock

by [predominant] end use / by origin	Year	In agriculture	In census industry	In small scale industry	In transport and communications	In trade	In housing stock Rural	In housing stock Urban	In stock for social purposes	Total entered into stock	Total distributed in consumer's prices
A	B	66	67	68	69	70	71	72	73	74	75
Total for the economy	1928	2177.6	1332.1	23.4	746.4	61.3	931.4	625.5	443.8	6368.5	71597.6
	1929	1678.8	1884.9	27.7	976.8	138.8	858.2	658.1	507.8	6793.6	81712.8
	1930	2436.4	2876.1	28.5	1586.1	278.9	559.6	763.5	567.7	9096.8	98498.6
a) Products of building	1928	677.2	656.4	11.8	349.9	42.0	931.4	652.5	356.1	3677.3	5295.8
	1929	758.4	943.0	13.5	426.6	84.2	858.2	658.1	455.7	4197.7	6643.8
	1930	929.4	1431.8	15.4	855.5	158.5	559.6	763.5	420.7	5134.4	9141.2
b) Industrial products	1928	632.1	673.3	11.6	396.5	19.3	-	-	87.7	1820.5	39248.4
	1929	798.0	938.9	14.2	550.2	54.6	-	-	115.1	2471.0	45590.3
	1930	1110.4	1443.0	13.1	730.6	120.4	-	-	147.0	3564.5	54967.3
c) Agricultural products and products of hunting	1928	868.3	2.4	-	-	-	-	-	-	870.7	27053.4
	1929	121.9	3.0	-	-	-	-	-	-	124.9	29478.7
	1930	396.6	1.3	-	-	-	-	-	-	397.9	34390.1
A. Means of production	1928	2166.4	1308.1	23.4	715.3	61.3	-	-	87.7	4362.2	39969.0
	1929	1666.4	1854.2	27.7	933.0	138.8	-	-	115.1	4735.2	45867.9
	1930	2418.4	2834.2	28.5	1509.6	278.9	-	1	147.0	7216.6	55266.9
a) Products of building	1928	677.2	656.4	11.8	349.9	42.0	-	-	-	1737.3	2866.2
	1929	758.4	943.0	13.5	426.6	84.2	-	-	-	2225.7	3926.2
	1930	929.4	1431.8	15.4	855.5	158.5	-	-	-	3390.6	6115.4
b) Industrial products	1928	620.9	649.3	11.6	365.4	19.3	-	-	87.7	1754.2	20186.4
	1929	786.1	908.2	14.2	506.4	54.6	-	-	115.1	2384.6	23802.4
	1930	1092.4	1401.1	13.1	654.1	120.4	-	-	147.0	3428.1	28800.0
c) Agricultural products and products of hunting	1928	868.3	2.4	-	-	-	-	-	-	870.7	16916.4
	1929	121.9	3.0	-	-	-	-	-	-	124.9	18139.3
	1930	396.6	1.3	-	-	-	-	-	-	397.9	20351.5

Table 4. (cont'd)

Input of products into the economy
Stocks at beginning of year

by [predominant] end-use / by origin	Year	In agri-culture	In census industry	In small-scale industry	In trans-port	In forestry	In building						Total in building	In channels of circ-ulation	Total stocks at start of year
							Rural	Indus-trial	Trans-port	Trade	Housing	Social purposes			
A	B	1	2	3	4	5	6	7	8	9	10	11	12	13	14
1. Fixed means of production	1928	-	143.3	-	64.7	-	-	880.4	105.7	42.2	-	-	1028.3	101.5	1337.8
	1929	-	159.3	-	63.0	-	-	1280.6	259.2	49.0	-	-	1588.8	100.9	1912.0
	1930	-	176.4	-	39.5	-	9.1	1822.4	440.5	64.4	-	-	2336.4	125.3	2677.6
a) Products of building	1928	-	-	-	-	-	-	563.4	105.7	42.2	-	-	711.3	-	711.3
	1929	-	-	-	-	-	-	820.7	259.2	49.0	-	-	1128.9	-	1128.9
	1930	-	-	-	-	-	9.1	1186.5	440.5	64.4	-	-	1700.5	-	1700.5
b) Industrial products	1928	-	143.3	-	64.7	-	-	317.0	-	-	-	-	317.0	101.5	626.5
	1929	-	159.3	-	63.0	-	-	459.9	-	-	-	-	459.9	100.0	782.2
	1930	-	176.4	-	39.5	-	-	635.9	-	-	-	-	635.9	125.1	976.9
c) Agricultural products	1928	-	-	-	-	-	-	-	-	-	-	-	-	-	-
	1929	-	-	-	-	-	-	-	-	-	-	-	-	0.9	0.9
	1930	-	-	-	-	-	-	-	-	-	-	-	-	0.2	0.2

Table 4. (cont'd)

Input of products into the economy

Production per year at producer's prices

A by [predominant] end-use by origin	B Year	In agri-culture 15	In census industry 16	In small-scale industry 17	In forestry 18	Hunting 19	In fishing 20	In domestic produc-tion 21	In building 22	In other branches of the economy 23	Total produc-tion per year 24	Imports 25	Transport and trade mark-up 26	Customs duties 27	Excise 28	Total ent-ered, in consumer's prices 29
1. Fixed means of production	1928	2807.7	1418.4	229.4	-	-	-	-	2154.9	-	6610.2	235.1	169.7	35.9	-	8398.7
	1929	2448.6	2046.4	262.3	-	-	-	-	2797.3	-	7554.6	245.2	228.8	37.5	-	9978.1
	1930	2976.2	2933.7	240.6	-	-	-	-	4414.9	-	10565.4	476.8	330.1	121.8	-	14171.2
a) Products of building	1928	-	-	-	-	-	-	-	2154.9	-	2154.9	-	-	-	-	2866.2
	1929	-	-	-	-	-	-	-	2797.3	-	2797.3	-	-	-	-	3926.2
	1930	-	-	-	-	-	-	-	4414.9	-	4414.9	-	-	-	-	6115.4
b) Industrial products	1928	-	1418.2	229.4	-	-	-	-	-	-	1647.6	231.8	169.7	35.9	-	2711.5
	1929	-	2046.4	262.3	-	-	-	-	-	-	2308.7	212.9	228.8	37.5	-	3600.1
	1930	-	2933.7	240.6	-	-	-	-	-	-	3174.3	475.2	330.1	121.8	-	5078.3
c) Agricultural products	1928	2807.7	-	-	-	-	-	-	-	-	2807.7	3.3	-	-	-	2811.0
	1929	2448.6	-	-	-	-	-	-	-	-	2448.6	2.3	-	-	-	2451.8
	1930	2976.2	-	-	-	-	-	-	-	-	2976.2	1.1	-	-	-	2977.5

Table 4. (cont'd)

Distribution of products in the economy

by origin A	Year B	Consumed in production										Transport 40	Housing, social purposes and trade 41	Total building 42	Total consumed in production 43
		In agriculture 30	In census industry 31	In small-scale industry 32	In transport 33	In forestry 34	In fishing 35	In domestic production 36	In trade enterprises 37	Industrial 38	Rural 39				
1. Fixed means of production	1928	1939.4	183.2	12.4	22.6	–	–	–	–	2.0	–	–	–	2.0	2159.6
	1929	2326.7	244.6	14.0	40.3	–	–	–	–	3.0	–	–	–	3.0	2628.6
	1930	2579.6	387.7	16.6	67.0	–	–	–	–	5.0	–	–	–	5.0	3055.9
a) Products of building	1928	–	–	–	–	–	–	–	–	–	–	–	–	–	–
	1929	–	–	–	–	–	–	–	–	–	–	–	–	–	–
	1930	–	–	–	–	–	–	–	–	–	–	–	–	–	–
b) Industrial products	1928	–	183.2	12.4	22.6	–	–	–	–	2.0	–	–	–	2.0	220.2
	1929	–	244.6	14.0	40.3	–	–	–	–	3.0	–	–	–	3.0	301.9
	1930	–	387.7	16.6	67.0	–	–	–	–	5.0	–	–	–	5.0	476.3
c) Agricultural products	1928	1939.4	–	–	–	–	–	–	–	–	–	–	–	–	1939.4
	1929	2326.7	–	–	–	–	–	–	–	–	–	–	–	–	2326.7
	1930	2579.6	–	–	–	–	–	–	–	–	–	–	–	–	2579.6

by [predominant] end-use

Table 4. (cont'd)

Distribution of products in the economy
Consumed by institutions and by
the population

Stocks at beginning of year

by [predominant] end-use by origin	Year	Institutions and social organis-ations	Population Agricul-tural	Non-agricul-tural	Total consumed by inst-itutions and pop-ulation	Losses In stor-age in agricul-ture	In channels of circ-ulation	Total	Exports	In agric-ulture	In census industry	In small-scale industry	In trans-port	In forestry
A	B	44	45	46	47	48	49	50	51	52	53	54	55	56
1. Fixed means of production	1928	12.6	–	–	12.6	–	2.6	2.6	0.9	–	159.3	–	63.0	–
	1929	15.7	–	–	15.7	–	4.6	4.6	2.0	–	176.4	–	39.5	–
	1930	16.0	–	–	16.0	–	–	–	2.1	–	202.2	–	37.5	–
a) Products of building	1928	–	–	–	–	–	–	–	–	–	–	–	–	–
	1929	–	–	–	–	–	–	–	–	–	–	–	–	–
	1930	–	–	–	–	–	–	–	–	–	–	–	–	–
b) Industrial products	1928	12.6	–	–	12.6	–	2.6	2.6	0.9	–	159.3	–	63.0	–
	1929	15.7	–	–	15.7	–	4.6	4.6	2.0	–	176.4	–	39.5	–
	1930	16.0	–	–	16.0	–	–	–	2.1	–	202.2	–	37.5	–
c) Agricultural products	1928	–	–	–	–	–	–	–	–	–	–	–	–	–
	1929	–	–	–	–	–	–	–	–	–	–	–	–	–
	1930	–	–	–	–	–	–	–	–	–	–	–	–	–

Table 4. (cont'd)

Distribution of products in the economy
Stocks at end of year

by [predominant] end-use

by origin	Year	Rural	Indus-trial	Trans-port	Trade	Housing	Social purposes	Total in building	In channels of circ-ulation	Total stocks at end of year
A	B	57	58	59	60	61	62	63	64	65
1. Fixed means of production	1928	-	1280.6	259.2	49.0	-	-	1588.8	100.9	1912.0
	1929	9.1	1822.4	440.5	64.4	-	-	2336.4	125.3	2677.6
	1930	6.0	2994.1	515.9	126.1	-	-	3642.1	131.3	4013.1
a) Products of building	1928	-	820.7	259.2	49.0	-	-	1128.9	-	1128.9
	1929	9.1	1186.5	440.5	64.4	-	-	1700.5	-	1700.5
	1930	6.0	2076.8	515.9	126.1	-	-	2724.8	-	2724.8
b) Industrial products	1928	-	459.9	-	-	-	-	459.9	100.0	782.2
	1929	-	635.9	-	-	-	-	635.9	125.1	976.9
	1930	-	917.3	-	-	-	-	917.3	131.3	1288.3
c) Agricultural products	1928	-	-	-	-	-	-	-	0.9	0.9
	1929	-	-	-	-	-	-	-	0.2	0.2
	1930	-	-	-	-	-	-	-	-	-

Table 4. (cont'd)

Distribution of products in the economy
Entered into fixed capital stock

by [predominant] end-use / by origin	Year	In agriculture	In census industry	In small-scale industry	In transport and communications	In trade	In housing stock Rural	In housing stock Urban	In stock for social purposes	Total entered into stock	Total distributed in consumer's prices
A	B	66	67	68	69	70	71	72	73	74	75
1. Fixed means of production	1928	2159.1	1272.2	21.9	712.7	58.8	-	-	76.3	4301.0	8388.7
	1929	1658.6	1808.8	25.6	929.8	128.5	-	-	98.3	4649.6	9978.1
	1930	2406.6	2771.5	26.5	1503.7	256.2	-	-	119.6	7084.1	14171.2
a) Products of building	1928	677.2	656.4	11.8	349.9	42.0	-	-	-	1737.3	2866.2
	1929	758.4	943.0	13.5	426.6	84.2	-	-	-	2225.7	3926.2
	1930	929.4	1431.8	15.4	855.5	158.5	-	-	-	3390.6	6115.4
b) Industrial products	1928	613.6	613.4	10.1	362.8	16.8	-	-	76.3	1693.0	2711.5
	1929	778.3	862.8	12.1	503.2	44.3	-	-	98.3	2299.0	3600.1
	1930	1080.6	1338.4	11.1	648.2	97.7	-	-	119.6	3295.6	5078.3
c) Agricultural products	1928	868.3	2.4	-	-	-	-	-	-	870.7	2811.0
	1929	121.9	3.0	-	-	-	-	-	-	124.9	2451.8
	1930	396.6	1.3	-	-	-	-	-	-	397.9	2977.5

Table 4. (cont'd)

Input of products into the economy
Stocks at beginning of year

by [predominant] end-use — by origin (A)	Year (B)	In agriculture (1)	In census industry (2)	In small-scale industry (3)	In transport (4)	In forestry (5)	In building							In channels of circulation (13)	Total stocks at start of year (14)
							Rural (6)	Industrial (7)	Transport (8)	Trade (9)	Housing (10)	Social purposes (11)	Total in building (12)		
2. Circulating means of production	1928	3786.4	2458.0	5.0	188.9	39.4	-	83.8	37.4	-	-	-	121.2	565.1	7164.0
	1929	4605.6	2336.6	5.4	201.1	52.0	-	89.0	43.4	-	-	-	132.4	718.0	8051.1
	1930	4686.6	2684.9	6.3	160.7	187.7	-	117.6	37.6	-	-	-	155.2	1267.8	9149.2
a) Industrial products	1928	23.8	2160.6	5.0	188.9	39.4	-	83.8	37.4	-	-	-	121.2	380.3	2919.2
	1929	35.1	2060.2	5.4	201.1	52.0	-	89.0	43.4	-	-	-	132.4	420.2	2906.4
	1930	16.2	2396.2	6.3	160.7	187.7	-	117.6	37.6	-	-	-	155.2	432.1	3354.4
b) Agricultural products	1928	3762.6	295.5	-	-	-	-	-	-	-	-	-	-	184.8	4242.9
	1929	4570.5	272.8	-	-	-	-	-	-	-	-	-	-	297.8	5141.1
	1930	4670.4	282.0	-	-	-	-	-	-	-	-	-	-	835.7	5788.1
c) Products of hunting	1928	-	1.9	-	-	-	-	-	-	-	-	-	-	-	1.9
	1929	-	3.6	-	-	-	-	-	-	-	-	-	-	-	3.6
	1930	-	6.7	-	-	-	-	-	-	-	-	-	-	-	6.7
B. Consumer goods	1928	1478.5	523.5	-	62.1	81.0	-	-	-	-	197.3	148.1	345.4	1219.0	3709.5
	1929	1813.9	507.5	-	69.9	80.1	-	-	-	-	277.6	212.0	489.6	1438.4	4399.4
	1930	1917.0	444.4	-	63.2	137.0	-	-	-	-	419.9	326.1	745.6	1577.1	4884.3
a) Products of building	1928	-	-	-	-	-	-	-	-	-	197.3	148.1	345.4	-	345.4
	1929	-	-	-	-	-	-	-	-	-	277.6	212.0	489.6	-	489.6
	1930	-	-	-	-	-	-	-	-	-	419.5	326.1	745.6	-	745.6
b) Industrial products	1928	467.6	517.5	-	62.1	81.0	-	-	-	-	-	-	-	1209.0	2337.2
	1929	572.3	501.8	-	69.9	80.1	-	-	-	-	-	-	-	1430.1	2654.2
	1930	535.6	438.4	-	63.2	137.0	-	-	-	-	-	-	-	1518.0	2692.2
c) Agricultural products	1928	1010.9	6.0	-	-	-	-	-	-	-	-	-	-	10.0	1026.9
	1929	1241.6	5.7	-	-	-	-	-	-	-	-	-	-	8.3	1255.6
	1930	1381.4	6.0	-	-	-	-	-	-	-	-	-	-	59.1	1446.5

Table 4. (cont'd)

Input of products into the economy
Stocks at beginning of year

by [predominant] end-use / by origin	Year	In agriculture (15)	In census industry (16)	In small-scale industry (17)	In forestry (18)	Hunting (19)	In fishing (20)	In domestic production (21)	In building (22)	In other branches of the economy (23)	Total production per year (24)	Imports (25)	Transport and trade mark-up (26)	Customs duties (27)	Excise (28)	Total entered, in consumer's prices (29)
2. Circulating means of production	1928	9141.7	10793.9	886.1	703.3	87.7	-	309.7	-	36.4	21958.8	593.5	1611.2	177.8	75.0	31580.3
	1929	9750.6	13029.6	927.5	946.0	82.3	-	350.1	-	42.4	25128.5	518.5	1949.8	151.9	90.0	35889.8
	1930	10692.2	15572.4	890.8	1077.1	129.1	-	385.2	-	85.5	28832.3	431.7	2355.8	190.2	136.5	41095.7
a) Industrial products	1928	-	10793.1	886.1	703.3	-	-	309.7	-	36.4	12728.6	401.6	1213.3	135.2	75.0	17474.9
	1929	-	13828.5	927.5	946.0	-	-	350.1	-	42.4	15294.5	364.6	1434.0	112.8	90.0	20202.3
	1930	-	15571.0	890.8	1077.1	-	-	385.2	-	85.5	18009.6	322.8	1746.6	151.8	136.5	23721.7
b) Agricultural products	1928	9141.7	0.7	-	-	-	-	-	-	-	9142.4	188.0	373.9	42.6	-	13989.8
	1929	9750.6	1.0	-	-	-	-	-	-	-	9751.6	152.0	480.9	39.1	-	15564.7
	1930	10692.2	1.3	-	-	-	-	-	-	-	10693.5	107.8	578.5	38.4	-	17206.3
c) Products of hunting	1928	-	0.1	-	-	87.7	-	-	-	-	87.8	1.9	24.0	-	-	115.6
	1929	-	0.1	-	-	82.3	-	-	-	-	82.4	1.9	34.9	-	-	122.8
	1930	-	0.1	-	-	129.1	-	-	-	-	129.2	1.1	30.7	-	-	167.7
B. Consumer goods	1928	7291.9	7032.9	4753.2	708.0	-	235.8	842.5	2084.2	-	22958.5	124.5	3400.3	57.8	1388.0	31628.6
	1929	8135.0	8285.8	5157.1	795.9	-	272.3	843.0	2228.0	-	25717.1	116.9	3859.6	64.2	1687.7	25844.9
	1930	10438.8	10179.9	5461.1	746.2	-	335.2	987.4	2280.8	-	30428.8	150.8	4789.1	91.7	2887.0	43231.7
a) Products of building	1928	-	-	-	-	-	-	-	2084.2	-	2084.2	-	-	-	-	2429.6
	1929	-	-	-	-	-	-	-	2228.0	-	2228.0	-	-	-	-	2717.6
	1930	-	-	-	-	-	-	-	2280.2	-	2280.2	-	-	-	-	3025.8
b) Industrial products	1928	-	7020.8	4667.9	708.0	-	235.8	153.9	-	-	12786.2	114.8	2378.4	57.4	1388.0	19062.0
	1929	-	8267.9	5058.2	795.9	-	272.3	136.5	-	-	14530.8	109.5	2742.1	63.6	1687.7	21787.9
	1930	-	10146.4	5386.3	746.2	-	335.2	109.9	-	-	16724.0	126.9	3645.9	91.3	2887.0	26167.3
c) Agricultural products	1928	7291.9	12.3	85.3	-	-	-	688.6	-	-	8078.1	9.7	1021.9	0.4	-	10137.0
	1929	8135.0	17.9	98.9	-	-	-	706.5	-	-	8958.3	7.4	1117.5	0.6	-	11339.4
	1930	10438.8	33.5	74.8	-	-	-	877.5	-	-	11424.6	23.9	1143.2	0.4	-	14038.6

Table 4. (cont'd)

Distribution of products in the economy

Consumed in production

by [predominant] end-use — by origin	Year	In agri-culture	In census industry	In small-scale industry	In trans-port	In forestry	In fishing	In domestic produc-tion	In trade enter-prises	In building Indus-trial	In building Rural	In building Trans-port	In building Housing, social purposes and trade	Total building	Total consumed in prod-uction
A	B	30	31	32	33	34	35	36	37	38	39	40	41	42	43
2. Circulating means of production	1928	4327.2	11302.2	3335.1	477.9	2.2	-	-	166.0	530.8	867.1	280.4	674.5	2352.8	21963.4
	1929	4781.7	12848.5	3712.9	529.3	3.0	-	-	210.5	740.1	865.7	338.4	800.1	2744.3	24830.2
	1930	5283.8	14213.3	3889.1	744.8	4.1	-	-	246.0	1302.8	816.7	523.0	1035.6	3678.6	28059.7
a) Industrial products	1928	341.5	9379.6	965.3	391.7	2.2	-	-	166.0	530.8	846.3	280.4	674.5	2332.0	13578.3
	1929	377.7	10863.0	1006.4	447.8	3.0	-	-	210.5	740.1	835.8	338.4	800.1	2714.4	15622.8
	1930	443.9	11775.5	1008.5	592.7	4.1	-	-	264.0	1302.3	771.7	523.0	1036.6	3633.6	17704.3
b) Agricultural products	1928	3985.7	1899.3	2360.1	86.2	-	-	-	-	-	20.8	-	-	20.8	8352.1
	1929	4404.0	1947.4	2694.6	81.5	-	-	-	-	-	29.9	-	-	29.9	9157.4
	1930	4839.9	2355.9	2866.5	152.1	-	-	-	-	-	45.0	-	-	45.0	10259.4
c) Products of hunting	1928	-	23.3	9.7	-	-	-	-	-	-	-	-	-	-	33.0
	1929	-	38.1	11.9	-	-	-	-	-	-	-	-	-	-	50.0
	1930	-	81.9	14.1	-	-	-	-	-	-	-	-	-	-	96.0
B. Consumer goods	1928	1331.3	1495.6	659.8	109.9	-	81.6	677.8	49.1	4.4	-	-	10.1	14.5	4419.6
	1929	1292.8	1944.8	725.3	139.6	-	90.5	750.4	57.5	3.5	-	-	8.2	11.7	5012.6
	1930	1267.9	2730.3	789.4	190.7	-	110.1	891.4	61.4	3.4	-	-	8.0	11.4	6052.6
a) Products of building	1928	-	-	-	-	-	-	677.8	-	-	-	-	-	-	-
	1929	-	-	-	-	-	-	750.4	-	-	-	-	-	-	-
	1930	-	-	-	-	-	-	891.4	-	-	-	-	-	-	-
b) Industrial products	1928	458.2	1376.0	536.9	109.9	-	81.6	-	49.1	4.4	-	-	10.1	14.5	2626.2
	1929	473.2	1788.8	588.6	139.6	-	90.5	-	57.6	3.5	-	-	8.2	11.7	3149.9
	1930	378.1	2507.7	624.4	190.7	-	110.1	-	61.4	3.4	-	-	8.0	11.4	3883.8
c) Agricultural products	1928	873.1	119.6	122.9	-	-	-	677.8	-	-	-	-	-	-	1793.4
	1929	819.6	156.0	136.7	-	-	-	750.4	-	-	-	-	-	-	1862.7
	1930	889.8	222.6	165.0	-	-	-	891.4	-	-	-	-	-	-	2168.8

Table 4. (cont'd)

Distribution of products in the economy
Consumed by institutions and by
the population

by [predominant] end-use / by origin	Year	Institutions and social organisations	Population Agricultural	Population Non-agricultural	Total consumed by institutions and population	Losses In storage in agriculture	Losses In channels of circulation	Losses Total	Exports	Stocks at end of year In agriculture	Stocks In census industry	Stocks In small-scale industry	Stocks In transport	Stocks In forestry
A	B	44	45	46	47	48	49	50	51	52	53	54	55	56
2. Circulating means of production	1928	202.9	404.5	258.4	865.8	52.2	68.3	120.5	518.3	4605.6	2336.6	5.4	201.1	52.0
	1929	232.6	461.8	317.5	1011.9	63.6	93.9	157.5	655.4	4686.6	2684.9	6.3	160.7	187.7
	1930	262.7	352.7	392.4	1007.8	91.3	287.8	379.1	796.6	4893.4	3838.0	7.6	108.8	274.4
a) Industrial products	1928	177.6	103.5	254.0	535.1	-	68.2	68.2	325.7	35.1	2060.2	5.4	201.1	52.0
	1929	198.5	101.8	308.2	608.5	-	93.7	93.7	437.3	16.2	2396.2	6.3	160.7	187.7
	1930	224.7	94.3	368.8	687.8	-	128.4	128.4	447.8	9.5	3504.8	7.6	108.8	274.4
b) Agricultural products	1928	25.3	301.0	4.4	330.7	52.2	0.1	52.3	113.6	4570.5	272.8	-	-	-
	1929	34.1	360.0	9.3	403.4	63.6	0.2	63.8	152.0	4670.4	282.0	-	-	-
	1930	38.0	258.4	23.6	320.0	91.3	136.8	228.1	308.2	4883.9	324.7	-	-	-
c) Products of hunting	1928	-	-	-	-	-	-	-	79.0	-	3.6	-	-	-
	1929	-	-	-	-	-	-	-	66.1	-	6.7	-	-	-
	1930	-	-	-	-	-	22.6	22.6	40.6	-	8.5	-	-	-
B. Consumer goods	1928	693.7	11437.0	8236.7	20367.4	140.5	15.1	155.6	280.3	1813.9	507.5	-	69.9	80.1
	1929	846.7	13232.2	9352.2	23431.1	171.5	20.7	192.2	266.3	1917.0	444.4	-	63.2	137.0
	1930	1071.2	14863.0	12895.6	28829.8	250.6	17.5	268.1	237.7	2016.8	919.3	-	44.0	171.2
a) Products of building	1928	-	-	-	-	-	-	-	-	-	-	-	-	-
	1929	-	-	-	-	-	-	-	-	-	-	-	-	-
	1930	-	-	-	-	-	-	-	-	-	-	-	-	-
b) Industrial products	1928	634.8	7228.2	5683.3	13546.3	-	3.8	3.8	165.2	572.3	501.8	-	69.9	80.1
	1929	772.5	8637.1	6263.9	15673.5	-	9.2	9.2	176.7	535.6	438.4	-	63.2	137.0
	1930	976.1	9647.2	8001.5	18624.8	-	6.4	6.4	202.7	746.2	612.4	-	44.0	171.2
c) Agricultural products	1928	58.9	4208.8	2553.4	6821.1	140.5	11.3	151.8	115.1	1241.6	5.7	-	-	-
	1929	74.2	4595.1	3088.3	7757.6	171.5	11.5	183.0	89.6	1281.4	6.0	-	-	-
	1930	95.1	5215.6	4891.1	10205.0	250.6	11.1	261.7	35.0	1270.6	6.9	-	-	-

Table 4. (cont'd)

Distribution of products in the economy
Stocks at end of year

by [predominant] end-use / by origin (A)	Year (B)	In building Rural (57)	Industrial (58)	Transport (59)	Trade (60)	Housing (61)	Social purposes (62)	Total in building (63)	In channels of circulation (64)	Total stocks at end of year (65)
2. Circulating means of production	1928	-	89.0	43.4	-	-	-	132.4	718.0	8051.1
	1929	-	117.6	37.6	-	-	-	155.2	1267.8	9149.2
	1930	-	180.0	35.0	-	-	-	215.0	1382.8	10720.0
a) Industrial products	1928	-	89.0	43.4	-	-	-	132.4	420.2	2906.4
	1929	-	117.6	37.6	-	-	-	155.2	432.1	3354.4
	1930	-	180.0	35.0	-	-	-	215.0	500.8	4620.9
b) Agricultural products	1928	-	-	-	-	-	-	-	297.8	5141.1
	1929	-	-	-	-	-	-	-	835.7	5788.1
	1930	-	-	-	-	-	-	-	882.0	6090.6
c) Products of hunting	1928	-	-	-	-	-	-	-	-	3.6
	1929	-	-	-	-	-	-	-	-	6.7
	1930	-	-	-	-	-	-	-	-	8.5
B. Consumer goods	1928	-	-	-	-	277.6	212.0	489.6	1458.4	4399.4
	1929	-	-	-	-	419.5	326.1	745.6	1577.1	4884.3
	1930	-	-	-	-	764.8	517.2	1282.0	1850.0	5963.3
a) Products of building	1928	-	-	-	-	277.6	212.0	489.6	-	489.6
	1929	-	-	-	-	419.5	326.1	745.6	-	745.6
	1930	-	-	-	-	764.8	517.2	1282.0	-	1282.0
b) Industrial products	1928	-	-	-	-	-	-	-	1450.1	2654.2
	1929	-	-	-	-	-	-	-	1518.0	2692.2
	1930	-	-	-	-	-	-	-	1739.4	3313.2
c) Products of hunting	1928	-	-	-	-	-	-	-	8.3	1255.6
	1929	-	-	-	-	-	-	-	59.1	1446.5
	1930	-	-	-	-	-	-	-	90.6	1368.1

Table 4. (cont'd)

Distribution of products in the economy

by [predominant] end-use by origin (A)	Year (B)	Entered into fixed capital stock									Total distributed in consumer's prices
		In agriculture 66	In census industry 67	In small-scale industry 68	In transport and communications 69	In trade 70	In housing stock Rural 71	Urban 72	In stock for social purposes 73	Total entered into stock 74	75
2. Circulating means of production	1928	7.3	35.9	1.5	2.6	2.5	-	-	11.4	61.2	31580.3
	1929	7.8	45.4	2.1	3.2	10.3	-	-	16.8	85.6	35889.0
	1930	11.8	62.7	2.0	5.9	22.7	-	-	27.4	132.5	48095.7
a) Industrial products	1928	7.8	35.9	1.5	2.6	2.5	-	-	11.4	61.2	17474.9
	1929	7.8	45.4	2.1	3.2	10.3	-	-	16.8	85.6	20202.9
	1930	11.8	62.7	2.0	5.9	22.7	-	-	27.4	132.5	23721.7
b) Agricultural products	1928	-	-	-	-	-	-	-	-	-	13989.8
	1929	-	-	-	-	-	-	-	-	-	15564.7
	1930	-	-	-	-	-	-	-	-	-	17206.3
c) Products of hunting	1928	-	-	-	-	-	-	-	-	-	115.8
	1929	-	-	-	-	-	-	-	-	-	122.8
	1930	-	-	-	-	-	-	-	-	-	167.7
B. Consumer goods	1928	11.2	24.0	-	31.1	-	931.4	652.5	356.1	2006.3	31628.6
	1929	11.9	30.7	-	43.8	-	858.2	658.1	455.7	2058.4	35844.9
	1930	18.0	41.9	-	76.5	-	559.6	763.5	420.7	1880.2	44231.7
a) Products of building	1928	-	-	-	-	-	931.4	652.5	356.1	1940.0	2429.6
	1929	-	-	-	-	-	858.2	658.1	455.7	1972.0	2717.6
	1930	-	-	-	-	-	559.6	763.5	420.7	1743.8	3025.8
b) Industrial products	1928	11.2	24.0	-	31.1	-	-	-	-	66.3	19062.0
	1929	11.9	30.7	-	43.8	-	-	-	-	86.4	21787.9
	1930	18.0	41.9	-	76.5	-	-	-	-	136.4	26167.3
c) Agricultural products	1928	-	-	-	-	-	-	-	-	-	10137.0
	1929	-	-	-	-	-	-	-	-	-	11339.4
	1930	-	-	-	-	-	-	-	-	-	14058.1

Table 5. Balance of distribution and redistribution of the national income, by classes and groups of the population, in 1928

Column headings (numbered 1–9):
- Incomes received through distribution
  - Wages of persons employed
    - 1. Wages of persons employed in production
    - 2. Wages of persons employed in circulation and serving production
  - 3. Entrepreneurial income
  - 4. Interest
- 5. Incomes of cooperative producers
- 6. Incomes of independent producers
- 7. Pensions and allowances
- 8. Value of free social cultural and medical services
- 9. Total basic incomes

A	1	2	3	4	5	6	7	8	9
A. Non-agricultural population	4189.8	1033.3	1047.7	30.5	475.0	1330.0	290.7	476.7	8873.7
I. Proletariat	4189.8	1033.3	-	30.5	-	196.7	250.4	402.9	6217.7
of which:							40.3	73.8	
1. Manual workers	3415.9	131.3	-	13.5	-	58.8	224.5	347.5	4213.4
2. Non-manual workers	666.4	875.3	-	16.1	-	42.9	23.8	43.9	1758.3
3. Other proletarian population	107.5	25.7	-	0.9	-	95.0	2.1	11.5	246.0
II. Cooperative producers	-	-	-	-	475.0	37.0	8.6	13.3	512.0
III. Artisans and craftsmen	-	-	-	-	-	1096.3	31.2	57.7	1096.3
IV. Capitalist group	-	-	1047.7	-	-	-	-	-	1047.7
of which: Traders	-	-	951.6	-	-	-	-	-	951.6
V. Other population	-	-	-	-	-	-	0.5	2.8	-
B. Agricultural population	2043.0	66.6	1182.8	-	251.5	10987.3	7.0	22.3	14560.5
1. Proletariat	396.6	12.6	-	-	-	91.6	7.0	22.3	530.1
2. Collective farmers	19.4	-	-	-	132.8	107.0	-	-	259.2
3. Individual peasants	1592.0	54.0	-	-	118.7	10788.7	-	-	12553.4
4. Kulaks	35.0	-	1182.8	-	-	-	-	-	1217.8
Total	6232.8	1099.9	2230.5	30.5	726.5	12317.3	297.7	499.0	23434.2
Income of socialised sector	-	-	-	-	-	-	-	-	3008.1
Total	-	-	-	-	-	-	-	-	26442.3

Table 5. (con'd)

Incomes received through redistribution

A	Wages in non-productive sphere	Income from sale of services	Insurance payments	Pensions and allowances	Value of free social cultural and medical services	Other receipts	Total derivative incomes	Total incomes	Received from sale of property	Total received
	10	11	12	13	14	15	16	17	18	19
A. Non-agricultural population	2001.1	597.2	9.9	365.0	306.4	636.5	3916.1	12789.8	174.3	12964.1
I. Proletariat	2001.1	205.5	3.2	358.6	206.4	152.9	2927.7	9145.4	174.3	9319.7
of which:										
1. Manual workers	248.0	68.2	1.7	16.2	25.1	20.1	379.3	4592.7	40.0	4632.7
2. Non-manual workers	1623.3	45.6	1.5	58.0	107.0	23.7	1859.1	3617.4	59.6	3677.0
3. Other proletarian population	129.8	91.7	-	284.4	74.3	109.1	689.3	935.3	74.7	1010.1
II Cooperative producers	-	-	-	-	31.0	6.5	37.5	549.5	-	549.5
III. Artisans and craftsmen	-	318.0	5.4	6.4	69.0	16.1	414.9	1511.2	-	1511.2
IV. Capitalist group	-	73.7	1.3	-	-	-	75.0	1122.7	-	1122.7
of which:										
Traders	-	-	-	-	-	-	-	951.6	-	951.6
V. Other population	-	-	-	-	-	461.0	461.0	461.0	-	461.0
B. Agricultural population	97.4	-	137.8	29.0	495.4	-	759.6	15320.1	-	15320.1
1. Proletariat	53.7	-	3.4	-	3.4	-	60.5	590.6	-	590.6
2. Collective farmers	-	-	-	-	8.7	-	8.7	267.9	-	267.9
3. Individual peasants	43.7	-	119.0	29.0	460.1	-	651.8	13205.2	-	13205.2
4. Kulaks	-	-	15.4	-	23.2	-	38.6	1256.4	-	1256.4
Total	2096.6	597.2	147.7	394.0	801.8	636.5	4675.7	28109.9	174.3	28294.2
Income of socialised sector	-	-	-	-	-	-	-	-	-	-
Total	-	-	-	-	-	-	-	-	-	-

Table 5. (cont'd)

Expenditure

A	Consumption of material goods (20)	Rent payment (21)	Purchase of services (22)	Value of free social cultural and medical services (23)	Taxes and dues (24)	Payments to social insurance (25)	Payments to state insurance (26)	Subscriptions to trade unions and social organisations (27)	Shares in cooperatives (28)	Total expended (29)	Residual[1] (30)	of which, state loans (31)	Income realised in the form of accumulation and consumption of material goods and services (32)	Income realised in the form of accumulation consumption of material goods (33)
A. Non-agricultural population	...	977.9	603.9	783.1	541.3	46.3	25.6	188.5	21.1	12674.0	...	212.4	11967.0	9602.1
I. Proletariat of which	6721.5	714.7	405.3	683.1	27.0	8.0	12.5	168.4	18.0	8758.4	387.0	196.4	8911.5	7108.5
1. Manual workers	3423.8	299.7	137.2	385.9	11.2	4.5	7.0	76.5	9.2	4355.0	237.7	103.7	4484.3	3661.5
2. Non-manual workers	2575.7	340.6	234.8	208.6	14.4	3.5	5.5	81.9	6.7	3471.7	145.7	88.0	3505.4	2721.4
3. Other proletarian population	722.0	74.4	33.2	88.6	1.4	-	-	10.0	2.1	931.7	3.6	4.7	921.8	725.6
II. Cooperative producers	...	27.7	15.4	31.0	44.0	-	-	-	-	614.9	...		505.5	431.4
III. Artisans and craftsmen	...	87.8	50.3	69.0	69.6	16.9	11.4	11.7	3.0	1687.2	...	16.0	1398.6	1191.5
IV. Capitalist group	...	143.0	130.4	-	400.7	21.4	1.7	8.0	-	1324.2	...		690.9	417.5
of which: Traders	...	...	...	-	-	-	...	...	-	...	...	...	...	...
V. Other population	453.2	4.7	2.6	-	-	-	-	0.4	0.1	461.0	...	-	460.5	453.2
B. Agricultural population	12408.2	...	140.0	517.0	387.6	7.3	113.8	2.1	36.0	13612.0	1708.1	96.0	14773.3	14116.3
1. Proletariat	...	...	...	...	...	...	...	...	...	...	...	...	...	...
2. Collective farmers	...	...	...	...	...	...	...	...	...	...	...	...	...	...
3. Individual peasants	...	...	...	...	...	...	...	...	...	...	...	...	...	...
4. Kulaks	...	...	...	...	...	...	...	...	...	...	...	...	...	...
Total	-	977.9	743.9	1300.1	928.9	53.6	139.4	190.6	57.1	26286.0	-	308.4	26740.3	23718.4
Income of socialised section	-	-	-	-	-	-	-	-	-	-	-	-	-	2723.9
Total	-	-	-	-	-	-	-	-	-	-	-	-	-	26442.3

1. The residual does not include receipts from sale of property, and so in certain cases the amount of loans exceeds the amount of residuals.

[... = no data available]

Table 5a. Balance of distribution and redistribution of the national income, by classes and groups of the population, in 1929

| A | Incomes received through distribution | | | | Incomes of cooperative producers | Incomes of independent producers | Pensions and allowances | Value of free social cultural and medical services | Total basic incomes |
| | Wages of persons employed in production | Wages of persons employed in circulation and serving production | Entrepreneurial income | Interest | | | | | |
	1	2	3	4	5	6	7	8	9
A. Non-agricultural population	5323.0	1310.9	874.8	43.9	661.0	1306.5	370.5	582.4	10473.0
I. Proletariat	5323.0	1310.9	-	43.9	-	392.6	314.6	496.7	7881.7
of which: 1. Manual workers	4303.3	151.5	-	19.4	-	95.6	276.1	434.8	5280.7
2. Non-manual workers	899.7	1131.2	-	23.2	-	159.3	36.4	54.7	2304.5
3. Other proletarian population	120.0	28.2	-	1.3	-	137.7	2.1	7.2	296.5
II. Cooperative producers	-	-	-	-	661.0	23.0	9.7	15.3	709.0
III. Artisans and craftsmen	-	-	-	-	-	893.1	45.7	68.7	1007.5
IV. Capitalist group	-	-	874.8	-	-	-	-	-	874.8
of which: Traders	-	-	800.0	-	-	-	-	-	800.0
V. Other population	-	-	-	-	-	-	0.5	1.7	-
B. Agricultural population	2308.2	83.7	1150.8	-	600.6	10807.6	11.6	26.2	14988.7
1. Proletariat	499.6	15.2	-	-	-	116.0	11.6	26.2	668.6
2. Collective farmers	52.8	-	-	-	466.4	208.8	-	-	728.0
3. Individual peasants	1719.5	68.5	-	-	134.2	10482.8	-	-	12405.0
4. Kulaks	36.3	-	1150.8	-	-	-	-	-	1187.1
Total	7631.2	1394.6	2025.6	43.9	1261.6	12114.1	382.1	608.6	25461.7
Income of socialised sector	-	-	-	-	-	-	-	-	4674.2
Total	-	-	-	-	-	-	-	-	30135.9

Table 5a. (cont'd)

Incomes received through redistribution

A	Wages in non-productive sphere	Income from sale of services	Insurance payments	Pensions and allowances	Value of free social cultural and medical services	Other receipts	Total derivative incomes	Total incomes	Received from sale of property	Total received
	10	11	12	13	14	15	16	17	18	19
A. Non-agricultural population	2322.0	667.3	9.9	433.4	350.2	694.4	4477.2	14950.2	228.6	15178.8
I. Proletariat	2322.0	270.0	3.5	426.3	233.2	184.3	3439.8	11321.5	228.6	11550.1
of which:										
1. Manual workers	255.0	79.6	1.7	16.3	25.7	23.3	401.6	5682.3	48.3	5730.6
2. Non-manual workers	1893.0	55.4	1.5	76.4	114.8	29.3	2170.4	4474.9	70.9	4545.8
3. Other proletarian population	174.0	135.0	0.3	333.6	92.7	132.2	867.8	1164.3	109.4	1273.7
II. Cooperative producers	-	-	-	-	39.0	9.0	48.0	757.0	-	757.0
III. Artisans and craftsmen	-	321.3	6.4	7.1	78.0	11.0	423.8	1431.3	-	1431.3
IV. Capitalist group	-	76.0	-	-	-	-	76.0	950.8	-	950.8
of which:										
Traders	-	-	-	-	-	-	-	800.0	-	800.0
V. Other population	-	-	-	-	-	489.6	489.6	489.6	-	489.6
B. Agricultural population	106.8	-	181.1	35.2	597.6	-	920.7	15909.4	-	15909.4
1. Proletariat	60.0	-	9.1	1.4	3.2	-	73.7	762.0	-	762.0
2. Collective farmers	1.1	-	10.0	1.1	21.8	-	34.0	742.3	-	742.3
3. Individual peasants	45.0	-	155.0	32.7	555.6	-	788.3	13193.3	-	13193.3
4. Kulaks	0.7	-	7.0	-	17.0	-	24.7	1211.8	-	1211.8
Total	2428.8	667.3	191.0	468.6	947.8	694.4	5397.9	30859.6	228.6	31088.2
Income of socialised sector	-	-	-	-	-	-	-	-	-	-
Total	-	-	-	-	-	-	-	-	-	-

Table 5a. (cont'd)

Expenditure

A	Consumption of material goods 20	Rent payment 21	Purchase of services 22	Value of free social cultural and medical services 23	Taxes and dues 24	Payments to social insurance 25	Payments to state insurance 26	Subscriptions to trade unions and social organisations 27	Shares in cooperatives 28	Total expended 29	Residual[1] 30	of which, state loans 31	Income realised in the form of accumulation and consumption of material goods and services 32	Income realised in the form of accumulation and consumption of material goods 33
A. Non-agricultural population	...	1048.1	725.6	932.6	654.8	43.7	27.4	289.0	119.2	12308.4	...	509.0	13816.1	11109.8
I. Proletariat of which	8160.8	815.7	586.7	815.6	51.0	9.2	12.9	267.8	110.0	10829.7	491.8	462.5	10870.6	8652.6
1. Manual workers	4076.5	349.3	190.8	475.8	19.7	5.2	7.0	123.0	80.9	5303.2	379.1	239.1	5446.5	4430.6
2. Non-manual workers	3142.4	389.2	350.7	238.2	30.6	4.0	5.9	135.0	20.8	4341.8	133.1	217.8	4278.6	3300.5
3. Other proletarian population	941.9	77.2	45.2	101.6	0.7	-	-	9.8	8.3	1184.7	-20.4	5.6	1145.5	921.5
II. Cooperative producers	...	36.3	18.5	39.0	68.0	-	11.7	17.0	8.8	161.8	...		689.0	595.2
III. Artisans and craftsmen	...	80.3	38.5	78.0	110.1	12.2	2.8	3.5	-	356.6	...	46.5	1271.5	1074.7
IV. Capitalist group of which, Traders	...	110.0	79.8	-	425.7	22.3	-	...	-	644.1	...	...	496.5	306.7
V. Other population	480.6	5.8	2.1	-	-	-	-	0.7	0.4	489.6	...	-	488.5	480.6
B. Agricultural population	14262.8	-	196.3	623.8	677.0	17.8	257.0	7.4	225.0	16267.1	357.7	18.1	14725.2	13905.1
1. Proletariat	-	-	6.7	29.4	-	-	-	5.1	3.0	...	...	5.9	734.2	695.3
2. Collective farmers	-	-	9.5	21.8	11.0	-	14.0	-	7.0	...	...	0.5	730.0	701.5
3. Individual peasants	-	-	168.8	555.6	469.0	4.5	231.0	0.6	215.0	...	...	11.0	12273.2	11548.8
4. Kulaks	-	-	11.3	17.0	197.0	13.3	12.0	1.7	-	...	...	0.7	987.8	959.5
Total	-	1048.1	921.9	1556.4	1331.8	61.5	284.4	296.4	344.2	28575.5	...	527.1	28541.3	25014.9
Income of socialised sector	-	-	-	-	-	-	-	-	-	-	-	-	-	5121.0
Total	-	-	-	-	-	-	-	-	-	-	-	-	-	30135.9

1. The residual does not include receipts from sale of property, and so in certain cases the amount of loans exceeds the amount of residuals.
[... = no data available]

Table 5b. Balance of distribution and redistribution of the national income, by classes and groups of the population, in 1930

A	Incomes received through distribution						Pensions and allowances	Value of free social cultural and medical services	Total basic incomes
	Wages of persons employed		Entrepre-neurial income	Interest	Incomes of cooperative producers	Incomes of independent producers			
	Wages of persons employed in production	Wages of persons employed in circulation and serving production							
	1	2	3	4	5	6	7	8	9
A. Non-agricultural population	7264.7	1625.7	567.7	81.5	1003.0	1197.4	401.5	839.4	12980.9
I. Proletariat	7264.7	1625.7	–	81.5	–	311.6	349.5	743.1	10524.4
of which: 1. Manual workers	5965.0	190.8	–	34.7	–	108.8	312.2	675.6	7318.7
2. Non-manual workers	1217.2	1416.4	–	44.9	–	67.3	35.7	63.3	2960.1
3. Other proletarian workers	82.5	18.5	–	1.9	–	135.5	1.6	4.2	245.6
II. Cooperative producers	–	–	–	–	1003.0	55.0	10.0	21.6	1058.0
III. Artisans and craftsmen	–	–	–	–	–	830.8	41.6	73.7	830.8
IV. Capitalist group	–	–	567.7	–	–	–	–	–	567.7
of which: Traders	–	–	511.2	–	–	–	–	–	511.2
V. Other population	–	–	–	–	–	–	0.4	1.0	–
B. Agricultural population	2460.5	93.8	431.4	–	2783.9	11753.2	11.5	42.1	17576.4
1. Proletariat	622.4	18.9	–	–	–	125.3	11.5	42.1	820.2
2. Collective farmers	321.0	–	–	–	2656.9	1079.9	–	–	4057.8
3. Individual peasants	1500.5	74.9	–	–	127.0	10548.0	–	–	12250.0
4. Kulaks	17.0	–	431.4	–	–	–	–	–	448.4
Total	9725.2	1719.5	999.1	81.5	3786.9	12950.6	413.0	881.5	30557.3
Income of socialised sector	–	–	–	–	–	–	–	–	7775.9
Total	–	–	–	–	–	–	–	–	38333.2

Table 5b. (cont'd)

Incomes received through redistribution

A	Wages in non-productive sphere	Income from sale of services	Insurance payments	Pensions and allowances	Value of free social cultural and medical services	Other receipts	Total derivative incomes	Total incomes	Received from sale of property	Total received
	10	11	12	13	14	15	16	17	18	19
A. Non-agricultural population	3478.1	853.0	15.9	434.1	368.4	765.6	5915.1	18896.0	413.9	19331.0
I. Proletariat	3478.1	395.8	13.4	431.8	263.4	234.5	4817.0	15341.4	413.9	15776.4
of which:										
1. Manual workers	328.9	100.3	6.7	17.3	37.5	62.0	552.7	7871.4	83.0	7954.4
2. Non-manual workers	2977.4	77.4	3.8	87.6	155.1	38.8	3340.1	6300.2	101.0	6401.2
3. Other proletarian population	171.8	218.1	2.9	326.9	70.8	133.7	924.2	1169.8	229.0	1420.8
II. Cooperative producers	–	–	–	–	54.7	15.7	70.4	1128.4	–	1128.4
III. Artisans and craftsmen	–	375.0	2.5	2.3	50.3	26.4	456.5	1287.3	–	1287.3
IV. Capitalist group	–	82.2	–	–	–	–	82.2	649.9	–	649.9
of which: Traders	–	–	–	–	–	–	–	511.2	–	511.2
V. Other population	–	–	–	–	–	489.0	489.0	489.0	–	489.0
B. Agricultural population	130.1	–	126.7	56.9	779.9	–	1093.6	18670.0	–	18670.0
1. Proletariat	80.0	–	7.7	1.5	5.6	–	94.8	915.0	–	915.0
2. Collective farmers	10.0	–	34.0	20.0	155.4	–	219.4	4277.2	–	4277.2
3. Individual peasants	40.1	–	81.0	35.4	609.9	–	766.4	13016.4	–	13016.4
4. Kulaks	–	–	4.0	–	9.0	–	13.0	461.4	–	461.4
Total	3608.2	853.0	142.6	491.0	1148.3	765.6	7008.7	37566.0	413.9	38001.0
Income of socialised sector	–	–	–	–	–	–	–	–	–	–
Total	–	–	–	–	–	–	–	–	–	–

Table 5b. (cont'd)

Expenditure

A	Consumption of material goods (20)	Rent payment (21)	Purchase of services (22)	Value of free social cultural and medical services (23)	Taxes and dues (24)	Payments to social insurance (25)	Payments to state insurance (26)	Subscriptions to trade unions and social organisations (27)	Shares in cooperatives (28)	Total expended (29)	Residual[1] (30)	of which, state loans (31)	Income realised in the form of accumulation, consumption of material goods and services (32)	Income realised in the form of accumulation and consumption of material goods (33)
A. Non-agricultural population	...	1125.1	850.9	1207.8	677.3	30.9	18.6	335.1	217.1	16185.3	...	431.6	17617.0	14433.3
I. Proletariat of which	11405.3	903.7	709.9	1102.8	52.0	9.2	12.5	321.1	205.0	14720.9	620.5	406.4	14741.6	12025.8
1. Manual workers	5873.5	391.8	239.2	734.7	19.8	5.2	7.0	151.2	110.4	7532.8	338.6	203.1	7577.8	6212.1
2. Non-manual workers	4398.8	432.6	418.7	292.1	31.6	4.0	5.5	161.0	87.7	5832.0	468.2	198.3	6010.4	4867.0
3. Other proletarian population	1133.0	78.7	52.0	76.0	0.6	-	-	8.9	6.9	1356.1	186.3	5.0	1153.4	946.7
II. Cooperative producers	...	63.9	30.7	54.7	135.8	-	-	-	-	285.1	...		992.6	843.3
III. Artisans and craftsmen	...	76.8	46.6	50.3	175.6	6.9	4.0	13.5	12.1	385.8	...	25.0	1075.2	901.5
IV. Capitalist group	...	76.3	61.1	-	312.5	14.8	2.1	0.5	-	467.3	...		320.0	182.7
of which: Traders	...	...	...	...	...	...	...	...	...	...	...	...	...	...
V. Other population	480.0	5.0	2.6	-	1.4	-	-	-	-	489.0	...	-	487.6	480.0
B. Agricultural population	15793.5	-	151.0	822.0	693.1	7.0	303.0	10.0	410.0	18189.6	1445.8	171.7	17246.9	16273.9
1. Proletariat	...	-	5.9	47.7	1.6	-	-	8.0	9.6	-	-	41.0	895.8	842.2
2. Collective farmers	...	-	31.1	155.4	60.0	-	96.0	-	128.9	-	-	11.2	3992.3	3805.8
3. Individual peasants	...	-	110.7	609.9	463.3	3.0	198.0	0.5	271.5	-	-	112.7	12080.1	11359.5
4. Kulaks	...	-	3.3	9.0	168.2	4.0	9.0	1.5	-	-	-	6.8	278.7	266.4
Total	...	1125.1	1001.9	2029.8	1370.4	37.9	321.6	345.1	627.1	34374.9	-	603.3	34863.9	30707.2
Income of socialised sector	-	-	-	-	-	-	-	-	-	-	-	-	-	7626.0
Total	-	-	-	-	-	-	-	-	-	-	-	-	-	38333.2

1. The residual does not include receipts from sale of property, and so in certain cases the amount of loans exceeds the amount of residuals.

[... = no data available]

3. Tables and notes

IV EXPLANATORY NOTES ON THE CALCULATION OF ARTICLES IN THE BALANCE

CONTENTS

IV   EXPLANATORY NOTES ON THE CALCULATION OF ARTICLES IN THE
BALANCES

[A]   Methods and sources for estimating national income and its distribution

1.   THE DISTRIBUTION AND REDISTRIBUTION OF THE NATIONAL INCOME BY
CLASSES AND GROUPS OF THE POPULATION [pp. 162, 247–9]

The data of social statistics are used to determine the size of the population.[1] Seasonal workers have been excluded from the group 'industrial proletariat', and are included, together with their incomes, in the 'agricultural population'. The proletarian population includes day-labourers, casual labourers, domestic servants, unemployed, pensioners and grant-aided students (living on their own). 'Cooperative producers' include members of cooperative organisations in census industry [see Glossary], cooperative transport workers, and some other types of cooperative organisations. The group 'artisans and handicraftsmen' covers persons not organised in cooperatives, and includes: (*a*) artisans and handicraftsmen in the strict sense, who do not employ hired labour at all, or not more than two persons; (*b*) transport workers who do not employ hired labour; (*c*) members of the free professions; and (*d*) a group of 'other persons' (persons who let rooms and premises and whose income from letting does not exceed 1,200 rubles a year).

The group 'bourgeoisie' ['capitalist groups'] includes: (*a*) industrialists employing more than two persons; (*b*) transport workers employing hired labour; (*c*) all traders; and (*d*) a group of 'other persons' – this includes rentiers and persons who let rooms whose income exceeds 1,200 rubles a year. Thus 'capitalist groups' in these estimates covers a wider circle of persons than in the estimates of consumption, where traders who do not employ hired labour are not included in the 'bourgeoisie'.

'Other population' covers persons on the pay-roll of the state, and *declassé* persons.

The estimates of the incomes of the proletariat are based on the following three sources of data: (1) data from labour statistics on wage funds, corrected on the basis of data from Gosbank [the State Bank], (2) data from the [family] budget studies of manual and office workers, and (3) data from reports of TsUSStrakh [Central Administration of Social Insurance] and other government departments concerning the amount of expenditure on services to the proletariat.

In addition to its basic sources of income – wages – the proletariat is also a recipient of other types of income: (*a*) from handicrafts and agriculture; these have been included with 'incomes of producers'; (*b*) receipts from the financial system (interests, winnings on state loans, etc.); (*c*) pensions and allowances, socio-cultural and medical services in kind; (*d*) income from the sale of services and property and from the resale of products; (*e*) travelling expenses and some other items. Excluding social, cultural and medical services in kind, these additional sources of income account for 12–13 per cent of total income in the case of workers.

The estimates of the incomes of cooperative craftsmen are based on data from industrial statistics on the volume of production by artisan and handicraft industry and on data on profits deductions paid by cooperative craftsmen.

In addition to their basic source of income – from artisan and handicraft activities – cooperative craftsmen are also recipients of other incomes. Urban craftsmen received an additional 10 per cent of their income from other sources and rural craftsmen received an additional 25 per cent. In the latter case almost all additional income came from agricultural activities. (All these figures exclude the value of social, cultural and medical services received in kind.)

The incomes of artisans and handicraftsmen not organised in cooperatives have been estimated on the basis of data from the statistics of small-scale industry which show the volume of production by small-scale industry in the private sector. Apart from its income from industry (net production minus wages paid), this group also has other sources of income. For the urban craftsmen these sources amount to ten per cent of their income from artisan and handicraft activities, and for rural craftsmen to 25 per cent. The additional income in the latter case comes from agricultural activities. Apart from these sources this group is also a recipient of income in the form of social, cultural and medical services in kind.

The incomes of transport workers, members of the free professions and persons who let premises were estimated on the basis of tax data.

Estimates of the incomes of the capitalist groups were based on data showing the volume of net production created in the capitalist sector (after deduction of wages) and on taxation data.

The incomes of the agricultural proletariat were calculated from data of labour statistics on wage funds. 'Other incomes', obtained from their own personal agriculture, comprised 20 per cent of their total income in 1928 and 1929 and 18 per cent in 1930.

The incomes of collective farmers are made up as follows: income from the collective and the individual sectors of agriculture; income from the processing of agricultural produce; income from haulage, fishing, hunting and from handicraft industries; income from their own building work (collective and individual) and from procurement of timber (not to be confused with wages received for timber procurement in the state sector); and, finally, income in the form of wages received for timber-procurement, seasonal activities, etc. Their incomes also include pensions, allowances, insurance payments, and social, cultural and medical services received in kind. Incomes from the collective sector of agriculture were estimated on the basis of data on the net production of the collective farm sector. To facilitate comparison with the incomes of individual peasants, the incomes of the collective farmers have been shown as including the entire net production of the collective farm sector and not just that part of which is received by collective farmers for their individual use.

The income of collective farmers from the individual sector of agriculture was obtained by dividing the data for gross production of agriculture in the private sector between individual peasants and collective farmers. However, for determining the net production of households a different coefficient was used in the case of collective farmer households than in the case of individual peasant households. (For collective farmers the ratio of net production to gross production is lower than for the private sector as a whole, because the structure of their gross production is different.)

The incomes of collective farmers from other branches of the economy were determined by dividing between the individual sector and the collective farmers the total volume of the income from these branches received by the agricultural population.

The total income from artisan and handicraft occupations was established as 32 per cent of the total volume of net production of craft industry in the countryside (from the statistics on small-scale industry). Income from forestry (obtained by activities of households on their own account) was obtained from the balance of production and consumption of timber and firewood [presumably based on data from peasant budget studies]. Incomes from haulage were estimated from the data on peasant budgets and on freight turnover in rural localities. 'Income from their own building work' was taken as equal to the net production of agricultural building work. In the case of collective farmers this is the net production of their building work both in the collective farm sector and on an individual basis.

Incomes from the processing of agricultural products were established from the balance of production and consumption for these products. Wages were estimated from the data of labour statistics with some corrections.

In order to establish the breakdown of income from a particular branch of the economy between the individual peasant sector and the collective sector it was necessary in certain cases to supplement reasonably reliable statistical data by more or less indirect indicators. Thus, in order to divide income from forestry work by sector, we considered data on the different level of collectivisation in forest areas in comparison with data for areas without forests.

The total sum of incomes of individual peasant households, including kulak households, was obtained by aggregating incomes from agriculture and 'other incomes' (these were as listed above for collective farmers). Agricultural income was obtained by deduction from the total net production of the private sector that part of it which is received by collective farmers from their ancillary individual agriculture, by the agricultural proletariat and by the non-agricultural population. Income from other branches is determined by dividing the total income of the branch between the individual sector and the collective farmers.

The income of the kulaks was obtained as a total amount, without distinguishing separate items. Consequently the incomes of non-kulak individual peasant households are also available only as a total amount, obtained by deducting kulak incomes from the total income of all individual peasant households.

After obtaining the total amount of the incomes of the several classes and groups of the population, estimates were then made of the total obligatory payments falling on each group, and the total incomes realised in the form of accumulation and consumption of material goods and services.

All types of obligatory payments are included in the estimates: taxes, payments to TsUSStrakh [Central Social Insurance Administration], payments to Gosstrakh [State Insurance], subscriptions to trade-union and other voluntary organisations, subscriptions to cooperatives, shares in Traktorotsentr [All-Union Centre for Machine Tractor Stations]. Loans normally appear as an item in 'accumulation', although in the table '[Balance of the] principal indicators of reproduction by sectors of the national economy' [p. 128] they appear with 'other obligatory payments'.

Incomes realised in the form of accumulation and consumption of material goods and services were obtained by deducting total obligatory payments from total incomes (i.e. basic incomes plus derived incomes). Incomes realised in the form of accumulation and consumption of material goods *excluding* services were obtained by deducting from the value of services 'incomes realised in the form of accumulation and consumption of material goods and services'. The assessed value of services included both paid for and free services, and also included expenditure on rent for accommodation. All rent for accommodation was treated as payment for services, although a very large part of it is in fact compensation for the depreciation of the accommodation, and should really be treated as compensation for material consumption.

2. EXPENDITURE OF THE NON-PRODUCTIVE SPHERE
The expenditure of the non-productive sphere was estimated on the basis of the reports of NKFin [People's Commissariat of Finance], Gosbank, TsUSStrakh, Gosstrakh, the trade unions, NKPros [People's Commissariat of Education], NKZdrav [People's Commissariat of Health], and other organisations.

[B]   *Methods and sources for estimating capital stocks and capital investments of branches of the economy [pp. 167–78, 405–36]*

[1]   INDUSTRY (INCLUDING ELECTRIC POWER)
[a]   *Fixed funds (osnovnye fondy)* [i.e. fixed capital, referred to here as 'capital stocks']. *Capital stocks* were estimated at their value net of depreciation. The balance of capital stocks consisted of the following items: (*a*) incomplete building work in progress at the beginning and the end of the year; (*b*) capital stocks at the beginning and the end of the year; (*c*) capital investment during the year; (*d*) entry into exploitation during the year; (*e*) decrease of capital stocks during the year (depreciation).

It was difficult to transfer the data on capital stocks in restoration prices from an economic year to a calendar year basis because there are no quarterly reports on the amount of investment entering into exploitation. The problem was solved by means of an estimation procedure using calendar year data for capital investments to derive capital stocks.

Since industrial statistics do not provide a direct record of capital stocks in terms of value net of depreciation, this value has been estimated in the following manner. For each year, beginning with 1 October 1925, the annual value of depreciation has been deducted from the value of capital stock, and the annual value of completed capital repairs has been added.

[b]   *Capital investments* were included in the balance of capital stocks only for those sums which enter into capital stocks. Capital investments in geological prospecting and in preparation of projects were therefore excluded, as they enter into value in proportion to the capital stock coming into exploitation.

As industrial statistics cover only the capital stock of industrial establishments and enterprises ('factory-method' statistics) the balance excludes capital investment in scientific research, outlays on the training of personnel and outlays on property held by trusts.

To transfer capital investment to a calendar-year basis, the current conjunctural accounts were used to establish the share of the first quarter in annual investment. In the economic year 1927/8 [1 October 1927, to 30 September 1928] the first quarter accounted for 17 per cent of annual investment, in 1928/9 for 16.7 per cent and in 1929/30 for 20 per cent. Data for the special quarter [October–December 1930] was obtained from preliminary current accounts. Capital investment in 1930 was taken from available reports of associations [*ob"edineniya*] for 'planned industry'; these covered 70 per cent of all industry.

The percentage of the capital investment plan for this part of industry was extrapolated to those parts of planned industry not presenting reports and also to the remaining unplanned part of state industry.

For industry under the control of VSNKh, capital investment figures were corrected from data in the VSNKh materials which were published for the XVII Party Conference [January 1932]. [11]

Data on capital investment for 1931 were obtained from the same VSNKh source.

For industries under the control of NKSnab, and for other industry, capital investment was estimated from the preliminary data of current reports on plan fulfilment.

[c]   *Entry into exploitation* of capital stock by economic years was obtained from industrial statistics. In the absence of quarterly reports on the entry of stock into exploitation, the transfer to a calendar-year basis was obtained by using data on investment by calendar years and relating entry into exploitation to the data for capital investment by economic years.

Data on entry into exploitation for 1930 were obtained from the reports of the associations covering the same group of industry as the capital investment data.

The relationship between entry into exploitation and capital investment in this part of industry was extrapolated to other state industry.

The VSNKh industry data was corrected on the basis of the materials published for the XVII Party Conference.

Data for VSNKh industry in 1931 were also taken from the XVII Party Conference materials. For Narkomsnab and for 'other state industry' estimates were made from the preliminary data of current (conjunctural) reports. These data must be regarded as extremely rough.

[d]   *Depreciation* by economic years is assumed in the industrial statistics to be the sum of the actual allocations to the depreciation fund. Consequently the depreciation rates have been calculated from this sum.

For the transfer to a calendar year basis, depreciation has been taken as being the same percentage as in the economic years. The level of depreciation in 1930 and 1931 has been calculated by using the 1929 percentage. Thus the norms of depreciation are: (1) 5 per cent of the restoration value for 1927/8, 5.2 per cent for 1928/9 and 5.2 per cent for 1929/30 and (2) 7.6 per cent of the value of stock net of depreciation in 1928, 7.7 per cent in 1929, 7.3 per cent in 1930 and 8.3 per cent in 1931. In addition the value of the decrease in stock for 1928 and 1929 also included an additional amount for property worn out through age and wear and tear, 12.0 million rubles in 1928 and 20.0 million rubles in 1929.

[*e*] The size of incomplete building work in progress was obtained for 1930 from the data in the reports and for other years was obtained by means of the balance method.

[*f*] Data by the types of property for all the above mentioned indicators were obtained for all these years from the data in the reports. Since the types of property listed in these data included installations in the 'transport' category, we have to resort to 'expert' evaluations to deduct the share of transport installations in the figures on capital stock, capital investment and entry into exploitation. The share of installations in capital investment in the transport category was estimated at 43 per cent in 1928, 40 per cent in 1929 and 33.9 per cent in 1930. The share of installations in the capital stock of transport at the beginning of 1928 was estimated at 39.2 per cent. Incomplete building work in progress in transport was all classified as 'installations'; given the nature of the rest of the transport property it was unlikely to provide any of the incomplete building work in progress. Using the data thus obtained for building work in progress and capital investment the value of entry into exploitation was estimated. An amortisation rate of 2 per cent was applied.

[2] TRANSPORT AND COMMUNICATIONS
Before 1930 the former Central Statistical Administration of the USSR did not carry out any systematic survey of the capital stock of transport. In 1930 a special study was therefore undertaken to estimate the capital stock in transport in 1927/8–1929/30, by using the available data collected by the different government departments.

[*a*] *The capital stock of railway transport*
[i] Owing to certain peculiarities in the records and accounts of NKPS [People's Commissariat of Transport] these materials cannot be fully used in determining the value and the changes in the capital stock of railway transport.
In order to estimate the capital stock we had to use the following sources: (*a*) materials from the statistics on transport and various kinds of other information compiled by NKPS for special purposes, describing the quantities, in kind, of the different elements of the capital stock of the railways; (*b*) the 'price-lists' of TsMIK [Central Inter-departmental Stocktaking Commission]; (*c*) expert evaluations of those types of property to which it would be difficult to apply the 'price-lists'; (*d*) in the operational records of the railroads, those sections dealing with outlay of the railroads for the acquisition, reconstruction, widening and capital repairs to property; and (*e*) materials of TsMIK showing detailed records of the inventory of three railway lines.
The operational reports of the railways, supplemented in certain cases with special reports from NKPS, provided the basic information for determining the receipt and loss of property. In these reports, expenditure on capital stock is often mixed in with current

expenditure, and it is therefore necessary to analyse each job separately in order to get accurate data. Where it was not possible to obtain an accurate breakdown of items of expenditure for a particular job we had to make an approximate breakdown using the advice of experts.

From the record of the inventory of the three railway lines investigated in detail we were able to obtain (*a*) data on the actual state, allowing for wear and tear (percentage of useful life remaining), of particular elements in the capital stock on 1 October 1927, and (*b*) the relative weights of particular elements, which were needed in order to calculate the value of the property as a whole. We also calculated (*c*) the value of a unit of 'artificial' and civil installations [see glossary] to be used as an average for the whole network. The capital stock (excluding workshops, depots and electric power stations, which were treated as industry) was broken down into the eight groups used in the railways' accounting practice: (1) the earth track-bed, (2) the 'artificial installations', (3) the superstructure of the railway, (4) the civil installations, (5) communications, (6) locomotives, (7) passenger rolling-stock, and (8) freight rolling-stock.

The value of the property on 1 October 1927 was determined on the basis of the data on the quantity of particular units of this property and the average value per unit. The quantity of the separate types of units were determined on the basis of the statistical and operational reports mentioned above. The average value of the separate units was established partly from 'price-lists' (*tsenniki*) and partly from the detailed investigation of the three railway lines. Valuation was made at restoration cost. The value of the stock net of depreciation was estimated from the 'percentages of useful life remaining', which were taken from the TsMIK materials.

[ii] *The recalculation of the capital stock of the railways into calendar years.* In view of the absence of quarterly accounts on the construction and acquisition of equipment, the relative share of the first quarter in capital investment in 1929/30 for the most important types of property was estimated by experts: (1) the earth track-bed, (2) the artificial installations, (3) the superstructure of the railway, (4) the civil installations, (5) communications, (6) rolling stock and (7) 'other property'. The share of the first quarter was estimated at 18.6 per cent of the capital investment in 1929/30 in the case of these seven types of property. This percentage was taken to apply to 1927/8 and to 1928/9 as well. Capital investments in the special quarter were estimated on the basis of the reports of NKPS.

Entry into exploitation by calendar years was determined, as in the case of capital investment, by using expert evaluations to identify the first quarters of 1927/8–1929/30. The special quarter of 1930 was estimated on the basis of NKPS reports. The stock on 1 January 1928 was established by deducting the amount of amortisation during one quarter (25 per cent of the annual amount for 1927/8) and by adding the value of the property entering into exploitation in the first quarter of 1928/9.

For 1931 the data on capital investment and entry into exploitation were calculated from the preliminary current accounts.

[*b*]   *The capital stock of sea and river transport*
   [i] For TsUMor (Central Administration of Maritime Transport), calculations were

made on the basis of the following data: (i) expert evaluations of the percentages of useful life and the average periods of service, and (ii) accounting records on the initial value, and on the receipt and loss of property. The materials from the 1923/4 stocktaking were also used, although these were extremely defective.

[ii] For Sovtorgflot (Soviet Merchant Navy) the basis for the calculation of the value of stock was the accounting reports and materials from the revaluation carried out on 1 January 1928. In determining the value of the stock net of depreciation in *chervonets* [current] rubles, the Soviet Merchant Navy proceeded from the original value in gold rubles, without converting it into *chervonets* rubles. Consequently, when we estimated the value of the stock, we attempted to eliminate these defects by using a variety of materials.

[iii] For 'Kaspar' (Caspian Sea Steamship Line), the calculation of stock values was carried out on the basis of materials from the stock revaluation of 1 January 1926, and from accounting records on the receipt and loss of property. Norms of amortisation were to a considerable extent determined by expert evaluation.

[iv] For Tsuvodput (Central Administration of Inland Waterways), the basis of the calculation was accounting records on receipts and losses of property, but the value of stock for 1 October 1927 was based on expert evaluations and the materials of the stock-taking of 1925. The scale of deductions for amortisation was fixed on the basis of the norms of TsMIK and expert evaluations.

[v] For Tsentroreka (Central Administration for River Transport) the basis of the calculation was the material from the accounts. In the initial balance [i.e. at the time of its creation] of Tsentroreka, part of the property was entered according to its actual value (value net of depreciation) in gold rubles, part at its original value [with no depreciation deducted] in gold rubles, and part in current prices. After separating the value of the property reckoned in gold rubles from the value in *chervonets* rubles, we estimated the change in each group of the property. Deductions for amortisation were determined on the basis of the TsMIK materials and of expert evaluations.

Estimates of capital stock and capital investments were made in terms of calendar years. The data for 1931 were established on the basis of the preliminary current conjunctural accounts.

[c]   The capital stock of surfaced and dirt roads
The basis for this calculation was provided by the reports for 1927/8, the plans for 1928/9, the estimates for 1929/30 and the expert evaluations of the staff of TsUdortrans (Central Administration for Road Transport).

The reports provided the following data for 1 October 1927: (i) the length and the type of road: (ii) the number of linear metres of artificial installations (bridges, tunnels, etc): (iii) the number of square metres of civil installations: and (iv) the number of mechanical devices.

Expert evaluations were used to determine the value of a unit of the different types of property as listed above. The value of the property net of depreciation was calculated on the basis of data from the reports on the state of the property according to a three-grade evaluation and an expert evaluation of the degree of useful life remaining. Amortisation was calculated on the basis of expert estimations of the lengths of service of each type of property. As a result, the following norms of amortisation were obtained: for roads of all types 5.1 per cent, for artificial installations 2.05 per cent, for civil installations 1.7 per cent, and for mechanical devices 10.8 per cent.

The recalculation of capital stock in terms of calendar years was carried out in the same way as for railway transport.

The share of the first quarter of 1929/30 in capital investment was determined by means of expert evaluation to be 12 per cent of the annual investment and this percentage was also used for the first quarters of 1927/8 and 1928/9. Data for the special quarter was obtained from the reports of TsUdortrans, and data for the year 1931 was estimated from preliminary materials.

[*d*] *Capital stock of communications [posts and telegraphs, etc.], (NKSvyaz) (People's Commissariat of Communications)*

The basis for the estimates was the material from stocktaking of the property of NKPT (NKSvyaz) for 1 March 1929. Capital investment, entry into exploitation and loss of property (depreciation) were estimated from financial and technical reports for 1927/8 and 1929/30.

The value of property on 1 March 1927 was taken to be roughly the same as on 1 January 1929. The share of the first quarter in 1928/9 and 1929/30 was estimated by expert evaluation to be 17 per cent of the investment in the economic year.

Depreciation was calculated on the basis of the norms of amortisation laid down in the instructions for stocktaking in the case of communications property.

For the special quarter of 1930 investment and entry into exploitation were calculated from the reports of NKSvyaz.

Data for 1931 were calculated from the preliminary materials of the current accounts of plan fulfilment.

[3] AGRICULTURE

The volume and changes in the capital stock of agricultural enterprises for 1928–1931 were calculated in two variants: (*a*) at their stocktaking (balance) value, net of depreciation, and (*b*) at their value net of depreciation in constant 1926/7 prices.

The stocktaking (balance) value of capital stock refers to the actual value of the stock at the time of entry into production, net of the value of technical depreciation recorded at the time the records were made (at the beginning or the end of the given year).

In order to establish the social and economic structure of the capital stock and its changes, all calculations were carried out with a breakdown of agriculture by social sector showing the main categories of agricultural enterprise, and with a breakdown for the separate types of capital stock, showing both productive stock (fixed means of production) and consumption stock.

The capital stock of the state sector includes the stock of state farms and other state agencies and of trusts and associations providing services (OBV [Organisation for Agricultural Pest Control] the 'Mineral Fertilizer' Joint-Stock Company, VET [All-Union Electrical Trust] etc.). A further problem is the absence of a sectoral breakdown of the data on the capital stock in irrigation and, to a considerable extent, in land improvement. In our tables the convention has been followed that the entire stock of irrigation installations, and a considerable part (the part not divided by social sector in the data) of the stock of land improvement installations, have been assigned to the state sector of agriculture.

The capital stock of the collective and cooperative sector includes the socialised stock of the collective farms and the agricultural producers' cooperatives, and also by the convention the stock of the MTS [Machine-Tractor Stations] and the MTK [Machine-Tractor Columns].

The capital stock of the private sector is defined as the stock of individual peasant households plus the non-socialised stock of the collective farms.

The size and the changes in capital stock of agricultural enterprises have been shown by type and group as listed below:

PRODUCTIVE STOCK (FIXED MEANS OF PRODUCTION)
  A. *Agricultural*
    1. Buildings for agricultural use.
    2. Land-improvement and irrigation works.
    3. Machines and implements:
      (*a*) agricultural machinery and tools
      (*b*) tractors
      (*c*) means of transport (mechanical and horse-drawn)
      (*d*) other agricultural implements.
    4. Animals, poultry and bees:
      (*a*) of which, working animals (of work age).
  B. *Other (non-agricultural) productive branches*
    5. Buildings, equipment and tools of industrial and subsidiary technical enterprises and establishments (including the personal craft implements of collective-farm members and individual peasant households).
    6. Buildings and equipment of rural electric power stations and electrical installations.

CONSUMPTION (NON-PRODUCTIVE) STOCK
    7. Dwellings.
Changes in the capital stock for all years covered were calculated as follows:
    1. The value of stock at the beginning of the year net of depreciation.
    2. Obtained during the year:
      (*a*) newly introduced; manufactured; extended; re-equipped; acquired; value of capital repairs.
      (*b*) transferred without compensation from other sectors and groups of households, through collectivisation and redistribution.
    3. Losses during the year:
      (*a*) depreciation (yearly amount for technical wear-and-tear);
      (*b*) fire; premature death of animals; losses and other natural damage;
      (*c*) as a result of replacement by more advanced means of production; other losses before the due date;
      (*d*) sold, and transferred without compensation, to other sectors and groups of household, through collectivisation and redistribution.
    4. The value of stock at the end of the year net of depreciation [1 + 2 − 3].

In calculating the changes in the capital stock in livestock and poultry, the volume of capital investment was obtained as the value of the gross increase in livestock and poultry during the year, minus the value of the livestock and poultry set aside for slaughter (for meat). The volume of capital investment in work-stock was obtained as the value of the gross increase in the level of work-stock during the year plus the value of the young animals transferred to the category of work-stock during the year, minus the value of work-stock set aside for slaughter (for meat).

Because of the state of statistical and operational departmental records in the case of the collective-cooperative and private sectors of agriculture, capital stock for the calendar years 1928–30 was estimated from the corresponding estimates for the 1927/8–1929/30 agricultural years (July–June) or economic years (October–September), which were then transferred to a calendar year basis. In the case of state farms, capital stock was estimated directly in calendar years.

Changes in capital stock during 1931 were estimated from data on the preliminary fulfilment of the capital investment plan for agriculture for the calendar year 1931. The figures for this year are not derived from the annual accounts of agricultural enterprises and must be regarded as approximate.

[a]   *Capital stock of state farms for 1928–30*

[i] *[1928–9].* The basic materials for determining the scale and change in capital stock of the state farms in 1928 and 1929 were taken from the comprehensive survey of state farms in 1926 and annual reports of the state farm trusts. These covered the years 1928 and 1929 in the case of Sovkhoztsentr [State Farm Centre], Ukrsovkhozob″edinenie [Ukrainian State Farm Association], Soyuzsakhar [State Sugar-Beet Farm Association] and the Ovtsevod [Sheep Farming] joint-stock company for 1928 and 1929, and the year 1929 for Zernotrest [State Grain Farm Trust]. Capital stock of those republican trusts which did not submit annual reports, and of state farms not organised into trusts, was estimated from data from the comprehensive survey of state farms in 1928. These results were extrapolated by using the rate of growth of stock for those republican trusts [which did submit annual reports]; the figures obtained were corrected with the help of data on the fulfilment of the financial plan for the years in question.

[ii] *[1930].* The change in the capital stock of state farms in 1930 was obtained from data in the annual reports both of all the associations of state farms of all-Union significance and of the most important republican trusts. For republican state farm trusts which did not submit annual reports, and for state farms not organised into trusts, we applied the rates of growth of capital stock in the case of those republican state farms which did submit annual reports. Certain all-Union and republican trusts which were separated out from the former Sovkhoztsentr submitted annual reports only for the period after they became separately organised (i.e. from 1 May 1930). In order to establish the annual data, these incomplete data were corrected by using information on the fulfilment of the plan for financing the state farm trusts from the Union and republican budget covering the whole of the 1930 calendar year.

In our estimate of the stock of the state farms we did not include the stock of state farms planned by NKSnab, except the state farms of Soyuzsakhar.

[*b*] *Capital stock of collective farms for 1928–30.* The size and changes in the capital stock of the collective farms were calculated for the agricultural years 1927/8–1929/30, and then recalculated into the corresponding calendar years by preparing half-yearly balances. The basic materials used to obtain the size and changes in the level of collective farm stock for the years in question were obtained from the comprehensive surveys of collective farms of 1 June 1928, 1 June 1929 and 1 June 1930, from the budget surveys of collective farms in 1927/8 (the latter were carried out in 1928 by the Scientific Research Institute for the Study of Large Agricultural Enterprises), from the accounts of Soyuzkolkhozbank [All-Union Collective Farm Bank] on the special credits to collective farms for those years, and from the annual reports of the collective farms for the calendar year 1930.

In recalculating capital stock onto a calendar year basis, the breakdown of capital investment into 'pure' building work and machines and implements for half-year periods took into account seasonal variations in building work and seasonal variations in the acquisition of particular types of implement. Corrections were applied to allow for the increased acquisitions of property and implements associated with the development of collectivisation. These annual estimates were also corrected by data on the half yearly distribution of the special credits to collective farms.

Socialised capital was divided into half-years for each year in accordance with the proportion of collectivised households in the given year, in relation to their total number for the year. The transfer of stock was estimated not on the basis of juridical ownership, but from the actual moment of the economic use of the stock. The socialisation of stock in the first half of the calendar year was defined as the amount of the stock handed over to the households which entered a collective farm, in the period from the time when the autumn sowing campaign of the previous year terminated until the end of the spring sowing campaign of the year in question (i.e. from October of the previous year to June of the year in question). Socialisation of stock in the second half of the calendar year is therefore defined as the amount of stock handed over to the households entering a collective farm in the period from the time when the spring sowing campaign terminated until the end of the autumn sowing campaign of the calendar year in question.

The changes in the stocks of animals were calculated for half years by estimating the half-yearly herd turnover, using seasonal data on the births and the slaughter contingent for the separate animals and on the progress of collectivisation.

The socialised capital stock of collective farms includes the capital stock of group associations (*kustovye ob"edineniya*) of collective farms in 1929 and 1930, obtained from the comprehensive survey of the group associations for the relevant years.

[*c*] *Capital stock of MTS and MTK* (state and cooperative) for the calendar years 1928–30. The basic material for calculating the stock of the MTS and MTK was obtained from the survey of 362 MTS and MTK carried out in the spring of 1930. The capital stock of the MTS and MTK for 1 January 1929, and 1 January 1930, and 1 October 1930, was estimated from the preliminary figures for the tractor stock on these dates, which were taken for all these dates as being in the same ratio to the other types of

capital stock (buildings, machinery and implements, and work-animals) as in the spring of 1930, when tractors accounted for 67 per cent of all capital stock in MTS and MTK.

The size of the capital stock of the MTS on 1 January 1931 was estimated on the basis of the stock figures for 1 October 1930 (estimated by the method described above) adjusted by data on the fulfilment of the capital investment plan in the special quarter of 1930, corrected by data from the summary balance of Traktorotsentr for 1 January 1931.

[*d*] *Capital stock of agricultural producers' cooperatives* in the calendar years 1928–30. The capital stock of the agricultural producers' cooperatives was calculated for the economic years 1927/8–1929/30 and then recalculated to a calendar year basis. Capital stock at the beginning of the 1927/8 economic year (1 October 1927) was the starting point for the estimates of the stock in subsequent years. This initial level was obtained from the comprehensive survey of the primary producers' cooperatives carried out by the former Central Statistical Administration in 1927. The amount of capital investment in each economic year was taken from the control figures, and corrected for each type of investment (machinery and implements; livestock; land-improvement work; electric installations), using departmental records of the sales of agricultural machinery and implements and of the issue of special credits. The annual transfer of the capital stock of agricultural producer cooperatives' into the collective farm sector was obtained as an approximation: the proportion of the total members of primary cooperative associations who joined collective farms during the year was taken as the proportion of the value of the stock at the beginning of the year which was transferred during the year. Cooperative membership was obtained from the data prepared by relevant cooperative centres and by the Council of the Unions of Agricultural Producers' Cooperatives.

[*e*] *Capital stock of individual peasant households and non-socialised stock of members of collective farms in the calendar years 1928–30.* Capital stock of individual peasant households and the non-socialised capital stock of collective farmers was calculated for the agricultural years 1927/28–1929/30 and recalculated into calendar years by preparing half-yearly balances of stock.

To obtain the stock of buildings two sources were used (i) a sample (5 per cent) survey (revaluation) of buildings was carried out by Gosstrakh (State Insurance agency) in 1927 and was systematised and elaborated by the former Central Statistical Administration, and (ii) peasant household budget surveys for 1925/6–1929/30. To obtain the stock of agricultural machinery and implements, transport, livestock, poultry and bees the following sources were used: (i) the spring sample (10 per cent) survey of peasant households in 1927, 1928 and 1929, corrected for underestimation, and (ii) data from the tax registers for 1930 and 1931. Stocks of other agricultural and craft implements and changes in stocks of buildings, machinery and implements, livestock, poultry and bees in 1927/8–1929/30 were obtained by applying norms calculated from peasant household budget surveys for each year. In the case of machinery and implements, these figures were corrected by the aid of departmental data on the annual sales of agricultural implements.

To recalculate capital stock from an economic year to a calendar year basis capital investment in agricultural building and in machinery and implements was broken down into half year periods on the basis of data on the seasonal acquisition of building materials and of separate types of machinery and implements. These data were obtained by preparing a break-down of the records of the receipts and expenditures of peasant households in 1927/8–1929/30 agricultural years, corrected for the reduced seasonal acquisition of building materials and reduced amount of building in the first half of the calendar years.

The stock of animals and its change in each half year was obtained by preparing data on the half yearly turnover of the herds, using seasonal information on births and slaughter for each separate type of livestock and on the progress of collectivisation.

Owing to the absence of any statistical or departmental data for the second half of 1930, the amount of capital investment in agriculture in this period was estimated by using expert evaluation based on the assumption that there was a simple reproduction of capital stock.

[f]   *Capital stock in land-improvement and irrigation in the 1928–30 calendar years.* The capital stock in land-improvement and irrigation at the beginning of the 1927/8 economic year and capital investment in 1927/8 and 1928/9 economic years were taken from the 1929/30 control figures. Capital investment in the 1929/30 economic year was taken from the data of the water-economy group of the agricultural sector of Gosplan USSR, and, for the last quarter of 1930, from data on the fulfilment of the plan for financing land improvement in that period.

The stock of land improvements and irrigation was recalculated from an economic year to a calendar year basis by calculating the share of capital investment in the first quarter of the economic year. This amounted to 20 per cent of the whole year in land improvement and 45 per cent in the case of irrigation.

[g]   *Norms of annual depreciation of capital stock.* The norms of depreciation for the separate types of capital stock were obtained as follows: (*a*) state farms – from the annual reports of state farm trusts for the calendar years 1928–30; (*b*) MTS – from the norms used by the main state farm trusts for each type of fixed capital; (*c*) collective farms – from the data of the collective farm budget surveys for 1927/8 and 1929/30; and (*d*) individual peasant households and non-socialised stock of collective-farm members – from the data of the budget surveys for 1926/7 and 1927/8. The norms established on the basis of the materials listed above were used for the whole period (1929–31). The norms for depreciation of stock in land-improvement, irrigation and electrical installations were taken from the 1929/30 control figures.

[h]   *Changes in capital stock in the calendar year 1931.* In the case of agricultural enterprises of the socialised sector (state farms, collective farms, MTS and agricultural producers' cooperatives), with the exception of the stock of animals, capital stock for the 1931 calendar year was calculated from the amount of capital investment, using preliminary data on the fulfilment of the plan for financing agriculture in that year. Capital investment was corrected to allow for investment from internal resources not included in

the plan for financing agriculture. These corrections were obtained on the basis of the actual proportion of this investment to outlays of the financial plan obtained from the annual reports for 1930.

The transfer of the capital stock of the agricultural producers' cooperatives into the collective farm sector was assessed for 1931 by the method used for 1930, explained above.

The extent to which the capital stock of the individual peasant holdings was socialised by means of collectivisation was obtained on the basis of the number of peasant holdings collectivised in 1931: (i) for buildings, in accordance with the average norms of socialisation for one collectivised household, obtained from the data for 1930 on the extent to which buildings are collectivised; (ii) for agricultural machinery and implements – by assuming that all complex agricultural machines and implements (for ploughing and reaping) are socialised; and (iii) for transport equipment – by assuming that all transport equipment associated with work animals socialised in 1931 was itself socialised.

The transfer of stock resulting from the estimation of kulak households was obtained from the spring 1930 comprehensive survey of collective farms.

The stock of animals was obtained on the basis of the number of animals in the spring of 1930, the spring of 1931 and on 1 January 1932 (using the plan figures), adjusted by estimating the half-year herd turnover. Data on the purchases of animals to build up the herds of the agricultural enterprises of the socialised sector were obtained from the preliminary data on the fulfilment of the plan for financing agriculture in 1931.

The capital stock of individual peasants and the non-socialised stock of collective farm members in 1931 were obtained by using the estimates of the amount of capital stock for 1 January 1931, and the data on the amount of capital investment in 1931.

In view of the absence of any statistical or departmental materials showing the amount of capital investment in the private sector of agricultural building in 1931, it was obtained by an approximation, as follows: (i) for house-building – the amount needed for simple reproduction of the housing stock of individual peasant households and of collective farm members, and (ii) for buildings for agricultural purposes – the amount needed for simple reproduction of the stock of economic structures but only for those individual peasant households which had not entered collective farms by the end of 1931 – no new building work is included for the households of collective farm members.

Capital investment in agricultural machines and implements was obtained from the preliminary data on the sales of agricultural machines and implements to individual peasant households in 1931, minus capital repairs to non-socialised equipment in the year, using the norms for capital repair in 1929/30. Capital investment in transport equipment was obtained approximately, using the average norms of investment in 1929/30 per unit of work stock not socialised by the end of the year. Finally capital investment in other agricultural equipment was assessed as the amount ensuring simple reproduction of the stock of individual peasant households at the end of 1931 and the simple reproduction of minor general equipment on the households of collective-farm members.

As already mentioned, the estimates of the changes in capital stock for the 1931 calendar years are based on preliminary reports, and to some extent on plan figures and even on expert assessment of capital investment in 1931, and are therefore only rough approximations. In particular, the data now available on the number of animals on 1 February 1932 show that the level of livestock on 1 January 1932, and therefore its change since 1931, have been somewhat under-estimated for the collective farm sector, and have been seriously over-estimated for the individual peasant households and for the holdings of collective farm members.

[4] HOUSING, THE MUNICIPAL ECONOMY, THE HEALTH SERVICE, EDUCATION AND ADMINISTRATION

[*a*]   *Capital stock.* Since no systematic record of these stocks has been kept, and since they have never been subject to a general stocktaking, their value can be established only by guesswork, using all sorts of indirect data. Estimates for several years were made by Gosplan USSR and published in the 1929/30 control figures. These estimates have been taken as the basis for our present further estimates. Capital stocks were given in the control figures in terms of economic years, and we have shifted them to a calendar year basis. The value of stock net of depreciation for 1 October 1927 was taken from the 1929/30 control figures, reduced by the amount of depreciation in the quarter October–December 1927 and increased by the amount of capital investment in this quarter. The quarterly amount of depreciation was assumed to be a quarter of the total depreciation for the year 1927/8 and the amount of capital investment in this quarter was assumed to be 16.2 per cent of the annual capital investment in 1927/8.

This established the value of stock on 1 January 1927, and data on depreciation, capital investment and entry into exploitation was used to obtain the value of stock on 1 January 1928, our starting date.

With the exception of municipal capital stock, the value of capital stock covered only the value of *buildings*. The capital stock of the municipal economy does not include electric power stations.

[*b*]   *Capital investment.* The recalculation of capital investment data into calendar years was based on data in the Gosplan control figures for 1929/30. [12]

Data from the 1928/9 control figures on capital investment (with the exception of investment in the municipal economy), and also from the 1927/8 control figures for investment in the public health service, were used with minor adjustments based on data from the Gosplan sector of capital works. Capital investments in the housing stock of industry, of the executive committees [of local soviets] and of housing cooperatives were estimated from the comprehensive records collected by TsSU and its successor TsUNKhU.

Capital investment in 1929/30 was obtained as follows. The 1929/30 plan was corrected by data from the Gosplan sector of capital works. The percentage by which the plan was fulfilled was estimated by this sector jointly with other sectors of Gosplan, and this percentage was then applied to the plan figure.

Capital investment plan for 1929/30 and its fulfilment (in million rubles)

	Plan 1929/30	Percentage fulfilled	Actual investment in 1929/30 [13]
Education	288	70	202
Public health	170	60	102
Administration	140	80	112
Municipal economy (with electric power stations)	489	65	318
Housing stock of the socialised sector:			
(a) industry	387	77	298.6
(b) Soviet executive committees and cooperatives	371	66.8	248.0

Capital investment in the housing stock of the private sector in 1927/8–1929/30 was estimated from the comprehensive survey of building.

As a result of the adjustments explained above, the following figures were taken as the basis for recalculating capital investment in terms of calendar years:

Capital investment (in million rubles in current prices)

	1927/8	1928/9	1929/30
Education	114	215	202
Public health	96	114	102
Administration	61	58	112
Municipal economy (with electric power stations)	220	286	318
Socialist sector housing stock:			
(a) industry	167.6	202.3	298.6
(b) Soviet executive committees and cooperatives	278.2	288.6	248.0
Private sector housing stock	238.1	242.9	109.8

The proportion of capital investment occurring in the first quarter of the economic year was established by the Gosplan sector of capital works on the basis of conjunctural reports. For 1927/8 and 1928/9 the first quarter accounted for 16.2 per cent of total investment, for 1929/30 the proportion was 20 per cent for education, public health, and administration, 19 per cent for the municipal economy, and 18 per cent for housing.

Investment in the 'special quarter' was estimated from the data of the conjunctural reports and from expert estimates.

Capital investment in public health in 1930 was further adjusted on the basis of additional material, and was established as 130.3 million rubles.

Capital investment in 1930 in the housing stocks of industry was established from the annual reports of the various associations and trusts. For the private sector housing stock, the value of new buildings was estimated from the comprehensive building survey, and the value of capital repair was estimated on the basis of an outlay of 1 per cent (72.4 million rubles) of the restoration value of the stock.

The estimates for the municipal economy included municipal power stations. In order to exclude the power stations in the final tables it was therefore necessary to establish the value of capital investment in these power stations. This was obtained from data from the municipal and housing sector of Gosplan USSR.

The estimate of capital investment in 1931 was based on State Bank materials on the fulfilment of the financial plan. The level of actual outlays was determined by the capital works sector of Gosplan.

Capital investment in the housing stock of industries was estimated from conjunctural reports.

The State Bank data on the housing of cooperatives and the executive committees of the local soviets refer only to new building. Investment in capital repair was estimated at 1 per cent of the restoration value of the stock at the beginning of the year (88.3 million rubles).

Capital investment in private sector housing stock was estimated by applying to data from the plan (see the 1931 control figures) [14] an expert estimate of the percentage fulfilment (80 per cent). Capital repairs were calculated by the same method as for 1930, the figure arrived at being 71.8 million rubles.

[c] *Capital investment in 'pure building'* [see Glossary]. Investment in 'pure building' was estimated from data of the Gosplan sector of capital works on the share of pure building in total investment.

Pure building as a percentage of total capital investment

	1928	1929	1930	1931
Education	100	90	85	85.3
Public health	100	90	85	87.1
Administration	100	100	95	96
Municipal economy	71	70	65	65

For education and public health the percentage of pure building for 1928 was corrected to 90 per cent. For the municipal economy, excluding the electric power stations, the percentage of pure building was estimated at 90 per cent for 1928 and 68.7 per cent in both 1930 and 1931.

For education, public health and the municipal economy the level of capital investment and entry into exploitation excluded expenditure included in the plans of other branches of the economy.

[d]   Entry into exploitation (completed construction). The proportion of total capital investment entering into exploitation was established from the comprehensive survey of building for 1928–30. This percentage was applied to the capital investment figures estimated as shown above.

For housing, the percentage of investment entering into exploitation was estimated only in relation to total capital investment in new buildings. The amount of investment in capital repairs was added to the amount entering into exploitation to give the full amount.

The amount of investment entering into exploitation in 1931 was estimated on the assumption that it was the same percentage of total capital investment as in 1930.

For the housing stock of industry, entry into exploitation was estimated from the annual reports of the associations and trusts, and, for 1931, from the data of conjunctural reports. The housing stock of VSNKh industry was corrected from the materials published by VSNKh for the XVII Party Conference [January 1932].

[e]   Incomplete building work. The comprehensive survey of building in 1930 was used to obtain the value of incomplete building work in progress (*ostatki nezakonchennogo stroitel'-stva*) at the the end of 1930 and the beginning of 1931. The proportion of capital investment used for incomplete building in progress revealed by the 1930 survey was applied to the total amount of capital investment as estimated by the method explained above. Using the balance method, from 1930 to 1929 and 1928, incomplete building work at the beginning and the end of 1928 and 1929 was estimated from the data for 1930.

For the private sector, incomplete building work in progress was obtained from data in the comprehensive survey of construction carried out in 1928. The ratio of incomplete building work in progress to capital investment thus obtained was applied to the capital expenditure data for 1925/6 and 1926/7, and from this the amount of incomplete building work in progress at the beginning of 1928 was estimated.

[f]   Depreciation. Amortisation norms as percentages of the restoration value of capital stock were taken from the control figures of the Gosplan USSR for 1929/30 (*loc. cit.* pp. 464 and 468): for education – 1.25 per cent, for public health – 1.22 per cent, for administration – 2.19 per cent, for the housing stock of the socialised sector – 2.19 per cent, for housing stock of the private sector – 2.53 per cent and for the municipal economy – 4.25 per cent.

[C]   Methods and sources for calculating indexes of the cost of building and capital investment

[I]   INDEX OF BUILDING COSTS
['pure building', p. 148]
For industry, power station construction, rail transport, [water and] other transport,

communications, housing construction in the socialist sector, municipal economy, education and public health we used the building cost indexes for the years 1926/7 to 1928/9 (1925/6 = 100) given in the control figures of the USSR Gosplan for 1929/30 (*loc. cit.* p. 578, table 88).

For later years, beginning with 1929/30, the indexes were calculated as follows:

[*a*] *Industry and power station construction (including the housing stock of industry).* The building cost index for 1929/30 was calculated from the cost index of one square metre of floor-space in a brick-and-concrete building constructed by the state. This index was estimated by the building sector of Gosplan from the annual reports. According to these reports building costs in 1930 were 7.8 per cent below the 1929/30 [*sic*- should be 1929] level. For industrial building, these figures are close to the figures given in the reports of Soyuzstroi [All-Union Building Trust].

The building costs index for 1931 was obtained from the data of the building sector of Gosplan and the qualitative indicators sector of TsUNKhU, which was based on the reports of Soyuzstroi, Ukrstroi [Ukrainian Building Trust], Rosstroi [Building Trust of the Russian Republic] and Khlebstroi [Grain Building Trust]. For these organisations the weighted index of cost increase in comparison with 1930 was 15.4 per cent. This increase was also used for all industry and for power station construction.

[*b*] *Rail transport.* In 1929/30 the index was calculated from the reports of the People's Commissariat of Transport (NKPS). In the case of newly constructed railway lines, these reports covered 46.5 per cent of the total value of new lines under construction in 1928/9 and 39.5 per cent in 1929/30. Costs were obtained from data on the following types of installations: the earth-bed, the superstructure, tunnels, piers of bridges, iron and concrete bridge superstructures, and other bridges. For each of these items we calculated the cost for a unit of building in kind. The overall change in the cost of a physical unit of building was calculated by weighting these unit costs according to the proportion of each type of installation work in the total capital investment of the Construction Department of the People's Commissariat of Transport in 1929/30 (the data for these calculations covered all investment in the Department).

To calculate the average cost of building in railways already in operation, we used the annual reports of the railways, from 1926/7 onwards. These showed reconstruction and restoration for the following items: the laying of ballast, sleepers, crossing timbers, rails, switch-points and frogs. The average cost in kind per unit of work in 1929/30 was evaluated by using data on the cost in money terms of the work in 1928/9. The year 1926/7 was taken as the basis for calculating the cost of a unit of building. The results obtained for the listed items were used for similar items of building: stations and junctions, secondary lines, the completion of lines and branch lines, the repairing of neglected lines, the strengthening of lines. The total amount covered, including the items for which cost data were available, was 225.5 million rubles.

For 1931 the building cost index was estimated by the sector of capital works of Gosplan on the basis of reports from the Construction Department of NKPS. The increase in the building costs thus obtained was 12.9 per cent above the 1930 level; this percentage was extrapolated to all pure building in rail transport.

[c]   *Water transport.* For the years 1926/7, the cost indexes for ports and waterways used by river and sea steamships were taken from the Central Planning Bureau of Gosplan.[2] Since these indexes did not provide a separate index for total 'pure construction', we had to assume that all expenditure on ports and waterways was 'pure construction'. The indexes were weighted by using the data for capital investment in ports and waterways given in the control figures for 1929/30 to obtain our costs index for 'pure construction' for the whole of water transport.

For 1929/30 there are no data on building costs in water transport. In the data of the building sector of Gosplan, the index for 1929/30 of capital investment costs in water transport is 100 (1928/9 = 100), and we took this for our index of building costs.

For 1931 the building costs index was taken as equal to the building costs index of Vodstroi [Waterways Building Trust] (an increase of 14.5 per cent), estimated by the building sector of Gosplan on the basis of Vodstroi reports.

[d]   *Other transport.* We have no reports for 1929/30. On the basis of the estimates of the building sector of Gosplan, we took building costs in that year as being 100 per cent of the 1928/9 level.

We are also lacking materials for 1931. As building in other transport is similar in nature to building on the railways, we used the same cost increase for 1931 (12.9 per cent).

[e]   *Municipal economy, education, administration, public health, exchange and distribution, communications.* In the case of these branches of the economy, we used for 1929/30 the index of the cost of building a cubic metre of the external volume of buildings for social use. As estimated by the building sector of Gosplan from the comprehensive survey, the 1929/30 cost index was 7.8 per cent below the 1929 level.

For 1931 the building costs index for the municipal economy was taken to be the same as the index for Kommunstroi [Municipal Economy Building Trust] (an increase of 18.3 per cent in comparison with 1929). This was estimated by the building sector of Gosplan on the basis of the reports of Kommunstroi.

For education, public health and communications in 1931, we took the increase in costs to be 15.4 per cent. The same consideration applied as in the case of house-building (see below).

As we have no materials with which to estimate a building costs index for administration, or for exchange and distribution, we used the same indexes as for education for all years.

[f]   *Building of housing in the socialist sector.* For 1929/30, we took the index for 1930 in relation to 1929 estimated by the building sector of Gosplan on the basis of the comprehensive survey of all types of building in the state sector. In this sector the index

of the cost of building one square metre of housing-space was 10.7 per cent below the 1929 level. This was used for all building of housing in the socialist sector.

For 1931 we had no reports on the cost of building of housing. All indirect data indicate that the cost increased, and we have assumed that the increase was the same as for industrial building (15.4 per cent). This is a conservative estimate.

[g] *Housing stock of industry.* When we separated out the housing stock of industry from the rest of capital investment in industry and electrification, we used the building cost indexes of the Central Planning Bureau of Gosplan for the years up to 1927/8. From 1928/9 we used the annual index for the building of housing in the socialist sector.

[h] *Building of housing in the private sector.* For 1928/9 we used the index calculated by the Central Planning Bureau of Gosplan. For 1929/30 the increase in building costs was taken as 6.9 per cent; this was obtained by the building sector of Gosplan, which used the comprehensive survey of building to estimate the cost of one cubic metre of the external volume of private building. For 1931, expert estimates gave the increase in costs as 20 per cent in comparison with 1930.

[2]   INDEX OF CAPITAL INVESTMENT COSTS [pp. 149–50]
[a]   *Industry and electric power stations.* The cost index for capital investment as a whole was obtained by weighting the separate cost indexes for building and equipment.

The cost index for equipment [pp. 149, table 10c] was obtained by weighting the cost indexes for imported and home-produced equipment, given in the publication *Basic Features of Industrial Reconstruction*.[3] The relative shares of imported and home produced equipment in total equipment was also taken from this publication for the years 1925/6–1928/9.

For 1929/30 the cost index for equipment was estimated in the following manner. In the absence of any materials on the costs of home-produced equipment in 1929/30 we assumed that costs were the same as in 1928/9. For imported equipment, on the basis of the cost [index] for total imports, we assume that there had been a 10 per cent decrease in costs in comparison with 1928/9. According to the estimates of the building sector of TsUNKhU imported equipment accounted for 38.3 per cent of all equipment.

For 1931, for home-produced equipment, we took the cost index as equal to the index of transfer prices for the engineering industry, estimated by the sectors of qualitative indicators and of industrial records [of TsUNKhU]. This gave a decrease in costs of 5.2 per cent in comparison with 1929/30. For imported equipment, on the basis of the cost index for total imports, we assumed a reduction in costs of 11 per cent in comparison with 1929/30. The share of imported equipment in 1931 was estimated on the basis of data on imports of equipment in 1931, together with data on the gap in 1929 between (a) the share of imported equipment in total capital investment (as given in building reports) and (b) the share of imported equipment (as given in import data) in total investment in equipment.

In order to estimate the weighted index for all capital investment, investment data (in current prices), for all the years 1927/8–1931, were used to obtain the relative shares of equipment and building.[4]

[*b*]   *Rail transport*. For 1926/7 and 1927/8 indexes for rail transport equipment were not calculated. Indexes for capital investment as a whole were taken from the data of the Central Planning Bureau of Gosplan. Indexes for 1928/9 and 1929/30 (1927/8 = 100) were estimated as follows. Changes in the value of rolling stock were calculated by applying data of the Central Planning Administration of NKPS on the acquisition of rolling stock in physical units to the contract prices for each year for each type of rolling stock. The number of units produced in 1929/30 was then evaluated in 1927/8 and 1928/9 prices. In order to estimate a sub-index for capital repairs to rolling stock we used material from the reports of railways from 1926/7 onwards. As the unit cost of repairs we took expenditure per locomotive-kilometre and per wagon-axle-kilometre.

To obtain the overall cost index of capital repairs to all types of rolling stock, we weighted these unit costs by the 1929/30 distances covered. For 1931 the cost index for rolling stock (equipment) was calculated from materials from the qualitative indicators sector and the industrial records sector of TsUNKhU on changes in the transfer prices for railway engineering in 1931 in comparison with 1930.

In order to obtain the weighted index for total capital investment, data in current prices on investment in pure building and rolling stock were used as weights.

[*c*]   *Water transport*. We used the indexes of the Central Planning Bureau of Gosplan. Data on investment in water transport given in the 1929/30 Control Figures were used as weights in establishing the weighted index for total capital investment in water transport. As mentioned above, costs in the year 1929/30 were assumed to be the same as in 1928/29.

For equipment in 1931 we used an index of transfer prices, which showed an increase of 4.1 per cent above 1930. The index for total capital investment was obtained by weighting the cost indexes for building and equipment.

[*d*]   *Other transport and communications*. Since the share of equipment in the investment of these branches is very small, we have applied the building costs index to total capital investment.

[*e*]   *Exchange and distribution*. In all years the equipment index was assumed to be the same as in the case of home-produced equipment in industry.

The index for total capital investment was obtained by weighting the cost indexes of equipment and building.

[*f*]   *Municipal economy, public health, education and administration*. The equipment costs index for all years was taken as equal to the index for home-produced equipment used for capital investment in industry. The cost index for total capital investment was obtained by weighting the cost indexes for building and equipment. For all the years 1927/8 to 1931 data on investment (in current prices) were used to weight equipment and building.

As no materials were available for the cost of total capital investment in the case of administration, we used the indexes for education.

[3] COST INDEXES FOR BUILDING AND TOTAL CAPITAL INVESTMENT IN AGRICULTURE

[a] *Building cost indexes.* State sector. For 1928–30 the estimates of the Central Planning Bureau of Gosplan were used to obtain the indexes. For 1931, as no reports were available, we concluded on the basis of expert estimates that costs were at the same level as in 1930.

Private sector. An index was estimated by the agricultural sector of TsUNKhU using the budget surveys for the relevant years.

Collective-farm and cooperative sector. For 1928-30 the index was estimated by the Central Planning Bureau of Gosplan by expert estimates on the basis of the indexes for the state and private sectors. For 1931 costs were estimated to have declined to 96 per cent of the 1930 level. The indexes for the whole socialised sector, and for all sectors, were obtained by weighting the indexes of the separate sectors.

[b] *Indexes of capital investment costs* [p. 150, table 10e].

(i) Indexes of investment in *machinery and implements* (agricultural machines and implements, tractors and transport equipment). State sector. For 1928–30 the estimates of the Central Planning Bureau of Gosplan were used; costs were equal to those in 1926/7. For 1931 expert estimates concluded that costs were at the same level as in 1930.

Private sector. Estimates were made by the agricultural sector of TsUNKhU using the peasant budget surveys for the corresponding years: costs in 1931 were taken as being the same as in 1930.

Collective-farm and cooperative sectors. The 1928–30 index of capital investment was established by the agricultural sector of TsUNKhU, on the basis of the indexes for the state and private sectors; costs in 1931 were taken as being the same as in 1930.

(ii) *Livestock* (including poultry). The index was obtained by means of valuing the number of livestock in both 1926/7 prices and in current prices. For the prices of 1926/7, 1927/8 and 1928/9 we used the average annual prices supplied to the sector of exchange and distribution by the network of correspondents of TsSU. For 1929/30 and 1931 animals procured to build up the socialised herds were valued at procurement prices, and animals set aside for slaughter were valued at the procurement prices for animals slaughtered for meat.

(iii) *Irrigation, land-improvement and electric power stations.* The 1928–30 indexes of capital investment costs were estimated by the agricultural sector of TsUNKhU jointly with the capital investment group of Gosplan on the basis of data from Vodkhoz and from the sector of electrification [of Gosplan]. The 1931 index was taken to be at the same level as the 1930 index. (The slight increase for the total socialised sector is explained by changes in weights.)

(iv) *Industrial enterprises.* The index was estimated as follows. The costs index for agricultural buildings for each sector was used for the costs index for buildings; the costs index of machinery and equipment for each sector was used for the costs index for equipment. A weighted index using these indexes of building costs and the costs of machinery and implements was then obtained as the costs index for total capital investment.

(v) *Other measures and investments, not differentiated by types.* The index was taken to be the average of the indexes for all the types of property mentioned above, except livestock.

[D] *Methods and sources for estimating production, consumption and stocks in industry*

[I] LARGE-SCALE (CENSUS) INDUSTRY

[a] *General observations.* The construction of the balance of the national economy requires a more than usually elaborate reworking of statistical material. The normal basis for grouping statistical materials is to take the industrial establishments, arranged according to their categories of production, or, in rare cases, according to some other indicators. For each category summary data are given in value terms concerning production, the use of raw materials and fuel, depreciation, wages, etc. A limited amount of information is also provided about the quantity produced (in kind) of the *most important* articles, the consumption of the most important types of raw material, and in a little more detail, on fuel consumption.

For the system of tables incorporated in the balance of the national economy it is necessary for data on specific products and their groups to be expressed both in value and in kind, and for there to be a complete breakdown of the entire mass of products of every sort which are manufactured and consumed and in hand at the beginning and the end of the year. This must be carried out according to a specific product classification (nomenclature).

Consequently, special investigations and special estimates are required in order to obtain the data required for the balance.

[b] *Gross turnover.* In practice, there are two methods for determining the outcome of the productive activity of industrial establishments: 'gross turnover' and 'gross production'. 'Gross turnover' refers to the whole mass of goods and semi-finished goods manufactured in a given period of time regardless of whether they are consumed in the establishment where they were manufactured or whether they were sent out from it. 'Gross production' refers to gross turnover minus semi-finished goods in the same establishment for further processing within the given period of time.

In the balance, production has been calculated by the gross turnover method. The balance of the national economy is constructed on the basis of the balances for particular products; in one enterprise these might be semi-finished goods, while in another the same goods might be finished goods. The amount of production reported would therefore be incomplete if we used the gross production method. For example, the output of pig iron would be reported only insofar as it was transferred in the form of pigs to other works; the remainder, the pig iron turned into steel in the same works, would not be recorded as production, since it had not entered into gross production.

Since the gross turnover method has been adopted in the balance, in consumption we have included not only the consumption of raw materials and auxiliary materials brought in from outside but also the consumption of semi-finished goods manufactured by an enterprise and already reported as part of its production and unfinished production.

[c] *Sources from which material was obtained.* The basic sources for calculating production, consumption and stocks were:

[i] The reworking of Form 'B'. For 1928/9 this was carried out at the centre in accordance with the special classification (nomenclature) used by the balance of the national economy. This reworking covered 96.6 per cent of all the industry reported on Form B in the case of gross turnover and 97.5 per cent in the case of consumption. Even with this work we were unable to classify all products according to the special nomenclature. Because a number of Forms B were inaccurately completed only 94.7 per cent of production and 93.1 per cent of consumption could be allocated to the different heads of the nomenclature.

[ii] For 1927/8 the processing of Form B was carried out locally by the agencies of the former TsSU, but only for those products for which balances in kind were being compiled at the time. The work enabled us to obtain data for those balances which required these particular items in kind, but not for the other items in the classification of our present balances. The material for 1926/7 also failed to provide data for compiling balances in value terms, so we had to resort to earlier material, for 1925/6.

[iii] The processing of Form B for 1925/6 was also carried out by the local agencies of the former TsSU, using a special classification (nomenclature) which was a somewhat abridged version of the full classification used on the forms themselves. As a result a considerable part of production, consumption and stocks was not allocated to the different items in the classification for the balance. Additional work was therefore undertaken at the centre in order to allocate the unallocated items. These allocations were made by using coefficients estimated on the basis of those Forms B which were properly filled in, and by expert estimates.

Thus, in order to obtain the items in the balances for 1927/8, we used the materials for 1925/6 and 1928/9. Each item in the classification of the balance was estimated by taking these two years as bench-marks, except of course those items which were reported in kind in 1927/8 (see Appendix D, pp. 438–40 below 'Nomenclature of products in the balance of production and consumption').

The transfer from economic years to calendar years was carried out by using the information summarised from the 'current report cards' (*kartochki 'srochnykh donesenii'*). These cards contained quarterly data on gross production reported in categories (according to the production classification), and also quarterly data in kind on the production of certain products and the consumption of certain types of raw materials. In some cases data from the industrial associations were also used, but the number of industrial establishments included in the reports of associations does not normally coincide with the number of establishments reported in Form B and it was therefore possible to use this information only in order to estimate coefficients of the rate of growth.

The summary information from the reports did not include any data on stocks, and it was therefore impossible in the case of most products to convert the October stock figure to a January figure. For certain products we were able to use quarterly data on changes in stocks from the Central Department of Statistics (TsOS) of VSNKh, and for some products stocks were estimated from data on changes in production and consumption. But in a number of cases the January stock figure was simply assumed to be the same as the October figure.[5]

[*d*]   *Estimates for 1930.* In the absence of reports covering the items needed to compile the 1930 balance, production, consumption and stocks were estimated as follows:

[i] *Items for which no data in kind were available.* Data for 1928–30 on changes in level of gross production by branches of industry provided the basis for estimating these items. These data were compiled with due allowance for changes in the criteria for 'census' industry and for changes in the classifications of branches of industry. All the items in the classification were in turn divided into two groups in this part of the work:

The *first* group contained products (or groups of products) for which changes in levels of production could be assumed to be the same as changes in the relevant branches of industry. The following products were assigned to this group:

(*a*) Machinery and equipment
(*b*) Firebricks
(*c*) Pulverised cement
(*d*) Paper
(*e*) Woodwork products
(*f*) Ready-made clothing
(*g*) Knitwear
(*h*) Other toiletries
(*i*) Publications

In 1929, the above products comprised 29 per cent of total production.

For these groups of products the coefficients for the rate of growth of gross production of the corresponding branches of industry were used.

The *second* group contained products manufactured and consumed in several branches of industry.

The summaries of Form B for 1928/9 were used to obtain data on the amount of a particular product which was manufactured and consumed in various branches of industry. Hence the weight of the various branches of industry in the production and consumption of the given product (product group) was obtained. The indicator of the rate of growth of each branch of industry was multiplied by its weight for the given product (product group) and [summing these sub-items] we obtained the rate of growth for the product (product group). Absolute figures for 1930 were obtained by applying this rate of growth to the data for 1929.

Altogether, estimates using this method covered 33.7 per cent of production and 34.9 per cent of consumption.

In the case of products which are manufactured and consumed in very small quantities and which play a trivial role in the economy, a cruder method was employed for our estimates, using data from the industrial associations. These products accounted for 2.6 per cent of production and 6.6 per cent of consumption.

[ii] *Items for which data were available in kind.* All these items were also divided into two groups:

The *first* group contained industrial products. Their production was estimated from data on changes in the production of each product in kind, obtained from current report cards, and from the data of TsOS of VSNKh and of certain industrial associations. For these products, in order to co-ordinate the balances in kind, the material was analysed in detail using a large amount of data from the industrial associations. In addition, at the beginning of 1932, time series were prepared for the production of a number of specific products in kind. The results of this work were examined by a special commission of the industrial sector of TsUNKhU. The figures agreed as the result of the work of this commission also covered the earlier years. It was therefore necessary to alter some of the figures that had been estimated earlier for 1928 and 1929.

The *second* group contained agricultural products. The main source of data on the consumption of agricultural products came from the various associations. These data were used to construct coefficients of the rate of change and were supplemented by the agricultural balances in kind which were prepared in 1931.

[iii] Stocks on 1 January 1931 were estimated primarily from the coefficients of growth of production and consumption. In a small number of cases, stocks on 1 January 1931 were assumed to have been at the same level as on 1 January 1930. For some products, mainly agricultural, it was possible to obtain data on changes in the level of stocks from the associations.

[e] *Corrections in the course of coordinating the balances.* As mentioned above, the most complete processing of the data of Form B for 1928/9 covered only 96.6 per cent of gross turnover and only 97.5 per cent of the consumption reported on Form B. In addition it has to be borne in mind that not all the industrial establishments required to return Form B in fact did so. This became apparent once the balances had been set up, as production and consumption were lower than that shown by an analysis of expenditure items. Corrections were therefore required for several balances. The balances which were estimated both in physical and in value terms were examined with particular care. The simultaneous compilation of a balance in both physical and value terms made it possible to compare and analyse prices. This very clearly revealed defects in certain items in the balances (in particular, the production, consumption and stocks in industry). As a result, the corrections made in these balances were based on a much more thorough analysis than was possible for balances available only in value terms. The correction procedure was as follows. The first stage was that the balance of production and consumption in physical terms was co-ordinated, and then it was transferred to a value basis by applying the prices. In the process of coordinating the balance in value terms, inaccuracies were often disclosed in the already-coordinated balance in physical terms.

Products for which data were available in physical terms accounted for 41.5 per cent of all production and 29.4 per cent of all consumption in 1928; 38.2 per cent and 27.6 per cent in 1929; and 32.9 per cent and 25.1 per cent in 1930. The fall in the proportion of production covered by products for which data are available in physical terms is due to the reduction in the share of textiles and food products in the total; these items were most fully covered by reports in physical terms.

[f] Comparison with data from other sources. There is a rather significant difference between the rates of growth of gross production published in connection with the control figures for 1932 and the rates of growth given by the balance (in 1926/7 prices). The control figures' data show a rate of growth of gross production of 25.4 per cent from 1928 to 1929 and 22.3 per cent from 1929 to 1930 – that is, a certain decline in the overall rate of growth. The balance data indicate a growth of 21.5 per cent from 1928 to 1929 and 24.3 per cent from 1929 to 1930 – i.e. an increasing rate of growth. The reasons for the difference are as follows:

[i] The control figures cover only industry planned by VSNKh and by the People's Commissariat of Supply (NKSnab), on the basis of enterprises comparable with those covered in 1928. In 1930 the production of these comparable enterprises was 19,923.0 million rubles as compared with a total for all enterprises planned by these two departments of 21,460.9 million rubles. For our balances, however, we used data for all 'census' industry (using the old 'census' classification of TsSU); according to a TsUNKhU handbook[6] the rate of growth for this coverage was 24.3 per cent in 1929 and 25.8 per cent in 1930. Thus the rate of growth for all census industry was increasing, as is the case with our balance data.

[ii] Both the control figures' data and the data in the TsUNKhU handbook refer to gross production, whereas in the balances we are dealing with gross turnover. According to the 1928/9 data, gross turnover was 129.1 per cent of gross production, and of course this could affect the growth rates.

[iii] TsUNKhU did not have direct materials at its disposal when making estimates for the 1930 balance, and was obliged to use data on the rates of growth for particular branches of industry or associations. Although attempts were made to eliminate errors in these estimates, it is possible that for some products the rates of growth from 1929 to 1930 were overestimated or underestimated. These errors would arise through the transfer of certain industrial establishments (*a*) from one association to another, (*b*) from small-scale industry to large scale (census) industry, as a result of their growth in size or (*c*) from the non-socialised sector to the socialised sector, or from management by cooperatives to management by People's Commissariats. However, this would merely have redistributed the amount of production between large-scale and small-scale industry, without affecting the total amount of all industrial production.

Comparisons of data for Group 'A' production in different sources are impossible. This is because the entire intra-factory turnover of establishments placed in Group 'B' consists of means of production, and is therefore assigned in the balances to Group A. Consequently these rates of growth are also substantially different. Thus from the balances the growth of Group A was 24.8 per cent in 1929 and 26.2 per cent in 1930, while the statistical handbook showed that Group A increased by 24.8 per cent in 1929 and 43.9 per cent in 1930.

The differences in growth rates are due to the fact that the rate of growth of Group B is lower than that of Group A, and so when intra-factory turnover of Group B is placed in Group A in our balance, this lowers the rate of growth of Group A as compared with the gross production data. For example, in the case of the textile industry (see below for more detail), products were transferred to Group A to the value of 1,658.5 million rubles in 1928, 1,887.4 million rubles in 1929, and 1,833.5 million rubles in 1930. The figures from just this one example reduce the rate of growth of gross production to 26.8 per cent in 1929 and 33.3 per cent in 1930.

It might seem that comparison and analysis could be made with greater success for Group B, since it might be supposed that by far the greater part of the gross production of Group B consists of consumer goods and only an insignificant part of means of production (which in some cases can to some extent be estimated). In the industrial establishments of Group A only a comparatively trivial proportion of all consumer goods are manufactured. Consequently, after making a few corrections, gross production in Group B ought to correspond roughly with the figure for Group B obtained by aggregating specific products (consumer goods) in the balances, and the rate of growth ought to be the same. According to the latest available data for gross production in 1926/7 prices, gross production of Group B was 8,581.6 million rubles in 1928, 10,625.4 million rubles in 1929, and 12,349.0 million rubles in 1930. According to the balance data, however, the figures were 7,427.2 million rubles in 1928, 8,587.4 million rubles in 1929, and 10,392.6 million rubles in 1930. But it must be borne in mind that for textiles, gross production was 3,515.6, 3,998.6 and 3,694.3 million rubles in the respective years, as against the balance for textiles which showed 1,857.1, 2,111.2 and 1,860.8 million rubles. These figures show that gross production of textiles must include a whole series of products which appear in the balances as means of production (unbleached linen, thread, etc.).[7]

After the application of the necessary corrections to the data on gross production, we get the following production for Group B: 7,034.7 million rubles (1928), 8,868.5 (1929) and 10,641.1 (1930). The remaining difference can be explained by other facts similar to those mentioned above. If the analysis is pursued further and the output of distilleries (except for grain spirit) is excluded from the gross production of Group B we get a growth of gross production by 24 per cent in 1929 and 22 per cent in 1930. It is not possible to undertake further comparisons of this kind owing to the absence of the necessary materials, but such corrections could certainly be made, and they would substantially affect the rate of growth, tending to reduce it. An example of this is that the rates of growth of manufactured meat in current prices is 34 per cent. As this meat is a product of slaughterhouses, it is included in gross industrial production, but in the balance calculations it is assigned to agriculture. On the other hand, it will be seen from the accompanying table that, in the case of nearly all branches of industry where it is possible to compare the products, the percentage of growth from 1928 to 1929 was higher for gross production than in the balance. When translated into absolute figures the differences between the two measurements of growth in the sugar industry and the oil milling industry alone amount to 100 million rubles; this alters the growth rate by 1.2 per cent.

Comparison between the balance data and the data of the industrial sector for gross production of Group B in 1926/7 prices

Branch (group of products)	1929 (1928 = 100)		1930 (1929 = 100)	
	Balance data	Gross production	Balance data	Gross production
Flour-milling	93.3	103.5	96.5	96.2
Sugar	93.3	108.4	123.7	127.7
Oil-milling	108.2	126.2	83.7	90.4
Tobacco	115.0	117.2	106.9	109.4
Makhorka	90.1	106.3	88.3	101.0
Textiles	113.7	113.7	88.1	92.0
Clothing	155.2	169.0	170.3	176.7
Knitwear	133.6	147.5	160.9	161.0
Leather footwear	164.9	180.6	155.7	182.0
Confectionery	151.0	158.4	187.4	187.2
Total for Group B	115.6	124.1	121.1	117.8

All the above indicates that, although it appears possible to compare the data for Group B in the balance and in the gross production data, in reality the assortment of output was affected by the increasing share of means of production, and consequently a comparison with other sources of data is possible only for industry as a whole.

[g] *Methods for revaluing production in constant prices.* For revaluation in constant 1928 prices, production was divided into two groups.

[i] *Industrial products expressed only in value terms.* In order to revalue products belonging to this group, a price index of branches of industry was used; this was obtained by comparing for each branch growth of its gross production in current prices with its growth in constant 1926/7 prices.

In this group, 34 balances were revalued. For 18 of these balances price indexes for appropriate branches of industry were used:

Balances	*Branches of industry*
1. Rail transport	Other engineering and metal-work
2. Water transport	Other engineering and metal-work
3. Other transport	Other engineering and metal-work
4. Engines and machines	Other engineering and metal-work
5. Other equipment	Other engineering and metal-work
6. Agricultural machinery	Agricultural engineering
7. Firebricks	Production of firebricks and building bricks
8. Pulverised cement	Cement industry
9. Paper	Paper industry
10. Woodwork products	Production of wooden articles

11. Pig-iron scrap	Metallurgy
12. Section-iron	Metallurgy
13. Chemical fertilisers	Other chemicals
14. Charcoal	Other chemicals
15. Other mineral fuels	Coal industry
16. Fish industry products	Other food industries
17. Clothing and underwear	Garment industry
18. Other footwear	Leather footwear

In the case of the remaining 16 balances, the products in each balance were manufactured by various branches of industry, and so a weighted price index was used derived from the indexes of the different branches. As a basis for the weights we used the summaries of Form B data for 1928/9, taken from the section giving data on the distribution of specific products among the branches of industry which produced them. The coefficients of growth of gross production in current prices for each branch were then multiplied by the weights of the branch and aggregated in order to obtain weights for 1927, 1928 and 1930. The branch indexes weighted by this method were used for revaluing production in fixed prices. These weighted indexes were used in the case of the following balances:

1. Other building materials,
2. Other minerals and ores,
3. Other products of textile raw material,
4. Other products of vegetable raw material,
5. Other products of animal raw material processing,
6. Other products of metal-working,
7. Other products of mineral working,
8. Other chemical products,
9. Articles of confectionery and other food products,
10. Other alcoholic drinks,
11. Other textiles,
12. Other toilet articles,
13. Furniture and other articles of interior decoration,
14. Crockery and utensils,
15. Sanitary and hygienic goods,
16. Other consumer goods.

[ii] *Industrial products with balances in both value and physical terms.*

For revaluing this group of balances – the balances in physical terms – we took directly 1928 prices for revaluation in 1928 prices, and 1926/7 prices for revaluation in 1926/7 prices. The 1928 prices were derived from the balances, and the 1926/7 prices from the summary data from Form B for 1926/7.

Stocks in census industry were revalued using the same coefficient as for production, the stocks at the end of a year being revalued in accordance with the index for that year: thus, stocks at 1 January 1931 were revalued with the 1930 index, those of 1 January 1930 with the 1929 index, those of 1 January 1929 with the 1928 index, and those of 1 January 1928 with the 1927 index.

In those cases where data in physical terms were available, *agricultural products and stocks* were revalued by applying the corresponding 1928 prices. In those cases where such data were not available we used the price indexes used for revaluing agricultural production (see the explanatory note: 'Methods of evaluating agricultural production and balances').

[2] SMALL-SCALE (NON-CENSUS) INDUSTRY

Small-scale industry refers to all industrial enterprises which do not satisfy the census requirements of the former TsSU for large-scale enterprises, both in the socialist sector (i.e. state and cooperative enterprises and enterprises of voluntary organisation) and in the private sector (this includes establishments of the artisan-handicraft type).

Production and consumption in small-scale industry were established as follows:

For 1928 they were estimated on the basis of the growth of small-scale industry in the data of the sample survey of 1926/7 and the full census of 1928/9.

The 1926/7 survey contained a sample of dispersed industry and a full census of clusters (i.e. typical areas of more advanced small-scale industry).

In the survey production and consumption were recorded both in value terms and in physical terms. In order to establish the total number of persons employed in small-scale industry, the materials of the 1926 population census were specially reworked. The conclusions arrived at on the basis of the 1926/7 sample survey were then extended to the total number of persons employed in small-scale industry.

Other materials used were the results of the 1928/9 all-union census of small-scale industry, processed by the industrial records section of TsUNKhU.

Data for 1929 were obtained directly from the materials of the 1928/9 census of small-scale industry. Data for 1930 were estimated by expert estimates on the basis of a questionnaire-survey of the private sector and a survey of the socialist sector of small-scale industry. This survey was carried out as follows:

For the private sector, the district planning commission compiled lists of handicraftsmen and artisans, and established the amount of time they worked (in man-weeks). For the socialist sector the planning commissions carried out a comprehensive census. The estimates of production and consumption in the private sector were made in the regional planning commissions. The material was summarised at a local level in the regions and the republics, and centrally for the USSR as a whole.

The data on production and productive consumption thus obtained was corrected by comparison with other materials in the course of compiling and coordinating each balance.

[E] Methods and sources for estimating agricultural production

[I GENERAL OBSERVATIONS]

Agricultural production figures for 1928–30 in the balances of the national economy were estimated by the 'gross turnover' method. They therefore differ somewhat from the normal estimates of the agricultural records sector of TsUNKhU which are closer to 'gross production', although not fully corresponding to it.

In estimating agricultural production in the balances, all products were divided into groups according to their end-use:

(*a*) means of production, fixed and circulating, and
(*b*) consumer goods.

The estimates covered the following products:

A. MEANS OF PRODUCTION
    (*a*) *Fixed*
        1. Livestock
        2. Poultry and bees in hives
    (*b*) *Circulating*
        1. Cereals (by crops)[8]
        2. Industrial crops (by crops)
        3. Fodder products (by types)
        4. Raw materials of animal origin (by products)
        5. Unfinished products (in arable farming)
B. CONSUMER GOODS
    1. Potatoes, vegetables and melons, fruit and grapes
    2. Meat and fat
    3. Dressed poultry
    4. Milk
    5. Eggs

The differences between these estimates and those of the agricultural records sector are as follows. The latter include livestock and poultry in its estimates only as the natural increase less the number sent for slaughter. It also includes the growth in unfinished production in arable farming between the beginning and the end of the year. The estimates for the balances, on the other hand, include in production the total production of livestock, and all unfinished production in arable farming at the end of the year. Subsequently, when the balances were constructed, livestock sent for slaughter were assigned to productive consumption for the production of slaughter-house products, and unfinished production at the beginning of the year, recorded in the balance as stocks at the beginning of the year, was listed as productive consumption for the production of the corresponding products of arable farming.

All the estimates of production were broken down by social sectors – state farms, collective farms and the private sector. (Production on the individual holdings of the collective farmers was assigned to the private sector.)

As may be seen from the list of products given above, only raw products[9] were included in agricultural production (the inclusion of meat is somewhat questionable). The domestic production by agricultural producers of products of primary processing (i.e. butter, cottage cheese, sour cream, other dairy products, wine from grapes, etc.) was recorded as domestic production and included in the balance tables published in the present volume as 'other' branches of the economy. Products of primary processing which were produced within agricultural enterprises, but in separate industrial units (industrial enterprises of state farms), were classified as industrial production.

[2 THE PRODUCTION OF SEPARATE PRODUCTS AND GROUPS OF PRODUCTS]

[a] *Production of grain and fodder crops.* Production of grain and fodder crops was estimated for the balances by multiplying the 'sown areas consolidated by spring' (i.e. total area sown less the winter loss of winter-sown crops) by the average yields per hectare. The sown area of state farms was classified with the sown area of agricultural enterprises, institutions and organisations.

[i] *Sown area.* State farms. For 1928 sown areas were taken from the comprehensive survey of state farms. For 1929 the areas of those state farms organised in trusts were taken from the figures supplied by the trusts; for other state farms the 1928 figures were used. For 1930, state farm sown area figures were taken from the data of Sovkhozob''e-dinenie (State Farm Association).

Collective farms. For 1928 and 1929 sown areas were taken from the comprehensive survey of collective farms, corrected for underestimation. For 1930, the figures from the regional authorities were used; these were derived from taxation records, but were corrected on the basis of a 2 per cent sample survey of sown areas.

Individual households and individual cultivation by collective farmers. In 1928 and 1929 sown areas were based on the results of the spring 10 per cent sample questionnaire, corrected for under-estimation. The corrections were estimated with the aid of the results of control measurements by aerial photographic surveys of sown areas, and of comparisons between the results of the spring questionnaire and those of budget surveys for the same households. For 1930, the sown areas for individual households and the individual sowings of collective-farm members were estimated by local authorities on the basis of the tax records for 1930, with a correction based on the 2 per cent sample measurement of areas.

[ii] *Yield.* The average yield for state farms and collective farms for 1928 and 1929 was obtained by expert estimates which used materials obtained from a special questionnaire and local data.

For 1930 the average yield for state farms was based on the grain-fodder balances specially constructed by the state farms. The yields for collective farms were based on the figures supplied by the statistical plenipotentiaries, corrected by local commissions of experts using data from large-scale [control] samples of reaping and threshing.

The average yield of individual households for 1928 and 1929 was based on the results of the autumn questionnaire, corrected by the results of control reapings and threshings and by peasant budgets. For 1930 yield of individual households was taken from the same source as for collective farms (see above).

1930 production, as estimated from sown area and average yield, was included in the balance of the national economy only after a deduction was made for the 1930 harvest losses. The level of deduction was established by the Expert Council for Evaluation of Production for the 1930/1 grain-fodder balance.

[b] *Production of industrial and special crops*

[i] *Sugar-beet, cotton, tobacco and makhorka.* The sown area, yield and gross production of these crops was taken for all years from the data of the appropriate organisations (Soyuzsakhar [All-Union Sugar Association], the Chief Cotton Administration

attached to NKZem (USSR), and Tabaksyr'e [All-Union Tobacco Association]). Since these organisations record only the marketed crop, in order to estimate total sugar-beet and cotton production, an addition had to be made for the part of the crop retained by the peasants. For 1928 and 1929, the amount of the crop retained by the peasants was estimated from the results of questionnaires. For 1930 these amounts were established by expert estimates.

[ii] *Flax, hemp, sunflowers, potatoes.* For 1928 and 1929, sown area and yield data for these crops were taken from the data of the former TsSU. Sown area was taken from the data of the spring questionnaires, corrected for underestimation. Yield data for individual peasant households were taken from questionnaires with corrections based on the balance method (in the course of compiling balances for the agricultural years). The 1928 and 1929 yields for the collective farm and state farm sector were established by expert estimates (by applying an estimated addition to the yields of individual peasants).

For 1930 sown area and yield data were taken from the data of the local expert commissions.

[iii] *New oil-yielding crops.* The sown area, yield and gross production for all these crops were taken from the data of Soyuzrasmaslo [All-Union Association for Vegetable Oil].

[iv] *Vegetables and melons.* For 1928 and 1929, sown areas were taken from the spring questionnaires, corrected for underestimates. Yields for individual peasant households were taken from the autumn questionnaire, corrected by the balance method. Yields for state farms and collective farms were corrected by an estimated addition provided by expert estimates. The 1930 figures were obtained from the data of local expert commissions.

[v] *Fruit.* Areas were based on the spring questionnaires for earlier years, and yields were established by means of a special questionnaire.

[vi] *Vines.* Areas were taken from the data of the Phylloxera Commission. The distribution between different sectors was based on data of the former TsSU. Yields were established by means of special questionnaires.

[c] *Livestock products*

[i] *Number of livestock.* In 1928 and 1929 the number of livestock in the state and collective farms in 1928 and 1929 was based on the results of comprehensive surveys. (An additional estimate was made for state farms in 1929, owing to the incompleteness of the survey.)

In 1928 and 1929, the number of livestock in individual use (belonging to collective farms and individual peasants) was taken from the results of the spring 10 per cent sample questionnaire, corrected for underestimation by comparing the results of the spring questionnaire with the results of budget surveys for the same households.

For 1930/1 livestock numbers were taken from the tax assessment records made by Narkomfin agencies via the local soviets. The number of individual livestock was corrected for underestimation (see above).

[ii] *Products of animal husbandry.* It is impossible to make a direct calculation of the products of animal husbandry in calendar years because of the absence of the appropriate statistical material (number of animals and norms for conversion into products of

animal husbandry). The products of animal husbandry have therefore, as a rule, to be estimated for agricultural years and can then be split into half-years to obtain the calendar-year figures.

Meat and hides production for agricultural years was estimated by the 'herd-turnover method'.

For the 1927/8 and 1928/9 agricultural years, the norms needed for estimating products of animal husbandry (norms of herd turnover, weight of livestock carcasses, norms of milk yield, wool-clip, etc.) were established mainly from the peasant budget data and partly from correspondents' reports. For norms of animal loss (for cattle over a year old and for full-grown horses), we also used materials from Gosstrakh [State Insurance Administration]; for norms of carcass weight we used slaughterhouse data.

For 1929/30 and 1930/1, the norms for estimating animal husbandry production were usually obtained by expert evaluation, owing to the absence of adequate statistical materials. These estimates were based on the data for earlier years.

The division of the production of an agricultural year into half-years was carried out for meat and hides on the basis of the following half-yearly data: (*a*) procurements data from NKSnab [People's Commissariat of Supply], Soyuzmyaso [All-Union Association for Meat] and Soyuzkozh [All-Union Association for Leather], (*b*) sales of livestock and meat products from peasant budgets, and (*c*) consumption data for meat for the rural population from peasant budget records. In order to divide milk and egg production into half-years we used materials from the correspondents' network on seasonal variations in milk yields and egg yields.

It proved possible to calculate wool production directly in calendar years.

To estimate livestock production in the socialised sector in 1930 we drew upon materials and estimates from Skotovod [Cattle Farming Association], Ovtsevod [Sheep Farming Association], Svinovod [Pig Farming Association], Tsentrosoyuz [All-Union Central Union of Consumers' Societies] and Kolkhoztsentr [All-Union Centre of Agricultural Collectives].

So far we have been considering only the main products of animal husbandry (meat, milk, eggs, dressed poultry, hides, wool). Other products were estimated for 1928–30 directly in value terms. For this purpose we used reports of the expenditure of these items in the balances for these products (data on consumption by industry, exports, etc.), and we also used data on the relative value of the basic and secondary forms of animal husbandry production obtained from budget and other materials.

For the main products listed above, production was estimated in physical terms, and then estimated in value terms by prices prepared specially for the balance (see explanatory notes on the methodology of evaluating agricultural production and balances of agricultural products, pp. 458–9).

In addition we also estimated the gross production of animals (net increase in the size and weight of the herd) in value terms.

Statistical and departmental reports for 1928–30 are insufficient to enable us to make a direct assessment of the gross production of animals in agriculture for these years, in terms of the value of the net increase in the size and weight of the herd. These quantities had to be estimated by guesswork as the sum of net increases in the weight [including births] of the herd, less the value of livestock lost through premature death, and the amount slaughtered and sold in the course of the year.

Data are available on the number of livestock in the spring of each year from 1927 to 1931 by type and age-group. Estimates can also be made of the number lost through premature death and set aside for slaughter in the agricultural years 1927/8 to 1930/1, and of the number of livestock transferred from one sector to another through collectivisation and through purchase and sale between agricultural enterprises in different sectors. From these data we were able to value the total animal stock at the beginning and the end of the corresponding year, and also to determine the value of the stock that died or were set aside for slaughter, or were transferred from one sector to another.

Livestock at the beginning and the end of the year was valued at the average annual prices for the sale of an animal of a given type and age-group. Separate evaluations were made of livestock in the productive herd and livestock set aside for slaughter. The livestock present at the beginning of the year (minus those set aside for slaughter during the year) and the livestock present at the end of the year (minus those set aside for slaughter in the following year), were valued at the average annual prices pertaining to the year concerned for livestock acquired to supplement the herd. Livestock set aside for slaughter in the year concerned from the stock at the beginning of the year, and livestock set aside for slaughter in the following year from the stock at the end of the year, were valued at the average annual prices in the given year for the slaughter contingent.

In 1930 there was a mass transfer into the state and collective farms from peasant households of animals that were of a poorer pedigree than the animals already in the socialist sector. Consequently, in valuing the livestock of the state and collective farms at the end of the year, we considered separately those animals that had been transferred from the private to the socialist sector.

Livestock losses were evaluated at the weighted prices established for valuing the entire animal stock at the beginning of the year. Animals transferred from one sector to another through collectivisation were valued at the prices for the acquisition of livestock to supplement the herds. Purchases and sales of animals between agricultural enterprises in different sectors were valued at their actual prices. Assuming that the quality of the animals in the different age-groups shown in the statistics did not undergo any substantial changes during the year concerned, the value of the natural increase in the number of animals was obtained by aggregating (i) the value of the animal stock at the end of the year, (ii) the value of animal losses in the year concerned, (iii) the value of animals set aside for slaughter in the year concerned, (iv) the value (plus or minus) of animals transferred from one sector to another, and then deducting from the total of (i)–(iv) the value of animal stock in existence at the beginning of the year.

Livestock was valued at average prices for the USSR, calculated as the weighted average of prices for areas or regions. For 1928 and 1929 livestock in the state and collective farm sectors was valued at prices taken from the annual reports of the state farms and from the comprehensive surveys of collective farms in the corresponding years. For the private sector in these years livestock was valued at the market prices for livestock sales by agricultural producers. In 1930 livestock was valued at procurement prices, with an allowance for prices on the private market for those animals set aside for slaughter and sold on the private market, and also with a correction for the higher quality of animals in state farms.

[*d*]   *Unfinished production.* As explained above, our estimates of the amount of agricultural production in a year include not only the value of the finished products produced by agriculture in that year, but also the value of semi-products still in process of production, the 'value of unfinished production' in agriculture.

In the estimates made for the balance, agricultural production included the value of unfinished production only in the case of arable farming. This was assessed as the value of work performed in sowing winter cereals and in preparation for the spring sowing of subsequent years.

The value of unfinished arable production was measured on the basis of the sales value of the finished product, by assessing the share of the total amount of living labour and embodied labour expended on the finished product which had been expended on unfinished production.

Using this method, the value of unfinished production was not measured at cost; it amounted to that part of the difference between the cost of the finished product and its value when sold which corresponded to the share of unfinished production in finished production.

Moreover, with this method of calculation, the value of unfinished production is determined not only by the size of the expenditure but also by the level of productivity in the years concerned (by the size of the harvest). Consequently a larger outlay which is transferred to the following year's harvest may be valued at a lower level than in the previous year if the harvest is smaller.

The amount of living labour and embodied labour in unfinished production and its share in the total amount of outlays on the production of the finished product were estimated separately for the winter and spring sowings, on the basis of the following two sources:

(*a*)   data on the area sown to winter crops and the area ploughed in the autumn for the following year's harvest, broken down by social sectors;
(*b*)   the norms of outlay of living labour and embodied labour (i) expended in the autumn per unit area of winter and spring sowing for the harvest of the following year, and (ii) expended in the spring and summer of the year concerned for the spring sowings and the reaping and processing of the winter and spring sowings.

The norms of outlay of living labour and embodied labour per unit area of winter and spring sowings were obtained as follows:

(*a*)   state farms: from the annual reports of Sovkhoztsentr for 1927, 1928 and 1929, and of Zernotrest for 1929 and 1930;
(*b*)   private sector: from the data on time expended for agricultural production per unit area cultivated for winter and spring crops worked out from the budget surveys of the individual peasants;
(*c*)   collective farms: owing to the absence of the necessary materials, we used the average norms of expenditure estimated for the state-farm and private sectors of agriculture.

[3] METHODS OF VALUING AGRICULTURAL BALANCES

The balances of agricultural products in physical terms were valued at current prices in accordance with the actual sales prices at each stage of their circulation, allowing for the dates at which products were sold in each year concerned.

In view of the general design of the balances of agricultural products in physical terms, we had first to value the products consumed in agricultural enterprises, and then to value marketed production as distributed between the different categories of consumer.

Procurement prices were the basis for our estimates of agricultural production, except for that part of production sold by agricultural enterprises on the private market. Only sales on the urban private market appear in the balance, and no account has been taken of private intra-rural turnover. Private urban sales were valued at 'bazaar prices', the prices at which producers sold their products on the private extra-rural market.

The marketed part of production was therefore valued at the prices at which products were actually disposed of: procurement and private market prices were weighted according to the relative shares of state procurements and private sales, with due attention being paid to seasonal differences in these patterns of sales.

The part of production which was consumed by the agricultural enterprises themselves in kind, and never entered market circulation, was valued at procurement prices, with a deduction for overhead expenses incurred in preparing and transporting the product to the delivery point.

The value of these transport deductions as an average for the whole USSR was established from transport statistics on the value of the average level of agricultural products in terms of a percentage of the actual procurement prices paid to the producer: 7 per cent for cereals, 15 per cent for vegetables and potatoes, 25 per cent for hay, and 40 per cent for both spring and winter straw.

No deduction was made for the remaining agricultural products, which are more valuable and more easily transportable.

On the basis of these general principles separate items of the balance, concerning the production and distribution of agricultural production within agricultural enterprises, were valued as follows:

[a] *Stocks of agricultural products held by the producers.* Marketable stocks were valued at a weighted average of 'realisation prices' (procurement and private-market prices, weighted according to the relative share of procurements and extra-rural private-market sales). Stocks for domestic consumption within the household or enterprise were valued at procurement prices less deductions for transport expenses. Stocks at the beginning of a given calendar year were valued at the prices current in the first half of that year, and stocks at the end of the year were valued at the prices of the first half of the following year.

[b] *Production.* Stocks carried forward to the following year were valued as indicated above for stocks held by producers at the end of the year. Production that was distributed within the given calendar year was valued at actual realisation prices for the marketed part of production and at procurement prices, with a deduction for transport expenses,

for production distributed in kind. Arable production distributed in kind was valued at the prices of the second half of the given calendar year, and products of animal husbandry were valued at the average annual prices for the given calendar year.

[c] *Productive and personal consumption* [by the agricultural population]. The productive and personal consumption by the agricultural population of the products of their own households, and their losses in production, were valued at the procurement prices of the corresponding half of the calendar year, with a deduction for transport expenses. Their consumption of purchased agricultural products was valued at the actual purchase-prices. But the balance covers only purchases of agricultural products by producers which are made through planned supply, and does not include purchases on the private urban or intra-rural markets. This part of consumption [included in the balance] was therefore valued at the transfer prices of the supply organisation.

Expenditure items of the balance forming part of marketed production were valued at actual consumer prices, as follows:

[d] *Productive consumption and stocks in industry.* These were valued at actual consumer prices, obtained from the reports of industrial enterprises, with the exception of the processing of agricultural products to orders placed by the agricultural population; these were valued at procurement prices, with a deduction for transport expenses.

[e] *Personal consumption by the non-agricultural population.* This was valued at the average prices established by the sector of labour records of TsUNKhU. The consumption of the non-agricultural population was estimated from budget survey data.

[f] *Consumption by institutions and organisations.* This was valued at the transfer prices of the supply organisations, and, in cases where these organisations made their own procurements, at the procurement prices actually paid by these organisations.

[g] *Exports and imports.* These were valued at the prices of the organisations exporting and importing agricultural products.

[h] *Stocks in the channels of circulation.* These were valued at procurement prices with a mark-up for circulation costs: (i) stocks at the beginning of the year were valued at the prices of the second half of the previous year; and (ii) stocks at the end of the year were valued at the prices of the second half of the current year.

The value of those primary processed products using agricultural raw materials, which were either (i) processed on orders from the agricultural population (grain processing products) or (ii) the products of domestic production (dairy products), were assessed at the value of raw materials, valued at procurement prices, with a deduction for transport costs,[10] and the addition of the value of the processing. The amount of the latter was taken to be 10 per cent of the value of the raw material in the case of milled products and 20 per cent in the case of dairy products.

[F]   Methods and sources for estimating consumption

The estimates of personal consumption which underpin the balance of production and consumption for 1928–1930 are the result of work carried out in May–June 1931. The coordination of the balances, in which the estimates of consumption played a major part, was basically completed in September 1931 (subsequently only a few corrections were made). Since then, more recent estimates by sectors of TsUNKhU have resulted in modifications to the norms of consumption (more accurate estimates of consumption by the non-agricultural population in 1930 were completed by the labour sector at the end of June 1932); and they have also resulted in changes in the data on the number and social composition of the population. However, these modifications were made at a time when statistical work on the balance had already been completed, and were consequently not included in the balance estimates. This must be borne in mind when using the tables relating to the consumption, number and social composition of the population.

[I]   THE NUMBER AND SOCIAL COMPOSITION OF THE POPULATION
The fundamental division of the population adopted for the consumption estimates is into 'agricultural' and 'non-agricultural' (the latter includes the population engaged in industry, trade, the socio-cultural sphere, administration, etc.). The criterion used as the basis for this division was the principal source of income. The population whose principal source of income was agriculture was assigned to the agricultural division, and all the rest to the non-agricultural division. In practice, however, it proved impossible to apply this principle strictly when estimating consumption. There were no data whatsoever for determining the norms of consumption of the rural handicraftsmen, and for this group of the population it was impossible to undertake any estimates at all. Moreover, rural handicraftsmen in our initial count of different groups of the population were assigned to the non-agricultural population, but the peasant budget surveys, which were used for estimating consumption in 1928 and 1929, included the households of rural craftsmen among the households of the agricultural population, with no distinction between them. Consequently if we continued to classify rural crafts separately from the agricultural population, it would be impossible to use the budget data to derive the consumption of the agricultural population as such. These considerations compelled us to depart from our general principle and include the bulk of rural craftsmen (those not employing hired labour) in the agricultural population for the purpose of calculating consumption.

It is especially necessary to point out that in the present estimates, unlike the estimates of TsUNKhU for later years (1931), seasonal workers in the industrial branches of the economy are included in the agricultural population.

The estimates of the number and social composition of the population used in the construction of the balance were made in the spring of 1931 by the sector for population records of TsUNKhU (which was then the sector of labour and lifestyle [*byt*] of Gosplan). The total population of the USSR as a whole was estimated for the mid-point of each calendar year, starting with the population census data for 1926, and extending the figures by using the records of the natural increase of the population. For the social composition of the population, the first stage of the estimate was to determine the size of the different groups of the non-agricultural population. We started by determining the size of the active population in each group and obtained the total number of persons in each group by multiplying the number of active population in the group by the coefficient of dependents for that group.

The distribution of the active population between groups was determined in the following way:

[a]   [*Proletariat*]

(i) The average annual number of workers and employees was established from the labour statistics records. Minor servicing personnel were classified as employees in the case of institutions and trading enterprises and as workers in the case of productive enterprises.

Deductions were made from the number of workers and employees thus obtained to allow for seasonal workers. For the railways, the number of seasonal workers was estimated from the data of NKPS, and for other branches of the economy their numbers were estimated as the difference between the average annual number of persons working in the branch and the minimum number in any one month.

In addition to this deduction of seasonal workers, a further conventional deduction of 50 per cent was made from the number of employees working in trading enterprises in rural areas and in rural administrative institutions. The number thus deducted were treated as though they belonged to the agricultural population and had agriculture as their principal source of income.

(ii) The number of unemployed was established on the basis of the 1926 census data together with coefficients of changes in the level of unemployment obtained from the reports of the labour exchanges.

(iii) The number of students in receipt of grants and the number of pensioners were established from the appropriate departmental data.

[b]   [*Non-proletariat*] For the non-proletarian groups of the population the following sources were used: the 1926 population census, the 1929 census of small-scale industry and the 1929 comprehensive survey of trade. In order to establish changes in the size of these groups, data were used from the survey of income-tax payers by TsSU and from reports of NKFin on the number of patents [see glossary] taken out. It must be mentioned that the method used here to separate out the capitalist group from the rest of the non-proletarian population differs from the method used in later TsUNKhU estimates, and from the method used in estimating distribution of the national income. In the present estimate traders who do not employ hired labour are not included in the capitalist group, while in later estimates they are included.

(i) For the *declassé* population, the 1926 census figures were used for all years, without any changes.

As already mentioned the total number of persons in each group was obtained by multiplying the number of the independent population in the group by its dependency coefficient. The dependency coefficients were established from the 1926 census data and the budgets of workers and employees with various corrections estimated by experts.

The size of the non-agricultural population thus obtained was used as the basis for estimating consumption in 1928–30. However some changes were made in the population groupings in order to make the groups correspond more closely to family groups. This was necessary since the budgets of workers and employees used for income and consumption estimates show the consumption of the *family*. Consequently certain groups of the population – pensioners, students in receipt of grants, and the unemployed – were divided according to whether they were living on their own or in families assigned to other groups of the population. This division was carried out primarily in accordance with the results of the 1926 census, with some corrections. Those living in families of the groups of the population were assigned to those groups.

(ii) Apart from these groups of the non-agricultural population, for which consumption estimates were made directly, we also established from the data of the relevant departments the number of persons living in institutions and receiving collective supplies (children in children's homes, prisoners, disabled, the army). The consumption of these groups was included in the balance in the section for institutional consumption.

(iii) The size of the agricultural population was estimated as a residual by deducting the number of persons in the listed groups from the total number of the population. This figure for the agricultural population thus includes workers and employees in agriculture and forestry for both the socialised and the private sector, and includes both collective farm peasants and individual peasants (together with seasonal workers). As already mentioned we have included those rural craftsmen who did not employ hired labour as part of the agricultural population for purposes of estimating consumption.

[2] CONSUMPTION

The study of personal consumption is an aspect of our work which particularly suffers from very poor data. The available materials (data on the retail turnover of socialised trade, the despatch of goods etc.) are insufficient to provide a correct estimate even of the total size of the market fund placed at the disposal of the population. This is because the data are for the most part incomplete, either as regards the trading system or the goods covered (they cover planned goods only or predominantly only those goods that are distributed through centralised supply). Hardly any information is available for decentralised funds. And even where we do possess full information concerning a particular group of goods, the amount consumed by the population remains unknown, because the goods can be acquired from the retail trade network by institutions of the socialist sector.

Reports on state trade are most unsatisfactory and this has become particularly important in recent years, when state trade has developed extensively. For private trade (including private sales by the peasants) there is absolutely no information, even though this trade plays a considerable role in the personal consumption of certain groups of goods (especially when valued in money terms).

Furthermore, the available data are very defective in their breakdown by types of goods, and in particular lack data in physical terms. This makes it extremely difficult to use these materials for estimating personal consumption and for constructing balances in physical terms. This is especially the case in the conditions of recent years, with the existence of different prices for the same goods (for the commercial fund (see glossary)).

The situation becomes even more difficult as we attempt to move from estimating the total retail trade fund to its division between urban and rural purchases. In the first place, the available data on goods despatched to urban and rural areas do not indicate how the fund was actually distributed, because the reports were not compiled at the lowest level of operation and do not take into account the variations from the original distribution which took place as the goods passed through the various levels of the trade network. But even if these reports were satisfactory they would still not provide all the material needed, since, for example, it is difficult to record such a widespread phenomenon as the purchasing of goods by the rural population in the towns.

It is virtually impossible to estimate consumption by different social groups with the records available. No material at all is available for this task. The defects in existing records listed above, which result partly from their unsatisfactory organisation and partly from the complexity of the problem, make it impossible to use them for an estimate of consumption with a detailed breakdown by type of product, or for a breakdown between agricultural and non-agricultural population, or for a breakdown by social groups. All this compels us to base our estimates of consumption (at least for the non-agricultural population) on the budget survey data and to use statistical records only for correcting these results.

[a]   *Estimates of consumption by the non-agricultural population* in the balance of the national economy for 1928–30 were based on the budget surveys which have been carried out for a number of years by the sector of labour records of TsUNKhU (formerly TsSU), and which have normally inevitably been used by everyone working on consumption.

The budget surveys for workers and employees provide the most satisfactory information for estimating the amount and growth of consumption. The number of budgets of worker and employee families are quite large, amounting to 10,000 in 1931. Moreover, the labour sector has greatly improved the quality of the data by moving from a system of enquiring about the whole previous year's consumption in its November enquiries, to one of enquiring only about current consumption. This change took place in November 1928.

As regards other groups of the population, no systematic investigation of them has been made. In 1929 a mass budget survey was carried out which covered not only workers and employees but also other groups of the non-agricultural population (craftsmen, bourgeoisie, unemployed, pensioners, etc.). Data from the survey provided the basis for estimating norms of consumption in 1929 (in both money and physical terms) which were then used to estimate consumption for the balance of the national economy for 1928–30. This survey covered 10,000 families and was carried out in October 1929. The investigators enquired into consumption in the previous month. For a small number of items, including the main elements of the family budget, they also enquired into consumption in the whole previous year.

Various corrections were made in the consumption norms obtained from this survey by using data on the current budgets of workers and employees. The mass survey did not cover persons living alone. These persons had a very different pattern of consumption from family members, and accordingly corrections were made using the results of the budgets of November 1927 and November 1928.

The 1928 and 1930 consumption norms were estimated as follows:

(i) For workers and employees the results of budget surveys for the years concerned were used to establish the rate of change in consumption from 1928 to 1929 and from 1929 to 1930. The increase in public catering was included with food products. Data from Vsekoopit were used to establish the product structure of consumption in public catering, since this information was not available from the budget surveys.

(ii) For the other groups of the non-agricultural population the position was considerably worse. There were no current budget studies and no adequate data on changes in consumption by these groups. For our 1928 estimate we used the results of a questionnaire on the acquisition of industrial goods, carried out by the labour statistics sector of TsSU, and growth coefficients based on the budgets of workers and employees corrected by expert estimates. The corrections for the capitalist group were especially important since these had markedly different levels and changes of levels of income, different conditions of acquisition, and so on. A number of corrections were made here to the changes both in norms and in prices; for 1930, prices were corrected in line with changes in private trade prices.

The estimates based on these sources cover all acquisitions of products in exchange for money, in both socialised and private trade, and also purchases from the peasants and consumption through public catering, as well as all forms of receipt of products without money payment (wages paid in kind, products obtained from one's own household and so on).

Consumption obtained from social and cultural services provided without payment by the state and by social organisations was not included in the estimates. The omitted items included, for example, material consumption while residing in rest-homes and sanatoria, consumption connected with cultural services (newspapers, books, etc.), and medical services.

As the estimate covers only the consumption of material goods entering into budgets of individuals, the growth in consumption norms in this estimate is somewhat under-estimated because the increase in services without payment was considerably more rapid than the increase in expenditure from the budgets of individuals.

[Once the norms have been estimated in physical terms they have to be valued in money terms in order to obtain a figure for consumption.] The budgets show actual expenditure on every purchase, and so calculations based on the budgets provide the actual prices of products, taking into account the actual weight of the different trade sectors and the difference in the level of their prices.

The products entering into public catering were valued at cooperative prices. As regards products received otherwise than in exchange for money: (i) products of a person's own household were valued at the average price paid for these products in monetary transactions; (ii) wages paid in kind were valued according to the valuation made by the enterprise, or, if this was not available, in cooperative prices. Products obtained through barter were valued at the value of the goods given in exchange.

After consumption norms per head had been estimated both in money and in kind by the methods and sources described above, they were then multiplied by the number of the population in order to establish the size of the consumption funds.

[b] *Estimates of consumption by the agricultural population* were based upon much weaker evidence than the estimates for the non-agricultural population, especially for the year 1930. For 1928 and 1929 estimates were based on the results of the 1927/8 and 1928/9 peasant budgets transferred to a calendar-year basis. For industrial goods, these calendar year adjustments were based on the quarterly data of Tsentrosoyuz on changes in sales in rural areas. The results of the budget surveys of 1929/30 were also used to some extent, but the full use of these materials was impossible due to the defects in certain parts. These materials served as the basis for our estimates for preparing certain balances, but as work progressed it became clear that very substantial corrections were called for, both in the total amount consumed and in the rate of change, especially in relation to industrial goods. These corrections were considerably larger than those introduced in setting up the balances of consumption by the non-agricultural population. It was sometimes necessary to construct the consumption of the agricultural population completely from scratch, using our evaluations of the total consumption fund for the entire population, the more precise figures for the towns, and reported data on the sale of industrial goods. Thus, the present estimates of consumption by the agricultural population are to a large extent speculative (*konstruktivnyi*) in character, as is the case for all the estimates we have on this matter, owing to the lack of good quality material for earlier years and the almost total absence of any data for very recent years. This unfavourable situation with the data made it impossible for us to include in the balances any kind of division of the agrarian population into social groups. We were unable to provide even the fundamental division of consumption between collective farm peasants and individual peasants. A rough estimate of the division of consumption between these social groups was made only for the balance showing principal indicators of reproduction of the sectors, and no division in terms of particular goods could be made.

Consumption by the agricultural population was evaluated as follows. Purchased industrial goods and agricultural products were valued at the prices at which they were acquired. Agricultural products produced by the consumer, and products processed domestically, or received from processing carried out by industry to orders from the rural population, were valued at the prices of the non-marketed part of agricultural production, with the addition of the value of processing for products subjected to primary processing (see explanatory note on the methods of valuing the balances of agricultural products [pp. 299–300]).

The level of consumption of about 70 goods and groups of goods was estimated from these sources and by these methods. For the majority of these goods, consumption was estimated in both physical and monetary terms, but for some groups of goods estimates were made only in terms of rubles. The goods for which estimates were made in physical as well as monetary terms accounted for 82 per cent of total consumption in the case of the non-agricultural population and 90 per cent in the case of the agricultural population.

In addition to these estimates in current prices *consumption was also estimated in constant prices of 1928.* The conversion of consumption in 1929 and 1930 into constant prices of 1928 was carried out, as a rule, by directly revaluing consumption in physical terms in these years in the prices of 1928. As may be seen from the figures above, between 82 per cent and 90 per cent of goods could be revalued by this method. The remaining groups of goods, for which no data in physical terms were available, were revalued by applying indexes based on the growth of retail prices of one or several goods which form part of the group being revalued. In certain cases we lacked any data on consumption in physical terms for any commodity in the group, and had to use direct estimates of consumption made by the labour sector of TsUNKhU. Corrections for the group of goods as a whole were made in the course of coordinating the balance. In these cases the index was constructed by directly revaluing the goods belonging to this group, using the estimates of the labour sector. These were then applied to the balance figure with appropriate corrections. In fact this was almost equivalent to a direct revaluation. This method was used for goods which covered about 7 per cent of the consumption of the agricultural population. Therefore altogether about 89 per cent of the consumption of the agricultural population was converted into 1928 prices by means of direct revaluation of data in physical terms, or by a method approximating to such a revaluation.

The revaluation of consumption in 1928 prices enabled us to trace the growth in physical terms of consumption by the agricultural and non-agricultural population. We also revalued the consumption of those agricultural products and industrial goods which were processed domestically by the agricultural population into the 1928 consumers' prices paid by the non-agricultural population. This estimate was made in order to enable us to compare the levels of consumption of these two groups of the population, since the prices used in the balance to value the consumption of agricultural products by the agricultural population were obtained by a special method which gave them an extremely low value (see the explanatory note on methods of evaluating the balances of agricultural products [on pp. 299–300]). Even this revaluation into urban prices [prices of the non-agricultural population] gives a somewhat misleading idea of the level of consumption in the countryside as compared with the town. It does not take account of differences in quality for a number of agricultural products, and it does not include industrial goods (except for products processed domestically), since the assortment and quality of the goods differ greatly in town and country and it was therefore impossible to revalue them at urban prices. Nevertheless this revaluation does enable us to make an approximate comparison between the levels of consumption of these two groups of the population, though it must be borne in mind that for the reasons stated the consumption level of the agricultural population has been somewhat overestimated in this estimation.

All these estimates of personal consumption, which constitute one of the basic elements in the balance of production and consumption, included only the consumption of material goods. In order to find the general welfare level of particular groups of the population and its changes over time, a special estimate was made which included services as well as the consumption of material goods. The results of this estimate differ substantially from those for the consumption of material goods alone (see tables 15, 15a, 15b and 15c, in the section on 'Consumption'). Data on free social and cultural services and on services for which a charge was made were taken from the relevant tables of the estimates of the national income department of the sector of balances of TsUNKhU.

[G]   Methods for estimating stocks in the channels of circulation, trade and transport mark-ups

[1]   STOCKS IN THE CHANNELS OF CIRCULATION

The lack of a complete survey of stocks in the channels of circulation made it difficult to obtain the information needed for the balance of the national economy and compelled us to resort to some rough estimates, especially of the breakdown by type of good. But this did not seriously affect the results, since it applied to fields which covered a relatively insignificant share of total stocks (e.g. hunting cooperatives, disabled-persons cooperatives, agricultural cooperatives etc.).

The data sources for stocks are as follows: (*a*) in the case of agricultural products, centralised records are available and (*b*) in the case of industrial products, independent information is available on stocks in state and private trade.

(*a*)   *Agricultural products.* From 1927 the former TsSU carried out through its local agencies surveys of stocks of agricultural raw materials and cereals, using its own nomenclature of goods. This survey was made on the first day of each quarter. The local statistical agencies obtained information on the quantity of stocks in the warehouses of state collection agencies, in cooperative agencies and in the hands of private traders.

These surveys provided data on stocks of raw materials and cereals on 1 January 1928, 1929 and 1930. Because of the reorganisation of the local statistical agencies in 1930, the information for 1 January 1931 was incomplete, and it was necessary to check and supplement it with the aid of information from government departments.

Stocks in transit were obtained from the survey by NKPS, although it must be borne in mind that before 1 January 1931 this included only cereals and oilseeds. The survey for 1 January 1931 covered a considerably larger number of products. All the information received from this survey was in physical terms, and it was converted into the appropriate procurement and other prices at the centre.

(*b*) *Industrial products.* Stocks in state and private trade were obtained from the 'detailed survey of trade' for 1926/7 to 1928/9. Data for cooperative trade were taken from the cooperative annual balances.

To establish the total amount of stocks in the country, the only rough estimate which had to be made involved extrapolating the results for the RSFSR to the USSR as a whole. The degree of error here was relatively small, as this procedure was used only for minor branches of trade. It was more difficult to establish the size of the stocks of particular commodities. For the stocks covered by the 'detailed survey of trade' the commodity breakdown was perfectly satisfactory: the nomenclature was uniform and fairly complete and consistent from year to year. But there was no unified nomenclature in cooperative trade, and some systems of cooperatives (disabled persons, agricultural and hunting cooperatives) merely recorded the total stock balance figure, with no breakdown at all by type of good.

In such cases we had to resort to using data on the structure of the assortment of stocks in similar types of trade, data from sample surveys, and coefficients of the rate of circulation of goods.

The stock figures for particular goods were corrected and adjusted when we put the balance together in terms of economic years.

The size of stocks on 1 January was not shown in the records, and the balances for calendar years were prepared by adjusting the 1 October stock figures to obtain 1 January figures. Total stocks in the channels of circulation were estimated by using quarterly data on turnover and conjunctural materials on monthly goods turnover. Quarterly turnover was itself estimated from the current records of NKTorg RSFSR [People's Commissariat of Trade of RSFSR] and quarterly reports of Tsentrosoyuz on procurements, and the detailed survey of private trade. From these materials it was possible to establish the monthly changes in the ratio of stocks to turnover, and thus obtain correction coefficients for wholesale and retail trade for each sector of trade.

The re-estimates of stocks of particular goods on a calendar-year basis were derived mainly from the materials of the consumer cooperatives (the main holders of stocks for most goods), and in addition from the materials of the associations.

For the consumer cooperatives the data for the year 1930 were the most reliable, since conjunctural data on the level of stocks were available for January in comparison with October. For 1929 wholesale trade data are available on a quarterly basis, but retail stock levels had to be estimated from data on the turnover of specific goods, corrected by conjunctural data. For 1928, owing to the lack of data, a very crude method had to be adopted: the correction coefficients for 1929 were used for 1928, and merely corrected for the change in overall stock levels in 1928 as compared with 1929. As a result of the above operations we obtained a table of correction coefficients by means of which we adjusted the October stocks shown in the balance to obtain the stocks on 1 January.

Total stocks on 1 January 1931 were obtained from the annual balances. In order to estimate the stocks of specific commodities the following data were used: (*a*) for consumer cooperatives, the level of stocks on 1 January 1931, covering 30 per cent of the network, and also stocks on 8 November 1930, and 1 April 1931; (*b*) for *snabtorgi* – the level of stocks on 1 January 1931, covering 50 per cent of the network. These data were then extrapolated to obtain stocks in the system as whole.

In order to obtain stocks in physical terms, we used the prices for the relevant goods and trade systems obtained from the department of prices and indexes of TsUNKhU.

[2]   TRADE AND TRANSPORT MARK-UPS

The total size of the trade and transport mark-up was established on the basis of the following material: (*a*) the reports of NKPS and NKVod (People's Commissariat of Waterways) on the gross receipts of freight transport; (*b*) the estimates by the sector of balances of the gross receipts of road transport; and (*c*) data on the trade mark-up estimated by the 'real' method. The 'real' method of estimating the trade and transport mark-up is to aggregate the mark-ups actually obtained in each trade system at each level.

To establish the trade and transport mark-ups for specific goods we had to make rough estimates. For the balances in physical terms, which constitute 66 per cent of the total number of balances, the trade and transport mark-up was obtained by subtracting producers' prices from the prices paid by the consumers. For some balances of industrial goods in physical terms we used the estimates of trade and transport mark-ups for types of commodity made by the sector of circulation [trade] records of TsUNKhU, using the 'real' method.

To estimate the mark-up for the balances compiled only in value terms, we used the following materials: materials on the gap between producer prices and consumer prices, the standard unit-costs as estimated by the consumer cooperatives, trade and transport mark-ups estimated by the 'real' method for economic years, and transport mark-ups estimated by the transport sector of TsUNKhU on the basis of NKPS data on freight turnover, average length of haul, and average freight charges.

The total mark-up obtained by aggregating the mark-ups for the separate goods was then allocated to 'trade' and 'transport'. The following method was used. From the total amount of the mark-up we deducted the mark-up on means of production not entering into intermediate trade (which was simply the transport mark-up on these goods). The remainder was the trade and transport mark-up on goods entering into intermediate trade; and was identical in concept to the trade and transport mark-up as estimated by the 'real' method, and was in fact close to it in magnitude.

On the basis of the above operations the trade and transport mark-ups were divided into 'trade' and 'transport'. The transport mark-up on all goods was obtained by adding together the transport mark-up on goods entering into intermediate trade and the mark-up on goods not entering into intermediate trade.

A comparison of the total mark-up (gross receipts of transport plus the trade mark-up) and the mark-up shown in the balance shows that the transport mark-up in the balance was somewhat lower than the total receipts from freight transport. This is for two reasons. First, gross production was overestimated in our estimates for road transport. Secondly, in our estimates of the transport mark-up a certain amount of transport costs (in particular for raw materials) was included not in the mark-up but in the price paid by the producer.

In order to avoid double counting, we have therefore used the mark-up shown in the balance.

NOTES

1 For more details, see the explanatory note on the calculation of consumption (pp. 301–3).
2 The cost index of building work and capital investment was calculated by the Central Planning Bureau in 1929/30 for the revised variant of the Five-Year Plan. This index is meant, wherever subsequently the index of the Central Planning Bureau is mentioned. [This note, taken in conjunction with the text, seems to imply that these indexes were used for 1927/8 and 1928/9 as well as 1926/7.]

3 *Osnovnye momenty rekonstruktsii promyshlennosti,* published by the economic statistics sector of Gosplan in 1930.

4 Where it was necessary to use the relative share of equipment and building as measured in current prices in order to estimate the weighted index, we have used a reverse index for these weights.

5 'Industrial stocks' refers to the stocks in the stores belonging to industrial establishments. Stocks held in base stores and in stores of industrial associations and trusts are treated as 'stocks in the channels of circulation.'

6 See *Narodnoe khozyaistvo SSSR: statisticheskii spravochnik 1932 g,* Sotsekgiz, 1932, p. 5.

7 On the other hand the gross production of the rubber industry was assigned to group A, despite the fact that this industry manufactured galoshes to the value of 111.6 million rubles in 1928, 130.5 million rubles in 1929 and 125.6 million rubles in 1930.

8 Cereals were classified as means of production since they were consumed almost exclusively in production (seed, fodder, the milling industry). Grain consumption by the population appears in the balance of milling and groat grinding products which is included with the consumer goods' balances; these are then included as products of the milling and groat-grinding industry in the balance of industrial goods.

9 In the case of flax and hemp fibre, production was included with the products of primary processing (scutched fibre).

10 The marketed part of the products of milk processing are an exception; the value of the raw material was established from the value of the processed products which was actually realised.

[11] [*Itogi raboty promyshlennosti VSNKh za 1931g i perspektivy tyazheloi promyshlennosti na 1932g: materialy k dokladu tov. Ordzhonikidze XVII vsesoyuznoi konferentsii VKP (b), Narkomtyazhprom,* 1932]

[12] [*Kontrol'nye Tsifry Narodnogo Khozyaistva SSSR na 1929/30 god,* 1930, pp. 459–60.]

[13] [Original source mistakenly states '1929'.]

[14] [*Narodno-Khozyaistvennyi plan SSSR na 1931 god,* 1931, p. 154.]

3. Tables and notes

V APPENDICES (TABLES)

CONTENTS

Section V

Appendix A. Balances of products of industry

Table 1. Tractor balance

A Num-bers	B Des-ignat-ion of prod-uct	C Year	D Unit of measurement	1 Stocks at beg-inning of year in industry	2 Produc-tion per year in industry	3 Imports	4 Customs duties	5 Total input	6 Distributed In industry Produced in USSR	7 Imported	8 Total	9 In agriculture Produced in USSR	10 Imported	11 Total	12 Total distrib-uted	13 Stocks at end of year in industry	14 Losses due to selling tractors below cost	15 Total output
1		1928	a) horse power	2050	14910	27250	-	44210	420	-	420	10630	27250	37880	38300	5910	-	44210
2		"	b) numbers of tractors	205	1491	2558	-	4254	42	-	42	1063	2558	3621	3663	591	-	4254
3		"	c) thousand rubles	622	4520	4960	1170	11272	75	-	75	1903	4878	6781	6856	1792	2624	11272
4		"	d) price per tractor in thousand rubles	3.0	3.0	1.9	-	2.6	1.8	-	1.8	1.8	1.9	1.9	1.9	3.0	-	2.6
5		1929	a) horse power	5910	54828	171706	-	232444	10373	2312	12685	42720	169394	212114	224799	7645	-	232444
6	Trac-tors	"	b) numbers of tractors	591	4569	10250	-	15410	251	57	308	4272	10193	14465	14773	637	-	15410
7		"	c) thousand rubles	1792	17376	27615	2115	48928	3646	747	4393	7645	30321	37966	42359	1979	4590	48928
8		"	d) price per tractor in thousand rubles	3.6	3.8	2.7	-	3.2	14.5	13.1	14.3	1.8	3.0	2.6	2.9	3.1	-	3.2
9		1930	a) horse power	7645	159087	418140	-	584872	30735	10840	41575	127445	407300	534745	576320	8552	-	584872
10		"	b) numbers of tractors	637	12727	21588	-	34952	596	271	867	12029	21317	33346	34213	739	-	34952
11		"	c) thousand rubles	1979	45197	56779	8080	112035	10010	3501	13511	22813	72907	95720	109231	2804	-	112035
12		"	d) price per tractor in thousand rubles	3.1	3.6	2.6	-	3.2	16.8	12.9	15.6	1.9	3.4	2.9	3.2	3.8	-	3.2

Appendix A
Table 2. Electrical power balance

				Production per year						Consumed						
Numbers	Designation of product	Year	Unit of measurement	District stations and stations working on district network	Local stations in general use	Factory stations	Rural stations	Special purpose stations (NKPS and NKSvyaz.)	Total input	By census industry	By railway transport and communication	For municipal and everyday needs	By agriculture	Total	Losses in district networks and local stations and natural consumption	Total output
A	B	C	D	1	2	3	4	5	6	7	8	9	10	11	12	13
1		1928	a) million kilowatt hours	2002	690	2160	40	111	5003	3268	111	1039	45	4463	540	5003
2		"	b) thousand rubles	140140	95220	259830	4860	16650	516700	298203	16650	196467	5380	516700	–	516700
3		"	c) price of 1,000 kwh	70.0	138.0	120.3	121.5	150.1	103.1	91.2	150.0	189.1	119.5	115.8	–	103.2
4	Electric-	1929	a) million kilowatt hours	2785	879	2560	45	117	6386	4300	119	1277	50	5746	640	6386
5	al pow-	"	b) thousand rubles	181025	115149	277850	4962	16950	595936	359990	17000	213526	5500	595936	–	595936
6	er	"	c) price of 1,000 kwh.	55.0	131.0	108.5	110.3	144.9	93.3	83.7	142.9	167.2	110.0	103.7	–	93.3
7		1930	a) million kilowatt hours	4380	957	2715	55	124	8231	5600	136	1472	78	7286	945	8231
8		"	b) thousand rubles	262800	119625	284000	5722	17400	689547	439600	20400	221447	8100	689547	–	689547
9		"	c) price of ,000 kwh	60.0	125.0	104.6	104.0	140.3	83.8	78.5	150.0	150.4	103.8	94.6	–	83.8

Appendix A

Table 3. Fuel balance

Numbers	Designation of product	Year	Unit of measurement	Stocks at beginning of year					Production per year					Imports	Excises	Customs duties	Trade and transport mark-up	Total input	Numbers
				In census industry	In channels of circulation	In transport	Others	Total	Census industry	Non-census industry	Self procurement	Obtained after processing	Total						
A	B	C	D	1	2	3	4	5	6	7	8	9	10	11	12	13	14	15	A
1		1928	a) thousand tonnes	2137.0	155.0	1630.0	425.0[1]	4347.0	35631.4[2]	-	-	13318.0[3]	48949.4	56.2	-	-	-	53352.6	1
2		"	b) thousand tonnes of conventional fuel	2023.7	146.8	1543.6	402.5	4116.6	33742.9	-	-	12612.2	46355.1	53.2	-	-	-	50524.9	2
3		"	c) thousand rubles	35179	1546	17050	8096[1]	61871	316681[2]	-	-	130569[3]	447250	509	-	-	130233	639863	3
4		"	d) price per tonne	16.46	9.97	10.46	19.05	14.23	8.89	-	-	9.80	9.14	9.06	-	-	11.99		4
5		1929	a) thousand tonnes	3258.9	152.0	1944.0	480.0[1]	5834.9	41165.0[2]	-	-	13540.0[3]	54705.0	66.0	-	-	-	60605.9	5
6		"	b) thousand tonnes of conventional fuel	3086.2	143.9	1841.0	454.6	5525.7	38983.3	-	-	12822.4	51805.7	62.5	-	-	-	57393.9	6
7	Coal	"	c) thousand rubles	48804	1519	20279	9149[1]	79761	371114[2]	-	-	128076[3]	499190	599	-	-	140737	720277	7
8		"	d) price per tonne	14.98	9.99	10.43	19.06	13.67	9.02	-	-	9.46	9.13	9.08	-	-	11.88		8
9		1930	a) thousand tonnes	3978.2	175.0	1926.0	600.0[1]	6679.2	48944.0[2]	-	-	15600.0[3]	64544.0	63.6	-	-	-	71286.8	9
10		"	b) thousand tonnes of conventional fuel	3769.4	165.7	1823.9	568.2	6325.2	46349.9	-	-	14773.2	61123.1	60.2	-	-	-	67508.5	10
11		"	c) thousand rubles	60601	1750	20082	11496[1]	93929	441256[2]	-	-	150220[3]	591476	601	-	-	142180	828186	11
12		"	d) price per tonne	15.23	10.0	10.43	19.16	14.06	9.03	-	-	9.63	9.17	9.45	-	-	11.62		12

Appendix A
Table 3. (cont'd)

Num-bers (A)	Des-ignation of product (B)	Year (C)	Unit of measurement (D)	Consumed in production						Consumed by the population and by institutions				Num-bers (A)
				Census industry	Non-census industry	Transport	In agriculture	Sent for processing	Total	Agricultural population	Non-agricultural population	Institutions and social organisation	Total	
				16	17	18	19	20	21	22	23	24	25	A
1		1928	a) thousand tonnes	17774.2	242.0	11699.3[4]	–	13770.0[5]	43485.7	–	1903.0[6]	988.7	2891.7	1
2		"	b) thousand tonnes of conventional fuel	16832.4	229.2	11079.2	–	13040.2	41181.0	–	1802.1	936.3	2738.4	2
3		"	c) thousand rubles	252041	11000	125670[4]		118363[5]	507074		28996[6]	18877	47873	3
4		"	d) price per tonne	14.18	45.45	10.46	–	8.00	9.79	–	15.24	19.09	16.56	4
5		1929	a) thousand tonnes	19179.0	259.0	13092.9[4]	–	16090[5]	48620.9	–	2250.0[6]	1098.1	3348.1	5
6		"	b) thousand tonnes of conventional fuel	18162.5	245.3	12399.0	–	15237.2	46044.0	–	2130.7	1039.9	3170.6	6
7	Coal	"	c) thousand rubles	266967	11779	140273[4]		138866[5]	557885	–	34964[6]	21113	56077	7
8		"	d) price per tonne	13.92	45.48	10.42		6.63	11.47	–	11.10	19.23	16.75	8
9		1930	a) thousand tonnes	24552.0	326.5	16726.0[4]	–	18360.0[5]	59964.5	–	2840.0[6]	374.0	42140	9
10		"	b) thousand tonnes of conventional fuel	23250.7	309.2	15839.5	–	17386.9[5]	56786.3	–	2689.4	1301.2	3990.6	10
11		"	c) thousand rubles	327027	14900	172900[4]	–	162300	677127	–	44250[6]	26000	70250	11
12		"	d) price per tonne	13.32	45.64	10.34	–	10.03	11.29	–	15.05	18.92	16.66	12

Appendix A
Table 3. (cont'd)

Num-bers A	Desig-nation of products B	Year C	Unit of measurement D	Losses 26	Exports 27	Stocks at end of year				Total 32	Total output 33	Num-bers A
						In census industry 28	In channels of circulation 29	In transport 30	Others 31			
1		1928	a) thousand tonnes	535.0	605.3	3258.9	152.0	1944.0	480.0	5834.9	53352.6	1
2		"	b) thousand tonnes of conventional fuel	506.6	573.2	3086.2	143.9	1841.0	454.6	5525.7	50524.9	2
3		"	c) thousand rubles	-	5165	48804	1519	20279	9149[1]	79751	639863	3
4		"	d) price per tonne	-	8.53	14.93	9.99	10.43	19.06	13.67	11.99	4
5		1929	a) thousand tonnes	620.0	1337.7	3978.2	175.0	1926.0	600.0	6679.2	60605.9	5
6		"	b) thousand tonnes of conventional fuel	587.3	1266.9	3767.3	165.7	1823.9	568.2	6325.1	57393.9	6
7	Coal	"	c) thousand rubles	-	12386	60601	1750	20082	11496	93929	720277	7
8		"	d) price per tonne	-	9.26	15.23	10.0	10.43	19.16	14.06	11.88	8
9		1930	a) thousand tonnes	720.0	1856.3	2994.0	200.0	1038.0	300.0	4532.0	71286.8	9
10		"	b) thousand tonnes of conventional fuel	681.9	1757.9	2835.3	189.4	983.0	284.1	4291.8	67508.5	10
11		"	c) thousand rubles	-	16780	45419	2000	10850	5760[1]	64029	828186	11
12		"	d) price per tonne	-	9.04	15.17	10.00	10.45	19.20	14.13	11.62	12

Appendix A
Table 3. (cont'd)

Num-bers (A)	Des-ignation of product (B)	Year (C)	Unit of measurement (D)	Stocks at beginning of year					Production per year					Imports	Excises	Customs duties	Trade and transport mark-up	Total input	Num-bers (A)
				In census industry (1)	In channels of circulation (2)	In transport (3)	Others (4)	Total (5)	Census industry (6)	Non-census industry (7)	Self procurement (8)	Obtained after processing (9)	Total (10)	(11)	(12)	(13)	(14)	(15)	
13		1928	a) thousand tonnes	281.0	19.0	6.0	-	306.0	4149.0	-	-	-	4149.0	-	-	-	-	4455.0	13
14		"	b) thousand tonnes of conventional fuel	261.3	17.7	5.6	-	284.6	3858.6	-	-	-	3858.6	-	-	-	-	4143.2	14
15		"	c) thousand rubles	6900	330	142	-	7372	73023	-	-	-	73023	-	-	-	13960	94355	15
16		"	d) price per tonne	24.56	17.37	23.67	-	24.09	17.60	-	-	-	17.60	-	-	-	-	21.92	16
17		1929	a) thousand tonnes	292.8	23.0	5.0	-	320.8	5000.0	-	-	-	5000.0	-	-	-	-	5320.8	17
18	Coke	"	b) thousand tonnes of conventional fuel	272.3	21.4	4.6	-	298.3	4650.0	-	-	-	4650.0	-	-	-	-	4948.3	18
19		"	c) thousand rubles	7933	405	126	-	8464	86500	-	-	-	86500	-	-	-	15935	110899	19
20		"	d) price per tonne	27.09	17.61	25.20	-	26.38	17.30	-	-	-	17.30	-	-	-	-	21.58	20
21		1930	a) thousand tonnes	204.0	28.0	2.0	-	234.0	6120.3	-	-	-	6120.3	-	-	-	-	6354.3	21
22		"	b) thousand tonnes of conventional fuel	189.7	26.0	1.9	-	217.6	5691.9	-	-	-	5691.9	-	-	-	-	5909.5	22
23		"	c) thousand rubles	5266	467	58	-	5791	103927	-	-	-	103927	-	-	-	22763	132481	23
24		"	d) price per tonne	25.81	16.68	29.00	-	24.75	16.98	-	-	-	16.98	-	-	-	-	21.38	24

Appendix A
Table 3. (cont'd)

Numbers (A)	Designation of product (B)	Year (C)	Unit of measurement (D)	Consumed in production						Consumed by the population and by institutions				Numbers (A)
				Census industry	Non-census industry	Transport	In agriculture	Sent for processing	Total	Agricultural population	Non-agricultural population	Institutions and social organisations	Total	
				16	17	18	19	20	21	22	23	24	25	A
13		1928	a) thousand tonnes	3886.0	5.0	18.0	-	-	3909.0	-	-	-	-	13
14		"	b) thousand tonnes of conventional fuel	3614.0	4.6	16.7	-	-	3635.3	-	-	-	-	14
15		"	c) thousand rubles	85067	400	419	-	-	85886	-	-	-	-	15
16		"	d) price per tonne	21.89	80.0	23.28	-	-	21.97	-	-	-	-	16
17		1929	a) thousand tonnes	4776.2	5.0	25.0	-	-	4806.2	-	-	-	-	17
18		"	b) thousand tonnes of conventional fuel	4441.9	4.6	23.2	-	-	4469.7	-	-	-	-	18
19	Coke	"	c) thousand rubles	104073	415	609	-	-	105097	-	-	-	-	19
20		"	d) price per tonne	21.79	83.0	24.36	-	-	21.86	-	-	-	-	20
21		1930	a) thousand tonnes	5808.4	5.0	25.0	-	-	5838.4	-	-	-	-	21
22		"	b) thousand tonnes of conventional fuel	5401.8	4.6	23.2	-	-	5429.6	-	-	-	-	22
23		"	c) thousand rubles	126449	435	600	-	-	127484	-	-	-	-	23
24		"	d) price per tonne	21.77	87.0	24.00	-	-	21.67	-	-	-	-	24

Appendix A
Table 3. (cont'd)

Num-bers (A)	Desig-nation of products (B)	Year (C)	Unit of measurement (D)	Losses (26)	Exports (27)	Stocks at end of year – In census industry (28)	In channels of circulation (29)	In transport (30)	Others (31)	Total (32)	Total output (33)	Num-bers (A)
13		1928	a) thousand tonnes	225.0	0.2	292.8	23.0	5.0	–	320.8	4455.0	13
14		"	b) thousand tonnes of conventional fuel	209.4	0.2	272.3	21.4	4.6	–	298.3	4143.2	14
15		"	c) thousand rubles	–	5.0	7933	405	126	–	8464	94355	15
16		"	d) price per tonne	–	25.0	27.09	17.61	25.20	–	26.38	21.92	16
17		1929	a) thousand tonnes	280.0	0.6	204.0	28.0	2.0	–	234.0	5320.8	17
18	Coke	"	b) thousand tonnes of conventional fuel	260.4	0.6	189.7	26.0	1.9	–	217.6	4948.3	18
19		"	c) thousand rubles	–	11	5266	467	58	–	5791	110899	19
20		"	d) price per tonne	–	18.33	25.81	16.68	29.00	–	24.75	21.58	20
21		1930	a) thousand tonnes	310.0	0.6	169.7	33.6	2.0	–	205.3	6354.3	21
22		"	b) thousand tonnes of conventional fuel	288.4	0.6	157.8	31.2	1.9	–	190.9	5909.5	22
23		"	c) thousand rubles	–	9	4400	540	48	–	4988	132481	23
24		"	d) price per tonne	–	15.0	25.93	16.07	24.00	–	24.30	21.38	24

Appendix A
Table 3. (cont'd)

Num-bers (A)	Des-ignat-ion of prod-uct (B)	Year (C)	Unit of measurement (D)	Stocks at beginning of year					Production per year					Imports	Excises	Cust-oms duties	Trade and trans-port mark-up	Total input	Num-bers (A)
				In census industry (1)	In channels of circul-ation (2)	In transport (3)	Others (4)	Total (5)	Census industry (6)	Non-census indus-try (7)	Self pro-cure-ment (8)	Obtained after process-ing (9)	Total (10)	(11)	(12)	(13)	(14)	(15)	
25	1928		a) thousand tonnes	55.3	438.9	3.1	-	497.3	1985.7	-	-	-	1985.7	-	-	-	-	2483.0	25
26	"		b) thousand tonnes of conventional fuel	81.3	645.2	4.6	-	731.1	2919.0	-	-	-	2919.0	-	-	-	-	3650.1	26
27	"		c) thousand rubles	1900	35000	300	-	37200	62600	-	-	-	62600	-	41100	-	80700	221600	27
28	"		d) price per tonne	34.36	79.74	96.78	-	74.80	31.53	-	-	-	31.53	-	-	-	-	89.29	28
29	Kero-sene	1929	a) thousand tonnes	46.1	391.3	3.2	-	440.6	2503.7	-	-	-	2503.7	-	-	-	-	2944.3	29
30	"	"	b) thousand tonnes of conventional fuel	67.8	575.2	4.7	-	647.7	3680.4	-	-	-	3680.4	-	-	-	-	4328.1	30
31	"	"	c) thousand rubles	1400	36400	300	-	38100	71600	-	-	-	71600	-	50100	-	105100	264900	31
32	"	"	d) price per tonne	30.37	93.02	93.75	-	86.47	28.66	-	-	-	28.66	-	-	-	-	89.87	32
33	1930		a) thousand tonnes	49.2	398.8	2.7	-	450.7	3256.4	-	-	-	3256.4	-	-	-	-	3707.1	33
34	"		b) thousand tonnes of conventional fuel	72.3	586.2	4.0	-	662.5	4786.9	-	-	-	4786.9	-	-	-	-	5449.4	34
35	"		c) thousand rubles	1300	36900	200	-	38400	94400	-	-	-	94400	-	73300	-	145000	351100	35
36	"		d) price per tonne	26.42	92.53	74.07	-	85.20	28.99	-	-	-	28.99	-	-	-	-	94.71	36

Appendix A
Table 3. (cont'd)

Num-bers	Des-ignation of prod-uct	Year	Unit of measurement	Consumed in production						Consumed by the population and by institutions				Num-bers
				Census industry	Non-census industry	Transport	In agri-culture	Sent for processing	Total	Agricul-tural population	Non-agri-cultural population	Institut-utions and social organ-isations	Total	
A	B	C	D	16	17	18	19	20	21	22	23	24	25	A
25		1928	a) thousand tonnes	6.0	9.7	13.7[7]	153.6	-	183.0	487.1	605.6	20.3	1113.0	25
26		"	b) thousand tonnes of conventional fuel	8.8	14.3	20.1	225.8	-	269.0	716.0	890.2	29.8	1636.0	26
27		"	c) thousand rubles	500	1500	1200	14800		18000	65100	72100	2000	139200	27
28		"	d) price per tonne	83.33	154.63	87.59	96.35		98.36	133.65	119.06	98.52	123.93	28
29	Kero-	1929	a) thousand tonnes	9.5	7.8	15.4[7]	310.1	-	342.8	454.8	849.9	19.2	1323.9	29
30	sene	"	b) thousand tonnes of conventional fuel	14.0	11.5	22.6	455.8	-	503.9	668.6	1249.4	28.2	1946.2	30
31		"	c) thousand rubles	800	1300	1600	30900		34600	60300	101000	1900	1632 0	31
32		"	d) price per tonne	84.21	166.66	103.90	99.65		100.93	132.59	118.84	98.96	122.33	32
33		1930	a) thousand tonnes	14.0	7.7	21.7[7]	626.1	-	669.5	371.1	1174.2	23.2	1568.5	33
34		"	b) thousand tonnes of conventional fuel	20.6	11.3	31.9	920.4	-	984.2	545.5	1726.1	34.1	2305.7	34
35		"	c) thousand rubles	1100	1300	2000	67700		72100	45900	143500	2300	191700	35
36		"	d) price per tonne	78.57	168.83	92.17	108.13		107.69	123.69	122.21	99.14	121.12	36

Appendix A
Table 3. (cont'd)

Num-bers	Desig-nation of products	Year	Unit of measurement	Losses	Exports	Stocks at end of year					Total output	Num-bers
						In census industry	In channels of circulation	In transport	Others	Total		
A	B	C	D	26	27	28	29	30	31	32	33	A
25		1928	a) thousand tonnes	30.2	716.2	46.1	391.3	3.2	-	440.6	2483.0	25
26		"	b) thousand tonnes of conventional fuel	44.5	1052.9	67.8	575.2	4.7	-	647.7	3650.1	26
27		"	c) thousand rubles	-	26300	1400	36400	300	-	38100	221600	27
28		"	d) price per tonne	-	36.72	30.37	93.02	93.75	-	86.47	89.29	28
29		1929	a) thousand tonnes	39.1	787.8	49.2	398.8	2.7	-	450.7	2944.3	29
30	Kerosene	"	b) thousand tonnes of conventional fuel	57.5	1158.0	72.3	586.2	4.0	-	662.5	4328.1	30
31		"	c) thousand rubles	-	28700	1300	36900	200	-	38400	264900	31
32		"	d) price per tonne	-	36.43	26.42	92.53	74.07	-	85.20	89.87	32
33		1930	a) thousand tonnes	38.8	781.2	150.9	496.8	1.4	-	649.1	3707.1	33
34		"	b) thousand tonnes of conventional fuel	57.0	1148.3	221.8	730.3	2.1	-	954.2	5449.4	34
35		"	c) thousand rubles	-	27700	4100	55400	100	-	59600	351100	35
36		"	d) price per tonne	-	35.46	27.17	111.51	71.43	-	91.82	94.71	36

Appendix A
Table 3. (cont'd)

A Num-bers	B Des-ignat-ion of prod-uct	C Year	D Unit of measurement	Stocks at beginning of year					Production per year										A Num-bers
				1 In census industry	2 In channels of circul-ation	3 In transport	4 Others	5 Total	6 Census industry	7 Non-census indus-try	8 Self pro-cure-ment	9 Obtained after process-ing	10 Total	11 Imports	12 Excises	13 Cust-oms duties	14 Trade and trans-port mark-up	15 Total input	
37		1928	a) thousand tonnes	1068.1	1710.6	379.6	-	3158.3	12600.0	-	-	4735.5	17335.5	-	-	-	-	20493.8	37
38		"	b) thousand tonnes of conventional fuel	1527.4	2446.2	542.8	-	4516.4	18018.0	-	-	6771.8	24789.8	-	-	-	-	29306.2	38
39		"	c) thousand rubles	29266	48005	9890	-	87161	193410	-	-	93763[8]	287173	-	-	-	70380	444714	39
40		"	d) price per tonne	27.40	28.06	26.05	-	27.2	15.35	-	-	19.80	16.05	-	-	-	-	21.70	40
41	1929		a) thousand tonnes	1050.5	1737.9	386.1	-	3174.5	14800.0	-	-	6850.9	21650.9	-	-	-	-	24825.4	41
42	Oil fuel	"	b) thousand tonnes of conventional fuel	1502.2	2485.2	552.1	-	4539.5	21164.0	-	-	9796.8	30960.8	-	-	-	-	35500.3	42
43		"	c) thousand rubles	31410	50225	10922	-	92557	201576	-	-	121261[8]	322837	-	-	-	72673	488067	43
44		"	d) price per tonne	29.90	28.89	28.29	-	29.16	13.62	-	-	17.70	14.91	-	-	-	-	19.66	44
45		1930	a) thousand tonnes	1471.1	1990.1	346.0	-	3807.2	18864.9	-	-	8762.9	27627.8	-	-	-	-	31435.0	45
46		"	b) thousand tonnes of conventional fuel	2103.7	2845.8	494.8	-	5444.3	26976.8	-	-	12530.9	39507.7	-	-	-	-	44952.0	46
47		"	c) thousand rubles	32413	42862	9808	-	85083	228277	-	-	184021[8]	412298	-	-	-	103471	600852	47
48		"	d) price per tonne	22.03	21.54	28.35	-	22.35	12.11	-	-	21.00	14.92	-	-	-	-	19.11	48

Appendix A
Table 3. (cont'd)

Num-bers (A)	Des-ignation of product (B)	Year (C)	Unit of measurement (D)	Consumed in production						Consumed by the population and by institutions				Num-bers (A)
				Census industry	Non-census industry	Transport	In agri-culture	Sent for processing	Total	Agricul-tural population	Non-agri-cultural population	Institutions and social organ-isations	Total	
				16	17	18	19	20	21	22	23	24	25	
37		1928	a) thousand tonnes	3085.5	155.4	2855.0	-	9559.7	15655.6	-	-	233.8	233.8	37
38		"	b) thousand tonnes of conventional fuel	4412.3	222.2	4082.6	-	13670.4	22387.5	-	-	334.3	334.3	38
39		"	c) thousand rubles	106172	5405	84280	-	133836	329693	-	-	4354	4354	39
40		"	d) price per tonne	34.41	34.78	29.52	-	14.00	21.06	-	-	16.70	18.70	40
41	Oil fuel	1929	a) thousand tonnes	3737.6	157.4	3090.5	-	11658.8	18644.3	-	-	319.4	319.4	41
42		"	b) thousand tonnes of conventional fuel	5344.8	225.1	4419.4	-	16672.1	26661.4	-	-	456.7	456.7	42
43		"	c) thousand rubles	134516	5039	90088	-	146901	376544	-	-	5369	5369	43
44		"	d) price per tonne	35.99	32.01	29.15	-	12.60	20.20	-	-	16.81	16.81	44
45		1930	a) thousand tonnes	3857.2	158.9	3448.4	-	16201.8	23666.3	-	-	350.0	350.0	45
46		"	b) thousand tonnes of conventional fuel	5515.8	227.2	4931.2	-	23168.6	33842.8	-	-	500.5	500.5	46
47		"	c) thousand rubles	141027	5085	125671	-	171739	443522	-	-	6628	6628	47
48		"	d) price per tonne	36.56	32.00	36.44	-	10.60	18.74	-	-	18.94	18.94	48

Appendix A
Table 3. (cont'd)

Num- bers A	Desig- nation of products B	Year C	Unit of measurement D	Losses 26	Exports 27	Stocks at end of year		In transport 30	Others 31	Total 32	Total output 33	Num- bers A
						In census industry 28	In channels of circulation 29					
37		1928	a) thousand tonnes	433.7	996.2	1050.5	1737.9	386.1	–	3174.5	20493.8	37
38		"	b) thousand tonnes of conventional fuel	620.3	1424.6	1502.2	2485.2	552.1	–	4539.5	29306.2	38
39		"	c) thousand rubles	–	18110	31410	50225	10922	–	92557	444714	39
40		"	d) price per tonne	–	18.18	29.90	28.90	28.29	–	29.16	21.70	40
41	Oil fuel	1929	a) thousand tonnes	625.1	1429.4	1471.1	1990.1	346.0	–	3807.2	24825.4	41
42		"	b) thousand tonnes of conventional fuel	893.9	2044.0	2103.7	2845.8	494.8	–	5444.3	35500.3	42
43		"	c) thousand rubles	–	21071	32413	42862	9808	–	85083	488067	43
44		"	d) price per tonne	–	14.74	22.03	21.54	28.35	–	22.35	19.66	44
45		1930	a) thousand tonnes	803.8	1741.6	2081.2	2323.4	468.7	–	4873.3	31435.0	45
46		"	b) thousand tonnes of conventional fuel	1149.4	2490.5	2976.1	3322.5	670.2	–	6968.8	44952.0	46
47		"	c) thousand rubles	–	25799	50781	56584	17538	–	124903	600852	47
48		"	d) price per tonne	–	14.83	24.40	24.35	37.42	–	25.63	19.11	48

Appendix A
Table 3. (cont'd)

Numbers (A)	Designation of product (B)	Year (C)	Unit of measurement (D)	Stocks at beginning of year					Production per year					Imports (11)	Excises (12)	Customs duties (13)	Trade and transport mark-up (14)	Total input (15)	Numbers (A)
				In census industry (1)	In channels of circulation (2)	In transport (3)	Others (4)	Total (5)	Census industry (6)	Non-census industry (7)	Self procurement (8)	Obtained after processing (9)	Total (10)						
49		1928	a) thousand tonnes	28.7	54.8	0.3	-	83.8	963.0	-	-	-	963.0	-	-	-	-	1046.8	49
50		"	b) thousand tonnes of conventional fuel	43.0	82.2	0.5	-	125.7	1444.5	-	-	-	1444.5	-	-	-	-	1570.2	50
51		"	c) thousand rubles	2464	12489	77	-	15030	114597	-	-	-	114597	-	13350	-	4298	147275	51
52		"	d) price per tonne	85.9	227.9	256.7	-	180.5	119.0	-	-	-	119.0	-	-	-	-	140.7	52
53	Gaso-line	1929	a) thousand tonnes	24.9	69.8	0.3	-	95.0	1302.3	-	-	-	1302.3	-	-	-	-	1397.3	53
54		"	b) thousand tonnes of conventional fuel	37.3	104.7	0.5	-	142.5	1953.5	-	-	-	1953.5	-	-	-	-	2096.0	54
55		"	c) thousand rubles	3084	15984	77	-	19145	157578	-	-	-	157578	-	17480	-	5295	199498	55
56		"	d) price per tonne	123.8	229.0	256.7	-	201.5	121.0	-	-	-	121.0	-	-	-	-	142.8	56
57		1930	a) thousand tonnes	39.6	88.6	0.2	-	128.4	1961.7	-	-	-	1961.7	-	-	-	-	2090.1	57
58		"	b) thousand tonnes of conventional fuel	59.4	132.9	0.3	-	192.6	2942.6	-	-	-	2942.6	-	-	-	-	3135.2	58
59		"	c) thousand rubles	5188	20378	51	-	25617	235404	-	-	-	235404	-	30700	-	8876	300597	59
60		"	d) price per tonne	131.0	230.0	225.0	-	199.3	120.0	-	-	-	120.0	-	-	-	-	143.8	60

Appendix A
Table 3. (cont'd)

A Numbers	B Designation of product	C Year	D Unit of measurement	Consumed in production						Consumed by the population and by institutions				Numbers
				Census industry 16	Non-census industry 17	Transport and trade 18	In agriculture 19	Sent for processing 20	Total 21	Agricultural population 22	Non-agricultural population 23	Institutions and social organisations 24	Total 25	
49		1928	a) thousand tonnes	10.0	0.7	70.9	3.0	–	84.6	–	13.2	18.3	31.5	49
50		"	b) thousand tonnes of conventional fuel	15.0	1.1	106.4	4.5	–	127.0	–	19.8	27.4	47.2	50
51		"	c) thousand rubles	2280	190	18200	474	–	21144		3986	4603	8589	51
52		"	d) price per tonne	228.8	271.4	256.7	158.0	–	249.93		302.0	251.5	307.9	52
53	Gas-	1929	a) thousand tonnes	17.3	1.0	109.1	10.4	–	137.8	–	9.5	11.3	20.8	53
54	oline	"	b) thousand tonnes of conventional fuel	26.0	1.5	163.6	15.6	–	206.7	–	14.3	16.9	31.2	54
55		"	c) thousand rubles	3944	246	28366	2194	–	34750	–	2869	3474	6343	55
56		"	d) price per tonne	228.0	246.0	260.0	211.0	–	252.2	–	302.0	307.4	305.0	56
57		1930	a) thousand tonnes	23.3	1.6	215.4	159.9	–	400.2	–	6.9	22.6	29.5	57
58		"	b) thousand tonnes of conventional fuel	35.0	2.4	323.1	239.8	–	600.2	–	10.4	33.9	44.3	58
59		"	c) thousand rubles	5381	394	53136	25424	–	84335	–	2341	6820	9161	59
60		"	d) price per tonne	230.9	246.3	246.7	159.0	–	210.7	–	301.0	301.8	301.6	60

Appendix A
Table 3. (cont'd)

Num-bers	Designation of product	Year	Unit of measurement	Losses	Exports	In census industry	Stocks at end of year In channels of circulation	In transport	Others	Total	Total output	Num-bers
A	B	C	D	26	27	28	29	30	31	32	33	A
49		1928	a) thousand tonnes	8.9	826.8	24.9	69.8	0.3	-	95.0	1046.8	49
50		"	b) thousand tonnes of conventional fuel	13.4	1240.2	37.3	104.7	0.4	-	142.4	1570.2	50
51		"	c) thousand rubles	-	98397	3084	15984	77	-	19145	147275	51
52		"	d) price per tonne	-	119.0	123.8	229.0	256.7	-	201.5	140.7	52
53	Gasoline	1929	a) thousand tonnes	12.9	1097.4	39.6	88.6	0.2	-	128.4	1397.3	53
54		"	b) thousand tonnes of conventional fuel	19.4	1646.1	59.4	132.9	0.3	-	192.6	2096.0	54
55		"	c) thousand rubles	-	132788	5188	20378	51	-	25617	199498	55
56		"	d) price per tonne	-	121.0	131.0	230.0	255.0	-	199.5	142.8	56
57		1930	a) thousand tonnes	27.0	1453.6	81.9	97.7	0.2	-	179.8	2090.1	57
58		"	b) thousand tonnes of conventional fuel	40.5	2180.4	122.8	146.6	0.3	-	269.7	3135.2	58
59		"	c) thousand rubles	-	174441	10729	21880	51	-	32660	300597	59
60		"	d) price per tonne	-	120.0	131.0	207.4	255.0	-	175.9	143.8	60

Appendix A
Table 3. (cont'd)

Num-bers A	Des-ignation of prod-uct B	Year C	Unit of measurement D	Stocks at beginning of year — In census industry 1	In channels of circulation 2	In transport 3	Others 4	Total 5	Production per year — Census industry 6	Non-census industry 7	Self procurement 8	Obtained after processing 9	Total 10	Imports 11	Ex-cises 12	Cust-oms duties 13	Trade and transport mark-up 14	Total input 15	Num-bers A
61		1928	a) thousand tonnes	10525	-	5814	30000[9]	46339	60224[10]	9805[11]	154660[12]	-	224689	2	-	-	-	271030	61
62		"	b) thousand tonnes of conventional fuel	1831.4	-	1011.6	5220.0	8063.0	10479.0	1706.1	26910.8	-	39095.9	0.3	-	-	-	47159.2	62
63		"	c) thousand rubles	34732	-	25699	81000[9]	141431	163563[10]	26767	518574	-	708904	19	-	-	123607	973961	63
64		"	d) price per cubic metre	3.30	-	4.42	2.70	3.05	2.73	2.73	3.35	-	3.15	9.50	-	-	-	3.59	64
65	Fire-wood	1929	a) thousand tonnes	11330	-	6918	29358[9]	47586	87603[10]	9190[11]	147260[12]	-	244053	2	-	-	-	291641	65
66		"	b) thousand tonnes of conventional fuel	1971.4	-	1203.7	5104.8	8279.9	15242.9	1599.1	25623.2	-	42465.2	0.3	-	-	-	50745.4	66
67		"	c) thousand rubles	40678	-	30490	80090[9]	151258	265817[10]	27754[11]	508978	-	800549	15	-	-	163635	1115457	67
68		"	d) price per cubic metre	3.59	-	4.41	2.73	3.18	2.70	3.02	3.46	-	3.28	7.50	-	-	-	3.82	68
69		1930	a) thousand tonnes	10700	-	6573	45352[9]	62625	92393[10]	3500[11]	136168[12]	-	232061	-	-	-	-	294686	69
70		"	b) thousand tonnes of conventional fuel	1861.8	-	1143.7	7891.2	10896.7	16076.4	609.0	23693.2	-	40378.6	-	-	-	-	51275.3	70
71		"	c) thousand rubles	40339	-	28970	136963[9]	206272	294128[10]	11200[11]	445066	-	750394	-	-	-	203377	1160043	71
72		"	d) price per cubic metre	3.77	-	4.41	3.02	3.29	3.18	3.20	3.27	-	3.66	-	-	-	-	3.94	72

Appendix A
Table 3. (cont'd)

Numbers (A)	Designation of product (B)	Year (C)	Unit of measurement (D)	Consumed in production						Consumed by the population and by institutions				Numbers (A)
				Census industry (16)	Non-census industry (17)	Transport and trade (18)	In agriculture (19)	Sent for processing (20)	Total (21)	Agricultural population (22)	Non-agricultural population (23)	Institutions and social organisations (24)	Total (25)	
61		1928	a) thousand tonnes	35881.0	11350	8854[13]	11220	–	67305	100980	49583	5556	156119	61
62		"	b) thousand tonnes of conventional fuel	6243.3	1974.9	1540.6	1952.3	–	11711.1	17570.5	8627.4	966.7	27164.6	62
63		"	c) thousand rubles	129200	31703	42199	30743		233845	276685	280640	31392	588717	63
64		"	d) price per cubic metre	3.60	2.79	4.49	2.74		3.47	2.74	5.66	5.65	3.77	64
65	Firewood	1929	a) thousand tonnes	38823	11491	9533[13]	11400		71247	102600	49583	5463	157646	65
66		"	b) thousand tonnes of conventional fuel	6755.2	1999.4	1658.7	1983.6		12396.9	17852.4	8627.4	950.6	27430.4	66
67		"	c) thousand rubles	147527	35782	45251	31692		260252	285228	332797	30556	648581	67
68		"	d) price per cubic metre	3.80	3.11	4.49	2.78		3.65	2.78	6.71	5.59	4.14	68
69		1930	a) thousand tonnes	38047	10674	14101[13]	11420		74242	102780	42266	5447	150493	69
70		"	b) thousand tonnes of conventional fuel	6620.2	1857.3	2453.6	1987.1		12918.2	17883.7	7354.3	947.8	26185.8	70
71		"	c) thousand rubles	137100	37161	67675	31748		273684	285728	335631	29733	651092	71
72		"	d) price per cubic metre	3.60	3.48	4.67	2.78		2.90	2.78	4.94	5.46	2.60	72

Appendix A
Table 3. (cont'd)

Num-bers	Designation of product	Year	Unit of measurement	Losses	Exports	In census industry	In channels of circulation	In transport	Others	Total	Total output	Num-bers
A	B	C	D	26	27	28	29	30	31	32	33	A
61		1928	a) thousand tonnes	–	20	11330	–	6918	29338	47586	271030	61
62		"	b) thousand tonnes of conventional fuel	–	3.6	1971.4	–	1203.7	5104.8	8279.9	47159.2	62
63		"	c) thousand rubles	–	141	40678	–	30490	80090	151258	973961	63
64		"	d) price per cubic metre	–	7.50	3.59	–	4.41	2.73	3.18	3.59	64
65	Firewood	1929	a) thousand tonnes	–	123	10700	–	6573	45352	62625	291641	65
66		"	b) thousand tonnes of conventional fuel	–	21.4	1861.8	–	1143.7	7891.2	10896.7	50745.4	66
67		"	c) thousand rubles	–	352	40339	–	28970	136963[9]	206272	1115457	67
68		"	d) price per cubic metre	–	2.86	3.77	–	441	3.02	3.29	3.82	68
69		1930	a) thousand tonnes	–	133	9104	–	7219	53495	69818	294686	69
70		"	b) thousand tonnes of conventional fuel	–	23.0	1584.1	–	1256.1	9308.1	12148.3	51275.3	70
71		"	c) thousand rubles	–	485	31409	–	32189	171184[9]	234782	1160043	71
72		"	d) price per cubic metre	–	3.64	3.45	–	4.45	3.20	3.36	3.94	72

Stocks at end of year
In

Appendix A

Table 3. (cont'd)

Numbers (A)	Designation of product (B)	Year (C)	Unit of measurement (D)	Stocks at beginning of year					Production per year					Imports	Excises	Customs duties	Trade and transport mark-up	Total input	Numbers (A)
				In census industry	In channels of circulation	In transport	Others	Total	Census industry	Non census industry	Self procurement	Obtained after processing	Total						
				1	2	3	4	5	6	7	8	9	10	11	12	13	14	15	A
73		1928	a) thousand tonnes	3979.2	-	-	-	3979.2	5344.2	-	839.5	-	6183.7	-	-	-	-	10162.9	73
74		"	b) thousand tonnes of conventional fuel	1830.4	-	-	-	1830.4	2458.3	-	386.2	-	2844.5	-	-	-	-	4674.9	74
75		"	c) thousand rubles	4531.0	-	-	-	4531.0	55150	-	2518	-	57668	-	-	-	-	102978	75
76		"	d) price per tonne	11.39	-	-	-	11.39	10.32	-	3.00	-	9.33	-	-	-	-	10.13	76
77	Peat	1929	a) thousand tonnes	5221.1	-	-	-	5221.1	5450.0	-	1000.4	-	6450.4	-	-	-	-	11671.5	77
78		"	b) thousand tonnes of conventional fuel	2401.7	-	-	-	2401.7	2507.0	-	460.2	-	2967.2	-	-	-	-	5368.9	78
79		"	c) thousand rubles	53860	-	-	-	53860	50090	-	3006	-	53096	-	-	-	-	106956	79
80		"	d) price per tonne	10.32	-	-	-	10.32	9.19	-	3.00	-	8.23	-	-	-	-	9.16	80
81		1930	a) thousand tonnes	5708.1	-	-	-	5708.1	6400.0	-	1899.9	-	8299.9	-	-	-	-	14008.0	81
82		"	b) thousand tonnes of conventional fuel	2625.7	-	-	-	2625.7	2944.0	-	874.0	-	3818.0	-	-	-	-	6443.7	82
83		"	c) thousand rubles	54286	-	-	-	54286	61440	-	7086	-	68526	-	-	-	-	122812	83
84		"	d) price per tonne	9.51	-	-	-	9.51	9.60	-	3.73	-	8.26	-	-	-	-	8.77	84

Appendix A
Table 3. (cont'd)

Num-bers (A)	Designation of product (B)	Year (C)	Unit of measurement (D)	Consumed in production						Consumed by the population and by institutions				Num-bers (A)
				Census industry	Non-census industry	Transport and trade	In agri-culture	Sent for processing	Total	Agricultural population	Non-agricultural population	Institutions and social organisations	Total	
A	B	C	D	16	17	18	19	20	21	22	23	24	25	A
73		1928	a) thousand tonnes	4498.4	3.0	-	-	-	4501.4	323.3	-	0.7	324.0	73
74		"	b) thousand tonnes of conventional fuel	2069.3	1.4	-	-	-	2070.7	148.7	-	0.3	149.0	74
75		"	c) thousand rubles	48110	30	-	-	-	48140	970	-	8	978	75
76		"	d) price per tonne	10.69	10.00	-	-	-	10.69	3.00	-	11.43	3.02	76
77	Peat	1929	a) thousand tonnes	5250.6	3.3	-	-	-	5253.9	561.7	-	0.8	562.5	77
78		"	b) thousand tonnes of conventional fuel	2415.3	1.5	-	-	-	2416.8	258.4	-	0.4	258.8	78
79		"	c) thousand rubles	50944	33	-	-	-	50977	1685	-	8	1693	79
80		"	d) price per tonne	9.70	10.00	-	-	-	9.70	3.00	-	10.00	3.01	80
81		1930	a) thousand tonnes	6762.7	3.3	-	-	-	6766.0	1310.0	-	1.0	1311.0	81
82		"	b) thousand tonnes of conventional fuel	3110.8	1.5	-	-	-	3112.3	602.6	-	0.5	603.1	82
83		"	c) thousand rubles	62571	33	-	-	-	62604	4700	-	13	4713	83
84		"	d) price per tonne	9.25	10.00	-	-	-	9.25	3.59	-	13.00	3.59	84

Appendix A
Table 3. (cont'd)

Num-bers (A)	Designation of product (B)	Year (C)	Unit of measurement (D)	Losses (26)	Exports (27)	Stocks at end of year — In census industry (28)	In channels of circulation (29)	In transport (30)	Others (31)	Total (32)	Total output (33)	Num-bers (A)
73		1928	a) thousand tonnes	116.5	-	-	-	-	-	5221.0	10162.9	73
74		"	b) thousand tonnes of conventional fuel	53.5	-	-	-	-	-	2401.7	4674.9	74
75		"	c) thousand rubles	-	-	-	-	-	-	53860	102978	75
76		"	d) price per tonne	-	-	-	-	-	-	10.32	10.13	76
77	Peat	1929	a) thousand tonnes	147.0	-	-	-	-	-	5708.1	11671.5	77
78		"	b) thousand tonnes of conventional fuel	67.6	-	-	-	-	-	2625.7	5368.9	78
79		"	c) thousand rubles	-	-	-	-	-	-	54486	106956	79
80		"	d) price per tonne	-	-	-	-	-	-	9.51	9.16	80
81		1930	a) thousand tonnes	231.0	-	-	-	-	-	5700.0	14008.0	81
82		"	b) thousand tonnes of conventional fuel	106.3	-	-	-	-	-	2622.0	6443.7	82
83		"	c) thousand rubles	-	-	-	-	-	-	55495	122812	83
84		"	d) price per tonne	-	-	-	-	-	-	9.74	8.77	84

Appendix A
Table 3. (cont'd)

Notes

1. Stocks in non-productive sphere.
2. Coal and ordinary anthracite.
3. Including (thousands of tonnes).

	Sorted	Washed	Rubble and slurry
1928	10220.0	9000.0	10300.0
1929	2010.0	2820.0	3320.0
1930	1088.0	1720.0	9980.0

4. Including in commercial enterprises (thousands of tonnes)

1928	382.3
1929	436.9
1930	576.0

5. Ordinary coal was sent for sorting and washing.
6. Including for own needs (thousands of tonnes)

1928	682.0
1929	741.0
1930	930.0

7. Including in trade (thousands of tonnes)

1928	5.1
1929	5.1
1930	7.1

8. Fuel oil and "engine fuel".
9. Stocks of large-scale procurement agencies.
10. Including large-scale procurement agencies (thousands of cubic metres)

1928	59582
1929	83803
1930	90593

11. Small-scale procurement agencies.
12. Self-procurement by agricultural and non-agricultural population, including towns (thousands of rubles)

1928	4660
1929	4660
1930	1968

13. Including in trade (thousands of cubic metres)

1928	2106
1929	2199
1930	2290

Appendix A
Table 4. Building materials balance

Numbers of products	Designation of products	Year	Unit of measurement	Stocks at beginning of year					Production per year				Imports	Trade and transport mark-up	Total input	Numbers
				In industry	In channels of circulation	In transport	In building	Total	Census industry	Non-census industry	Self procurement	Total				
A	B	C	D	1	2	3	4	5	6	7	8	9	10	11	12	A
1		1928	a) thousand tonnes	9.7	58.1	12.2	11.9	91.9	389.5	–	–	389.5	–	–	481.4	1
2		"	b) thousand rubles	2078	14600	2102	3102	21882	80532	–	–	80532	–	19558	121972	2
3	Roofing iron	"	c) price per tonne	224.5	250.0	172.3	260.7	238.1	206.8	–	–	206.8	–	–	253.4	3
4		1929	a) thousand tonnes	14.2	71.5	12.2	15.5	113.4	390.5	–	–	390.5	–	–	503.9	4
5		"	b) thousand rubles	3036	18000	2045	3944	27025	79507	–	–	79507	–	18358	124890	5
6		"	c) price per tonne	213.8	250.2	167.6	254.5	238.3	205.0	–	–	205.0	–	–	247.8	6
7		1930	a) thousand tonnes	17.1	50.8	10.9	21.0	99.8	320.6	–	–	320.6	–	–	420.4	7
8		"	b) thousand rubles	3889	12500	1826	4964	23179	65275	–	–	65275	–	12313	100767	8
9		"	c) price per tonne	227.4	246.7	167.5	236.1	232.2	203.6	–	–	203.6	–	–	239.7	9
10		1928	a) thousand tonnes	52.9	–	35.1	90.1	178.1	1907.1	–	–	1907.1	1.3	–	2086.5	10
11		"	b) thousand rubles	1630	–	1090	4480	7200	69159	–	–	69159	34	12899	89292	11
12	Cement	"	c) price per tonne	30.8	–	31.1	49.7	42.8	36.3	–	–	36.3	26.2	–	42.8	12
13		1929	a) thousand tonnes	62.8	–	36.4	103.3	202.5	2368.3	–	–	2368.3	1.1	–	2571.9	13
14		"	b) thousand rubles	1874	–	1059	4080	7013	78719	–	–	78719	36	17045	102813	14
15		"	c) price per tonne	29.8	–	29.1	39.5	34.6	33.2	–	–	33.2	32.7	–	40.0	15
16		1930	a) thousand tonnes	91.7	–	29.9	149.3	270.9	3170.0	–	–	3170.0	1.4	–	3442.3	16
17		"	b) thousand rubles	2652	–	870	6542	10064	106354	–	–	106354	46	23814	140278	17
18		"	c) price per tonne	28.9	–	29.1	43.8	37.2	33.5	–	–	33.5	32.5	–	40.8	18

Appendix A
Table 4. (cont'd)

Num-bers (A)	Designation of products (B)	Years (C)	Unit of measurement (D)	Consumed in production			In building		Transport				Num-bers
				Census industry (13)	Non-census industry (14)	Transport and trade (15)	Industrial (16)	Agricultural (17)	Transport (18)	Other (19)	Total (20)	TOTAL (21)	(A)
1		1928	a) thousand tonnes	80.9	12.8	22.4	58.6	91.1	–	102.2	251.9	368.0	1
2		"	b) thousand rubles	17496	4390	3915	13237	26117	–	29792	69146	94947	2
3		"	c) price per tonne	217.9	343.0	174.8	228.0	286.7	–	291.5	274.5	258.0	3
4	Roofing iron	1929	a) thousand tonnes	100.0	10.3	29.4	70.7	86.5	–	107.2	264.4	404.1	4
5		"	b) thousand rubles	21300	4000	4927	16042	24000	–	30842	71484	101711	5
6		"	c) price per tonne	213.1	400.0	167.6	226.0	284.6	–	288.1	270.4	251.7	6
7		1930	a) thousand tonnes	75.0	10.4	34.3	102.9	34.9	–	87.5	225.3	345.0	7
8		"	b) thousand rubles	16100	4931	5748	20382	11035	–	24864	56281	83060	8
9		"	c) price per tonne	215.2	474.7	167.6	222.0	316.7	–	284.2	249.8	240.8	9
10		1928	a) thousand tonnes	52.6	2.7	30.3	880.0	91.0	186.5	570.6	1728.1	1813.7	10
11		"	b) thousand rubles	2158	170	1006	39830	4277	5819	27673	77599	80933	11
12		"	c) price per tonne	41.0	63.0	33.2	45.3	47.0	31.2	48.5	44.9	44.6	12
13	Cement	1929	a) thousand tonnes	45.6	2.7	42.5	1163.7	81.9	273.7	612.4	2131.7	2222.5	13
14		"	b) thousand rubles	1788	170	1228	46938	3441	7991	29702	88072	91258	14
15		"	c) price per tonne	37.0	63.0	28.9	40.3	42.0	29.2	48.5	41.3	41.1	15
16		1930	a) thousand tonnes	54.8	2.7	96.0	1643.8	68.5	342.5	743.2	2798.0	2951.5	16
17		"	b) thousand rubles	2114	170	2765	68301	2875	10000	36492	117668	122717	17
18		"	c) price per tonne	38.6	63.0	28.8	41.6	42.0	29.2	49.1	42.2	41.6	18

Appendix A
Table 4. (cont'd)

Numbers of products (A)	Designation of products (B)	Years (C)	Unit of measurement (D)	Losses (22)	Exports (23)	Stocks at end of year					Total output (29)	Numbers (A)
						In industry (24)	In channels of circulation (25)	In transport (26)	In building (27)	Total (28)		
1	Roofing iron	1928	a) thousand tonnes	-	-	14.2	71.5	12.2	15.5	113.4	481.4	1
2		"	b) thousand rubles	-	-	5036	18000	2045	3944	72025	121972	2
3		"	c) price per tonne	-	-	213.8	251.7	167.5	254.5	238.3	253.4	3
4		1929	a) thousand tonnes		-	17.1	50.8	10.9	21.0	99.8	503.9	4
5		"	b) thousand rubles		-	3889	12500	1826	4964	23179	124890	5
6		"	c) price per tonne		-	227.4	246.1	167.5	236.4	232.3	247.8	6
7		1930	a) thousand tonnes			19.8	36.1	1.5	18.0	75.4	420.4	7
8		"	b) thousand rubles			4492	8747	251	4217	17707	100767	8
9		"	c) price per tonne			226.9	242.4	167.5	234.3	234.8	239.7	9
10		1928	a) thousand tonnes	-	70.3	62.8	-	36.4	103.3	202.5	2086.5	10
11		"	b) thousand rubles	-	1346	1874	-	1059	4080	7013	89292	11
12		"	c) price per tonne	-	19.1	29.8	-	29.1	39.5	34.6	42.8	12
13	Cement	1929	a) thousand tonnes	-	78.5	91.7	-	29.9	149.3	270.9	2571.9	13
14		"	b) thousand rubles	-	1491	2652	-	870	6542	10064	102813	14
15		"	c) price per tonne	-	20.0	28.9	-	29.1	43.8	37.2	40.0	15
16		1930	a) thousand tonnes	-	71.0	118.9	-	24.5	276.4	419.8	3442.3	16
17		"	b) thousand rubles	-	1350	3414	-	688	12109	16211	140278	17
18		"	c) price per tonne	-	19.0	28.7	-	28.1	43.8	38.6	40.8	18

Appendix A
Table 4. (cont'd)

Num-bers (A)	Designation of products (B)	Year (C)	Unit of measurement (D)	Stocks at beginning of year — In industry (1)	In channels of circulation (2)	In transport (3)	In building (4)	Total (5)	Production per year — Census industry (6)	Non-census industry (7)	Self procurement (8)	Total (9)	Imports (10)	Trade and transport mark-up (11)	Total input (12)	Num-bers (A)
19		1928	a) million units	403.3	-	66.5	128.0	597.8	2048.6	714.9	655.0	3418.5	-	-	4016.3	19
20		"	b) thousand rubles	14118	-	2453	6304	22875	70006	26450	22462	118918	-	20931	162724	20
21		"	c) price per unit	35.0	-	36.9	39.3	38.3	34.2	37.0	34.5	34.8	-	-	40.5	21
22	Bricks (for building)	1929	a) million units	399.0	-	66.8	145.5	611.3	2361.0	918.9	1090.1	4370.0	-	-	4981.3	22
23		"	b) thousand rubles	13066	-	2144	6645	21855	75663	31976	35124	142763	-	30237	194855	23
24		"	c) price per unit	32.7	-	32.1	45.7	35.8	32.0	33.8	32.2	32.7	-	-	39.1	24
25		1930	a) million units	496.0	-	41.4	186.7	724.1	3349.4	1126.7	1172.5	5648.6	-	-	6372.7	25
26		"	b) thousand rubles	15102	-	1329	8805	25236	93838	39322	37778	170938	-	56119	252293	26
27		"	c) price per unit	30.4	-	32.1	47.2	34.9	28.0	34.9	32.2	30.3	-	-	39.6	27
28	Window glass	1928	a) thousand square metres	1207	8473	421	2341	12442	34242	-	-	34242	145	-	46829	28
29		"	b) thousand rubles	1611	11100	724	3184	16619	45884	-	-	45884	143	8340	70986	29
30		"	c) price per square metre	1.33	1.31	1.72	1.36	1.34	1.34	-	-	1.34	0.99	-	1.5	30
31		1929	a) thousand square metres	1891	9753	383	2644	14671	40320	-	-	40320	284	-	55275	31
32		"	b) thousand rubles	2524	13756	663	3596	20539	53667	-	-	53667	294	9003	83503	32
33		"	c) price per square metre	1.33	1.41	1.73	1.36	1.40	1.33	-	-	1.33	1.04	-	1.51	33
34		1930	a) thousand square metres	3222	9698	310	3757	16987	43094	-	-	43094	14	-	60095	34
35		"	b) thousand rubles	4301	13674	533	5147	23655	57370	-	-	57370	18	7015	88058	35
36		"	c) price per square metre	1.53	1.41	1.72	1.37	1.39	1.33	-	-	1.33	1.28	-	1.47	36

Appendix A
Table 4. (cont'd)

Num-bers	Designation of products	Years	Unit of measurement	Consumed in production Census industry	Non-census industry	Transport and trade	In building Industrial	Agricultural	Transport	Other	Total	TOTAL	Num-bers
A	B	C	D	13	14	15	16	17	18	19	20	21	A
19		1928	a) million units	77.8	2.7	69.0	675.5	459.9	215.5	1904.6	3255.5	3405.0	19
20		"	b) thousand rubles	3651	99	2916	29248	15591	8038	81326	134203	140869	20
21		"	c) price per unit	46.9	36.7	42.3	43.3	33.9	37.3	42.7	41.2	41.4	21
22	Bricks (for building)	1929	a) million units	125.3	3.5	81.3	926.1	462.6	305.1	2353.3	4047.1	4257.2	22
23		"	b) thousand rubles	4399	121	2800	42509	14895	9824	95071	162299	169619	23
24		"	c) price per unit	35.1	34.6	34.4	45.9	32.2	40.4	40.4	40.1	39.8	24
25		1930	a) million units	139.3	3.0	87.8	1648.1	330.2	543.7	2646.9	5168.9	5399	25
26		"	b) thousand rubles	4889	106	2995	75648	10344	17453	105613	209058	217048	26
27		"	c) price per unit	35.1	35.3	34.1	45.9	31.3	32.1	39.9	40.4	40.2	27
28		1928	a) thousand square metres	1160	91	220	4748	11960	713	11376	28797	30268	28
29		"	b) thousand rubles	3120	272	378	6505	21866	1241	16834	46446	50216	29
30		"	c) price per square metre	2.69	2.98	1.72	1.37	1.83	1.74	1.48	1.61	1.66	30
31	Window glass	1929	a) thousand square metres	1164	77	273	6866	14136	888	12321	34211	35725	31
32		"	b) thousand rubles	3181	228	457	9269	26828	1563	18012	55672	59518	32
33		"	c) price per square metre	2.73	2.96	1.60	1.35	1.90	1.76	1.46	1.63	1.67	33
34		1930	a) thousand square metres	1346	76	221	11225	9383	1442	12547	34597	36240	34
35		"	b) thousand rubles	3680	224	413	15135	18395	2451	18552	54533	58850	35
36		"	c) price per square metre	2.73	2.95	1.87	1.35	1.96	1.70	1.48	1.58	1.62	36

Appendix A
Table 4. (cont'd)

Num-bers	Designation of products	Years	Unit of measurement	Losses	Exports	Stocks at end of year					Total output	Num-bers
						In industry	In channels of circulation	In transport	In building	Total		
A	B	C	D	22	23	24	25	26	27	28	29	A
19	Bricks (for building)	1928	a) million units	-	-	399.0	-	66.8	145.5	611.3	4016.3	19
20		"	b) thousand rubles	-	-	13066	-	2144	6645	21855	162724	20
21		"	c) price per unit	-	-	32.7	-	32.1	45.7	35.8	40.5	21
22		1929	a) million units	-	-	496.0	-	41.4	186.7	724.1	4981.3	22
23		"	b) thousand rubles	-	-	15102	-	1329	8805	25236	194855	23
24		"	c) price per unit	-	-	30.4	-	32.1	47.2	34.9	39.1	24
25		1930	a) million units	-	-	574.1	-	80.8	318.8	973.7	6372.7	25
26		"	b) thousand rubles	-	-	17998	-	2647	14600	35245	252293	26
27		"	c) price per unit	-	-	31.3	-	32.8	45.8	36.2	39.6	27
28	Window glass	1928	a) thousand square metres	1712	178	1891	9753	383	2644	14671	46829	28
29		"	b) thousand rubles	-	231	2524	13756	663	3596	20539	70986	29
30		"	c) price per square metre	-	1.30	1.33	1.41	1.73	1.36	1.40	1.52	30
31		1929	a) thousand square metres	2303	260	3222	9698	310	3757	16987	55275	31
32		"	b) thousand rubles	-	330	4301	13674	533	5147	23655	83503	32
33		"	c) price per square metre	-	1.27	1.33	1.41	1.72	1.37	1.39	1.51	33
34		1930	a) thousand square metres	2638	957	3586	10053	209	6412	20260	60095	34
35		"	b) thousand rubles	-	1215	4780	14475	382	9856	27993	88058	35
36		"	c) price per square metre	-	1.27	1.33	1.41	1.83	1.35	1.38	1.47	36

Appendix A
Table 4. (cont'd)

Num-bers (A)	Designation of products (B)	Year (C)	Unit of measurement (D)	Stocks at beginning of year — In industry (1)	In channels of circulation (2)	In transport (3)	In building (4)	Total (5)	Production per year — Census industry (6)	Non-census industry (7)	Self procurement (8)	Total (9)	Imports (10)	Trade and transport mark-up (11)	Total input (12)	Num-bers (A)
37		1928	a) thousand cubic metres	1091	–	1284	873	3248	13771	1161	11100	26032	2	–	29282	37
38		"	b) thousand rubles	26511	–	37673	25605	89789	356807	20492	238814	616113	315	79569	785786	38
39		"	c) price per cubic metre	24.3	–	28.3	29.3	27.6	25.9	17.7	21.5	23.7	157.5	–	26.8	39
40		1929	a) thousand cubic metres	1419	–	1502	798	3719	16783	1272	10782	28837	2	–	32558	40
41	Sawn timber	"	b) thousand rubles	34907	–	42296	21450	98653	414204	24829	231191	670224	184	86578	855639	41
42		"	c) price per cubic metre	24.6	–	28.2	26.9	26.5	24.7	19.5	21.4	23.3	92.0	–	26.3	42
43		1930	a) thousand cubic metres	1992	–	1459	858	4309	22365	1310	9197	32872	2	–	37183	43
44		"	b) thousand rubles	47290	–	40414	24350	112054	530945	21641	185842	738428	164	131714	982360	44
45		"	c) price per cubic metre	23.7	–	27.7	28.4	26.0	23.7	16.5	20.2	22.5	82.0	–	26.4	45
46		1928	a) thousand cubic metres	13148	–	1140	1685	15973	45400	5432	37600	88432	39	–	104444	46
47	Rough timber	"	b) thousand rubles	111575	–	20896	19640	152111	325972	39002	301552	666526	403	221686	1040720	47
48		"	c) price per cubic metre	8.49	–	18.33	11.66	9.59	7.18	7.18	8.02	7.54	10.33	–	9.90	48
49		1929	a) thousand cubic metres	16699	–	1174	1731	19604	85086	2300	32100	119486	3	–	13903.6	49
50		"	b) thousand rubles	148562	–	19113	24096	191771	631338	17066	258084	906488	16	265552	1361827	50
51		"	c) price per cubic metre	8.90	–	16.28	13.92	9.78	7.42	7.42	8.04	7.57	5.33	–	9.79	51
52		1930	a) thousand cubic metres	40835	–	679	1635	43149	112254	1759	24700	138713	2	–	181867	52
53		"	b) thousand rubles	342472	–	11020	19849	373341	812719	12735	199082	1024536	11	281963	1679857	53
54		"	c) price per cubic metre	8.39	–	16.23	12.14	8.65	7.24	7.24	8.06	7.39	5.50	–	9.24	54

Appendix A
Table 4. (cont'd)

Num-bers A	Designation of products B	Years C	Unit of measurement D	Consumed in production			In building					TOTAL	Num-bers
				Census industry 13	Non-census industry 14	Transport and trade 15	Industrial 16	Agricultural 17	Transport 18	Other 19	Total 20	21	A
37		1928	a) thousand cubic metres	3151	1054	1308	4177	5532	2241	4837	16787	22300	37
38		"	b) thousand rubles	83596	27762	36119	121968	120044	63331	148496	453839	601316	38
39		"	c) price per cubic metre	26.5	26.3	27.6	29.2	21.7	28.3	30.7	26.0	27.0	39
40	Sawn timber	1929	a) thousand cubic metres	4491	885	1112	5287	5099	3028	4336	17750	24238	40
41		"	b) thousand rubles	110793	27798	28377	145551	110645	78304	130210	464710	631678	41
42		"	c) price per cubic metre	24.7	31.4	25.3	27.5	20.7	25.9	30.1	26.2	26.1	42
43		1930	a) thousand cubic metres	5515	973	615	9737	3429	2775	4158	20099	27202	43
44		"	b) thousand rubles	130926	30562	15443	268060	70974	71401	124407	534842	711773	44
45		"	c) price per cubic metre	23.7	31.4	25.1	27.5	20.6	25.7	29.5	26.6	29.8	45
46		1928	a) thousand cubic metres	26580	3463	423	6694	38106	1710	5787	52297	82763	46
47		"	b) thousand rubles	271116	25407	8473	87758	294559	34251	94097	510665	815661	47
48		"	c) price per cubic metre	10.20	7.34	20.03	13.11	7.73	20.03	16.26	9.76	9.86	48
49	Rough timber	1929	a) thousand cubic metres	37195	3300	479	9400	33187	2237	6566	51390	92364	49
50		"	b) thousand rubles	377157	25968	7793	123140	256536	36396	110374	526446	937364	50
51		"	c) price per cubic metre	10.14	7.87	16.27	13.10	7.73	16.27	16.81	10.24	10.15	51
52		1930	a) thousand cubic metres	54046	3105	560	15763	28552	2242	6500	53057	110768	52
53		"	b) thousand rubles	491278	28565	9061	187580	219565	36275	110500	553920	1082824	53
54		"	c) price per cubic metre	9.11	9.20	16.18	11.90	7.69	16.18	17.00	10.44	9.78	54

Appendix A
Table 4. (cont'd)

Num-bers	Designation of products	Years	Unit of measurement	Losses	Exports	Stocks at end of year		In transport	In building	Total	Total output	Num-bers
						In industry	In channels of circulation					
A	B	C	D	22	23	24	25	26	27	28	29	A
37		1928	a) thousand cubic metres	-	3263	1419	-	1502	798	3719	29282	37
38		"	b) thousand rubles	23200	62617	34907	-	42296	21450	98653	785786	38
39		"	c) price per cubic metre	-	19.2	23.6	-	28.2	26.9	26.5	26.8	39
40	Sawn timber	1929	a) thousand cubic metres	-	4011	1992	-	1459	858	4309	32558	40
41		"	b) thousand rubles	29481	82426	47290	-	40414	24350	112054	855639	41
42		"	c) price per cubic metre	-	20.6	23.7	-	27.7	28.4	26.0	26.3	42
43		1930	a) thousand cubic metres	-	4100	2492	636	1032	1721	5881	37183	43
44		"	b) thousand rubles	34356	84253	57914	13072	33684	47328	151998	982360	44
45		"	c) price per cubic metre	-	20.6	23.2	20.6	32.6	27.5	25.9	26.4	45
46		1928	a) thousand cubic metres	-	2077	16699	-	1174	1731	19604	104444	46
47		"	b) thousand rubles	-	33234	148562	-	19113	24096	191771	1040726	47
48		"	c) price per cubic metre	-	16.03	8.90	-	16.28	13.92	7.78	9.96	48
49	Rough timber	1929	a) thousand cubic metres	-	3580	40835	-	679	1635	43149	139093	49
50		"	b) thousand rubles	-	51122	342472	-	11020	19849	373341	1361827	50
51		"	c) price per cubic metre	-	14.28	8.37	-	16.23	12.14	8.65	9.79	51
52		1930	a) thousand cubic metres	-	4575	63203	-	557	2761	66521	181864	52
53		"	b) thousand rubles	-	57005	498070	-	9096	32856	540022	1679851	53
54		"	c) price per cubic metre	-	12.46	7.88	-	16.33	11.90	8.12	9.24	54

Appendix A

Table 5. Balance of ores, pig-iron and textile raw material

Num-bers	Desig-nation of products	Years	Unit of measurement	Stocks at beginning of year			Production per year					Imports	Cus-toms duties	Trade and trans-port mark-up	Total input	Num-bers
A	B	C	D	In industry	In channels of circul-lation	Other	Total	Census industry	Non-census industry	Obtained after pro-cessing	Total					A
				1	2	3	4	5	6	7	8	9	10	11	12	A
1	Ores and pig-iron	1928	a) thousand tonnes	234.5	2.7	-	237.4	1396.5	-	828.8	2225.3	-	-	-	2462.5	1
2		"	b) thousand rubles	1209	13	-	1222	6284	-	9564	15848	-	-	9159	26229	2
3		"	c) price per tonne	5.16	5.00	-	5.15	4.50	-	11.54	7.12	-	-	-	10.66	3
4	Manganese ore	1929	a) thousand tonnes	270.6	2.1	-	272.7	2690.2	-	1312.6	4002.8	-	-	-	4275.5	4
5		"	b) thousand rubles	2162	10	-	2172	12806	-	16050	28856	-	-	7659	38687	5
6		"	c) price per tonne	7.99	4.95	-	7.97	4.76	-	12.23	7.20	-	-	-	9.05	6
7		1930	a) thousand tonnes	301.5	3.8	-	305.3	2721.0	-	1376.0	4097.0	-	-	-	4402.3	7
8		"	b) thousand rubles	2410	19.0	-	2429	12217	-	16911	29128	-	-	2882	34439	8
9		"	c) price per tonne	7.99	5.00	-	7.96	4.49	-	12.29	7.11	-	-	-	7.94	9
10	Iron ore	1928	a) thousand tonnes	2387.0	21.0	-	2408.0	6331.7	-	452.5	6784.2	-	-	-	9192.2	10
11		"	b) thousand rubles	10974	97	-	11071	35901	-	3158	39059	-	-	18919	69049	11
12		"	c) price per tonne	4.60	4.60	-	4.60	5.67	-	6.98	5.76	-	-	-	7.55	12
13		1929	a) thousand tonnes	2230.7	19.7	-	2250.4	8076.0	-	468.5	8544.5	-	-	-	10794.9	13
14		"	b) thousand rubles	9593	90	-	9683	43126	-	3270	46396	-	-	26075	82154	14
15		"	c) price per tonne	4.30	4.59	-	4.30	5.34	-	6.98	5.43	-	-	-	7.65	15
16		1930	a) thousand tonnes	2012.9	24.5	-	2037.4	10991.0	-	672.7	11663.7	-	-	-	13701.1	16
17		"	b) thousand rubles	8656	100	-	8756	56100	-	4700	60800	-	-	29405	98961	17
18		"	c) price per tonne	4.30	4.09	-	4.30	5.10	-	6.99	5.21	-	-	-	7.24	18

Appendix A
Table 5. (cont'd)

Numbers	Designation of products	Years	Unit of measurement	Consumed in production — In census industry	In non-census industry	Sent for processing	Other	Total	Losses	Exports	Stocks at end of year — In industry	In circulation	Other	Total	Total output	Numbers
A	B	C	D	13	14	15	16	17	18	19	20	21	22	23	24	A
1	Ores and pig-iron	1928	a) thousand tonnes	268.8	–	1379.8	–	1648.6	26.4	514.8	270.6	2.1	–	272.7	2462.5	1
2		"	b) thousand rubles	4067	–	6209.0	–	10276	–	13781	2162	10	–	2172	26229	2
3		"	c) price per tonne	15.13	–	4.50	–	6.23	–	26.77	7.99	4.95	–	7.97	10.66	3
4	Manganese ore	1929	a) thousand tonnes	262.3	–	2616.8	–	2879.1	54.0	1037.1	301.5	3.8	–	305.3	4275.5	4
5		"	b) thousand rubles	3990	–	11828	–	15818	–	20440	2410	19	–	2429	38687	5
6		"	c) price per tonne	15.21	–	4.52	–	5.49	–	9.71	7.99	5.00	–	7.96	9.05	6
7		1930	a) thousand tonnes	350.0	–	2761.0	–	3111.0	60.9	754.2	472.6	3.6	–	476.2	4402.3	7
8		"	b) thousand rubles	5296	–	12452	–	17748	–	12896	3777	18	–	3795	34439	8
9		"	c) price per tonne	15.13	–	4.51	–	5.70	–	17.10	7.97	5.00	–	7.95	7.94	9
10		1928	a) thousand tonnes	5851.1	–	549.0	–	6400.1	62.0	479.7	2230.7	19.7	–	2250.4	9192.2	10
11		"	b) thousand rubles	52660	–	1570	–	54230	–	5136	9593	90	–	9683	69049	11
12		"	c) price per tonne	9.00	–	2.86	–	8.47	–	10.71	4.30	4.59	–	4.30	7.55	12
13	Iron ore	1929	a) thousand tonnes	7519.9	–	615.6	–	8135.5	76.8	545.2	2012.9	24.5	–	2037.4	10794.9	13
14		"	b) thousand rubles	66401	–	1514	–	67915	–	5483	8656	100	–	8756	82154	14
15		"	c) price per tonne	8.83	–	2.46	–	8.35	–	10.6	4.30	4.09	–	4.30	7.65	15
16		1930	a) thousand tonnes	8970.0	–	890.0	–	9860.0	90.0	466.6	3256.0	28.5	–	3284.5	13701.1	16
17		"	b) thousand rubles	77430	–	2200	–	79630	–	4114	15100	117	–	15217	98961	17
18		"	c) price per tonne	8.63	–	2.47	–	8.08	–	8.82	4.61	4.11	–	4.60	7.24	18

Appendix A
Table 5. (cont'd)

Num-bers (A)	Desig-nation of products (B)	Years (C)	Unit of measurement (D)	Stocks at beginning of year — In industry (1)	In circul-lation (2)	Other (3)	Total (4)	Production per year — Census industry (5)	Non-census industry (6)	Obtained after pro-cessing (7)	Total (8)	Imports (9)	Cust-oms duties (10)	Trade and trans-port mark-up (11)	Total input (12)	Num-bers (A)
19		1928	a) thousand tonnes	376.6	-	13.0	389.6	3375.0	-	-	3375.0	0.6	-	-	3765.2	19
20		"	b) thousand rubles	24405	-	803	25208	209209	-	-	209209	167	-	8099	242683	20
21		"	c) price per tonne	64.8	-	61.8	64.7	62.0	-	-	62.0	278.3	-	-	64.5	21
22	Pig-iron	1929	a) thousand tonnes	322.5	-	11.8	334.3	4346.8	-	-	4346.8	0.4	-	-	4681.5	22
23		"	b) thousand rubles	20889	-	700	21589	258271	-	-	258271	33	-	9025	288918	23
24		"	c) price per tonne	64.8	-	59.3	64.6	59.4	-	-	59.4	82.5	-	-	61.7	24
25		1930	a) thousand tonnes	346.1	-	7.9	354.0	5017.0	-	-	5017.0	0.1	-	-	5371.1	25
26		"	b) thousand rubles	23217	-	409	23626	298010	-	-	298010	9	-	11417	333062	26
27		"	c) price per tonne	67.1	-	51.8	66.7	59.4	-	-	59.4	90.0	-	-	62.1	27
28	Textile raw material	1928	a) thousand tonnes	102.2	-	-	102.2	478.6	3.2	-	481.8	-	-	-	584.0	28
29		"	b) thousand rubles	5948	-	-	5948	20053	134	-	20187	-	-	3094	29229	29
30		"	c) price per tonne	58.18	-	-	58.18	41.90	41.88	-	41.90	-	-	-	50.05	30
31	Cotton seed	1929	a) thousand tonnes	130.8	-	-	130.8	507.8	2.0	-	509.8	-	-	-	640.6	31
32		"	b) thousand rubles	7613	-	-	7613	20007	84	-	20091	-	-	3628	31332	32
33		"	c) price per tonne	58.20	-	-	58.20	39.40	42.00	-	39.41	-	-	-	48.91	33
34		1930	a) thousand tonnes	142.3	-	-	142.3	512.2	1.9	-	514.1	-	-	-	656.4	34
35		"	b) thousand rubles	8268	-	-	8268	20181	80	-	20261	-	-	3426	31955	35
36		"	c) price per tonne	58.10	-	-	58.10	39.40	41.10	-	39.41	-	-	-	48.68	36

Appendix A
Table 5. (cont'd)

350 — *Materialy*

| Num-bers A | Desig-nation of products B | Years C | Unit of measurement D | Consumed in production | | | | | Losses | Exports | Stocks at end of year | | | | Total output | Num-bers |
				In census industry 13	In non-census industry 14	Sent for pro-cessing 15	Other 16	Total 17	18	19	In industry 20	In circul-lation 21	Other 22	Total 23	24	A
19		1928	a) thousand tonnes	3399.0	4.6	-	25.2	3428.8	-	2.1	322.5	-	11.8	334.3	3765.2	19
20		"	b) thousand rubles	219003	307	-	1586	220896	-	198	20889	-	700	21589	242683	20
21		"	c) price per tonne	64.43	66.7	-	62.9	64.4	-	94.3	64.8	-	59.3	64.6	64.5	21
22	Pig-iron	1929	a) thousand tonnes	4288.8	5.7	-	32.7	4327.2	-	0.3	346.1	-	7.9	354.0	4681.5	22
23		"	b) thousand rubles	262972	360	-	1941	265273	-	19	23217	-	409	23626	288918	23
24		"	c) price per tonne	61.32	63.2	-	59.4	61.3	-	63.3	67.1	-	51.8	66.7	61.7	24
25		1930	a) thousand tonnes	4955.4	6.2	-	47.7	5009.3	-	2.1	359.1	-	0.6	359.7	5371.1	25
26		"	b) thousand rubles	302775	393	-	2851	305999	-	95	26932	-	36	26968	333062	26
27		"	c) price per tonne	61.10	64.4	-	59.4	61.2	-	45.2	75.0	-	60.0	75.0	62.1	27
28	Textile raw material	1928	a) thousand tonnes	385.3	7.7	-	60.2	453.2	-	-	130.8	-	-	130.8	584.0	28
29		"	b) thousand rubles	18571	390	-	2649	21610	-	-	7619	-	-	7619	29229	29
30		"	c) price per tonne	48.20	50.65	-	46.00	47.68	-	-	58.25	-	-	58.25	50.05	30
31	Cotton seed	1929	a) thousand tonnes	422.6	8.6	-	67.1	498.6	-	-	142.3	-	-	142.3	640.6	31
32		"	b) thousand rubles	19862	424	-	2778	23064	-	-	8268	-	-	8268	31332	32
33		"	c) price per tonne	47.00	49.30	-	42.40	46.29	-	-	58.10	-	-	58.10	48.91	33
34		1930	a) thousand tonnes	399.2	5.8	-	101.8	506.8	-	-	149.6	-	-	149.6	656.4	34
35		"	b) thousand rubles	18762	286	-	4215	23263	-	-	8692	-	-	8692	31955	35
36		"	c) price per tonne	48.00	49.31	-	42.40	47.90	-	-	58.10	-	-	58.10	48.68	36

Appendix A
Table 5. (cont'd)

Num-bers	Desig-nation of products	Years	Unit of measurement	Stocks at beginning of year — In industry (1)	In channels of circulation (2)	Other (3)	Production per year — Total (4)	Census industry (5)	Non-census industry (6)	Obtained after processing (7)	Total (8)	Imports (9)	Customs duties (10)	Trade and transport mark-up (11)	Total input (12)	Num-bers
37	Ginned cotton	1928	a) thousand tonnes	50920	-	-		255500	1731	-	257231	144165	-	-	452316	37
38		"	b) thousand rubles	59500	-	-		242725	1766	-	244491	160611	20	75339	539961	38
39		"	c) price per tonne	1168	-	-		950	1020	-	954	1114	-	-	1194	39
40		1929	a) thousand tonnes	75185	-	-		282500	1054	-	283554	115031	-	-	473770	40
41		"	b) thousand rubles	88841	-	-		290975	1075	-	292050	117269	16	81424	579600	41
42		"	c) price per tonne	1182	-	-		1030	1075	-	1030	1019	-	-	1223	42
43		1930	a) thousand tonnes	74258	-	-		278000	1032	-	279032	57876	-	-	411166	43
44		"	b) thousand rubles	87960	-	-		286340	1054	-	287394	55992	8	72439	503793	44
45		"	c) price per tonne	1184	-	-		1030	1021	-	1130	967	-	-	1225	45
46	Cotton yarn	1928	a) thousand tonnes	15.6	-	-	15.6	339.4	1.6	-	341.0	-	-	-	356.6	46
47		"	b) thousand rubles	39706	-	-	39706	785949	4450	-	790399	-	-	73116	903221	47
48		"	c) price per tonne	2545.3	-	-	2545.3	2315.7	2781.3	-	2317.9	-	-	-	2532.9	48
49		1929	a) thousand tonnes	12.4	-	-	12.4	365.9	1.0	-	366.9	-	-	-	379.3	49
50		"	b) thousand rubles	31533	-	-	31533	825470	3820	-	829290	-	-	75893	936716	50
51		"	c) price per tonne	2543.0	-	-	2543.0	2256.0	3820.0	-	2260.3	-	-	-	2469.6	51
52		1930	a) thousand tonnes	12.3	-	-	12.3	290.6	1.0	-	291.6	-	-	-	303.9	52
53		"	b) thousand rubles	32616	-	-	32616	604448	3820	-	608268	-	-	51858	692742	53
54		"	c) price per tonne	2651.7	-	-	2651.7	2080.0	3820.0	-	2086.0	-	-	-	2279.9	54

Appendix A
Table 5. (cont'd)

Numbers (A)	Designation of products (B)	Years (C)	Unit of measurement (D)	Consumed in production					Losses	Exports	Stocks at end of year				Total output	Numbers
				In census industry (13)	In non-census industry (14)	Sent for processing (15)	Other (16)	Total (17)	(18)	(19)	In industry (20)	In channels of circulation (21)	Other (22)	Total (23)	(24)	(A)
37		1928	a) thousand tonnes	375400	1731	–	–	377131	–	–	75185	–	–	75185	452316	37
38		"	b) thousand rubles	449354	1766	–	–	451120	–	–	88841	–	–	88841	539961	38
39		"	c) price per tonne	1197	1020	–	–	1196	–	–	1182	–	–	1182	1194	39
40	Ginned cotton	1929	a) thousand tonnes	396000	1054	–	–	397054	–	2458	74258	–	–	74258	473770	40
41		"	b) thousand rubles	487674	1675	–	–	489349	–	2291	87960	–	–	87960	579600	41
42		"	c) price per tonne	1231.5	1020	–	–	1232	–	932	1184	–	–	1184	1223	42
43		1930	a) thousand tonnes	309000	1032	–	–	310032	–	10134	91000	–	–	91000	411166	43
44		"	b) thousand rubles	384860	1054	–	–	385914	–	6981	110898	–	–	110898	503793	44
45		"	c) price per tonne	1245.5	1021	–	–	1295	–	689	1219	–	–	1219	1225	45
46		1928	a) thousand tonnes	325.2	19.0	–	–	344.2	–	–	12.4	–	–	12.4	356.6	46
47		"	b) thousand rubles	809748	61940	–	–	871688	–	–	31533	–	–	31533	903221	47
48		"	c) price per tonne	2490.0	3260.0	–	–	2532.5	–	–	2543.0	–	–	2543.0	2532.9	48
49	Cotton yarn	1929	a) thousand tonnes	348.0	19.0	–	–	367.0	–	–	12.3	–	–	12.3	379.3	49
50		"	b) thousand rubles	842160	61940	–	–	904100	–	–	32616	–	–	32616	936716	50
51		"	c) price per tonne	2420.0	3260.0	–	–	2465.5	–	–	2651.7	–	–	2651.7	2469.6	51
52		1930	a) thousand tonnes	280.1	13.9	–	–	294.0	–	–	9.9	–	–	9.9	303.9	52
53		"	b) thousand rubles	624623	41700	–	–	666323	–	–	26419	–	–	26419	692742	53
54		"	c) price per tonne	2230.0	3000.0	–	–	2266.7	–	–	2668.6	–	–	2668.6	2279.9	54

Appendix A

Table 6. Balance of consumer goods

Num-bers (A)	Desig-nation of products (B)	Years (C)	Unit of measurement (D)	Stocks at beginning of year — In industry (1)	In channels of circulation (2)	port (3)	Total (4)	Production per year — Census industry (5)	Non-census industry (6)	Obtained through processing (7)	Total (8)	Imports (9)	duties (10)	Excises (11)	Trade and transport mark-up (12)	Total input (13)	Num-bers (A)
1	**Food products**	1928	a) thousand tonnes	801.6	144.2	-	945.8	1221.2	-	545.7	1766.9	-	-	-	-	2712.7	1
2		"	b) thousand rubles	306200	96800	-	403000	375200	-	201900	577100	-	-	299200	89600	1368900	2
3		"	c) price per tonne	381.9	671.7	-	426.1	307.2	-	370.2	326.6	-	-	-	-	504.6	3
4	Sugar	1929	a) thousand tonnes	711.3	179.1	-	890.4	957.9	-	656.7	1614.6	36.4	-	-	-	2541.4	4
5		"	b) thousand rubles	278000	117600	-	395600	289400	-	231300	520700	3800	2900	258300	114300	1295600	5
6		"	c) price per tonne	390.8	656.6	-	443.8	302.1	-	352.2	322.5	104.4	-	-	-	509.8	6
7		1930	a) thousand tonnes	461.1	278.4	-	739.5	1489.5	-	566.4	2055.9	290.0	-	-	-	3085.4	7
8		"	b) thousand rubles	183600	160300	-	343900	449700	-	199500	649200	49300	23300	287600	483500	1836800	8
9		"	c) price per tonne	398.2	574.8	-	465.0	301.9	-	352.2	315.8	170.0	-	-	-	595.3	9
10		1928	a) centners	19933	62900	-	82833	3139	-	-	3139	292980	-	-	-	378952	10
11		"	b) thousand rubles	6134	35727	-	41861	938	-	62582	63520	36858	32749	31942	43582	250512	11
12		"	c) price per centner	308	568	-	506	299	-	-	299	126	-	-	-	661	12
13	Tea	1929	a) centners	17220	91315	-	108535	3799	-	-	3799	285900	-	-	-	398234	13
14		"	b) thousand rubles	4352	51867	-	56219	1268	-	72931	74199	28810	35361	37733	46546	274868	14
15		"	c) price per centner	253	568	-	518	334	-	-	334	101	-	-	-	690	15
16		1930	a) centners	39434	101112	-	140546	4328	-	-	4328	242270	-	-	-	387144	16
17		"	b) thousand rubles	12094	56522	-	68616	1506	-	68835	70341	20611	37234	41328	43454	281584	17
18		"	c) price per centner	307	559	-	488	348	-	-	348	85	-	-	-	727	18

Appendix A
Table 6. (cont'd)

Numbers	Designation of products	Years	Unit of measurement	Consumed in production					Consumed by the population and by institutions — By the non-agricultural population							Numbers
A	B	C	D	In census industry	In non-census industry	Other	Sent for processing	Total	Manual workers	Non-manual workers	Other proletarians	Independent producers	Capitalist group	Other population	Total	A
				14	15	16	17	18	19	20	21	22	23	24	25	A
	Food products															
1	Sugar	1928	a) thousand tonnes	559.4	32.0	90.7	–	682.1	194.2	167.0	19.4	89.8	3.9	30.6	504.9	1
2		"	b) thousand rubles	171700	22500	53300	–	247500	130100	108300	13500	60000	2600	21100	335600	2
3		"	c) price per tonne	306.9	703.2	587.7	–	362.9	669.9	648.5	695.9	668.2	666.7	689.5	664.7	3
4		1929	a) thousand tonnes	672.5	30.5	93.2	–	796.2	195.9	136.9	23.0	50.0	1.5	39.6	446.9	4
5		"	b) thousand rubles	203000	21400	54800	–	279200	133200	95700	15300	46500	2000	26700	319400	5
6		"	c) price per tonne	301.9	701.6	588.0	–	350.7	679.9	699.1	665.2	930.0	1333.3	674.2	714.7	6
7		1930	a) thousand tonnes	580.0	41.0	198.7	–	819.7	263.5	144.3	19.7	47.1	1.1	33.3	509.0	7
8		"	b) thousand rubles	174300	33700	116800	–	324800	205800	132700	16000	53400	4000	27500	439400	8
9		"	c) price per tonne	300.5	821.9	587.2	–	396.2	781.0	916.6	812.2	1133.8	3636.4	825.8	863.3	9
10	Tea	1928	a) centners	–	–	–	–	47924	38230	32570	3580	17880	580	6090	98930	10
11		"	b) thousand rubles	47924	–	–	–	47924	27287	24723	2387	12785	549	4068	71799	11
12		"	c) price per centner	–	–	–	–	–	771	759	666	715	916	668	726	12
13		1929	a) centners	–	–	–	–	–	35660	31570	4360	12560	290	8530	92970	13
14		"	b) thousand rubles	60498	–	–	–	60498	26247	22700	3200	9300	300	6400	68147	14
15		"	c) price per centner	–	–	–	–	–	734	719	733	740	1034	750	733	15
16		1930	a) centners	–	–	–	–	–	41870	24800	2780	8800	160	5500	83910	16
17		"	b) thousand rubles	57352	–	–	–	57352	33173	20500	2300	7500	400	4700	68573	17
18		"	c) price per centner	–	–	–	–	–	793	827	827	852	2500	855	817	18

Appendix A
Table 6. (cont'd)

Num-bers	Designation of products	Years	Unit of measurement	Consumed by the population and by institutions			Losses	Exports	Stocks at end of year			Total output	Num-bers
				Agricultural population	Institutions and organisations	Total			In industry	In channels of circulation	Total		
A	B	C	D	26	27	28	29	30	31	32	33	34	A
	Food products												
1		1928	a) thousand tonnes	477.9	21.8	1003.8	–	136.4	711.3	179.1	890.4	2712.7	1
2		"	b) thousand rubles	343600	12300	691500	–	34300	278000	117600	395600	1368900	2
3		"	c) price per tonne	719.0	585.7	688.9	–	251.5	390.8	656.6	444.3	504.6	3
4	Sugar	1929	a) thousand tonnes	409.3	22.8	879.0	–	126.7	461.1	278.4	739.5	2541.4	4
5		"	b) thousand rubles	305400	13300	658100	–	34400	185600	160300	343900	1295600	5
6		"	c) price per tonne	746.4	583.3	725.9	–	271.5	398.2	575.8	465.0	509.8	6
7		1930	a) thousand tonnes	419.0	36.3	964.3	–	101.9	845.6	353.9	1199.5	3085.4	7
8		"	b) thousand rubles	434600	21400	895400	–	27000	309300	280300	589600	1836800	8
9		"	c) price per tonne	1037.2	589.5	928.4	–	265.0	365.8	792.0	491.5	595.3	9
10		1928	a) centners	158000	13435	270365	–	52	17220	93315	108535	378952	10
11		"	b) thousand rubles	67308	7249	146356	–	13	4352	51867	56219	250512	11
12		"	c) price per centner	426	540	541	–	250	253	568	517	661	12
13	Tea	1929	a) centners	148000	16688	257658	–	30	39434	101112	140546	398234	13
14		"	b) thousand rubles	68524	9071	145742	–	12	12094	56522	68616	274868	14
15		"	c) price per centner	453	544	550	–	400	306	559	488	690	15
16		1930	a) centners	149000	19902	252812	–	610	37383	96339	133722	387144	16
17		"	b) thousand rubles	79300	10989	158862	–	52	11465	53853	65318	281584	17
18		"	c) price per centner	531	552	622	–	85	307	559	488	727	18

Appendix A
Table 6. (cont'd)

Numbers (A)	Designation of products (B)	Years (C)	Unit of measurement (D)	Stocks at beginning of year — In industry (1)	In channels of circulation (2)	In transport (3)	Total (4)	Production per year — Census industry (5)	Non-census industry (6)	Obtained through processing (7)	Total (8)	Imports (9)	Customs duties (10)	Excises (11)	Trade and transport mark-up (12)	Total input (13)
19		1928	a) thousand tonnes	23.8	21.3	-	45.1	418.9	286.0	-	704.9	-	-	-	-	750.0
20		"	b) thousand rubles	10100	10400	-	20500	171500	166700	-	338200	-	-	-	29600	388300
21		"	c) price per tonne	424.4	488.3	-	454.5	409.4	582.9	-	479.8	-	-	-	-	517.7
22	Vegetable oil	1929	a) thousand tonnes	27.1	46.1	-	73.2	453.0	263.9	-	716.9	-	-	-	-	790.1
23		"	b) thousand rubles	11700	20900	-	32600	197600	184400	-	382000	-	-	-	41100	455700
24		"	c) price per tonne	431.7	453.4	-	445.4	436.4	698.7	-	532.8	-	-	-	-	576.8
25		1930	a) thousand tonnes	27.5	30.5	-	58.0	379.2	247.4	-	626.6	-	-	-	-	684.6
26		"	b) thousand rubles	11900	13900	-	25800	167700	209700	-	377400	-	-	-	135200	538400
27		"	c) price per tonne	432.7	455.7	-	444.8	442.2	847.6	-	602.3	-	-	-	-	786.4
28		1928	a) thousand tonnes	824	569	-	1393	2453	-	-	2453	-	-	-	-	3816
29		"	b) thousand rubles	3316	11408	-	14724	16656	-	-	16656	-	-	-	71860	103240
30		"	c) price per tonne	4.02	20.05	-	10.56	6.79	-	-	6.79	-	-	-	-	26.84
31	Salt	1929	a) thousand tonnes	866	624	-	1490	2868	-	-	2868	-	-	-	-	4358
32		"	b) thousand rubles	2952	11794	-	14746	20607	-	-	20607	-	-	-	73780	109133
33		"	c) price per tonne	4.36	18.90	-	9.89	7.22	-	-	7.22	-	-	-	-	25.04
34		1930	a) thousand tonnes	872	881	-	1753	3205	-	-	3205	-	-	-	-	4958
35		"	b) thousand rubles	3383	16651	-	20034	23108	-	-	23108	-	-	-	78808	121950
36		"	c) price per tonne	3.88	18.90	-	11.42	7.21	-	-	7.21	-	-	-	-	21.59

Appendix A
Table 6. (cont'd)

Num-bers A	Desig-nation of products B	Years C	Unit of measurement D	Consumed in production					Consumed by the population and by institutions / By the non-agricultural population							Num-bers A
				In census industry 14	In non-census industry 15	Other 16	Sent for processing 17	Total 18	Manual workers 19	Non-manual workers 20	Other proletarians 21	Independent producers 22	Capitalist group 23	Other population 24	Total 25	
19	Vegetable oil	1928	a) thousand tonnes	214.8	13.6	32.0	-	260.4	41.4	21.9	4.5	19.0	0.6	7.7	95.1	19
20		"	b) thousand rubles	91100	7200	14500	-	112800	25200	13000	2800	11500	400	4900	57800	20
21		"	c) price per tonne	424.1	529.4	453.1	-	433.2	608.7	593.6	622.2	605.3	666.6	636.4	607.8	21
22	Vegetable oil	1929	a) thousand tonnes	240.2	9.8	25.3	-	275.3	51.2	29.7	5.3	16.9	0.4	8.2	111.7	22
23		"	b) thousand rubles	103600	5900	11700	-	121200	37200	19600	3900	20100	500	6100	87400	23
24		"	c) price per tonne	415.7	602.0	462.5	-	440.2	726.6	659.9	783.8	1189.3	1250.0	743.9	782.6	24
25		1930	a) thousand tonnes	220.2	8.6	24.0	-	252.8	47.3	20.8	3.0	10.9	0.2	4.5	86.7	25
26		"	b) thousand rubles	93300	5300	11400	-	110000	54800	61600	9900	56700	900	14900	198800	26
27		"	c) price per tonne	423.7	616.3	475.0	-	435.1	1179.7	2961.5	3300.0	5201.8	4500.0	3311.1	2293.0	27
28	Salt	1928	a) thousand tonnes	175	35	590	-	800.0	70.9	38.2	9.8	31.9	1.1	14.1	166.0	28
29		"	b) thousand rubles	3340	1652	19959	-	24931	3269	1904	440	1479	54	696	7842	29
30		"	c) price per tonne	19.09	47.19	33.79	-	31.16	46.10	49.84	45.37	46.36	49.01	49.36	47.19	30
31	Salt	1929	a) thousand tonnes	257	42	645	-	944	71.8	38.6	1.0	29.0	0.7	14.9	165.0	31
32		"	b) thousand rubles	4883	2022	19368	-	26273	3349	1969	465	1411	38	720	7952	32
33		"	c) price per tonne	19.00	48.15	30.02	-	27.83	46.64	51.01	46.50	48.65	54.28	48.32	48.15	33
34		1930	a) thousand tonnes	326	57	830	-	1213	80.0	47.2	9.8	31.0	0.6	14.4	183.0	34
35		"	b) thousand rubles	6194	2739	23770	-	32703	3932	2418	462	1545	32	707	9096	35
36		"	c) price per tonne	19.00	48.05	28.64	-	26.96	49.15	51.23	47.14	49.83	53.33	49.09	49.70	36

Appendix A
Table 6. (cont'd)

Num bers (A)	Desig-nation of products (B)	Years (C)	Unit of measurement (D)	Consumed by the population and by institutions — Agricultural population (26)	Institutions and organisations (27)	Total (28)	Losses (29)	Exports (30)	Stocks at end of year — In industry (31)	In channels of circulation (32)	Total (33)	Total output (34)	Num bers (A)
19		1928	a) thousand tonnes	298.2	7.0	400.3	-	16.1	27.1	46.1	73.2	750.0	19
20		"	b) thousand rubles	176500	3300	237600	-	5300	11700	20900	32600	388300	20
21		"	c) price per tonne	591.9	471.1	593.6		329.2	431.7	453.4	445.4	517.7	21
22	Vegetable oil	1929	a) thousand tonnes	305.3	7.1	424.1	-	32.7	27.5	30.5	58.0	790.1	22
23		"	b) thousand rubles	208600	3400	299400	-	9300	11900	13900	25800	455700	23
24		"	c) price per tonne	683.3	478.8	706.0		287.5	432.7	455.7	444.8	576.8	24
25		1930	a) thousand tonnes	286.7	8.6	382.0	-	8.6	21.2	20.0	41.2	681.6	25
26		"	b) thousand rubles	203100	4100	406000	-	2400	9200	10800	20000	538400	26
27		"	c) price per tonne	708.4	506.2	1062.8		279.2	434.0	540.0	485.4	786.4	27
28		1928	a) thousand tonnes	1217	25	1408	73	75	866	624	1490	3846	28
29		"	b) thousand rubles	54290	518	62650	-	913	2952	11794	14746	103240	29
30		"	c) price per tonne	44.61	20.72	44.50		12.17	4.36	18.90	9.90	26.86	30
31	Salt	1929	a) thousand tonnes	1310	26	1501	92	68	872	881	1753	4358	31
32		"	b) thousand rubles	53828	533	62313	-	513	3383	16651	20034	109133	32
33		"	c) price per tonne	41.09	20.65	41.51		7.54	3.88	18.90	11.43	25.04	33
34		1930	a) thousand tonnes	1339	34	1556	102	75	958	1054	2012	4958	34
35		"	b) thousand rubles	55033	894	65023	-	568	3736	19920	23656	121950	35
36		"	c) price per tonne	41.10	26.29	41.78		8.74	3.90	18.90	11.75	24.59	36

Appendix A
Table 6. (cont'd)

A Numbers	B Designation of products	C Years	D Unit of measurement	Stocks at beginning of year			Production per year					9 Imports	10 Customs duties	11 Excises	12 Trade and transport mark-up	13 Total input	A Numbers
				1 In industry	2 In channels of circulation	3 port	4 Total	5 Census industry	6 Non-census industry	7 Obtained through processing	8 Total						
37	Beverages and narcotics	1928	a) million litres	17.5	26.4	-	43.9	549.8			549.8	-	-	-	-	593.7	37
38		"	b) thousand rubles	6000	41100	-	47100	224500	-	-	224500	-	-	744300	112500	1128400	38
39		"	c) price per litre	0.34	1.56	-	1.07	0.41	-	-	0.41	-	-	-	-	1.90	39
40	Vodka	1929	a) million litres	15.3	23.3	-	38.6	525.3	-	-	525.3	-	-	-	-	563.9	40
41		"	b) thousand rubles	5200	37800	-	43000	205800	-	-	205800	-	-	1038600	82700	1370100	41
42		"	c) price per litre	0.34	1.62	-	1.11	0.39	-	-	0.39	-	-	-	-	2.43	42
43		1930	a) million litres	14.3	22.3	-	36.6	613.4	-	-	613.4	-	-	-	-	650.0	43
44		"	b) thousand rubles	5400	51800	-	57200	171700	-	-	171700	-	-	2054600	94000	2377500	44
45		"	c) price per litre	0.38	2.32	-	1.56	0.28	-	-	0.28	-	-	-	-	3.66	45
46	Makhorka	1928	a) centners	80390	237400	-	317790	837260	-	-	837260	-	-	-	-	1155050	46
47		"	b) thousand rubles	5761	25900	-	31661	45487	-	-	45487	-	-	43200	18957	139305	47
48		"	c) price per centner	71.7	108.7	-	99.3	84.4	-	-	84.4	-	-	-	-	120.6	48
49		1929	a) centners	53660	226900	-	280560	754020	-	-	754020	-	-	-	-	1034580	49
50		"	b) thousand rubles	3845	24100	-	27945	42452	-	-	42452	-	-	37751	27316	135464	50
51		"	c) price per centner	71.7	106.2	-	99.6	56.3	-	-	56.3	-	-	-	-	130.9	51
52		1930	a) centners	52670	168000	-	220670	665400	-	-	665400	-	-	-	-	886070	52
53		"	b) thousand rubles	3774	19000	-	22774	37595	-	-	37595	-	-	42283	27999	130651	53
54		"	c) price per centner	71.7	113.1	-	108.0	56.0	-	-	56.0	-	-	-	-	147.4	54

Appendix A
Table 6. (cont'd)

Num-bers	Desig-nation of products	Years	Unit of measurement	Consumed in production			Sent for pro-cessing	Total	Consumed by the population and by institutions By the non-agricultural population						Total	Num-bers
				In census industry	In non-census industry	Other			Manual workers	Non-manual workers	Other prolet-arians	Inde-pendent producers	Capit-alist group	Other popu-lation		
A	B	C	D	14	15	16	17	18	19	20	21	22	23	24	25	A
Beverages and narcotics																
37	Vodka	1928	a) million litres	0.2	-	-	-	0.2	102.7	27.6	3.6	46.4	2.8	7.8	190.9	37
38		"	b) thousand rubles	100	-	-	-	100	227100	50500	8000	102300	6300	16700	410900	38
39		"	c) price per litre	0.50	-	-	-	0.50	2.21	1.83	2.22	2.20	2.25	2.14	2.15	39
40		1929	a) million litres	1.6	-	-	-	1.6	79.2	20.1	4.9	35.6	1.5	9.6	150.9	40
41		"	b) thousand rubles	600	-	-	-	600	238900	55700	14400	104800	4500	28700	447000	41
42		"	c) price per litre	0.38	-	-	-	0.38	3.02	2.77	2.94	2.94	3.00	2.99	2.96	42
43		1930	a) million litres	1.6	-	-	-	1.6	112.0	27.4	5.4	43.1	1.4	10.3	199.6	43
44		"	b) thousand rubles	400	-	-	-	400	444900	99700	20900	167200	5600	40400	778700	44
45		"	c) price per litre	2.50	-	-	-	2.50	3.97	3.64	3.87	3.88	4.00	3.92	3.90	45
46	Makhorka	1928	a) centners	-	-	-	-	-	103740	21240	7290	14090	190	14440	160990	46
47		"	b) thousand rubles	-	-	-	-	-	13972	3012	1007	2068	25	2088	22172	47
48		"	c) price per centner	-	-	-	-	-	135.0	142.0	138.0	147.0	131.0	145.0	137.7	48
49		1929	a) centners	-	-	-	-	-	83580	20060	6890	11020	110	13700	135360	49
50		"	b) thousand rubles	-	-	-	-	-	13900	3000	1000	1700	-	2200	21800	50
51		"	c) price per centner	-	-	-	-	-	166.0	149.0	145.0	154.0	-	161.0	160.8	51
52		1930	a) centners	-	-	-	-	-	117200	22100	6150	10840	80	12110	168480	52
53		"	b) thousand rubles	-	-	-	-	-	22828	3900	1100	2000	-	2200	32028	53
54		"	c) price per centner	-	-	-	-	-	195.0	176.0	179.0	185.0	-	182.0	194.7	54

Appendix A
Table 6. (cont'd)

Num-bers (A)	Desig-nation of products (B)	Years (C)	Unit of measurement (D)	Consumed by the population and by institutions			Losses (29)	Exports (30)	Stocks at end of year			Total output (34)	Num-bers (A)
				Agricultural population (26)	Institutions and organisations (27)	Total (28)			In industry (31)	In channels of circulation (32)	Total (33)		
37	Beverages and narcotics	1928	a) million litres	358.6	0.0	549.5	5.4	0.0	15.3	23.3	38.6	593.7	37
38		"	b) thousand rubles	674200	100	1085200	-	100	5200	37800	43000	1128400	38
39		"	c) price per litre	1.88	1.59	1.97	-	2.95	0.34	1.62	1.11	1.90	39
40	Vodka	1929	a) million litres	369.6	0.0	520.5	5.2	0.0	14.3	22.3	36.6	563.9	40
41		"	b) thousand rubles	864900	100	1312000	-	300	5400	51800	57200	1370100	41
42		"	c) price per litre	2.34	1.97	2.52	-	1.86	0.38	2.32	1.56	2.43	42
43		1930	a) million litres	399.9	0.0	599.5	6.2	0.0	16.7	26.0	42.7	650.0	43
44		"	b) thousand rubles	1495600	100	2274400	-	200	6300	96200	102500	2377500	44
45		"	c) price per litre	3.74	2.89	3.79	-	1.86	0.38	3.70	2.63	3.66	45
46		1928	a) centners	713500	-	874490	-	-	53660	226900	280560	1155050	46
47		"	b) thousand rubles	89188	--	111360	-	-	3845	24100	27945	139305	47
48		"	c) price per centner	125.0	-	124.3	-	-	71.7	106.2	99.6	120.6	48
49	Makhorka	1929	a) centners	678550	-	813910	-	-	52670	168000	220670	1034580	49
50		"	b) thousand rubles	90890	-	112690	-	-	3774	19000	22774	135464	50
51		"	c) price per centner	134.0	-	138.5	-	-	71.7	113.1	103.2	130.9	51
52		1930	a) centners	622150	-	790630	-	-	27440	68000	95440	886070	52
53		"	b) thousand rubles	85857	-	117885	-	-	1966	10800	12766	130651	53
54		"	c) price per centner	138.0	-	149.1	-	-	71.7	158.1	133.8	147.4	54

Appendix A
Table 6. (cont'd)

Numbers	Designation of products	Years	Unit of measurement	Stocks at beginning of year				Production per year				Imports	Customs duties	Excises	Trade and transport mark-up	Total input	Numbers
				In industry	In circulation	In transport	Total	Census industry	Non-census industry	Obtained through processing	Total						
A	B	C	D	1	2	3	4	5	6	7	8	9	10	11	12	13	A
55	Tobacco and cigarettes	1928	a) millions of smoking units	430	9107	-	9537	51649	-	-	51649	2	-	-	-	61188	55
56		"	b) thousand rubles	862	45000	-	45862	127960	-	-	127960	18	-	145872	72651	392363	56
57		"	c) price per smoking unit	2.00	4.99	-	4.81	2.48	-	-	2.48	6.02	-	-	-	6.41	57
58		1929	a) millions of smoking units	381	10495	-	10876	60504	-	-	60504	5	-	-	-	71385	58
59		"	b) thousand rubles	764	52200	-	52964	138424	-	-	138424	33	-	173072	83253	447746	59
60		"	c) price per smoking unit	2.01	4.07	-	4.87	2.29	-	-	2.29	6.02	-	-	-	6.28	60
61		1930	a) millions of smoking units	94	10561	-	10455	64680	-	-	64680	5	-	-	-	75140	61
62		"	b) thousand rubles	189	34896	-	35085	195980	-	-	195980	31	-	248763	94184	574043	62
63		"	c) price per smoking unit	2.01	3.37	-	3.36	3.03	-	-	3.03	6.02	-	-	-	7.62	63
	Footwear and fabrics																
64	Leather footwear	1928	a) thousand pairs	438	7900	148	8486	29588	70434	-	100022	8	-	-	-	108516	64
65		"	b) thousand rubles	3585	99800	1865	105250	231229	957841	-	1189070	58	-	-	78000	1372378	65
66		"	c) price per pair	8.2	12.6	12.5	12.4	7.8	11.0	-	10.0	7.0	-	-	-	12.6	66
67		1929	a) thousand pairs	291	13942	161	14394	48780	48349	-	97129	3	-	-	-	111526	67
68		"	b) thousand rubles	2381	124000	2010	128591	394232	883757	-	1277989	22	-	-	90000	1496402	68
69		"	c) price per pair	8.2	8.9	12.5	8.9	8.1	13.8	-	10.9	7.0	-	-	-	13.4	69
70		1930	a) thousand pairs	204	9873	122	10199	75447	37225	-	112582	7	-	-	-	122888	70
71		"	b) thousand rubles	1716	95100	1532	98348	609794	977239	-	1587033	47	-	-	120000	1805428	71
72		"	c) price per pair	8.4	9.6	12.5	9.6	8.1	18.1	-	11.2	7.0	-	-	-	14.7	72

Appendix A
Table 6. (cont'd)

Numbers (A)	Designation of products (B)	Years (C)	Unit of measurement (D)	Consumed in production					Consumed by the population and by institutions — By the non-agricultural population							Numbers (A)
				In census industry (14)	In non-census industry (15)	Other (16)	Sent for processing (17)	Total (18)	Manual workers (19)	Non-manual workers (20)	Other proletarians (21)	Independent producers (22)	Capitalist group (23)	Other population (24)	Total (25)	A
55	Tobacco and cigarettes	1928	a) millions of smoking units	–	–	–	–	–	17021	13332	1769	5231	240	3844	41427	55
56		"	b) thousand rubles	–	–	–	–	–	110506	96910	10407	36645	4181	23054	281703	56
57		"	c) price per smoking unit	–	–	–	–	–	6.49	7.27	5.88	7.00	17.42	6.00	6.80	57
58		1929	a) millions of smoking units	–	–	–	–	–	18733	14714	2025	4801	187	4396	44856	58
59		"	b) thousand rubles	–	–	–	–	–	123777	108683	11793	34132	2755	26124	307264	59
60		"	c) price per smoking unit	–	–	–	–	–	6.61	7.39	5.82	7.11	14.73	5.94	6.85	60
61		1930	a) millions of smoking units	–	–	–	–	–	26323	16242	1811	4722	145	3814	53057	61
62		"	b) thousand rubles	–	–	–	–	–	203429	140396	12348	39348	2472	26463	421456	62
63		"	c) price per smoking unit	–	–	–	–	–	7.73	8.64	6.82	8.54	17.05	6.94	8.00	63
	Footwear and fabrics															
64	Leather footwear	1928	a) thousand pairs	4238	–	290	–	4528	16664	10225	1469	5909	697	2156	37150	64
65		"	b) thousand rubles	53386	–	3667	–	57053	137340	93722	13910	60731	8768	18862	415436	65
66		"	c) price per pair	12.6	–	12.6	–	12.6	8.2	9.1	9.5	10.3	12.6	8.7	9.0	66
67		1929	a) thousand pairs	5457	–	372	–	5829	16884	11403	1508	3696	273	2317	36081	67
68		"	b) thousand rubles	68210	–	4653	–	72863	158300	114500	14300	35100	3000	2160	432055	68
69		"	c) price per pair	12.5	–	12.5	–	12.5	9.4	10.0	9.5	9.5	11.0	9.3	9.6	69
70		1930	a) thousand pairs	8924	–	526	–	9450	21444	11683	1253	3378	194	1879	39831	70
71		"	b) thousand rubles	111547	–	6578	–	118125	201100	109500	11100	29900	2000	16800	496114	71
72		"	c) price per pair	12.5	–	12.5	–	12.5	9.4	9.4	8.9	8.9	10.3	8.9	9.3	72

Appendix A
Table 6. (cont'd)

Num-bers	Desig-nation of products	Years	Unit of measurement	Consumed by the population and by institutions			Losses	Exports	Stocks at end of year			Total output	Num-bers
				Agricultural population	Institutions and organisations	Total			In industry	In channels of circulation	Total		
A	B	C	D	26	27	28	29	30	31	32	33	34	A
55	Tobacco and cigarettes	1928	a) millions of smoking units	7311	1421	50159	-	153	381	10495	10876	61188	55
56		"	b) thousand rubles	47668	9109	338480	-	919	764	52200	52964	392363	56
57		"	c) price per smoking unit	6.52	6.41	6.75	-	6.02	2.01	4.97	4.87	6.41	57
58		1929	a) millions of smoking units	14347	1475	60678	-	252	94	10361	10455	71385	58
59		"	b) thousand rubles	94260	9617	411141	-	1520	189	34896	35085	447746	59
60		"	c) price per smoking unit	6.57	6.52	6.78	-	6.02	2.01	3.37	3.36	6.28	60
61		1930	a) millions of smoking units	17421	1500	71978	-	322	23	2817	2840	75140	61
62		"	b) thousand rubles	116572	11033	551861	-	1936	46	20200	20246	574043	62
63		"	c) price per smoking unit	6.68	7.36	7.65	-	6.02	2.00	7.17	7.18	7.62	63
64	Footwear and fabrics / Leather footwear	1928	a) thousand pairs	49617	2810	89577	-	17	291	14103	14394	108516	64
65		"	b) thousand rubles	739843	31544	1186823	-	111	2381	126010	128391	1372378	65
66		"	c) price per pair	12.8	11.2	11.2	-	6.5	8.2	8.9	8.9	12.6	66
67		1929	a) thousand pairs	56593	2771	95445	-	53	204	9995	10199	111526	67
68		"	b) thousand rubles	857959	34903	1324917	-	274	1716	96632	98348	1496402	68
69		"	c) price per pair	12.8	12.6	11.6	-	5.2	8.4	9.7	9.6	13.4	69
70		1930	a) thousand pairs	64986	3250	108067	-	106	204	5061	5265	122888	70
71		"	b) thousand rubles	1098809	40954	1635877	-	550	1716	49160	50876	1805428	71
72		"	c) price per pair	13.9	12.0	12.2	-	5.2	8.4	9.7	9.7	11.7	72

Appendix A
Table 6. (cont'd)

A Numbers	B Designation of products	C Years	D Unit of measurement	Stocks at beginning of year — 1 In industry	2 In channels of circulation	3 In transport	4 Total	Production per year — 5 Census industry	6 Non-census industry	7 Obtained through processing Total	8 Total	9 Imports	10 Customs duties	11 Excises	12 Trade and transport mark-up	13 Total input	A Numbers
73	Galoshes	1928	a) thousand pairs	2178	4961	–	7139	37717	–	–	37717	–	–	–	–	44856	73
74		"	b) thousand rubles	4421	15496	–	19917	85995	–	–	85995	–	–	23436	28147	157495	74
75		"	c) price per pair	2.0	3.1	–	2.8	2.3	–	–	2.3	–	–	–	–	3.5	75
76		1929	a) thousand pairs	4333	5394	–	9727	44080	–	–	44080	–	–	–	–	53807	76
77		"	b) thousand rubles	9033	18016	–	27049	108878	–	–	108878	–	–	27454	38023	201404	77
78		"	c) price per pair	2.3	3.3	–	2.8	2.5	–	–	2.5	–	–	–	–	3.7	78
79		1930	a) thousand pairs	4168	5449	–	9617	42421	–	–	42421	–	–	–	–	52038	79
80		"	b) thousand rubles	13100	18560	–	31460	115385	–	–	115385	–	–	27959	27610	202414	80
81		"	c) price per pair	3.1	3.4	–	3.3	2.7	–	–	2.7	–	–	–	–	3.9	81
82	Cotton fabrics	1928	a) million metres	17.3	427.7	–	445.0	2742.3	80.7	–	2823.0	1.6	–	–	–	3269.6	82
83		"	b) thousand rubles	12200	226700	–	238900	1384900	41300	–	1426200	800	200	–	216000	1882100	83
84		"	c) price per metre	0.71	0.53	–	0.54	0.51	0.52	–	0.51	0.50	–	–	–	0.58	84
85		1929	a) million metres	18.0	423.2	–	441.2	3068.2	69.3	–	3137.5	7.0	–	–	–	3685.7	85
86		"	b) thousand rubles	12700	224500	–	237000	1503600	34700	–	1538300	3400	1300	–	272000	2152000	86
87		"	c) price per metre	0.71	0.53	–	0.54	0.49	0.50	–	0.49	0.49	–	–	–	0.60	87
88		1930	a) million metres	28.4	466.4	–	494.8	2352.7	71.0	–	2423.7	2.4	–	–	–	2920.9	88
89		"	b) thousand rubles	16000	243900	–	259900	1150500	35500	–	1186000	1200	700	–	347800	1795600	89
90		"	c) price per metre	0.56	0.52	–	0.52	0.49	0.51	–	0.49	0.50	–	–	–	0.61	90

Appendix A
Table 6. (cont'd)

Numbers	Designation of products	Years	Unit of measurement	Consumed in production					Consumed by the population and by institutions — By the non-agricultural population							Numbers
				In census industry	In non-census industry	Other	Sent for processing	Total	Manual workers	Non-manual workers	Other proletarians	Independent producers	Capitalist group	Other population	Total	
A	B	C	D	14	15	16	17	18	19	20	21	22	23	24	25	A
73		1928	a) thousand pairs	-	-	-	-	-	7356	4557	668	2721	307	936	16545	73
74		"	b) thousand rubles	-	-	-	-	-	24153	15322	2404	9219	1032	3366	55496	74
75		"	c) price per pair	-	-	-	-	-	3.3	3.4	3.6	3.4	3.4	3.6	3.4	75
76	Galoshes	1929	a) thousand pairs	-	-	-	-	-	7932	5004	745	2462	117	1166	17426	76
77		"	b) thousand rubles	-	-	-	-	-	27059	17727	2228	9305	410	3788	60517	77
78		"	c) price per pair	-	-	-	-	-	3.4	3.5	3.0	3.8	3.5	3.2	3.5	78
79		1930	a) thousand pairs	-	-	-	-	-	9095	5514	666	2416	90	1046	18827	79
80		"	b) thousand rubles	-	-	-	-	-	33003	20759	2117	9712	334	3735	69660	80
81		"	c) price per pair	-	-	-	-	-	3.6	3.8	3.2	4.0	3.7	3.6	3.7	81
82		1928	a) million metres	229.7	201.1	15.1	-	445.9	222.1	107.3	22.5	100.4	3.5	28.0	483.8	82
83		"	b) thousand rubles	141100	120500	8000	-	269600	134800	71700	13100	61000	3200	15900	299700	83
84		"	c) price per metre	0.61	0.60	0.53	-	0.63	0.61	0.69	0.58	0.6	0.91	0.57	0.62	84
85	Cotton fabrics	1929	a) million metres	280.1	192.5	16.5	-	489.1	231.3	145.2	15.7	87.4	2.5	29.6	511.7	85
86		"	b) thousand rubles	171900	123200	8700	-	303800	142300	96800	8700	53800	1700	16700	320000	86
87		"	c) price per metre	0.51	0.64	0.53	-	0.62	0.62	0.67	0.55	0.62	0.68	0.56	0.63	87
88		1930	a) million metres	457.7	179.9	16.8	-	654.4	192.3	79.5	7.0	42.6	0.9	13.4	335.7	88
89		"	b) thousand rubles	281000	112000	8900	-	401900	115100	49900	3700	24600	600	7200	201100	89
90		"	c) price per metre	0.61	0.62	0.53	-	0.61	0.60	0.64	0.53	0.58	0.67	0.61	0.60	90

Appendix A
Table 6. (cont'd)

Numbers	Designation of products	Years	Unit of measurement	Consumed by the population and by institutions			Losses	Exports	Stocks at end of year				Total output	Numbers
A	B	C	D	Agricultural population 26	Institutions and organisations 27	Total 28	29	30	In industry 31	In channels of circulation 32	Total 33		34	A
73	Galoshes	1928	a) thousand pairs	15884	-	32429	-	2700	4333	5394	9727		44856	73
74		"	b) thousand rubles	63536	-	119032	3743	7671	9033	18016	27049		157495	74
75		"	c) price per pair	4.0	-	3.7	-	2.8	2.1	3.3	2.8		3.5	75
76	Galoshes	1929	a) thousand pairs	22665	-	40091	-	4099	4168	5449	9617		53807	76
77		"	b) thousand rubles	92473	-	152990	9210	7744	13100	18360	31460		201404	77
78		"	c) price per pair	4.1	-	3.8	-	1.9	3.1	3.4	3.3		3.7	78
79		1930	a) thousand pairs	19895	-	38722	-	3600	3184	6532	9716		52038	79
80		"	b) thousand rubles	85549	-	155209	6379	6450	11591	22785	34376		202414	80
81		"	c) price per pair	4.3	-	4.0	-	1.8	3.6	3.5	3.5		3.9	81
82	Cotton fabrics	1928	a) million metres	1661.3	115.4	2260.5	-	122.0	18.0	423.2	441.2		3269.6	82
83		"	b) thousand rubles	973500	46200	1319400	-	56100	12700	224300	237000		1882100	83
84		"	c) price per metre	0.59	0.40	0.58	-	0.46	0.71	0.53	0.54		0.58	84
85	Cotton fabrics	1929	a) million metres	1828.2	142.4	2482.3	-	119.5	28.4	466.4	494.8		3585.7	85
86		"	b) thousand rubles	1170000	54100	1544100	-	44200	16000	243900	259900		2152000	86
87		"	c) price per metre	0.64	0.38	0.62	-	0.37	0.56	0.52	0.53		0.60	87
88		1930	a) million metres	1299.5	176.7	1811.9	-	127.4	33.8	293.4	327.2		2920.9	88
89		"	b) thousand rubles	908400	62000	1171500	-	47100	19000	156100	175100		1795600	89
90		"	c) price per metre	0.70	0.35	0.65	-	0.37	0.56	0.53	0.54		0.61	90

Appendix A
Table 6. (cont'd)

Num-bers (A)	Desig-nation of products (B)	Years (C)	Unit of measurement (D)	Stocks at beginning of year				Production per year				Imports	Customs duties	Excises	Trade and transport mark-up	Total input	Num-bers
				In industry (1)	In channels of circulation (2)	In transport (3)	Total (4)	Census industry (5)	Non-census industry (6)	Obtained through processing (7)	Total (8)	(9)	(10)	(11)	(12)	(13)	(A)
91		1928	a) million metres	2.7	8.5	–	11.2	91.2	9.3	–	100.5	0.2	–	–	–	111.9	91
92		"	b) thousand rubles	8900	34300	–	43200	339300	20700	–	360000	800	900	–	83100	488000	92
93		"	c) price per metre	3.30	4.03	–	3.85	3.72	2.22	–	3.58	4.00	–	–	–	4.36	93
94	Woollen fabrics	1929	a) million metres	3.0	9.3	–	12.3	101.9	8.1	–	110.0	1.7	–	–	–	124.0	94
95		"	b) thousand rubles	9900	38000	–	47900	427000	19100	–	446100	7000	6400	–	85700	593100	95
96		"	c) price per metre	3.30	4.09	–	3.89	4.19	2.35	–	4.06	4.13	–	–	–	4.78	96
97		1930	a) million metres	3.9	9.8	–	13.7	112.1	7.3	–	119.4	0.7	–	–	–	123.8	97
98		"	b) thousand rubles	16900	40100	–	57000	469700	17200	–	486900	2900	3500	–	123900	674200	98
99		"	c) price per metre	4.33	4.09	–	4.16	4.16	2.36	–	4.08	4.14	–	–	–	5.05	99
	Clothing in fabric equivalent																
100	Cotton fabric	1928	a) million metres	22.5	454.9	–	477.4	2742.3	80.7	–	2823.0	1.6	–	–	–	3302.0	100
101		1929	a) million metres	22.0	461.0	–	483.0	3068.2	69.3	–	3137.5	7.0	–	–	–	3628.5	101
102		1930	a) million metres	31.7	497.3	–	529.0	2352.7	71.0	–	2423.7	2.4	–	–	–	2955.1	102
103	Woollen fabric	1928	a) million metres	3.5	12.6	–	16.1	91.2	9.3	–	100.5	0.2	–	–	–	116.8	103
104		1929	a) million metres	3.6	15.0	–	18.6	101.9	8.1	–	110.0	1.7	–	–	–	130.3	104
105		1930	a) million metres	4.7	17.3	–	22.0	112.1	7.3	–	119.4	0.7	–	–	–	142.1	105

Appendix A
Table 6 (cont'd)

Num-bers	Desig-nation products	Years	Unit of measurement	Consumed in production					Consumed by the population and by institutions								Num-bers
									By the non-agricultural population								
				In census industry	In non-census industry	Other	Sent for pro-cessing	Total	Manual workers	Non-manual workers	Other prolet-arians	Inde-pendent producers	Capit-alist group	Other popu-lation	Total	
A	B	C	D	14	15	16	17	18	19	20	21	22	23	24	25	A
91	Woollen fabrics	1928	a) million metres	28.5	27.9	–	–	56.4	6.8	4.6	0.5	2.9	0.3	0.6	15.7	91
92		"	b) thousand rubles	140600	105700	–	–	246300	31300	26300	2400	20100	4200	2700	87000	92
93		"	c) price per metre	4.93	3.79	–	–	4.37	4.60	5.72	4.80	6.93	14.00	4.50	5.54	93
94	Woollen fabrics	1929	a) million metres	53.9	20.1	–	–	74.0	4.5	3.7	0.2	1.7	0.06	0.44	10.6	94
95		"	b) thousand rubles	299200	81800	–	–	381000	20400	19500	900	7700	300	2000	50800	95
96		"	c) price per metre	5.55	4.09	–	–	5.15	4.53	5.27	4.50	4.53	5.00	4.55	4.79	96
97		1930	a) million metres	76.9	13.0	–	–	89.9	3.3	1.6	0.1	0.7	0.03	0.17	5.9	97
98		"	b) thousand rubles	426800	52900	–	–	479700	16400	9600	400	3500	100	900	30900	98
99		"	c) price per metre	5.55	4.06	–	–	5.34	4.97	6.00	4.00	5.00	5.00	6.43	5.24	99
	Clothing in fabric equivalent															
100	Cotton fabric	1928	a) million metres	127.0	22.0	28.8	–	177.8	260.3	136.9	26.3	122.8	7.7	32.6	586.8	100
101		1929	a) million metres	153.3	25.1	32.6	–	211.0	274.1	175.1	21.1	103.3	3.4	36.1	613.1	101
102		1930	a) million metres	182.2	25.5	35.4	–	243.1	268.2	118.1	12.3	61.3	1.6	20.2	481.7	102
103	Woollen fabric	1928	a) million metres	0.2	–	1.1	–	1.3	18.2	11.2	1.4	11.1	1.1	1.7	44.7	103
104		1929	a) million metres	0.3	–	1.3	–	1.6	17.0	11.2	1.3	6.4	0.3	1.9	38.1	104
105		1930	a) million metres	0.4	–	1.2	–	1.6	19.4	7.8	0.8	4.1	0.1	1.2	33.4	105

Appendix A
Table 6. (cont'd)

Num-bers	Desig-nation of products	Years	Unit of measurement	Consumed by the population and by institutions			Losses	Exports	Stocks at end of year			Total output	Num-bers
				Agricultural population	Institutions and organisations	Total			In industry	In channels of circulation	Total		
A	B	C	D	26	27	28	29	30	31	32	33	34	A
91		1928	a) million metres	19.2	8.0	42.9	–	0.3	3.0	9.3	12.3	111.9	91
92		"	b) thousand rubles	73200	32900	193100	–	700	9900	38000	47900	488000	92
93		"	c) price per metre	3.81	4.11	4.50	–	2.33	3.30	4.09	3.89	4.36	93
94	Woollen fabrics	1929	a) million metres	16.5	9.0	36.1	–	0.2	3.9	9.8	13.7	124.0	94
95		"	b) thousand rubles	66800	37000	154600	–	500	16900	40100	57000	593100	95
96		"	c) price per metre	4.06	4.11	4.29	–	2.50	4.33	4.09	4.16	4.78	96
97		1930	a) million metres	13.9	12.4	32.2	–	0.2	4.3	7.2	11.5	133.8	97
98		"	b) thousand rubles	63200	51100	145200	–	500	19100	29700	48800	674200	98
99		"	c) price per metre	4.55	4.12	4.51	–	2.50	4.44	4.13	4.24	5.05	99
	Clothing in fabric equivalent												
100	Cotton	1928	a) million metres	1794.7	137.7	2519.2	–	122.0	22.0	461.0	483.0	3302.0	100
101		1929	a) million metres	1984.4	170.4	2768.0	–	119.5	31.7	497.3	529.0	3627.5	101
102	fabric	1930	a) million metres	1514.6	219.0	2215.3	–	127.4	39.1	330.2	369.3	2955.1	102
103		1928	a) million metres	42.1	9.8	96.6	–	0.3	3.6	15.0	18.6	116.8	103
104	Woollen	1929	a) million metres	57.1	11.2	106.5	–	0.2	4.7	17.3	220	130.3	104
105	fabric	1930	a) million metres	71.1	15.2	119.7	–	0.2	5.5	15.1	20.6	142.1	105

Appendix A
Table 6. (cont'd)

Numbers (A)	Designation of products (B)	Years (C)	Unit of measurement (D)	Stocks at beginning of year — In industry (1)	In channels of circulation (2)	In transport (3)	Total (4)	Census industry (5)	Non-census industry (6)	Obtained through processing (7)	Total (8)	Imports (9)	Customs duties (10)	Excises (11)	Trade and transport mark-up (12)	Total input (13)	Numbers (A)
106	**Other consumer goods** / Domestic soap	1928	a) tonnes	2599	17900	3600	24099	195000	38632	-	233632	-	-	-	-	257731	106
107		"	b) thousand rubles	901	9300	1296	11497	79922	18757	-	98659	-	-	-	21072	131228	107
108		"	c) price per tonne	347	520	360	477	410	485	-	422	-	-	-	-	509	108
109	Domestic soap	1929	a) tonnes	4941	19500	3800	28241	221614	27558	-	249172	-	-	-	-	277413	109
110		"	b) thousand rubles	1713	9700	1368	12781	90485	14001	-	104489	-	-	-	42942	160212	110
111		"	c) price per tonne	347	497	360	453	410	507	-	419	-	-	-	-	578	111
112		1930	a) tonnes	5929	15100	3100	24129	189923	22183	-	212106	-	-	-	-	236235	112
113		"	b) thousand rubles	2428	7200	1116	10744	77868	14284	-	92152	-	-	-	39040	141936	113
114		"	c) price per tonne	410	477	360	445	410	644	-	431	-	-	-	-	501	114
115		1928	a) boxes	173842	919000	-	1092842	5833000	-	-	5833000	-	-	-	-	6925842	115
116		"	b) thousand rubles	932	11304	-	12236	36143	-	-	36143	-	-	28547	12247	89175	116
117		"	c) price per box	5.36	12.30	-	11.20	6.20	-	-	6.20	-	-	-	-	12.88	117
118	Matches	1929	a) boxes	290221	931000	-	1221221	7574038	-	-	7574038	-	-	-	-	8795259	118
119		"	b) thousand rubles	1557	11451	-	13008	45700	-	-	45700	-	-	35010	13206	106924	119
120		"	c) price per box	5.36	12.30	-	10.65	6.03	-	-	6.03	-	-	-	-	12.16	120
121		1930	a) boxes	96820	1215000	-	1311820	9407000	-	-	9407000	-	-	-	-	10718820	121
122		"	b) thousand rubles	510	14945	-	15455	56724	-	-	56724	-	-	51467	9982	133628	122
123		"	c) price per box	5.27	12.30	-	11.78	6.03	-	-	6.03	-	-	-	-	12.33	123

Appendix A
Table 6. (cont'd)

Num-bers (A)	Desig-nation of products (B)	Years (C)	Unit of measurement (D)	Consumed in production					Consumed by the population and by institutions / By the non-agricultural population							Num-bers (A)
				In census industry (14)	In non-census industry (15)	Other (16)	Sent for pro-cessing (17)	Total (18)	Manual workers (19)	Non-manual workers (20)	Other prolet-arians (21)	Inde-pendent producers (22)	Capit-alist group (23)	Other popu-lation (24)	Total (25)	
Other consumer goods																
106		1928	a) tonnes	6000	–	5800	–	11800	33969	21211	2866	14052	1155	6228	79481	106
107		"	b) thousand rubles	2922	–	2088	–	5010	15331	9575	1293	6339	737	2810	36084	107
108		"	c) price per tonne	487	–	360	–	425	451	451	451	451	637	451	454	108
109	Domestic soap	1929	a) tonnes	10000	–	7200	–	17200	39249	25767	3741	14049	640	7344	90790	109
110		"	b) thousand rubles	4870	–	2592	–	7462	17799	11686	1697	6372	412	3334	41300	110
111		"	c) price per tonne	487	–	360	–	434	453	453	453	453	644	454	455	111
112		1930	a) tonnes	16544	–	10400	–	26944	35241	22273	2620	10837	373	5200	76544	112
113		"	b) thousand rubles	8057	–	3744	–	11801	19652	12421	1461	6044	769	2900	43247	113
114		"	c) price per tonne	467	–	360	–	438	558	558	558	558	2009	558	565	114
115	Matches	1928	a) boxes	–	–	–	–	–	561244	427346	60442	192963	9195	118529	1369719	115
116		"	b) thousand rubles	–	–	–	–	–	8509	6337	943	3272	156	1872	21089	116
117		"	c) price per box	–	–	–	–	–	15.16	14.83	15.27	16.96	10.96	15.79	15.40	117
118	Matches	1929	a) boxes	–	–	–	–	–	705920	539783	76646	228796	7646	151175	1709966	118
119		"	b) thousand rubles	–	–	–	–	–	10886	8158	1218	3505	130	2436	26333	119
120		"	c) price per box	–	–	–	–	–	15.42	15.11	15.89	15.31	17.00	16.11	15.40	120
121		1930	a) boxes	–	–	–	–	–	989601	594586	68455	224877	5849	134886	2018234	121
122		"	b) thousand rubles	–	–	–	–	–	15265	8992	1088	3448	104	2184	31081	122
123		"	c) price per box	–	–	–	–	–	15.42	15.12	15.89	15.33	17.78	16.19	15.40	123

Appendix A
Table 6. (cont'd)

Num-bers (A)	Desig-nation of products (B)	Years (C)	Unit of measurement (D)	Consumed by the population and by institutions			Losses (29)	Exports (30)	Stocks at end of year				Total output (34)	Num-bers (A)
				Agricultural population (26)	Institutions and organisations (27)	Total (28)			In industry (31)	In channels of circulation (32)	Total (33)			
	Other consumer goods													
106		1928	a) tonnes	130231	6671	216383	–	1307	4941	23300	28241		257731	106
107		"	b) thousand rubles	73581	3249	112914	–	523	1713	11068	12781		131228	107
108		"	c) price per tonne	565	487	522	–	400	347	475	453		509	108
109	Domestic soap	1929	a) tonnes	134795	7875	233460	–	2624	5929	18200	24129		277413	109
110		"	b) thousand rubles	95704	3835	140839	–	1167	2428	8316	10744		160212	110
111		"	c) price per tonne	710	487	603	–	445	410	457	445		578	111
112		1930	a) tonnes	105846	11161	193551	–	2552	4488	8700	13188		236235	112
113		"	b) thousand rubles	74163	6284	123694	–	764	2081	3596	5677		141936	113
114		"	c) price per tonne	710	564	639	–	299	464	413	430		501	114
115		1928	a) boxes	3316189	60000	4745908	–	958713	290221	931000	1221221		6925842	115
116		"	b) thousand rubles	49743	888	71720	–	4445	1557	11451	13008		89173	116
117		"	c) price per box	15.00	14.80	15.11	–	4.64	5.36	12.30	10.65		12.88	117
118	Matches	1929	a) boxes	3780987	60000	5550953	–	1932486	96820	1215000	1311820		8795259	118
119		"	b) thousand rubles	56715	888	83936	–	7533	510	14945	15455		106924	119
120		"	c) price per box	15.00	14.80	15.12	–	3.90	5.27	12.30	11.70		12.16	120
121		1930	a) boxes	4291420	60000	6369654	–	1071464	96820	3180882	3277702		10718820	121
122		"	b) thousand rubles	64571	888	96340	–	3831	510	32947	33457		133628	122
123		"	c) price per box	15.00	14.80	15.12	–	3.60	5.27	10.35	10.20		12.33	123

Appendix A
Table 7. Balance of milling and grinding products

Numbers (A)	Designation of products (B)	Years (C)	Unit of measurement (D)	Stocks at beginning of year				Produced	Imports	Customs duties	Trade and transport mark-ups	Total input	Consumed in production				Numbers (A)
				In agriculture (1)	In industry (2)	In channels of circulation (3)	Total stocks (4)	(5)	(6)	(7)	(8)	(9)	In industry[1] (10)	In agriculture (11)	In transport (12)	Total (13)	
1	Rye flour	1928	a) thousand centners	46284	311	1270	47865	145946	–	–	–	193811	7144	27850	630	35624	1
2		"	b) thousand rubles	233271	2457	11367	247095	927425	–	–	101114	1275634	73991	165186	6319	245496	2
3		"	c) price per centner	5.0	7.9	9.0	5.2	6.4	–	–	–	6.6	10.4	5.9	10.0	6.9	3
4	Rye flour	1929	a) thousand centners	40321	339	1053	41713	129054	–	–	–	170767	8213	22121	341	30675	4
5		"	b) thousand rubles	275392	2909	10846	289147	960955	–	–	66852	1316954	149757	89109	3751	242617	5
6		"	c) price per centner	6.8	8.6	10.3	6.9	7.4	–	–	–	7.7	18.2	4.0	11.0	7.9	6
7		1930	a) thousand centners	24499	262	2618	27379	162975	–	–	–	190354	18800	17101	–	35901	7
8		"	b) thousand rubles	175167	2405	28615	206187	1250506	–	–	125125	1581818	218764	115432	–	334196	8
9		"	c) price per centner	7.1	9.2	10.9	7.5	7.7	–	–	–	8.3	11.6	6.8	–	9.3	9
10		1928	a) thousand centners	21685	581	2169	24435	144192	–	–	–	168627	15775	2366	–	18141	10
11		"	b) thousand rubles	154831	6745	25377	186953	1454562	–	–	363507	2005022	258362	18313	–	276675	11
12		"	c) price per centner	7.1	11.6	11.7	7.7	10.1	–	–	–	11.9	16.4	7.7	–	15.3	12
13	Wheaten flour	1929	a) thousand centners	22143	557	2927	25627	144942	–	–	–	170569	18814	2073	–	20887	13
14		"	b) thousand rubles	195080	7391	42939	245410	1676452	–	–	352502	2274364	333106	17828	–	350934	14
15		"	c) price per centner	8.8	13.3	14.7	9.6	11.6	–	–	–	13	17.7	8.6	–	16.8	15
16		1930	a) thousand centners	28305	618	3836	32759	137287	–	–	–	170046	24107	541	–	24648	16
17		"	b) thousand rubles	263237	9326	57195	329758	1485371	–	–	219331	2034460	422324	4604	–	426928	17
18		"	c) price per centner	9.3	15.1	14.9	0.1	10.8	–	–	–	12.0	17.5	8.5	–	17.3	18

Appendix A
Table 7. (cont'd)

Num- bers (A)	Desig- nation of products (B)	Years (C)	Unit of measurement (D)	Consumed by institutions and by the population				Losses in channels of circu- lation (18)	Exports (19)	Stocks at end of year						Total output (24)	Num- bers (A)
				Non agri- cultural population[1] (14)	Agri- cultural population (15)	Insti tutions and social organ- isations (16)	Total (17)			In agri- culture (20)	In industry (21)	In channels of circu- lation (22)	Total (23)				
1	Rye flour	1928	a) thousand centners	4261	110486	1663	116410	50	14	40321	339	1053	41713		193811	1
2		"	b) thousand rubles	54956	677507	10410	740873	-	118	275392	2909	10846	289147		1275634	2
3		"	c) price per centner	12.9	6.1	6.3	6.4	-	8.4	6.8	8.6	10.3	6.9		6.6	3
4	Rye flour	1929	a) thousand centners	4152	106333	2046	112531	182	-	24499	262	2618	27379		170767	4
5		"	b) thousand rubles	93610	759225	15325	868150	-	-	175167	2405	28615	206187		1316954	5
6		"	c) price per centner	22.5	7.1	7.5	7.7	-	-	7.1	9.2	10.9	7.5		7.7	6
7		1930	a) thousand centners	7012	106030	2203	115245	380	4	34040	262	4522	38824		190354	7
8		"	b) thousand rubles	141900	798595	16545	957030	-	49	242024	2575	45944	290543		1581818	8
9		"	c) price per centner	20.2	7.5	7.5	8.3	-	12.3	7.1	9.8	10.2	7.5		8.3	9
10	Wheaten flour	1928	a) thousand centners	14972	108964	698	124634	61	164	22143	557	2927	25627		168627	10
11		"	b) thousand rubles	391967	1079833	8062	1479862	-	3075	195080	7391	42939	245410		2005022	11
12		"	c) price per centner	26.2	9.9	11.6	11.9	-	18.8	8.8	13.3	14.7	9.6		11.9	12
13	Wheaten flour	1929	a) thousand centners	9761	104473	2166	116400	395	128	28305	618	3836	32759		170569	13
14		"	b) thousand rubles	280100	1285018	25407	1590525	-	3147	263237	9326	57195	329758		2274364	14
15		"	c) price per centner	28.7	12.3	11.7	13.7	-	24.6	9.3	15.1	14.9	10.1		13.3	15
16		1930	a) thousand centners	7806	100781	2509	111096	422	155	27805	789	5131	33725		170016	16
17		"	b) thousand rubles	232000	1000260	29906	1261766	-	3078	254752	11843	76093	342688		2034460	17
18		"	c) price per centner	29.7	9.9	11.8	11.4	-	19.9	9.2	15.0	14.8	10.2		12.0	18

Appendix A
Table 7. (cont'd)

				Stocks at beginning of year									Consumed in production				
Num-bers	Desig-nation of products	Years	Unit of measurement	In agri-culture	In industry	In channels of circul-ation	Total stocks	Produced	Imports	Cust-oms dut-ies	Trade and trans-port mark-ups	Total input	In industry[1]	In agri-culture	In trans-port	Total	Num-bers
A	B	C	D	1	2	3	4	5	6	7	8	9	10	11	12	13	A
19		1928	a) thousand centners	4495	-	368	4863	63157	-	-	-	68020	-	34047	296	34343	19
20		"	b) thousand rubles	26476	-	2535	29011	474956	-	-	6035	510002	-	221299	3256	224555	20
21		"	c) price per centner	5.9	-	6.9	6.0	7.5	-	-	-	7.5	-	6.5	11.0	6.5	21
22	Other flour	1929	a) thousand centners	5310	-	520	5830	75127	-	-	-	80957	1045	35877	2466	39388	22
23		"	b) thousand rubles	37170	-	4508	41678	604114	-	-	29597	675389	11338	253889	27619	292846	23
24		"	c) price per centner	7.0	-	8.7	7.1	8.0	-	-	-	8.3	10.8	7.1	11.2	7.4	24
25		1930	a) thousand centners	3833	-	754	4587	81334	-	-	-	85921	451	30068	2227	32746	25
26		"	b) thousand rubles	27290	-	6718	34008	601743	-	-	20430	656181	5245	207357	28973	241575	26
27		"	c) price per centner	7.1	-	8.9	7.4	7.4	-	-	-	7.6	11.6	6.9	13.0	7.4	27
28		1928	a) thousand centners	6330	23	231	6584	14604	-	-	-	21188	-	412	1	413	28
29		"	b) thousand rubles	40449	205	2973	43627	107549	-	-	33776	184952	-	2706	17	2723	29
30		"	c) price per centner	6.4	8.9	12.9	6.6	7.4	-	-	-	8.7	-	6.6	17.0	6.6	30
31	Millet groats	1929	a) thousand centners	6403	8	608	7019	13453	-	-	-	20472	5	360	-	305	31
32		"	b) thousand rubles	46486	76	8330	54892	105519	-	-	37737	198148	49	254	-	2591	32
33		"	c) price per centner	7.3	9.5	13.7	7.8	7.8	-	-	-	9.7	9.8	7.1	-	7.1	33
34		1930	a) thousand centners	6721	55	473	7249	14779	-	-	-	22028	9	401	-	410	34
35		"	b) thousand rubles	47249	562	6480	54291	109780	-	-	47935	212006	92	2695	-	2787	35
36		"	c) price per centner	7.0	10.2	13.7	7.5	7.4	-	-	-	9.6	10.2	6.7	-	6.8	36

Appendix A
Table 7. (cont'd)

A Num-bers	B Desig-nation of products	C Years	D Unit of measurement	Consumed by institutions and by the population						Stocks at end of year						24 Total output	A Num-bers
				14 Non agri-cultural population [1]	15 agri-cultural population	16 Instit-utions and social organ-isations	17 Total	18 Losses in channels of circu-lation	19 Exports	20 In agri-culture	21 In industry	22 In channels of circu-lation	23 Total		
19	Other flour	1928	a) thousand centners	628	27195	4	27827	9	11	5310	-	520	5830	68020	19
20		"	b) thousand rubles	17176	226418	73	243667	-	102	37170	-	4508	41678	510002	20
21		"	c) price per centner	27.4	8.3	18.3	8.8	-	9.3	7.0	-	8.7	7.1	7.5	21
22		1929	a) thousand centners	629	36321	-	36950	32	-	3833	-	754	4587	80957	22
23		"	b) thousand rubles	25588	322947	-	348535	-	-	27290	-	6718	34008	675389	23
24		"	c) price per centner	40.7	8.9	-	9.4	-	-	7.1	-	8.9	7.4	8.3	24
25		1930	a) thousand centners	564	30490	26	31080	17	-	21920	-	158	22078	85921	25
26		"	b) thousand rubles	24700	227836	411	252947	-	-	160291	-	1368	161659	656181	26
27		"	c) price per centner	43.8	7.5	15.8	8.1	-	-	7.3	-	8.7	7.3	7.6	27
28	Millet groats	1928	a) thousand centners	796	12740	195	13731	20	5	6403	8	608	7019	21188	28
29		"	b) thousand rubles	14699	110490	2043	127232	-	105	46486	76	8350	54892	184952	29
30		"	c) price per centner	18.5	8.7	10.5	9.3	-	21.0	7.3	9.5	13.7	7.8	8.7	30
31		1929	a) thousand centners	2122	10481	205	12808	33	17	6721	55	473	7249	20472	31
32		"	b) thousand rubles	52286	86571	2216	140873	-	393	47249	562	6480	54291	198148	32
33		"	c) price per centner	24.6	8.2	10.8	11.0	-	23.1	7.0	10.2	13.7	7.5	9.7	33
34		1930	a) thousand centners	2042	14299	192	16533	34	36	4354	60	601	5015	22028	34
35		"	b) thousand rubles	61913	106257	2327	170497	-	710	29959	633	8120	38012	212006	35
36		"	c) price per centner	30.3	7.4	12	10.3	-	19.7	6.7	10.6	13.5	7.6	9.6	36

Appendix A
Table 7. (cont'd)

Num-bers (A)	Desig-nation of products (B)	Years (C)	Unit of measurement (D)	Stocks at beginning of year — In agri-culture (1)	In industry (2)	In channels of circul-ation (3)	Total stocks (4)	Produced (5)	Imports (6)	Customs duties (7)	Trade and trans-port mark-ups (8)	Total input (9)	Consumed in production — In industry[1] (10)	In agri-culture[1] (11)	In trans-port (12)	Total (13)	Num-bers (A)
37	Buckwheat groats	1928	a) thousand centners	1205	10	261	1476	4038	-	-	-	5514	-	73	6	79	37
38		"	b) thousand rubles	10447	117	4215	14779	44554	-	-	18883	78216	-	703	120	823	38
39		"	c) price per centner	8.7	11.7	16.1	10.0	11.0	-	-	-	14.2	-	9.6	20.0	10.4	39
40		1929	a) thousand centners	1315	6	356	1677	4089	-	-	-	5766	62	61	-	123	40
41		"	b) thousand rubles	13965	76	6020	20061	53026	-	-	20353	93440	822	657	-	1479	41
42		"	c) price per centner	10.6	12.7	16.9	12.0	13.0	-	-	-	16.2	13.3	10.8		12.0	42
43		1930	a) thousand centners	1386	19	173	1578	3160	-	-	-	4738	75	17	-	92	43
44		"	b) thousand rubles	16840	261	2955	20056	36883	-	-	9782	66721	1043	164	-	1207	44
45		"	c) price per centner	12.2	13.7	17.1	12.7	11.7	-	-	-	14.1	13.9	9.8		13.1	45
46	Other groats	1928	a) thousand centners	251	25	129	405	8872	345	-	-	9622	-	528	4	532	46
47		"	b) thousand rubles	2206	337	3023	5566	90146	10293	-	75442	181447	-	5236	87	5323	47
48		"	c) price per centner	8.8	13.5	23.4	13.7	10.2	29.8	-	-	18.9	-	9.9	21.8	10.0	48
49		1929	a) thousand centners	413	78	314	805	9708	403	500	-	10916	26	440	-	466	49
50		"	b) thousand rubles	4130	1056	8092	13278	102357	9598		25168	150901	383	4778	-	5161	50
51		"	c) price per centner	10.0	13.5	25.8	16.5	10.5	23.8	-	-	13.8	14.7	10.9		11.1	51
52		1930	a) thousand centners	559	145	345	1049	16786	277	100	-	18112	6	212	-	218	52
53		"	b) thousand rubles	5875	2124	9063	17062	148613	5490		80673	251938	90	1694	-	1784	53
54		"	c) price per centner	10.5	14.6	26.3	16.3	8.9	19.8	-	-	13.9	15.0	8.0		8.2	54

Appendix A
Table 7. (cont'd)

Num-bers (A)	Desig-nation of products (B)	Years (C)	Unit of measurement (D)	Non agri-cultural population[1] (14)	Agri-cultural population (15)	Instit-utions and social organ-isations (16)	Total (17)	Losses in channels of circu-lation (18)	Exports (19)	In agri-culture (20)	In industry (21)	In channels of circu-lation (22)	Total (23)	Total output (24)	Num-bers (A)
				Consumed by institutions and by the population						Stocks at end of year					
37		1928	a) thousand centners	947	2604	197	3718	10	-	1315	6	356	1677	5514	37
38		"	b) thousand rubles	23460	31782	2090	57332	-	-	13965	76	6020	20061	78216	38
39		"	c) price per centner	24.7	12.2	10.6	15.3		-	10.6	12.7	16.9	12.0	14.2	39
40	Buckwheat groats	1929	a) thousand centners	1554	2275	215	4044	21	-	1386	19	173	1578	5766	40
41		"	b) thousand rubles	40637	28881	2387	71905	-	-	16840	261	2955	20156	93440	41
42		"	c) price per centner	26.1	12.7	11.1	17.8		-	12.2	13.7	17.1	12.7	16.2	42
43		1930	a) thousand centners	645	1761	246	2652	13	3	1666	20	292	1978	4738	43
44		"	b) thousand rubles	19344	21968	2866	44178		30	16077	288	4941	21306	66721	44
45		"	c) price per centner	30.0	12.5	11.7	16.7		10.0	9.7	14.4	16.3	10.6	14.1	45
46		1928	a) thousand centners	1763	6474	37	8274	9	2	413	78	314	805	9622	46
47		"	b) thousand rubles	92124	69200	1442	162766		80	4130	1056	8092	13278	181417	47
48		"	c) price per centner	52.3	10.7	39.0	19.7		40.0	10.0	13.5	25.8	16.5	18.9	48
49	Other groats	1929	a) thousand centners	620	8670	91	9381	16	4	559	145	345	1049	10916	49
50		"	b) thousand rubles	27962	97277	3275	128514		164	5875	2124	9063	17062	150901	50
51		"	c) price per centner	45.1	11.2	36.0	13.7		41.0	10.5	14.6	26.3	16.3	13.8	51
52		1930	a) thousand centners	1867	9352	121	11340	39	34	5122	141	1218	6481	181 2	52
53		"	b) thousand rubles	81913	87071	1866	170880		1340	43822	2115	31997	77934	251938	53
54		"	c) price per centner	43.9	9.3	15.4	15.1		39.4	8.6	15.0	26.3	12.0	13.9	54

Appendix A
Table 7. (cont'd)

Num-bers (A)	Desig-nation of products (B)	Years (C)	Unit of measurement (D)	Stocks at beginning of year				Produced	Imports	Cust-oms dut-ies	Trade and trans-port mark-ups	Total input	Consumed in production				Num-bers (A)
				In agri-culture (1)	In industry (2)	In channels of circul-ation (3)	Total stocks (4)	(5)	(6)	(7)	(8)	(9)	In industry (10)	In agri-culture[1] (11)	In trans-port (12)	Total (13)	
55		1928	a) thousand centners	8755	212	-	8967	32545	-	-	-	41512	-	31564	1207	32771	55
56		"	b) thousand rubles	23814	693	-	24507	118962	-	-	27076	170545	-	126566	8087	134653	56
57		"	c) price per centner	2.7	3.3	-	2.7	3.7	-	-	-	4.1		4.0	6.7	4.1	57
58	Bran	1929	a) thousand centners	8534	96	104	8734	22130	-	-	-	30864	4	26267	476	26747	58
59		"	b) thousand rubles	35075	333	44	35849	94066	-	-	14138	144053	19	122824	3618	126461	59
60		"	c) price per centner	4.1	3.5	4.2	4.0	4.3	-	-	-	4.7	4.8	4.7	7.6	4.7	60
61		1930	a) thousand centners	3770	64	245	4079	20983	-	-	-	25062	17	20774	816	21607	61
62		"	b) thousand rubles	16173	223	1176	17572	72522	-	-	20535	110629	79	92008	5957	98044	62
63		"	c) price per centner	4.3	3.5	4.8	4.3	3.5	-	-	-	4.4	4.6	4.4	7.3	4.5	63

1. Including bakings

Appendix A
Table 7. (cont'd)

Num-bers	Desig-nation products	Years	Unit of measurement	Consumed by institutions and by the population				Losses in channels of circu-lation	Exports	Stocks at end of year				Total output	Num-bers
				Non agri-cultural population[1]	Agri-cultural population	Instit-utions and social organ-isations	Total			In agri-culture	In industry	In channels of circu-lation	Total		
A	B	C	D	14	15	16	17	18	19	20	21	22	23	24	A
55		1928	a) thousand centners	-	-	-	-	-	7	8534	96	104	8734	41512	55
56		"	b) thousand rubles	-	-	-	-	-	43	35075	333	441	35849	170545	56
57		"	c) price per centner	-	-	-	-	-	6.1	4.1	3.5	4.2	4.1	4.1	57
58	Bran	1929	a) thousand centners	-	-	-	-	35	3	3770	64	245	4079	30864	58
59		"	b) thousand rubles	-	-	-	-	-	20	16173	223	1176	17572	144053	59
60		"	c) price per centner	-	-	-	-	-	6.7	4.3	3.5	4.8	4.3	4.7	60
61		1930	a) thousand centners	-	-	2	2	69	-	2707	64	613	3384	25062	61
62		"	b) thousand rubles	-	-	9	9	-	-	9474	221	2881	12576	110629	62
63		"	c) price per centner	-	-	4.5	4.5	-	-	3.5	3.5	4.7	3.7	4.4	63

1. Excluding purchases of bread in baked form.

Appendix B. Balances of products of agriculture

Table 1. Grain balance

Designation of products	Years	Unit of measurement	Stocks at beginning of year				Production per year	Imports	Customs duties	Trade and transport mark-up	Total input	Consumed in production			In industry	In transport	Total	Numbers
												In agriculture						
			In agriculture	In industry	In channels of circulation	Total						Seed	Cattle fodder	Total				
A	B C	D	1	2	3	4	5	6	7	8	9	10	11	12	13	14	15	A
Rye grain	1928	a) thousand centners	74083	2383	1910	78376	191217	-	-	-	269593	36400	5287	41687	154866	-	196553	1
	"	b) thousand rubles	331192	12368	10448	354008	1125574	-	-	12738	1492320	217166	26594	243760	836759	-	1080519	2
	"	c) price per centner	4.5	5.2	5.5	4.5	5.9	-	-	-	5.5	6.0	5.0	5.8	5.4	-	5.5	3
	1929	a) thousand centners	64538	1055	2068	67661	203591	-	-	-	271252	38116	4202	42318	135148	-	177466	4
	"	b) thousand rubles	365963	6530	13483	385976	1296442	-	-	23077	1705495	238783	24792	263575	855480	-	1119055	5
	"	c) price per centner	5.6	6.2	6.5	5.7	6.4	-	-	-	6.3	6.3	5.9	6.2	6.3	-	6.3	6
	1930	a) thousand centners	66472	1079	22365	89916	219177	-	-	-	309093	37640	3804	41444	174612	-	216056	7
	"	b) thousand rubles	392828	6852	166619	566299	1327417	-	-	55592	1949308	234746	22484	257230	1124190	-	1381420	8
	"	c) price per centner	5.9	6.4	7.4	6.3	6.1	-	-	-	6.3	6.2	5.9	6.2	6.4	-	6.4	9
Wheat grain	1928	a) thousand centners	93055	2179	5786	101020	219798	2452	-	-	323270	36292	6800	43092	169192	-	212284	10
	"	b) thousand rubles	565007	18129	42238	625374	1650475	27336	-	46888	2350073	231050	43248	274298	1258203	-	1532501	11
	"	c) price per centner	6.1	8.3	7.3	6.2	7.5	11.1	-	-	7.3	6.4	6.4	6.4	7.4	-	7.2	12
	1929	a) thousand centners	95022	1745	10287	107054	188778	214	-	-	296046	38121	5418	43539	159053	-	202592	13
	"	b) thousand rubles	692670	14676	90217	797563	1561809	1337	-	65321	2426030	279890	40418	320308	1341353	-	1661661	14
	"	c) price per centner	7.3	8.4	8.8	7.5	8.3	6.2	-	-	8.2	7.3	7.5	7.4	8.4	-	8.2	15
	1930	a) thousand centners	64157	2206	24230	90573	246108	69	-	-	336750	39014	4376	43390	155559	-	198949	16
	"	b) thousand rubles	48983	19192	239877	748900	1940977	564	-	49054	2739495	304385	33514	337899	1294330	-	1632229	17
	"	c) price per centner	7.6	8.7	9.9	8.3	7.9	8.2	-	-	8.1	7.8	7.7	7.8	8.3	-	8.2	18

Table 1. (cont'd)

Num-bers (A)	Designa-tion of products (B)	Years (C)	Unit of measurement (D)	Consumed by the population and by institutions				Losses In storage and in channels of circu-lation	In prices	Exports	Stocks at end of year				Total output	Num-bers
				Agri-cultural popu-lation (16)	Non agri-cultural popu-lation (17)	Instit-utions and social organ-isations (18)	Total (19)	(20)	(21)	(22)	In agri-culture (23)	In industry (24)	In channels of circu-lation (25)	Total (26)	(27)	(A)
1	Rye grain	1928	a)thousand centners	4950	–	–	4950	331	–	98	64538	1055	2063	67661	269593	1
2		"	b)thousand rubles	24998	–	–	24998	–	–	827	365963	6530	13483	385976	1492320	2
3		"	c)price per centner	5.1	–	–	5.1	–	–	8.4	5.7	6.2	6.5	5.7	5.5	3
4		1929	a)thousand centners	3419	–	–	3419	440	–	11	66472	1079	22365	89916	271352	4
5		"	b)thousand rubles	20035	–	–	20035	–	–	106	392828	6852	166619	566299	1705495	5
6		"	c)price per centner	5.9	–	–	5.9	–	–	9.6	5.9	6.4	7.4	6.3	6.3	6
7		1930	a)thousand centners	–	–	–	–	780	–	6456	59452	1079	25270	85801	309093	7
8		"	b)thousand rubles	–	–	–	–	–	16463	20982	348734	6841	174868	530443	1949308	8
9		"	c)price per centner	–	–	–	–	–	–	3.3	5.9	6.3	6.9	6.2	6.3	9
10	Wheat grain	1928	a)thousand centners	3075	–	–	3075	824	–	33	95022	1745	10287	107054	323270	10
11		"	b)thousand rubles	19741	–	–	19741	–	–	268	692670	14676	90217	797563	2350073	11
12		"	c)price per centner	6.4	–	–	6.4	–	–	8.1	7.3	8.4	7.8	8.5	7.3	12
13		1929	a)thousand centners	2119	–	–	2119	762	–	–	64137	2206	24230	90573	296046	13
14		"	b)thousand rubles	15469	–	–	15469	–	–	–	489831	19192	239877	748900	2426030	14
15		"	c)price per centner	7.3	–	–	7.3	–	–	–	7.6	8.7	9.9	8.3	8.2	15
16		1930	a)thousand centners	–	–	–	–	1147	–	25309	79525	2206	29614	111345	336750	16
17		"	b)thousand rubles	–	–	–	–	–	77193	130341	610495	18861	270376	899732	2739495	17
18		"	c)price per centner	–	–	–	–	–	–	5.1	7.7	8.5	9.1	8.1	8.1	18

Appendix B
Table 1. (cont'd)

Num-bers	Designation of products	Years	Unit of measurement	Stocks at beginning of year				Production per year	Imports	Customs duties	Trade and transport mark-up	Total input	Consumed in production						Num-bers
				In agriculture	In industry	In channels of circulation	Total						In agriculture			In industry	In transport	Total	
													Seed	Cattle fodder	Total				
A	B	C	D	1	2	3	4	5	6	7	8	9	10	11	12	13	14	15	A
19		1928	a) thousand centners	25626	252	560	26438	56717	-	-	-	83155	9099	10308	19407	28774	1706	49887	19
20		"	b) thousand rubles	142263	2001	3114	147378	331988	-	-	19486	498852	50122	63213	113335	186293	10859	310478	20
21		"	c) price per centner	5.6	7.9	5.6	5.6	5.9	-	-	-	6.0	5.5	6.1	5.8	6.5	6.4	6.2	21
22	Barley grain	1929	a) thousand centners	30745	521	1069	32335	72135	-	-	-	104470	9948	9172	19120	40717	506	60343	22
23		"	b) thousand rubles	172255	3934	7394	183583	441543	-	-	41737	666863	55257	60474	115731	270959	3258	389948	23
24		"	c) price per centner	5.6	7.6	6.9	5.7	6.1	-	-	-	6.4	5.6	6.6	6.1	6.7	6.4	6.5	24
25		1930	a) thousand centners	30169	1496	9868	41533	64631	-	-	-	106164	8649	8052	16701	44939	468	62108	25
26		"	b) thousand rubles	177577	13225	72925	263727	394258	-	-	15021	672986	48648	55732	104380	277441	15116	396937	26
27		"	c) price per centner	5.9	8.8	7.4	6.3	6.1	-	-	-	6.3	5.6	6.9	6.2	6.2	32.3	6.4	27
28		1928	a) thousand centners	90533	49	2038	92620	164012	-	-	-	256632	28622	80254	108876	22429	4541	135846	28
29		"	b) thousand rubles	381426	248	9864	391538	827514	-	-	54624	1273676	118495	388948	507443	134728	24703	666874	29
30		"	c) price per centner	4.2	5.1	4.8	4.2	5.0	-	-	-	5.0	4.1	4.8	4.7	6.0	5.4	4.9	30
31	Oats grain	1929	a) thousand centners	113479	173	4480	118132	157393	-	-	-	275525	31173	88454	119627	28012	4601	152240	31
32		"	b) thousand rubles	566260	984	27462	594706	859172	-	-	79988	1533866	154316	477628	631944	181606	25950	839500	32
33		"	c) price per centner	5.0	5.7	6.1	5.0	5.5	-	-	-	5.6	5.0	5.4	5.3	6.5	5.6	5.5	33
34		1930	a) thousand centners	96715	667	22249	119631	153949	-	-	-	273580	27558	85186	113744	28078	4658	146480	34
35		"	b) thousand rubles	526050	4636	145286	675972	640537	-	-	45221	1561730	151931	482483	634434	176393	42481	853308	35
36		"	c) price per centner	5.4	7.0	6.5	5.7	5.5	-	-	-	5	5.5	5.6	5.6	6.3	9.1	5.8	36

Appendix B
Table 1. (cont'd)

Numbers (A)	Designation of products (B)	Years (C)	Unit of measurement (D)	Agricultural population (16)	Non-agricultural population (17)	Institutions and social organisations (18)	Total (19)	Losses In storage and in channels of circulation (20)	In prices (21)	Exports (22)	In agriculture (23)	In industry (24)	In channels of circulation (25)	Total (26)	Total output (27)	Numbers (A)
19		1928	a)thousand centners	842	–	–	842	91	–	–	30745	521	1069	32335	83155	19
20		"	b)thousand rubles	4791	–	–	4791	–	–	–	172255	3934	7394	183583	498852	20
21		"	c)price per centner	5.7	–	–	5.7	–	–	–	5.6	7.6	6.9	5.7	6.0	21
22	Barley grain	1929	a)thousand centners	781	–	–	781	228	–	1585	30169	1496	9868	41533	104470	22
23		"	b)thousand rubles	4413	–	–	4413	–	–	8775	177577	13235	72925	263727	666863	23
24		"	c)price per centner	5.7	–	–	5.7	–	–	5.5	5.9	8.8	7.4	6.3	6.4	24
25		1930	a)thousand centners	–	–	–	–	324	–	11814	24142	1496	6280	31918	106161	25
26		"	b)thousand rubles	–	–	–	–	–	30480	36742	152980	12955	42892	208827	672986	26
27		"	c)price per centner	–	–	–	–	–	–	3.1	6.3	8.7	6.8	6.5	6.3	27
28		1928	a)thousand centners	–	–	2415	2415	235	–	4	113479	173	4480	118132	256632	28
29		"	b)thousand rubles	–	–	12074	12074	–	–	22	566260	984	27462	594706	1273676	29
30		"	c)price per centner	–	–	5.0	5.0	–	–	5.5	5.0	5.7	6.1	5.0	5.0	30
31	Oats grain	1929	a)thousand centners	–	–	3104	3104	471	–	79	96715	667	22249	119631	275525	31
32		"	b)thousand rubles	–	–	18003	18003	–	–	391	526050	4636	145286	675972	1533866	32
33		"	c)price per centner	–	–	5.8	5.8	–	–	4.9	5.4	7.0	6.5	5.7	5.6	33
34		1930	a)thousand centners	–	–	2766	2766	613	–	3525	92795	667	26734	120196	273580	34
35		"	b)thousand rubles	–	–	15822	15822	–	6345	11245	507504	4696	162810	675010	1561730	35
36		"	c)price per centner	–	–	5.7	5.7	–	–	3.2	5.5	7.0	6.1	5.6	5.7	36

Appendix B
Table 1. (cont'd)

Numbers (A)	Designation of products (B)	Years (C)	Unit measurement (D)	In agriculture (1)	In industry (2)	In channels of circulation (3)	Total (4)	Production per year (5)	Imports (6)	Customs duties (7)	Trade- and transport mark-up (8)	Total input (9)	Seed (10)	Cattle fodder (11)	Total (12)	In industry (13)	In transport (14)	Total (15)	Numbers (A)
				Stocks at beginning of year									Consumed in production						
													In agriculture						
37		1928	a) thousand centners	7666	137	347	8150	16238	-	-	-	24388	3388	768	4156	11314	-	15470	37
38		"	b) thousand rubles	36947	830	2186	39923	93988	-	-	2721	136672	15788	3986	19774	65022	-	84796	38
39		"	c) price per centner	4.8	6.1	6.3	4.9	5.8	-	-	-	5.6	4.7	5.2	4.8	5.7	-	5.5	39
40	Buck- wheat grain	1929	a) thousand centners	8365	63	452	8880	15138	-	-	-	24018	3258	721	3979	11514	-	15493	40
41		"	b) thousand rubles	48330	386	3160	51876	95991	-	-	4484	152351	18538	4508	23046	78739	-	101785	41
42		"	c) price per centner	5.8	6.1	7.0	5.8	6.3	-	-	-	6.3	5.7	6.3	5.8	6.8	-	6.6	42
43		1930	a) thousand centners	7472	99	915	8486	11461	-	-	-	19947	2426	770	3196	9871	-	13067	43
44		"	b) thousand rubles	43096	653	6817	50566	70888	-	-	1925	123379	13961	4501	18462	60943	-	79405	44
45		"	c) price per centner	5.8	6.6	7.5	6.0	6.2	-	-	-	6.2	5.8	5.8	5.8	6.2	-	6.1	45
46		1928	a) thousand centners	11600	64	228	11892	29833	-	-	-	41725	1651	2376	4027	25122	-	29149	46
47		"	b) thousand rubles	46853	278	1188	48319	136763	-	-	2781	187863	6621	10265	16886	114366	-	131152	47
48		"	c) price per centner	4.0	4.3	5.2	4.1	4.6	-	-	-	4.5	4.0	4.3	4.2	4.6	-	4.5	48
49	Millet grain	1929	a) thousand centners	11615	88	832	12535	31127	-	-	-	43662	1629	2111	3740	24661	-	28401	49
50		"	b) thousand rubles	51299	436	4876	56611	144870	-	-	6082	20756	7004	9367	16371	119468	-	135839	50
51		"	c) price per centner	4.4	5.0	5.9	4.5	4.7	-	-	-	4.8	4.3	4.4	4.4	4.8	-	4.8	51
52		1930	a) thousand centners	12194	495	2494	15183	26976	-	-	-	42159	1385	2556	3941	25218	-	29159	52
53		"	b) thousand rubles	53646	2490	15588	71724	124368	-	-	1435	197527	6076	11112	17188	117502	-	132690	53
54		"	c) price per centner	4.4	5.0	6.3	4.7	4.6	-	-	-	4.7	4.4	4.3	4.4	4.7	-	4.6	54

Appendix B
Table 1. (cont'd)

Num-bers (A)	Designation of products (B)	Years (C)	Unit of measurement (D)	Consumed by the population and by institutions				Losses In storage and in channels of circulation (20)	In prices (21)	Exports (22)	Stocks at end of year				Total output (27)	Num-bers (A)
				Agri-cultural population (16)	Non-agri-cultural population (17)	Institutions and social organisations (18)	Total (19)				In agri-culture (23)	In industry (24)	In channels of circulation (25)	Total (26)		
37		1928	a) thousand centners	-	-	-	-	38	-	-	8365	63	452	8880	24588	37
38		"	b) thousand rubles	-	-	-	-	-	-	-	48330	386	3160	51876	136672	38
39		"	c) price per centner	-	-	-	-	-	-	-	5.8	6.1	7.0	5.8	5.6	39
40	Buckwheat grain	1929	a) thousand centners	-	-	-	-	39	-	-	7472	99	915	8496	24018	40
41		"	b) thousand rubles	-	-	-	-	-	-	-	43096	653	6817	50566	152351	41
42		"	c) price per centner	-	-	-	-	-	-	-	5.8	6.6	7.5	6.0	6.3	42
43		1930	a) thousand centners	-	-	-	-	33	-	-	5388	113	1346	6847	19947	43
44		"	b) thousand rubles	-	-	-	-	-	-	-	33124	782	10068	43974	123379	44
45		"	c) price per centner	-	-	-	-	-	-	-	6.1	6.9	7.5	6.4	6.2	45
46		1928	a) thousand centners	-	-	-	-	41	-	-	11615	88	832	12535	41725	46
47		"	b) thousand rubles	-	-	-	-	-	-	-	51299	436	4876	56611	187863	47
48		"	c) price per centner	-	-	-	-	-	-	-	4.4	5.0	5.9	4.5	4.5	48
49	Millet grain	1929	a) thousand centners	-	-	-	-	78	-	-	12194	495	2494	15183	43662	49
50		"	b) thousand rubles	-	-	-	-	-	-	-	53646	2490	15588	71724	207563	50
51		"	c) price per centner	-	-	-	-	-	-	-	4.4	5.0	6.3	4.7	4.8	51
52		1930	a) thousand centners	-	-	-	-	81	-	-	9954	620	2345	12919	42159	52
53		"	b) thousand rubles	-	-	-	-	-	-	-	45568	3199	14070	62837	197527	53
54		"	c) price per centner	-	-	-	-	-	-	-	4.6	5.2	6.0	4.9	4.7	54

Appendix B
Table 1. (cont'd)

Num-bers prod-ucts (A)	Des-igna-tion of prod-ucts (B)	Years (C)	Unit of measurement (D)	Stocks at beginning of year				Prod-uction per year	Imports	Trade Customs duties	Trade-and trans-port mark-up	Total input	Consumed in production						Num-bers (A)
				In agri-culture	In industry	In channels of circu-lation	Total						In agriculture			In industry	In trans-port	Total	
													Seed	Cattle fodder	Total				
				1	2	3	4	5	6	7	8	9	10	11	12	13	14	15	A
55		1928	a) thousand centners	16249	446	926	17621	33402	–	–	–	51023	898	13035	13933	18357	–	32290	55
56		"	b) thousand rubles	65343	2961	4509	72813	145055	–	–	11202	229070	3601	52428	56029	88792	–	144821	56
57		"	c) price per centner	4.0	6.6	4.9	4.1	4.3	–	–	–	4.1	4.0	4.0	4.0	4.8	–	4.5	57
58	Maize	1929	a) thousand centners	17169	557	881	18607	30187	–	–	–	48794	744	11549	12293	17807	–	30100	58
59	grain	"	b) thousand rubles	76227	2857	4713	83797	144760	–	–	14230	242787	3229	50584	53813	95370	–	149183	59
60		"	c) price per centner	4.4	5.1	5.3	4.5	4.8	–	–	–	5.0	4.3	4.4	4.4	5.4	–	5.0	60
61		1930	a) thousand centners	15536	875	2113	18524	25695	–	–	–	44219	767	10330	11097	21694	–	32791	61
62		"	b) thousand rubles	75607	4681	12720	93008	137541	–	–	4762	235311	3531	57724	61255	109554	–	170809	62
63		"	c) price per centner	4.9	5.3	6.0	5.0	5.4	–	–	–	5.3	4.6	5.6	5.5	5.0	–	5.2	63
64		1928	a) thousand centners	3559	14	366	3939	19508	257	–	–	23704	4406	1219	5625	9143	–	14768	64
65		"	b) thousand rubles	22785	219	3843	26847	137937	4769	1000	5844	176397	27934	8280	36214	73460	–	109674	65
66		"	c) price per centner	6.4	15.6	10.5	6.8	7.1	18.6	–	–	7.4	6.3	6.8	6.4	8.0	–	7.4	66
67	Other	1929	a) thousand centners	7640	20	566	8226	19066	316	–	–	27608	5560	1346	6706	7779	–	14485	67
68	grain	"	b) thousand rubles	50653	12	5943	56721	140954	4587	1600	5651	207913	34679	8799	43478	53259	–	96737	68
69		"	c) price per centner	6.6	6.3	10.5	6.9	7.4	14.5	–	–	7.5	6.5	6.5	6.5	6.8	–	6.7	69
70		1930	a) thousand centners	10950	68	1179	12197	23698	440	–	–	36335	3762	3213	6975	16345	–	23320	70
71		"	b) thousand rubles	82968	515	13063	96546	164906	9249	1000	21990	293691	29713	23308	53021	117561	–	170582	71
72		"	c) price per centner	7.6	7.6	11.1	7.9	7.0	21.0	–	–	8.1	7.9	7.3	7.6	7.2	–	7.3	72

Appendix B
Table 1. (cont'd)

Numbers	Designation of products	Years	Unit of measurement	Consumed by the population and by institutions				Losses In storage and in channels of circulation	In prices	Exports	Stocks at end of year				Total output	Numbers
				Agricultural population	Non-agricultural population	Institutions and social organisations	Total				In agriculture	In industry	In channels of circulation	Total		
A	B	C	D	16	17	18	19	20	21	22	23	24	25	26	27	A
55	Maize grain	1928	a)thousand centners	-	-	-	-	62	-	64	17169	557	881	18607	51023	55
56		"	b)thousand rubles	-	-	-	-	-	-	452	76227	2857	4713	83797	229070	56
57		"	c)price per centner	-	-	-	-			7.1	4.4	5.1	5.3	4.5	4.5	57
58		1929	a)thousand centners	-	-	-	-	64	-	106	15536	875	2113	18524	48794	58
59		"	b)thousand rubles	-	-	-	-	-	-	596	75607	4681	12720	93008	242787	59
60		"	c)price per centner	-	-	-	-			5.6	4.9	5.3	6.0	5.0	5.0	60
61		1930	a)thousand centners	-	-	-	-	69	493	536	8027	199	2597	10823	44219	61
62		"	b)thousand rubles	-	-	-	-	-		1994	46457	1093	14465	62015	235311	62
63		"	c)price per centner	-	-	-	-			3.7	5.8	5.5	5.6	5.7	5.3	63
64	Other grains	1928	a)thousand centners	-	-	-	-	25	-	685	7640	20	566	8226	23704	64
65		"	b)thousand rubles	-	-	-	-	-		10002	50653	125	5943	56721	176397	65
66		"	c)price per centner	-	-	-	-			14.6	6.6	6.3	10.5	6.9	7.4	66
67		1929	a)thousand centners	-	53	26	78	28	-	820	10950	68	1179	12197	27608	67
68		"	b)thousand rubles	-	1888	162	2050	-		12580	82968	515	13063	96546	207913	68
69		"	c)price per centner	-	35.6	6.5	26.3			15.3	7.6	7.6	11.1	7.9	7.5	69
70		1930	a)thousand centners	-	450	85	535	47	-	779	9510	71	2073	11654	36335	70
71		"	b)thousand rubles	-	23598	1692	25290	-	771	4877	66350	530	25291	92171	293691	71
72		"	c)price per centner	-	52.4	19.9	47.3			6.3	7.0	7.5	12.2	7.9	8.1	72

Appendix B
Table 2. Balance of technical crops

A	B Designation of products	C Years	D Unit of measurement	Stocks at beginning of year				5 Production	6 Imports	7 Customs duties	8 Trade and transport mark-up	9 Total input	Consumed in production				14 In industry	15 In transport	16 Total consumed in industry	A Numbers
				1 In agriculture	2 In industry	3 In channels of circulation	4 Total stocks						In agriculture							
													10 Seed	11 Cattle fodder	12 Other items	13 Total				
1	Sunflower seeds	1928	a) thousand centners	7147	3258	1517	11922	21275	–	–	–	33197	570	–	–	570	18530	–	19100	1
2		"	b) thousand rubles	55461	27139	11924	92524	172659	–	–	11366	278549	4372	–	–	4372	155792	–	160164	2
3		"	c) price per centner	7.8	8.3	7.9	7.9	8.1	–	–	–	8.4	7.7	–	–	7.7	8.4	–	8.4	3
4		1929	a) thousand centners	5169	4189	1602	10960	17655	–	–	–	28595	530	–	–	530	18007	–	18537	4
5		"	b) thousand rubles	41558	38080	13601	93239	156236	–	–	12909	262384	4161	–	–	4161	172655	–	176816	5
6		"	c) price per centner	8.0	9.1	8.5	8.5	8.9	–	–	–	9.2	7.9	–	–	7.9	9.6	–	9.5	6
7		1930	a) thousand centners	2567	3441	1177	7185	15753	–	–	–	22938	530	–	–	530	14967	–	15497	7
8		"	b) thousand rubles	20025	29042	9287	58354	167311	–	–	8887	234582	4129	–	–	4129	169440	–	173569	8
9		"	c) price per centner	7.8	8.4	7.9	8.1	10.6	–	–	–	10.2	7.8	–	–	7.8	11.3	–	11.2	9
10	Flax seeds	1928	a) thousand centners	2737	707	252	3696	6018	–	–	–	9714	1474	69	–	1543	3681	–	5227	10
11		"	b) thousand rubles	28492	8766	2875	40133	75132	–	–	3671	118936	14859	731	–	15590	45762	–	61352	11
12		"	c) price per centner	10.4	12.4	11.4	10.9	12.5	–	–	–	12.2	10.1	10.6	–	10.1	12.4	–	11.7	12
13		1929	a) thousand centners	2808	1117	561	4486	7127	–	–	–	11613	1755	68	–	1823	4598	–	6421	13
14		"	b) thousand rubles	35265	15119	7186	57570	94450	–	–	10242	162262	20165	800	–	20965	72402	–	93367	14
15		"	c) price per centner	12.6	13.5	12.8	12.8	13.3	–	–	–	14.0	11.5	11.8	–	11.5	15.7	–	14.5	15
16		1930	a) thousand centners	2882	1253	1057	5192	6778	–	–	–	11970	1915	–	–	1915	4413	–	6328	16
17		"	b) thousand rubles	36463	18945	13487	68895	85594	–	–	7802	162291	22763	–	–	22763	63742	–	88505	17
18		"	c) price per centner	12.7	15.1	12.8	13.3	12.6	–	–	–	13.6	11.9	–	–	11.9	19.3	–	14.0	18

Appendix B
Table 2 (cont'd)

Num-bers	Designa-tion of products	Years	Unit of measurement	Consumed by the population and by institutions — Non agricultural population	Agri-cultural population	Instit-utions and social organi-sations	Total	Losses In storage — In agri-culture	In industry and in chan-nels of circu-lation	In prices	Exports	Stocks at end of year — In agri-culture	In industry	In chan-nels of circu-lation	Total	Total output	Num-bers
A	B	C	D	17	18	19	20	21	22	23	24	25	26	27	28	29	A
1	Sunflower	1928	a) thousand centners	500	2549	-	3049	49	-	-	39	5169	4189	1602	10960	33197	1
2		"	b) thousand rubles	4415	19805	-	24220	382	-	-	544	44558	38080	13601	93239	278549	2
3		"	c) price per centner	8.8	7.8	-	7.9	7.8	-	-	13.9	8.0	9.1	8.5	8.5	8.4	3
4	Sunflower seeds	1929	a) thousand centners	400	2336	-	2736	68	-	-	69	2567	3441	1177	7185	28595	4
5		"	b) thousand rubles	7440	18361	-	25801	534	-	-	879	20025	29042	9287	58354	262384	5
6		"	c) price per centner	18.6	7.9	-	9.4	7.9	-	-	12.7	7.8	8.4	7.9	8.1	9.2	6
7		1930	a) thousand centners	-	650	-	650	-	-	-	47	3073	1997	1674	6744	22938	7
8		"	b) thousand rubles	-	5167	-	5167	-	-	-	542	24634	17194	13476	55304	234582	8
9		"	c) price per centner	-	7.9	-	7.9	-	-	-	11.5	8.0	8.6	8.1	8.2	10.2	9
10		1928	a) thousand centners	-	-	-	-	-	-	-	1	2808	1117	561	4486	9714	10
11		"	b) thousand rubles	-	-	-	-	-	-	-	14	35265	15119	7186	57570	118936	11
12		"	c) price per centners	-	-	-	-	-	-	-	14.0	12.6	13.5	12.8	12.8	12.2	12
13	Flax seeds	1929	a) thousand centners	-	-	-	-	-	-	-	-	2882	1253	1057	5192	11613	13
14		"	b) thousand rubles	-	-	-	-	-	-	-	-	36463	18945	13487	68895	162262	14
15		"	c) price per centner	-	-	-	-	-	-	-	-	12.7	15.1	12.8	13.3	14.0	15
16		1930	a) thousand centners	-	-	-	-	-	-	-	7	4232	478	925	5635	11970	16
17		"	b) thousand rubles	-	-	-	-	-	-	-	107	53781	7170	12728	73679	162291	17
18		"	c) price per centner	-	-	-	-	-	-	-	15.3	12.7	15.0	13.8	13.1	13.6	18

Appendix B
Table 2. (cont'd)

Num-bers (A)	Designa-tion of prod-ucts (B)	Years (C)	Unit of measurement (D)	Stocks at beginning of year				Prod-uction	Im-ports	Cust-oms du-ties	Trade and trans-port mark-up	Total input	Consumed in production						Total consumed in industry	Num-bers (A)
				In agri-culture	In industry	In channels of circu-lation	Total stocks						In agriculture				In industry	In trans-port		
				1	2	3	4	5	6	7	8	9	Seed 10	Cattle fodder 11	Other items 12	Total 13	14	15	16	A
19		1928	a)thousand centners	3080	170	74	3324	5610	-	-	-	8934	1348	92	-	1440	3995	-	5435	19
20		"	b)thousand rubles	28767	1740	687	31194	52906	-	-	637	84737	12159	822	-	12981	38347	-	51328	20
21		"	c)price per centner	9.3	10.2	9.3	9.4	9.4	-	-	-	9.5	9.0	8.9	-	9.0	9.6	-	9.4	21
22	Hemp seeds	1929	a)thousand centners	3069	175	105	3349	4086	-	-	-	7455	1272	79	-	1351	3467	-	4818	22
23		"	b)thousand rubles	29092	1899	1063	32054	40718	-	-	2519	75291	11702	734	-	12436	37764	-	50200	23
24		"	c)price per centner	9.5	10.9	10.1	9.6	10.0	-	-	-	10.1	9.2	9.3	-	9.2	10.9	-	10.4	24
25		1930	a)thousand centners	2071	259	180	2510	3678	-	-	-	6188	1071	-	-	1071	2834	-	3905	25
26		"	b)thousand rubles	19216	2950	1930	24096	39381	-	-	3905	67382	9950	-	-	9950	35741	-	45691	26
27		"	c)price per centner	9.3	11.4	10.7	9.6	10.7	-	-	-	10.9	9.3	-	-	9.3	12.6	-	11.7	27
28		1928	a)thousand centners	1712	338	289	2339	3238	-	-	-	5577	-	-	-	-	1093	-	1093	28
29		"	b)thousand rubles	69093	15149	12054	96296	155616	-	-	22918	274830	-	-	-	-	52915	-	52915	29
30		"	c)price per centner	40.4	44.8	41.7	41.2	48.1	-	-	-	49.3	-	-	-	-	48.4	-	48.4	30
31	Flax fibre	1929	a)thousand centners	2171	336	507	3014	3606	-	-	-	6620	-	-	-	-	1500	-	1500	31
32		"	b)thousand rubles	103055	18898	27024	148977	178040	-	-	13360	340377	-	-	-	-	78342	-	78342	32
33		"	c)price per centner	47.5	56.2	53.3	49.4	49.4	-	-	-	51.4	-	-	-	-	52.2	-	52.2	33
34		1930	a)thousand centners	1938	601	725	3264	4100	-	-	-	7364	-	-	-	-	1472	-	1472	34
35		"	b)thousand rubles	93319	33482	38236	165087	205045	-	-	6686	376768	-	-	-	-	82455	-	82455	35
36		"	c)price per centner	48.2	55.7	52.7	50.6	50.0	-	-	-	51.2	-	-	-	-	56.1	-	56.1	36

Appendix B
Table 2. (cont'd)

Num-bers (A)	Designation of products (B)	Years (C)	Unit of measurement (D)	Consumed by the population and by institutions — Non agricultural population (17)	Agricultural population (18)	Institutions and social organisations (19)	Total (20)	Losses, In storage — In agriculture (21)	In industry and in channels of circulation (22)	In prices (23)	Exports (24)	Stocks at end of year — In agriculture (25)	In industry (26)	In channels of circulation (27)	Total (28)	Total output (29)	Num-bers (A)
19		1928	a)thousand centners	-	149	-	149	-	-	-	1	3069	175	105	3349	8934	19
20		"	b)thousand rubles	-	1332	-	1332	-	-	-	23	29092	1899	1063	32054	84737	20
21		"	c)price per centner	-	8.9	-	8.9	-	-	-	23.0	9.5	10.9	10.1	9.6	9.5	21
22	Hemp seeds	1929	a)thousand centners	-	107	-	107	-	-	-	-	2071	259	180	2510	7435	22
23		"	b)thousand rubles	-	992	-	992	-	-	-	3	19216	2950	1930	24096	75291	23
24		"	c)price per centner	-	9.3	-	9.3	-	-	-	-	9.3	11.4	10.7	9.6	10.1	24
25		1930	a)thousand centners	-	-	-	-	-	-	-	-	2005	97	181	2283	6188	25
26		"	b)thousand rubles	-	-	-	-	-	-	-	-	18636	1118	1937	21691	67382	26
27		"	c)price per centner	-	-	-	-	-	-	-	-	9.3	11.5	10.7	9.5	10.9	27
28		1928	a)thousand centners	-	1189	-	1189	-	-	-	281	2171	336	507	3014	5577	28
29		"	b)thousand rubles	-	51075	-	51075	-	-	-	21863	103055	18898	27024	148977	274830	29
30		"	c)price per centner	-	43.0	-	43.0	-	-	-	77.8	47.5	56.2	53.3	49.4	49.3	30
31	Flax fibre	1929	a)thousand centners	-	1291	-	1291	-	-	-	565	1938	601	725	3264	6620	31
32		"	b)thousand rubles	-	60290	-	60290	-	-	-	36708	93219	33482	38236	165037	340377	32
33		"	c)price per centner	-	46.7	-	46.7	-	-	-	65.0	48.2	55.7	52.7	50.6	51.4	33
34		1930	a)thousand centners	-	1242	-	1242	700	-	-	530	2420	252	748	3420	7364	34
35		"	b)thousand rubles	-	59184	-	59184	32151	-	3528	22748	123358	14044	39300	176702	376768	35
36		"	c)price per centner	-	47.7	-	47.7	45.9	-	-	42.9	51.0	55.7	52.5	51.7	51.2	36

Appendix B
Table 2. (cont'd)

| | | | | Stocks at beginning of year | | | | | | | | | Consumed in production | | | | | | | |
| | | | | | | | | | | | | | In agriculture | | | | | | | |
Num-bers (A)	Des-igna-tion of prod-ucts (B)	Years (C)	Unit of measurement (D)	In agri-culture (1)	In industry (2)	In channels of circu-lation (3)	Total stocks (4)	Prod-uction (5)	Im-ports (6)	Cust-oms dut-ies (7)	Trade and trans-port mark-up (8)	Total input (9)	Seed (10)	Cattle fodder (11)	Other items (12)	Total (13)	In industry (14)	In trans-port (15)	Total consumed in industry (16)	Num-bers (A)
37		1928	a)thousand centners	3714	209	43	3966	5178	-	-	-	9144	-	-	3664	3664	1201	‹	4865	37
38		"	b)thousand rubles	131833	9634	1881	143348	190933	-	-	2612	336893	-	-	129739	129739	46698	-	176437	38
39		"	c)price per centner	35.5	46.1	43.7	36.1	36.9	-	-	-	36.8	-	-	35.4	35.4	38.9	-	36.3	39
40	Hemp	1929	a)thousand centners	4051	83	63	4197	4649	-	-	-	8846	-	-	3448	3448	1234	-	4682	40
41	fibre	"	b)thousand rubles	151378	3595	2566	157539	185708	-	-	7222	350469	-	-	122301	122301	55042	-	177343	41
42		"	c)price per centner	37.4	43.3	40.7	37.5	39.9	-	-	-	39.6	-	-	35.5	35.5	44.6	-	37.9	42
43		1930	a)thousand centners	3790	120	135	4045	4142	-	-	-	8187	-	-	3310	3310	1152	-	4462	43
44		"	b)thousand rubles	158194	5137	5574	168905	249858	-	-	7866	426629	-	-	131217	131217	89643	-	220860	44
45		"	c)price per centner	41.7	42.8	41.3	41.8	60.3	-	-	-	52.1	-	-	39.6	39.6	77.8	-	40.5	45
46		1928	a)thousand centners	674	3910	-	4584	8215	-	-	-	12799	-	-	-	-	8351	-	8351	46
47		"	b)thousand rubles	18985	117300	-	136285	231504	-	-	20036	387825	-	-	-	-	257064	-	257064	47
48		"	c)price per centner	28.2	30.0	-	29.7	28.2	-	-	-	30.3	-	-	-	-	30.8	-	30.8	48
49	Raw	1929	a)thousand centners	1174	2978	-	4152	8640	-	-	-	12792	-	-	-	-	8834	-	8834	49
50	cotton	"	b)thousand rubles	33089	89328	-	122417	243325	-	-	18737	384479	-	-	-	-	274109	-	274109	50
51		"	c)price per centner	28.2	30.0	-	29.5	28.2	-	-	-	30.1	-	-	-	-	31.0	-	31.0	51
52		1930	a)thousand centners	890	2711	-	3601	11132	-	-	-	14733	-	-	-	-	9107	-	9107	52
53		"	b)thousand rubles	25097	75203	-	100300	332846	-	-	32733	465879	-	-	-	-	299803	-	299803	53
54		"	c)price per centner	28.2	27.7	-	27.9	29.9	-	-	-	31.6	-	-	-	-	32.9	-	32.9	54

Appendix B
Table 2. (cont'd)

Num-bers	Designa-tion of products	Years	Unit of measurement	Consumed by the population and by institutions				Losses			Exports	Stocks at end of year				Total output	Num-bers
								In storage									
				Non agri-cultural popu-lation	Agri-cultural popu-lation	Instit-utions and social organi-sations	Total	In agri-culture	In industry and in chan-nels of circu-lation	In prices	Exports	In agri-culture	In industry	In chan-nels of circu-lation	Total	Total output	
A	B	C	D	17	18	19	20	21	22	23	24	25	26	27	28	29	A
37		1928	a)thousand centners	-	-	-	-	-	-	-	82	4051	83	63	4197	9144	37
38		"	b)thousand rubles	-	-	-	-	-	-	65	2842	151378	3595	2566	157529	336893	38
39		"	c)price per centner	-	-	-	-	-	-	-	34.8	37.4	43.3	40.7	37.5	36.8	39
40	Hemp fibre	1929	a)thousand centners	-	-	-	-	-	-	-	119	3790	120	135	4045	8846	40
41		"	b)thousand rubles	-	-	-	-	-	-	213	4008	158194	5137	5574	168905	350469	41
42		"	c)price per centner	-	-	-	-	-	-	-	33.7	41.7	42.8	41.3	41.8	39.6	42
43		1930	a)thousand centners	-	-	-	-	-	-	-	59	3409	63	194	3666	8187	43
44		"	b)thousand rubles	-	-	-	-	-	-	982	1597	190277	3238	9675	203190	426629	44
45		"	c)price per centner	-	-	-	-	-	-	-	27.1	55.8	51.4	49.9	55.4	52.1	45
46		1928	a)thousand centners	-	296	-	296	-	-	-	-	1175	2977	-	4152	12799	46
47		"	b)thousand rubles	-	8344	-	8344	-	-	-	-	33089	89328	-	122417	387825	47
48		"	c)price per centner	-	28.2	-	28.2	-	-	-	-	28.2	30.0	-	29.5	30.3	48
49	Raw cotton	1929	a)thousand centners	-	357	-	357	-	-	-	-	890	2711	-	3601	12792	49
50		"	b)thousand rubles	-	10070	-	10070	-	-	-	-	25097	75203	-	100300	384479	50
51		"	c)price per centner	-	28.2	-	28.2	-	-	-	-	28.2	27.7	-	27.6	30.1	51
52		1930	a)thousand centners	-	343	-	343	-	-	-	-	1197	4086	-	5283	14733	52
53		"	b)thousand rubles	-	9912	-	9912	-	-	-	-	35790	120374	-	156164	465879	53
54		"	c)price per centner	-	28.9	-	28.9	-	-	-	-	29.9	29.5	-	29.9	31.6	54

Materialy

Appendix B
Table 2. (cont'd)

Num-bers (A)	Designa-tion of prod-ucts (B)	Years (C)	Unit of measurement (D)	Stocks at beginning of year				Prod-uction	Im-ports	Cust-oms dut-ies	Trade and trans-port mark-up	Total input	Consumed in production							Num-bers (A)
				In agri-culture	In industry	In channels of circu-lation	Total stocks						In agriculture				In industry	In trans-port	Total consumed in industry	
													Seed	cattle fodder	Other items	Total				
				1	2	3	4	5	6	7	8	9	10	11	12	13	14	15	16	A
55		1928	a)thousand centners	279	93	284	656	330	-	-	-	986	-	-	-	-	297	-	297	55
56		"	b)thousand rubles	21367	14145	28655	64167	25466	-	-	19282	108915	-	-	-	-	39912	-	39912	56
57		"	c)price per centner	76.6	152.1	100.9	97.8	77.2	-	-	-	110.5	-	-	-	-	134.4	-	134.4	57
58	Raw tobac-co	1929	a)thousand centners	250	89	267	606	315	-	-	-	921	-	-	-	-	328	-	328	58
59		"	b)thousand rubles	19212	12706	29102	61020	18969	-	-	22117	102106	-	-	-	-	46164	-	46164	59
60		"	c)price per centner	76.8	142.8	109.0	100.7	60.2	-	-	-	110.9	-	-	-	-	140.7	-	140.7	60
61		1930	a)thousand centners	212	13	240	465	391	-	-	-	856	-	-	-	-	356	-	356	61
62		"	b)thousand rubles	13390	1973	28485	43848	39561	-	-	32950	116359	-	-	-	-	57601	-	57601	62
63		"	c)price per centner	63.2	151.8	118.7	91.3	101.2	-	-	-	135.9	-	-	-	-	161.8	-	161.8	63
64		1928	a)thousand centners	168	188	435	791	846	-	-	-	1657	-	-	-	-	946	-	946	64
65		"	b)thousand rubles	2544	4464	8964	15972	13218	-	-	5552	34742	-	-	-	-	21794	-	21794	65
66		"	c)price per centner	15.1	23.7	20.6	20.2	15.6	-	-	-	21.2	-	-	-	-	23.0	-	23.0	66
67	Raw Mak-hor-ka	1929	a)thousand centners	234	135	274	643	875	-	-	-	1518	-	-	-	-	833	-	833	67
68		"	b)thousand rubles	3655	3008	5794	12457	17933	-	-	6129	36519	-	-	-	-	21384	-	21384	68
69		"	c)price per centner	15.6	22.3	21.1	19.4	20.5	-	-	-	24.1	-	-	-	-	25.7	-	25.7	69
70		1930	a)thousand centners	187	120	283	590	902	-	-	-	1492	-	-	-	-	837	-	837	70
71		"	b)thousand rubles	4446	2820	6328	13594	28319	-	-	17012	58925	-	-	-	-	36057	-	36057	71
72		"	c)price per centner	23.8	23.5	22.4	23.0	31.4	-	-	-	39.5	-	-	-	-	43.1	-	43.1	72

Appendix B
Table 2. (cont'd)

Numbers	Designation of products	Years	Unit of measurement	Consumed by the population and by institutions — Non agricultural population (17)	Agricultural population (18)	Institutions and social organisations (19)	Total (20)	Losses In storage — In agriculture (21)	In industry and in channels of circulation (22)	In prices (23)	Exports (24)	Stocks at end of year — In agriculture (25)	In industry (26)	In channels of circulation (27)	Total (28)	Total output (29)	Numbers
A	B	C	D	17	18	19	20	21	22	23	24	25	26	27	28	29	A
55		1928	a)thousand centners	-	18	-	18	-	7	-	58	250	89	267	606	986	55
56		"	b)thousand rubles	-	1676	-	1676	-	-	-	6307	19212	12706	29102	61020	108915	56
57		"	c)price per centner	-	93.1	-	93.1	-	-	-	108.7	76.8	142.8	109.2	100.7	110.5	57
58	Raw tobacco	1929	a)thousand centners	-	30	-	30	-	6	-	92	212	13	240	465	921	58
59		"	b)thousand rubles	-	2250	-	2250	-	-	-	9844	13390	1973	28485	43848	102106	59
60		"	c)price per centner	-	75.0	-	75.0	-	-	-	107.0	63.2	151.8	118.7	94.3	110.9	60
61		1930	a)thousand centners	-	26	-	26	-	7	-	91	216	38	122	376	856	61
62		"	b)thousand rubles	-	2034	-	2034	-	-	-	11460	21827	6703	16734	45264	116359	62
63		"	c)price per centner	-	78.2	-	78.2	-	-	-	125.9	101.1	176.4	137.2	120.4	135.9	63
64		1928	a)thousand centners	-	37	-	37	-	11	-	-	234	135	274	643	1657	64
65		"	b)thousand rubles	-	491	-	491	-	-	-	-	3655	3008	5794	12457	34742	65
66		"	c)price per centner	-	13.3	-	13.3	-	-	-	-	15.6	22.3	21.1	19.4	21.2	66
67	Raw Makhorka	1929	a)thousand centners	-	85	-	85	-	10	-	-	187	120	283	590	1518	67
68		"	b)thousand rubles	-	1541	-	1541	-	-	-	-	4446	2820	6328	13594	36519	68
69		"	c)price per centner	-	18.1	-	18.1	-	-	-	-	23.8	23.5	22.4	23.0	24.1	69
70		1930	a)thousand centners	-	99	-	99	-	11	-	-	104	55	386	545	1492	70
71		"	b)thousand rubles	-	2451	-	2451	-	-	-	-	3250	2446	14741	20437	58925	71
72		"	c)price per centner	-	24.8	-	24.8	-	-	-	-	31.3	44.5	38.2	37.5	39.5	72

Appendix B
Table 2. (cont'd)

Numbers	Designation of products	Years	Unit of measurement	Stocks at beginning of year				Production	Imports	Customs duties	Trade and transport mark-up	Total input	Consumed in production				In industry	In transport	Total consumed in industry	Numbers
				In agriculture	In industry	In channels of circulation	Total stocks						In agriculture							
													Seed	Cattle fodder	Other items	Total				
A	B	C	D	1	2	3	4	5	6	7	8	9	10	11	12	13	14	15	16	A
73		1928	a) thousand centners	4789	12780	-	17569	101450	-	-	-	118999	-	6655	-	6655	98561	-	105216	73
74		"	b) thousand rubles	5268	20448	-	25716	111573	-	-	44692	181981	-	7155	-	7155	155726	-	162881	74
75		"	c) price per centner	1.1	1.6	-	1.5	1.1	-	-	-	1.5	-	1.1	-	1.1	1.6	-	1.5	75
76	Sugar beet	1929	a) thousand centners	5906	7877	-	13783	62478	-	-	-	76261	-	6828	-	6828	65149	-	71977	76
77		"	b) thousand rubles	6497	12603	-	19100	68101	-	-	26602	113803	-	7443	-	7443	102935	-	110378	77
78		"	c) price per centner	1.1	1.6	-	1.4	1.1	-	-	-	1.5	-	1.1	-	1.1	1.6	-	1.5	78
79		1930	a) thousand centners	2888	174	-	3062	140188	-	-	-	143250	-	5813	-	5813	106732	-	112545	79
80		"	b) thousand rubles	3147	278	-	3425	218695	-	-	101226	323346	-	7710	-	7710	251888	-	259598	80
81		"	c) price per centner	1.1	1.6	-	1.1	1.6	-	-	-	2.3	-	1.3	-	1.3	2.4	-	2.3	81
82		1928	a) thousand centners	247132	3500	-	250632	464409	-	-	-	715041	71921	143043	-	214964	10347	-	225311	82
83		"	b) thousand rubles	585703	5705	-	591408	1104149	-	-	67456	1763013	165418	332805	-	498223	22932	-	521155	83
84		"	c) price per centner	2.4	1.6	-	2.4	2.4	-	-	-	2.5	2.3	2.3	-	2.3	2.2	-	2.3	84
85	Potatoes	1929	a) thousand centners	258690	2822	-	261512	456297	-	-	-	717809	72022	125366	-	197388	14541	-	211929	85
86		"	b) thousand rubles	591909	5221	-	597130	1390352	-	-	98130	2085613	157008	302885	-	459893	37868	-	497761	86
87		"	c) price per centner	2.3	1.9	-	2.3	3.0	-	-	-	2.9	2.2	2.4	-	2.3	2.6	-	2.3	87
88		1930	a) thousand centners	264690	2558	-	267248	471004	-	-	-	738252	69088	110863	-	179951	22049	-	202000	88
89		"	b) thousand rubles	796064	5627	-	801691	1492947	-	-	123536	2418174	192756	298024	-	490780	55771	-	546551	89
90		"	c) price per centner	3.0	2.2	-	3.0	3.2	-	-	-	3.3	2.8	2.7	-	2.7	2.5	-	2.7	90

Appendix B
Table 2. (cont'd)

Num bers	Designa-tion of products	Years	Unit of measurement	Consumed by the population and by institutions				Losses In storage			Exports	Stocks at end of year				Total output	Num bers
				Non agri-cultural popu-lation	Agri-cultural popu-lation	Institutions and social organi-sations	Total	In agri-culture	In industry and in chan-nels of circu-lation	In prices		In agri-culture	In industry	In chan-nels of circu-lation	Total		
A	B	C	D	17	18	19	20	21	22	23	24	25	26	27	28	29	A
73		1928	a) thousand centners	–	–	–	–	–	–	–	–	5906	7877	–	13783	118999	73
74		"	b) thousand rubles	–	–	–	–	–	–	–	–	6497	12603	–	19100	181981	74
75		"	c) price per centner	–	–	–	–	–	–	–	–	1.1	1.6	–	1.4	1.5	75
76	Sugar beet	1929	a) thousand centners	–	–	–	–	–	1222	–	–	2888	174	–	3062	76261	76
77	beet	"	b) thousand rubles	–	–	–	–	–	–	–	–	3147	278	–	3425	113803	77
78		"	c) price per centner	–	–	–	–	–	–	–	–	1.1	1.6	–	1.1	1.5	78
79		1930	a) thousand centners	–	–	–	–	–	2835	–	–	4300	23570	–	27870	143250	79
80		"	b) thousand rubles	–	–	–	–	–	–	–	–	6709	57039	–	63748	323346	80
81		"	c) price per centner	–	–	–	–	–	–	–	–	1.6	2.4	–	2.3	2.3	81
82		1928	a) thousand centners	26086	171600	983	198669	26750	2120	–	679	258690	2822	–	261512	715041	82
83		"	b) thousand rubles	179413	396396	5450	581259	61792	–	526	1151	591909	5221	–	597130	1765013	83
84		"	c) price per centner	6.9	2.3	5.5	2.9	2.3	–	–	1.7	2.3	1.9	–	2.3	2.5	84
85	Potatoes	1929	a) thousand centners	34074	180494	1347	215915	19874	2800	–	43	264690	2568	–	267248	717809	85
86		"	b) thousand rubles	278003	448320	9752	736075	49939	–	72	75	796064	5627	–	801691	2085613	86
87		"	c) price per centner	8.2	2.5	7.2	3.4	2.5	–	–	1.7	3.0	2.2	–	3.0	2.9	87
88		1930	a) thousand centners	50087	182139	1837	234063	31144	4400	–	–	256288	2707	7650	266645	738252	88
89		"	b) thousand rubles	514007	460329	19472	993809	77929	–	–	–	740658	6443	52785	799886	2418174	89
90		"	c) price per centner	10.3	2.5	10.6	4.2	2.5	–	–	–	2.9	2.4	6.9	3.0	3.3	90

Appendix B

Table 3. Balances of livestock products

Num-bers (A)	Designation of products (B)	Years (C)	Unit of measurement (D)	Stocks at beginning of year				Production per year	Imports	Customs duties	Trade and transport mark-up	Total input	Consumed in production			Num-bers (A)
				In agriculture (1)	In industry (2)	In channels of circulation (3)	Total (4)	(5)	(6)	(7)	(8)	(9)	In agriculture (10)	In industry (11)	Total (12)	
1	Large raw hides	1928	a) thousands of hides	1350	428	1469	3247	16932	1500	-	-	21679	500	16137	16637	1
2		"	b) thousands of rubles	12496	4836	16188	33520	154676	38513	1800	27909	2564 8	4403	202550	206933	2
3		"	c) price per hide	9.3	11.3	11.0	10.3	9.1	25.7	-	-	1 .8	8.8	12.6	12.4	3
4		1929	a) thousands of hides	2114	646	2222	4982	21027	1320	-	-	27329	440	18854	19294	4
5		"	b) thousands of rubles	18390	7106	23553	49049	183261	31006	1500	46417	311233	3472	236401	239873	5
6		"	c) price per hide	8.7	11.0	10.6	9.8	8.7	23.5	-	-	11.4	7.9	12.5	12.4	6
7		1930	a) thousands of hides	4216	848	2859	7923	17150	893	-	-	25966	350	19267	19617	7
8		"	b) thousands of rubles	37706	8480	25311	70897	163126	15609	1200	66964	317796	2855	255106	257961	8
9		"	c) price per hide	8.8	10.0	8.9	8.9	9.5	17.5	-	-	12.2	8.2	13.2	13.1	9
10	Small raw hides	1928	a) thousands of hides	9300	783	4999	15082	66085	3063	-	-	84230	-	57115	57115	10
11		"	b) thousands of rubles	23576	2271	12847	38694	164613	10877	500	17564	232248	-	161151	161151	11
12		"	c) price per hide	2.5	2.9	2.6	2.6	2.5	3.6	-	-	9.8	-	2.8	2.8	12
13		1929	a) thousands of hides	1000	1080	6502	17590	83658	3032	-	-	104280	-	66145	66145	13
14		"	b) thousands of rubles	25275	3564	16580	45419	204832	14775	600	25454	291080	-	186548	186548	14
15		"	c) price per hide	2.5	3.3	2.5	2.6	2.4	4.9	-	-	2.8	-	2.8	2.8	15
16		1930	a) thousands of hides	18725	1082	7110	26917	75475	3193	-	-	105585	-	64662	64662	16
17		"	b) thousands of rubles	46254	3354	18346	67954	180047	9451	800	32213	298465	-	187840	187840	17
18		"	c) price per hide	2.5	3.1	2.6	2.5	2.5	3.0	-	-	2.3	-	2.9	2.9	18

Appendix B
Table 3. (cont'd)

Num-bers (A)	Desig-nation of products (B)	Years (C)	Unit of measurement (D)	Institutions and social organisations (13)	Agricultural population (14)	Non-agricultural population (15)	Total (16)	Exports (17)	Losses In storage and in channels of circulation (18)	In prices (19)	In agriculture (20)	In industry (21)	In channels of circulation (22)	Total (23)	Total output (24)	Num-bers (A)
1		1928	a) thousands of hides	–	–	–	–	60	–	–	2114	646	2222	4982	21679	1
2		"	b) thousands of rubles	–	–	–	–	436	–	–	18590	7106	23553	49049	256418	2
3		"	c) price per hide	–	–	–	–	7.3	–	–	8.7	11.0	10.6	9.8	11.8	3
4	Large raw	1929	a) thousands of hides	–	–	–	–	112	–	–	4216	848	2859	7923	27329	4
5	hides	"	b) thousands of rubles	–	–	–	–	463	–	–	37106	8480	25311	70897	311233	5
6		"	c) price per hide	–	–	–	–	4.1	–	–	8.8	10.0	8.9	8.9	11.4	6
7		1930	a) thousands of hides	–	–	–	–	284	–	–	2800	848	2417	6065	25966	7
8		"	b) thousands of rubles	–	–	–	–	2167	–	–	25849	9413	22406	57668	317796	8
9		"	c) price per hide	–	–	–	–	7.6	–	–	9.2	11.1	9.3	9.5	12.2	9
10		1928	a) thousands of hides	–	5100	–	5100	4425	–	–	10008	1080	6502	17590	84230	10
11		"	b) thousands of rubles	–	12442	–	12442	13236	–	–	25275	3564	16580	45419	232248	11
12		"	c) price per hide	–	2.4	–	2.4	3.0	–	–	2.5	3.3	2.5	2.6	2.8	12
13	Small	1929	a) thousands of hides	–	6252	–	6252	4966	–	–	18725	1082	7110	26917	104280	13
14	raw	"	b) thousands of rubles	–	15165	–	15165	21413	–	–	46254	3354	18346	67954	291080	14
15	hides	"	c) price per hide	–	2.4	–	2.4	4.3	–	–	2.5	3.1	2.6	2.5	2.8	15
16		1930	a) thousands of hides	–	9275	–	9275	4000	–	–	18840	1085	7723	27648	105585	16
17		"	b) thousands of rubles	–	22258	–	22258	17400	–	–	47338	3472	20157	70967	298465	17
18		"	c) price per hide	–	2.4	–	2.4	4.4	–	–	2.5	3.2	2.6	2.6	2.8	18

Appendix B
Table 3. (cont'd)

Numbers	Designation of products	Years	Unit of measurement	Stocks at beginning of year				Production per year	Imports	Customs duties	Trade and transport mark-up	Total input	Consumed in production			Numbers
A	B	C	D	In agriculture	In industry	In channels of circulation	Total						In agriculture	In industry	Total	A
				1	2	3	4	5	6	7	8	9	10	11	12	
19	Meat and	1928	a) thousands of centners	–	–	–	–	45220	130	–	–	45350	–	1960	1960	19
20	fat	"	b) thousands of rubles	–	–	–	–	1884111	6137	–	362928	2253176	–	106826	106826	20
21		"	c) price per centner	–	–	–	–	42.6	47.2	–	–	49.7	–	54.5	54.5	21
22	Meat and	1929	a) thousands of centners	–	–	–	–	52420	90	–	–	52510	–	2010	2010	22
23	fat	"	b) thousands of rubles	–	–	–	–	2106170	4055	–	420344	2530569	–	122562	122562	23
24		"	c) price per centner	–	–	–	–	40.2	45.1	–	–	48.2	–	61.0	61.0	24
25		1930	a) thousands of centners	750	–	730	1480	37520	420	–	–	39420	–	1980	1980	25
26		"	b) thousands of rubles	42202	–	52618	94820	2321256	22580	–	269342	2707998	–	168157	168157	26
27		"	c) price per centner	56.3	–	72.1	64.1	61.9	53.8	–	–	68.7	–	84.9	84.9	27
28		1928	a) millions of eggs	–	–	–	–	10770	1	–	–	10771	561	33	594	28
29		"	b) thousands of rubles	–	–	–	–	340715	55	–	60529	401299	17136	1104	18240	29
30		"	c) price per thousand	–	–	–	–	31.6	55.0	–	–	37.3	30.5	33.5	30.7	30
31	Eggs	1929	a) millions of eggs	–	–	–	–	10109	0.3	–	–	10109	525	26	551	31
32		"	b) thousands of rubles	–	–	–	–	395768	20	–	88300	484088	19928	1060	2098	32
33		"	c) price per thousand	–	–	–	–	39.2	66.7	–	–	47.9	88.0	40.8	38.1	33
34		1930	a) millions of eggs	–	–	–	–	7193	1	–	–	7194	374	21	395	34
35		"	b) thousands of rubles	–	–	–	–	438841	76	–	79393	518310	17155	1808	18963	35
36		"	c) price per thousand	–	–	–	–	61.0	76.0	–	–	72.1	45.9	86.1	48.0	36

Tables and notes   403

Appendix B
Table 3. (cont'd)

Num-bers A	Designation of products B	Years C	Unit of measurement D	Consumed by institutions and by the population				Exports 17	Losses In storage and in channels of circulation 18	Stocks at end of year					Total output 24	Num-bers A
				Institutions and social organisations 13	Agricultural population 14	Non-agricultural population 15	Total 16			In prices 19	In agriculture 20	In industry 21	In channels of circulation 22	Total 23		
19	Meat and fat	1928	a) thousands of centners	810	27740	13470	42020	370	1000	-	-	-	-	-	45350	19
20		"	b) thousands of rubles	43302	1145621	937118	2126041	20309	-	-	-	-	-	-	2253176	20
21		"	c) price per centner	53.5	41.3	62.5	50.6	54.9	-	-	-	-	-	-	49.7	21
22	Meat and fat	1929	a) thousands of centners	840	33680	12720	47240	280	1500	-	750	-	730	1480	52510	22
23		"	b) thousands of rubles	49527	1263701	983414	2296642	16545	-	-	42202	-	52618	94820	2530569	23
24		"	c) price per centner	59.0	37.5	77.3	48.5	59.1	-	-	56.3	-	72.1	64.1	48.2	24
25		1930	a) thousands of centners	860	26130	9550	36340	100	1000	-	-	-	-	-	39420	25
26		"	b) thousands of rubles	55479	1210427	1268027	2533933	5908	-	-	-	-	-	-	2707998	26
27		"	c) price per centner	64.5	46.3	135.6	69.7	59.1	-	-	-	-	-	-	68.7	27
28	Eggs	1928	a) millions of eggs	19	5478	3422	8919	1258	-	-	-	-	-	-	10771	28
29		"	b) thousands of rubles	768	167642	173423	341833	41226	-	-	-	-	-	-	401299	29
30		"	c) price per thousand	40.4	30.6	50.7	38.3	32.8	-	-	-	-	-	-	37.3	30
31	Eggs	1929	a) millions of eggs	22	5517	3441	8980	578	-	-	-	-	-	-	10109	31
32		"	b) millions of rubles	880	209260	229005	439145	23955	-	-	-	-	-	-	484088	32
33		"	c) price per thousand	40.0	37.9	66.6	48.9	41.4	-	-	-	-	-	-	47.9	33
34	Eggs	1930	a) millions of eggs	16	4034	2620	6670	129	-	-	-	-	-	-	7194	34
35		"	b) thousands of rubles	825	185017	307700	493542	3740	-	2065	-	-	-	-	518310	35
36		"	c) price per thousand	51.6	45.9	117.4	74.0	29.0	-	-	-	-	-	-	72.1	36

Appendix B
Table 3. (cont'd)

Num-bers	Desig-nation of products	Years	Unit of measurement	Stocks at beginning of year				Produc-ion per year	Imports	Cust-oms duties	Trade and trans-port mark-up	Total input	Consumed in production			Num-bers
				In agri-culture	In industry	In chan-nels of circu-lation	Total						In agri-culture	In industry	Total	
A	B	C	D	1	2	3	4	5	6	7	8	9	10	11	12	A
37	Milk and dairy products conver-	1928	a) thousand centners	-	-	-	-	304890	-	-	-	304890	17210	2566	19776	37
38	ted to	1929	a) thousand centners	-	-	-	-	293350	-	-	-	293350	16630	2963	19593	38
39	milk eq-uivalent	1930	a) thousand centners	-	-	-	-	265720	-	-	-	265720	15340	3515	18855	39
40	Wool conver-ted to its	1928	a) thousand centners	-	92	51	143	1066	297	-	-	1506	-	916	916	40
41	washed	1929	a) thousand centners	-	113	59	172	1072	312	-	-	1586	-	939	939	41
42	equiv-alent	1930	a) thousand centners	-	163	70	233	883	237	-	-	2353	-	994	994	42

Appendix B
Table 3. (cont'd)

Num-bers	Desig-nation of products	Years	Unit of measurement	Consumed by institutions and by the population				Exports	Losses In storage and in channels of circu-lation	Stocks at end of year					Total output	Num-bers
				Instit-utions and social organi-isations	Agri-cultural popu-lation	Non-agri-cultural popu-lation	Total			In prices	In agri-culture	In industry	In chan-nels of circu-lation	Total		
A	B	C	D	13	14	15	16	17	18	19	20	21	22	23	24	A
	Milk and dairy products conver-ted to milk eq-uivalent															
37		1928	a) thousand centners	533	227003	51667	279203	5911	-	-	-	-	-	-	304890	37
38		1929	a) thousand centners	624	216190	52314	269158	4599	-	-	-	-	-	-	293350	38
39		1930	a) thousand centners	618	194945	49395	244958	1907	-	-	-	-	-	-	265720	39
	Wool conver-ted to its washed equiv-alent															
40		1928	a) thousand centners	-	418	-	418	-	-	-	-	113	59	172	1506	40
41		1929	a) thousand centners	-	414	-	414	-	-	-	-	163	70	233	1586	41
42		1930	a) thousand centners	-	212	-	212	-	-	-	-	92	55	147	1353	42

Appendix C. Fixed capital stock

Table 1. Fixed capital stock of branches of the economy in terms of value, allowing for depreciation (in current prices, in millions of rubles)

Branches of the economy	Stock at beginning of year						As % of previous year				1932 in relation to 1928
	1928	1929	1930	1931 including small-scale industry	1931 excluding small-scale industry	1932[3]	1929	1930	1931	1932	
A	1	2	3	4	5	6	7	8	9	10	11
Total economy											
a) excluding livestock	56029.8	58111.9	61083.9	65751.2	65014.4	72519.4	103.7	105.1	107.6	111.5	129.4
b) including livestock	64327.1	66471.3	69159.1	75401.9	74665.1	86444.7	103.3	103.2	105.3	108.8	131.4
		66972.1	71635.4	80210.0	79473.2						
Socialist sector											
a) excluding livestock	30926.7	32557.1	35305.7	41309.7	40757.1	49816.4	105.2	108.5	117.0	122.2	161.1
b) including livestock [1]	31009.9	32667.4	35694.6	43047.6	42495.0	55644.7	105.3	109.3	120.1	128.2	179.4
		32671.0	35852.3	43961.0	43408.4						
Private sector											
a) excluding livestock	25103.1	25574.8	25778.2	24441.5	24257.	22703.0	101.9	100.8	94.8	93.6	90.4
b) including livestock [1]	33317.2	33803.9	33444.5	32354.3	32170.1	30800.0	101.5	97.5	90.4	85.4	92.4
		34301.1	35783.1	36249.0	36064.8						
1. Census industry	5273.8	5887.6	6907.0	8734.3		11483.1	111.6	117.3	126.5	131.5	217.7
of which: planned by VSNKh and NKSnab	4634.7	5245.0	6074.6	7734.6		9983.5	113.1	115.9	127.3	129.1	215.4
group "A"	2531.2	3009.3	3718.3	5188.7		7270.3	118.9	123.6	139.5	140.1	287.2
group "B"	2103.5	2233.7	2356.3	2545.9		2713.2	106.2	105.5	108.0	106.6	129.0
2. District and municipal electric power stations	458.3	548.4	640.9	834.5		1250.6	125.1	116.9	130.2	147.5	280.8
of which: electric power stations of Energotsentr	284.5	383.3	459.5	635.4		1005.9	134.7	119.9	138.3	158.3	353.6
3. Power stations in agriculture	10.2	14.5	23.7	37.8		61.7	142.2	163.4	159.5	163.2	604.9
4. Small-scale industry	769.2	755.1	756.8	736.8			98.2	100.2	97.4	–	–
socialist sector	130.8	168.4	267.9	552.6			128.7	159.1	206.3	–	–
private sector	638.4	586.7	488.9	184.2			91.9	83.3	37.7	–	–

Appendix C
Table 1. (cont'd)

A — Branches of the economy	Stock at beginning of year						As % of previous year				1932 in relation to 1928
	1928	1929	1930	1931 including small-scale industry	1931 excluding small-scale industry	1932³	1929	1930	1931	1932	
	1	2	3	4	5	6	7	8	9	10	11
5. Agriculture (less housing stock and power stations)											
a) excluding livestock	9655.0	10037.2	10620.7	11553.3	–	12966.8	104.0	105.8	108.8	112.2	134.3
b) including livestock¹	17952.3	18396.6	18675.9	21204.0	–	26892.1	102.5	98.8	100.2	103.4	149.8
		18897.4	21172.2	26012.1							
socialist sector											
a) excluding livestock	1200.4	1355.6	1824.0	3376.9	–	6059.1	112.9	134.6	185.1	179.4	504.8
b) including livestock¹	1283.6	1485.9	2212.9	5114.8	–	11887.4	115.8	148.6	215.8	197.2	926.1
		1489.5	2370.6	6028.2							
private sector											
a) excluding livestock	8454.6	8681.6	8796.7	8176.4	–	6907.7	102.7	101.3	92.4	84.5	81.7
b) including livestock	16668.7	16910.7	16463.0	16089.2	–	15004.7	101.5	94.6	85.6	75.1	90.0
		17407.9	18801.6	19983.9							
6. Transport²	10520.8	10674.9	10996.6	11886.7	–	13295.9	101.5	103.0	108.1	111.9	126.4
a) railway	9575.7	9717.6	9954.0	10575.6	–	11482.5	101.5	102.4	106.2	108.6	119.9
b) river	300.2	294.4	308.6	372.4	–	465.5	98.1	104.8	120.7	125.0	155.1
c) maritime	276.9	284.9	326.7	398.1	–	486.9	102.9	114.7	121.9	122.3	175.8
d) surfaced and dirt roads	368.0	378.0	407.3	540.6	–	861.0	102.7	107.8	132.7	159.3	234.0
7. Communications	229.6	259.7	301.7	370.4	–	516.5	113.1	116.2	122.8	139.4	225.0
8. Exchange and distribution	425.9	464.3	577.1	823.9	–	1299.8	109.0	124.3	142.8	157.8	305.2

Appendix C
Table 1. (cont'd)

Branches of the economy	Stock at beginning of year						As % of previous year				1932 in relation to 1928
	1928	1929	1930	1931	including small-scale industry / excluding small-scale industry	1932³	1929	1930	1931	1932	
A	1	2	3	4	5	6	7	8	9	10	11
9. Stock assigned for social purposes	5454.1	5698.0	6053.0	6359.6	-	6709.6	104.5	106.2	105.1	105.5	123.0
a) education	1810.5	1878.6	2004.1	2097.1	-	2190.7	103.8	106.7	104.6	104.5	121.0
b) public health	939.0	997.9	1064.9	1134.1	-	1195.3	106.3	106.7	106.5	105.4	127.3
c) administration	545.3	580.8	622.0	652.2	-	735.9	106.5	107.1	104.9	112.8	135.0
d) municipal economy	2159.3	2240.7	2362.0	2476.2	-	2587.7	103.8	105.4	104.8	104.5	119.8
10. Urban housing stock	12204.6	12424.6	12642.0	12932.7	-	13324.9	101.8	101.7	102.3	103.0	109.2
Socialist sector (housing stock of industry, executive committees, cooperatives)	7162.8	7363.0	7577.0	7943.3	-	8441.2	102.8	102.9	104.8	106.3	117.8
Private sector	5041.8	5061.6	5065.0	4989.4	-	4888.7	100.4	100.1	98.5	97.9	96.9
11. Rural housing stock	11048.3	11347.6	11564.4	11481.2	-	11630.5	102.7	101.9	99.3	101.3	105.3
Socialist sector	80.0	102.7	136.8	389.7	-	718.9	128.4	133.2	284.9	184.5	898.6
Private sector	10968.3	11244.9	11427.6	11091.5	-	10911.6	102.5	101.6	97.1	98.4	99.5

Notes: 1.   The numerator shows the stock at the end of the previous year, and the denominator those at the beginning of the year indicated. This difference between the stock at the end and at the beginning of the following year is due to the fact that, in agriculture, livestock have been revalued in the average-yearly prices of each year.

2.   The transport stock are given with the housing stock and buildings serving social purposes.

3.   Without small-scale industry.

Appendix C

Table 2. Fixed capital stock of the national economy, by economic categories and sectors (in current prices, in millions of rubles)

Sectors and economic categories	Stock at beginning of year										1932 as % of 1928
	1928	1929	1930	1931 including small-scale industry	1931 excluding small-scale industry	1932[3]	1929	1930	1931	1932	
A	1	2	3	4	5	6	7	8	9	10	11
A. Total economy											
a) excluding livestock	56029.8	58111.9	61083.9	65751.2	65014.4	72519.4	103.7	105.1	107.6	111.5	129.4
b) including livestock[1]	64327.1	66471.3	69139.1	75401.9	74665.1	86444.7	103.3	103.2	105.3	108.8	134.4
of which:											
1. Productive stock											
a) excluding livestock	26896.9	28177.4	30247.4	34153.8	33417.0	39554.6	104.8	107.3	112.9	118.4	147.1
b) including livestock[1]	35194.2	36536.8	38302.6	43804.5	43067.7	53479.9	103.8	103.4	107.4	114.7	152.0
2. Distributive stock	425.9	464.3	577.1	823.9	823.9	1299.8	109.0	124.3	142.8	157.8	305.2
3. Consumption stock	28707.0	29470.2	30259.4	30773.5	30773.5	31665.0	102.7	102.7	101.7	102.9	110.3
B. Socialist sector											
a) excluding livestock	30926.7	32537.1	35305.7	44309.7	40757.1	49816.4	105.2	108.5	117.0	122.2	161.1
b) including livestock[1]	31009.9	32667.4	35694.6	43047.6	42495.0	55644.7	105.3	109.3	120.1	128.2	179.4
of which:											
1. Productive stock[2]											
a) excluding livestock	17803.9	18909.1	10961.8	25793.2	25240.6	32646.9	106.2	110.9	123.0	129.3	193.4
b) including livestock[1]	17887.1	19039.4	21350.7	27531.1	26978.5	38475.2	106.4	112.1	128.0	137.9	215.1
2. Distributive stock	425.9	464.3	577.1	823.9	823.9	1299.8	109.0	124.3	142.8	157.8	305.2
3. Consumption stock	12696.9	13163.7	13766.8	14692.6	14692.6	15869.7	103.7	104.6	106.7	108.0	125.0

Appendix C
Table 2. (cont'd)

Sectors and economic categories	Stock at beginning of year										1932 as % of 1928
	1928	1929	1930	1931 including small-scale industry	excluding small-scale industry	1932[3]	1929	1930	1931	1932	
A	1	2	3	4	5	6	7	8	9	10	11
C. Private sector											
a) excluding livestock	25103.1	25574.8	25778.2	24441.5	24257.3	22703.0	101.9	100.8	94.8	93.6	90.4
b) including livestock	33317.2	33803.9 / 34301.1	33444.5 / 35783.1	32334.3	32170.1	30800.0	101.5	97.5	90.4	85.4	92.4
of which:											
1. Productive stock:											
a) excluding livestock	9093.0	9268.3	9285.6	8360.6	8176.4	6907.7	101.9	100.2	90.0	84.5	76.0
b) including livestock[1]	17307.1	17497.4 / 17994.6	16951.9 / 19290.5	16273.4	16089.2	15004.7	101.1	94.2	84.4	75.1	86.7
2. Distributive stock	-	-	-	-	-	-	-	-	-	-	-
3. Consumption stock	16010.1	16306.5	16492.0	16680.9	16680.9	15795.3	101.9	101.1	97.5	98.2	98.7

Notes: 1. The numerator shows the stock at the end of the previous year, and the denominator those at the beginning
            of the year indicated. This difference between the stock at the end and at the beginning of the following
            year is due to the fact that, in agriculture, the livestock have been revalued in the average-yearly prices
            of each year.

         2. The productive stock of transport includes dwelling houses and buildings serving social purposes.

         3. Excluding small-scale industry.

Appendix C

Table 2a. Active fixed capital stock of the economy, by economic categories and sectors (in 1928 prices, in millions of rubles)

Sectors and economic categories	Stock at beginning of year						As % of previous year				1932 as % of 1928
	1928	1929	1930	1931 including small-scale industry	excluding small-scale industry	1932[2]	1929	1930	1931	1932	
A	1	2	3	4	5	6	7	8	9	10	11
A. Total economy											
a) excluding livestock	56029.8	58111.9	61192.7	66482.9	65746.1	73462.0	103.7	105.3	108.6	111.7	131.1
b) including livestock	64327.1	66471.3	68841.0	73381.5	72644.7	79917.2	103.3	103.6	106.6	110.0	124.2
of which:											
1. Productive stock											
a) excluding livestock	26896.9	28177.4	30321.3	34648.8	33912.0	40235.8	104.8	107.6	114.3	118.6	149.6
b) including livestock	35194.2	36536.8	37969.6	41547.4	40810.6	46691.0	103.8	103.9	109.4	114.4	132.7
2. Distributive stock	425.9	464.3	582.6	854.8	854.8	1332.1	109.0	125.5	146.7	155.8	312.8
3. Consumption stock	28707.0	29470.2	30288.8	30979.3	30979.3	31894.1	102.7	102.8	102.3	103.0	111.1
B. Socialist sector											
a) excluding livestock	30926.7	32537.1	35470.2	42081.3	41528.7	50789.5	105.2	109.0	118.6	122.3	164.2
b) including livestock	31009.9	32667.4	35839.0	43305.6	42753.0	53396.2	105.3	109.7	120.8	124.9	172.2
of which:[1]											
1. Productive stock											
a) excluding livestock	17803.9	18909.1	21067.1	26297.9	25745.3	33318.8	106.2	111.4	124.9	124.9	187.1
b) including livestock	17887.1	19039.4	21430.5	27522.2	26969.6	35925.5	106.4	112.6	128.4	133.2	200.8
2. Distributive stock	425.9	464.3	582.6	854.8	854.8	1332.1	109.0	125.5	146.7	155.8	312.8
3. Consumption stock	12696.9	13163.7	13825.9	14928.6	14928.6	16158.6	103.7	105.0	108.0	108.1	127.1

Appendix C
Table 2a. (cont'd)

Sectors and economic categories	Stock at beginning of year						As % of previous year				1932 as % of 1928
	1928	1929	1930	1931 including small-scale industry	1931 excluding small-scale industry	1932[2]	1929	1930	1931	1932	
A	1	2	3	4	5	6	7	8	9	10	11
C. Private sector											
a) excluding livestock	25103.1	25574.8	25722.5	24401.6	24217.4	22672.5	101.9	100.6	94.9	93.6	90.3
b) including livestock	33317.2	33803.9	33002.0	30075.9	29891.7	26521.0	101.5	97.6	91.1	88.7	79.6
of which:											
1. Productive stock:											
a) excluding livestock	9093.0	9268.3	9259.6	8350.9	8166.7	6917.0	101.9	99.9	90.2	84.7	76.1
b) including livestock	17307.1	17497.4	16539.1	14025.2	13841.0	10765.5	101.1	94.5	84.8	77.8	62.2
2. Distributive stock	-	-	-	-	-	-	-	-	-	-	-
3. Consumption stock	16010.1	16306.5	16462.9	16050.7	16050.7	15755.5	101.9	101.0	97.5	98.2	98.4

Notes: 1. The productive stock of transport includes dwelling houses and buildings serving social purposes.

          2. Excluding small-scale industry.

Appendix C

Table 3. Structure of fixed capital stock by sectors (in current prices)   -   a) excluding livestock
b) including livestock

Types of funds	As % of total 1928	1929	1930	1931 including small-scale industry	1932 excluding small-scale industry	including small-scale industry
A	1	2	3	4	5	6
Total economy a)	100.0	100.0	100.0	100.0	100.0	100.0
b)	100.0	100.0	100.0	100.0	100.0	100.0
of which, socialist sector a)	55.2	56.0	57.8	62.8	62.7	68.7
b)	48.2	48.8	50.0	54.8	54.6	64.4
" " private sector a)	44.8	44.0	42.2	37.2	37.3	31.3
b)	51.8	51.2	50.0	45.2	45.4	35.6
Productive stock a)	100.0	100.0	100.0	100.0	100.0	100.0
b)	100.0	100.0	100.0	100.0	100.0	100.0
of which, socialist sector a)	66.2	67.1	69.3	75.5	75.5	82.5
b)	50.8	51.4	52.7	58.5	58.3	71.9
" " private sector a)	33.8	32.9	30.7	24.5	24.5	17.5
b)	49.2	48.6	47.3	41.5	41.7	28.1
Non-productive stock	100.0	100.0	100.0	100.0	100.0	100.0
of which, socialist sector	45.0	45.5	46.5	49.1	49.1	52.1
" " private sector	55.0	54.5	53.5	50.9	50.9	47.9

Appendix C

Table 3a. Structure of fixed capital stock by sectors (in 1928 prices)   -   a) excluding livestock
b) including livestock

Type of funds	As % of total 1928	1929	1930	1931 including small-scale industry	1932 excluding small-scale industry	including small-scale industry
A	1	2	3	4	5	6
Total national economy a)	100.0	100.0	100.0	100.0	100.0	100.0
b)	100.0	100.0	100.0	100.0	100.0	100.0
of which, socialist sector a)	55.2	56.0	58.0	63.3	63.2	69.1
b)	48.2	49.1	52.1	59.0	58.9	66.8
" " private sector a)	44.8	44.0	42.0	36.7	36.8	30.9
b)	51.8	50.9	47.9	41.0	41.1	33.2
Productive stock a)	100.0	100.0	100.0	100.0	100.0	100.0
b)	100.0	100.0	100.0	100.0	100.0	100.0
of which, socialist sector a)	66.2	67.1	69.5	75.9	75.9	82.8
b)	50.8	52.1	56.4	66.2	66.1	76.9
" " private sector a)	33.8	32.9	30.5	24.1	24.1	17.2
b)	49.2	47.9	43.6	33.8	33.9	23.1
Non-productive stock	100.0	100.0	100.0	100.0	100.0	100.0
of which, socialist sector	45.0	45.5	46.7	49.6	49.6	52.6
" " private sector	55.0	54.5	53.3	50.4	50.4	47.4

Appendix C

Table 4. Balance of fixed capital stock of branches of the economy (in value terms, net of depreciation, in current prices, in millions of rubles)

Branches of the economy	1928 Stock at 1 Jan 1928 (1)	1928 Residue of incomplete building at 1 Jan 1928 (2)	1928 Capital investment (3)	1928 Stock entered into exploitation (4)	1929 Residue of incomplete building at 1 Jan 1929 (5)	Deprec-[2] iation (6)	Stock at 1 Jan 1929 (7)	1929 Residue of incomplete building at 1 Jan 1929 (8)	1929 Capital investment (9)	Stock entered into exploitation (10)	Residue of incomplete building at 1 Jan 1930 (11)	Deprec-[2] iation (12)	Stock at 1 Jan 1930 (13)
Total economy													
a) excluding livestock	56029.8	1380.8	5975.4	5318.2	2038.0	3173.3 / 62.8	58111.9	2038.0	7293.1	6369.2	2961.9	3310.5 / 86.7	61083.9
b) including livestock[1]	64327.1	1380.8	6843.7	6186.5	2038.0	3460.8 / 581.5	66471.3 / 66972.1	2038.0	7692.6	6768.7	2961.9	3577.1 / 1024.6	69139.1 / 71635.4
1. Census industry (with power stations)	5712.1	880.4	1525.5	1171.4	1234.5	435.5 / 12.0	6436.0	1234.5	2091.2	1624.3	1701.4	492.4 / 20.0	7547.9
2. Small-scale industry	769.2	-	35.4	35.4	-	49.5	755.1	-	47.7	47.7	-	46.0	756.8
of which, socialist sector[4]	130.8	-	25.0	25.0	-	8.4	168.4	-	38.4	38.4	-	10.3	267.9
" " private sector	638.4	-	10.4	21.0	-	41.1 / 21.0	586.7	-	71.4	71.4	-	35.7 / 71.4	488.9
3. Agriculture													
a) excluding livestock	9665.2	-	1309.4	1309.4	-	905.1 / 17.8	10051.7	-	1556.4	1556.4	-	933.5 / 30.2	10644.4
b) including livestock[1]	17962.5	-	2177.7	2177.7	-	1192.6 / 536.5	18411.1 / 18911.9	-	1955.9	1955.9	-	1200.1 / 968.1	18699.6 / 21195.6
4. Transport[3]	10520.8	124.6	901.8	738.4	288.0	584.3	10674.9	288.0	1146.6	939.9	494.7	618.2	10996.6
a) railway	9575.7	100.8	731.0	577.5	254.3	435.6	9717.6	254.3	873.0	699.5	427.8	463.1	9954.0
b) river	300.2	10.0	49.0	45.0	14.0	50.8	294.4	14.0	86.0	63.9	36.1	49.7	308.6
c) maritime	276.9	10.8	45.8	45.7	10.9	37.7	284.9	10.9	81.6	82.2	10.3	40.4	326.7
d) surfaced and dirt roads	368.0	3.0	76.0	70.2	8.8	60.2	378.0	8.8	106.0	94.3	20.5	65.0	407.3
5. Communications	229.6	5.9	53.5	44.7	14.7	14.6	259.7	14.7	70.3	57.0	28.0	15.0	301.7

Appendix C
Table 4. (cont'd)

Branches of the economy (A)	Residue of incomplete building at 1 Jan 1930 (14)	Capital investment (15)	Stock entered into exploitation (16)	Residue of incomplete building at 1 Jan 1931 (17)	Depreciation (18)	Stock at 1 Jan 1931 Including small-scale industry (19)	Excluding small-scale industry (20)	Residue of incomplete building at 1 Jan 1931 (21)	Capital investment (22)	Stock entered into exploitation (23)	Residue of incomplete building at 1 Jan 1932 (24)	Depreciation (25)	Stock at 1 Jan 1932 (26)
Total economy													
a) excluding livestock	2961.9	9960.3	8280.5	4641.7	3504.4 / 108.8	65751.2	65014.4	4641.7	14781.6	11583.4	7859.9	3834.8 / 193.6	72519.4
b) including livestock [1]	2961.9	10533.6	8853.8	4641.7	3783.0 / 1285.6	75401.9	74665.1	4641.7	15823.2	12625.0	7859.9	4557.1 / 1276.8	86444.7 [5]
1. Census industry (with power stations)	1701.4	3613.0	2574.6	2739.8	553.7	9568.8	–	2739.8	5904.3	3940.7	4703.4	795.8	12713.7
2. Small-scale industry	–	28.5	28.5	–	48.5	36.8	–	–	–	–	–	–	–
of which socialist sector [4]	–	26.1	26.1	–	26.3	552.6	–	–	–	–	–	–	–
private sector	–	2.4	2.4	–	22.2 / 284.9	184.2	–	–	–	–	–	–	–
3. Agriculture													
a) excluding livestock	–	2039.8	2039.8	–	1022.0 / 71.1	11591.1	–	–	2730.0	2730.0	–	1135.2 / 157.4	13028.5
b) including livestock [1]	–	2613.1	2613.1	–	1300.6 / 1247.9	21241.8 [5]	–	–	3771.6	3771.6	–	1607.5 / 1240.6	26953.8 [5]
4. Transport [3]	494.7	1624.7	1528.7	590.7	638.6	11886.7	–	590.7	2499.4	2086.0	1004.1	676.8	13295.9
a) railway	427.8	1112.2	1097.9	442.1	476.3	10575.6	–	442.1	1715.6	1410.8	746.9	503.9	11482.5
b) river	36.1	152.1	115.2	73.0	51.4	372.4	–	73.0	221.8	146.0	148.8	52.9	465.5
c) maritime	10.3	136.2	115.6	30.9	44.2	398.1	–	30.9	163.8	138.0	56.2	49.2	486.9
d) surfaced and dirt roads	20.5	224.2	200.0	44.7	66.7	540.6	–	44.7	398.7	391.2	52.2	70.8	861.0
5. Communications	28.0	94.4	86.0	36.4	17.3	370.4	–	36.4	180.0	165.8	50.6	19.7	516.5

Appendix C
Table 4. (cont'd)

Branches of the economy	1928							1929					
	Stock at 1 Jan 1928	Residue of incomplete building at 1 Jan 1928	Capital invest-ment	Stock entered into exploit-ation	Residue of incomplete building at 1 Jan 1929	Deprec-[2] iation	Stock at 1 Jan 1929	Residue of incomplete building at 1 Jan 1929	Capital invest-ment	Stock entered into exploit-ation	Residue of incomplete building at 1 Jan 1930	Deprec-[2] iation	Stock at 1 Jan 1930
A	1	2	3	4	5	6	7	8	9	10	11	12	13
6. Exchange and distribution	425.9	42.2	68.1	61.3	49.0	22.9	464.3	49.0	154.2	138.8	64.4	26.0	577.1
7. Stock assigned for social purposes	5454.1	144.7	461.1	402.5	203.3	158.6	5698.0	203.3	627.3	519.4	311.2	164.4	6053.0
a) education	1810.5	34.1	117.0	100.6	50.5	32.5	1878.6	50.5	198.9	158.9	90.5	33.4	2004.1
b) public health	939.0	45.8	89.1	76.4	58.5	17.5	997.9	58.5	104.4	85.2	77.7	18.2	1064.9
c) administration	545.3	29.2	61.0	52.3	37.9	16.8	580.8	37.9	71.0	58.8	50.1	17.6	622.0
d) municipal economy	2159.3	35.6	194.0	173.2	56.4	91.8	2240.7	56.4	253.0	216.5	92.9	95.2	2362.0
8. Urban housing stock	12204.6	183.0	689.2	623.7	248.5	403.7	12424.6	248.5	741.2	627.5	362.2	410.1	12642.0
of which, socialist sector	7162.8	109.0	452.9	421.3	140.6	221.1	7363.0	140.6	517.9	441.0	217.5	227.0	7577.0
" " private sector	5041.8	74.0	236.3	202.4	107.9	182.6	5061.6	107.9	223.3	186.5	144.7	183.1	5065.0
9. Rural housing stock	11048.3	-	931.4	931.4	-	599.1 / 33.0	11347.6	-	858.2	858.2	-	604.9 / 36.5	11564.4
In addition, capital investment in unrecorded funds and not passed into capital stock	-	-	432.4	-	-	-	-	-	758.0	-	-	-	-
of which: in unrecorded stock	-	-	193.9	-	-	-	-	-	322.6	-	-	-	-

Notes: 1. In the stock columns the numerator shows the stock at the end and the denominator at the beginning of the year. This difference between the stocks at the end and and at the beginning of the year is due to the fact that, in agriculture, the livestock were revalued in the average-yearly stock of each year.

2. In the "depreciation" column the denominator shows, for census industry, the property lost through age and wear-and-tear; for small-scale industry transference through socialisation; for agriculture and the rural housing stock other losses (premature death of livestock, losses through fires etc.)

3. The transport stock includes the stock of dwelling houses and buildings serving social purposes.

4. The denominator in the "capital investment" and "stock entered into exploitation" columns shows the property transferred from the private sector through socialisation.

Appendix C
Table 4. (cont'd)

Branches of the economy	1930					Stock at 1 Jan 1931		1931					
	Residue of incomplete building at 1 Jan 1930	Capital investment	Stock entered into exploitation	Residue of incomplete building at 1 Jan 1931	Depreciation	Including small-scale industry	Excluding small-scale industry	Residue of incomplete building at 1 Jan 1931	Capital investment	Stock entered into exploitation	Residue of incomplete building at 1 Jan 1932	Depreciation	Stock at 1 Jan 1932
A	14	15	16	17	18	19	20	21	22	23	24	25	26
6. Exchange and distribution	64.4	340.6	278.9	126.1	32.1	823.9	–	126.1	595.2	522.0	199.3	46.1	1299.8
7. Stock assigned to social purposes	311.2	670.4	479.4	502.2	172.8	6359.6	–	502.2	768.1	530.4	739.9	180.4	6709.6
a) education	90.5	201.1	127.9	163.7	34.9	2097.1	–	163.7	205.9	129.7	237.9	36.1	2190.7
b) public health	77.7	110.8	88.2	100.3	19.0	1134.1	–	100.3	101.9	81.1	121.1	19.9	1195.3
c) administration	50.1	90.8	48.7	92.2	18.5	652.2	–	92.2	191.9	102.9	181.2	19.2	735.9
d) municipal economy	92.9	267.7	214.6	146.0	100.4	2476.2	–	146.0	270.4	216.7	199.7	105.2	2587.7
8. Urban housing stock	362.2	989.3	705.0	646.5	414.3	12932.7	–	646.6	1307.6	811.5	1142.6	419.3	13324.9
of which: socialist sector	217.5	864.8	597.5	484.8	231.2	7943.3	–	484.8	1195.8	736.0	944.6	238.1	8441.2
" private sector	144.7	124.5	107.5	161.7	183.1	4989.4	–	161.7	111.8	75.5	198.0	181.2	4883.7
9. Rural housing stock	–	559.6	559.6	–	605.1 / 37.7	11481.2	–	–	797.0	797.0	–	611.5 / 36.2	11630.5
In addition, capital investment in unrecorded stock and not passed into capital stock	–	1146.6	–	–	–	–	–	–	1080.1	–	–	–	–
of which: in unrecorded stock	–	441.6	–	–	–	–	–	–	–	–	–	–	–

Notes: 5. The imbalance of 18.7 million rubles in 1930 and of 19.6 million rubles in 1931 is due to the fact that livestock to these amounts were transferred from agriculture to the suburban holdings of Tsentrosoyuz; where they were not recorded as stock, just as these amounts were not recorded in the stock of the economy as a whole.

Appendix C

Table 4a. Balance of fixed capital stock of branches of the economy (in value terms, net of depreciation, in 1928 prices, in millions of rubles)

Branches of the economy	1928 Stock at 1 Jan 1928	Residue of incomplete building 1 Jan 1928	Capital investment	Stock entered into exploitation	Residue of incomplete building at 1 Jan 1929	Depreciation[1]	Stock at 1 Jan 1929	1929 Residue of incomplete building at 1 Jan 1929	Capital investment	Stock entered into exploitation	Residue of incomplete building at 1 Jan 1930	Depreciation[1]	Stock at 1 Jan 1930
A	1	2	3	4	5	6	7	8	9	10	11	12	13
Total economy													
a) excluding livestock	56029.8	1380.8	5975.4	5318.2	2038.0	3173.3 / 62.8	58111.9	2038.0	7432.9	6473.5	2997.4	3309.4 / 83.3	61192.7
b) including livestock	64327.1	1380.8	6843.7	6186.5	2038.0	3460.8 / 581.5	66471.3	2038.0	7874.2	6914.8	2997.4	3581.5 / 963.6	68841.0
1. Census industry (with power stations)	5712.1	880.4	1525.5	1171.4	1234.5	435.5 / 12.0	6436.0	1234.5	2187.4	1699.0	1722.9	492.4 / 20.0	7622.6
2. Small-scale industry	760.2	-	35.4	35.4	-	49.5	755.1	-	47.7	47.7	-	46.0	756.8
of which, socialist sector[3]	130.8	-	25.0	25.0	-	8.4	168.1	-	38.4	38.4	-	10.3	267.9
" " private sector	638.4	-	10.4	10.0	-	41.1 / 21.0	586.7	-	71.4	71.4	-	35.7 / 71.4	488.9
3. Agriculture													
a) excluding livestock	9665.2	-	1309.4	1309.4	-	905.1 / 17.8	10051.7	-	1541.0	1541.0	-	932.5 / 26.8	10633.4
b) including livestock	17962.5	-	2177.7	2177.7	-	1192.6 / 536.5	18411.1	-	1982.3	1982.3	-	1204.6 / 907.1	18281.7
4. Transport[2]	10520.8	124.6	901.8	738.4	288.0	584.3	10674.9	288.0	1154.8	947.4	495.4	618.2	11004.1
a) railway	9575.7	100.8	731.0	577.5	254.3	435.6	9717.6	254.3	867.8	695.3	426.8	463.1	9949.8
b) river	300.2	10.0	49.0	45.0	14.0	50.8	294.4	14.0	90.7	67.4	37.3	49.7	312.1
c) maritime	276.9	10.8	45.8	45.7	10.9	37.7	284.9	10.9	86.1	86.7	10.3	40.4	331.2
d) surfaced and dirt roads	368.0	3.0	76.0	70.2	8.8	60.2	378.0	8.8	110.2	98.0	21.0	65.0	411.0
5. Communications	229.6	5.9	53.5	44.7	14.7	14.6	259.7	14.7	73.6	59.7	28.6	15.0	304.4

Appendix C
Table 4a. (cont'd)

Branches of the economy	1930					Stock at 1 Jan 1931		1931					
	Residue of incomplete building at 1 Jan 1930	Capital investment	Stock entered into exploitation	Residue of incomplete building at 1 Jan 1931	Depreciation[1]	Including small-scale industry	Excluding small-scale industry	Residue of incomplete building at 1 Jan 1931	Capital investment	Stock entered into exploitation	Residue of incomplete building at 1 Jan 1932	Depreciation[1]	Stock at 1 Jan 1932
A	14	15	16	17	18	19	20	21	22	23	24	25	26
Total economy													
a) excluding livestock	2997.4	10823.6	8909.0	4912.0	3508.9 / 109.9	66482.9	65746.1	4912.0	15171.5	11845.2	8238.3	3929.6 / 199.7	73462.0
b) including livestock	2997.4	11312.4	9397.8	4912.0	3772.7 / 1075.0	73381.5[4]	72644.7	4912.0	15666.1	12339.8	8238.3	4179.1 / 879.2	79917.2[4]
1. Census industry (with power stations)	1722.9	4429.1	2942.4	2909.6	556.4	10008.6	-	2909.6	6281.2	4192.2	4998.6	830.7	13370.1
2. Small-scale industry	-	28.5	28.5	-	48.5	736.8	-	-	-	-	-	-	-
of which: socialist sector[3]	-	26.1	26.1	-	26.3	552.6	-	-	-	-	-	-	-
" " private sector	-	2.4	2.4	-	22.2	184.2	-	-	-	-	-	-	-
	-	284.9	284.9	-	284.9	-	-	-	-	-	-	-	-
3. Agriculture													
a) excluding livestock	-	2076.1	2076.1	-	1014.4 / 72.9	11622.2	-	-	2793.1	2793.1	-	1127.7 / 163.6	13124.0
b) including livestock	-	2564.9	2564.9	-	1278.2 / 1036.0	18520.8[4]	-	-	3287.7	3287.7	-	1377.2 / 843.1	19579.2[4]
4. Transport[2]	495.4	1633.9	1534.0	595.3	641.7	11896.4	-	595.3	2401.6	1997.5	999.4	679.8	13214.1
a) railway	426.8	1096.8	1082.7	440.9	477.6	10554.9	-	440.9	1613.9	1327.2	727.6	502.8	11379.3
b) river	37.3	160.4	121.5	76.2	52.0	381.6	-	76.2	242.4	159.6	159.0	54.2	487.0
c) maritime	10.3	143.7	121.9	32.1	44.7	408.4	-	32.1	178.5	150.8	59.8	50.6	508.6
d) surfaced and dirt roads	21.0	233.0	207.9	46.1	67.4	551.5	-	46.1	366.8	359.9	53.0	72.2	839.2
5. Communications	28.6	107.3	97.7	38.2	17.3	384.8	-	38.2	177.2	163.2	52.2	20.4	527.6

Appendix C
Table 4a. (cont'd)

Branches of the economy	Stock at 1 Jan 1928	Residue of in-complete building at 1 Jan 1928	Capital invest-ment	Stock entered into exploit-ation	Residue of in-complete building at 1 Jan 1929	Deprec-iation [1]	Stock at 1 Jan 1929	Residue of in-complete building at 1 Jan 1929	Capital invest-ment	Stock entered into exploit-ation	Residue of in-complete building at 1 Jan 1930	Deprec-iation [1]	Stock at 1 Jan 1930
A	1	2	3	4	5	6	7	8	9	10	11	12	13
								1929						
6. Exchange and distribution	425.9	42.2	68.1	61.3	49.0	22.9	464.3	49.0	160.3	144.3	65.0	26.0	582.6
7. Stock assigned to social purposes	5454.1	144.7	461.1	402.5	203.3	158.6	5698.0	203.3	656.9	543.9	316.3	164.4	6077.5
a) education	1810.5	34.1	117.0	100.0	50.5	32.5	1878.6	50.5	209.1	167.1	92.5	33.4	2012.3
b) public health	939.0	45.8	89.1	76.4	58.5	17.5	997.9	58.5	109.1	89.0	78.5	18.2	1068.7
c) administration	545.3	29.2	61.0	52.3	37.9	16.8	580.8	37.9	74.6	61.8	50.7	17.6	625.0
d) municipal economy	2159.3	35.6	194.0	173.2	56.4	91.8	2240.7	56.4	264.1	226.0	94.5	95.2	2371.5
8. Urban housing stock	12204.6	183.0	689.2	623.7	248.5	403.7	12424.6	248.5	787.7	667.0	369.2	410.1	12681.5
of which, socialist sector	7162.8	109.0	452.9	421.3	140.6	221.1	7363.0	140.6	557.5	474.7	223.4	227.0	7610.7
" " private sector	5041.8	74.0	236.3	202.4	107.9	182.6	5061.6	107.9	230.2	192.3	145.8	183.1	5070.8
9. Rural housing stock	11048.3	-	931.4	931.4	-	599.1 / 33.0	11347.6	-	823.5	823.5	-	604.8 / 36.5	11529.8

Appendix C
Table 4a. (cont'd)

A	1930 Residue of incomplete building at 1 Jan 1930	Capital investment	Stock entered into exploitation	Residue of incomplete building at 1 Jan 1931	Depreciation[1]	Stock at 1 Jan 1931 Including small-scale industry	Excluding small-scale industry	1931 Residue of incomplete building at 1 Jan 1931	Capital investment	Stock entered into exploitation	Residue of incomplete building at 1 Jan 1932	Depreciation[1]	Stock at 1 Jan 1932
Branches of the economy	14	15	16	17	18	19	20	21	22	23	24	25	26
6. Exchange and distribution	65.0	372.2	304.8	132.4	32.6	854.8	-	132.4	598.8	525.2	206.0	47.9	1332.1
7. Stock assigned to social purposes	316.3	745.1	532.5	528.9	174.9	6435.1	-	528.9	763.5	527.1	765.3	181.7	6780.5
a) education	92.5	224.9	143.1	174.3	35.0	2120.4	-	174.3	202.9	129.0	248.2	36.5	2212.9
b) public health	78.6	122.8	97.8	103.6	19.2	1147.3	-	103.6	100.7	80.1	124.2	20.7	1206.7
c) administration	50.7	101.6	54.5	97.8	18.7	660.8	-	97.8	190.9	102.4	186.3	19.2	744.0
d) municipal economy	94.5	295.8	237.1	153.2	102.0	2506.6	-	153.2	269.0	215.6	206.6	105.3	2616.9
8. Urban housing stock	369.2	1162.0	823.6	707.6	419.2	13085.9	-	707.6	1358.1	828.9	1216.8	430.6	13484.2
of which: socialist sector	223.4	1042.0	719.9	545.5	235.9	8094.7	-	545.5	1248.2	768.2	1025.5	250.9	8612.0
" " private sector	145.8	120.0	103.7	152.1	183.3	4991.2	-	162.1	89.9	60.7	191.3	179.7	4872.2
9. Rural housing stock	-	569.4	569.4	-	603.9 / 37.0	11458.3	-	-	818.0	818.0	-	610.8 / 36.1	11629.4

Notes:
1. In the "depreciation" stock the denominator shows, for small-scale industry transference through socialisation, and, for agriculture and the rural housing stock, other losses (premature death of livestock, losses from fire, etc.)
2. The transport stock includes stock of dwelling houses and buildings serving social purposes.
3. The denominator in the "capital investment" and "stock entered into exploitation" columns show property transferred from the private sector through socialisation.
4. The imbalance of 11.6 million rubles in 1930 and 9.0 million rubles in 1931 is due to the fact that livestock of these amounts were transferred from agriculture to the suburban holdings of Tsentrosoyuz, where they were not recorded as stock, just as these amounts were not recorded in the stock of the economy as a whole.

Appendix C

Table 5. Balance of fixed capital stock of agriculture, by sectors (in current prices, in millions of rubles)

Economic categories	Years	Socialist sector						Private sector					All sectors				
		Stock at beginning of year	Through capital construction	Through socialisation	Total	Lost in year (depreciation)	Stock at end of year	Stock at beginning of year	Received in year (capital construction)	Depreciation	Transferred through socialisation	Total	Stock at end of year	Stock at beginning of year	Received in year (capital construction)	Lost in year (depreciation)	Stock at end of year
1	2	3	4	5	6	7	8	9	10	11	12	13	14	15	16	17	18
Total fixed capital stock (production and consumption)																	
excluding livestock	1928	1290.6	227.0	38.1	265.1	82.2 / 0.1	1472.8	19422.9	2013.8	1421.4 / 50.7	38.1	1421.4 / 88.8	19926.5	20713.5	2240.8	1504.2 / 50.8	21399.3
	1929	1472.8	510.1	117.7	627.8	115.6 / 0.5	1984.5	19926.5	1904.5	1422.8 / 62.2	117.7	1422.8 / 185.9	20224.3	21399.3	2414.6	1538.4 / 66.7	22208.8
	1930	1984.5	1550.1	528.0	2078.0	257.1 / 1.0	3804.4	20224.3	1049.4	1370.0 / 107.8	528.0	1370.0 / 635.8	19267.9	22208.8	2599.5	1627.1 / 108.8	23072.3
	1931	3804.4	2519.2	1017.8	3537.0	500.1 / 1.6	6839.7	19267.9	1007.8	1246.6 / 192.0	1017.8	1246.6 / 1209.8	17819.3	23072.3	3527.0	1746.7 / 193.6	24659.0
including livestock[5]	1928	1373.8	275.3	45.9	321.2	87.3 / 4.6	1603.1	27657.0	2866.2	1704.4 / 564.9	45.9	1704.4 / 645.2	28155.6	29010.8[4]	3109.1[4]	1791.4 / 569.5	29758.7
	1929	1606.7	659.8	239.6	899.4	125.1 / 7.6	2373.4	28652.8	2260.2	1679.9 / 997.0	239.6	1679.9 / 1342.5	27890.6	30259.5	2814.1[4]	1805.0 / 1004.6	30264.0
	1930	2531.1	2133.1	1217.2	3350.3	1300.3 / 38.8	5542.3	30229.2	1450.5	1605.4 / 1246.8	1217.2	1605.4 / 2893.6	27180.7	32760.3	3172.7[4]	1905.7 / 1285.6	32723.0[3]
	1931	6455.7	3555.0	3514.9	7069.9	721.7 / 135.9	12668.0	31075.4	1556.1	1497.3 / 1140.9	3514.9	1497.3 / 5217.9	25916.3	37531.1	4568.6[4]	2219.0 / 1276.8	38584.3[3]
a) Productive stock																	
excluding livestock	1928	1210.6	206.7	30.9	237.6	78.0 / 0.1	1370.1	8454.6	1102.7	827.1 / 17.7	30.9	827.1 / 48.6	8681.6	9665.2	1309.4	905.1 / 47.8	10051.7
	1929	1370.1	486.2	100.8	587.0	109.1 / 0.3	1847.7	8681.6	1070.2	824.4 / 29.9	100.8	824.4 / 130.7	8796.7	10051.7	1556.4	933.5 / 30.2	10644.4
	1930	1847.7	1442.2	371.3	1813.5	246.0 / 0.5	3414.7	8796.7	597.6	776.0 / 70.6	371.3	776.0 / 441.9	8176.4	10644.4	2039.8	1022.0 / 71.1	11591.1
	1931	3414.7	2343.2	840.8	3184.0	477.0 / 0.9	6120.8	8176.4	386.8	658.2 / 156.5	840.8	658.2 / 997.3	6907.7	11591.1	2730.0	1135.2 / 157.4	13028.5

Appendix C
Table 5. (cont'd)

Economic categories	Years	Socialist sector						Private sector						All sectors			
		Stock at beginning of year	Through capital construction	Through socialisation	Total	Lost in year (deprec- iation)	Stock at end of year	Stock at beginning of year	Received in year (capital construction)	Deprec- iation[1]	Transferred through socialis- ation[1]	Total	Stock at end of year	Stock at beginning of year	Received in year (capital construction)	Lost in year (deprec- iation)	Stock at end of year
		2	3	4	5	6	7	8	9	10	11	12	13	14	15	16	17	18
including livestock[5]	1928	1293.8	255.0	38.7	293.7	82.5 / 4.6	1500.4	16668.7	1955.1	1110.1 / 531.9	38.7 / 32.4[2]	1110.1 / 603.0	16910.7	17962.5	2177.7	1192.6 / 536.5	18411.1
	1929	1504.0	635.9	222.7	858.6	118.6 / 7.4	2236.6	17407.9	1425.9	1081.5 / 960.7	222.7[2] / 105.9	1081.5 / 1289.3	16463.0	18911.9	1955.9	1200.1 / 968.1	18699.6
	1930	2394.3	2025.3	1060.5	3085.4	289.2 / 38.3	5152.6	18801.6	998.7	1011.4 / 1209.6	1060.5 / 429.6[2]	1011.4 / 2699.7	16089.2	21195.9	2613.1	1300.6 / 1247.9	21241.8[3]
	1931	6066.0	3379.0	3337.9	6716.9	698.6 / 135.2	11949.1	19983.9	935.1	908.9 / 1105.4	3337.9 / 562.1[2]	908.9 / 5005.4	15004.7	26049.9	3771.6	1607.5 / 1240.6	26953.8[3]
b) Consumption stock (rural housing stock)	1928	80.0	20.3	7.2	27.5	4.8	102.7	10968.3	911.1	594.3 / 33.0	7.2 / 42.0	594.3 / 42.0	11244.9	11048.3	931.4	599.1 / 33.0	11347.6
	1929	102.7	23.9	16.9	40.8	6.5 / 0.2	136.8	11244.9	834.3	598.4 / 36.3	16.9 / 53.2	598.3 / 53.2	11427.6	11347.6	858.2	604.9 / 36.5	11564.4
	1930	136.8	107.8	156.7	264.5	11.1 / 0.5	389.7	11427.6	451.9	594.0 / 37.2	156.7 / 193.9	594.0 / 193.9	11091.5	11564.4	559.6	605.1 / 37.7	11481.2
	1931	389.7	176.0	177.0	253.0	23.1 / 0.7	718.9	11091.5	621.0	588.4 / 35.5	177.0 / 212.5	588.4 / 212.5	10911.6	11481.2	797.0	611.5 / 36.2	11630.5

Notes:
1. The denominator in the depreciation column shows other losses (premature death of livestock, losses through fire, etc.)
2. The denominator shows sale of livestock from the stock of the private sector to the socialist sector.
3. The imbalance of 18.7 million rubles in 1930 and of 19.6 million rubles in 1931 is due to the fact that stock of these amounts was transferred from the private sector to the suburban holdings of Tsentrosoyuz, where they were not recorded as stock.
4. The disparity between the total and the sum of the separate sectors is due to the fact that the socialist sector includes purchases of livestock from the stock of the private sector, and investments in agriculture for livestock in the total of the sectors include the natural increase of the livestock. Consequently, the transference of livestock from one sector to another does not affect the natural increase of the livestock in agriculture as a whole. For the amount of purchases see note 2.
5. The difference between the stock at the end and at the beginning of the year is due to the fact that the livestock was revalued in the average-yearly prices of each year.

Appendix C

Table 6. Net increase in fixed capital stock and in incomplete buildings by branches of the economy (in current prices, in millions of rubles)

Branches of the economy	Increase in active fixed capital stock				Increase in incomplete building[2]				Total increase			
	1928	1929	1930	1931	1928	1929	1930	1931	1928	1929	1930	1931
A	1	2	3	4	5	6	7	8	9	10	11	12
Total economy												
a) excluding livestock	2082.1	2972.0	4667.3	7505.0	657.2	923.9	1679.8	3198.2	2739.3	3895.9	6347.1	10703.2
b) including livestock	2144.2	2167.0	3766.5	6971.5	657.2	923.9	1679.8	3198.2	2801.4	3090.9	5446.3	10169.7
Socialist sector												
a) excluding livestock	1610.4	2768.6	6004.0	9058.3	623.3	887.1	1662.8	3161.9	2233.7	3655.7	7666.8	12221.2
b) including livestock	1657.5	3023.6	7195.3	12236.3	623.3	887.1	1662.8	3161.9	2280.8	3910.7	8858.1	15398.2
Private sector												
a) excluding livestock	471.7	203.4	-1336.7	-1554.3	33.9	36.8	17.0	36.3	505.6	240.2	-1319.7	-1518.0
b) including livestock	486.7	-856.8	-3428.8	-5264.8	33.9	36.8	17.0	36.3	520.6	-819.8	-3411.8	-5228.5
1. Census industry, with power stations	723.9	1111.9	2020.9	3144.9	354.1	466.9	1038.4	1963.6	1078.0	1578.8	3059.3	5108.5
2. Power stations in agriculture	4.3	9.2	14.1	23.9	-	-	-	-	4.3	9.2	14.1	23.9
3. Small-scale industry	-14.1	+1.7	-20.0	-	-	-	-	-	-14.1	+1.7	20.0	-
socialist sector	37.6	99.5	284.7	-	-	-	-	-	37.6	99.5	284.7	-
private sector	-51.7	-97.8	-304.7	-	-	-	-	-	-51.7	-97.8	-304.7	-
4. Agriculture (less housing stock and power stations)												
a) excluding livestock	382.2	583.5	932.6	1413.5	-	-	-	-	382.2	583.5	932.6	1413.5
b) including livestock	444.3	-221.5	31.8	880.0	-	-	-	-	444.3	-221.5	31.8	880.0
socialist sector												
a) excluding livestock	155.2	468.4	1552.9	2682.2	-	-	-	-	155.2	468.4	1552.9	2682.2
b) including livestock	202.3	723.4	2744.2	5859.2	-	-	-	-	202.3	723.4	2744.2	5859.2
private sector												
a) excluding livestock	227.0	115.1	-620.3	-1268.7	-	-	-	-	227.0	115.1	-620.3	-1268.6
b) including livestock	242.0	-944.9	-2712.4	-4919.2	-	-	-	-	242.0	-944.9	-2712.4	-4979.2
5. Transport[1]	154.1	321.7	890.1	1409.2	163.4	206.7	96.0	413.4	317.5	528.4	986.1	1822.6
of which: railway	141.9	236.4	621.6	906.9	153.5	173.5	14.3	304.8	295.4	409.9	635.9	1211.7
river	-5.8	14.2	63.8	93.1	4.0	22.1	36.9	75.8	-1.8	36.3	100.7	168.9
maritime	8.0	41.8	71.4	88.8	0.1	-0.6	20.6	25.3	8.1	41.2	92.0	114.1
surfaced and dirt roads	10.0	29.3	133.3	320.4	5.8	11.7	24.2	7.5	15.8	41.0	157.5	327.9

Appendix C
Table 6. (cont'd)

Branches of the economy	Increase in active fixed capital stock				Increase in incomplete building[2]				Total increase			
	1928	1929	1930	1931	1928	1929	1930	1931	1928	1929	1930	1931
A	1	2	3	4	5	6	7	8	9	10	11	12
6. Communications	30.1	42.0	68.7	146.1	8.8	13.3	8.4	14.4	38.9	55.3	77.1	160.3
7. Exchange and distribution	38.4	112.8	246.8	475.9	6.8	15.4	61.7	73.2	45.2	128.2	308.5	549.1
8. Stock assigned to social purposes	243.9	335.0	306.6	350.0	58.6	107.9	191.0	237.7	302.5	462.9	497.6	587.7
a) education	68.1	125.5	93.0	93.6	16.4	40.0	73.2	74.2	84.5	165.5	166.2	167.8
b) public health	58.9	67.0	69.2	61.2	12.7	19.2	22.6	20.8	71.5	86.1	91.8	82.0
c) administration	35.5	41.2	30.2	83.7	8.7	12.2	42.1	89.0	44.2	53.4	72.3	172.7
d) municipal economy	81.4	121.3	114.2	111.5	20.8	36.5	53.1	53.7	102.2	157.8	167.3	165.2
9. Urban housing stock	220.0	217.4	290.7	392.2	65.5	113.7	284.3	496.1	285.5	331.1	575.0	888.3
Socialist sector (housing stock of industry, executive committees and cooperatives)	200.2	214.0	366.3	497.9	31.6	76.9	267.3	459.8	231.8	290.9	633.6	957.7
Private sector	19.8	3.4	-75.6	-105.7	33.9	36.8	17.0	36.3	53.7	40.2	-58.6	-69.4
10. Rural housing stock	299.3	216.8	-83.2	149.3	-	-	-	-	299.3	216.8	-83.2	149.3
Socialist sector	22.7	34.1	252.9	329.2	-	-	-	-	22.7	34.1	252.9	329.2
Private sector	276.6	182.7	-336.1	-179.9	-	-	-	-	276.6	182.7	-336.1	-179.9
In addition, capital investments and increase of incomplete buildings in unrecorded stock, passed into the balance:												
Socialist sector	193.9	322.6	441.6	-	47.5	79.7	162.3	-	241.4	402.3	603.9	-
Total for the economy, including capital investments in unrecorded stock (including livestock)	2338.1	2489.6	4208.1	-	704.7	1003.6	1842.1	-	3042.8	3493.2	6050.2	-
of which: Socialist sector	1851.4	3346.2	7636.9	-	670.8	966.8	1825.1	-	2522.2	4313.0	9462.0	-
Private sector	486.7	-856.6	-3425.8	-	33.9	36.8	17.0	-	520.6	-819.8	-3411.8	-

Notes: 1. Including increase in stock and residues of incomplete buildings of the housing stock and buildings serving social purposes.
         2. Included in incomplete building work is not only pure building work but also equipment not yet installed.

Appendix C

Table 7. Rate of growth of capital investment and pure building work (in current prices)

Branches of the economy	In millions of rubles								Capital investment as % of previous year			Coefficient of pure building work			
	1928		1929		1930		1931		1929	1930	1931	1928	1929	1930	1931
	Capital invest-ment	Of which pure building work	Capital invest-ment	Of which pure building work	Capital invest-ment	Of which pure building work	Capital invest-ment	Of which pure building work							
A	1	2	3	4	5	6	7	8	9	10	11	12	13	14	15
Socialist sector															
I. Industry including stock of industry															
1) Planned by VSNKh	1347.7	-	1903.5	-	3650.6	2306.5	5604.8	3566.2	141.2	191.8	153.5	-	-	63.2	63.6
2) Planned by NKSnab	163.7	-	199.0	-	270.2	166.8	362.9	230.9	121.6	135.8	134.3	-	-	61.7	63.6
Total	1511.4	-	2102.5	-	3920.5	2473.3	5967.7	3797.1	139.1	186.5	152.2	-	-	63.1	63.6
of which: Group "A"	995.4	-	1545.8	-	3340.2	2110.5	5391.3	3430.7	155.3	216.1	161.2	-	-	63.2	63.6
" " Group "B"	456.4	-	491.4	-	580.6	362.8	575.9	366.4	112.6	118.1	99.2	-	-	62.5	63.6
3) Other industry	159.4	-	204.6	-	232.0	145.4	466.0	292.6	128.4	113.4	200.9	-	-	62.7	62.8
Total for state sector	1670.8	-	2307.1	-	4152.8	2618.7	6433.7	4089.7	138.1	180.0	154.9	-	-	63.1	63.6
4) Cooperative industry	32.7	-	61.9	-	127.1	77.7	229.5	142.8	189.3	205.3	180.6	-	-	61.1	62.2
a) Tsentrosoyuz	12.2	-	21.9	-	31.8	19.5	115.0	71.6	179.5	145.2	361.6	-	-	61.3	62.3
b) Industrial and disabled persons' cooperatives	20.5	-	40.0	-	95.3	58.2	114.5	71.2	195.1	238.3	120.1	-	-	61.2	62.2
Total for industry with housing stock	1703.5	975.3	2369.0	1373.1	4279.9	2696.4	6663.2	4232.5	139.1	180.7	155.7	57.3[3]	58.0[3]	63.0	63.5
of which: housing stock	173.1	173.1	223.9	223.9	611.6	611.6	875.7	875.7	129.3	273.2	143.2	100.0	100.0	100.0	100.0
" " less housing stock	1530.4	802.2	2145.1	1149.2	3668.3	2084.8	5787.5	3356.8	140.2	171.0	157.8	52.4	53.6	56.8	58.0
II. Power stations	217.8	112.6	308.1	162.0	457.0	267.5	510.9	303.3	141.5	148.3	111.8	51.7	52.6	58.5	59.4
District stations	176.2	92.3	250.9	134.4	394.5	234.6	444.8	269.8	142.4	157.2	112.8	52.4	53.6	59.5	60.7
Municipal stations	36.7	19.2	47.1	25.2	46.9	26.7	39.6	23.0	128.3	99.6	84.4	52.4	53.6	56.8	58.0
Power stations in agriculture	4.9	1.1	10.1	2.4	15.6	6.2	26.5	10.5	206.1	154.5	169.9	22.4	23.8	39.7	39.7

Appendix C
Table 7. (cont'd)

In millions of rubles

Branches of the economy	1928		1929		1930		1931		Capital investment as % of previous year			Coefficient of pure building work			
	Capital invest- ment	Of which pure building work	Capital invest- ment	Of which pure building work	Capital invest- ment	Of which pure building work	Capital invest- ment	Of which pure building work	1929	1930	1931	1928	1929	1930	1931
A	1	2	3	4	5	6	7	8	9	10	11	12	13	14	15
III. Transport	915.0	519.8	1151.0	620.1	1647.1	941.4	2510.9	1645.0	125.8	143.1	152.4	56.8	53.9	57.2	65.5
a) railway	731.0	418.6	873.0	472.4	1112.2	638.5	1715.6	1139.8	119.4	127.4	154.3	57.3	54.1	57.4	66.4
b) river	49.0	12.1	86.0	21.2	152.1	37.5	221.8	109.5	175.5	176.9	145.8	24.7	24.7	24.7	49.4
c) maritime	59.0	16.1	86.0	23.5	158.6	41.2	174.8	51.0	145.8	184.4	110.2	27.3	27.3	26.0	34.9
d) surfaced and dirt roads	76.0	73.0	106.0	103.0	224.2	224.2	398.7	344.7	139.5	211.5	177.8	96.1	97.2	100.0	86.5
IV. Communications	53.5	40.0	70.3	50.6	99.8	64.5	180.0	116.3	131.4	142.0	180.4	74.8	72.0	64.6	64.6
V. Civil aviation	3.5	2.4	9.9	5.9	35.0	19.9	90.0	54.0	282.9	353.5	257.1	68.6	59.6	56.9	60.0
VI. Exchange and distribution (less industrial)	68.1	48.8	154.2	99.6	340.6	220.2	595.8	38.1	226.4	220.9	174.8	71.7	64.6	64.7	64.7
NKSnab	20.1	-	60.6	-	163.8	-	250.7	-	301.5	270.3	153.1	-	-	-	-
NKVnesh Torg	48.0	-	93.6	-	176.8	-	344.5	-	195.0	188.9	194.9	-	-	-	-
VII. Education	130.0	117.0	221.0	198.9	236.6	201.1	239.0	203.9	170.0	107.1	101.0	90.0	90.0	85.0	85.3
VIII. Public health[2]	99.0	89.1	116.0	104.4	130.3	110.8	117.0	101.9	117.2	112.3	80.8	90.0	90.0	85.0	87.1
IX. Administration	61.0	61.0	71.0	71.0	95.6	90.8	202.0	191.9	116.4	134.6	211.1	100.0	100.0	95.0	95.0
X. Municipal economy	194.0	137.7	253.0	177.1	267.7	184.4	270.4	186.3	130.4	105.8	101.0	71.0	70.0	68.9	68.9
XI. Urban housing stock[1]	279.8	279.8	294.0	294.0	253.2	253.2	320.1	320.1	105.1	86.1	126.4	100.0	100.0	100.0	100.0

Notes: 1. Less the urban housing stock conventionally assigned to the cooperative sector.

2. Not included are investments passed through the plan of other branches, which in 1931 came to 35.0 million rubles.

3. For 1928 and 1929 pure building work is given for industry as a whole, because the coefficient of pure building work which were used excluded the housing stock. There were no data for distinguishing the housing stock by sections of industry (VSNKh, NKSnab,etc.)

4. For river transport in 1928-1929 we have applied the coefficient of pure building for 1930, since there are accounts data for 1930.

Appendix C
Table 7. (cont'd)

Branches of the economy	In millions of rubles								Capital investment as % of previous year			Coefficient of pure building work			
	1928		1929		1930		1931								
	Capital invest-ment	Of which pure building work	Capital invest-ment	Of which pure building work	Capital invest-ment	Of which pure building work	Capital invest-ment	Of which pure building work	1929	1930	1931	1928	1929	1930	1931
A	1	2	3	4	5	6	7	8	9	10	11	12	13	14	15
XII. Agriculture (less power stations)															
1. State sector [7]	177.0	89.9	420.5	182.2	1411.3	513.2	2122.1	840.3	237.6	335.6	150.4	50.8	43.3	36.4	39.6
of which: housing stock	18.1	18.1	27.9	27.9	126.5	126.5	182.7	182.7	154.1	453.4	144.4	100.0	100.0	100.0	100.0
a) financed under the heading of NKZem[5]	143.6	72.9	358.6	155.3	1262.7	459.6	2015.1	798.0	249.7	352.1	159.6	50.8	43.3	36.4	39.6
b) ditto, less purchases of livestock and rearing of young animals	131.9	72.9	329.8	155.3	1028.3	459.6	1561.1	798.0	250.0	311.8	151.9	55.3	47.1	44.7	51.1
2. Collective farm and cooperative sector	215.2	48.0	423.7	81.8	1211.0	283.0	1957.2	593.5	196.9	285.8	161.6	22.5	19.3	23.4	30.3
of which: housing stock	2.2	2.2	4.5	4.5	32.8	32.8	24.5	24.5	204.5	728.9	74.1	100.0	100.0	100.0	100.0
a) financed under the heading of NKZem[5]	209.5	46.5	399.2	77.4	1000.0	234.0	1413.4[8]	422.6	190.5	250.5	141.3	22.3	19.4	23.4	29.9
b) ditto, less purchases of livestock and rearing of young animals	193.8	46.5	331.3	77.4	836.7	234.0	1219.8	422.6	170.9	252.6	145.7	24.0	23.4	28.0	34.7
3. Total for socialist sector	392.2	137.9	844.2	264.1	2622.3	796.2	4079.3	1433.8	215.2	310.6	155.6	35.2	31.3	30.4	35.1
of which: housing stock	20.3	20.3	32.4	32.4	159.3	159.3	207.0	207.0	159.6	491.7	129.9	100.0	100.0	100.0	100.0
a) financed by NKZem[5]	353.1	119.4	757.8	232.7	2262.7	693.6	3428.5	1220.6	214.6	298.7	151.5	33.8	30.7	30.7	35.6
b) financed by NKZem net of purchases of livestock and rearing of young animals	325.7	119.4	661.1	232.7	1865.0	693.6	2780.9	1220.6	203.0	282.1	149.1	36.7	35.2	37.2	43.9

Appendix C

Table 7. (cont'd)

In millions of rubles

Branches of the economy	1928 Capital investment	Of which pure building work	1929 Capital investment	Of which pure building work	1930 Capital investment	Of which pure building work	1931 Capital investment	Of which pure building work	Capital investment as % of previous year 1929	1930	1931	Coefficient of pure building work 1928	1929	1930	1931
A	1	2	3	4	5	6	7	8	9	10	11	12	13	14	15
Total for the economy															
State sector	3537.1	-	4980.8	-	8689.1	-	12921.1	-	140.8	174.5	148.7	-	-	-	-
of which:															
a) for agriculture financed only by NKZem	3503.7	-	4918.9	-	8540.5	-	12814.1	-	140.4	173.6	150.0	-	-	-	-
b) for agriculture financed only by NKZem, less purchases of livestock and rearing of young animals	3492.0	-	4890.1	-	8306.1	-	12360.6	-	140.0	169.9	148.8	-	-	-	-
Cooperative sector	580.3	-	880.9	-	1766.0	-	2856.9	-	151.8	201.6	160.9	-	-	-	-
of which:															
a) for agriculture financed only by NKZem	574.6	-	856.4	-	1565.0	-	2313.1	-	149.0	182.7	147.8	-	-	-	-
b) for agriculture financed only by NKZem, less purchases of livestock and rearing of young animals	558.9	-	788.5	-	1401.7	-	2119.0	-	141.1	177.8	151.2	-	-	-	-
Total for socialist sector	4117.4	2521.4	5861.7	3420.8	10465.1	5846.4	15778.0	9174.1	142.4	178.0	150.8	61.2	58.4	55.9	58.1
of which:															
a) for agriculture financed only by NKZem	4078.3	2502.9	5775.3	3389.4	10105.5	5743.8	15127.2	8960.9	141.6	175.0	149.7	61.4	58.7	56.8	59.2
b) for agriculture financed only by NKZem, less purchases of livestock and rearing of young animals	4050.9	2502.9	5678.6	3389.4	9707.8	5743.8	14479.6	8960.9	140.2	171.0	149.2	61.8	59.7	59.2	61.9

Appendix C
Table 7. (cont'd)

A															
	In millions of rubles								Capital investment as % of previous year			Coefficient of pure building work			
	1928		1929		1930		1931								
Branches of the economy	Capital invest-ment	Of which pure building work	Capital invest-ment	Of which pure building work	Capital invest-ment	Of which pure building work	Capital invest-ment	Of which pure building work	1929	1930	1931	1928	1929	1930	1931
	1	2	3	4	5	6	7	8	9	10	11	12	13	14	15
In addition, private sector															
1. Industry	18.0	9.5	22.0	11.9	19.0	10.9	-	-	122.2	86.4	-	52.7	54.1	57.4	-
2. Urban housing stock	236.3	236.3	223.3	223.3	124.5	124.5	111.8	111.8	94.5	55.6	87.8	100.0	100.0	100.0	100.0
3. Agriculture	2901.4	1469.6	2401.8	1367.7	1454.0	735.0	1556.0	846.0	82.8	60.5	107.0	50.7	56.9	50.6	54.4
4. of which, housing stock	911.1	911.1	834.3	834.3	451.8	451.8	621.0	621.0	91.6	54.2	137.5	100.0	100.0	100.0	100.0
a) financed by NKZem[5]	247.9	123.0	342.8	195.7	109.0	53.6	29.0	14.2	138.3	31.8	26.6	49.6	57.1	49.2	49.1
b) financed by NKZem, less purchases of livestock and rearing of young animals	226.9	123.0	328.8	195.7	109.0	53.6	29.0	14.2	144.9	33.2	26.6	54.2	59.5	49.2	49.1
Total for private sector	3155.7	1715.4	2647.1	1602.9	1597.5	870.4	1667.8	957.8	83.9	60.3	104.4	54.4	60.6	54.5	57.4
Total for economy[6]	7240.7	4236.8	8402.9	5023.7	11651.7	6716.8	16903.3	10131.9	116.1	138.7	145.1	58.5	59.8	57.6	59.9
in addition, small-scale industry	35.4	11.8	47.7	13.5	28.5	15.4	-	-	134.7	59.7	-	33.3	28.3	54.0	-

Notes: 5. Excluding own resources not provided for by financing.

6. The disparity between the total and the sum of the separate sectors is due to the fact that, for agriculture in the socialist sector, we have excluded purchases of livestock from the stock of the private sector, and investment for agriculture in livestock excludes the natural increase of the herd. Consequently, the transfer of livestock from one sector to another does not alter the natural increase of livestock in the economy as a whole. The amount of these purchases was, in 1928 32.4 million rubles, in 1929 105.9 million rubles, and in 1931 542 million rubles.

7. Excluding investment in the state farms of the People's Commissariat of Trade (except Soyuzsakhar) and in the suburban holdings of Tsentrosoyuz, which are listed under exchange and distribution. The state farms of the People's Commissariat of Trade (except Soyuzsakhar) constituted: in 1928 3.4 million rubles, in 1929 20.9 million rubles, in 1930 36.2 million rubles, and in 1931 54.8 million rubles. The suburban holdings of Tsentrosoyuz constituted in 1929 16.7 million rubles, in 1930 126.0 million rubles and in 1931 165.0 million rubles.

8. Excluding the labour of collective farmers, provided for by the financial plan for 1928-30.

Appendix C

Table 7a. Rate of growth of capital investment and pure building work (in 1928 prices)

A	In millions of rubles								Capital investment as % of previous year			Coefficient of pure building work			
	1928		1929		1930		1931		1929	1930	1931	1928	1929	1930	1931
Branches of the economy	Capital invest-ment	Of which pure building work	Capital invest-ment	Of which pure building work	Capital invest-ment	Of which pure building work	Capital invest-ment	Of which pure building work							
	1	2	3	4	5	6	7	8	9	10	11	12	13	14	15
Socialist sector															
I. **Industry** (including housing stock of industry)															
1) Planned by VSNKh	1347.1	-	1989.0	-	4167.4	2716.7	5962.6	3642.7	147.6	209.5	143.1	-	-	65.2	61.1
2) Planned by NKSnab	163.7	-	207.9	-	308.4	196.5	386.0	235.8	127.0	148.9	125.2	-	-	63.7	61.1
Total	1511.4	-	2196.9	-	4475.8	2913.2	6348.6	3878.5	145.4	203.7	141.8	-	-	65.1	61.1
of which: Group "A"	995.4	-	1615.3	-	3813.0	2485.9	5735.9	3504.3	162.3	236.1	150.4	-	-	65.2	61.1
Group "B"	463.4	-	513.5	-	662.8	427.3	612.7	374.2	117.7	129.1	92.4	-	-	64.5	61.1
3) Other industry	159.4	-	213.8	-	264.8	171.3	495.7	298.9	134.1	123.9	187.2	-	-	64.7	60.3
Total for state sector	1670.8	-	2410.7	-	4740.6	3084.5	6844.3	4177.4	144.3	196.6	165.5	-	-	65.1	61.0
4) Cooperative industry	32.7	-	64.7	-	145.1	91.5	244.1	145.9	197.9	224.3	168.2	-	-	63.0	59.8
a) Tsentrosoyuz	12.2	-	22.9	-	36.4	23.0	122.3	73.1	187.7	158.9	336.0	-	-	63.2	59.8
b) Industrial and disabled persons' cooperatives	20.5	-	41.8	-	108.7	68.5	121.8	72.8	203.9	260.0	112.1	-	-	63.0	59.8
Total for industry, with housing stock	1703.5	975.3	2475.4	1492.5	4885.7	3176.0	7088.4	4323.3	145.3	197.4	145.1	57.3[3]	60.0[3]	65.0	61.0
of which: housing stock	173.1	173.1	241.0	241.0	736.9	736.9	914.1	914.1	139.2	305.8	124.0	100.0	100.0	100.0	100.0
" less housing stock	1530.4	802.2	2234.4	1251.5	4148.6	2439.1	6174.3	3409.2	146.0	185.7	148.8	52.4	56.0	58.8	55.2
II. **Power stations**	217.8	112.6	325.3	179.5	524.1	320.6	550.0	315.8	148.4	162.1	104.9	51.7	55.5	61.2	57.4
District stations	176.2	92.3	264.1	149.2	454.5	282.3	480.9	281.3	149.9	172.1	105.8	52.4	56.5	62.1	58.5
Municipal stations	36.7	19.2	49.6	28.0	54.0	32.1	42.8	24.0	135.1	108.9	79.3	52.3	56.5	59.4	56.1
Power stations in agriculture	4.9	1.1	9.6	2.8	15.6	6.2	26.3	10.5	195.9	162.5	168.6	22.4	24.0	39.7	39.9

Appendix C
Table 7a. (cont'd)

Branches of the economy	In millions of rubles								Capital investment as % of previous year			Coefficient of pure building work			
	1928		1929		1930		1931		1929	1930	1931	1928	1929	1930	1931
	Capital investment	Of which pure building work	Capital investment	Of which pure building work	Capital investment	Of which pure building work	Capital investment	Of which pure building work							
	1	2	3	4	5	6	7	8	9	10	11	12	13	14	15
III. Transport	915.0	519.8	1159.4	652.9	1657.6	964.4	2414.1	1491.3	126.7	143.0	145.6	56.8	56.3	58.2	62.2
a) railway	731.0	418.6	867.7	498.8	1096.8	649.5	1613.9	1026.8	118.7	126.4	147.1	57.4	57.5	57.2	63.0
b) river	49.0	12.1	90.7	22.3	160.4	39.0	242.4	100.6	185.1	176.8	151.1	24.7	24.6	24.3	41.5
c) maritime	59.0	16.1	90.7	24.7	167.3	42.8	191.0	46.8	153.7	184.5	114.2	27.3	27.2	25.6	24.5
d) surfaced and dirt roads	76.0	73.0	110.2	107.1	233.1	233.1	366.8	317.1	145.0	211.5	157.4	96.1	97.2	100.0	86.5
IV. Communications	53.5	40.0	73.6	73.0	113.4	73.7	177.2	114.5	137.6	154.1	156.3	74.8	72.0	64.6	64.6
V. Civil aviation	3.5	2.5	10.3	6.4	40.0	23.4	95.7	55.2	294.3	388.3	239.3	68.6	62.1	58.5	57.7
VI. Exchange and distribution (less industrial)	68.1	48.8	159.1	104.8	372.2	251.6	598.8	380.9	233.6	233.9	160.9	61.7	65.9	67.6	63.0
NKSnab	20.1	-	62.5	-	179.0	-	252.2	-	310.9	286.4	140.9	-	-	-	-
NKVnesh Torg	48.0	-	96.6	-	193.2	-	346.6	-	201.2	200.0	179.4	-	-	-	-
VII. Education	130.0	117.0	212.4	209.4	264.6	229.8	237.8	201.9	178.8	113.8	89.9	90.0	90.1	86.8	84.9
VIII. Public health[2]	99.0	89.1	121.2	109.4	144.4	125.9	115.6	100.3	122.4	119.1	80.0	90.0	90.3	87.2	86.8
IX. Administration	61.0	61.0	74.7	74.7	106.9	103.8	201.0	190.0	122.4	143.1	188.0	100.0	100.0	97.1	94.5
X. Municipal economy	194.0	137.7	264.1	186.4	293.8	210.7	209.1	179.8	136.1	112.0	91.0	71.0	70.6	71.2	66.8
XI. Urban Housing stock[1]	279.8	279.8	316.5	316.5	305.1	305.1	334.1	334.1	113.1	96.4	109.5	100.0	100.0	100.0	100.0

Notes: 1. Excluding housing stock, conventionally assigned to the cooperative sector.
2. Not included are the investments passed through the plan of other branches, which amounted in 1931 to 35.0 million rubles, in 1931 prices.
3. For 1928 and 1929 pure building work is given for industry as a whole, because the coefficients of building work which were used excluded the housing stock. No data were available for distinguishing the housing stock by sections of industry (VSNKh, NKSnab, etc.)

Appendix C
Table 7a. (cont'd)

Branches of the economy	In millions of rubles								Capital investment as % of previous year			Coefficient of pure building work			
	1928		1929		1930		1931		1929	1930	1931	1928	1929	1930	1931
	Capital invest-ment	Of which pure building work	Capital invest-ment	Of which pure building work	Capital invest-ment	Of which pure building work	Capital invest-ment	Of which pure building work							
A	1	2	3	4	5	6	7	8	9	10	11	12	13	14	15
XII. Agriculture (less power stations) [6]															
1. State sector	177.0	89.9	416.7	185.0	1353.1	567.2	1913.5	930.6	235.4	324.7	141.4	50.8	44.4	41.9	48.6
of which: housing stock	18.1	18.1	28.8	28.8	144.2	144.2	208.3	208.3	159.1	500.7	144.5	100.0	100.0	100.0	100.0
a) financed under the heading of NKZem[4]	143.6	72.9	355.4	157.8	1210.6	507.2	1817.0	883.1	247.5	340.6	150.1	50.8	44.4	41.9	48.6
b) ditto, less purchases of livestock and rearing of young animals	131.9	72.9	326.9	157.8	985.9	507.2	1407.7	883.1	247.8	301.6	142.8	55.3	48.3	51.4	62.7
2. Collective farm and cooperative sector	215.2	48.0	415.0	80.7	1132.8	285.8	1691.6	614.7	192.8	273.0	149.3	24.5	19.4	25.2	36.3
of which: housing stock	2.2	2.2	4.4	4.4	33.0	33.0	25.2	25.2	200.0	750.0	76.4	100.0	100.0	100.0	100.0
a) financed under the heading of NKZem[4]	209.5	46.5	391.0	75.9	935.5	235.7	1221.6[7]	443.4	186.6	239.3	130.6	24.5	19.4	25.2	36.3
b) ditto, less purchases of livestock and rearing of young animals	193.8	46.5	324.5	75.9	782.7	235.7	1053.8	443.4	167.4	241.2	134.6	24.0	23.4	30.1	42.1
3. Total for socialist sector	392.2	137.9	831.7	265.7	2485.9	853.0	3605.1	1545.3	212.1	298.9	145.0	35.2	31.9	34.3	42.9
of which: housing stock	20.3	20.3	33.2	33.2	177.2	177.2	233.5	253.5	163.5	533.7	131.8	100.0	100.0	100.0	100.0
a) financed by NKZem[4]	353.1	119.4	746.4	233.7	2146.1	742.9	3038.6	1326.5	211.4	287.5	141.	33.8	31.3	34.6	43.7
b) financed by NKZem net of purchases of livestock and rearing of young animals	325.7	119.4	651.4	233.7	1768.6	742.9	2461.5	1326.5	200.0	271.5	139.2	36.6	35.9	42.0	53.9

Appendix C

Table 7a. (cont'd)

Branches of the economy	In millions of rubles								Capital investment as % of previous year			Coefficient of pure building work			
	1928 Capital investment	Of which pure building work	1929 Capital investment	Of which pure building work	1930 Capital investment	Of which pure building work	1931 Capital investment	Of which pure building work	1929	1930	1931	1928	1929	1930	1931
A	1	2	3	4	5	6	7	8	9	10	11	12	13	14	15
Total for the economy															
State sector	3537.1	–	5141.6	–	9411.6	–	13065.0	–	145.4	183.0	138.8	–	–	–	–
of which:															
a) for agriculture financed only by NKZem	3503.7	–	5080.3	–	9269.1	–	12968.5	–	145.0	182.4	139.9	–	–	–	–
b) for agriculture financed only by NKZem, less purchases of livestock and rearing of young animals	3492.0	–	5051.8	–	9044.4	–	12559.2	–	144.7	179.0	138.9	–	–	–	–
Cooperative sector	580.3	–	900.1	–	1784.1	–	2621.9	–	154.6	198.6	147.2	–	–	–	–
of which:															
a) for agriculture financed only by NKZem	574.6	–	876.1	–	1586.8	–	2151.9	–	152.0	181.4	135.8	–	–	–	–
b) for agriculture financed only by NKZem, less purchases of livestock and rearing of young animals	558.9	–	809.6	–	1434.0	–	1984.1	–	144.4	177.4	138.6	–	–	–	–
Total for socialist sector	4117.4	2521.4	6041.7	3651.2	11195.7	6637.6	15686.9	9232.4	146.7	185.3	140.2	61.2	60.4	59.3	58.9
of which:															
a) for agriculture financed only by NKZem	4078.3	2502.9	5956.4	3619.2	10855.9	6527.5	15120.4	9013.6	146.0	182.3	139.3	61.4	60.8	60.0	59.6
b) for agriculture financed only by NKZem, less purchases of livestock and rearing of young animals	4050.9	2502.9	5861.4	3619.2	10478.4	6527.5	14543.3	9018.6	144.6	178.8	138.8	61.8	61.7	62.3	62.0

Appendix C
Table 7a. (cont'd)

Branches of the economy	In millions of rubles								Capital investment as % of previous year			Coefficient of pure building work			
	1928		1929		1930		1931		1929	1930	1931	1928	1929	1930	1931
	Capital invest-ment	Of which pure building work	Capital invest-ment	Of which pure building work	Capital invest-ment	Of which pure building work	Capital invest-ment	Of which pure building work							
A	1	2	3	4	5	6	7	8	9	10	11	12	13	14	15
In addition, private sector															
1. Industry	18.0	9.5	23.0	12.4	21.8	12.4	-	-	127.8	94.8	-	52.8	53.9	56.9	-
2. Urban housing stock	236.3	236.3	230.2	230.2	120.1	120.1	89.9	89.9	97.4	60.9	74.9	100.0	100.0	100.0	100.0
3. Agriculture	2901.4	1469.6	2357.0	1310.2	1429.7	733.5	1276.5	844.3	81.2	60.6	89.3	50.6	55.6	51.3	66.1
4. of which, housing stock[4]	911.1	911.1	799.1	799.1	450.9	450.9	619.8	619.8	88.8	56.4	137.5	100.0	100.0	100.0	100.0
a) financed by NKZem	247.9	123.0	336.4	187.0	107.2	55.0	23.8	15.7	135.7	31.9	22.2	50.6	55.6	51.3	66.1
b) financed by NKZem, less purchases of livestock and rearing of young animals	226.9	123.0	322.7	187.0	107.2	55.0	23.8	15.7	142.2	33.2	22.2	54.2	57.9	51.3	66.1
Total for private sector	3155.7	1715.4	2610.2	1552.8	1571.6	866.0	1366.4	934.2	82.7	60.2	86.9	54.4	59.5	55.1	68.4
Total for economy[5]	7240.7	4236.8	8554.5	5204.0	12507.7	7503.6	16853.7	10166.6	118.1	146.2	134.7	58.5	60.8	60.0	60.3

Notes: 4. Excluding housing stock, conventionally assigned to cooperative sector.

5. The disparity between the total and the sum of the separate sectors is due to the fact that, for agriculture included in the state and collective farm sectors are purchases of livestock from the stock of the private sector, which amounted in 1928 to 32.4 million rubles, in 1929 to 97.4 million rubles, in 1930 to 259.6 million rubles and in 1931 to 199.6 million rubles.

6. Excluding investments in the state farms of the People's Commissariat of Trade (except Soyuzsakhar) and in the suburban holdings of Tsentrosoyuz, which were listed under exchange and distribution.

7. Excluding the labour of collective farmers, provided for by the financial plan for 1928-30.

Appendix C

Table 8. Structure of active fixed capital stock, by branches and sectors (in value terms, net of depreciation, in current prices)

Branches of the economy	Stock at beginning of year 1928 Excluding livestock	1928 Including livestock	1929 Excluding livestock	1929 Including livestock	1930 Excluding livestock	1930 Including livestock	1931 Excluding livestock	1931 Including livestock	1932 Excluding livestock	1932 Including livestock
A	1	2	3	4	5	6	7	8	9	10
Total economy	100.0	100.0	100.0	100.0	100.0	100.0	100.0	100.0	100.0	100.0
1. Census industry	9.4	8.2	10.1	8.8	11.3	9.6	13.3	10.9	15.8	13.3
of which, planned by VSNKh and										
NKSnab	8.3	7.2	9.0	7.8	9.9	8.5	11.8	9.6	13.8	11.5
Group "A"	4.5	3.9	5.2	4.5	6.1	5.2	7.9	6.5	10.1	8.4
Group "B"	3.8	3.8	3.8	3.3	3.8	3.3	3.9	3.2	3.7	3.1
2. Power stations (district and municipal) of which: power	0.8	0.7	0.9	0.8	1.0	0.9	1.3	1.0	1.7	1.4
stations of Energotsentr.	0.5	0.4	0.7	0.6	0.8	0.6	1.0	1.1	1.4	1.2
3. Power stations in agriculture	0.02	0.01	0.02	0.02	0.03	0.03	0.05	0.06	0.09	0.07
4. Small-scale industry	1.4	1.2	1.3	1.1	1.2	1.1	1.1	0.9	-	-
Socialist sector	0.2	0.2	0.3	0.9	0.4	0.4	0.8	0.7	-	-
Private sector	1.2	1.0	1.0	0.8	0.8	0.7	5.3	0.2	-	-
5. Agriculture	17.2	27.9	17.3	28.9	17.4	29.6	17.6	32.4	17.9	31.1
Socialist sector	2.1	2.0	2.3	2.2	3.0	3.3	5.1	7.5	8.4	13.8
Private sector	15.1	25.9	15.0	26.0	14.4	26.3	12.5	24.9	9.5	17.3
6. Transport[1]	18.8	16.4	18.4	15.9	18.0	15.4	18.1	14.8	18.3	15.4
railway	17.1	14.9	16.7	14.5	16.3	13.9	16.1	13.2	15.8	13.3
river	0.5	0.5	0.5	0.4	0.5	0.4	0.6	0.	0.6	0.5
maritime	0.5	0.4	0.5	0.4	0.5	0.5	0.6	0.5	0.7	0.6
surfaced and dirt roads	0.7	0.6	0.7	0.6	0.7	0.6	0.8	0.7	1.2	1.0
7. Communications	0.4	0.4	0.4	0.4	0.5	0.4	0.6	0.5	0.7	0.6
8. Exchange and distribution	0.8	0.7	0.8	0.7	0.9	0.8	1.3	1.0	1.8	1.5
9. Stock assigned to social purposes	9.8	8.5	9.8	8.5	9.9	8.5	9.7	7.9	9.3	7.8
education	3.2	2.8	3.2	2.8	3.3	2.8	3.2	2.6	3.0	2.5
public health	1.7	1.5	1.7	1.5	1.7	1.5	1.7	1.4	1.7	1.4
administration	1.0	0.8	1.0	0.9	1.0	0.9	1.0	0.8	1.0	0.9
municipal economy	3.9	3.4	3.9	3.3	3.9	3.3	3.8	3.1	3.6	3.0
10. Urban housing stock	21.8	18.9	21.4	18.6	20.7	17.7	19.7	16.1	18.4	15.4
Socialist sector	12.8	11.1	12.7	11.0	12.4	10.6	12.1	9.9	11.7	9.8
Private sector	9.0	7.8	8.7	7.6	8.3	7.1	7.6	6.2	6.7	5.6
11. Rural housing stock	19.6	17.2	19.5	16.9	18.9	16.1	17.5	14.3	16.0	13.5
Socialist sector	0.1	0.1	0.2	0.2	0.2	0.2	0.6	0.5	1.0	0.8
Private sector	19.5	17.1	19.3	16.7	18.7	15.9	16.9	13.8	15.0	12.7

Note: 1. Including housing and buildings serving social purposes.

Appendix C

Table 9. Rate of growth of fixed capital stock and investment in fixed capital stock of agriculture
a) excluding livestock
b) including livestock

Type of funds		Stock at beginning of year, as % of previous year					Capital investment as % of previous year			
		1929	1930	1931	1932	1932 as relative to 1928	1929	1930	1931	1931 as relative to 1928
A		1	2	3	4	5	6	7	8	9
Total capital stock	a)	103.3	103.8	103.9	106.9	119.0	107.8	107.7	135.7	157.4
	b)	102.6	100.0	99.9	102.8	133.0	90.5	112.7	144.0	146.9
Socialist sector [1]	a)	114.1	134.7	191.7	179.8	530.0	224.7/170.2	303.9/331.0	162.5/236.8	1109.8/1334.2
	b)	116.7	147.7	219.0	196.2	922.1	239.7/280.0	323.3/372.5	166.7/211.0	1291.3/2201.1
Private sector	a)	102.6	101.5	95.3	92.5	91.7	91.6	55.1	96.0	50.0
	b)	101.9	97.3	89.9	83.4	93.8	78.9	64.2	107.3	54.3
A. Productive stock	a)	104.0	105.9	108.9	112.4	134.8	118.9	131.1	133.8	208.5
	b)	102.5	98.9	100.2	103.5	150.1	89.8	133.6	144.3	173.2
Socialist sector [1]	a)	113.2	134.9	184.8	179.2	505.6	235.2/247.1	286.6/308.9	162.5/175.6	1133.6/1340.1
	b)	116.0	148.7	215.2	197.0	923.6	249.4/292.3	318.5/359.4	166.8/217.7	1325.1/2287.0
Private sector	a)	102.7	101.3	92.9	81.5	81.7	97.1	55.8	64.7	35.1
	b)	101.5	94.6	85.6	75.1	90.0	72.9	70.0	93.6	47.8
B. Consumption stock (rural housing stock)		102.7	101.9	99.3	101.3	105.3	92.1	65.2	142.6	85.6
Socialist sector [1]		128.4	133.2	284.8	184.5	898.6	117.7/148.4	451.0/648.3	163.3/133.5	867.0/1283.6
Private sector		102.5	101.6	97.1	98.4	99.5	91.6	54.2	137.5	68.2

Note: 1. In the socialist sector, for the growth of capital investment, the numerator shows only the growth of capital investment and the denominator the growth of capital investment together with receipts through socialisation from the stock of the private sector.

Appendix D.

Nomenclature of products in the balance of production and consumption in 1928-30

1. Nomenclature of products of building work
    Ia) <u>Fixed means of production</u>
        i) Productive buildings
            1. Industrial   3. Agricultural
            2. Transport   4. Commercial
        ii) Other constructions
            1. Industrial   3. Agricultural
            2. Transport   4. Commercial
        iii) Installation of machinery and equipment
    II <u>Consumer goods</u>
            1. Urban housing
            2. Rural housing
            3. Buildings with a social purpose

2. <u>Nomenclature of products of industry</u>
    I. <u>Means of production</u>
    a) <u>Fixed means of production</u>
        i) Machinery and equipment not installed
            1. Industrial-productive
            2. Transport, including
                railway
                tractor*
                other transport machinery
            3. Agricultural
        ii) Other products of industry
    b) Raw materials and auxiliary materials
            1. Iron ore*
            2. Manganese ore*
            3. Other mineral raw material
            4. Pig-iron*
            5. Section iron
            6. Other metals and metalware
            7. Scrap-iron
            8. Rough timber*
            9. Sawn-timber*
            10. Roofing iron*
            11. Bricks*
            12. Cement*
            13. Window-glass*
            14. Firebricks
            15. Other building materials
            16. Mineral fertilisers
            17. Other products of the chemical industry
            18. Paper, other than writing paper
            19. Other products of wood processing
            20. Products of forestry (other than rough timber and firewood)
            21. Cleaned cotton*
            22. Cotton thread*
            23. Cotton-seed*
            24. Other products of the processing of textile raw materials.
            25. Bran*
            26. Oilcake*
            27. Other products of the processing of vegetable raw materials.

28. Products of the processing of other animal raw materials

29. Products of the processing of minerals.

30. Unfinished production

c) Fuel and power

1. Coal*

2. Coke*

3. Oil fuel*

4. Benzine and gasoline*

5. Kerosine*

6. Peat*

7. Charcoal

8. Other fuel (except wood)

9. Electric power*

II. Consumer goods

1. Rye flour*

2. Wheaten flour*

3. Other flour*

4. Buckwheat groats*

5. Millet*

6. Other groats*

7. Baked rye bread*

8. Baked wheaten bread*

9. Refined and unrefined sugar*

10. Tea*

11. Vegetable Oil*

12. Fresh fish*

13. Salted, dried and smoked fish

14. Salt*

15. Confectionery and other food products

16. Vodka*

17. Other alcoholic beverages

18. Tobacco and articles made from tobacco*

19. Makhorka*

20. Cotton fabrics*

21. Woollen fabrics*

22. Other fabrics

23. Ready-made clothes [*]

24. Leather footwear*

25. Rubber footwear*

26. Other footwear

27. Wood fuel*

28. Furniture and objects of interior decoration

29. Crockery and utensils

30. Matches*

31. Domestic soap*

32. Other articles of hygiene, sanitation and medicine

33. Other consumer goods

34. Life-saving equipment

35. Water

36. Gas for lighting purposes

3. Nomenclature of products of agriculture

I. Means of production

a) Fixed means of production

1. Livestock

2. Poultry and bees in hives

b) Raw materials

    1. Rye*

    2. Wheat*

    3. Oats*

    4. Barley*

    5. Maize*

    6. Millet*

    7. Buckwheat*

    8. Other cereals*

    9. Flax seed*

   10. Hemp seed*

   11. Sunflower seed*

   12. Other oilseeds*

   13. Flax fibre*

   14. Hemp fibre*

   15. Raw cotton*

   16. Sugar beet*

   17. Raw tobacco*

   18. Raw makhorka*

   19. Tea*

   20. Other vegetable raw material

   21. Fodder root-crops*

   22. Hay*

   23. Straw and residues from threshing*

   24. Hides raw material (large)*

   25. Hides raw material (small)*

   26. Wool*

   27. Other animal raw material

   28. Unfinished production

II. Consumer goods

    1. Potatoes*

    2. Market garden products and melons*

    3. Fruits and berries*

    4. Grapes*

    5. Meat and fat*

    6. Dressed poultry*

    7. Milk*

    8. Butter*

    9. Other dairy products*

   10. Eggs*

4. Nomenclature of products of hunting

   I. Means of production

   a) Raw materials

    1. Undressed furs

    2. Technical products of hunting

Note: * Balances marked with an asterisk were also composed in kind.

3. Tables and notes

VI   NOTES TO TABLES

CONTENTS

[A]   *Notes to tables on 'General results of the balance of the national economy'*
[Materialy, 3.I, pp. 127–50]

TABLES I AND I A

(*a*)   *The national income* as calculated in the balance of the national economy differs from previously published estimates of Gosplan USSR in two ways: (i) national income does not include excises, which were included in the Gosplan estimates (see the general note on method on pp. 105–6); furthermore (ii) the estimates in the balance do not include the net production of public catering and communications, but do include the net production of the domestic processing of a number of agricultural products of commercial importance (butter, 'other dairy products', grape wine) and the self-procurement of building materials and peat by the rural population. Gosplan does not include these products in its estimates.

(*b*)   Since the national income has been estimated net of excise, the consumption fund is therefore also net of excises in both tables.

(*c*)   In table 1a, national income in 1928 prices is given in two variants. The first variant shows the amount of net production by the branches of the economy in constant prices (created national income [national income by sector of origin]), and the second variant shows consumption and accumulation in constant prices [national income by end-use]. Differences in the methods of estimation make it impossible to compare consumption and accumulation as estimated in the second variant with national income as estimated in the first variant. (On this point see the general note on pp. 100–24.)

(*d*)   The slight difference between national income for 1928 in 1928 prices as given in the first variant in table 1a and the national income for 1928 in current prices given in table 1 is due entirely to the different methods used in the revaluation of agricultural produce into constant prices.

(*e*)   The differences in the level of real accumulation in 1928 in the two tables were due to the following reason. Accumulation as measured in current prices (the difference in stocks and in the stock of fixed capital between the beginning and the end of the year) reflects the change in prices in the course of the year. The evaluation in table 1a was made at the beginning and end of the year in identical prices, and hence figures for the amount of real accumulation differ.

TABLE 2.   BALANCE OF THE PRINCIPAL INDICATORS OF REPRODUCTION BY SECTORS

(*a*)   Gross production in consumer prices is given net of excises and includes the total quantity of products produced in the various branches plus the total amount of trade and transport mark-ups and customs duties.

When gross and net production are divided by social sector, the production of the individual economy of collective farmers is assigned to the production of the private sector. This is the practice throughout this work.

(*b*)   Line 4 shows only transfers from one sector to another via direct distribution. Line 4a shows wages received in the socialist sector (from building work, timber procurement, etc.) by the population of the private sector (mostly by individual peasants). Line 4b shows the incomes received by the collective farmers from their individual economy, and by the proletariat in the socialist sector from their own agricultural activity.

(*c*)   Line 6, accumulation, is obtained as the difference between the sector's primary income (line 5) and consumption (line 9).

(*d*)   Line 7, like line 4, shows only the transfers from one sector to another, but line 7 shows transfers via redistribution: (*a*) transfers from the private sector through direct taxes and loans obtained from the private sector, etc.; (*b*) excises charged on consumption by the private sector of the population, and, with the opposite sign, (*c*) pensions and allowances received by the population of the private sector, and their free social, cultural and medical services.

(*e*)   Line 11 shows a surplus of imports over exports as (+) and a surplus of exports as (−).

(*f*)   Line 13 shows the amount of real accumulation resulting from the redistribution of property between the sectors – principally the transfer of fixed capital and stocks through collectivisation.

TABLE 3 AND 3A.   NATIONAL INCOME AND REAL ACCUMULATION
The increase in stocks shown in these tables does not coincide with the figures given in table 1 of section III. In the present tables the increase in stocks is shown net of the increase in incomplete building work in progress, but in table 1 of section III incomplete building work in progress is included in stocks.

TABLES 4, 4A AND 4B.   MATERIAL STRUCTURE OF ACCUMULATION
(*a*)   In these tables, as in the preceding ones, net increase in stocks is shown net of incomplete building work in progress.

(*b*)   In table 4b, line IV, 'total increase in stocks of raw materials, auxiliary materials, fuel, and consumer goods', the total increase in consumer goods is given, including not only the increase in stocks but also the increase in consumption funds.

(*c*)   In all three tables incomplete building work in progress, both productive and non-productive, is wholly assigned to means of production (by analogy with unfinished production in industry and agriculture). In the basic integrated tables (section III) incomplete non-productive building work in progress is assigned to stocks in consumer goods.

TABLE 5. PRODUCTION OF MATERIAL GOODS

(*a*)   The production of material goods is given in producers' prices, i.e. net of trade and transport mark-ups, excises and customs duties. It is therefore less than the amount of production shown in table 2 (see note (a) to table 2), by the trade and transport mark-up and by customs duties, and it is less than the amount shown in table 6 by the sum of mark-ups, customs duties and excises (see note 1 to table 6).

(*b*)   Products are grouped by economic end-use in these tables according to the predominant end-use, as means of production or as consumer goods, that is, the principle of grouping is the same as that employed in the basic integrated balance tables (see the general note on pp. 100–1).

TABLE 6. PRODUCTION OF MATERIAL GOODS

(*a*)   In this table, production is given in consumer prices. It includes both the total amount of production by the branches of material production in producer prices given in table 5, and also trade and transport mark-ups, excises and customs duties.

(*b*)   The economic grouping of products in this table differs from the grouping in table 5, since production is here broken down into producer and consumer goods on the basis not of predominant end-use but of actual utilisation. Sugar, for example, being predominantly an item of consumer goods is wholly assigned to 'consumer goods' in table 5 and in the basic integrated tables (section III), but in the present table 6 that part of sugar production which was actually consumed in production (for confectionery, etc.) is assigned to 'means of production'.

TABLE 7. THE INTER-BRANCH DISTRIBUTION OF ANNUAL PRODUCTION

(*a*)   This table is a brief excerpt from the table 'Distribution of annual production by branches of the national economy' included in section III ('Basic integrated tables in the balance of the national economy'). (See notes on pp. 448–51).

(*b*)   Production is given in consumer prices, which include trade and transport mark-ups and excises.

(*c*)   Col. 2 – 'retained in own branch' – includes that part of the production of a given branch which went into productive consumption or the accumulation of stocks in the branch, or became part of the capital stock of the branch.

[*d*]   Col. 3 – 'disposed of outside own branch, in productive sphere' – includes that part of production which entered into productive consumption and accumulation of stocks in other productive branches, or became part of the capital stock of these branches.

[*e*]   Col. 10 – 'disposed of in non-productive consumption' – includes both what was consumed in the non-productive sphere and what became part of consumption funds.

[*f*]   The sum of col. 11 and 12 does not give us col. 10, because these columns only include consumption and do not include production which enters into consumption funds.

TABLE 8.   ACTUAL GROSS PRODUCTION OF THE NATIONAL ECONOMY
'Actual gross production' is production estimated by the usual method of aggregating the production of the various branches (and, within these, of the various enterprises), net of double-counting of products created in the given year. Thus the normal method of estimating production includes agricultural raw materials first as part of the production of agriculture and for a second time as part of the production of those branches of industry which process agricultural materials.

In the present estimate all this double counting is avoided, and consequently actual production includes only : (*a*) the transferred value of consumed means of production which were created in previous years, and (*b*) the value created exclusively in the given year.

In practice the estimate was made by calculating the following elements:

	1928	1929	1930
	(in million rubles at current prices)		
1. Non-productive consumption (in consumer prices excluding excises)	21305.7	24218.8	28462.8
2. Losses from current production	278.7	354.3	647.2
3. Exports	799.5	923.7	1036.4
4. Production of capital invested in stock	6368.5	6793.6	9096.8
5. Increase in capital stock	574.2	765.6	1335.6
6. Increase in stocks of consumer goods	504.9	409.9	904.0
7. Stocks of circulating means of production at end of year	8821.1	9994.2	11740.0
8. Total	38652.6	43460.1	53222.7
Minus			
9. Imports: (*a*) fixed means of production	235.1	245.2	476.3
(*b*) consumer goods	124.5	116.9	150.8
Total actual gross production of the national economy (col. 8 minus col. 9)	38293.0	43098.0	52595.6

TABLES 10 AND 10A.   INDEXES OF PRODUCERS' PRICES AND CONSUMER PRICES
No independently calculated indexes have been constructed for converting production and consumption as a whole into constant 1928 prices. Estimates in 1928 prices were

made for particular products or groups of products by direct revaluation of them in kind where this was possible; revaluation was made with the use of indexes for those groups of products for which data in kind were not available. Less than 10 per cent of agricultural production needed to be revalued with the use of indexes. A higher percentage of industrial production was revalued through indexes.

The indexes in tables 10 and 10a were obtained from the above estimates in current prices and 1928 prices.

[B] *Notes to tables on 'Consumption'* [*Materialy*, 3.II.D., pp. 192–219]

1.   In the tables in this section consumption is estimated in two variants. The first, basic variant is identical to that which appears in the balance tables (see table 1 of section III: 'Basic integrated tables in the balance of the national economy'). Consumption here includes consumption of dwellings in a sum equivalent to their annual depreciation. However, suitable material on the depreciation of dwellings is available only for the non-agricultural population as a whole and for the agricultural population as a whole; it is impossible to estimate depreciation for separate classes and groups of the non-agricultural population. When this break-down is required an alternative variant is adopted: consumption of dwellings is measured not in terms of depreciation but by the sum paid in rent after deducting the value of electricity, fuel, water and gas (which already appear under the consumption of the product concerned).

These two variants differ considerably. In 1928, depreciation of dwellings amounted to 14.5 rubles per head on average for the non-agricultural population as a whole, but rent minus municipal services amounted to 32.7 rubles. In the case of consumption of institutional buildings, only the first variant is used.

The two variants are given in summary table 1, 'Consumption fund of material goods': the first variant, with the depreciation of housing, as the basic variant, and the second variant, by groups of the non-agricultural population, for purposes of comparison with other tables.

In other tables, the first variant is used only in tables 14a and 14b where the purpose is to provide comparable figures for the consumption of the agricultural and non-agricultural population as a whole.

In the remaining tables consumption of dwellings by the non-agricultural population is given in terms of rent minus municipal services.

2.   In the balance tables (see tables 1 and 4 of section III, 'Basic integrated tables in the balance of the national economy') all products are divided into three main groups according to origin – industrial products, agricultural products, and products of building work. Grain products (flour, groats, bread) are included here with industrial products. However, grain products have been given as a separate item in the consumption tables, because they are acquired by methods similar to the methods by which agricultural products are acquired. ([This requires taking into account] the role of the private market and price indexes.)

Consequently, the figures for industrial products in all the consumption tables are lower than those in the balance tables by the value of grain products.

3.   In the case of the non-agricultural population the only agricultural products consumed are food products; all other products consumed are industrial products. In the case of the agricultural population, however, agricultural products also appear in several other product groups besides food (see table 12). Consequently the total amount of agricultural products consumed (37.07 rubles per head in 1928, 40.08 rubles per head in 1929 and 44.19 rubles per head in 1930 – current prices) is larger than the total amount of agricultural products recorded as food products (34.7 rubles in 1928, 37.33 rubles in 1929 and 42.14 rubles in 1930). This difference is due to the fact that domestic processing of certain forms of raw material was not recorded in the balance; instead, the raw materials concerned were recorded directly, either as personal consumption by the agricultural population or as productive consumption in agriculture. In the case of personal consumption, each kind of raw material was assigned to that item of consumption to which the product domestically processed from it belonged. Thus: (*a*) flax fibre, cotton, wool and small hides were included in the clothing and footwear group, (*b*) home-distilled vodka and raw tobacco in the drink and tobacco group, and (*c*) straw in the fuel group.

4.   In a number of tables, consumption by the agricultural population in 1928 prices is given in two variants. In the first variant it is revalued in 1928 consumer prices for the agricultural population. In the second variant the data on consumption by the agricultural population are presented for comparison with consumption by the non-agricultural population, and therefore consumption of agricultural and grain products by the agricultural population was revalued in 1928 consumer prices for the non-agricultural population (see the explanatory note on methods of estimating consumption, pp. 301–7).

In the case of industrial goods, only the following groups of products were revalued: those products which had been processed domestically (e.g. wine), those which had been processed by industry as a result of orders placed by the agricultural population (vegetable oil), and those which the agricultural population had acquired for their own consumption (firewood).

In the present consumption tables the first variant is headed 'valued in rural prices' and the second 'valued in urban prices'. The first variant (in rural prices) is shown in table 1, in the rest of the tables it is indicated which variant is being used.

Where consumption by the agricultural population is shown in both variants, the rate of growth of consumption is different in the two variants (see tables 12a, 15b and 15c). Thus in table 12a, the growth in per capita consumption between 1928 and 1930 is +2.4 per cent in rural prices but −1 per cent in urban prices. At first sight these differences might seem anomalous. However, the urban and rural prices of agricultural products used in the balances differ very sharply: in 1928 per capita consumption of agricultural products plus grain products by the agricultural population amounted to 55.1 rubles in rural prices, but 129.2 rubles in urban prices. For this reason, revaluation in urban prices increases very considerably the relative share of agricultural products in consumption: agricultural products plus grain products in 1930 accounted for 50 per cent of total consumption in rural prices, and 69 per cent in urban prices. But in the case of agricultural and grain products, in contrast to industrial products, consumption actually fell: the consumption of grain products between 1928 and 1930 fell by 4.1 per cent and that of agricultural products by 5.4 per cent, while the consumption of industrial products increased by 12.3 per cent. In consequence, consumption grows less rapidly when estimated in urban prices than in rural prices.

5.   Tables 1 to 14a show the consumption of material goods, using the method of evaluation used in the balance estimates. Tables 15, 15a, 15b and 15c also include the consumption of services, both those paid for and free social, cultural and medical services. In these tables the value of the consumption of material goods includes the value of the preparation of food in public catering, since in the balance of consumption the amount of public catering recorded is only the value of the products used in the consumed food, excluding the value added by the preparation of the food in public catering enterprises.

6.   The grouping of the population in the consumption tables differs from the grouping given in the tables showing the distribution of the national income (see the explanatory note on the methods of estimating consumption, pp. 301–7) as follows:

(*a*)   in the consumption tables rural craftsmen who do not employ hired labour are included among the agricultural population, but in the tables showing the distribution of the national income those craftsmen whose craft enterprise is their principal source of income are assigned to the non-agricultural population;

(*b*)   in the consumption tables traders who do not employ hired labour are included in the group 'craftsmen, artisans and small traders', but in the tables showing the distribution of the national income they appear in the capitalist group;

(*c*)   in the consumption tables we have not included consumption by persons maintained by the state [servicemen, prisoners, etc.]: their consumption is recorded with the consumption by institutions. In the national income tables they are recorded among 'other population'.

[C]   *Notes to tables in section 'Basic integrated tables in the balance of the national economy'*
[*Materialy*, 3.III tables 1–4, pp. 222–46, for notes to table 5 see below [F] p. 460]

TABLES 1, 2 AND 4
Table 1, 'The balance of production, consumption and accumulation'; table 2, 'Extract from balance of production and consumption'; and table 4, 'The balance of production and consumption'. Tables 2 and 4 show the distribution of annual production and stocks

at the beginning of each year, but table 1 also shows the active capital stock at both the beginning and the end of the year, and also shows the whole turnover for the year including that of the capital stock, and its consumption (depreciation) and accumulation. Thus only table 1 shows the whole of accumulation – the increase in capital stock (of capital goods and consumer goods) as well as that of stocks; tables 2 and 4 show only the accumulation of stocks. Table 1 enables us to arrive at a figure for net production, by deducting productive consumption from total production.

In the three tables different groupings of goods are shown. Table 4 shows the most complete categorisation, both by origin (industrial, agricultural, building work) and by [predominant] economic end-use (means of production, both fixed and circulating, and consumer goods). In table 2, which is a brief excerpt from table 4, goods are categorised only according to their [predominant] economic end-use. In table 1, they are categorised only according to origin.

For individual items of the balance, the differences between these tables are as follows:

1. *Capital stock* at the beginning and the end of the year is shown only in table 1.
2. *Consumed in production.*   (*a*) In tables 2 and 4 this row includes the consumption of raw materials, auxiliary materials and fuels, but it does not include the consumption of capital stock (depreciation). In table 1 all productive consumption is shown, including depreciation of capital stock. (*b*) In table 1, 'consumption in agricultural production' also includes the residual value of working animals written off through depreciation and of dead livestock, i.e. the value of utilised hides. This amounted to 47.4 million rubles in 1928, 45.4 million rubles in 1929, and 53.5 million rubles in 1930. Since this portion of the value of the livestock is included in capital stock at the beginning of each year, and enters neither into the depreciation of the working animals or into losses during the year, it needs to be included in order to ensure a balance. But when it is included in productive consumption it corresponds to the equivalent quantity of hides which appears under agricultural production on the other side of the balance. (*c*) In tables 2 and 4 for technical reasons no breakdown could be given for the consumption of transport as between freight and passenger use, and the total consumption of transport is included in the row 'consumed in production'. In table 1 the equivalent row includes freight consumption only, and passenger consumption appears with non-productive consumption in the row 'consumed by the population and by institutions'.
3. *Consumption by the population and by institutions.*   In table 1 this includes depreciation of consumption funds (dwellings, funds for public purposes), but this is not included in table 2. (On the difference relating to passenger transport, see above).
4. *Losses*
(*a*)   In table 1 this row includes losses from stocks which are not included in tables 2 and 4. Losses from stocks include uncompensated losses from natural causes (premature death of livestock, fire) but do not include such 'losses' as, for example, the wilful slaughter of livestock; this could not be shown in the balance as losses but was treated as productive consumption, since it corresponds on the production side of the balance to the production of meat, hides and other products of slaughter.
(*b*)   Losses are included only in the case of agriculture. Losses of livestock are shown in a separate row, and other losses are given in a summary form for both the production fund and the consumption fund of agriculture.
5. *Entered into capital stocks*
(*a*)   This row is included only in tables 2 and 4, which show how annual production was

distributed. Entry into capital stock approximates to the concept of 'entry into exploitation', but does not fully coincide with it in practice (see Appendix C, 'Fixed capital stock'). This is because it was not possible, for technical reasons, in the case of certain small branches of the economy, to separate out in the balance precisely what was 'entered into exploitation' from 'incomplete building work in progress'. For these branches the value 'entered into exploitation' was taken as equal to total capital investment, and this was included in the row 'entered into capital stock'. Consequently the column 'entered into capital stock' partly includes incomplete building work in progress, though as a general rule this appears as part of stocks.

(*b*)   In table 1 there is no row 'entered into capital stock'; this amount appears in the table as part of capital stock at the end of the year.

(*c*)   In tables 2 and 4, for technical reasons transport is given in the row 'Entered into capital stock' together with communications. Communications are therefore included in total 'production funds', while in table 1 they are treated as consumption funds.

6.   *Capital investment in non-recorded stock* is shown only in table 1. This row shows all those capital investments which have not been recorded in capital stock at the end of the year. This includes: (*a*) certain minor branches of the economy for which investments are recorded, but no assessment of capital stock is possible due to lack of information, (*b*) certain special kinds of investment which do not result in the formation of [physical] stocks (geological prospecting work, preparing of capital projects etc.).

7.   *Increase in fixed capital and other stocks*, i.e. accumulation. This is of course shown only in table 1.

It follows from the above observations that if we add depreciation (plus the value of the utilised hides of discarded working animals) and losses from capital stock (plus the value of the utilised hides of dead livestock) to the row 'increase in capital stock' in table 1 the result will be a value equal to that given in the row 'entered into capital stock' in tables 2 and 4. There are minor disparities in particular branches, due to the fact that the changes in capital stock in these branches between the beginning and the end of the year (as shown in table 1) are affected by transfer of stock from one branch to another, which is not shown in table 2. But the amounts involved are insignificant. The most important of these transfers was from census industry to small-scale industry, and totalled only 12.1 million rubles in 1928 and 20.0 million rubles in 1929. In the remaining branches these transfers were entirely insignificant.

TABLE 3.   THE DISTRIBUTION OF ANNUAL PRODUCTION

This is intended to give a picture of the inter-connection between *branches* in annual production and in its distribution. The table is a modification of table 4, incorporating the following changes:

(*a*)   Table 3 does not include the categorisation of goods by [predominant] economic end-use.

(*b*)   In the rows of table 4, goods are categorised by origin in three basic groups – industrial products, products of agriculture and products of building. Each product was assigned to a particular category in accordance with the branch in which it was predominantly produced. Butter, for example, was mainly produced in this period in agricultural enterprises, and it was therefore treated entirely as a product of agriculture, although a certain proportion of it was also produced in the enterprises of both census and small-scale industry. The share of products produced other than in the main branch by origin can be found in the columns of the table: where for instance, the production of butter is distributed between the domestic holdings of agricultural producers and the enterprises of census and small-scale industry.

In the present table 3 we are concerned with the *branches* of the economy, as such, and with the distribution of production *between branches*. Consequently the rows here do not show the three groups of goods which appear in table 4, but instead list all those branches whose production was included in the balance. Thus the row 'Industry' shows the distribution of the *whole* of industrial production, including those products which were treated as agricultural products in table 4 (butter, *tvorog* [cottage cheese], *smetana* [sour cream], etc.). Consequently, there was no need to give a further breakdown of production by branches in the columns of the table, and it is all given in a single column. The trade and transport mark-ups appertaining to the production of particular branches were also distributed in a similar manner.

(*c*)   The present table 3 shows the distribution of *annual production of the USSR*, whereas the basic balance tables (2 and 4) also include the distribution of stocks as at the beginning of the year, and of the total quantity of commodities imported into the country during the year. Consequently, total consumption by each type of consumer shown in table 3 does not coincide with the totals of consumption shown in tables 2 and 4, since it does not include imported commodities or consumption from stocks.

(*d*)   All the estimates mentioned in (*a*)–(*c*) above were very approximate since, of course, no precise figures exist on the distribution of consumed stocks or of particular imports by type of consumer. When the rows are regrouped by branches it is also difficult to determine precisely which consumer receives, say, butter produced in industrial enterprises, and which receives butter produced domestically.

The way in which the rough estimates were made depended on the nature of the product. Thus imported industrial machinery was deducted from the total entering into the capital stock of industry included in table 4; imports of tractors and agricultural machinery were deducted from the total entering into agricultural capital stock; stocks of raw materials expended and not replaced were deducted from industrial consumption; and so on. The whole estimate is approximate, but it does provide us with a picture of the connections between branches in the distribution of annual production.

[D]   *Notes to the tables of Appendix A 'Balances of products of industry'*
[*Materialy*, 3.V.A., pp. 314–18]

I.   TABLE I. THE TRACTOR BALANCE
(*a*)   Only completed tractors are included in the balance; spare parts are not included.

(*b*)   'Distributed' is taken to refer to the moment when tractors are transferred by the distribution agencies to the place of work (depreciation of tractors is not included in the balance).

The distribution or transfer of tractors to agriculture was established from the data of the People's Commissariat of Agriculture. The data on the distribution of tractors to industry also include tractors distributed to other branches of the national economy apart from agriculture.

(*c*) The loss (*raznitsa*) due to the sale of tractors at less than their cost was obtained from the difference between prices of production or import prices and the prices obtained in distribution.

2. TABLE 2. ELECTRIC POWER BALANCE

(*a*) Consumption for municipal and everyday needs refers to consumption by institutions, by the population, by trade, and also for purely municipal requirements.

(*b*) Where factory power stations are concerned the cost of production of power is shown, and not the transfer price.

3. TABLE 3. FUEL BALANCE

(*a*) Coal balance
  (i) The coal balance includes all grades of coal, anthracite and brown coal;
  (ii) Stocks in the 'non-productive sphere' refers to stocks held by institutions and organisations;
  (iii) Losses were estimated on the basis of norms [standard losses];
  (iv) Consumption for own needs refers, principally, to consumption for heating workers' dwellings, offices and other buildings classified as non-productive which are attached to the mines;
  (v) To convert coal into 7,000-calorie conventional fuel we used a conversion coefficient of 0.947, which corresponds to 6.5 million calories per tonne.

(*b*) Coke balance
  (i) The coke balance includes only coke derived from coal; peat-coke is not included;
  (ii) To convert coke into 7,000-calorie conventional fuel we used a coefficient of 0.930, which corresponds to 6.5 million calories per tonne.

(*c*) Kerosene balance
  (i) The kerosene balance includes kerosene and pyronaphtha: distillates are not included;
  (ii) To convert kerosene into 7,000-calorie conventional fuel we used a coefficient of 1.470, which corresponds to 10.3 million calories per tonne.

(*d*) Oil-fuel balance
  (i) The oil-fuel balance includes: petroleum, natural gas derived from petroleum, boiler fuel, engine fuel, diesel fuel (*gazoil'*) and solar oil;
  (ii) 'Sent for processing' refers to petroleum sent for processing and blending, and also to boiler fuel sent for blending in order to produce engine fuel;

(iii) The amount lost was calculated on the basis of norms. Losses also included the draining-off of water and mud (sediment);

(iv) Estimates of the amount of oil extracted and sent for processing were made in terms of cost-prices;

(v) A coefficient of 1.430 was used to convert oil-fuel into 7,000-calorie conventional fuel. This corresponds to 10 million calories per tonne.

(*e*) Petroleum distillates balance

(i) The petroleum distillates balance includes benzine, gasoline and ligroin;

(ii) Agricultural consumption was calculated from data of Soyuzneft' [the industrial association responsible for oil production];

(iii) Losses were calculated on the basis of norms;

(iv) A coefficient of 1.500 was used in order to convert benzine into 7,000-calorie conventional fuel. This corresponds to 10.5 million calories per tonne.

(*f*) Firewood balance

(i) The firewood balance includes both firewood obtained as a result of timber-procurement and firewood obtained as an industrial by-product;

(ii) The balance was compiled in Raum-metres [1 Raum-metre = 0.64 Fest-metres];

(iii) 'Large-scale procurement agencies' refers to the procurement agencies of VSNKh, NKPS, NKZem and other departments covered by the special study of TsUNKhU;

(iv) Procurement of firewood in census industry refers to the by-products of saw-milling and wood-processing;

(v) 'Small procurement agencies' refers to state institutions, cooperatives (other than forestry cooperatives), private persons and enterprises;

(vi) 'Procurement by the agricultural population' refers to: (1) procurement for consumption within own household; (2) procurement for sale; and (3) procurement by rural craftsmen for production purposes;

(vii) The trade and transport mark-up includes also the cost of planting the timber;

(viii) 'Productive consumption in agriculture' refers to the consumption of firewood for economic needs – the heating of farm buildings, etc.;

(ix) To convert firewood into 7,000-calorie conventional fuel we used a coefficient of 0.174 which corresponds to 1.22 million calories per cubic metre.

(*g*) Peat balance

(i) The peat balance includes all forms of peat: cut peat, hydrolysed water peat, peat-litter, peat coke and peat briquettes;

(ii) A coefficient of 0.460 was used to convert peat into 7,000-calorie conventional fuel. This corresponds to 3.2 million calories per tonne.

4. TABLE 4. BUILDING MATERIALS BALANCE

(*a*) Balance of roofing iron

(i) Stocks in the channels of circulation include stocks for building work (for urban, municipal, agricultural and social purposes), with the exception of industrial building work, the stocks of which are recorded with stocks for building work;

(ii) Consumption in industrial building work also includes consumption in the building of dwellings in industry.

(b)   Cement balance

(i) The cement balance includes all forms of cement: natural cements (Parker's cement), Portland, clinker, etc., in packed form and also unpacked cement which is despatched from factories in that form;

(ii) All barrels of cement have been taken as equivalent to 155 kg, and all sacks as equivalent to 75 kg.

(c)   Building bricks balance

(i) Old bricks from dismantled structures were included in determining the level of consumption of building bricks in building work, but were not included in the balance.

(d)   Window glass balance

(i) The stocks of glass in all kinds of building work with the exception of industrial building work were included in stocks in the channels of circulation. Stocks of glass in industrial building work were reported with stocks for building work;

(ii) The following coefficients were used to convert the production of window glass in tonnes into square metres: for 1928 – 232, 1929 – 215 and 1930 – 202;

(iii) Losses were assumed to be 5 per cent of production.

(e)   Sawn-timber balance

(i) The sawn-timber balance includes all forms of saw-mill products, including sleepers;

(ii) Self-procurement refers to production by manual methods wherever this takes place: the production of sawn-timber by the rural population, and the self-procurement of sleepers by NKPS. The latter amounted to 2,303 thousand cubic metres in 1928, 2,069 thousand cubic metres in 1929 and 1,403 thousand cubic metres in 1930.

(f)   Unsawn-timber balance

(i) Unsawn-timber balance includes all forms of rough working timber: logs, blocks, beams, trunks, etc.;

(ii) The stocks of unsawn-timber held by industry includes the stocks held by procurement organisations which amounted to 5,500,000 cubic metres on 1 January 1928, 7,000,000 cubic metres on 1 January 1929, 25,293,000 cubic metres on 1 January 1930 and 37,903,000 cubic metres on 1 January 1931;

(iii) The production of census industry refers to procurements by large-scale procurement agencies (see the note to the firewood balance);

(iv) The production of non-census industry refers to procurement by small-scale procurement agencies (see the note to the firewood balance);

(v) Self-procurement refers to procurement by the rural population.

5. TABLE 5. BALANCES OF ORE, PIG-IRON AND TEXTILE RAW MATERIALS

(*a–b*) Balances of iron and manganese ores:

(i) The production of census industry refers to the gross production of ore, both that requiring and that not requiring concentration;

(ii) 'Obtained after processing' refers to ore which has undergone concentration;

(iii) 'Sent for processing' refers to ore sent for concentration.

(*c*) Pig-iron balance

(i) 'Other stocks' and 'other consumption' refers to stocks and consumption in transport.

(*d*) Balance of cotton seeds

(i) 'Other consumption' of cotton seeds refers to consumption in agriculture for sowing.

(*e*) Cotton yarn balance

(i) The cotton yarn balance includes primary yarn (including waste) but does not include twisted or dyed thread.

6. TABLE 6. BALANCES OF CONSUMER GOODS

(*a*) Sugar balance

(i) The sugar balance includes both raw and refined sugar;

(ii) The production of census industry refers to the production of raw sugar;

(iii) 'Obtained after processing' refers to the production of refined sugar;

(iv) The consumption of raw sugar for turning into refined sugar is shown in the group 'consumption by census industry'; the consumption of sugar in other branches of industry (confectionery, etc.) is shown in the group 'other consumption'.

(*b*) Tea balance

(i) The tea balance includes all varieties of tea, both leaf tea and tea in brick form;

(ii) Stocks of undistributed tea in the customs storehouses are included in stocks in the channels of circulation;

(iii) The production of census industry refers to the production of tea from the raw state (produced by the Georgian tea association Chaigruziya);

(iv) 'Obtained after processing' refers to the amount of packaged tea as weighed in the tea packing factories;

(v) Consumption by census industry refers to the weight of tea entering the tea-packing factory. Since the quantity of tea remains the same during its weighing and packaging, the production and consumption of tea in this operation are expressed in value terms only.

(*c*) Vegetable oil balance

(i) 'Other consumption' refers to consumption in building work (as a drying agent).

(*d*)   Salt balance

   (i) 'Other productive consumption' refers to consumption in the fishing industry (for salting) and in agriculture.

(*e*)   Makhorka balance

   (i) The amount of growth of stocks of makhorka in the channels of circulation differ substantially from the figures given by Soyuztabak, because the latter do not take into account stocks held in the lower trading network.

(*f*)   Cigarette and tobacco balance

   (i) The following coefficients have been used to convert weight of tobacco into 'smoking units': 1928 and 1929 – 1,000 smoking units per 0.573 kg., 1930 – 1,000 smoking units per 0.535 kg.

(*g*)   Leather footwear balance

   (i) The leather footwear balance includes all forms of leather footwear, from boots to sandals, slippers, etc.;

   (ii) Production of non-census industry refers both to production of footwear and to repairs. Repairs were recorded only in value terms and were equivalent to 186,846 thousand rubles in 1928, 218,815 thousand rubles in 1929 and 321,259 thousand rubles in 1930;

   (iii) Productive consumption refers to the consumption of special protective footwear;

   (iv) Consumption by the non-agricultural population includes the value of repairs to footwear which amounted to 82,103 thousand rubles in 1928, 85,255 thousand rubles in 1929 and 125,750 thousand rubles in 1930. It was not possible to provide a breakdown of these amounts by classes of the population and they have consequently only been included as totals (col. 25). For this reason the values in col. 25 are larger than the sum of columns 19 to 24;

   (v) The value of consumption by the agricultural population includes both the value of footwear purchased and the value of repairs, amounting to 104,743 thousand rubles in 1928, 133,559 thousand rubles in 1929 and 195,509 thousand rubles in 1930;

   (vi) The value of repairs has not been taken into account in calculating the price of a pair of shoes or other footwear.

(*h*)   Cotton fabric balance

   (i) Consumption by census industry includes consumption by the garments industry: 154.7 million metres in 1928, 184.1 millions in 1929, and 343.7 millions in 1930;

   (ii) Consumption by non-census industry includes consumption by the garments industry: 181.1 million metres in 1928, 170.8 millions in 1929 and 158.0 millions in 1930;

   (iii) Other consumption refers to consumption in transport.

(*j*)   Balance of woollen fabrics

   (i) Consumption by census industry includes consumption by the garments industry: 28.3 million metres in 1928, 53.6 millions in 1929 and 76.5 millions in 1930;

(ii) All the consumption of non-census industry was consumed by the garments industry.

(*k*) Balance of ready-made clothes (in terms of fabrics)
'Consumers of fabrics' refers to the ultimate consumers, so that the intermediate stage (sewing of garments) is not included in the balances. Consumption of ready-made clothes by the population is recorded in terms of the amount of fabrics used in their manufacture. Owing to the approximate nature of these estimates they are given in quantitative terms only.

(*l*) Household soap balance:
   (i) Other stocks and other consumption refers to consumption in transport;
   (ii) Consumption in census industry refers to soap issued to workers.

7. TABLE 7. BALANCES OF MILLING AND GRINDING PRODUCTS
(*a*) The balance of milling and grinding products gives us the distribution of the total production of the milling and grinding industry and includes both marketed products and products produced to the orders of the agricultural population.

(*b*) Col. 11, 'Consumed in agricultural production', covers consumption as livestock fodder.

(*c*) Col. 12, 'Consumed in transport', covers the fodder given to draft animals in urban haulage.

(*d*) Col. 10, 'Consumed in industrial production', includes both consumption in the production of macaroni, confectionery, etc., and consumption in the baking of bread. In this balance consumption in bread making refers to the amount of bread consumed by the non-agricultural population. Consumption by the agricultural population is given in terms of flour, as it was not possible to determine the amount of baked bread purchased. Consequently bread-baking has not been fully accounted for.

(*e*) In accordance with [p. 446] above, col. 14, 'consumed by the non-agricultural population', includes under flour only purchases of flour, and not purchases of bread, as the latter amount has been recorded in industrial consumption. These amounts were:

	1928	1929	1930
		in thousands of tsentners	
Rye flour	7144	8204	18767
Wheat flour	15148	18049	20682
Other flour	–	1045	441
Total	22292	27298	39890

(*f*) Col. 18, 'Losses', includes losses in storage in the channels of circulation. The losses are not given in value terms as they already form part of the estimated selling price.

[E] *Notes for the tables of Appendix B: 'Balances of products of agriculture'*
[*Materialy*, 3.V.B., pp. 382–405]

TABLE I. GRAIN BALANCE

(*a*) This table is a balance of 'grain' and not a balance of grain products 'converted into grain equivalents'. Consequently the expenditure part of the balance includes only the expenditure of grain as such: expenditure of processed products (flour, groats and bran) is given in the balance of milling and grinding products.

The amount of grain corresponding to the quantity of flour and groats recorded in the milling and grinding balance appears in the grain balance under the heading 'consumed in production: industry'.

(*b*) Col. 2 of the balance, 'stocks in industry', includes the total amount of stocks both in the milling and grinding industry and in other branches (distilling, brewing, etc).

(*c*) Col. 3, 'stocks in the channels of circulation', includes stocks in the procurement agencies and grain in transit.

(*d*) Col. 11, 'cattle fodder', includes only that part of the fodder which consists of grain; flour and bran used for fodder are excluded. This column covers fodder for all rural livestock and for urban productive livestock: fodder for urban horses (haulage) is included in col. 14, 'consumed in transport'.

(*e*) Col. 13, 'consumed in production: industry', includes grain processed both in the milling and grinding industry and in other branches (distilling, brewing, etc.). Other branches accounted for 6,539 thousand tsentners in 1928, 4,416 thousands in 1929, and 8,975 thousands in 1930.

Processing by industry is shown for both census and small-scale industry, and includes processing carried out to the orders of the agricultural population.

(*f*) Cols. 16-19, 'consumed by the population and institutions', do not include the consumption of flour and groats (see (a) above). For the agricultural population, the figures given in col. 16 include expenditure of grain on home-distilled spirits.

(*g*) Col. 20, 'losses in the channels of circulation', is expressed only in physical terms: these losses (shrinkage, spillage, etc.) in value terms are allowed for in estimating the cost of the remaining part of the product, and are therefore included in the consumer price. Col. 21, conversely, is given only in value terms; this item covers losses on the prices when the trading organisations sell below cost price.

2. TABLE 2. BALANCE OF TECHNICAL CROPS [INCLUDING POTATOES]
(*a*) The balance of flax and hemp fibre is given in terms of scutched fibre.

(*b*) Domestic processing of raw material ('On-farm consumption of own product') is included in the balances as a rough estimate either as personal consumption by the agricultural population, or as consumption in agricultural production, depending on the nature of the product. The products of domestic processing of certain kinds of raw material (flax and hemp fibre) can be used for both personal consumption and economic consumption. Since it is not possible to establish the relative proportion of these two categories of consumption, total domestic processing of each kind of raw material was somewhat arbitrarily assigned either to personal or to economic consumption: (*a*) the domestic processing of hemp fibre was assigned to economic consumption (for ropes, sacks, etc.), and (*b*) the domestic processing of flax fibre, cotton, tobacco and makhorka was assigned to personal consumption.

(*c*) Col. 14 includes all industrial consumption (census and small-scale). This includes processing carried out to the orders of the agricultural population, as follows (in thousand tsentners):

	1928	1929	1930
Sunflower seeds	5373	5500	5668
Flax seeds	1354	1396	1306
Hemp seeds	2677	2326	2006

(*d*) The personal consumption of sunflower seed includes those chewed by the agricultural and the non-agricultural population.

(*e*) Col. 21 includes losses in storage in agriculture, expressed both in physical and in value terms. For losses in the channels of circulation [and on prices] (cols. 22 and 23), see the explanation given in the notes on the grain balance, point (g), p. 458.

3. TABLE 3. BALANCE OF LIVESTOCK PRODUCTS

(*a*) The production of slaughter goods (meat and hides) includes the amount of products obtained from the contingent of livestock slaughtered in the given year. The production of hides also includes the hides of livestock that died or were discarded during this period, including working animals. The production of meat and fat includes offal (on both the production and the expenditure side).

(*b*) 'On-farm consumption of own produce', in the case of large hides is included with productive consumption by agriculture, while in the case of small hides and wool it is included in the personal consumption of the agricultural population (see note to table 2,

'Balances of technical crops', (b), p. 459). Only domestic processing is included here: that part of the raw material which was processed by small-scale industry to the orders of the agricultural population is included in col. 16, 'consumed by industry', in the following amounts (in thousands):

	1928	1929	1930
Large raw hides (numbers)	2000	1760	1300
Small raw hides (numbers)	28900	35445	28475
Wool, converted to washed conditions (thousand tsentners)	298	278	300

(c)   In the balance of meat and fat (including offal), col. 11 gives the consumption by industry for the production of sausages, preserved meat (smoked), etc. Accordingly the personal consumption of the population is given net of these processed products.

(d)   The milk balance includes other dairy products (butter, cottage cheese, sour cream, etc.), in terms of milk equivalents. In the production column only milk is shown, but in the consumption column all dairy products are shown, in terms of milk. Col. 10 shows the milk used for feeding calves. Col. 11 shows butter consumed in the food industry in the production of confectionery, etc. in terms of milk.

[F] *Notes to the tables; 'Balance of distribution and redistribution of the national income',*
[*Materialy*, 3.III table 5, pp. 247–55]

1. The tables examine the movement of national income, and so exclude such items as receipts from the sale of property. Such items are excluded from both incomes and expenditures. As a result, in certain cases, the total of these additional items is less than the total of loans.

2. In certain cases total consumption is not balanced by incomes. This is the case for employees in 1929 for instance.

3. For a number of elements statistical data were lacking, and so the corresponding columns remained incomplete. Hence the estimates as a whole should be considered as, to some extent, preliminary.

Glossary

AGRICULTURAL YEAR (*sel'skokhozyaistvennyi god*): an accounting period from harvest to harvest, 1 July–30 June.

ARTIFICIAL INSTALLATIONS (*iskusstvennye sooruzheniya*): for railways and roads. This item includes such installations as embankments, cuttings, tunnels and bridges.

ASSOCIATIONS (*ob"edineniya*): combinations of state enterprises often covering a whole industry.

BUDGET SURVEYS (*byudzhetnye obsledovaniya*): sample surveys of the income and expenditure of individual households.

CATTLE FODDER (*furazh*): fodder for all animals.

CENSUS INDUSTRY (*tsenzovaya promyshlennost'*): generally those industrial units which used mechanical power and at least 16 workers or, in the case of industrial units without mechanical power, at least 30 workers. There were however numerous exceptions.

CHAIGRUZIYA Georgian Tea Association.

'CHERVONETS' the more stable gold-backed currency introduced into the Soviet economy by the currency reform of 1923–4 that halted the earlier rapid inflation.

CIVIL INSTALLATIONS (*grazhdanskie sooruzheniya*): for railways – this term includes such installations as stations.

COMMERCIAL FUND (*kommercheskii fond*): goods sold off the ration through state retail trade at higher 'commercial prices'.

CONSTANT PRICES OF 1928 (*po tsenam 1928g.*): evaluated in fixed prices of the year 1928.

CONTROL FIGURES (*kontrol'nye tsifry*): the planning figures and targets used in the middle and late 1920s.

CURRENT PRICES (*po tsenam sootvetstvyushchikh let*): evaluated in prices of the given year.

CURRENT REPORT CARDS (*kartochki srochnykh donesenii*): current report cards used for gathering current economic statistics.

DUTIES (*poshlina*): mainly customs duties but also other minor duties.

ECONOMIC YEAR (*khozyaistvennyi god*): an accounting period from 1 October–30 September.

FIXED CAPITAL STOCK (*osnovnye fondy*): fixed funds or fixed capital stock.

GOSBANK (Gosudarstvennyi Bank): State Bank.

461

GOSPLAN   (Gosudarstvennaya Planovaya Komissiya): State Planning Commission.

GOSSTRAKH   (*Gosudarstvennoe strakhovanie*): State Insurance.

GROSS PRODUCTION   (*valovoe proizvodstvo*): gross production refers to gross turnover minus semi-finished goods used in the same establishment for further processing within the given period of time.

GROSS TURNOVER   (*valovoi oborot*): gross turnover refers to the whole mass of goods and semi-finished goods manufactured in a given period of time regardless of whether they are consumed in the establishment where they were manufactured or whether they were sent out from it.

GROUP 'A'   one of the two Soviet classifications of industrial production covering the production of means of production – the capital goods sector.

GROUP 'B'   one of the two Soviet classifications of industrial production covering the production of consumer goods.

INCOMPLETE BUILDING WORK   (*ostatki nezakonchennogo stroitel'stva*): unfinished construction in progress.

KASPER   Caspian Sea Steamship Line.

KHLEBSTROI   Building Trust for Grain.

KOLKHOZ   (*kollektivnoe khozyaistvo*): Collective farm.

KOLKHOZTSENTR   All-Union Union of Agricultural Collective Farms.

'KUSTOVYE OB"EDINENIYA'   group associations of collective farms.

MINOR SERVICING PERSONNEL   (*mladshii obsluzhivayushchii personal*) (MOP): cleaners, porters, watchmen etc.

MTK   (Mashinno-Traktornaya Kolumna): Machine Tractor Column.

MTS   (Mashinno-Traktornaya Stantsiya): Machine Tractor Station.

NKFIN   (Narodnyi Komissariat Finansov): People's Commissariat of Finance.

NKPROS   (Narodnyi Komissariat Prosveshcheniya): People's Commissariat of Education (of the RSFSR).

NKPS   (Narodnyi Komissariat Putei Soobshcheniya): People's Commissariat of Transport.

NKPT   (Narodnyi Komissariat Pocht i Telegrafov): People's Commissariat of Posts and Telegraph – renamed NKSvyaz in 1932.

NKSNAB   (Narodnyi Komissariat Snabzheniya): People's Commissariat of Supply formed in November 1930 when NKVVTorg – People's Commissariat of Internal and External Trade – was divided into NKSnab, for internal trade, and NKTVnesh Torg, for external trade.

NKSVYAZ   (Narodnyi Komissariat Svyazi): People's Commissariat of Communications. Before January 1932 it was named NKPT – People's Commissariat of Posts and Telegraph.

NKTORG   (Narodnyi Kommissariat Vneshnei i Vnutrennei Torgovli): People's Commissariat of Trade.

NKVNESHTORG   (Narodnyi Komissariat Vneshnei Torgovli): People's Commissariat of External Trade.

NKVOD   (Narodnyi Komissariat Vodnogo Transporta): People's Commissariat of Waterways.

NKZDRAV (Narodnyi Komissariat Zdravookhraneniya): People's Commissariat of Health.

NKZEM (Narodnyi Komissariat Zemledeliya): People's Commissariat of Agriculture.

OFFICE WORKERS (*sluzhashchie*): office workers (all grades).

OVTSEVOD Sheep-farming Association.

PATENTS (*patenty*): licences for operating private trade and industrial enterprises.

PREMATURE DEATH (*padezh*): premature death of livestock, i.e. non-productive slaughter, normally due to disease or other disorders.

PRICE LISTS (*tsenniki*): lists of unit costs of component elements.

PURE BUILDING (*chistoe stroitel'stvo*): capital construction, exclusive of installations and machinery.

'RABOCHIE' manual workers.

RAUM-METRES 1 Raum-metre = 0.64 Fest-metres.

REAL ACCUMULATION actual increase in accumulation including changes in stock levels, losses and net imports.

ROSSTROI Building Trust of RSFSR.

RSFSR (Rossiskaya Sovetskaya Federativnaya Sotsialisticheskaya Respublika): Russian Soviet Federative Socialist Republic.

SKOTOVOD Cattle Farming Association: (including dairy farming).

SMALL-SCALE INDUSTRY (*melkaya promyshlennost'*): industry other than census industry (*see* census industry).

SNABTORG regional state trading agency primarily selling producer goods to state enterprises.

'SOVKHOZ' (*sovetskoe khozyaistvo*): state farm.

SOVKHOZOB"EDINENIE State Farm Association.

SOVKHOZTSENTR (Vserossiiskii Soyuz Sovkhozov): State Farm Centre.

SOVTORGFLOT Soviet Merchant Navy.

SOWN AREA CONSOLIDATED BY SPRING This refers to the total area sown less the winter loss of winter-sown crops.

SOYUZKOLKHOZBANK All-Union Collective Farm Bank.

SOYUZKOZH All-Union Association for Leather Goods.

SOYUZMYASO All-Union Association for Meat Products.

SOYUZNEFT' Industrial Association for Oil Production.

SOYUZRASMASLO All-Union Association for Vegetable Oil.

SOYUZSAKHAR All-Union Sugar Association.

SOYUZSTROI All-Union Building Trust.

SOYUZTABAK All-Union Tobacco Trust.

SPECIAL QUARTER October–December 1930: this was designated a special quarter because it appears as a special accounting period during the transition from record-keeping in economic years 1 October–30 September to calendar years 1 January–31 December. Economic records were kept in calendar years from 1 January 1931.

STANDARD COMMODITY PRODUCTION (*uslovnaya tovarnaya produktsiya*): the share of agricultural and industrial production in all production used outside its own branch.

SVINOVOD   Pig-farming Association.

TABAKSYR'E   All-Union Tobacco Association.

TOTAL INCOME   (*sovokupnyi dokhod*).

TRAKTOROTSENTR   (Vsesoyuznyi Tsentr Mashinno-Traktornykh Stantsii): All-Union Centre for Machine Tractor stations.

TSENTROSOYUZ   (Vsesoyuznyi tsentral'nyi soyuz potrebitelskikh obshchestv): All-Union Central Union of Consumers' Cooperatives.

TsMIK   (Tsentral'naya Mezhduvedomstvennaya Inventarizatsionnaya Komissiya): Central Inter-departmental Stocktaking Commission.

TsOS VSNKh   Central Department of Statistics of VSNKh.

TsSU   (Tsentral'noe Statisticheskoe Upravlenie): Central Statistical Administration, abolished in December 1929, when its functions were transferred to Gosplan.

TsUDORTRANS   (Tsentral'noe Upravlenie Dorozhnogo Transporta): Central Administration for Road Transport.

TsUMOR   (Tsentral'noe Upravlenie Morskogo Transporta): Central Administration for Maritime Transport.

TsUNKhU   (Tsentral'noe Upravlenie Narodno-Khozyaistvennogo Ucheta): Central Administration for National Economic Records attached to Gosplan, formed in January 1932 (equivalent of TsSU).

TsUSStrakh   (Tsentral'noe Upravlenie Sotsial'nogo Strakhovaniya): Central Administration for Social Insurance.

TsUVP   (Tsentral'noe Upravlenie Vodnykh Putei): Central Administration of Inland Waterways.

UKRSOVKHOZOB"EDINENIE   Ukrainian State Farm Association.

UKRSTROI   Building Trust of Ukrainian Republic.

VET   All–Union Electrical Trust.

VODSTROI   Waterways Building Trust.

VSEKOOPIT   (Vsesoyuznaya avtonomnaya sektsiya po obshchestvennomu pitaniyu Tsentrosoyuza): All-Union autonomous section for public catering in the Consumer Cooperatives Union.

VSNKh   (Vysshii Sovet Narodnogo Khozyaistva): Supreme Council of the National Economy. Originally after the revolution this was intended to cover the work of all the branches of the economy but in practice was concerned primarily with industry. It lost control over some food industries to NKSnab in November 1930, and in January 1932 it was divided further.

ZERNOTREST   (Vsesoyuznyi trest zernovykh sovkhozov): State Grain Farm Trust.

Index